The Evolution of Modern Demand Theory

The Evolution of Modern Demand Theory

A Collection of Essays

Edited by

R. B. Ekelund, Jr.
E. G. Furubotn
W. P. Gramm

Texas A&M University

Lexington Books
D.C. Heath and Company
Lexington, Massachusetts
Toronto London

Published simultaneously in Canada.

Printed in the United States of America.

International Standard Book Number: 0-669-62547-7.

Library of Congress Catalog Card Number: 72-158679.

Table of Contents

Foreword

No theory is born as complete as Pallas Athena springing from the head of Zeus. Even a theory dealing with as seemingly simple and immediately accessible concept as "demand" for goods and services had to undergo a long and sometimes tortuous line of development. After almost 150 years, since Cournot laid its foundations, the end of this road is not yet in sight. What at first seemed obvious and commonplace was shown to harbor a large set of problems whose solutions were completely out of reach even for those to whom significant advances in our understanding are due. The reason for the emergence of a multitude of new problems was, of course, that it was necessary to go beyond the rather trivial surface phenomena. The fact that men want things and services and want different quantities at different prices, to which they react in various ways, must all be fitted into a consistent theory.

This process of continuing questioning of premises, of widening of the field under investigation is, of course, typical for any scientific endeavour. From time to time it seems that all has been said that can be said and the ordinary textbooks certainly give this impression, no matter what their vintage, until suddenly entirely new problems emerge. We are in this situation now. In viewing the history it is fascinating to see the long lead time of new ideas, to observe their earliest manifestation and to witness how they had to wait for that strange factor, "the right moment in time," when they could become powerful.

Thus an anthology as the present one, which is far from being a mere collection of readings, has singular value. It not only presents some of the most important papers on demand theory that one might want to view together. It does more: it gives a lesson in the history of science since it shows the emergence of problems and methods in the sense of the above remark. It is singularly interesting to observe how the seeming triviality of the first statements about demand nevertheless contain the root of problems with which we have not finished to this day. One of the reasons why they were not enunciated earlier is, no doubt, due to the fact that the right language was lacking in which to describe them. And scientific language develops slowly; even the proper mathematical language germane to the subject matter may have to be created together with the subject matter.

For example, there is no demand theory without a theory of value and utility, and we know how elusive these two notions are. The theory of utility, seemingly firmly in hand only a few decades ago, is undergoing an almost explosive development because of the consideration of uncertainty and the attendant questions relating to probability. These new vistas have changed things in ways unanticipated even by the foremost writers of earlier eras. What once were milestones can now be seen as stumbling blocks which the new theory has learned to avoid.

FOREWORD

There is no part of economics where demand does not enter, so that it almost becomes impossible to separate demand theory from the rest of economics. This is evident from the range of the papers here collected and is amply illustrated in the penetrating and informative essay of the three editors. Without that study the reader would find it hard to make his way through the often difficult material that is reprinted. In fact, if it were not written for this anthology, their study ought to be one of its most important papers.

No reader will put this book down without being astonished at how long it took until we arrived at our present understanding of what "demand" means and how many turns and twists this road has had. Even in our present position we can see unresolved issues, such as finding the true distinction between static and dynamic theory, determining the role of expectations, reassessing markets whose structure is not adequately described by the naive summation of individual demand, dealing with the interaction of individual demands, etc. The question even arises whether all demand can be expressed in terms of demand functions of the type we now analyze, for example, the problem changes significantly when we encounter various types of auctions or the transactions on the stock exchange.

To be confronted with this book and to be introduced so ably to its subject matter by the brilliant first essay by Messrs Ekelund, Furubotn, and Gramm will offer welcome challenge and guidance to the new generation of economists.

Oskar Morgenstern

March 1971
New York University

Preface

Henry James once remarked that it takes an endless amount of history to make even a little tradition. Almost two centuries of writings on demand theory, if anything, lend strong support to James' observation. History has certainly not produced unanimity on the subject of demand, but it has yielded an incredibly rich literature on this fundamental tool of economic analysis.

The purpose of this collection of essays is to bring together, under one cover, a good sample of the diverse literature dealing with demand theory. In making our selection of essays we have attempted to present, given an obvious space constraint, papers that have not heretofore been readily accessible in a single source. Since a number of seminal papers on demand theory have been reprinted elsewhere, it was thought justifiable to omit them and to include, instead, some less familiar contributions to the literature of demand theory. To provide some guidance through the maze of existing writings we have attempted to chronicle some of the important developments in demand theory in an introductory essay that considers contributions from Charles Davenant through contemporary writings.

Acknowledging debts owed to others is always hazardous business since one always risks inadvertent omissions. However, several influences on this book cannot be ignored. We are grateful for the consistently efficient typing services of our secretary, Mrs. Shirley Minor. Her quiet efficiency made the project easier than it would otherwise have been. We should like to acknowledge the constructive criticisms and suggestions of Professors Alfred Chalk, Robert F. Hebert, and James P. Payne on various parts of our essay. But, most particularly, we wish to express a debt of gratitude to Professor Oskar Morgenstern for his encouragement, evaluations, and suggestions at all stages of the preparation of this volume. We are, of course, solely responsible for the final product which, we hope, will provide a convenient reference and introduction to the literature on demand theory.

R. B. Ekelund, Jr.
E. G. Furubotn
W. P. Gramm

April, 1971
College Station, Texas

Part I
The Evolution and State of Contemporary Demand Theory

1 Early Developments in the Theory of Demand

Introduction

The purpose of this essay is to survey contributions to demand theory from the writings of Gregory King and Charles Davenant through the contemporary period. As with excerpts from Shakespeare, one must make apologies not for what is included but rather for what is left out. In any event, a few caveats seem in order at the outset.

First, we have arbitrarily limited our coverage of demand theory to an (approximate) 300-year span beginning with the King–Davenant "law of demand." But utterances on demand (loosely defined, of course) are clearly evident in the writings of much earlier periods, among them, those of Greek, Roman, and medieval authors and pamphleteers.[1] As Professor Stigler puts the matter:

> The first recognition of an inverse relationship between the price and quantity of a commodity must have occurred thousands of years ago, and—to move somewhat closer to the present—the relationship has been known to every economist in the history of the science. [Stigler (1950) 1965, p. 213]

Yet, an investigation of primitive writers, while of genuine interest, is unlikely to yield many new insights into demand theory. It is probable that most primitive statements of the relationship between price and quantity demanded were (again to use Professor Stigler's apt description) "adventitious." Second, it is difficult to pinpoint, even within the range of this essay, the exact origin of scientific demand theory, i.e., the point at which the concept of demand is used as a tool to analyze consumer behavior as it relates to and influences (along with supply) price formation in practical or theoretical problems. Thus, many writers of the

1. Plato, for example, found the origin of the ideal State in needs, wants, and specialization which are manifest in the demand for goods. Identifying the basic wants and traditional necessities, Plato discussed how the "city will be able to supply this great demand." In doing so he presented what was perhaps the first coherent discussion of specialization and division of labor [Plato, pp. 60–65; Aristotle, bk. V, ser. 3]. In spite of Plato's incredible insights into the role of specialization, however, his concept of demand seems to be limited to a general and vague desire to purchase goods on the part of *individuals* comprising the polis. As such, Plato's treatment is of small interest as a tool of analysis. The same is true of the overwhelming majority of prenineteenth century writers on the subject.

English classical period covered in this essay are omitted, not because they did not consider demand (or supply), but because they presented confused and ambiguous treatments of the issue. Indeed, if the present essay were confined solely to demand theory of the "Marshallian" type, one would begin in 1838 with the writings of Cournot [Schumpeter 1954, p. 976; Fry and Ekelund 1971]. It would begin much later if one equated the origins of demand theory with *organized* and *cumulative* efforts to establish a body of theory dealing with consumer utility maximization and the attendant theory of demand [Stigler (1950) 1965, p. 213].

While either of these approaches might be defended, we prefer to focus upon a sample of individuals who were either possessed of analytic prevision in the area of demand or who contributed directly to "scientific" demand theory. Some of the writers we have selected are well known and others are relatively obscure. We are not concerned specifically with the early development of utility theory in the present essay. Professor Stigler's essay which chronicles utility theory has exhausted the topic [Stigler 1950]. Rather, we will concentrate on important attempts to establish a theory of demand with or without utility accouterments. Since the selection of contributors to be included in our essay is but one of many possible selections, we can but hope that our choices have produced a useful chronicle of the evolution of demand theory.

The Formative Period

The formative period of demand theory, for the purposes of this essay at least, extends roughly from the mercantilist period through the writings of Marshall's contemporaries. The term "formative" does not in any way imply that all of the writers considered here presented only tentative or incomplete formulations of demand. One could hardly consider Walras' treatment of demand primitive, for example. Rather, the term "formative" as used here has no other meaning than "pre-Marshallian" in time. Other nuances are neither intended nor implied.

Preclassical Contributions

The earliest statements of the "law of demand" were, without question, drawn from the observations of price and quantity relations of agricultural commodities. The relation between a "good" or a "bad" harvest and the market price of produce must have been known for many centuries. The incipient market system of the sixteenth and seventeenth centuries, together with the mercantilist fetish for improvement in the balance of trade and the increased emphasis upon accurate record keeping and data collection, must have increased the number of clear, even if adventitious, statements of the inverse relation between the quantity of a commodity *sold* and its price.

The best and most important example from the period of British mercantilism is that of the King-Davenant "law of demand."[2] "King's law," which was considerably refined by Davenant, appeared in Davenant's mercantilist treatise of 1699, *An Essay Upon the Probable Methods of Making a People Gainers in the Balance of Trade* [1771].[3] Davenant's version of the demand "law" follows:

> We take it, that a defect in the harvest may raise the price of corn in the following proportions:

Defect		above the common rate.
1 Tenth	raises the price	3 Tenths
2 Tenths		8 Tenths
3 Tenths		1.6 Tenths
4 Tenths		2.8 Tenths
5 Tenths		4.5 Tenths[4]

> So that when corn rises to treble the common rate, it may be presumed that we want above 1/3 of the common produce; and if we should want 5/10's, or half the common produce, the price would rise to near five times the common rate. [Davenant 1771, pp. 224–225]

King's actual statement of the demand relation was considerably less sophisticated, but it is clear that both Davenant and King were drawing upon observation of actual price and quantity behavior in their formulations.[5]

The Davenant-King statement is admirable in its clarity and it remains the best early statement of an inverse relation between price and quantity, but it is quite obviously simplistic either as demand theory or as an empirical demand curve. Neither King nor Davenant regarded the demand for corn as a function of

2. See the scholarly paper by G. Heberton Evans, Jr., [Evans, 1967].

3. We are not concerned with the *filiations* between King and Davenant on the issue of demand or with the related matter of priority in the statement of "King's Law." But Professor Evans has marshalled a convincing brief which places Davenant in a starring, rather than in a supporting, role to King on the issue of demand. After weighing the textual evidence, Evans concludes that ". . . it seems appropriate henceforth to refer to the 'King-Davenant Law of Demand' – or even the 'Davenant-King Law of Demand.' Perhaps on the basis of the above evidence some will want to go so far as to write of 'Davenant's Law of Demand' and to let King's fame rest upon contributions that are more clearly his" [Evans 1957, p. 492]. Given the evidence presented by Evans, we lean to the latter two alternatives.

4. As Evans points out, "the last three lines in the last column of Davenant's table must be read '1 and 6 tenths,' '2 and 8 tenths' and '4 and 5 tenths'" [Evans 1957, p. 489]. Yule made the point earlier, as noted by Evans [Yule 1915, p. 296].

5. King's statement did not appear in his *Natural and Political Observations and Conclusions upon the State and Condition of England* (1696), [see King (1696) 1936, p. 6]. His statement of the "law of demand" appeared in his working journal of 1696. King there noted that "in England if ȳ produce be but a 4th pt of its ordinary produce, the price will be 4 times its ordinary price." The important page [1936, p. 234] of King's working journal on which the statement appears is reproduced by Evans [Evans 1967, p. 487].

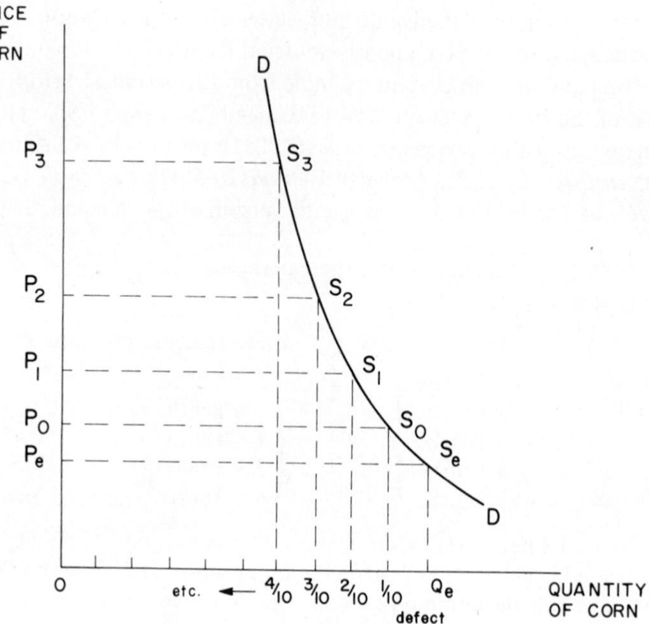

Figure 1-1.

income, wealth, and the price of other alimentary commodities. The Davenant-King "law of demand" is arrived at circuitously by considering either natural or contrived "defects" in supply. In functional terms, the Davenant-King formulation may be assessed as in Figure 1-1.

If P_e is the "common" or equilibrium price, it is apparent that, with defects in the normal harvest of corn, as in Figure 1-1, the price of corn rises. Thus, by inference, the Davenant-King formulation is *consistent* with the traditional negatively sloped demand curve. But the empirical information supplied by Davenant is also consistent with a demand curve consisting of the loci of supply-demand equilibrium points.[6] Although an inverse relation between price and quantity is posited by Davenant, the theoretical basis for such a proposition, as well as any concept of an *individual's* demand, as a tool for investigation, is entirely lacking. The Davenant-King law of demand (neither, of course, used the term) was, thus, empirically derived. Its importance for the evolution of demand theory rests in the not inconsiderable influence that King and Davenant exerted upon later writers [King (1696) 1936, pp. 6-7]. The "law" was a first step in the orientation of thought along lines vital to the development of a theoretical concept of demand.

6. Such a set of demand curves need not be negatively sloped, in addition.

Another early contribution to demand theory, that of Comte Pietro Verri (1728–1797), deserves special mention. Verri, in his *Meditazioni sull èconomia politica,* which was published five years before the appearance of Smith's *Wealth of Nations,* verbally posited a demand curve of specific form [Verri 1771]. Verrí's proposition is that quantity demanded is inversely proportional to changes in price [Manfra 1932, pp. 156–157]. The Italian mathematician, Paolo Frisi, gave Verri's proposition the algebraic form $pq = c$, where p = price, q = quantity, and c = a constant [Robertson 1949, p. 526].[7] The two-dimensional geometric representation is, of course, the hyperbolic demand curve of unit elasticity.

Although Verri did not speak of demand determinants or of other fundamental aspects of demand theory, his formulation appears to be the first clear expression. Further, he used the relation to condemn the monopoly of grain distribution and to support greater freedom in commerce [Robertson 1949, p. 526]. Verri, moreover, collected statistics on grain prices [Manfra 1932, pp. 129–134], from which he probably derived the theoretical demand curve expressed in his writings. Regardless of the source of his inspiration, however, Verri's concept of demand was, in its generality, definitely "above its time."

British Classical Contributions: Malthus and J. S. Mill

A glorious profusion of demand concepts existed in British classical writings on economics [Smith 1951, pp. 242–257]. Even a cursory review of those portions of Smith, Ricardo, James Mill, Senior, and others dealing with the topic reveals a confusion on definitions of the term. Most writers were neither consistent nor clear in their usage of the term within their own works. Senior's abstruse comments on demand are representative. In the *Outline* Senior notes that:

> . . . the force of the causes which give utility to a commodity is generally indicated by the word *Demand*. . . .
>
> Thus the common statement that commodities exchange in proportion to the Demand and Supply of each, means that they exchange in proportion to the force or weakness of the causes which give utility to them respectively and to the weakness or force of the obstacles by which they are respectively limited in supply.
>
> But though the vagueness with which the word Demand has been used renders it an objectionable term, it is too useful and concise to be given up; but we shall endeavour never to use it in any other signification than as expressing the utility of a commodity; or, what is the same, for we have seen that all utility is relative, the degree in which its possession is desired. [Senior 1836, pp. 14–15]

7. Robertson's formulation [Robertson 1949] of Verri's law of demand (after Frisi) differs somewhat from Schumpeter's [Schumpeter 1954, p. 307], which is used here.

Senior's statements are representative of the hopeless confusion in classical writings on demand. "Demand" to Senior seemed to connote a subjective degree of desire to possess a commodity, but he provided no framework in which to link utility with demand.[8] Absent from Senior, and other classical writers, is a clear distinction between the now-familiar force which changes quantity demanded (however labeled) and the factors underlying a change in demand (however labeled), or between demand as price-determining. The simple truth is that classical writers, with only several possible exceptions, were unable to extricate themselves from the terminological quagmire that surrounded the concept.

Malthus, as Schumpeter [1954, p. 602] suggested, may have been an exception. His rejection of Ricardo's explanation of value in terms of labor time and his disavowal of Say's Law may at least partially explain his interest in demand as an important determinant of value. Yet, Malthus' interest in demand is obvious in his earliest writings, including the *First Essay on Population* published in 1798. In the *First Essay's* diatribe against the Poor Laws, Malthus brought the efficacy of the transfer of funds from rich to poor into question. He argued:

> Suppose, that by a subscription of the rich, the eighteen pence a day which men earn now was made up five shillings, it might be imagined, perhaps, that they would then be able to live comfortably and have a piece of meat every day for their dinners. But this would be a very false conclusion. The transfer of three shillings and sixpence a day to every labourer would not increase the quantity of meat in the country. There is not at present enough for all to have a decent share. What would then be the consequence? The competition among the buyers in the market of meat would rapidly raise the price from six pence or seven pence, to two or three shillings in the pound, and the commodity would not be divided among many more than it is at present. [Malthus 1960, p. 30]

Thus, assuming an inelastic supply of meat, Malthus used demand analysis to demonstrate that the money price of meat would be driven up through the

8. Senior did not understand the role of diminishing marginal utility in demand theory or in price formation. A somewhat better understanding of utility theory was exhibited earlier by William F. Lloyd. E. R. A. Seligman advanced Lloyd's case as "the first thinker in any country to advance what is known today as the marginal theory of value" [Seligman 1903, p. 363]. Seligman's article is replete with quotations from Lloyd's "Lecture on the Notion of Value as Distinguishable Not Only from Utility, But Also from Value in Exchange" (delivered before the University of Oxford in Michaelmas Term, 1833). It is clear that Lloyd understood the fact that marginal satisfaction diminished with quantity, but little else can be said for his exposition. His ideas, verbally expressed, are disjointed and he presented no rigorous demonstration of them. Moreover, he did not relate his concept of diminishing marginal utility to demand, see [Stigler 1965, pp. 78–79; Gordon 1966].

operation of competitive forces.[9] Implicit in his explanation is a conception of demand as determined by money income and the number of purchasers in the market. By using a conception of shifting market demand price Malthus was able to demonstrate the futility of augmenting the incomes of the poor. Thus, although his formal definitions of demand did not appear until the *Principles* (1820), Malthus presented the concept with considerable lucidity more than twenty years earlier.[10]

In the *Principles* Malthus noted the imprecision with which the terms demand and supply are used and he proposed to clarify the concepts since ". . . of all the principles of political economy, there is none which bears so large a share in the phenomena which come under its consideration as the principle of supply and demand" [Malthus 1836, p. 61].[11]

At this point Malthus acknowledged that prices are formed by the relation between supply and demand. Changes in prices, moreover, are determined by changes in these relations. In order to discuss price formation he introduced the original concepts of "extent" and "intensity" of demand. Malthus noted that one correct use of the terms demand and supply–one which had been employed by previous writers–implied an equilibrium of quantity supplied and quantity demanded. As he noted:

> The actual *extent* of the demand, compared with the actual *extent* of the supply are always nearly equal to each other. If the supply be ever so small, the *extent* of the demand cannot be greater; and if the supply be ever so great, the *extent* of the demand will in most cases increase in proportion to the fall of price occasioned by the desire to sell, and the consumption will finally equal the production. It cannot, therefore, be in this sense that a change in the proportion of demand to supply takes place; because in this sense demand and supply always bear nearly the same relation to each other. [Malthus 1836, p. 62]

9. Malthus assumed a fixed resource supply for he noted that "If we can suppose the competition among the buyers of meat to continue long enough for a greater number of cattle to be reared annually, this could only be done at the expense of corn, which would be a very disadvantageous exchange . . ." [Malthus 1960, pp. 30–31]. He did admit that the increased demand would provide a goal to productive industry, but he argued that there would be counter balancing forces in the form of a wealth effect reducing the supply of labor [Malthus, 1960 p. 31].

10. In an essay published in 1800, *An Investigation of the Cause of the Present High Price of Provisions,* Malthus again argued against the poor laws using only a slightly more sophisticated analysis than in the *First Essay.* Malthus' *Investigation* is reprinted *en toto* in [Johnson 1949, pp. 190–202}. Smith correctly concludes that "the technical apparatus used in this argument . . . is clearly a rudimentary market demand schedule, the equivalent of that in Böhm-Bawerk's horse-market example" [Smith 1951, p. 248].

11. Quotations are taken from the 2nd edition of the *Principles:* Malthus' treatment of the issue in the second edition is essentially identical to that of the first (1820), see [Smith 1951, pp. 248–249]. Malthus was almost alone among the classical writers in emphasizing the importance of demand considerations in value formulation in both the long run and the short run.

Here Malthus is describing the equilibration of quantity demanded with quantity supplied, or in modern terms, the equilibrium quantity bought and sold determined by the intersection of supply and demand schedules. Assuming an "ever so great" quantity supplied of the commodity, the *extent* of demand (or quantity demanded) will be larger, with accompanying diminution in the price of the commodity, in order to achieve market clearance.

Malthus, however, thought that this conception of demand was an insufficient explanation of the determinants of demand and of price formation. He continued:

> Demand has been defined to be the will to purchase, combined with the means of purchasing.
>
> The greater is the degree of this will, and of these means of purchasing when directed to any particular commodity wanted, the greater or the more intense may be said to be the demand for it. But, however great this will and these means may be among the demanders of a commodity, none of them will be disposed to give a high price for it, if they can obtain it at a low one; and as long as the means and competition of the sellers continue to bring the quantity wanted to market at a low price, the whole intensity of the demand will not show itself.
>
> . . . if while money is considered as of the same value, certain commodities, either from scarcity, or the greater cost of production become more difficult of acquisition, as they will certainly not be acquired except by those who are willing and able to sacrifice a greater amount of money in order to obtain them, such a sacrifice, if made, must be considered as an evidence of greater intensity of demand.
>
> In fact, it may be said, that the giving a greater price for a commodity, while the difficulty of obtaining money remains the same, necessarily implies a greater intensity of demand; and that the real question is, what are the causes which determine the increase or diminution of this intensity of demand, which shows itself in a rise or fall of prices. [Malthus 1836, p. 63]

Thus Malthus introduces the concept of "intensity" of demand and it appears to have two meanings. At first Malthus is discussing an increased sacrifice on the part of certain demanders—the purchasing power of money assumed constant—in response to a reduction in the supply of a commodity due to an increase in scarcity or in costs of production. A change in supply induces a change in the quantity demanded of the commodity. "Intensity" in this sense connotes a movement along a demand schedule.[12]

But Malthus implied a second meaning to the term "intensity" when he noted that the "real question" concerning price formation is the investigation of

12. Demand (quantity demanded) is not here considered as directly price determined. Shifts in supply are the *cause* of change in quantity demanded. Thus Malthus was not describing a functional relation between price and quantity demanded.

the determinants of demand intensity. Here Malthus has demand shifts in mind, as the following quotation clearly indicates.

> It has been justly stated that the causes which tend to raise the price of any article estimated in some commodity named, and supposed, for short periods, not essentially to vary in the difficulty of its production, or the state of its supply compared with the demand, are, an increase in the number, wants, and means of the demanders, or a deficiency in the supply; and the causes which lower the price are a diminution in the number, wants, and means of the demanders, or an increased abundance in its supply.
>
> Now the first class of these causes is obviously calculated to call forth the expression of a greater intensity of demand, and the other of a less. [Malthus 1836, pp. 63-64].

Also, Malthus understood the distinction between *ex ante* and *ex post* conceptions of demand.[13]

His second conception of "intensity of demand" clearly approaches the modern concept of demand, and it amplifies the reasoning underlying his conception of demand shifts in the *First Essay* of 1798. His *ceteris paribus* assumptions include the number of purchasers, tastes (wants), and the means or income of the demanders. Not only did Malthus identify important parameters of the demand function, but he indicated (at least implicitly) that the demand-supply apparatus was to be understood in *real terms.* Although ambiguity remained in the concept of "intensity," Malthus must be credited, at the least, with the best explicit *theoretical* conception of demand among British classical writers of his period.[14]

John Stuart Mill, who also used purely verbal analysis, advanced the theory of demand on several fronts.[15] Mill recognized the necessity for simplification and abstraction in devising a manageable process for analyzing the functional

13. See [Malthus 1836, note, p. 64] and [Smith 1951, note 61, p. 250].

14. One result of Malthus' two conceptions of "intensity" is that so defined, as Smith points out, the concept "is incapable of distinguishing price-determining from price-determined changes in demand" [Smith 1951, p. 249]. Malthus also did not investigate demand theory from the individual's point of view; see Johnson's comments [Johnson 1949, pp. 190-191]. Yet his exposition was remarkable, especially in view of the fact that he did not employ quantitative tools.

15. It is difficult to agree, however, with Schumpeter's assessment that Mill's main contribution was "to develop the supply-and-demand analysis so fully that, as Marshall himself was to indicate, there remained not so very much to do beyond removing loose ends and adding rigor in order to arrive at something not far distant from Marshallian analysis" [Shumpeter 1954, p. 603]. The links which Marshall posited between utility and demand were certainly not derived from Mill, but rather from Dupuit, see [Ekelund and Gramm 1970, pp. 279-285]. Marshall's development of utility-based demand function was hardly a matter of simply "adding rigor" to Mill's discussion. In addition his use of mathematical functions, which Marshall derived from Cournot, was a considerable advance on Mill's method of presentation. Although Schumpeter seems to overstate the debt owed by Marshall to Mill he does note that Mill "did not achieve perfect clarity or in fact a complete and correct theory of supply and demand" [Schumpeter 1954, p. 603].

relation between price and quantity demanded. He noted, for example, that "in considering exchange value scientificially, it is expedient to abstract from it all causes except those which originate in the very commodity under consideration" [Mill 1965, pp. 438–439]. A concept of demand as a schedule showing a functional relationship between price and quantity demanded, given *ceteris paribus* assumptions, was the outcome of Mill's proposed method of abstraction. Noting the terminological confusion which had existed in previous writers, Mill sought to clarify the concept of demand and supply equilibrium:

> A ratio between demand and supply is only intelligible if by demand we mean quantity demanded, and if the ratio intended is that between the quantity demanded and the quantity supplied. But again, the quantity demanded is not a fixed quantity, even at the same time and place; it varies according to the value; if the thing is cheap, there is usually a demand for more of it than when it is dear. [Mill 1965, p. 446]

Mill's insistence that demand be understood as quantity demanded and that demand, thus defined, depended on value resulted in an abstract and schedular concept of demand which was a terminological improvement over that presented by Malthus.

Mill knew, however, that circular reasoning was involved if the term was improperly understood. It could be alleged that demand depended in part upon value, but that value was determined by demand. Mill's solution was to demonstrate that

> . . . the idea of a *ratio,* as between demand and supply, is out of place, and has no concern in the matter: the proper mathematical analogy is that of an *equation.* Demand and supply, the quantity demanded and the quantity supplied, will be made equal. If unequal at any moment, competition equalizes them, and the manner in which this is done is by an adjustment of the value. If the demand increases, the value rises; if the demand diminishes, the value falls: again, if the supply falls off, the value rises; and falls if the supply is increased. [Mill 1965, p. 448]

Mill thus broke the circularity contained in most early formulations of value and demand theory. If "demand increase (diminution)" is read as a rightward (leftward) *shift* in demand, Mill's compact statement is almost entirely analogous to modern explanations of the mechanics of price changes. Mill presents a perfectly adequate distinction between price-determined and price-determining changes in demand.

Despite the clarity of Mill's abstract conception of demand—and indeed his use of the term *ceteris paribus*—the exact parameters held constant when using a demand schedule are ambiguous. Mill explicitly notes the necessity for abstraction "from an alteration in public taste or in the number or wealth of the consumers" [Mill 1965, p. 445]. Thus it is clear that constant taste and wealth were two of Mill's parameters. Yet, he stated the assumption "that money itself

. . . not vary in its general purchasing power, but that the prices of all things, other than that which we happen to be considering, remain unaltered," without noting the inconsistency of the statement [Mill 1965, p. 439]. If the prices of all other goods remained unchanged and the price of the good under analysis varies, the general purchasing power of a given quantity of money cannot remain constant.[16]

Mill's formulation of a system of abstraction to analyze price-quantity relations, which enabled him to break the circuitousness of earlier arguments, was elegant and represented a clear advance in demand theory. It appears, in retrospect, to have been an even greater achievement in view of Mill's refusal to use mathematical tools to illumine his theory. Yet, Mill's performance was marred precisely because of his penchant for verbal analysis in preference to formal argument. Had Mill viewed demand as a precise specification, he might have been drawn to a theory of demand from the individual's point of view and thereby made more substantive contributions to demand analysis. Mill's development of the concept along with Malthus' earlier and less sophisticated attempt stand, however, as the best two statements of demand theory in the British classical literature, 1776-1848.

Some Continental Contributions: Say, Cournot, Dupuit, and Bordas

Nineteenth-century continental writers, it would seem, were especially inventive regarding economic theory and in forging tools in advance of their contemporaries in England.[17] As early as 1803 J. B. Say demonstrated an understanding of economic theory in general, and of demand theory in particular, which would compare most favorably with other economists of his period. In Book II of his *Treatise on Political Economy* Say sought to explain current price as "the only fair criterion of the value of an object" [Say 1803, p. 285]. Current price was described by Say as being dependent upon supply and demand, which originates in culturally determined wants. Wants, in Say's methodology, were to be taken as given. Say's scientific orientation is revealed in his discussion of wants and their role in demand analysis. He notes that

> The want or desire of [sic] any particular object depends upon the physical and moral constitution of man, the climate he may live in, the laws, customs, and manners of the particular society, in which he may

16. While there is some justification for Frank Knight's contention that J. S. Mill held real income constant in order to deal with relative prices in the formulation of demand schedule, support for both the constant money income and constant utility demand schedule interpretations can be found in Mill's text, see [Knight 1944, note 9, p. 299].

17. J. A. Schumpeter is reputed, perhaps apocryphally, to have once said that of *the* four great economic theorists, three were French: Quesnay, Cournot, and Walras. The fourth presumably was Marshall, see [Samuelson 1963, pp. 3-4].

> happen to be enrolled. He has wants, both corporeal and intellectual, social and individual; . . . It is not our business here to inquire, wherein these wants originate; we must take them as existing *data,* and reason upon them accordingly. [Say 1803, p. 285]

Utility, which Say understood as "usefulness," stood as the basis for demand and value, but Say thought that value could not exceed costs of production, for if it did, the consumer would produce the commodity in question for himself. In spite of his faulty analysis of utility [Rambaud 1909, pp. 282-283], Say linked utility to a concept of intensity of demand. As he noted:

> The Utility of a product is not confined to one human being, but applies to a whole class of society.
>
> Even the individual demand of a specific product for individual consumption may be more or less urgent. Whatever be its intensity, it may be called by the general name of demand; and the quantity attainable at a given time, and ready for the satisfaction of those who are in want of the specific article, may be called the supply or amount in circulation. [Say 1803, pp. 287–288; 1816, pp. 27–28]

But Say immediately qualified his remarks, noting thst some bounds must exist to demand. Demand (quantity demanded in a schedular sense) varied inversely with price and was related to the income and wealth of consumers:

> Wealth is, in all countries, distributed in every degree of gradation, from the populous level of mediocrity to the solitary pinnacle of extreme affluence. Accordingly, the products most generally desirable are really demanded by a limited number only, because they alone have wherewithal to obtain them; and even their ability may be more or less according to circumstances. Whence it may be further concluded, that the same product or products may be in greater demand at a lower scale of price, and when attainable by less productive exertion, although nowise increased in utility, merely because accessible to a greater number of consumers; and, on the contrary, less in demand at a higher scale of price, because accessible to a smaller number. [Say 1803, p. 288]

Thus, although the inverse relation between price and quantity is not established in a functional sense, Say appears to have had a grasp of the essential meaning of the "law of demand." Say supplemented his reason for the inverse relation by noting that given an increase in price, "not only is the number of consumers diminished, but the consumption of each consumer is reduced also" [Say 1803, p. 289]. Copious examples of the law are provided and Say concluded that

> . . . whatever be the general or particular causes, that operate to determine the relative intensity of supply and demand, it is that intensity, which

> is the ground-work of price on every act of exchange; for price, it will be remembered, is merely the current value estimated in money. The demand for all objects of pleasure, or utility, would be unlimited, did not the difficulty of attainment, or price, limit and circumscribe the supply. On the other hand, the supply would be infinite, were it not restricted by the same circumstance, the price, or difficulty of attainment: for there can be no limited quantity, so long as it could find purchasers at any price at all. Demand and supply are the opposite extremes of the beam, whence depend the scales of dearness and cheapness: the price is the point of equilibrium, where the momentum of the one ceases, and that of the other begins.
>
> This is the meaning of the assertion, that, at a given time and place, the price of a commodity rises in proportion to the increase of the demand and the decrease of the supply, and vice versa; or in other words, that the rise of price is in direct ratio to the demand, and inverse ratio to the supply. [Say 1803, p. 290]

The view of demand and supply as "opposite extremes of the beam" is reminiscent of Marshall's "pair of sizzers" analogy. Say's theory not only explains demand (quantity demanded) as price-determined, in a schedular sense, but it also explains price as the result of the forces of supply and demand.

Although Say, at several points, attempted to distinguish the concept of individual demand from the aggregate concept, he appears to do so without understanding the theoretical significance of the dichotomy. In addition, he did not provide a coherent discussion of the determinants of demand (excepting the wealth parameter) or of the relations between utility and consumer behavior or demand. His neglect and misuse of utility as a demand determinant stemmed from a belief, shared later by Cournot, that utility was an unscientific concept which was in the province of the "moral sciences." But, notwithstanding the tentative nature of his analysis of demand, Say's clear scientific conception of fundamental demand theory goes far in explaining the phenomenal advances made by his French successors, Cournot and Dupuit. It must be remembered, moreover, that it was not until Mill's *Principles* that demand theory progressed as far in England.

In 1838 Augustin Cournot published his *Recherches sur les Principes Mathematiques de la Theorie des Richesses,* which–in retrospect– revolutionized economics [Cournot 1960].[18] Cournot, with bold and unprecedented originality, introduced the differential and integral calculus into economic theory. In the process he fashioned the modern conception of the theory of the firm, not only in its competitive form, but for monopoly and duopoly environments as

18. A centennial reprint of the original *Recherches* has been published with an introduction by George Lutfulla (Paris: Revière, 1938). Page references are to the Bacon translation unless otherwise indicated. The interpretation of Cournot's demand curve contained in the present paper is essentially that found in [Fry and Ekelund 1971].

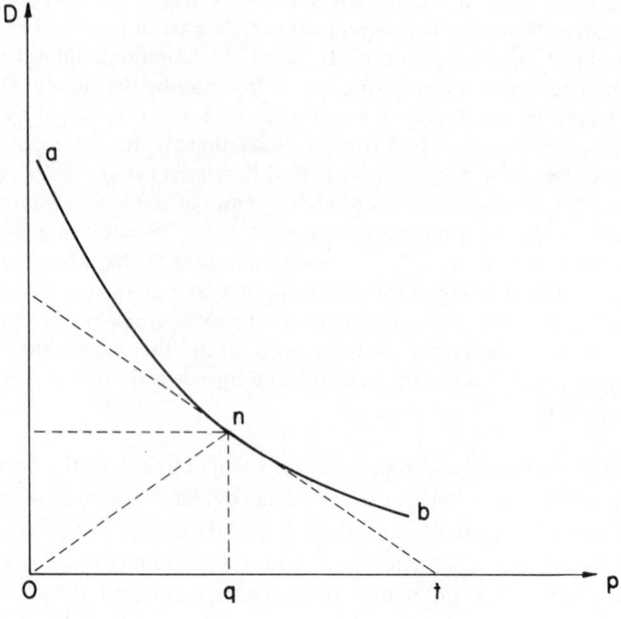

Figure 1-2.

well.[19] Underlying Cournot's analysis of firm behavior, however, is an amazing exposition of demand.

In 1838 Cournot drew a demand schedule (see Figure 1-2), but he gave it what was essentially an "empirical" definition. His *loi du débit* or "law of sales" was specified:

> Let us admit, therefore, that the sales or the annual demand D is, for each article, a particular function $F(p)$ of the price p of such article. To know the form of this function would be to know what we call *the law of demand* or *of sales.* [Cournot 1960, p. 47]

Cournot, in addition, defined his demand curve as negatively sloped, and

19 Modern theorists dealing with problems of imperfect competition often use Cournot's mineral springs model (with conjectural variation of zero) as their point of departure, see [Chamberlin 1948, pp. 32, 221–222]. William Fellner finds that it was Augustin Cournot's great achievement to have discovered the distinctive feature of the oligopoly problem. The distinctive feature to which Fellner refers is that the kind of assumptions one makes concerning rivals' reactions determines the kind of solution one obtains in any given problem, see [Fellner 1965, p. 56]. Until recently, it has been thought that Cournot's model yielded indeterminant results in the absence of an assumed conjectural variation of zero. But Irwin M. Grossack, in an interesting interpretation of the Cournot model, has shown that the "conjectural variation of zero" assumption can be dropped with the model still yielding determinant and plausible results [Grossack 1966].

assumed that the function was continuous throughout (see Figure 1-2).[20] Yet, as Walras and other writers have noted, Cournot adhered to an empirical as opposed to an explicit theoretical conception of demand [Walras 1954, p. 199; Roy 1933, pp. 13-22]. Cournot himself lucidly pointed out:

> Observation must . . . be depended on for furnishing the means of drawing up between proper limits a table of the corresponding values of *D* and *p*; after which, by the well-known methods of interpolation or by graphic processes, an empiric formula or a curve can be made to represent the function in question; and the solution of problems can be pushed as far as numerical applications. [Cournot 1960, p. 47]

The non-Marshallian character of Cournot's demand formulation is further revealed in Cournot's view of the role of utility in demand analysis. Cournot clearly eschewed considerations of utility as a basis for demand. As he observed:

> The abstract idea of *wealth* or of *value in exchange*, a definite idea, and consequently susceptible of rigorous treatment in combinations, must be carefully distinguished from the accessory ideas of utility, scarcity, and suitability to the needs and enjoyments of mankind, which the word *wealth* still suggests in common speech. These ideas are variable, and by nature indeterminant, and consequently ill suited for the foundation of a scientific theory. [Cournot 1960, p. 10]

Thus Cournot shared Say's opinion that utility was a "variable and indeterminant idea" and he disclaimed any opinions as to truth or error in discussions on the utilityof things. Although he was not entirely repelled by the inclusion of the word "utility" in the taxonomy of economic theory, as Say had been, Cournot knew that accurate cardinal measurement of "utility" could not be achieved. As he pointed out, "we only mean that generally neither truth nor error is capable of proof; that these are questions of valuation, and not soluble by calculation, nor by logical argument" [Cournot 1960, p. 11, note]. And, although Cournot identified utility as one of the determinants of demand when he noted that the law of demand "depends evidently on the kind of utility of the article" [Cournot 1960, p. 47], he did so with the understanding that there was neither a specified nor a quantifiable link between utility and demand. Indeed, there is no evidence that Cournot perceived of utility as meaning anything other than the standard classical interpretation of the term which was simply "usefulness."

Thus, given his remarks on utility, Cournot's demand curve cannot be strictly identified with Marshall's.[21] His explicit definition moreover, was empirical in nature. So much is clear from his textual specifications.

20. Cournot did note the possibility of a positively sloped function, however, but he seems to have been describing the "Veblen good", see [Cournot 1863, p. 95; Fry and Ekelund 1971].

21. Henry Schultz, for example, identifies a "Cournot-Marshall law of demand" [Schultz 1938, pp. 6–7] as does Schumpeter [Schumpeter 1954, p. 960].

It is possible nonetheless, and without reading very much into Cournot's actual remarks, to find a quasi-theoretical conception of demand in his writings. Cognizant of what would now be called the identification problem in the specification of empirical demand functions, Cournot establishes a set of *ceteris paribus* assumptions to be invoked when drawing up a demand function. In 1838, for example, he writes that the *loi du débit* depends on

> . . . the kind of utility of the article, on the nature of the services it can render or the enjoyments it can procure, on the habits and customs of the people, on the average wealth, and on the scale on which wealth is distributed. [Cournot 1960, p. 47]

In his 1863 work, *Principes de la Théorie des Richesses,* Cournot strengthened his development of demand parameters, noting that the law of demand

> . . . rests essentially on population, on the distribution of wealth, on general wellbeing, on tastes, on the habits of the consuming population, on the multiplication of markets, on the extension of the market resulting from transport improvements. All these conditions relative to demand remain the same; . . . If, . . . prices change because the law of demand has itself changed, due to a change in causes which no longer influence production but consumption, the construction of our tables will be made impossible since they must show how demand changes by virtue of a change in price and not by virtue of other causes. [Cournot 1863, p. 100]

Cournot, in order to have specified the determinants of the demand function as well as to have analyzed the effects of demand *shifts,* must have perceived some organizing principles. Cournot's demand specification, in other words, may be a prime example of Schumpeter's "pre-analytic vision."[22] It appears, at the very least, to have been a fascinating interation of inductive and deductive reasoning in the design of an economic theory

In whatever manner one interprets Cournot's specification of the demand function, however, it is clear that he *used* it as a *theoretical tool* to derive

22. In the Introduction to his *History of Economic Analysis* Schumpeter explained the process he called Vision. He noted that

> . . . in order to be able to posit to ourselves any problems at all, we should first have to visualize a distinct set of coherent phenomena as a worth-while object of our analytic efforts. In other words, analytic effort is of necessity preceded by a preanalytic cognitive act that supplies the raw material for the analytic effort. In this book, this preanalytic cognitive act will be called Vision.
>
> Analytic effort starts when we have conceived our vision of the set of phenomena that caught our interest, no matter whether this set lies in virgin soil or in land that had been cultivated before. The first task is to verbalize the vision or to conceptualize it in such a way that its elements take their places, with names attached to them that facilitate recognition and manipulation, in a more or less orderly schema or picture. [Schumpeter 1954, pp. 41–42].

Schumpeter's example is that of Keynes and the genesis of the *General Theory,* but a case could also be formulated for Cournot and the theory of the firm.

important and now well-known theorems concerning the competitive, monopolistic, and duopolistic firms. In addition, Cournot used a theoretical conception of demand to explain elasticity both mathematically and geometrically. As he argued:

> Since the function $pF(p)$ at first increases, and then decreases as p increases, there is therefore a value of p which makes this function a maximum, and which is given by the equation,
>
> $$F(p) + pF'(p) = 0 \tag{1.1}$$
>
> in which F, according to Lagrange's notation, denotes the differential coefficient of function F.
>
> If we lay out the curve *anb* [Figure 1-2], of which the abscissas Oq and the ordinates qn represent the variables p and D, the root of equation [1.1] will be the abscissa of the point n from which the triangle Ont, formed by the tangent nt and the radius vector On, is isosceles, so that we have $Oq = qt$. [Cournot 1960, p. 53]

Although the discussion of elasticity centered upon the theoretical aspects of the problem, and though he noted that it was "impossible to determine the function $F(p)$ empirically for each article," [Cournot 1960, p. 53], Cournot presented a lengthy discussion of the empirical problems faced by the firm attempting to maximize gross revenue. Indeed, he seemed to view the question of elasticity as *essentially* a statistical problem. He noted, for example, that "Commercial statistics should . . . be required to separate articles of high economic importance into two categories, according as their current prices are above or below the value which makes a maximum of $pF(p)$" [Cournot 1960, p. 54]. But, as with his explicit empirical specification of the demand function, Cournot's discussion of elasticity is marked by a felicitous blend of empiricism and theory.

Utility theory entered the theory of demand for the first time in the writings of Jules Dupuit, a French engineer and contemporary of Cournot.[23] Considerations of economic welfare and social well-being directed Jules Dupuit's attention to the study of political economy in the early 1840s. As chief engineer of bridges and highways, Dupuit required analytical tools which could give some

23. The economic writings of Dupuit are largely composed of journal contributions in the *Annales des Ponts et Chaussées* and in the *Journal des Economistes.* A collection of Dupuit's major articles (in French) was published in Italy under the editorship of Mario de Bernardi entitled *De l'Utilité et sa Mesure: Ecrits Choisis et Republies* [Dupuit 1934]. Two of these articles are in published translation: "On the Measurement of the Utility of Public Works" [Dupuit 1844] and "On Tolls and Transport Charges" [Dupuit 1849b]. Unpublished translations of other major economic works by Dupuit are available in the library of Louisiana State University, Baton Rouge. Dupuit's contributions to demand theory are given fuller treatment in [Ekelund and Gramm 1970].

measure of the desirability of all public projects. Moreover, the desire to devise tariffs and railroad rates for the "public good" led him into an investigation of political economy. The quest for sound public policy in these matters required an economic definition of, in his words, "the conditions which these [public] works must fulfill in order to be really useful" [Dupuit 1844, p. 83]. Dupuit, however, found contemporary economic theory wanting of such a measure and at the same time recognized that the key to the problem lay in the psychological concept of utility. Dupuit believed that all earlier utility theories were "vague, incomplete, and often inaccurate" [Dupuit 1844, p. 83], and consequently of little value in the measurement of public welfare. Accordingly, he reshaped the concept of utility into a tool of practical import.

Although the development of utility theory is not basically at issue here, it is important to note that Dupuit's discovery of the marginal principle as related to utility was the result of a dispute over the meaning that J. B. Say had ascribed to the term. Say treated utility as the faculty which things possess to be able to serve man in any possible way, and cited the example of the court mantle cloak (*manteau de cour*), to Say an apparently useless item, having utility *if* a price could be attached to it. Say thought further that "this price is the measure of the utility which men judge the thing to have . . ." and that "this price is the basis of the *demand* for products and consequently of their value" [Say quoted in Dupuit 1844, p. 83]. But Say thought that value could not exceed costs of production, for if it did, it would pay the consumer to produce it for himself. In sum, utility was the basis for demand and value, and price (or value in exchange) was a measure of utility. Say approved and accepted Smith's distinction between value in use and value in exchange, which amounted to asserting that *all* goods could not be treated under one theory of value. Water, in this familiar paradox, possessed much value in use, but no exchange value. Diamonds, on the other hand, had an abundance of exchange value, but were of little use. Say, attempting not to become embroiled in the confusion, noted that it would be preferable to reserve to the word "value" only the meaning implied by the phrase "value in exchange." He thought that the term "utility" was too capricious to use as a synonym for the word "value."

It is clear that Say thought that "real value," or value in exchange, was determined by costs of production and that the resultant market price was in fact a measure of the utility of that product. In this he followed the general notions of Adam Smith. But Say hastened to add that "one should not draw the absurd conclusion that, by raising the price by force, one increases . . . utility" [Dupuit 1853, pp. 6–7]. To illustrate, he used a wine-tax case in which he indicated that a tax of 5 cents (*sous*) per 10-cent bottle merely shifted 5 cents per bottle from the consumer or producer to the tax collector. Here Say regarded the 10 cents, or cost of production as the "real value" of the wine, and the 5 cents as contributing nothing to utility.

With respect to the wine-tax example, Dupuit readily accepted the fact that the 5 cents tax on wine added no utility to the product. But at the same time it was equally obvious to Dupuit that the product had to have at least 15 cents worth of utility, or the consumer simply would not buy wine. To substantiate this view, Dupuit invoked the fundamentals of consumers' surplus theory. To wit, with reference to the wine-tax example, he said that "all those who attach to the purchase of wine a value greater than 15 sous will buy, and will derive a kind of profit which will vary according to the significance which they put upon their acquisition" [Dupuit 1844, p. 85]. Thus, in arguing that market price and cost of production are not measures of utility, Dupuit arrived at his own measure—a measure not given by value in exchange, but by the *highest price* that one would offer for a quantity of a good. Carried to its logical end, this concept inevitably led Dupuit to the notion of *utilité relative* or "consumers' surplus," that is, that the difference between this *highest price* one would pay, and the price actually paid (value of exchange) for *fixed quantity* of output accrued to the consumer in the form of a surplus or net gain in satisfaction. The utility afforded by a product, thus conceived, is not measured by market price, as in Say's scheme, but it is related to maximum-offer price, and this maximum-offer price, to Dupuit, was determined by taste, income, and individual circumstances.

The fundamental relationship between marginal utility, total utility, and price are given repeatedly in Dupuit's writings [Dupuit 1853, p. 42]. It is clear from these examples and formulations that Dupuit understood the relationships between total and marginal utility. Total utility for any given quantity was the area under the marginal utility curve up to that quantity. If price is always equal to marginal utility, it follows that when price becomes zero, total utility is at a maximum and total revenue is zero. Dupuit was the first French economist, if not the *first* economist [Stigler (1950) 1965, pp. 78-79], to have clearly explained this relationship.

The marginal utility curve *is* Dupuit's *courbe de consommation,* and although most of his examples are concerned with transportation and communication, it is certain that the same laws applied to all goods and services. He provided explicit directions in his article on *Toll* on the manner in which a demand curve should be constructed:

> If, in a table of two columns, one inserts in the first all the prices, from 0, the one which corresponds to the greatest consumption, up to the price that stops all consumption and in the second, regarding the price, the corresponding quantity consumed, we will have the exact representation of what we call the law of consumption. [Dupuit 1852–1853, p. 8]

Dupuit neatly constructed such a demand curve in 1844, six years after Cournot's *Researches* was published. His construction, however, was apparently independent of Cournot's [Edgeworth 1923-1926, p. 654].[24] Like Cournot,

24. Additional corroboration on this point was given by René Roy in his centenary estimate of Cournot [Roy 1939, p. 143].

Dupuit gave the equation for the curve of consumption as

$$y = f(x),$$

or alternatively,

$$Q_d = f(p).$$

Additionally, Dupuit, as Walras was later to do, placed the independent variable (price) on the *x*-axis and the dependent variable (quantity) on the *y*-axis. Modern microeconomic diagrams, following Marshallian tradition, reverse this procedure because Marshall treated marginal demand price as a function of quantity. Dupuit's construction is reproduced as Figure 1-3. He described his construction as follows:

> If . . . along a line OP, Op', Op'' . . . represent various prices for an article, and that the verticals pn, $p'n'$, $p''n''$ . . . represent the number of articles consumed corresponding to these prices, then it is possible to construct a curve $Nn'n''P$ which we shall call the curve of consumption. ON represents the quantity consumed when the price is zero, and OP the price at which consumption falls to zero. [Dupuit 1844, p. 106]

It is obvious that this curve is conceptually identical to a marginal utility curve. Dupuit made his meaning clear, with reference to Figure 1-3, by stating that "the utility of . . . *np* articles is at least *OP* and . . . for almost all of them the

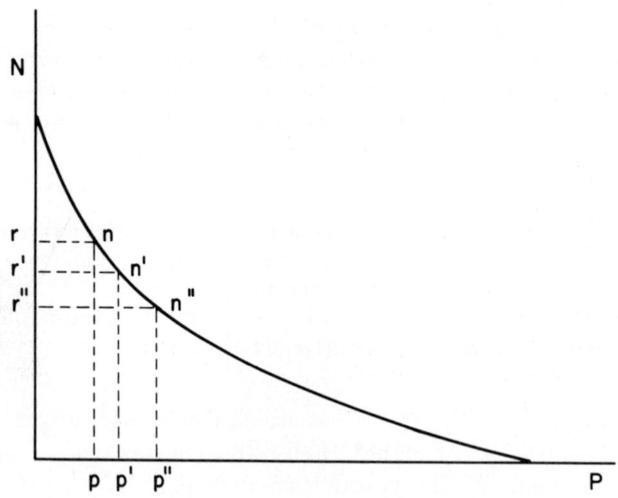

Figure 1-3.

utility is greater than *Op*" [Dupuit 1844, p. 106]. Since the relation between price and quantity is an inverse one, the demand curve drawn by Dupuit has a negative slope.

Dupuit considered total revenue by supposing that the demand curve in Figure 1-3 is one for a bridge. He then explained that if it is wished to raise a fixed sum of money (A), by levying a toll on the bridge it is necessary to solve the equation $xy = A$, where $y = f(x)$. He continued: "if it is wished to raise the greatest revenue, we must solve the equation $dyx/dx = 0$" [Dupuit 1844, p. 107]. Dupuit said that total revenue is at a maximum when marginal revenue is zero; alternatively, when the derivative of total revenue *with respect to price* is zero, total receipts are maximized.

It is important to collect some of the characteristics of Dupuit's demand curve and to consider some of the assumptions which he did (or did not) make in his construction as well.

1. Dupuit's demand curve was derived from observation. As chief engineer of bridges and highways, Dupuit observed an "operative" law of demand in all of his everyday activities. This was not new. Six years earlier Cournot had commented on the mathematical relationship between price and quantity demanded. But Dupuit's analysis was richer in the sense that he drew from his profession examples illustrating his theoretical contentions. He was under no illusion with respect to the problem of identification, however, since he candidly admitted that his "series of relationships [demand] is not known for any commodity since it depends on the volatile will of human beings; it is today no longer what it was yesterday" [Dupuit 1844, p. 103]. Thus he knew that the problem of obtaining an empirical function was compounded since the variables were constantly changing. But the demand curve was nevertheless a "fact of experience" to Dupuit "which has been verified statistically" [Dupuit 1844, p. 103].

2. Dupuit pushed demand theory toward Marshall's formulation by correctly distinguishing the law of marginal utility and by *identifying* the marginal utility curve with the demand curve itself. Additionally, Dupuit described the relation between total and marginal utility (demand) in tabular form.

3. Dupuit assumed that the price consumers would offer for a quantity of any good is determined by the *utility of that good alone* and not by the utility of other goods. Dupuit of course assumed that the utility function for the good could shift; for, he said, the demand curve "would not only be different for each bridge, each canal, each railway, each object but even different for the same bridge, the same canal, the same railroad and the same object with time which modifies use, habits, needs and caprices of man" [Dupuit 1852-1853, p. 9]. But nowhere did he indicate that the demand or marginal utility function might shift due to a change in the utility afforded by other goods in the consumer's collection. Consequently, it must be concluded that Dupuit assumed that all utility functions were independent (additive) since he gave no information to the contrary.

4. In a reply to criticisms made by M. Bordas, a fellow engineer [Bordas, 1847], Dupuit specified a number of demand *determinants* for a particular good.[25] Dupuit there included the following parameters in his *ceteris paribus* assumptions:

a. the wealth or income of the consumer;
b. the price of related commodities;
c. tastes or intensity of desire
d. and, implicitly, the constancy of the marginal utility of money.

Thus, given the set of explicit and implicit assumptions, Dupuit would be formally correct in identifying the demand curve with the marginal utility curve only in the case of a unitarily elastic demand function for all *independent* demands. All of his numerical examples, however, depicted demand curves of varying elasticity. The curves are more elastic in the upper reaches and less elastic in the lower portions. Moreover, if Dupuit were assuming unit elasticity ubiquitously, there would be little point in giving the condition $dxy/dx = 0$ for maximizing total revenue.[26]

Dupuit does not appear to have been aware of the results yielded by his assumptions and, in any case, chose to ignore their implications. His neglect of the logical ramifications of the budget constraint upon elasticity probably resulted from a primitive concept of elasticity. It is most likely that he sensed that in partial equilibrium analysis small price changes would have little effect on demand functions for other goods and on the marginal utility of money, and could thus be safely ignored. In short, he appears to have taken—at least implicitly—a Marshallian view of the matter.

Whatever Dupuit's intent on the matter of the specific relation between demand and utility, it is clear that demand theory (in the manner in which Marshall conceived of it) took a giant stride forward. The composite work of Cournot and Dupuit on demand theory represents a benchmark which was not to be surpassed in England for almost fifty years.

Another French engineer, M. Bordas, should be mentioned briefly in connection with the development of demand theory [Ekelund and Gramm, 1970, pp. 281-283]. Bordas, in a comment on Dupuit's 1844 paper, made what is probably the first reference to an "income effect" [Bordas, 1847, p. 16]. In the most important passage of the comment Bordas assumed that, because of a new

25. Dupuit's most complete specification of demand parameters is to be found in the first three sections of his "De l'Influence des Péages sur l'Utilité des Voies de Communication" [Dupuit 1849a]. The determinants specified in Dupuit's formulation of demand are considered in greater detail by [Ekelund and Gramm 1970, pp. 281-283].

26. It is easily shown that, given a demand curve of unitary elasticity, the total revenue function has a slope equal to zero.

process in the manufacture of stockings, the price of stockings falls from 6 francs to 3 francs. Bordas then suggests that if the buyer sets aside 24 francs a year in order to buy 4 pair when the price was 6 francs per pair, after the price decrease he will be able to buy 8 pair. However, as Bordas noted:

> In order to consume as many before, he would have been obliged to set aside a sum of 48 francs for the acquisition of this product, and to subtract 24 francs from his other consumptions. His situation, in relation to the former state of things, is then the same as though he were making an annual gain of 24 francs, or that his income had been increased by this sum. If, instead of consuming 8 pairs of stockings, he only consumed 7 and used the 3 francs left over to buy other objects of which the price would not have varied, his relative gain would not be more than 21 francs. [Bordas 1847, p. 16]

Bordas discovered that, with a constant money income, a consumer's real income increases with price declines. In the first part of the example the consumer chooses to receive the entire increase in real income in stockings. In the second example Bordas calculates the amount of the gains on stockings at 21 francs, but he points out that some of the real income increase may be realized by allocating expenditures in other directions, i.e., on other commodities.

Thus, Bordas presented an intuitive understanding of "income effect" for the individual consumer. His grasp, in 1847, of this fundamental concept places him among the earliest anticipators of the demand theory of J. R. Hicks and E. Slutsky.

Early Engineers and the Demand Function

Although the well-known British and American contemporaries of Say, Cournot, and Dupuit did not progress far in their analysis of demand, a subculture of economic literature was developing in the writings of professional engineers in the United States and in England. As with the writings of Cournot and Dupuit, the work of these individuals exerted little, if any, influence on the reigning economists of their day, although the tools they used to analyze economic questions were considerably more sophisticated than those of most first-rate academic or professional economists of the 1830s, 1840s, and 1850s. Use of the calculus and, more generally, a scientific view of fundamental economic relations was the hallmark of this literature, which included several important expositions of demand.

An American civil engineer, Charles Ellet, Jr., presented an advanced analysis of economic questions in 1839. In his *Essay on the Laws of Trade* [Ellet 1839] published in that year, Ellet applied the tools of calculus to the practical problems of monopoly profit maximization and to many other economic questions including duopoly and optimum intermodal rates between competing freight carriers.[27]

Ellet established a demand function as the foundation for his theory of the firm and revenue maximization. His best exposition of demand theory occurred in a discussion of the profit maximizing principles to be followed by a railroad carrying passenger traffic [Ellet, 1840].

Each passenger, in Ellet's view, will make a marginal cost-marginal revenue calculation in deciding whether to travel. In Ellet's terminology, a passenger will balance the opportunity and other "costs" of the journey against the "hope of gain."

> The profits of business, curiosity, or the prospect of pleasure, incites to embark on the voyage; and the *cost of the journey,* whether it consists of the value of his time, the importance of his personal attemtion to his home-affairs, the desire to yield to the dictates of indolence, or the amount of his traveling expenses, urges the party to remain. [Ellet 1840, p. 372]

The individual's decision will turn on whether the toll actually charged by the railway is below, equal to, or above the maximum price which–after all calculations, including the individual's means–the individual would be disposed to pay for the journey.

Among the large number of possible tariffs the hypothetical railroad company must select the profit maximizing rate. The demand function facing the firm is specified by Ellet:

> . . . Assume . . . that in every town on the line . . . there is a certain number of persons who can afford to make an excursion to some given point on the railroad . . . providing the cost of the trip shall not exceed a given sum. That there is another number that can afford to pay twice that amount–others three times that sum, and so on, until we arrive at the limit which would almost preclude traveling. . . . [Further] . . . it may be assumed that for every increase of the cost of reaching the point in question, the number of passengers will be diminished; and that the diminution of the number will be proportional to the augmentation of the cost. [Ellet 1840, p. 373]

Ellet thus presented a general specification for the demand function for traffic. He noted, however, that the question of profit maximization was too complex to be treated without the aid of mathematical analysis. Retaining his previous assumption of a linear relation between price and quantity demanded, he pre-

27. For a survey of Ellet's contributions to the theory of the monopoly firm see C. D. Calsoyas [Calsoyas 1950, pp. 162–170]. Ellet's interests included an immense range of topics and activities, including the design of the (then) largest suspension bridge in the world, see Gene D. Lewis's excellent biography [Lewis 1968].

sented an expression representing the *whole* number of passengers to make use of the line in functional terms:

$$T - \zeta h t \tag{1.2}$$

where T represents the total number of travelers at a zero toll; ζ represents the *gross* charge per mile on the railroad; h represents the distance under consideration and t represents a coefficient such that "for every increase of one cent in the charge, the number would be reduced some quantity," or further that "there are three times as many [passengers] who cannot afford to pay three dollars as there are of those who are unable to pay one—the number of persons excluded being directly as the sum which represents their grade" [Ellet 1840, p. 373].

Ellet's demand equation, then, can be stated in functional form as

$$q = f(p, h) \tag{1.3}$$

or conforming to his notation,

$$q = T - t(\zeta h) \tag{1.4}$$

where $t > 0$ is the constant slope of the function and ζh is the gross charge for any journey. When $\zeta = 0$, the total number of passengers carried equals T. Distance traversed, h, may of course relate to the toll, ζ, but if h is assumed to be a given journey (as between "Philadelphia and Baltimore"), a linear demand function for passage is generated.

Ellet, himself, raises an important objection to his demand function—that it assumes that the decrease in quantity demanded is proportional to an increase in ζ, i.e., that t is assumed to be constant.[28] In a discussion of a possible relation between ζ and t, Ellet acknowledged that the coefficient t would vary greatly at price extremes. His statement very nearly approaches a concept of elasticity:

> Indeed, it is probable that a given variation of the charge would produce very different values for the coefficient t, at the extreme limits of the sums designating the elevation of the grades. [Ellet 1840, p. 374]

Ellet's justification for neglecting variations in t was that the monopolist under analysis was assumed to be constrained by costs of production on the one hand, and by potential competition on the other. Within these not very well defined bounds, he noted, "it appears safe to assume that the *increase* or *decrease* of

28. If Ellet's numerical example is taken seriously and $t = 3$, his conclusion does indeed follow: there will be three times as many who will be excluded from passage at three dollars as will be excluded at one dollar.

travel (not the travel) will be proportional to the elevation or depression of the charges [Ellet 1840, p. 374].

Thus in analyzing profit maximization for passenger service on a hypothetical rail line Ellet developed a theoretical superstructure of demand theory. Although he did not relate utility to demand, his analysis identified wealth, tastes, and opportunity cost to the individual passengers as *ceteris paribus* assumptions in specifying his demand equation.

An early British engineer, along with Ellet, deserves mention in connection with demand theory. Perusal of Dionysius Lardner's *Railway Economy* [1850] can leave little doubt that Lardner's performance was just as Jevons [1957], p. xviii] described and perhaps even more.

Lardner's analysis including the graphics of profit maximization for the railway firm is not of direct interest here, although we might note that a negatively sloped demand function can be easily deduced from the bell-shaped total revenue function [Lardner 1850, p. 249]. But Lardner, as Ellet had done, supported his reasoning with mathematical arguments. Using goods traffic as his example, Lardner set out an algebraic analysis of the conditions for profit maximization. Lardner's demand function may be discussed in these terms: If, with Lardner, we let

r = the tariff imposed per mile on each ton of goods carried

D = the average distance in miles to which each ton of goods is carried

N = the number of tons booked

R = gross receipts from goods transport

then total receipts may be expressed as

$$R = NDr \tag{1.5}$$

The demand equation is, then, essentially identical with Ellet's. As Lardner specified:

> Any diminution of r (the tariff) must produce an increase either of D (the distance to which the traffic is carried), or of N (the quantity of traffic) or of both of these. [Lardner 1850, pp. 253–254]

Clearly, then, Lardner's demand function contains three mutually related variables, the tariff, distance, and the quantity of goods carried. Unlike Ellet, Lardner does not specify the form of the equation, but his function may be written in implicit form as

$$g(N, r, D) = 0 \tag{1.6}$$

or explicitly as

$$N = f(r, D) \quad \text{and} \quad \frac{\delta N}{\delta r} < 0; \frac{\delta N}{\delta D} < 0 \tag{1.7}$$

Thus Lardner's theoretical insight—coupled with a keen *practical* perception of detail—produced a useful and important tool of economic analysis. Although he neglected important demand parameters which had received varying degrees of attention by Cournot, Dupuit, and—to some extent—Ellet, the theoretical sophistication of his discussion seems noteworthy. As Schumpeter remarked, "The concepts [of supply and demand], so familiar to every beginner of our own days . . . proved unbelievably hard to discover" [Schumpeter 1954, p. 602]. Ellet and Lardner (and one might include Dupuit) were clear and important exceptions, at least in the area of demand analysis.

Jenkin and the Demand Curve (1870)

Fleeming Jenkin, in refuting W. T. Thornton's [1870] bizarre assault on the wages-fund theory and the laws of supply and demand, presented a persuasive, but wholly graphical, explanation of the principles of supply and demand [Jenkin 1870]. Jenkin, with graphical clarity, unlocks the circularity of many previous discussions of price determination. He defines demand at a price as "the *quantity* which, then and there, buyers would purchase at that price." He says, further, that both demand and supply "may be said to be functions of price" [Jenkin 1870, p. 77]. "Supply at a price" is defined similarly. Equilibrium price is graphically established by Jenkin and the explanation of its establishment by competitive forces would compare favorably with any modern textbook discussion of the subject.

An interesting facet of Jenkin's discussion results from his view of supply and demand in a real market situation (wheat trading). Jenkin assumes that an equilibrium is established in the market for wheat. In terms of the dashed supply and demand curves of Figure 1-4, s* represents equilibrium price and q* represents the equilibrium quantity of wheat traded. *After* the market has cleared itself, in Jenkin's example, the demand and supply curves for wheat appear as the solid functions in Figure 1-4. "Whole supply" is regarded to be the *whole* quantity to be offered for sale, which, as Jenkin notes, is a measurable quantity. Thus, in Figure 1-4 Jenkin has described a situation of zero excess demand and supply for wheat. His "demand at the conclusion of sales" is a primitive concept of a positive excess demand for wheat at prices below equilibrium.

While Jenkin takes great pains to distinguish between changes in quantity demanded and changes in demand, the parameters he identifies as causing shifts in the demand function are nebulous. He notes, for instance, that:

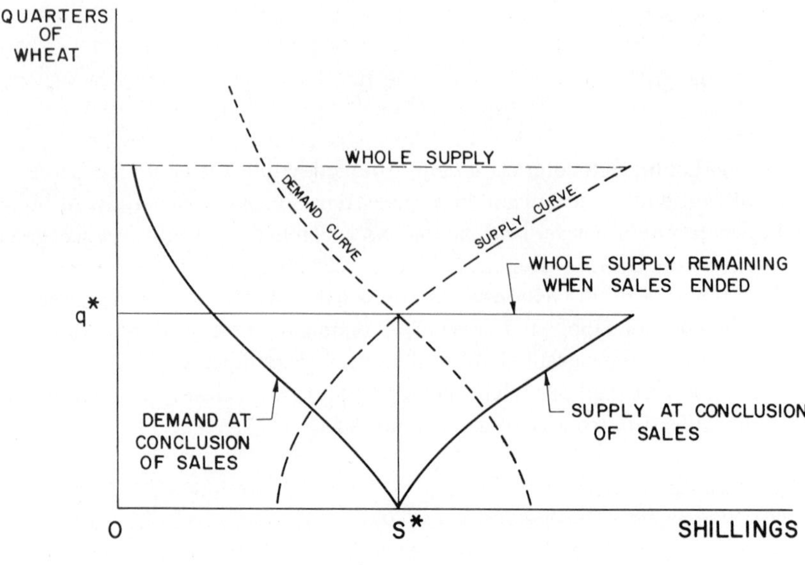

Figure 1-4.

> . . . the demand curve has a limit, which in this case is a limit at each price. The funds available for purchase at any price are limited, and this, which may be called the purchase fund, at each price limits the possible demand . . . the whole supply in the market may be constant, and the funds available to support demand may be constant, yet the market price of the commodity may vary immensely, as men's minds vary. [Jenkin 1870, pp. 79–80]

Thus, Jenkin identifies price of the good, a purchase fund *for the good in question* and the condition of "men's mind" as parameters of the demand function. Clearly Jenkin's aggregated "purchase fund" for a single good is ambiguous. Expenditures devoted by the individual demander to the purchase of any single good must be determined simultaneously with expenditures on all other goods, given an income constraint. Since Jenkin refers neither to the existence of other goods nor to an income constraint, his aggregated "purchase fund" has no analytical value.

The "condition of men's mind" parameter, moreover, has small theoretical merit. Although Jenkin does acknowledge that demand curves will vary "with every cause which can affect the desire of men for the article in question" [Jenkin 1870, p. 87], his discussion never penetrates to the nature of these causes. A large *portmanteau* variable is of course acceptable and useful in dealing with demand functions, but it must be accompanied by other explicit and important parameters which nowhere appear in Jenkin's essay. For these reasons it appears that Jenkin's *theoretical statement* of the demand function does not surpass earlier expositions in completeness or in importance. Jenki does allude, however, to the concept of elasticity: He notes the importance of whether "the curve be nearly horizontal—the total demand being little affected by price—or whether it is sharply inclined, showing that the demand increases rapidly as price is lowered, and *vice versa*" [Jenkin 1870, p. 90]. Although the possibilities of establishing statistical demand curves is also suggested by Jenkin, he, like Cournot, appeared to have been unaware of the problem of identification in dealing with these functions. Certainly Jenkin's penchant for graphical exposition of economic principles influenced both Jevons and Marshall [1961, note 1, p. 394]; and his essay remains at least for its day, a benchmark in the development of the graphics of partial equilibrium price analysis in England.

Marshall's Contemporaries on Demand

A minority of Marshall's contemporaries, notably the three leading members of the Austrian School (Carl Menger, Friedrich von Wieser and Eügen von Böhm-Bawerk) and W. S. Jevons, did not seek to apply the then-current speculations on consumer behavior to the theory of demand.

Although W. S. Jevons pioneered in the area of utility theory and in the rise of the mathematical method, he never ventured into demand or firm theory per se. (The same may be said of Gossen with respect to utility theory.) Jevons' neglect of demand and supply theory is all the more curious in view of the fact that he, more than any of his contemporaries, sought out the work of his predecessors [see the preface to the 2nd edition of *The Theory of Political Economy*, 1957]. Robertson attributes these gaps in Jevons' analysis to the fact that he considered "work of the sort performed by Lardner and Jenkin as being simply descriptive, as being in the area of applied economics rather than the legitimate subject matter of pure theory" [Robertson 1951, p. 248].

Another and far larger international group of economic theorists were directly concerned with the development of demand theory, among them, Velfredo Pareto; Rudolph Auspitz and Richard Lieben; Leon Walras; Maffeo Pantaleoni and Francis Y. Edgeworth. Within this period, for example, we find the invention of indifference curves [Edgeworth 1881], as well as the use of indifference curves in the establishment of conditions for consumer optimization [Pareto 1927]. In addition to the writings of Edgeworth and Pareto, an elegant approach to general equilibrium in consumption was being developed by Léon Walras and partial equilibrium analysis was undergoing further refinements at the hands of Pantaleoni, Auspitz and Lieben, and others. Space unfortunately constrains the present discussion to a sample composed of these latter writers.

Léon Walras: Demand and General Equilibrium. In 1874, merely four years after Jenkin's graphic exposition of supply and demand curves in partial equilibrium analysis, Léon Walras' *Elements D'Economie Politique Pure* appeared. The book, as history has shown, was unmatched for sheer originality and depth of economic understanding. Demand theory was among the many concepts boldly altered by Walras' conception of general equilibrium. Partial equilibrium demand analysis, while of great usefulness in analyzing some questions, was, according to Walras, ill conceived by the majority of its formulators.[29] Rather, Walras chose to build an interrelated system of demand relations from a simplified model of effective offer and demand. In the m-commodity case as in the 2- and 3-commodity cases, every individual is assumed to maximize a utility function which assumes diminishing marginal utility, and to possess a fixed quantity of a commodity $(A, B, C, D, \ldots, m)$ to trade. Total quantities of $A, B, C, D, \ldots, m$, both before and after exchange, are assumed to be fixed. The demand functions of an individual offering a quantity determined by the conditions of "maximum satisfaction" of commodity B in trade for other goods may then be represented by a set of equations:

$$
\begin{aligned}
d_{a,b} &= f_{a,b}(p_{a,b}, p_{c,b}, p_{d,b}, \ldots) \\
d_{c,b} &= f_{c,b}(p_{a,b}, p_{c,b}, p_{d,b}, \ldots) \\
d_{d,b} &= f_{d,b}(p_{a,b}, p_{c,b}, p_{d,b}, \ldots) \\
&\cdots\cdots\cdots\cdots\cdots\cdots \\
d_{m,b} &= f_{n,b}(p_{a,b}, p_{c,b}, p_{d,b}, \ldots) \qquad (1.8)
\end{aligned}
$$

The demand of an individual for each good, therefore, is a function not only of the price of the good in question, but of the price of all goods traded (in terms of good b). By summing up the equations of individual demand, we obtain $m - 1$ equations of "effective demand" for each separate good in terms of the good traded. In terms of the exchanged good A:

$$
\begin{aligned}
D_{b,a} &= F_{b,a}(p_{b,a}, p_{c,a}, p_{d,a}, \ldots) \\
D_{c,a} &= F_{c,a}(p_{b,a}, p_{c,a}, p_{d,a}, \ldots) \\
D_{d,a} &= F_{d,a}(p_{b,a}, p_{c,a}, p_{d,a}, \ldots) \\
&\cdots\cdots\cdots\cdots\cdots\cdots \qquad (1.9a)
\end{aligned}
$$

29. In the course of his review of *Untersuchungen über die Theorie des Preises* [Auspitz and Lieben 1889] in which Auspitz and Lieben develop a theory of partial equilibrium similar to that presented by Dupuit, Marshall, and Cournot, Walras insisted that "these two curves [partial equilibrium demand and supply] cannot serve as a starting point for a complete and rigorously exact theory of the determination of prices" [Walras 1954, p. 488].

In terms of good B, the $m - 1$ equations are

$$D_{a,b} = F_{a,b}(p_{a,b}, p_{c,b}, p_{d,b}, \ldots)$$

$$D_{c,b} = F_{c,b}(p_{a,b}, p_{c,b}, p_{d,b}, \ldots)$$

$$D_{d,b} = F_{d,b}(p_{a,b}, p_{c,b}, p_{d,b}, \ldots)$$

$$\ldots\ldots\ldots\ldots\ldots\ldots \qquad (1.9b)$$

There are, in short, $m - 1$ equations of effective demand for *each* of the m commodities considered two at a time or $m(m - 1)$ demand equations in all.

There are, in addition, $m - 1$ equations of exchange (or equilibrium equations) for each of the m commodities in terms of all other commodities. For equilibrium, in other words, the effective offer of, say, commodity A in terms of B must be equal to the effective demand for B in terms of A multiplied by the price of B in terms of A, and so on. The $m - 1$ equations of exchange of A for $B, C, D, \ldots$ may be written:

$$D_{a,b} = D_{b,a}p_{b,a} \qquad D_{a,c} = D_{c,a}p_{c,a} \qquad D_{a,d} = D_{d,a}p_{d,a} \qquad (1.10a)$$

The $m - 1$ equations of exchange of B for $A, C, D, \ldots$ are

$$D_{b,a} = D_{a,b}p_{a,b} \qquad D_{b,c} = D_{c,b}p_{c,b} \qquad D_{b,d} = D_{d,b}p_{d,b} \qquad (1.10b)$$

and so on. The $m(m - 1)$ equations of exchange when added to the $m(m - 1)$ equations of effective demand yield a total of $2m(m - 1)$ equations, which, as Walras notes, "connect precisely $2m(m - 1)$ unknowns, for there are $m(m - 1)$ total quantities exchanged when the m commodities are considered two at a time" [Walras 1954, p. 157].

In order to make the equilibrium described by the demand and exchange equation systems general, however, an additional condition must be satisfied. The condition required is that the price of either one or any two randomly chosen commodities expressed in terms of the other be equal to the ratio of the prices of each of these two commodities in terms of any third commodity. Arbitrage, in other words, is effectively ruled out by the following set of equations.

$$p_{a,b} = \frac{1}{p_{b,a}}, \qquad p_{c,b} = \frac{p_{c,a}}{p_{b,a}} \qquad p_{d,b} = \frac{p_{d,a}}{p_{b,a}} \qquad \ldots$$

$$p_{a,c} = \frac{1}{p_{c,a}} \qquad p_{b,c} = \frac{p_{b,a}}{p_{c,a}} \qquad p_{d,c} = \frac{p_{d,a}}{p_{c,a}} \qquad \ldots$$

$$p_{d,d} = \frac{1}{p_{d,a}} \qquad p_{b,d} = \frac{p_{b,a}}{p_{d,a}} \qquad p_{c,d} = \frac{p_{c,a}}{p_{d,a}} \qquad \ldots$$

$$\cdots\cdots\cdots\cdots\cdots\cdots \qquad (1.11)$$

These general equilibrium equations number $(m - 1)(m - 1)$ and implicitly contain $m(m - 1)/2$ equations expressing the reciprocal relationship between prices [Walras 1954, p. 161]. The commodity A serves the function of *numéraire.*

To reduce the number of equations in the equations of exchange which express the equality between offer and demand for each commodity traded, Walras establishes equations "expressing equality between the demand and offer of each commodity in terms of and in exchange for all the other commodities taken together," or in m equations:

$$D_{a,b} + D_{a,c} + D_{a,d} + \ldots = D_{b,a}p_{b,a} + D_{c,a}p_{c,a} + D_{d,a}p_{d,a} + \ldots$$

$$D_{b,a} + D_{b,c} + D_{b,d} + \ldots = D_{a,b}p_{a,b} + D_{c,b}p_{c,b} + D_{d,b}p_{d,b} + \ldots$$

$$D_{c,a} + D_{c,b} + D_{c,d} + \ldots = D_{a,c}p_{a,c} + D_{b,c}p_{b,c} + D_{d,c}p_{d,c} + \ldots$$

$$\cdots\cdots\cdots\cdots\cdots\cdots \qquad (1.12)$$

By expressing the prices of $B, C, D, \ldots$ in terms of A (the *numéraire*) p_b, p_c, $p_d, \ldots$, and by inserting the prices found in the general equilibrium equations in the above system, one obtains

$$D_{a,b} + D_{a,c} + D_{a,d} + \ldots = D_{b,a}p_b + D_{c,a}p_c + D_{d,d}p_d + \ldots$$

$$D_{b,a} + D_{b,c} + D_{b,d} + \ldots = D_{a,b}\frac{1}{p_b} + D_{c,b}\frac{p_c}{p_b} + D_{d,b}\frac{p_d}{p_b} + \ldots$$

$$D_{c,a} + D_{c,b} + D_{c,d} + \ldots = D_{a,c}\frac{1}{p_c} + D_{b,c}\frac{p_b}{p_c} + D_{d,c}\frac{p_d}{p_c} + \ldots$$

$$\cdots\cdots\cdots\cdots\cdots\cdots \qquad (1.13)$$

By algebraic manipulation [Walras 1954, p. 162, n. 8; p. 515], the first equation may be deleted from the above system yielding $(m - 1)$ equations of exchange. Adding the $(m - 1)$ equations of exchange to the $m(m - 1)$ demand equations and to the $(m - 1)(m - 1)$ general equations, a total of $2m(m - 1)$ equations are obtained. The roots of $2m(m - 1)$ equations are $m(m - 1)$ prices of m commodities and $m(m - 1)$ quantities of the m commodities exchanged. Thus, given fixed quantities, a constrained equality between offer and demand and the demand and offer functions for commodities, a set of equilibrium prices are established.

The relations between utility functions and demand functions are also demonstrated by Walras [Walras 1954, pp. 166–169]. Using one commodity (say A) as *numéraire* Walras demonstrates that maximum satisfaction is obtained by an individual when the ratio of the *raretés* (marginal utilities) of all the non-*numéraire* commodities held by the individual to the *rareté* of the commodity so used are equal to the prices of the non-*numéraire* commodities. In familiar definitional terms, maximum satisfaction is achieved when

$$\frac{r_b}{r_a} \equiv \frac{MU_b}{MU_a} = p_b \qquad \frac{r_c}{r_a} \equiv \frac{MU_c}{MU_a} = p_c \qquad \ldots \tag{1.14}$$

where the r's represent the *raretés* of the commodities.

For an individual who holds *several* commodities, the relation between the *raretés* and the separate demand functions can be developed assuming that his utility functions and original stocks of the separate commodities are known. Let the individual hold q_a of A, q_b of B, q_c of C, . . . and

$$r = \phi_a(q), \qquad r = \phi_b(q), \qquad r = \phi_c(q), \qquad \ldots$$

represent the separate utility or "want" functions for commodities A, B, C. . . . Let $p_b, p_c, p_d, \ldots$ be the commodity prices in terms of A, the *numéraire*, and let $x, y, z, w, \ldots$ be the quantities of $A, B, C, D, \ldots$ which the individual will add to q_a, q_b, q_c, q_d at prices $p_b, p_c, p_d, \ldots$. Quantities $x, y, z, w, \ldots$ may be positive or negative, but the individual faces the following equation.

$$x + yp_b + zp_c + wp_d + \ldots = 0 \tag{1.15}$$

Assuming maximum satisfaction to have been achieved, these quantities $(x, y, z, w, \ldots)$ will be related by the following $(m - 1)$ equations.

$$\begin{aligned}
\phi_b(q_b + y) &= p_b\phi_a(q_a + x) \\
\phi_c(q_c + z) &= p_c\phi_a(q_a + x) \\
\phi_d(q_d + w) &= p_d\phi_a(q_a + x) \\
\ldots\ldots\ldots&\ldots\ldots\ldots
\end{aligned} \tag{1.16}$$

The individual demand or offer for commodities *B, C, D,* . . . may be derived from the above m equations, i.e.,

$$
\begin{aligned}
y &= f_b(p_b, p_c, p_d, \ldots) \\
z &= f_c(p_b, p_c, p_d, \ldots) \\
w &= f_d(p_b, p_c, p_d, \ldots) \\
&\ldots\ldots\ldots\ldots\ldots\ldots
\end{aligned} \tag{1.17}
$$

and the demand or offer equation for the *numéraire* (A) is given as

$$x = -(yp_b + zp_c + wp_d + \ldots) \tag{1.18}$$

In addition to demonstrating the relation between *rareté* and demand for one individual Walras established the conditions under which prices and quantities in a system of m individuals are determinate, given the normal assumptions concerning the properties of utility functions [Wald 1936; Patinkin 1949]. Moreover, Walras shows the relation between the general equilibrium demand equations and the traditional "partial equilibrium" concept. A demand or "purchase" curve is generated for a new product which depicts quantity demanded in exchange for the *numéraire* [Walras 1954, pp. 194-196, 198-199]. Walras, however, seriously doubted whether the introduction of a new commodity or a change in the price of one already in existence would leave the equilibrium prices and quantities–including the one under consideraton–unchanged, especially if the commodity considered had close substitutes and complements. His indictment of the demand concepts of Dupuit and, especially, of Marshall [Walras 1965, letters 915 and 1051] exemplifies his view that demand curves could not be derived in simple fashion from utility functions. The foundation of economic theory including demand theory, in other words, required the inclusion of all the numerous variables affecting economic decisions and behavior. In Walras' view the methods used by earlier writers, as well as by his contemporaries, were at best approximations.

Pantaleoni, Auspitz, and Lieben: Demand Theory in 1889. In 1889, on the eve of the publication of Marshall's *Principles,* the prevailing exposition of demand theory was not that of Walras. In spite of Walras' criticisms, a number of continental economists were developing a partial equilibrium theory of price.

Empirical and theoretical aspects of demand, moreover, were being investigated by the French engineers of the Ecole des Ponts et Chaussées.[30]

The expositions of Maffeo Pantaleoni and of Rudolph Auspitz and Richard Lieben are typical of the period. The Italian Pantaleoni had read and was greatly influenced by Marshall's privately circulated *Pure Theory of Domestic Values* and *Pure Theory of Foreign Trade* (1879) and by the writings of W. S. Jevons. In his *Pure Economics* Pantaleoni identified the "law of demand" with the "scale of degrees of utility of a commodity" [Pantaleoni 1889, p. 166], although he did not draw welfare inferences from the identity.

Given that the law of demand remains constant, a "reduction in price renders the commodity accessible to more consumers, whilst a rise renders it accessible to fewer" [Pantaleoni 1889, p. 166]. Pantaleoni, in addition, investigated properties of the partial equilibrium conditions of supply and demand graphically. With great care, he set out the stability conditions for simple supply and demand equilibrium together with the rudiments of the theory of simple exchange based upon utility theory. Obviously under the influence of Marshall's graphic analysis of "offer curves" in international trade, Pantaleoni presented a technically sound and meticulous analysis of reciprocal demand between markets, including the necessary conditions for stability in the two-market, two-commodity case [Pantaleoni 1889, pp. 197–209]. Though not of great originality in view of its heavy dependence upon Marshall and Jevons' earlier treatment of utility and demand, Pantaleoni's scientific analysis of value theory was an important achievement in the development of partial equilibrium demand theory. Although the demand determinants of Marshall's *Principles* were more complete, Pantaleoni's presentation was more orderly. A penchant for theoretical nuance is evident throughout the *Pure Economics.*

Another important advance in demand theory was made in 1889 by two Austrian writers, Rudolf Auspitz and Richard Lieben, who published in that year their *Untersuchungen über die Theorie des Preises* [1889]. Auspitz and Lieben's book, as R. W. Houghton [Houghton 1958, p. 54] has noted, owed no debt to Marshall. Rather, it appears to have been a direct extension of Dupuit's discussion of demand and consumer surplus [Auspitz and Lieben 1889, p. xv]. Auspitz and Lieben, as did Dupuit, identified the demand curve with a utility function. Parameters to be held constant are more completely stated, however, in the *Untersuchungen* than in Dupuit's papers [Auspitz and Lieben 1889, pp. 5-16, 41-59]. Specifically, Auspitz and Lieben assumed that tastes, the prices of

30. Two French writers are of interest in connection with demand analysis. Emile Cheysson developed an econometric approach to demand similar in some respects to that discussed by Cournot [see Cheysson 1887; Hebert, 1970, pp. 86–91]. Clément Colson, who taught at the Ecole des Ponts et Chaussées, presented a theoretical analysis of demand in the manner of Dupuit, [see Colson 1901, p. 223].

related commodities, and the marginal utility of money are to be held constant in drawing up the demand curve for an individual good. Employing a rather bizarre diagrammatic technique, Auspitz and Lieben arrived at all of the familiar conclusions of partial equilibrium value theory. Their analysis and measurement of consumer surplus, moreover, as has been noted elsewhere [Houghton 1958, pp. 55-57], was considerably more general than that found in Marshall's *Principles.* Although the Auspitz-Lieben exposition of demand constituted a first-rate theoretical performance, the *Untersuchungen* had little impact on economic theorists of the day. The prime reason for the neglect, of course, was the appearance and tremendous influence of Marshall's *Principles.*

2 Demand Theory in Marshall's Tradition

As all western art is divided at Botticelli, so all demand theory is divided at Marshall. The importance and completeness of Marshall's demand curve is attested to by Hicks' statement that

> Marshall . . . remains classic; almost everything which Marshall says in his Book III retains its validity and requires, in some form or other, to be kept and the things which Marshall said were the really important things. . . . We have come, in some ways, to talk a different language; but the substance of what we have to say, over a central part of the field, is the same as what Marshall said. [Hicks 1956, pp. 1–2]

Marshall's work on demand theory is at once the first complete work and perhaps the last "primitive" work. The parameters held constant in the formulation of the demand curve are dispersed throughout his expositions; much of his theoretical framework is implicit; and the analysis of demand must be gleaned from general discussion and statements of "folk wisdom." The French were clearly more scientific in their expositions, while Marshall was more complete. Though demand theory was hardly born with Marshall much of that which has been passed on has come through Marshall. Yet it is also true that much of what Marshall originated or refined has not been carried over into modern literature. In extending and elaborating on Marshall's concepts, the literature has frequently glossed over important ideas. The legitimate function of historians of economic thought is to call attention to the neglected elements and assess them in light of more recent discoveries and methods.

The System of Abstraction

Marshall devoted a large portion of his writings to the analysis of demand. He attributed the prominence of demand theory in his study of economics to the following factors.

> (1) The growing belief that harm was done by Ricardo's habit of laying disproportionate stress on the side of cost of production, when analyzing the causes that determine exchange value.
>
> (2) The growth of exact habits of thought in economics is making people more careful to state distinctly the premises on which they reason.

> (3) The spirit of the age induces a closer attention to the question whether our increasing wealth may not be made to go further than it does in promoting the general wellbeing. [Marshall 1920, p. 84]

The methodological framework for Marshall's *ceteris paribus* assumptions in the construction of the demand curve is explicit.

> . . . we reduce to inaction all other forces by the phrase "other things being equal." We do not suppose that they are inert: but for the time we ignore their activity. This scientific device is a great deal older than science: it is the method by which, consciously or unconsciously, sensible men have dealt from time immemorial with every difficult problem of ordinary life. [Marshall 1961, p. 44]

While Marshall's schedule formulation and system of abstraction are clear, the variables he held constant in his list of "other things" are found only by assembling relevant passages from his texts, graphs, footnotes, and sections of his mathematical appendexes.

No other parameter of Marshall's demand curve receives so much attention as does time. To Marshall "time" is "the source of many of the greatest difficulties in economics" [Marshall 1920, p. 109]. Time is a necessary element in demand theory "for time is required to enable a rise in the price of a commodity to exert its full influence on consumption" [Marshall 1920, p. 110]. Time is also related to taste; and Marshall notes that "we do not suppose time to be allowed for any alteration in the character or taste of the man himself" [Marshall 1920, p. 94]. The time-taste relation seems to evolve from the fact that "use gives rise to acquired distaste as well as to acquired taste" [Marshall 1920, pp. 107-108]. Thus the dilemma: To allow too much time between an alteration in price and the measurement of the quantity demanded is to allow the distortions of taste change, but to fail to allow adequate time between a price change and the measurement of quantity demanded is to fail to measure the total effect of the price change. As Marshall expressed the problem:

> Thus while a list of demand prices represents the changes in the price at which a commodity can be sold consequent on changes in the amount offered for sale, *other things being equal*; yet other things seldom are equal in fact over periods of time sufficiently long for the collection of full and trustworthy statistics. There are always occurring disturbing causes whose effects are commingled with, and cannot easily be separated from, the effects of that particular cause which we desire to isolate. This difficulty is aggravated by the fact that in economics the full effects of a cause seldom come at once, but often spread themselves out after it has ceased to exist. [Marshall 1920, p. 109].

The specification of a time period of adjustment is thus a fundamental parameter of Marshallian demand theory. To vary the time period of adjustment is to alter the demand curve significantly and any formulation must carry a given adjustment time notation.

Marshall stated his taste parameter as follows: "There is . . . an implicit condition in this law which should be made clear. It is that we do not suppose time to be allowed for any alteration in the character or tastes of the man himself" [Marshall 1920, p. 94]. The necessity for holding tastes or customs and the prices of related goods constant in the formulation of the demand curve is made clear by Marshall's statement that

> The demand prices in our list are those at which various quantities of a thing can be sold in a market *during a given time and under given conditions.* If the conditions vary in any respect the prices will probably require to be changed; and this has constantly to be done when the desire for anything is materially altered by a variation of custom, or by a cheapening of the supply of a rival commodity, or by the invention of a new one. [Marshall 1920, p. 100]

In the specification of a long time period of adjustment "allowance must be made for changes in fashion, and taste and habit" [Marshall 1920, p. 110]. Taste change is inherent in most disturbances which displace equilibrium since the consumer finds "new activities giving rise to new wants" [Marshall 1920, p. 90]. While taste changes are generally to be abstracted from in theoretical analysis and minimized in empirical work by allowing only a short time elapse between disturbance and observation, Marshall noted the usefulness of allowing taste change in gauging a new type demand curve. As Marshall stated: "time may be also wanted for the growth of habits of familiarity with new commodities and the discovery of methods of economizing them" [Marshall 1920, p. 110].

Marshall's income parameter, the most controversial element of his theoretical construction, is stated explicitly several times in the exposition of his theory. In outlining the general premises of his analysis Marshall stated:

> . . . we may throughout this volume *neglect possible changes in the general purchasing power of money.* Thus the price of anything will be taken as representative of its exchange value *relatively* to things in general. [Marshall 1920, p. 62] (emphasis added)

In his analysis of marginal diminishing price, Marshall stated the assumed constancy of the purchasing power of money (or income) as follows:

> The larger the amount of a thing that a person has the less, other things being equal (i.e., *the purchasing power of money, and the amount of money at his command being equal*), will be the price which he will pay for a little more of it: or in other words his marginal demand price for it diminishes. [Marshall 1920, p. 95] (emphasis added)

Marshall explicitly noted the necessity of correcting for changes in both the purchasing power of money and real income or prosperity.

> The *purchasing power of money* is continually changing, and rendering necessary a correction of the results obtained on our assumption that money retains a uniform value. This difficulty can however be overcome fairly well, since we can ascertain with tolerable accuracy the broader changes in the purchasing power of money.
>
> . . . . . .
>
> [When *real income* ("prosperity") varies] the allowance to be made for it must be ascertained by comparing the prices and the consumption of as many things as possible. [Marshall 1920, p. 110] (emphasis added)

While Marshall explicitly included a constant purchasing power of money assumption in his analysis and noted "formal account could be taken of changes in the marginal utility of money," in practical uses such as the measurement of consumer surplus he concluded that "that task would be impracticable" [Marshall 1920, p. 132, note 1]. Therefore, we need note the presence of a continuum of levels of abstraction between operational approximations and rigorous formulations. In his theoretical statement of the demand curve, Marshall adhered rigidly to the exclusion of changes in the purchasing power of money. In application, "second order" movements in the purchasing power of money were permitted in order to make the demand curve more operational.

Marshall's "other things" held constant in gauging the functional relation between price and quantity demanded may be summarized as follows:

1. the time period of adjustment
2. the subject's tastes, preferences, and customs
3. the amount of money (income or wealth) at the subject's command
4. the purchasing power of money
5. the price and range of rival commodities

Whether the Marshallian demand curve falls into the category of the modern constant money income or the modern constant real income formulation depends on the interpretation given to the assumed constancy of the purchasing power of money and the importance which is attached to it. According to Friedman's interpretation, the only way the purchasing power of money can remain constant as the price of the good under analysis changes is for the subject to be compensated by changes in money income or counter movements in the prices of other goods he consumes to maintain the constancy of real income (in utility terms) [Friedman 1949, pp. 53-65]. According to the traditional interpretation, Marshall's assumption of the constancy of the purchasing power of money was a simplifying assumption that was, in rigorous terms, inconsistent with the rest of his formulation [Hicks 1946, pp. 38-41].

Viewed in retrospect, both interpretations appear correct though each refers to a different point on Marshall's continuum of levels of abstraction. The possibility of two distinct interpretations results from Marshall's failure to distinguish explicitly at what point on his continuum of levels of abstraction he was operating in various facets of his analysis. In the theoretical formulation of the demand curve, Marshall's formulation fits the constant real income classification and the Friedman interpretation appears valid. In practical applications such as consumer surplus, the constant money income interpretation, which assumes Marshall simply neglected changes in the purchasing power of money, seems more appropriate.

Giffen's Paradox and the Law of Demand

Marshall states Giffen's paradox as follows:

> There are, however, some exceptions. For instance, as Sir R. Giffen has pointed out, a rise in the price of bread makes so large a drain on the resources of the poorer labouring families and raises so much the marginal utility of money to them, that they are forced to curtail their consumption of meat and the more expensive farinaceous foods: and, bread being still the cheapest food which they can get and will take, they consume more, and not less of it [Marshall 1920, p. 132].

George Stigler's interpretation of Giffen's paradox is that: "One suspects that the paradox was a last minute addition to the *Principles,* for it stands in bold conflict with the law of demand" [Stigler 1947, p. 152]. Friedman follows the same line of reasoning.

> The possibility of interpreting Marshall in these two quite different ways arises in part from the vagueness of Marshall's exposition, from his failure to give precise and rigorous definitions. A more fundamental reason, however, is the existence of inconsistency in the third and later editions of the *Principles.* In that edition Marshall introduced the celebrated passage bearing on the Giffen phenomenon. [Friedman 1949, p. 56]

Within the above reconciliation, Giffen's paradox is neither a contradiction to the law of demand nor an inconsistency in Marshall's theory.[1] The paradox occurs in a section of Chapter VI that discusses the fact that in practical application it is seldom necessary to take account of changes in the purchasing power of money, "for there are very few practical problems, in which the corrections to be made under this head would be of any importance" [Marshall 1920, p. 132]. This point is clarified in a footnote with the statement that "In mathe-

1. The remainder of this section follows in large part from [Gramm 1970].

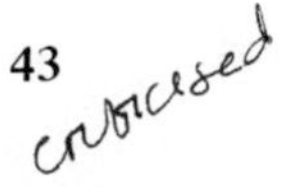

matical language the neglected elements would generally belong to the second order of small quantities" [Marshall 1920, p. 132, n. 1]. Giffen's paradox is not, therefore, as Stigler implies, an exception to the law of demand but an exception to the general case in which the neglect of the income effect results in an error of the second order of smallness.

Marshall's law of demand states:

> There is then one general *law of demand*: The greater the amount to be sold, the smaller must be the price at which it is offered in order that it may find purchasers; or, in other words, the amount demanded increases with a fall in price, and diminishes with a rise in price. [Marshall 1920, p. 99].

If the law of demand is viewed in the theoretical portion of Marshall's continuum of abstraction, Giffen's paradox is not a contradiction to this law. In Marshall's theoretical formulation of the demand curve the purchasing power of money, total money income, and, thus, real income are assumed constant. Friedman has shown that the only way the purchasing power of money can remain constant as the price of the good under analysis changes is for the subject to be compensated by changes in money income or counter movements in the prices of other goods he consumes, in order that his level of real income remain constant [Friedman 1949, pp. 53-56]. Thus Giffen's paradox exists only because the good under empirical observation, bread, makes up such a large part of the subject's budget that a change in its price greatly affects the marginal utility of money to him and thus his real income. This change in real income is abstracted from throughout the theoretical formulation of Marshall's demand curve [Marshall 1920, n. II, pp. 838-839; Friedman 1949, pp. 93-94]. The change in real income is present in the operational approximate of the demand curve employed in Marshall's consumer surplus discussion where Giffen's paradox occurs. The inclusion of Giffen's paradox, far from being a source of inconsistency, is a key to Marshall's framework of analysis.[2]

As is true of much of Marshallian demand theory, the constant purchasing power of money assumption is not without precedent. David Ricardo [Ricardo 1951, p. 46], Augustin Cournot [Cournot 1960, p. 26], Jules Dupuit [Dupuit 1844], John Stuart Mill [Mill 1965, p. 439], and numerous others had used the assumption before Marshall. The logical necessity for the constant purchasing power assumption is deeply woven into the fabric of the classical system. It is not an assumed parameter used solely to limit the domain of the demand curve, though this is the result of its application. Its logic is more basic. The constant purchasing power assumption is the product of the classical dichotomy.

2. Alford attributes the presence of Giffen's paradox in the Third Edition of *Principles* to a change in the factual material available to Marshall [Alford 1956, p. 42]. Marshall's additional factual material appears to have been Giffen's *Final Report of the Royal Commission on Agricultural Depression* [Prest 1948, p. 58].

Specifically, the theoretical division of economic analysis into a study of the value of money on the one hand and a study of relative values on the other forced its inclusion as a parameter in the study of demand. The constant purchasing power assumption was a simplification that dichotomized the economic system and made partial equilibrium analysis accessible. But the convenience it afforded was purchased by the imposition of a limited domain of applicability.[3] Giffen's paradox is an example of this limitation.

In general, Marshall developed tools to deal with actual market situations [Marshall 1920, p. 181], and dealt with examples in which the proportion of the individual's budget used in the purchase of a good was small and the income effect of a price change was negligible. As Marshall stated:

> . . . the assumption, which underlies our whole reasoning [is] that his expenditure on any one thing, as, for example, tea, is only a small part of his whole expenditure. [Marshall 1920, p. 842]

In most practical problems the income effect is of the "second order of small quantitites." Thus, Marshall's theoretical formulation of the demand curve was directly applicable to actual market situations. Only in the extreme case, Giffen's paradox, is the income effect present at so significant a level as to warrant formal recognition as an exception to the general case in which Marshall's formulation was a workable approximation of reality.

With the presentation of Giffen's paradox, Marshall had reached the limit beyond which the classical dichotomy was not an acceptable approximation of reality. He had reached the boundary of the classical methodological framework. While the income effect was outside the analysis of relative prices and was excluded in the classical dichotomy, the possible exception had to be acknowledged to denote the limited applicability of the theory. This did not mean, however, that the parameters of the Marshallian demand curve were inconsistent but only that the formulation had a limited domain of applicability.[4]

Current assessment of the law of demand was expressed by Henry Schultz when he stated:

> It is clear, therefore, that there is nothing "universal" about this law. But its extreme simplicity and the ease with which it can be manipulated, coupled with the good approximate description which it provides in many instances of actual economic behavior, have earned for it a secure place

3. For a similar account of Marshall's methodology, as it applied to the theory of the firm and the process of adjustment, see [Hicks 1965, pp. 49–57].

4. A modern vestige of this methodology is evident in Frank Knight's analysis of demand. Examining the Slutsky–Hicks demand curve he concludes: "The 'income effect' of Slutsky et al. is merely a particular case or mode of change in the purchasing power of money, or the price level; and it is this problem as a whole that should be isolated and reserved for separate treatment" [Knight 1944, p. 299].

> among the fundamental laws of economics. This is another illustration of the fact that in science it is often more important that a law be simple than it be true. [Schultz 1938, pp. 53-54]

Rejection of the law of demand has become a part of most expositions of demand theory [Hicks 1946, pp. 24-37; Samuelson 1947, pp. 90-122], and is predicated on the mathematical possibility of the positive income effect being larger in absolute magnitude than the negative substitution effect of the constant money income formulation.

Marshall's statement of the universal law of demand has been one of the most criticized parts of his theory [Marshall 1920, p. 99]. This criticism seems largely the result of a failure to recognize Marshall's general disbelief in "universal laws" except as *ceteris paribus* constructs. As Marshall stated:

> Some parts of economics are relatively abstract or *pure*, because they are concerned mainly with broad general propositions: for, in order that a proposition may be of broad application it must necessarily contain few details: it cannot adopt itself to particular cases; and if it points to any prediction, that must be governed by a strong conditioning clause in which a very large meaning is given to the phrase "other things being equal." [Marshall 1920, p. 37, n. 2]

The law of demand began as an empirical generalization of the inverse relation between price and quantity purchased. This idea is evident in the statement of "Gregory King's Law" and early writings on demand theory [Evans 1967]. Cournot stated the law of demand as follows: "The cheaper an article is, the greater ordinarily is the demand for it" [Cournot 1960, p. 46]. J. S. Mill followed the same line of analysis in stating: "if the thing is cheap, there is usually a demand for more of it than when it is dear" [Mill 1965, p. 446]. While J. S. Mill and Cournot expressed the law of demand as being "ordinarily" or "usually" true, Marshall stated it as a "general law" and "the one universal rule to which the demand curve conforms" [Marshall 1920, p. 99, note 2]. As pointed out above, Marshall conceived the demand schedule as a theoretical construction that was valid only if its *ceteris paribus* assumptions were met. The law of demand was the result of limitations placed on the formulation of the demand schedule due to the exclusion of the income effect which was beyond the domain of the analysis of relative prices in the classical system. As Marshall stated:

> . . . it follows that such a discussion of demand as is possible at this stage of our work, must be confined to an elementary analysis of an almost purely formal kind. The higher study of consumption must come after, and not before, the main body of economic analysis. [Marshall 1920, p. 90]

Thus, while the law of demand may have been an approximation or simplification prior to Marshall's analysis, to him it was a rigorous formulation resulting from *ceteris paribus* assumptions. Marshall's formal statement of the law of demand as a "universal rule" is further evidence that he viewed the demand curve as an abstract or pure construct.

The Formalization of the Marshallian Demand Curve

The development of demand theory since Marshall has consisted largely of a process of removing "those simplifications of genius, of which there are several instances in Marshall" [Hicks 1946, p. 32]. This idea is evident in Hick's statement that

> . . . the work of Marshall's successors may be regarded as the extension of his technique to cover more complicated problems than those with which he attempted to deal; this, in the end, was precisely what was to come of their efforts. [Hicks 1956, p. 2]

The alternative formulations of the demand curve developed since Marshall have been the product of an intensive analysis of the income parameter. Slutsky [1915] and Hicks and Allen [1934] isolated an income and substitution effect of a price change when the money income of the subject was held constant. Friedman [1949] interpreted Marshall's demand formulation to contain the assumed constancy of real income and elaborated on the properties of such a demand curve. Bailey [1954] integrated the production constraints of society into the parameters of demand theory.

The Slutsky Equation

Even by modern standards, Slutsky's "On the Theory of the Budget of the Consumer" is a scientific treatise. Its logical ordering and completeness would satisfy the most discriminating editor. Though its notation is somewhat difficult to follow and modern matrix theory greatly simplifies the results, Slutsky's work represents the most effective use of mathematics in demand theory up to its time.

Slutsky's formulation is lucid and complete. He specifies a constant money income demand curve which includes: (1) a constant taste parameter, (2) a given time period of adjustment, (3) constant money income, and (4) constant prices for all goods except the good under analysis [Slutsky 1915, pp. 30–31].

From the properties of maximizing behavior Slutsky derived the two expressions of the classic "Slutsky Equation,"

$$\frac{\partial X_i}{\partial p_i} = \frac{\partial X_i}{\partial p_i} + X_i \frac{\partial X_i}{\partial S} \tag{2.1a}$$

$$\frac{\partial X_j}{\partial p_i} = \frac{\partial X_j}{\partial p_i} + X_i \frac{\partial X_j}{\partial S} \tag{2.1b}$$

where X_i is the quantity of good i demanded, p_i is the price of good i, and S is income. The conditions for a utility maximum require that the substitution term of (2.1a) be negative.

From (2.1a) Slutsky deduced the following "laws of demand":

> I. The demand for a relatively indispensable good ($\partial X_i / \partial S > 0$) is necessarily always normal, that is, it diminishes if its price increases, and increases if its price decreases.
>
> II. The demand for a relatively dispensable good ($\partial X_i / \partial S < 0$) can be abnormal in certain cases, that is, it can increase with the increase of price and diminish with the decrease of price. [Slutsky 1915, p. 41]

Slutsky concluded that if $\partial X_i / \partial p_i$ and $\partial X_i / \partial S$ are of opposite sign the sign of (2.1a) is dependent on the absolute value of the two effects and two cases are possible.

Case I

$$\frac{\partial X_i}{\partial S} > 0 \qquad \frac{\partial X_i}{\partial p_i} < 0 \qquad \left| \frac{\dfrac{\partial X_i}{\partial p_i}}{\dfrac{\partial X_i}{\partial S}} \right| > X_i \tag{2.2}$$

Case II

$$\frac{\partial X_i}{\partial S} < 0 \qquad \frac{\partial X_i}{\partial p_i} > 0 \qquad \left| \frac{\dfrac{\partial X_i}{\partial p_i}}{\dfrac{\partial X_i}{\partial S}} \right| < X_i \tag{2.3}$$

The Hicksian Synthesis and Alternative Formulations of the Demand Curve

As Marshall's work on demand theory represented a synthesis of previous work, so Hick's writings, especially in *Value and Capital* (1939) [Hicks 1946, pp. 11-54], represented a point of demarcation from which later work on preferences and demand were to begin. In *Value and Capital* Hicks refines the work of Marshall, and to a large extent exhausts the Marshallian approach to demand theory. Hicks worked out the total effect of a price change given income and taste parameters. While there remained dispute over the income parameter which Marshall employed and the fecundity of various income parameters, the demand curve derived from a static preference function had yielded all the insight it could afford. Later work would have to question the assumptions of the static preference function to expand the frontiers of knowledge in demand theory.

The income effect and its economic interpretations were analyzed in some detail by Hicks and Allen [1934] some twenty years after Slutsky's paper though the works were independent. While Slutsky, Hicks and Allen, and Hicks viewed the income effect as a refinement of Marshall's analysis [Hicks 1946, pp. 26–41; 1956, pp. 136–148], Friedman and others have taken issue with this assessment [Friedman 1949, pp. 47–94]. In the ensuing discussion, the properties of various demand formulations have been specified and the result has been a definite enrichment of demand theory.

Throughout its evolution methodological disputes over demand analysis have been both numerous and inconclusive.[5] This development has been a natural occurrence, for as Frank Knight has observed: "The treatment of demand is the branch of economic theory in which methodological problems are most important and most difficult" [Knight 1944, p. 289]. Methodological disputes over the relevant parameters held constant in the derivation of the demand schedule date from 1847 when Bordas challenged Dupuit on the income effect of a price change [Ekelund and Gramm 1970, pp. 281-283] and in Britain from 1894 when F. Y. Edgeworth offered his interpretation of Marshall's demand curve [Edgeworth 1923–1926-a]. Such controversy was understandable, because Alfred Marshall, like John Stuart Mill and Augustin Cournot before him and J. R. Hicks and P. A. Samuelson after him, gave little explicit explanation of the exact variables held constant in his list of "other things" in the derivation of the demand curve. This failure to clarify exact parameters, that has so marked the development of demand theory, has been the result of three factors: first, an inadequate understanding of the important restrictions the *ceteris paribus* assumptions place on the theoretical construction of the demand schedule; second, as Samuelson has said, "Ambiguously defined assumptions are used to give a semblance of deriving theorems which are themselves inconclusive" [Samuelson 1947, p. 172]; and third, an excessive tendency to let context explain meaning [Marshall 1920, Book III].

Weintraub illustrated the extreme viewpoint when he stated: "We can proceed to draw demand curves of any shape whatever. The sole limitation seems to lie in the ingenuity of the analyst and the facts and reactions of the real world" [Weintraub 1942, p. 549]. Such an approach to methodology is the result of the idea, recently fostered by Leland Yeager, that methodological precepts con-

5. Recent discussions have been centered in the following articles: [Weintraub 1942; Knight 1944; Friedman 1949; Bailey 1954; Alford 1956; Buchanan 1958; Yeager 1960; and Gramm 1970].

nected with disputes over demand curves are solely matters of preference or convenience [Yeager 1960]. In the current literature *ceteris paribus* assumptions, other than the much disputed income parameter, place almost no limitations on the formulation or application of the demand curve.

In the formulation of the demand curve some combination of four parameters is generally specified as provisionally constant: (1) the tastes and preferences of the subject, (2) his income (money or real), (3) the prices of all other goods or only the prices of closely related goods, and (4) a time period of adjustment.[6] It will be helpful at this point to derive the basic demand curve formulations. Figures 2-1 and 2-2 will aid in this clarification process. Figure 2-1 presents a standard indifference map of which the 5 curves, I, II, III, IV, and V, which are directly relevant for this analysis, are shown. The slopes and positions of the indifference curves within the indifference map are dictated by the tastes of the subject. The indifference map conforms to the standard axioms of consumer behavior, and the following analysis is based on the assumption of utility maximization.

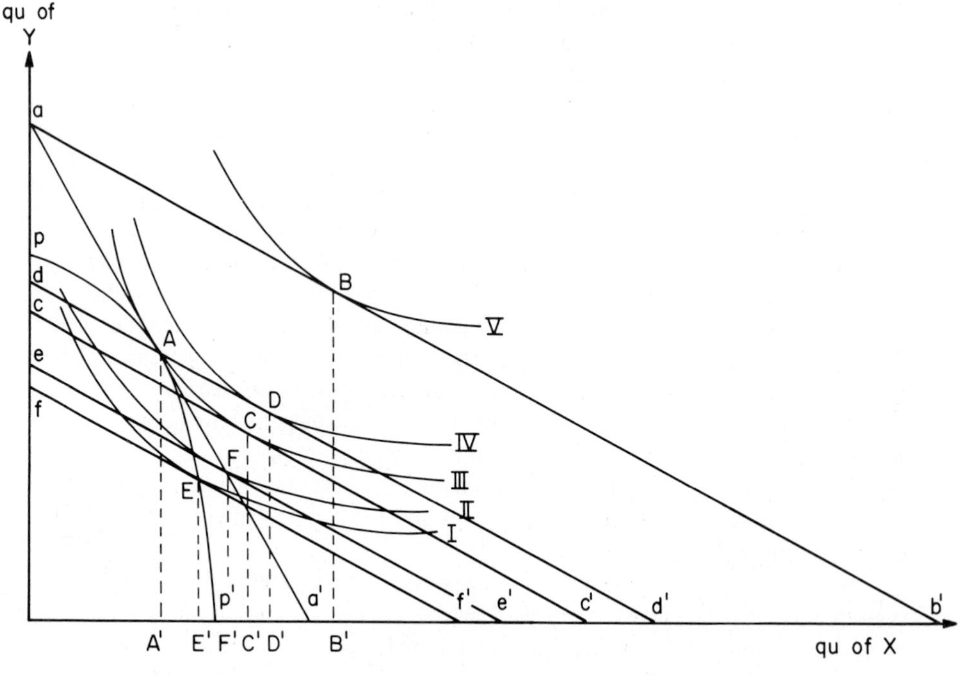

Figure 2-1

6. Some combination of these parameters is found in most modern textbooks. For example, see [Friedman 1962, pp. 12-55].

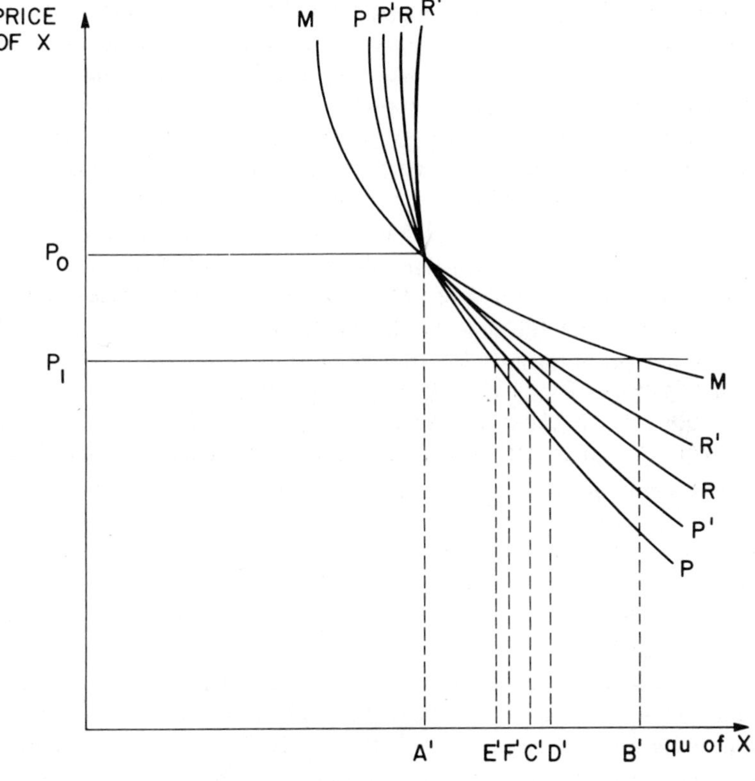

Figure 2-2

The formulation of the *constant money income* demand schedule requires the theoretical constancy of: (1) the tastes and preferences of the subject, (2) his money income, (3) the prices of all other goods, and (4) the time period of adjustment specified for the demand schedule. The geometric derivation begins, in Figure 2-1, with the subject in equilibrium at Point A where budget line aa' is tangent to indifference curve III. If the price of good X falls shifting the X intercept of the budget line from a' to b', the subject would be in equilibrium at point B where budget line ab' is tangent to indifference curve V. The original equilibrium point A and the newly attained equilibrium point B are points on the constant money income demand schedule for X, MM in Figure 2-2. The points on the constant money income demand curve are derived by varying the price of X and plotting the corresponding quantities demanded from equilibrium points between budget lines and indifference curves.

The *apparent real income* demand curve or *Slutsky* formulation of the demand curve holds constant: (1) the tastes and preferences of the subject, (2) his money income, (3) the prices of closely related goods and a price index containing the price of good *X* and all other goods, and (4) the time period of adjustment specified for the demand schedule. The derivation begins with the subject in equilibrium in Figure 2-1 at point *A* where budget line *aa′* is tangent to indifference curve III. If the price of *X* falls shifting the *X* intercept of the budget line from *a′* to *b′*, the subject would be in equilibrium at point *B* where budget line *ab′* is tangent to indifference curve V. However, the fall in the price of *X* raises real income which must be eliminated since the *ceteris paribus* assumptions of the apparent real income formulation limit it to an analysis in terms of relative prices. Thus the prices of other goods must rise to offset the fall in the price of *X* and maintain the constancy of the price index. This negative compensation is represented geometrically by rotating budget line *aa′* through point *A* parallel to budget line *ab′*. On budget line *dd′* the subject has the option to continue to consume the original combination of goods at point *A*. He is in equilibrium, however, at point *D* where budget line *dd′* is tangent to indifference curve IV. The demand schedule derived by this method of compensation is shown in Figure2-2 as curve *R′R′*. The apparent real income demand schedule is thus derived by varying the price of the good under analysis, compensating the subject to preserve his ability to purchase at the original equilibrium point, and plotting the resulting equilibrium points in a two-dimensional graph that relates price to quantity demand.

In the formulation of the *constant utility* demand schedule, given conditions include: (1) the tastes and preferences of the subject, (2) his level of utility (real income in the sense of constant total satisfaction), (3) the prices of closely related goods, and (4) the time period of adjustment specified for the demand schedule. The geometric derivation begins with the subject in equilibrium at point *A* in Figure 2-1 where budget line *aa′* is tangent to indifference curve III. A fall in the price of *X* shifts the *X* intercept of the budget line from *a* to *b′*. The subject would then be in equilibrium at *B* where budget line *ab′* is tangent to indifference curve V. However, the fall in the price of good *X* has raised the attainable utility level. To eliminate the income effect and analyze only the effect of the change in relative prices the Hicks compensation [Hicks 1946, p. 31] is used to compensate the subject to keep him at the original utility level. Hicks' compensation is theoretically accomplished by manipulating the subject's money income, while maintaining newly obtained relative prices, in such a way as to offset any change in utility level attainment that would result from a change in the price of the good under analysis. This compensation is demonstrated geometrically by constructing budget line *cc′* tangent to indifference curve III and parallel to budget line *ab′*. The constant utility demand curve is thus derived by allowing the price of *X* to vary, compensating the subject to keep him at the same level of utility, and plotting the resulting equilibrium points (point *C*) in a two-dimensional graph that relates price to quantity demanded. The demand schedule thus derived is shown in Figure 2-2 as curve *RR*.

The apparent real income demand schedule can best be thought of as an approximation of the constant utility formulation. In this light it should be recognized that the Slutsky, apparent real income, formulation does not completely eliminate the income effect of a price change. In most cases the difference between the constant utility and the apparent real income formulations is insignificant. This is evidenced by the fact that as ΔP approaches zero the difference between the results of the two formulations approaches zero more rapidly, and the two formulations can be considered comparable in the neighborhood about a position of equilibrium.[7] With the constant utility compensation the change in the quantity demanded from A' to B' (in Figure 2-1) may be divided into a substitution effect A'–C' and an income effect C'–B'. With the constant apparent real income compensation the substitution effect is A'–D' and the income effect is D'–B'.

While the constant utility demand curve purports to show the limitations on the demand curve imposed by production constraints, Bailey [1954] has shown that it is only an approximation of the true *constant production-possibilities* demand curve. In the constant production-possibilities demand curve, given conditions include: (1) taste and preferences, (2) a fixed production frontier, and (3) the time period of adjustment. In Figure 2-1, *pp* represents society's production-possibilities curve for the two-goods world composed of x and y; *pp* is tangent to indifference curve III at A; and competitive equilibrium requires a price line of aa', reflecting a relative price for X of p_o. If the price of X falls, the uncompensated budget constraint becomes ab'. Whereas the subject was compensated to keep him on indifference curve III in the constant utility demand curve, it is now necessary to extract a negative compensation from the individual so as to keep him on *pp*. Given the new relative price of $X(P_1)$ we need find a tangency between an indifference curve and a price line with the slope P_1 at a point on *pp*. Such a point is E on ff', *pp*, and I. Plotting P_1 against E', the quantity taken after the compensation, we obtain a second point on the constant production-possibilities demand curve *PP* in Figure 2-2.

PP requires a knowledge of the production-possibilities curve and therefore has limited empirical applicability. As was true of the constant utility formulation, however, an approximation of the constant production-possibilities demand curve is obtainable. Since the original budget line aa' is an approximation of *pp* at points near the original equilibrium point A, we may reconstruct the compensation so as to achieve tangency between a budget constraint with slope P_1 and some indifference curve on aa'. Such a point is F on ee', aa', and II. Plotting P_1 against F' we obtain a second point on the *constant apparent production-possibility* curve $P'P'$.

7. See [Friedman 1949, pp. 52–53]. The advantage of the Slutsky, apparent real income, compensation is that it can be computed directly from observable market data. The Hicks, constant utility, compensation is more rigorous but requires detailed knowledge of the subject's indifference map.

The essential properties of *PP*, *P′P′*, *RR*, and *R′R′* are that they are all tangent at P_o,A' in Figure 2-2 and *R′R′*, *RR*, and *P′P′* are successively better approximations of *PP*. *MM* is to the left of *PP* above P_o,A' and to the right of *PP* below P_o,A' when the good under analysis is normal and the income effect is negative.

We then obtain five formulations of the demand curve by varying the income parameter employed. *PP* can best be conceived of as a market experiment along which all points can be realized. *P′P′*, *RR*, *R′R′* are successively poorer approximations of the market experiment curve. *MM* on the other hand can be conceived of as an individual experiment showing what consumers expect to do if the price of *X* changes with the price of *Y* remaining constant. Given a constant production-possibilities curve, a change in the quantity of *X* supplied must affect the quantity of *Y* produced and thus its price. If taste and production possibilities are fixed only an outside force such as government can alter the relative price of *X* and *Y*. The price line *aa′* is dictated by the forces of taste and technology. Given a free market with no government intervention only point P_o,A' on *PP* is realizable. In most cases changes in prices will be proscribed by changes in taste or technology. In both these cases *PP* will shift. The total effect of a change in price generated by a taste change or a technological change must then be shown by successive points on different *PP* curves. Insofar as the individual experiment (constant money income formulation) and the market experiment (constant production-possibilities formulation) are two distinct facets in the spectrum of demand, one is no more useful than the other. The formulation to be employed depends on the problem at hand.[8]

To further clarify the distinctions between the *ceteris paribus* assumptions used in the five formulations of the demand schedule, Table 2-1 is given below. Note that this table refers only to stated methodological assumptions. As currently interpreted, constant taste means only that the utility function, and thus the indifference map, remains stable for all alternative points on the demand schedule. All five of the demand formulations explicitly assume constant taste.

Of the five formulations, only the constant utility demand schedule maintains constant utility for the subject at every point on the demand schedule. The level of utility attainment is different for every point on the constant money income formulation due to the lack of compensation to offset the effect price changes have on real income. The apparent real income formulation only partially offsets utility level changes produced by variations in the price of the good under analysis. The constant production-possibilities curve overcompensates from the point of view of utility level attainment.

Money income is held constant in the constant money income and apparent real income formulations. It is allowed to vary to offset price changes and thus maintain a constant level of utility in the constant utility demand schedule and

8. For a similar approach see [Yeager 1960].

Table 2–1
Assumed Constancies in Demand Schedule Formulation

	Taste	Total Utility	Money Income	Prices	Time	Production Possibilities
(*MM*) Constant Money Income	Yes	No	Yes	All	Yes	No
($R'R'$) Constant Apparent Real Income	Yes	No	Yes	Close Prices and Price Index	Yes	No
(*RR*) Constant Utility	Yes	Yes	No	All	Yes	No
(*PP*) Constant Production Possibilities	Yes	No	No	None	Yes	Yes
($P'P'$) Constant Apparent Production Possibilities	Yes	No	No	None	Yes	Approximately

to maintain constant production possibilities in the constant production-possibilities curve.

In the constant money income formulation, all prices except that of the good in question are held constant. In the apparent real income formulation, only the prices of complements and substitutes for the good in question and a price index containing the price of the good under analysis and the prices of all other goods are held constant. By holding a price index constant, the subject can still buy the old bundle of goods consumed before the variation in the price of the good being studied. Therefore, real income cannot be less, but it may be greater if the subject can consume on a higher indifference curve. In the constant utility formulation all prices except that for the good under analysis are held constant, and income is varied as the price of the good under analysis changes to maintain a constant level of utility.

The concept of the time period of adjustment is common to all five formulations of Table 2–1. The specified time period varies with the desired application of the theoretical system. The limitations placed on the length of the time period of adjustment are dictated by the fact that it cannot be shorter than the time needed for initial short-run adjustment nor longer than a period of time in which the assumptions of the schedule formulation lose all meaning. In general the demand schedule may be thought of as a short-run though not a static tool.

The constant production-possibilities demand curve maintains constant production possibilities by forcing the subject to move along the fixed production frontier. The constant apparent production possibilities formulation yields an approximation of constant production possibilities by forcing the subject to move along the original price line. The constant utility demand curve is a somewhat poorer approximation of the constant production-possibilities curve which forces the subject to move along the original indifference curve. The constant apparent real income formulation is yet a poorer approximation which allows a slight change in utility level attainment.

The above discussion represents an uncritical synthesis of the literature on the formulation of the demand curve within the Marshallian framework. In concluding this section, however, some evaluation seems in order. Hicks solidified Marshall's formulation by working out in detail the exact impact of a price change and also by dropping from the discussion problems, noted by Marshall, related to time and taste. While Marshall noted the possibility of a learning function: in the taste parameter [Marshall 1920, p. 110], Hicks made taste an exogenous factor and the demand curve became basically a static tool.

While disputes over the income parameter of demand theory have enriched the theory of demand, the problems introduced by more (empirically) confining income parameters have made the usefulness of the alternative formulations highly questionable. Viewing the production-possibilities curve as an aggregate tool means that all the aggregation problems of community indifference curves and production frontiers are encountered. The constant production-possibilities demand curve not only requires a knowledge of the production frontier of society but fails to take account of the distribution effects produced by moving along some production frontier. In an aggregate curve the distribution of income must be a parameter, but movements along the n-dimensional production surface generally produce changes in income distribution. The apparent production-possibilities curve avoids the necessity of knowing the production frontier but still requires knowledge of community indifference curves. While use of the budget line as an approximation for the production-possibilities curve has empirical advantages it still entails different income distributions at each point on the curve.

The constant utility demand curve requires knowledge of the subject's indifference map whereas the constant apparent real income demand curve does not. Since most price changes emanate from taste or technology changes, and not from nonmarket intervention, there are few empirical applications where the parameters of the constant apparent real income or constant utility demand curves are produced by market forces on the individual. For these reasons the constant money income demand curve, despite its deficiencies, is still the most useful curve for empirical analysis.

3 The State of Contemporary Demand Theory

Past Achievements and New Directions

The literature of demand theory has grown enormously since Hicks' classic exposition of the modern marginalist position in *Value and Capital.* Thus, the present brief survey can do no more than touch on major themes and consider what appear to be some of the more significant and interesting contributions to the field. Inevitably, the direction and emphasis of the discussion will reflect a subjective view of what has been happening during the past three decades. But it would seem that any observer must be struck by one central characteristic of the received work on the theory of the consumer—the tendency of so many studies to accept the objectives and basic preconceptions of earlier models without much change. While contributions to demand literature have covered a wide range of topics and have involved a number of methodological approaches, it remains true that the main thrust of postwar writing has been toward the extension and refinement of the classical theory of demand that has come down to us through Marshall, Hicks, et al.

It is both understandable and proper that efforts have been made to maintain the continuity of theory and preserve the traditional doctrine. Nevertheless, there is reason to believe that disproportionate attention has been given to the elementary model based on indifference curves. The conventional analysis has won the day too completely and, until quite recently, alternative approaches have been generally neglected by the profession. This bias in the direction of research seems especially important, moreover, because of the lack of convincing evidence to show that the predictive powers of conventional demand theory have been improving over time. By comparison to theories in the physical sciences, the operational significance of traditional demand analysis is still quite modest [Wold 1953, p. 1]; and the disparity in performance cannot all be attributed to the special difficulties that beset the development and testing of theories in the social sciences [Schoeffler 1955, ch. 2].

In part, the unimpressive predictive record of demand theory reflects the fact that a substantial proportion of the literature in the area has been concerned with models having very limited empirical content. Interest has focused primarily on logical problems and on the formulation of a rigorous, compact, and highly general theory of consumer choice [Strotz 1957, pp. 269-270]. The tendency to abstract theorizing probably had some effect in delaying a fundamental reappraisal of the static utility maximizing model but, in addition, the emphasis on formalism made it easier to ignore the poor predictive success of existing constructs [Lloyd 1965]. As Clarkson has asserted:

> . . . economic theories are normally judged on the basis of such criteria as their consistency with accepted doctrine, or their ability to be deduced from standard premises, all of which avoid any direct reference to empirical phenomena. This is certainly not to say that economists are uninterested in developing theories which explain and predict the course of economic events. It is rather that the notable poverty of predictive success has led them to adopt other criteria by which to appraise and reject contending theories. [Clarkson 1963, p. 3]

Clarkson's criticism may seem too sweeping in view of the many valuable econometric studies that have been completed in the postwar period. The point is however, that the advances made in estimating demand relations have come about largely because of improvements in statistical technique and computational capacity and not because of refinements in the conventional theory of demand as such.

If many contributions to the theory of demand over the past few decades have not been particularly helpful in furthering applied work, there is, nevertheless, little doubt that these writings have increased understanding of the true nature and limitations of the received doctrine. For example, the important discussions touched off by Samuelson's concept of revealed preference led to significant clarification of the logical foundations of demand theory. The revealed preference approach also gave impetus to another major development of the period—the movement away from formulations based on the infinitessimal calculus. To utilize modern mathematical tools and establish closer connections with observational quantities, Samuelson banished continuous functions and derivatives in favor of expressions involving finite differences (i.e., value sums). More generally, by recasting consumption theory in set-theoretic terms, writers like Debreu, Newman, Arrow, Uzawa, and others tried to purge conventional theory of faulty reasoning and achieve deeper understanding of choice and demand phenomena. The full impact of this "axiomatic revolution" has not yet been felt [Walsh 1970, ch. 1], but it is already clear that gains have been realized. Because the new techniques make it unnecessary to employ highly restrictive assumptions in the interest of mathematical manageability, certain artificial interpretations formerly made can now be avoided.

Perhaps the best assessment of traditionally oriented demand theory has been offered by Professor Shubik:

> My objection to all of the [conventional] material is not that it does not represent a contribution to economic knowledge, but that it is presented to students of microeconomics as though it were *the relevant*

way to study consumer behavior, rather than one partially explored path in almost virgin territory. [Shubik 1970, p. 410]

Given this interpretation, it follows that demand theory must be pushed in some fundamentally new directions. And, of course, certain promising new lines of research have already appeared [Theil 1965]. In particular, the importance of interdisciplinary studies has grown steadily [Suppes 1961], and attention has turned more and more to empirically based investigations of actual consumer behavior and decision-making processes. So far, work of this sort has provided no clear support for the traditional utility maximizing model; indeed, there are indications that the maximizing decision process is atypical [Simon 1968, pp. 4-8]. Moreover, current psychological theories of motivation rest on premises that are at variance with the concept of maximization. Motives for human action are explained in terms of psychological drives and the *satiation* of these drives; that is, action is required to satisfy certain innate drives but the need for action ends when the drives are satisfied and there is no reason to believe that a satisficing solution will always correspond to a maximizing solution. The situation is further complicated by the fact that the particular means or conditions for satisfying a drive are not fixed; human aspirations are likely to change over time as experience is accumulated. An individual's aspirations tend to rise when he is relatively successful in attaining his goals and fall when he is unsuccessful. Individual aspirations also tend to be linked so that each person's outlook is influenced by the observed achievements of others.

It is obvious that this line of thinking can lead to an adaptive model of demand that differs radically from the conventional static explanation [Weinstein 1968]. And, quite naturally, the proponents of the new behavioral approach claim significant advantages for it. For example, Simon has suggested that:

> Models of satisficing behavior are richer than models of maximizing behavior, because they treat not only of equilibrium but of the method of reaching it as well. Psychological studies of the formation and change of aspiration levels support propositions of the following kinds. (a) When performance falls short of the level of aspiration, search behavior (particularly search for new alternatives of action) is induced. (b) At the same time, the level of aspiration begins to adjust itself downward until goals reach levels that are practically attainable. (c) If the two mechanisms just listed operate too slowly to adapt aspirations to performance, emotional behavior—apathy or aggression, for example—will replace rational adaptive behavior. [Simon 1968, pp. 10–11].

The full potentialities of behavioral models have not yet been established. But since the ideas underlying these models link up with a number of other new developments in demand theory, it seems reasonable to say that future work will carry the analysis of demand a long way from the Hicksian model. The process of criticism and growth has been uninterrupted. As the inadequacies of the elementary theory became evident, various extensions and reformulations came into being. Thus, there are today substantial bodies of specialized theoretical literature on such problems as choice subject to risk, the formation of consumer expectations, the nature and cost of search, the influence of socio-economic variables on consumer behavior, etc. At the same time, much important empirical work has been stimulated by the theoretical discussions in these areas [Theil and Mnookin 1966]. In general, then, the situation is one where all the elements seem to be at hand for the generation of richer and more useful models of consumer demand.

Although we seem to be at a watershed in the development of demand theory, it is difficult to predict the type of model that will dominate professional thinking in the future. At least two major lines of innovation are clear at present. On the one hand, there is the inderdisciplinary approach just mentioned. Here, attempts are being made to synthesize new explanations of economic behavior by incorporating significant psychological and sociological findings. Because many of these models are adapted to the use of high speed computational methods and simulation techniques, their empirical content tends to be higher than that of the older analytical constructs. The consequence of introducing more institutional and other factual detail is, however, the emergence of a series of specialized models having somewhat restricted applicability. While the latter are by no means case studies, such empirically robust models contrast with the type of general choice theory that is being emphasized by another group of economists at work today.

Those concerned with the formulation of a general theory of choice are willing to carry abstraction to a very high level and seek a scheme for analyzing rational behavior in "all" choice situations. Thus:

> Everyone needs to know that at the core of today's mathematical economics lies a theory, not just of market decisions, but of all decisions subject to constraints. A theory not just of prices, or commodities, or conventional industry, but of all choices, all human and cybernetic optimizing activity, of all systems. A theory, moreover, for which it is claimed that behavior in conformity to its axiom set is behavior that merits the name "rational." [Walsh 1970, p. x]

The foregoing comments by Professor Walsh reveal, quite vividly, the ambitious nature of the new thinking. Choice theory in this sense represents the ultimate extension of the axiomatic analysis that grew out of traditional utility theory. Instead of focusing narrowly on demand phenomena, the objective now is to examine rational choice as it operates in an almost limitless variety of optimization problems. Thus, for economics, one immediate result has been the translation of consumption theory and production theory into common analytical terms–i.e., both areas are treated as particular models in the general theory of choice [Walsh 1970, p. 278].

The idea that quite diverse phenomena can be explained in the context of a single general theory has inherent intellectual appeal. Moreover, there need be no logical conflict between such a high-level model and the more limited traditional models. Controversy can arise, however, concerning the question of how scientific effort should be allocated [Rothenberg 1962]. In particular, not all economists accept the view that the general theory of choice represents the only valid approach to the development of a meaningful theory of demand. Since the general theory is based on maximizing behavior, it does not meet fully the requirements of those interested in the adaptive consumer behavior considered in satisficing models. Although, from a formal standpoint it may be possible to reconsider a satisficing problem and reformulate it as one of constrained maximization [Day 1967], this possibility does not necessarily mean that there is no real distinction between satisficing and maximizing models, or that satisficing models are always defective constructs. Actually, the translation of a satisficing model into a maximizing one may inhibit understanding of the operative decision process, and constitute nothing more than an ex post rationalization–in which case, of course, the predictive powers of the maximizing model are likely to be poor. Further, as the work of von Neumann and Morgenstern has made clear, many practically important economic situations cannot be interpreted as conventional problems of constrained optimization.

> Game theory on the other hand recognizes that there can be no maximum if the outcome of economic activities depends not only on the actions of the given individual consumer or entrepreneur (plus, perhaps, a chance factor– but also on the acts of others over which the former has no control. This, then, appears to be the normal condition in which an economy has to be viewed. It is, indeed, doubtful that this state can be approached by considering isolated, non-interacting Robinson Crusoes who face fixed conditions on which they never exercise any influence whatever. They represent nothing characteristic of reality, hardly a limiting case (though of some mathematical-formalistic interest). [Morgenstern 1964, p. 586]

While it is apparent that uniformity of opinion does not rule concerning the direction demand theory should take, there is no cause for alarm. Great vitality is reflected in current discussions; and, obviously, a number of promising avenues exist for future research. Little is to be gained by speculating about the precise nature of the demand models that will be forthcoming some decades hence; it is sufficient to recognize that they will be more sophisticated constructs and will, almost certainly, lead to more effective applied work. But, whatever the future may produce, some interest attaches to a review of past contributions and to the consideration of how the growing stock of ideas brought us to our present theoretical position. Thus, in what follows, an attempt will be made to trace the changing configuration of demand theory at both the technical and conceptual levels.

Technical Extensions of Classical Demand Theory

In discussing recent developments in the theory of demand, it is helpful to conceive of a fundamental demand model and, then, consider how various modifications and extensions of this basic formulation have been made over time to improve explanatory power. The version of demand theory that Hicks established so firmly and successfully in *Value and Capital* occupies a unique place in the literature and can be taken as the point of departure for modern theorizing [Houthakker 1961, p. 704]. The Hicksian or "classical" model represents a convenient benchmark, of course, because it deals with a highly simplified standard case and is generally familiar.

The major assumptions on which the Hicksian model rests deserve brief mention. The theory is static and treats the choice problems of a single consumer in situations where only small changes around an equilibrium point are considered. Each consumer is assumed to have well-defined and consistent preferences that can be represented by an ordinal utility function; interdependence between individual utility functions is ruled out. Although the time dimensions of the system are somewhat vague, the usual interpretation is that flow variables are employed; the consumer, who can neither borrow nor lend, has a given income each period which he expends fully on commodities to be consumed within the period. Then, by assuming further that the consumer possesses complete knowledge of market prices and the technical properties of the respective commodities, the choice problem is translated into a straightforward one of constrained maximization. The rational consumer is supposed to select the particular commodity combination that maximizes utility subject to the limitations imposed by fixed total expenditure [Anspach 1966].

On the basis of these and other assumptions to be discussed, a relatively comprehensive theory of demand could be formulated in terms of classical calculus methods. While Hicks confined his mathematical remarks to appendixes, the growing movement toward formal expression of theory shifted attention more and more to the mathematical structure of the demand model. And the emphasis on formal questions was important because it led to a series of technical extensions of the theory. That is to say, the inspiration for changes of this type came from the recognition of deficiencies or limitations in the *mathematical formulation* of the Hicksian model of demand. Revisions were made not because the standard explanation of consumer behavior was challenged in any basic way but, rather, because the technical requirements for meaningful utility maximization were not established satisfactorily, because more general and rigorous statements of demand theorems could be reached via reformulation, etc.

For example, in the case of nonnegativity restrictions, the existing model was reinterpreted to eliminate the possibility of an optimum solution implying negative consumption of certain commodities.

From an organizational standpoint, it will be convenient to begin systematic discussion with an account of some of the more important technical extensions of demand theory. The logic of such contributions is immediately apparent, and the development of theory in conformity with these technical themes has an "inevitable" quality. To say this, however, is not to suggest that the modifications are necessarily routine or trivial. The interesting thing is that reconsideration of the mathematical structure of a model frequently raises questions of the greatest significance for economic interpretation. In effect, we are forced to reexamine our assumptions about the real phenomena under investigation and make sure the economic problem is well posed.

It can be objected, of course, that if changes in mathematical treatment do, in fact, lead to major conceptual shifts, little virtue resides in a classification system that attempts to distinguish "technical" extensions of demand theory from other developments. This line of criticism has some justification; ultimately, the separation of a technical advance from a conceptual one rests on arbitrary judgement. Nevertheless, it remains true that a large part of the postwar literature on demand can reasonably be described as technically oriented. The central focus of these writings was on formal problems related to the classical model of utility maximization. Thus, the main accomplishments of the period arose from the elaboration of the conventional theory rather than from the exploration of fundamentally new types of models. Debreu's elegant and rigorous restatement of the choice problem in Chapter 4 of the *Theory of Value* (1959) has substantial advantages over earlier formulations, but the essential view of consumption contained here differs little from that in Hicks' *Value and Capital* (1939). Only in recent years has the pattern of research changed and serious interest been shown in radically different demand models based on game theory, behavioral analysis, etc. It may be, of course, that intensive technical investigation of the traditional model was a necessary prelude to more adventurous work.

Nonnegativity Restrictions

Use of classical calculus methods requires that an optimization problem be set up in a particular way; specifically, the objective and constraint functions must be continuous and differentiable, all functional constraints must appear in the form of equalities, and the system must be free of either explicit or implicit nonnegativity constraints on the variables. But when demand analysis is forced into this mold, problems arise and an economically meaningful solution is not assured. In other words, the logic of the economic application and the mathematical conditions may be at variance [Koopmans 1957, p. 6]. At equilibrium, a solution can arise where the optimum quantities of certain commodities are negative magnitudes.

Escape from the technical impasse just described is possible in several ways. Thus, if general knowledge of the economic situation leads to the conclusion that a particular operating point has only nonnegative coordinates, the usual consumption theory can hold for small changes around that point. Or, making an even bolder assumption, it can be accepted that, at *any* equilibrium, the optimum quantity of each commodity specified in the consumer's utility function is always positive [Wu and Pontney 1967, p. 172]. As Lancaster has observed:

> Traditional economic analysis has been based on the faith (often justified) that the functional constraints will always be effective and the direct constraints always ineffective in the region of the optimum. [Lancaster 1968, p. 61]

It is obvious, however, that the actual behavior of the consumer may be consistent with zero demand for one or more of the existing commodities. In short, nonnegativity restrictions have to be introduced explicitly. And the most straightforward approach is to reformulate the demand model as a nonlinear programming problem. The consumer's objective must be to maximize his utility function

$$U = \phi(q_1, q_2, \ldots, q_n) \tag{3.1}$$

subject to the budget constraint

$$\sum_{i=1}^{n} p_i q_i - y^o = 0 \tag{3.2}$$

and the inequality constraints

$$q_i \geqslant 0 \qquad (i = 1, 2, \ldots, n) \tag{3.3}$$

Then, use of the Kuhn-Tucker Theorem permits the derivation of revised equilibrium conditions which can rationalize both the decision to consume and the decision not to consume [Wu and Pontney 1967, ch. 8].

The mathematical procedures for treating this type of model have become familiar [Lancaster 1968, ch. 5]; [Houthakker 1960b], but the economic interpretation is less sure [Houthakker 1952; Theil 1952]. One significant problem concerns the way in which consumption choices vary with income. Practically, an individual is likely to consume only a small number of the numerous goods in the system and, as Duesenberry has emphasized, improvement in the consumer's income tends to be associated with movement to different and higher quality goods rather than to higher levels of consumption of the same goods [Duesenberry 1952, p. 22]. The Kuhn–Tucker demand model is broadly consistent with this type of behavior, but questions still exist about the properties the utility function must possess if the model is to yield meaningful solutions showing that any number of goods can be chosen within some reasonable range (greater than one and less than n) [Furubotn 1967].

Determination of the Global Optimum

Just as the classical calculus methods fail to insure a solution with appropriate sign (for economic interpretation), so these methods are also incapable of assuring a solution that represents a global optimum. Fortunately, this last limitation is not always of crucial significance for demand theory. Under some assumptions about the mathematical forms of the utility function (i.e., the maximand) and the budget constraint (i.e., the closed feasible set), the discovery of a local optimum immediately gives the global. In other words, every local optimum is also a global optimum if the utility function (3.1) is a positive monotonic transformation of a concave function, and the feasible set defined by (3.2) is a convex set [Lancaster 1968, pp. 17–19]. Since it is widely believed that the utility function conforms to the above specification, the real issue turns on whether equation (3.2) yields a convex set. And, for simple situations convexity does hold. When competition is assumed and the budget constraint (3.2) is linear, all the sufficient conditions are met; the global optimum is determinate via the classical procedures.

Although the classical formulation can be satisfactory in some applications, economists have shown concern with cases where local and global optima do not correspond. Professor Wold, for example, has noted this problem in his rigorous exposition of demand theory.

> What differs from other expositions is notably our stressing of one point, viz. that in the budget choice the consumer makes a simultaneous comparison between all budget alternatives he can afford, not only between alternatives in the vicinity of the optimal budget. . . . It is not sufficient to require, as is done in several earlier treatments, that the indifference surface should be convex in the vicinity of the tangent point q^o, for as indicated in [the diagram] it may then occur that there are budgets farther away in the balance plane that are preferred to q^o. [Wold and Jureen 1953, p. 90]

It should also be pointed out, of course, that the more recent adoption of the set-theoretic approach has had the effect of banishing forever the "myopic" predispositons inherent in the older theory [Koopmans 1957, p. 6]. As Debreu states:

> . . . it has been essentially a change from the calculus to convexity and topological properties, a transformation which has resulted in notable gains in the generality and in the simplicity of the theory. [Debreu 1959, p. viii]

Number of Commodities

Traditionally, consumption theory has involved utility and constraint functions based on a *finite* number of variables. But since it is possible to conceive of an infinite number of commodities, or commodity spectra, the demand problem can be generalized and reformulated as one in the calculus of variations [Court 1941]. The main justification for the extension is that:

> It is natural to think of the varieties or qualities of the various commodities (in which term we include the services of the factors of production) as constituting a continuous range. There are, at least conceptually, an infinite number of grades of wheat, sizes of shoe or types of labor. Any classification we may make into a finite number of homogeneous classes is bound to be arbitrary. [Graaff 1967, p. 11]

What ever the advantages that may be attributed to this approach, it seems clear that the introduction of infinitely many commodities leads to some relatively cumbersome mathematics. As Houthakker has pointed out, the problem of obtaining meaningful signs in the optimal solution is quite difficult in the case where an infinite number of commodities is assumed [Houthakker 1961, p. 723]. When a finite commodity set holds, economic logic can suggest the existence of a point where the quantities of all commodities must be nonnegative; but, in the infinite case, comparable reasoning is not possible. All that can be said, in general, is that the optimal commodity spectrum is likely to be highly discontinuous.

The study of systems with an infinity of commodities can have interest for more than technical reasons. Consideration of small variations in the characteristics of output introduces the broad issue of product quality and leads to questions concerning why particular goods are accepted or rejected by the consumer [Phlips 1964; Gabor and Granger 1966]. Despite the emphasis of product quality by Chamberlin, this area has not received as much attention as it deserves [Brems 1951; 1968, ch. 14; and Furubotn 1969] and both practical and conceptual problems remain unsolved.

Indivisibility of Commodities

Many situations arise in the theory of demand where meaningful economic interpretation requires the solution to be found in terms of nonnegative *integers* rather than fractional units. In other words, commodities must be viewed as indivisible entities, and the usual calculus methods based on continuous functions must be abandoned [Samuelson 1947, p. 77–81]. A comprehensive theory incorporating such changes has not yet been developed, but elements for this type of construction do exist [Harwitz 1968]. One suggestion has been to adapt the revealed-preference approach to the treatment of indivisible commodities [Wagner 1956], and another possibility is, of course, to use integer programming techniques.

The formal apparatus used to analyze consumer behavior has to meet some rather exacting standards. We are saying, in effect, that the satisfaction of non-negativity constraints is not enough; to secure results that are generally consistent with observed consumption choices, it is necessary to rule out the possibility of an individual purchasing fractional amounts of any good. While the latter behavior is conceivable, only slight loss of realism is sacrificed by adhering to the assumption of integral purchases. On the other hand, acceptance of the condition $q_i \geqslant 0 (i = 1, 2, \ldots, n)$, would admit cases where the optimum quantities of many (or all) goods could be very small. Then, at equilibrium, the consumer might be found choosing one tenth of a high quality cigar in preference to three cheaper cigars, half of an expensive suit, and so on.

The problem just mentioned can be interpreted to mean that the properties of the utility function have not been defined appropriately. If it is believed that infinitesimal purchases are impossible, representation of consumer preferences should be such that utility maximization can never lead to a solution calling for any optimum quantity to be nonintegral. But this line of reasoning suggests that other "common-sense" restrictions might be placed on the utility function. Since it is difficult to conceive of an individual spending his entire income on a single commodity no matter what the price set, the shapes of the indifference manifolds should be inconsistent with a maximizing solution of this type. Similarly, the utility function should not permit a solution where all n commodities (i.e., all goods in the system) are to be consumed simultaneously. Quadratic and other standard programming forms do not take account of these requirements. There is, therefore, reason to be skeptical about the worth of extending such methods to integer programming applications in the theory of demand.

Duality and the Indirect Utility Function

In the normal presentation, the utility function takes the form of equation (3.1) above, and the independent variables are understood to be the respective commodity flows $q_1, q_2, \ldots, q_n$. From a mathematical standpoint, however, it is clear that if the demand for each commodity is a function of prices and income, the latter variables can appear as arguments of the utility function. Utility, in other words, is indirectly a function of prices and income [Hotelling

1932], and the so-called "indirect" utility function can be established as

$$U = F(z_1, z_2, \ldots, z_n) \tag{3.4}$$

where the variables z_i represent price-income ratios:

$$z_i = \frac{p_i}{y} \qquad (i = 1, 2, \ldots, n)$$

The new formulation (3.4) differs from the ordinary utility function in superficial appearance, but can be manipulated in essentially familiar ways to yield indifference surfaces [Hicks 1958] and standard propositions of the classical theory of demand [Roy 1947].

The relation of the indirect utility function to the modern concept of duality was demonstrated by Houthakker [Houthakker 1952]. Thus, if equation (3.4) is *minimized* subject to the budget constraint

$$\sum_{i=1}^{n} p_i q_i^o - y = 0 \quad \text{or} \quad \sum_{i=1}^{n} z_i q_i^o - 1 = 0 \tag{3.5}$$

where the quantities of all commodities are specified, the result is equivalent to maximizing the "direct" utility function (3.1) subject to the usual constraint (3.2). The maximum value of ϕ is equal to the minimum value of F; and the situation here can be interpreted in terms of the duality theorem [Hadley 1964, pp. 238–240] familiar from programming literature:

> If either the primal or the dual problem has a finite optimum solution, then the other problem has a finite optimum solution, and the values of the objective functions are equal. [Naylor and Vernon 1969, p. 197]

Since parallel technical procedures are involved in the "direct" and "indirect" optimization problems, no fundamentally different conclusions about demand can be anticipated [Samuelson 1965]. It is true, nevertheless, that the changed perspective of the dual problem permits the standard theoretical statements to be seen with new insight; and Hicks has been able to utilize the "indirect" analysis (p theory) effectively in his work on *A Revision of Demand Theory* [Hicks 1956].

The Theory of Revealed Preference

There is rather general agreement that the development of the theory of revealed preference during the postwar years resulted in a major consolidation of knowledge. Houthakker's balanced assessment of the literature is typical of current thinking.

> Since Uzawa's contribution appears to settle the remaining problems concerning the relation between the classical approach to consumer's choice and the revealed preference approach (at least if everything is convex, continuous, and non-saturated), this is a suitable point for stock-taking. To what extent has the revealed preference approach satisfied the expectations which it raised? If we regard it primarily as an attempt at theoretical clarification, it has certainly been successful. As Samuelson (1950) pointed out, the longstanding question of integrability has at last been brought to a conclusion. As far as the foundations of the static theory of choice for a single consumer are concerned, we now know where we stand. [Houthakker 1961, p. 713]

In a real sense, then, the explication of revealed preference can be viewed as the capstone achievement of the line of thought that began with Pareto and Slutsky and continued unbroken to the modern era. Although the point of departure of revealed preference theory is entirely different from that of conventional utility analysis, there is no logical conflict between the two approaches. If the observed behavior of the consumer is consistent with certain postulates, it can be shown that he must possess an indifference map. Moreover, the properties of the latter can be established in as great detail as desired by considering the consumer's choices. We return, in other words, to the familiar model of utility maximization; and the revealed-preference doctrine emerges as a very sophisticated technical extension of the classical theory of demand.

The Analysis of Choice Behavior

Utility is not subject to direct observation or measurement; but, by contrast, the *choices* the consumer makes in the marketplace are clearly evident. Samuelson recognized the importance of this difference and went on to revolutionize thinking about demand [Samuelson 1938; 1947]. Stressing the desirability of empirical verification, he was able to develop a theory of consumption which avoided direct reliance on the utility concept and concentrated instead on observable price-quantity relations. By using value sums of the form

$$\sum_{i=1}^{n} p_i q_i$$

two objectives were accomplished. First, the new formulation permitted movement away from the artificialities of "instantaneous rates of change"; continuous demand functions could be replaced with empirically verifiable expressions based on finite differences. Second, the use of value sums provided a convenient means for organizing data on the consumer's reactions to different commodity bundles under different price conditions. Given two sets of quantities and two sets of prices, the sums

$$\sum_{i=1}^{n} p_i^1 q_i^1, \sum_{i=1}^{n} p_i^1 q_i^2, \sum_{i=1}^{n} p_i^2 q_i^1, \text{ and} \sum_{i=1}^{n} p_i^2 q_i^2$$

can be constructed. Inequality relations involving these value sums have significance for demand theory, and the revealed-preference logic is designed to make the interconnections clear.

To begin the analysis, it is assumed that a particular set of positive prices (p_i^1) is given.[1] In light of these prices, the consumer makes choices among the n commodities in existence; discommodities are ruled out. If the consumer buys the commodity set (q_i^1) his total expenditure is, of course, given by

$$\sum_{i=1}^{n} p_i^1 q_i^1$$

At the prevailing prices, however, some alternate set of commodities (q_i^2) could certainly have been purchased without exceeding this total expenditure level. Thus, it is possible to write:

$$\sum_{i=1}^{n} p_i^1 q_i^2 \leqslant \sum_{i=1}^{n} p_i^1 q_i^1 \tag{3.6}$$

Moreover, since q_i^1 was chosen by the consumer even though q_i^2 was attainable, the implication is that bundle q_i^1 is preferred to q_i^2. Action indicates preference; and, in the terminology employed here, the first bundle is revealed to be preferred to the second.

Assuming consistent behavior on the part of the consumer, a fundamental axiom of revealed preference is stated as follows: If the commodity set q_i^1 is revealed to be preferred to q_i^2, then q_i^2 must never be revealed to be preferred to q_i^1. Now, with a different set of prices p_i^2, the commodity bundle q_i^2 might be

1. The existence of a set of positive prices covering the n commodities in the system is taken for granted and not explained. The theory of exchange is able to explain the formation of the price structure, but the theory of exchange is based on indifference curves and the utility concept.

purchased. But the behavioral axiom just noted denies the possibility that $q_i^2 R q_i^1$ and, thus, the relation

$$\sum_{i=1}^{n} p_i^2 q_i^1 \leqslant \sum_{i=1}^{n} p_i^2 q_i^2 \tag{3.7}$$

cannot be true. The only acceptable explanation for the consumer's choice of q_i^2 is that

$$\sum_{i=1}^{n} p_i^2 q_i^1 > \sum_{i=1}^{n} p_i^2 q_i^2 \tag{3.8}$$

In other words, (3.6) implies (3.8) if two-term consistency holds. (If $\Sigma\, p^1 q^2 > \Sigma\, p^1 q^1$, q^1 is not revealed preferred to q^2 and nothing can be said concerning the cost $\Sigma\, p^2 q^1$ relative to $\Sigma\, p^2 q^2$.)

From these simple generalizations about demand, it was possible to establish many of the operational propositions of conventional utility analysis. Specifically, the weak axiom of revealed preference permitted demonstration that: demand functions are single-valued, the price change and the quantity change must have opposite signs when apparent real income is constant, demand functions are homogeneous of zeroth degree in prices and income, etc. [Samuelson 1938; Little 1949]. The fact that familiar theorems could be reached independently of any direct consideration of utility had interest. More important, however, was the question of whether the revealed-preference approach represented a means for inferring the essential properties of the consumer's indifference map. And it was this general theme that occupied demand theorists for some time thereafter.

The Relation Between Revealed Preference and Ordinal Preference

For a highly developed logical system, there is no fundamental distinction between assumptions and conclusions; the theorist has the freedom to decide which statements are to be considered as the assumptions and which as the derived conclusions. Thus, in demand theory, the work on revealed preference led to an extensive discussion of two axiom sets—one concerned with consumer preferences and the other with demand or choice functions.

> An alternative to making assumptions about Adam's preferences and then deducing restrictions on his choice functions is to place "reasonable"

> conditions directly on his choice behavior, and then to deduce those more complicated restrictions on choice functions that form the bulk of the theorems in demand theory. In doing this, however, we have to be careful not to place *stronger* conditions on choice behavior than are implied by the postulate that the individual chooses on the basis of a preference structure and an attainable set, for otherwise we could be constructing what is essentially a different theory. So an important aspect of this approach via choice behavior- which is due mainly to Samuelson- is to check that the assumptions placed on it are indeed implied by a preference structure. [Newman 1965, p. 130]

The search for a behavioral postulate in consonance with the traditional beliefs about preference structures ended with the introduction of the "strong axiom" of revealed preference [Afriat 1965]. This assumption requires the consumer's choices among commodity bundles to show consistency and transitivity. Specifically, if q_i^1 is revealed to be preferred to q_i^2, which is revealed to be preferred to q_i^3, . . . which is revealed to be preferred to q_i^m , then q_i^m must never be revealed to be preferred to q_i^1. Given the strong axiom, the analysis of the general n commodity case can go forward without difficulty; evidence of indirect preference (as q_i^1 over q_i^m) is meaningful because no contradictions can arise in comparisons among a series of bundles.

The technical discussions of axiom systems opened the way for rigorous demonstrations of how information on value sums could be used to derive the structure of preferences [Little 1949; Hicks 1956].[2] Thus, with the aid of the strong axiom and some assumptions about continuity and boundedness, Houthakker was able to secure a key proof [Houthakker 1950]. In essence, he showed that a consumer who always acts in accordance with the axioms of revealed preference must possess an indifference map and that the map can be reconstructed as closely as desired by observing the consumer's purchases at various price sets and making the proper inferences.

This result was, of course, a reflection of the fact that, under the conditions established, the set of axioms pertaining to choice or demand functions and the set pertaining to preferences are logically equivalent to one another. Apart from some cases of minor importance where no representation of preferences is possible even though choice behavior is manifest [Newman 1965, p. 151], the theory of revealed preference and the theory of utility are identical. It follows, then, that the respective axiom systems can be placed side by side for comparison; and the task performed by each axiom in its own system can be studied [Houthakker 1961, pp. 712-713; Newman 1965, pp. 150-151]. Uzawa's well-known paper was of special importance in clarifying the formal questions here; he carried out a comprehensive investigation of the equivalence of the alternative

2. Some of the significant contributions in this area are: [Corlett and Newman 1953; Newman 1955, 1965; Georgescu-Roegen 1954a; Rose 1958; Arrow 1959; Gale 1960; Green 1957; Mishan 1961].

axiom systems, and showed the relation between the Slutsky equations and choice functions [Uzawa 1960]. In general, of course, the theory of choice behavior (or revealed preference) can be used to derive all the properties of indifference and demand curves that were originally determined via utility theory.

These developments in axiomatic analysis represented a major intellectual achievement and led to deeper understanding of traditional demand theory [Richter 1966]. Nevertheless, the technical advances made did not result in any startling improvement in empirical research. Longstanding problems concerning aggregation and interaction have been mentioned as obstacles to applied work [Duesenberry 1952, pp. 17–19], but perhaps a more basic source of difficulty lies in the assumption of strict consumer rationality. Both utility theory and revealed-preference theory require that the consumer show highly consistent choice behavior. Thus, for example, if the consumer does not act in conformity with the strong axiom, he must be regarded as "irrational" and the whole system of revealed preference effectively breaks down.[3]

This rather rigid position relative to consistent preferences is ill adapted to the needs of an empirical science. Before observed consumer choices can be interpreted confidently it would seem essential to learn more about individual decision-making behavior under the conditions actually operative in the real world. This means, inter alia, that the process of human decision making itself and such factors as uncertainty, the cost of search, the social setting of choice, etc. must be taken into account by the demand model. Fortunately, there are indications that current research is, in fact, headed in this new direction.

The Interpretation of Consumer Preferences

During the neoclassical era, the approach to demand theory taken by writers like Jevons, Menger, and Walras placed strong emphasis on the role of utility in economic calculations. Utility was understood in a cardinal sense and quite specific properties were ascribed to the utility function. Thus, the latter could be written in the additive form.

$$U = {}_1f(q_1) + {}_2f(q_2) + \ldots + {}_nf(q_n) \tag{3.9}$$

Here, the contribution to total utility made by any commodity is assumed to be independent of the consumption rates of all other commodities.

$$\frac{\delta^2 U}{\delta q_i q_j} = 0$$

3. Note that violation of the axioms of revealed preference can be ascribed to changes in taste.

Further, the marginal utility yielded by any commodity is taken to be a diminishing function of the rate of consumption of that commodity.

$$\frac{\delta^2 U}{\delta q_i^2} < 0$$

On the basis of these axioms and the assertion of utility maximizing behavior, neoclassical theorists were able to derive a number of fundamental demand theorems. The rise of ordinal theory, however, did away with the need for these special restrictions on the form of the utility function [Stigler 1950]. The modern trend was to generalization; instead of insisting on universal independence, the ordinal model allows the cross-derivatives to show any relation between pairs of commodities [Samuelson 1947, pp. 174–189], and permits increasing, decreasing, or constant marginal utility to hold.

While the development of ordinal analysis reflected more sophisticated thinking about the problems of demand, the emphasis on generality had the effect of draining much of the empirical content from the theory [Rader 1963]. If any monotonic transformation of the utility function constitutes an acceptable index, distinctive properties must be few. The only real commitment is to the idea that the indifference manifolds are convex [Hicks 1946, pp. 20–24]; and even this presumption has been challenged [Graaff 1967, pp. 42–43; Gorman 1957; Rothenberg 1960].

The generalized ordinal model represented by an equation like (3.1) admits of complementarity and substitution, but because no specification is made of the internal structure of the utility function, little insight is conveyed into the nature or basis of consumer choice. In his argument justifying convexity of indifference curves, Hicks did introduce an empirical premise by suggesting that, with given market prices, the consumer normally reaches an equilibrium where a variety of different goods are consumed simultaneously. The notion that an individual does not specialize in the consumption of a single product (or a very limited number of products) is confirmed by casual observation; and as long as the focus is on the highly simplified geometric case involving two "commodities," the discussion has strong intuitive appeal. The trouble is, however, that the generalization of the elementary two-commodity case to an n-commodity model tends to be made in a purely mechanical fashion so that the general model does not differ in essentials from the simpler one.[4]

For example, when a family of indifference curves becomes a family of indifference hypersurfaces, are we to believe that, at equilibrium, all n commodities in the system are consumed at positive rates? As noted earlier, corner solutions are consistent with the assumption of convex hypersurfaces. But, then,

4. See [Henderson and Quandt 1958, pp. 30–32]. It might also be noted that the use of the composite commodity concept does not obviate the difficulties considered here.

are the shapes of the hypersurfaces such as to make complete specialization of consumption a possibility at certain price configurations? The implication of these questions seems clear: unless the utility function is defined in less general terms than (3.1), understanding of why certain of the n commodities are consumed and others are not must be quite limited.

The generalized Hicksian model leaves unanswered some fundamental questions about the reasons for consumer choice; but, in defense, it is often asserted that the ordinal utility function is designed merely to *describe* choices and not to *explain* them [Graaff 1967, p. 34]. Insofar as this position implies that there is no need to seek an ultimate psychological explanation of choice in terms of the utility or satisfactions derived from consumption, it is reasonable. What can be challenged, though, is the presumption that any attempts to explain the proximate forces shaping consumer preferences are vain [Morgenstern 1948]. If it were literally true that no hypotheses existed to rationalize the characteristics of the utility function, it would follow that no restrictions whatsoever could be placed on the function. The utility function would then be reduced to nothing more than the most general statement of a relation between an abstract index (U) and rates of commodity consumption; any mathematical form would be open.

Since such extreme purity of theory is not desired by many, recent literature has been directed more and more to the task of infusing greater empirical content into the classic ordinal utility function. The contributions vary considerably as to their objectives and the degree to which they actually incorporate new empirical premises, but all are concerned with the need to explain more fully the factors that shape consumer choice. At one extreme, the intent is merely to establish a more precise definition of the utility function in behavioral terms, but the literature also includes more radical departures from the basic Hicksian model. The latter consider such topics as the "technology" of consumption, the role of learning, the significance of externalities, the concept of commodity groups, etc. From the study of these separate themes there is emerging improved general understanding of how preferences are formed and why the consumer tends to choose one particular subset of commodities over another. We turn to this body of writings next in continuing the review of contemporary demand theory.

Behavior Lines and Lexicographic Preferences

It is said that a commodity bundle q_i^1 is preferred to q_i^2 if, *ceteris paribus*, the consumer freely *chooses* q_i^1 rather than q_i^2. From the standpoint of observable behavior, the preference relation is easily defined but the indifference relation is not. No simple test based on action can be associated with the concept of indifference [Little 1950, p. 23]. Little called attention to this difficulty and urged that the term "behavior line" be used in place of "indifference curve" [Little 1949]. He also argued that, given strict convexity and fixed competitive prices, only one point on an indifference curve can appear as an equilibrium point; thus, whether other points on the same indifference curve are preferred to the equilibrium point or not makes no difference to the actual choice. In general, it is only necessary to know that the points on any behavior line are preferred to any points on behavior lines closer to the origin, and dispreferred to any points on behavior lines further from the origin.

These considerations gave rise to the concept of a lexicographical preference ordering [Georgescu-Rogen 1958; Debreu 1954; Chipman 1960]. The latter is a hierarchical scheme which distinguishes, first, between points on higher and lower behavior lines, then, considers the ordering of points on a given behavior line, and so on for as many stages as are built into the lexicographical device. To each stage designated there corresponds a separate utility index; thus, one utility function holds for the primary ordering, another for the secondary ordering, etc.

It follows from this organization that the utility of any commodity bundle is not a scalar; rather, utility is a vector having as many components as there are separate orderings in the hierarchy. In principle, the comparison of two bundles would require sequential examination of the respective utility components—with the process being continued up to the stage where one bundle's superiority over another became apparent [Encarnacion 1964]. Practically, however, the higher-level utility comparisons are not relevant to market choices under competition, and are essential only in cases of monopolistic discrimination.

Utility Trees

General observation suggests that certain commodities are more closely related than others and can be grouped meaningfully into larger categories. The theoretical implications of commodity groups—a problem distinct from that considered by the composite commodity theorem [Hicks 1946, pp. 33-34; Leontief 1936]—have been studied in recent years, and work in the area is continuing [Green 1964]. Of special significance is the literature that considers the concept of functional separability.[5] Emphasis here is on the formal conditions for the separation of subsets of variables from a prime set representing the independent variables of a complicated function in many variables.

Thus, knowing only the mathematical properties of a utility function like (3.1), it is possible to determine the separable subsets (of various orders) and also to describe the characteristics of the intermediate functions consistent with

5. See [Leontief 1947; Sono 1961]. Professor Sono considered the problem of functional separability before Leontief, but the paper was not translated into English until 1961.

these sets. For example, under certain conditions, the utility function might translate into the form:

$$U = {}_of[{}_1f(q_{11},q_{12},\ldots,q_{1a}),\ {}_2f(q_{21},q_{22},\ldots,q_{2b}),\ldots,$$
$${}_mf(q_{m1},q_{m2},\ldots,q_{mz})] \qquad (a+b+\ldots+z=n) \tag{3.10}$$

According to this equation, which can be viewed as a utility tree, the n different commodities in (3.1) are partitioned among m mutually exclusive and exhaustive subsets.[6] Each subset represents a branch of the tree and the commodities within any branch, as $q_{11},\ldots,q_{1a}$, constitute the independent variables of a branch function, like ${}_1f(q_{11},q_{12},\ldots,q_{1a})$. Under this arrangement, utility is related, in an immediate sense, to a set of intermediate variables $(S_1,S_2,\ldots,S_m)$ but each of these, in turn, depends on certain of the n primary commodities in the manner indicated by the relevant branch function. In general, the order of a subset is defined by the number of other sets in the whole system from which it is separable: the subsets shown here are of the first order.

Various "principles of separation" can be conceived to justify the partitioning of commodities into a number of distinct groups (or branches). Thus, commodities may be related because they all contribute to the same general consumption purpose, as various foods provide protein in the diet; because they have common bonds of technical complementarity, as the goods which cooperate to produce a consumable service like transportation; or for other reasons. Note, however, that for any grouping established–i.e., any structure of subsets of q_1, $q_2,\ldots,q_n$ in the utility function (3.1)–there are corresponding rules of consumer behavior implied; and the mathematical expression of these rules is provided by the necessary and sufficient conditions stated for set separability. Therefore, an elementary requirement is that the rules of behavior implied by the commodity subsets be consistent with other significant generalizations about consumer behavior that have been verified by observation.

The so-called "strong" and "weak" definitions of separability, which are of central importance to the theory of utility trees, can be considered from the standpoint of the empirical premises they involve. Broadly stated, the effect of the weak definition is to leave room for complex association among the intermediate variables $(S_1,S_2,\ldots,S_m)$ in the "generation" of utility; some or all of the m intermediate variables can be interdependent.

$$\frac{\delta\left[\dfrac{\delta U/\delta S_h}{\delta U/\delta S_i}\right]}{\delta S_j} \neq 0 \tag{3.11}$$

6. This restriction is one of convenience. A utility tree can be conceived even when subsets intersect and the elements comprising each subset are not mutually exclusive.

By contrast, application of the strong definition of separability would require (3.11) to vanish. The latter condition implies that utility must depend additively on the variables $S_1, S_2, \ldots, S_m$; and, thus, in the limiting case, a function like (3.9) could emerge [Houthakker 1960; Green 1961].

The Integration of Consumption and Production Theory

Professor Hicks has made the suggestion that consumer preferences are established in terms of certain ends or objectives that are not, in general, commodities. Rather, commodities are seen as the *means* to the attainment of objectives [Hicks 1956, p. 166; Stigler 1945; Smith 1959]. Since this interpretation indicates an indirect linkage between utility and the individual commodities, it has formal similarity to the problems handled by separable functions. Morishima, seeing this, made the mathematical translation and extended the analysis in some interesting directions; it is to him we owe the neat generalization of production and consumption theory [Morishima 1959]. The latter work, however, was based on the strong definition of separability and assumed that all branch functions are homogeneous of degree one (i.e., reflect constant returns to scale in the production sense).

It is not clear that so rigid an interpretation is consistent with Hicks' original thinking on the issue. Thus, with a more general model than that used by Morishima, some additional insights into demand phenomena can be gained [Furubotn 1963]. For example, the extended utility-tree analysis makes some difference for the interpretation of the marginal utility of expenditure (MUE); following an approach which permits varying returns to scale in the branch functions, it becomes possible to explain increasing MUE without invoking special psychological assumptions concerning consumer behavior [Samuelson 1942; Friedman and Savage 1948]. That is, the MUE can be shown to increase whether the individual elements "consumed" afford the consumer increasing, decreasing, or constant marginal utility.

Further, the role of labor services can be introduced [Furubotn 1963, pp. 141-142]. The orthodox presentation of utility theory neglects any consideration of human effort in the consumption process; the utility tree, on the other hand, calls attention to the labor inputs and provides for a convenient formulation of these important variables [Muth, 1966]. Production of consumable products (i.e., $S_1, S_2, \ldots, S_m$) must involve the services of various types of labor. And, in a very real sense, the demand for any commodity depends on the amounts and costs of the complementary labor services which must be employed to utilize the commodity. For example, the great appeal of products such as instant coffee and frozen dinners for the American consumer implies that the services of hired cooks can only be secured at relatively high prices and that the consumer's own services are also valued highly. Thus, the rational consumer economizes on such costly inputs in "producing" this range of consumable products [Becker 1965].

The "technology of consumption" approach also has important application as a device for analyzing the process of new product acceptance. Lancaster has remarked:

> Traditional demand theory has never been able to handle satisfactorily the problem of introducing new goods. The consumer's preference map is given in terms of the original set of goods, and the new good requires that this be thrown away and replaced by a new preference map based on the new set of goods. All the information concerning preferences on the original set of goods is discarded in the process. [Lancaster 1969, pp. 218–219].

And, in an effort to circumvent the difficulties here, he has proposed that attention be turned from the commodities themselves to their intrinsic characteristics [Lancaster 1966a; 1966b]. Broadly, Lancaster's analysis does for consumption theory what Chenery's discussion of engineering production relations does for production theory. In the case of consumption, the key condition is that individual preferences relate to certain fundamental physical or aesthetic characteristics; commodities are merely the vehicles that convey the characteristics to the consumer [Georgescu-Roegen 1936; Quandt 1956]. Thus, the indifference map (drawn in terms of intrinsic characteristics) can be stable over time even though the array of specific commodities in the system is changing. By the systematic development of these ideas, Lancaster is able to explain, *inter alia,* how new goods embodying different proportions of the basic characteristics can gain acceptance with the public.

Noncomparable Consumption Alternatives

Ordinal utility analysis presumes that the consumer, in considering any two commodity bundles q_i^1 and q_i^2, can always make one and only one of the following statements: q_i^1 is preferred to q_i^2, q_i^2 is preferred to q_i^1, q_i^1 is indifferent to q_i^2. Taken together with the assumption of transitivity, this condition is often referred to as the postulate of rationality. The existence of such behavior is, of course, crucial to the theory of demand. It has been objected, however, that situations may easily arise where the individual is unable to say either that one alternative is preferred to another or that indifference holds. The two alternatives may simply not be comparable [Majumdar 1961, p. 7].

> It is a curiosity of the history of science that some of the most obvious and immediate of human experiences seem to require the very newest kind of formal expression. It must always have been obvious that there are

> things that cannot be compared. It is equally obvious that of any two such things it can correctly be said *neither* that they give the same amount of utility *nor* that one gives more. Likewise, it can be said *neither* that one is indifferent which one gets nor that one has a preference ordering between them. Yet the formal embodiment of this obvious truth is only now, as I write, taking place. [Walsh 1970, p. 33]

The existence of noncomparable alternatives must have significance for the purely formal structure of choice and demand theory, but the practical consequences of making the needed modifications in the standard doctrine may also be important. Relative to observed behavior, we might ask, for example, whether people actively seek to avoid choices of the noncomparable type and whether the ultimate equilibrium reached is strongly affected by such evasive tactics. Whatever the resolution of the basic problem of noncomparability, it would seem that the revised theory will have to possess greater empirical content and consider more carefully the social setting of choice.

The Decision-Making Unit

Demand theory is often vague about the nature of the ultimate decision-making unit responsible for commodity choice. There is discussion of both *individuals* and *households,* but the relation between the two is not always completely clear. Certainly, these terms cannot be used interchangeably in the theory. Unless all members of the household have homogeneous and identical preferences, it is essential to know whose preferences are determining commodity purchases. One way of rationalizing the situation is to assume that the choices of the head of the household dominate. Then, a paternalistic system exists and the head's choices are imposed on others in the household.

If individual preferences are to play a more active role in the choice process, however, the problem of aggregation must be faced. In effect, the household must find some systematic basis for reconciling the conflicting claims of household members on the limited financial resources available for consumption. Various schemes for achieving this objective are conceivable [Samuelson 1956], but the general theoretical solution would seem to depend on the application of welfare theory.

> The members of the household may have some common ethic, or *W* [social welfare function], which enables them to combine their individual preference-scales into a household scale. It is, indeed, more probable that a sufficient concilience of ethical valuations will exist within a small household than throughout a large nation—a clearly defined *W* is more likely to exist for one household than for a number of households. If this be granted, the "private indifference curves" of the household are nothing else than

> Bergson frontiers. They may not behave very well—especially since external effects are likely to be extremely important within a household—but if we assume the household to come into equilibrium at fixed prices on a competitive market, we can place various familiar restrictions on their shape in the neighbourhood of potential equilibrium points. [Graaf 1967, p. 52]

The Bergson contours, defined in commodity space, give a consistent representation of the social tastes of the household unit. Such a preference map is analogous to the conventional set of indifference curves which specifies individual tastes. Consequently, demand theory can proceed in essentially normal fashion. If, however, each member of the household acts independently so that behavior conforms to no sensible social welfare function, the successive choices of the household would appear irrational to an outside observer; and, e.g., the axioms of revealed preference must be violated.

Probabilistic Preferences

In an attempt to introduce greater empirical content, or realism, into classical demand theory, a number of writers have given explicit consideration to the probabilistic character of choice. The standard approach is rigidly deterministic. When confronted by alternative commodity bundles q_i^1 and q_i^2, the consumer is assumed to be capable of deciding which alternative is preferred (or indifferent). Then, having once revealed his choice, he is supposed to be consistent; *ceteris paribus,* the consumer considering q_i^1 and q_i^2 again should always choose the bundle regarded as preferable in the original experiment.

But, softening this case, one can argue [Georgescu-Roegen, 1936, 1958; Davidson and Marschak, 1959; Quandt, 1956] that the consumer's preference for, say, q_i^1 over q_i^2 does not necessarily mean that he will always choose q_i^1. Rather, it can be assumed that q_i^1 will be selected over q_i^2 with a probability that depends on the degree or strength of the consumer's preference for q_i^1 over q_i^2. In other words, if q_i^1 is only slightly preferred to q_i^2 (judged by a Neumann–Morgenstern utility index), the consumer might display fluctuating choices—selecting q_i^1 with one frequency and q_i^2 with another. True indifference would be reflected as apparent random selection with equal probability of q_i^1 or q_i^2 being purchased.

An interesting aspect of this line of investigation is that the conclusions reached for utility theory can be related to more straightforward psychological experiments involving human perception of phenomena like the weight of objects.

> When subjects are asked to decide which of two weights is heavier, the objectively heavier one is chosen more often than the lighter one, but the relative frequency of choosing the heavier approaches one-half as the

> two weights approach equality. The probability that a subject will choose the objectively heavier weight depends, in general, on the ratio of the two weights. [Simon 1968, p. 9]

Evidence of the type just noted is scarcely decisive [Stigler 1950], but does, perhaps, suggest that speculation about preference structures has some justification. In any event, the work on a probabilistic theory of utility [Luce 1957] seems to hold promise of advances at both the theoretical and applied levels of consumption research.

Choice Under Static Uncertainty

Classical demand analysis is based on certainty in the sense that it assumes each act of choice by the consumer is followed by an outcome that is known with certainty. Under the conventions adopted, the consumer is fully apprised of the technical properties of the various commodities in the system and is assured of receiving precisely the type or quality of good he chooses. Since this formulation of the choice problem is quite restrictive, the work of von Neumann and Morgenstern came as a major conceptual advance.[7] For the first time, it became possible to treat choice among *uncertain* alternatives within a well-defined analytical framework and, thus, to rationalize consumer behavior in situations comparable to those normally encountered in the real world.

The fundamental behavioral hypothesis underlying the Neumann-Morgenstern theory reduces to the following statement:

> In choosing among alternatives open to it, whether or not these alternatives involve risk, a consumer unit . . . behaves as if: (a) it had a consistent set of preferences; (b) these preferences could be completely described by a function attaching a numerical value—to be designated "utility"—to alternatives each of which is regarded as certain, (c) its objective were to make its expected utility as large as possible. [Friedman and Savage 1948, p. 70]

Granting that the consumer possesses a utility function of the type required, he can be conceived as choosing between generalized "lottery tickets"—where each alternative consists of a set of "prizes" whose occurrences are mutually exclusive but characterized by known probability values. For example, if lottery L_1 promises the outcomes $\overline{q}_1$ with probability p and q_1 with probability $(1 - p)$, the expected utility of this option is calculable. Then, the result $p \cdot U(\overline{q}_1) + (1 - p)U(q_1)$ can be compared with the expected utility yielded by another

7. Some leading contributions to the literature include: [von Neumann and Morgenstern 1947, ch. 1; Arrow 1951; 1958; Georgescu-Roegen 1954; Marschak 1950; Armstrong 1948; Friedman and Savage 1948; Alchian 1953; Ellsberg 1954; Herstein and Milnor 1953; Markowitz 1952; Morgenstern 1948].

option L_2, and the alternative offering the greater expected utility will, presumably, be preferred [Borch 1968; Hadar and Russell 1969]. Since the formal system established here implies that utilities can be combined meaningfully to calculate expected values and that utility differences can be ranked, the Neumann–Morgenstern utility index is unique up to a linear transformation.

A simple application of this analysis to demand theory might run as follows [Furubotn 1969]: Assume Q_1 and Q_2 represent the quantities of two distinct types of goods purchased by the consumer each period. Assume further that a unit of any good j ($j = 1,2$) can appear in either a standard (q_j) or a substandard ($\overline{q}_j$) form. Then, the nature of choice subject to risk is such that the consumer is never able to know in advance of actual purchase whether any commodity he is contemplating will come to him in the standard or the substandard form. The consumer is free to decide the general directions of his expenditures on goods and can regulate the variables Q_1 and Q_2, but his power to choose does not extend directly to the subproducts ($q_1, \overline{q}_1, q_2, \overline{q}_2$). Thus, once the levels for Q_1, Q_2 are established, the limit of effective control is reached.

It is clear on a priori grounds that, for given values of Q_1, Q_2, a finite number of distinct combinations of the subproducts $q_1, \overline{q}_1, q_2, \overline{q}_2$ is implied. But if the utility function

$$U = U(q_1,\overline{q}_1,q_2,\overline{q}_2) \tag{3.12}$$

exists, a utility number (U_i) can be associated with each conceivable mix. Moreover, assuming that the probability of drawing a substandard variant of good number 1 in any unit purchase is p and that the corresponding probability for good number 2 is P, it is possible to calculate the probability value (π_i) for the appearance of each different subproduct mix involving $q_1, \overline{q}_1, q_2, \overline{q}_2$ when any total purchase of Q_1, Q_2 is made. In other words, for each subproduct combination ($q_1, \overline{q}_1, q_2, \overline{q}_2$) and U_i, there exists a corresponding probability value of π_i and, therefore, the expected utility (U^*) of any purchase of Q_1, Q_2 can be determined.

$$U^* = \phi(Q_1,Q_2;p,P) \tag{3.13}$$

Although the variables Q_1 and Q_2 must be nonnegative integers, the expected utility function (3.13) can be used in essentially standard fashion to derive demand functions for the respective commodities. As logic would suggest, the demand curve for a product shifts systematically with a change in the probability of receiving a substandard commodity unit in any given draw [Wu and Pontney 1967, ch. 10].

By emphasizing the importance of uncertainty in decision making, the literature following the Neumann–Morgenstern analysis has contributed to a more adequate theory of consumption [Fellner 1961]. Nevertheless, questions have been raised concerning the assumption of maximizing behavior.[8] Even highly simplified psychological experiments, such as binary choice, have not confirmed the hypothesis that individuals typically pursue strategies designed to maximize expected utility. Rather, some of the evidence suggests that consumers may act as though they were playing games against nature; and theory is now being extended in this general direction with the development of game theoretic models of demand [Borch 1969, pp. 119-127].

Interdependence and Consumer Behavior

Economists have long been aware of the fact that external effects can be generated by consumption activity [Veblen 1899; Rae 1905], but the postwar years have seen a substantial rise of interest in the interpersonal apsects of utility and demand.[9] The basic theme underlying recent work is familiar; since there are plausible grounds for believing that the consumption behavior of an individual tends to be influenced by the consumption patterns of others, the literature emphasizes that externalities must be given explicit formulation in the demand model. The immediate problem is to explain how the shape and/or position of an individual's indifference map depend on variables other than the rates of commodity consumption maintained by the individual himself.

Once the influence of social forces on consumer choice is broached, however, fundamental questions arise concerning motivation and the formation of preferences. In this broader analytical context, an individual utility function cannot be defined meaningfully without reference to a general economic matrix. Thus, to understand preferences, it is essential to know something about social interaction. Within a modern industrial society, various types of group phenomena are distinguishable; and different social-psychological hypotheses can be constructed to rationalize such observed conditions as imitation, the desire for exclusiveness, altruism, envy, etc. Through the extension of the traditional theory along these lines, the system of endogenous economic relations has been enlarged [Duesenberry 1952, ch. 6] and useful insights have been gained into the relativity of demand and welfare. Yet, despite conceptual advances, the area is disappointing for its lack of firm empirical foundation. While the externalities discussed have real existence, they are elusive and extremely difficult to quantify. Hence, discussion of the effects of social interaction tends to be largely speculative.

Leibenstein's well-known paper is typical of the newer microeconomic approach [Leibenstein 1950]. Considering a static economic system, he attempts

8. The general flavor of the discussion is suggested by the following works: [Simon 1957, 1968; Edwards 1954; Davidson and Suppes 1957; Bush and Mostelle 1955; Papandreou et al, 1957; Luce 1957; Rose 1957].

9. See [Duesenberry 1952; Baumol 1952; Tintner 1946; Kemp 1955].

to classify the motivations behind consumer demand. First, a basic distinction is drawn between what is termed *functional* and *nonfunctional* demand; the former refers to "that part of the demand for a commodity which is due to the qualities inherent in the commodity itself," while the latter suggests that part of the demand for a commodity which is due to "the fact that others are purchasing and consuming the same commodity, or . . . the fact that the commodity bears a higher rather than a lower price tag" [Leibenstein 1950, p. 127]. Nonfunctional demand is, of course, the category of interest for the study of consumption externalities. The technical problem reduces, ultimately, to one of deciding how the conventional utility function is to be redefined to take account of new "social" variables such as the incomes or consumption rates of other individuals in the system [Kemp 1955], the levels of particular prices, the cumulative consumption of the community over some time interval [Wan 1966; Furubotn 1970], etc. Then, having appropriate utility functions, it is possible to consider the implications of the revised system for market demand curves [Duesenberry 1952, pp. 17-19]. The results may be artificial but, at least, represent movement in an important new direction.

Unfortunately, the consumption externalities that can be discussed within a static framework constitute only a small subset of conceivable effects. More fundamental social forces operate through time; thus, any serious study of preference formation must be conducted in terms of a comprehensive *dynamic* model of social processes. But since the latter undertaking would, presumably, involve broad-based interdisciplinary research, the prospects for any quick breakthroughs seem poor. The economist is left in an uneasy position. Having recognized social interaction, it is difficult to revert to the traditional model. If the preference systems in existence at any moment depend in a complex way on past economic and social events, preferences cannot be taken as given for the derivation of demand curves [Duesenberry 1952, p. 14]. Yet, so long as the process by which preferences evolve is only imperfectly understood, the best that can be done is to make crude corrections for the dynamics of preference formation.

Environment and Choice

If we abstract from dynamic processes of social interaction and consider the economy at a particular cross section of time, it is reasonable to say that consumer choice is shaped by the set of background conditions under which choice is made [Hoyt 1965]. In other words, the individual's (static) utility function may be so constituted that the utility number attaching to a given commodity bundle varies systematically with the "environment" in which consumption takes place. The concept of environment is, however, susceptible to very flexible interpretation. At one extreme, it can connote the system's entire institutional structure, including legal, ethical, and technological facets [Shaffer 1963], or it may refer, simply, to the immediate mood and circumstances influencing a particular act of choice. Environment in the latter sense has been discussed in the literature of decision making.

> Decision making deals primarily with conditions immediately surrounding a decision: what immediate alternatives are perceived; what forces are immediately acting on the decision makers; what goals the decision makers consider relative; and who takes the main responsibility or initiative in making this or that kind of decision. Within these limits the matter of decision making can be pursued without much knowledge of the broad fields of either psychology or economics. [Hoyt 1965, p. 107]

It would be misleading, though, to suggest that the narrow view of environment and decision making dominates thinking in this area of paraeconomics. Marketing researchers, in particular, have shown concern with the deeper psychological and sociological forces that help to determine consumer purchasing patterns. Unlike most economists, who avoid the question of how preferences are formed, marketing analysts have a keen interest in explaining *why* people buy given products. And, accordingly, they have provided some imaginative contributions which bring together the findings of varied specialists on human behavior. The following summary by Philip Kotler suggests how environment—in its very extended usage here—may operate to shape market demand.

> Marshallian man is concerned chiefly with economic cues—prices and income—and makes a fresh utility calculation before each purchase.
>
> Pavlovian man behaves in a largely habitual rather than thoughtful way; certain configurations of cues will set off the same behavior because of rewarded learning in the past.
>
> Freudian man's choices are influenced strongly by motives and fantasies which take place deep within his private world.
>
> Veblenian man acts in a way which is shaped largely by past and present social groups.
>
> And finally, Hobbesian man seeks to reconcile individual gain with organizational gain.
>
> Thus, it turns out that the "black box" of the buyer is not so black after all. Light is thrown in various corners by these models. Yet no one has succeeded in putting all these pieces of truth together into one coherent instrument for behavioral analysis. This, of course, is the goal of behavioral science. [Kotler 1965, p. 45]

More conventional use can be made of the concept of environment by emphasizing its relation to utility analysis [Gorman 1967]. For example, if an individual's choices depend on his background and his background changes with real income, the standard utility function requires reinterpretation. In effect, movement through utility space tends to modify the shapes and positions of the indifference curves [Peston 1967]. Under these circumstances, side conditions should be imposed on the utility function so that the latter is defined only for the limited range of real incomes consistent with a more or less fixed environmental position for the consumer; then, the preferences shown will reflect the choices the consumer will actually implement. Relevant to the general question of "environment" considered here is the concept of a time period of adjustment as a parameter of Marshallian demand theory.

The employment of advertising by business firms can be viewed as an organized effort to change the conditions under which consumer choices are made and, thus, to influence demand. Economists, however, have no carefully articulated explanation of the role of advertising. There is, of course, recognition that advertising activity can lead to some shifting of market demand curves, but the mechanism of change is not considered. While Chamberlin's theory of monopolistic competition [Chamberlin 1948, chs. 6, 7] directed attention to selling costs and the firm's adjustment to such costs [Brems 1951, pp. 5-9], the literature tends to avoid deeper questions and merely assumes the evidence of certain relations among advertising outlay, production costs and revenue [Buchanan 1942; Basmann 1956]. Again, this approach is in keeping with the traditional unwillingness of economists to explain the formation and content of preferences. Whatever the virtues of the position, it would seem that advertising phenomena cannot be integrated into the theory of demand unless consumer behavior is studied more intensively [Firestone 1967]. As long as some changes in taste cannot be accepted as autonomous and depend, instead, on the actions of others, it is necessary to consider the process by which changes in preferences develop.

The Level of Aggregation

Conventional utility theory has sought to avoid difficulties by reducing empirical content to a minimum and eschewing explanations of the motivations behind consumer behavior. But, at the same time, the theory attempts to present a detailed picture of demand; consideration is given to the contribution each individual in the system makes to the market outcome. It is important to note, though, that not all economists are convinced that demand phenomena should be approached through the investigation of individual behavior; that is, by the aggregation of microeconomic analysis into macroeconomic analysis. Partly because of the recognition of the social origin of preferences and the difficulties of explaining the dynamics of preference change, suggestions have been made to consider mass behavior. In other words, by focusing on the system of individuals as a whole, it is hoped to detect certain regularities of the system and to use these to characterize market demand.

Professor Duesenberry, for example, has described his methodological predilections as follows:

> We do not want to analyze every impulse affecting consumption decisions any more than anyone else. We try to solve the problem by being less ambitious. Instead of explaining every detail of consumption behavior, we try to explain the average behavior of a large group. Secondly, we are less wary. We shall make some definite commitments of a psychological and sociological nature. We may be wrong about them so that we take a certain risk which the preference system analysts avoided. On the other hand, we are compensated by being able to deal with the interdependence problem and by getting more definite results than can be obtained from the preference analysis. [Duesenberry 1952, p. 19]

There are, unquestionably, certain advantages in building demand models based on mass behavior rather than individual behavior. But no either-or choice need be made; it is possible for different groups of researchers to pursue both these lines of investigation simultaneously. Moreover, indications already exist that richer and more vital microeconomic constructs can be devised to deal with the longstanding problems that have plagued demand theory. As yet, the literature offers no hint that economists have given up on the possibility of creating a theory of consumption that has its roots in individual decision making.

Dynamic Models of Demand

The movement from static to dynamic theory represents a crucial, if extremely difficult, step in the development of an adequate theory of consumer demand. Logic is fully on the side of dynamic extension but, so far, the existence of formidable conceptual and technical problems has prevented the formulation of any generally accepted theory of consumption over time. The literature contains some useful preliminary discussion and offers a number of tentative and highly simplified formal models treating particular aspects of the dynamic case. The trouble is, however, that once serious consideration is given to intertemporal phenomena, virtually limitless complications can be introduced into a demand model. Both micro- and macro-level activities require attention and the boundaries between economic and other relevant social processes become more difficult to establish. Thus, an explanation of changing preferences may reduce to a complex study of social interaction involving political, sociological, and pyschological elements. In the limit, a "complete" theory of demand is likely to be coextensive with some grand theory of social dynamics.

From the standpoint of the present survey, it is also worth noting that the acceptance of dynamic demand models in place of static constructs will tend to reduce the significance of the one-period demand schedule that has been for so long, the focus of attention in traditional writings. This is not to say that an analogue of the standard demand schedule cannot be derived from a multiperiod model. The point is, rather, that when optimization over time is considered, major interest attaches to equilibrium time streams of consumption. Instantaneous or one-period configurations are not so significant in themselves but have importance largely because of the overall pattern to which they contribute. Thus, in a stock-flow model, it is true that even when prices, incomes, and preferences are fixed, the demand for goods can change over time within certain limits set by the conditions of dynamic equilibrium. Further, the more general the framework of analysis, the greater is the need for a model that gives active consideration to variables other than those stressed in the instantaneous price-quantity relation. An obvious example of the problem is found in the case of product innovation; for a dynamic economy, quality competition may be more important than price competition. In general, then, interest in any simple "law of demand" seems somewhat antiquated and unlikely to survive the transition to dynamic theorizing.

Some Elementary Conceptions

Perhaps the simplest extension of the conventional static model is represented by the multiperiod variant that treats the maximization of utility over time.[10] The consumer's utility index can be established in the following form:

$$U = G(q_{11}, q_{21}, \dots, q_{n1}; q_{12}, q_{22}, \dots, q_{n2}; \dots, q_{1T}, q_{2T}, \dots, q_{nT}) \tag{3.14}$$

where q_{it} is the (planned) rate of consumption of the ith good in the tth period. The implication is that the individual's satisfaction depends on his projected purchases and consumption of each of the n goods in the respective time periods to the planning horizon T. By assumption, the consumer will not accumulate commodity stocks in any period, but the model does provide for saving and investment decisions. The essential problem here is one of finding the optimal savings plan. Insofar as the consumer's given income stream $y_1, y_2, \dots y_T$ is different from his desired consumption stream, appropriate borrowing and lending policy can bring about an improvement in the timing of consumption and, thus, permit greater utility to be realized from the existing background conditions. The optimizing solution emerges from a standard constrained maximum problem based on (3.14) and suitable budget constraints.

The procedure employed is, of course, highly mechanical and fails to achieve a true dynamic analysis. With prices, interest rates, terminal position, etc. taken as data, the theoretical results reached are scarcely different from those of the

10. For example, see [Henderson and Quandt 1958, pp. 225–240; Wu and Pontney 1967, ch. 11; Tintner 1938; Yaari 1964; Koopmans et al. 1964; Puu 1965; Gutmann 1966; Liviatan 1966; Green 1967; Fama 1970].

normal static case. It should also be emphasized that the model is deterministic and makes no real provision for adaptive behavior. Nevertheless, some useful first thoughts on dynamic questions are established, and concepts like time preference [Lancaster 1963], intertemporal arbitrage, etc. can be formulated systematically in models of this general type.

A more sophisticated and satisfactory approach to dynamic theory is provided by stock-flow demand models [Bushaw and Clower 1957, ch. 5; Hadar 1965]. The latter are genuinely dynamic constructs and involve the time variable in an essential way.

> The distinctive characteristics of consumer stock-flow models can be said to derive from the fact that in such models the consumer's market behavior in any period of time determines not only his level of consumption in the current period, but also the size of his stock holdings at the end of that period. Thus, the consumer's behavior in the current period bears directly on his asset position as he enters the market in the following period, and this establishes a functional relationship between the consumer's actions in different periods of time. [Hadar 1965, p. 304]

Fundamental to the stock-flow explanation is the assumption that the consumer can derive utility from *holding* commodities as well as from consuming them. The utility function, therefore, differs from (3.14) and involves as arguments both stock and flow variables. But once the new form of utility function is defined and a plausible set of budget constraints is established, things proceed in familiar fashion. Specifically, utility maximizing solutions can be obtained for the desired levels of flows and stocks within the consumer's planning horizon. It is also possible to consider the pattern of consumption over time as the individual moves from one horizon to another.

There is little doubt that the relations between stock and flow variables must be explained in any acceptable dynamic theory of demand. But various hypotheses are conceivable and a great variety of models can be built around the basic stock-flow notions.[11] Broadly, we know that an ongoing economic process takes place in which today's decisions concerning consumption rates and stock accumulation depend on yesterday's consumption and stock determinations. Particularly in a world where durable commodities exist, current choice must grow out of the history of past actions [Miller 1961]. Nevertheless, the specific pattern of interaction (or cross-effects) between stock and flow variables depends on the assumptions made in defining the stock-flow utility function; and since

11. The mathematical tools developed in dynamic programming and control theory seem well adapted to problems in dynamic demand analysis, and an increasing flow of contributions embodying these formal methods can be expected, see [Kumar 1969]. The following works are representative of recent thinking on multiperiod utility and consumption: [Frisch 1964; Huang 1964; Yaari 1965; Wu 1965; Diamond 1965; Hakansson 1969].

real understanding of consumer preferences over time is limited, the form of the utility function is open [Morishima 1965].

Obvious questions arise about the simple maximizing models discussed above. Are multiperiod preferences best represented by a single deterministic equation, or a family of ordinal functions having stochastic properties? Is the utility function defined ex ante for all periods to some distant time horizon, or do preferences evolve in the course of actual choice-making behavior? From the standpoint of dynamic demand theory, it is not impossible to accept the idea that tastes adjust to the product mixes made available over time, rather than the converse. Further, there is the matter of the type of decision process followed.[12] Straightforward utility maximization is by no means assured even if an unambiguous maximization problem can be formulated for the multiperiod case. With a little flexibility, gaming behavior is conceivable; individuals may act as though they were playing games against nature or other parties. The list of possible revisions to the elementary stock-flow models could be extended, but the central conclusion that emerges is clear. Dynamic demand models face all the unresolved problems of the static theory and have, in addition, some rather special and abstruse complications of their own.

Other Themes

During the postwar period, attention has been given to topics which, while not narrowly related to microeconomic models of the type noted on pages 63–65, are important to the general development of dynamic demand theory. Some of the literature here has its roots in monetary theory,[13] in macroeconomic analysis, and in interdisciplinary behavioral studies [Rose 1963]; but the themes explored bear either directly or indirectly on the question of how households reach decisions concerning commodity purchases, savings, and wealth accumulation in an ongoing economic system.

Of special interest is the extensive set of writings, both theoretical and empirical, that have grown out of the original Keynesian conceptions of the consumption and savings functions [Thompson 1967; Heertje 1963]. Dissatisfaction with the early static formulations led to more sophisticated models based on a greater range of variables—with some of the latter relating to different points in time.[14] Friedman's permanent income hypothesis, in particular, has

12. As noted earlier, serious arguments can be raised against the assumption of a maximizing decision process. But behavioral models giving consideration to the learning process, information costs, search, habit formation, etc. have an inherently dynamic character and can form the basis for advanced theorizing about demand, see [Ferber 1968; 1954; Foote 1961; Juster 1960; Katona and Mueller 1953; March and Simon 1959].

13. For example, see [Archibald and Lipsey 1958; Clower 1963; Lloyd 1964; Archibald et al. 1960].

14. See [Modigliani and Ando 1960; Friend and Kravis 1957; Davis 1952; Morgan 1954].

provoked wide discussion [Gorman 1964] and has contributed to a more realistic theory of household behavior by emphasizing the time structure of consumption. In a dynamic world, economic variables like wealth, interest rates, price expectations, etc. must be accounted for, and Friedman's approach offers one possible rationalization of the way the household establishes a succession of consumption plans in the light of such data. Moreover, since the permanent income hypothesis has explicit links with Fisher's theory of rational saving [Friedman 1957, pp. 7-14], the new scheme is generally consistent with the traditional line of microeconomic thinking.

As the time horizon is extended, it is no longer defensible to assume that the set of forces normally taken as fixed background conditions in shorter-term analysis will, in fact, remain constant. Accordingly, the literature has placed increasing stress, in recent years, on investigating the influence on economic decisions of certain previously neglected variables. The variables singled out for closer consideration relate to the socioeconomic characteristics of the household, the financial or wealth position of the household, and the attitudes and expectations held by decision makers [Ferber 1968, pp. 126-141]. The logic here is straightforward. If the households deciding on consumption, savings, and investment plans are viewed individually, they are bound to show differences in respect to such things as education, family size, occupation, geographic location, etc. And these interhousehold differences can be expected to lead to dissimilarities in behavior which must be explained if the dynamic demand theory is to have predictive power. Another requirement is that the theory take into account the changing situation of the household over time as aging takes place and successive stages of the life cycle are reached. It is clear on a priori grounds that income, consumption, saving, etc. are likely to vary systematically as the household ages, and this presumption is confirmed by empirical observation.[15]

It should also be noted that numerous theoretical and empirical studies have been undertaken in the attempt to understand the patterns of change that occur through time in the household's income, wealth, liquidity, and asset holdings. Household decisions at any moment are conditioned by the current and past values of these variables, but the given values are, of course, the result of earlier decision stretching back through time.[16] Moreover, the complex interrelations present are made more difficult to interpret by the effects of consumer expectations. Knowledge of how motives, attitudes, and expectations are formed is still limited; while survey methods have been able to discover some empirical regularities and make assessments of the public's mood at given cross-sections of time, no solid theoretical formulation exists. In general, the work on the behavior

15. See [Modigliani and Brumberg 1954; Clark 1955; Strotz 1956; Brady 1956; Fisher 1952].

16. When we consider the possibility of the household having financial assets and liabilities, questions can be raised as to whether relative prices or absolute prices are relevant to the demand function, see [Patinkin 1956; Archibald et al. 1960].

of households appears to be at a preliminary stage and, therefore, this body of literature does not as yet provide an adequate basis for the construction of a dynamic theory of demand.

Postscript

It is apparent, given the manifold directions taken by demand theory over the past 200 years, that economists are far from unanimous in their conception of how demand phenomena should be treated. Indeed, the existence of very diverse approaches to demand theory at the present time underlines the fact that even the content of contemporary demand analysis is a matter for sharp debate. It is hoped that the present essay has helped to provide a clearer delineation of the areas of divergent opinion as well as an indication of the directions future research may take. Our examination of demand theory indicates, if anything, that great effort remains to be applied in this area which is so fundamental to the entire corpus of economic theory and policy.

Bibliography

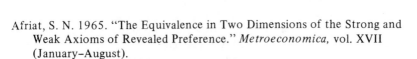

Afriat, S. N. 1965. "The Equivalence in Two Dimensions of the Strong and Weak Axioms of Revealed Preference." *Metroeconomica,* vol. XVII (January–August).

Alchian, A. A. 1953. "The Meaning of Utility Measurement." *American Economic Review,* vol. XLIII (March).

Alford, R. F. G. 1956. "Marshall's Demand Curve." *Economica,* vol. XXIII (February).

Anspach, R. 1966. "The General Incompatibility of the Traditional Consumer Equilibrium with Economic Rationality: An Exploratory Analysis." *Oxford Economic Papers,* vol. XVIII (March).

Archibald, G. C., and Lipsey, R. G. 1958. "Monetary and Value Theory: A Critique of Lange and Patinkin." *Review of Economic Studies,* vol. XXVI (October).

Archibald, G. C., et al. 1960. "A Symposium on Monetary Theory." *Review of Economic Studies,* vol. XXVIII (October).

Aristotle. *Ethics.* Edited by D. A. Rees. Oxford: Clarendon Press, 1951.

Armstrong, W. E. 1948. "Uncertainty and the Utility Function." *Economic Journal,* vol. LVIII (March).

Arrow, K. J. 1951. "Alternative Approaches to the Theory of Choice in Risk-Taking Situations." *Econometrica,* vol. XIX (October).

—— 1958. "Utilities, Attitudes, Choices: A Review Note." *Econometrica,* vol. XXVI (January).

—— 1959. "Rational Choice Functions and Orderings." *Economica,* vol. XXVI (May).

Auspitz, Rudolf, and Lieben, Richard. 1889. *Untersuchungen Uber die Theorie des Preises.* Leipsig: Verlag von Duncker and Humblot.

Bailey, M. J. 1954. "The Marshallian Demand Curve." *Journal of Political Economy,* vol. LXII (June).

Basmann, R. L. 1956. "A Theory of Demand with Variable Consumer Preferences." *Econometrica,* vol. XXIV (January).

Baumol, W. J. 1952. *Welfare Economics and the Theory of the State.* London: Harvard University Press.

Becker, G. S. 1965. "A Theory of the Allocation of Time." *Economic Journal,* vol. LXXV (September).

Borch, K. 1968. "Indifference Curves and Uncertainty." *Swedish Journal of Economics,* vol. LXX (March).

—— 1969. *The Economics of Uncertainty.* Princeton: Princeton University Press.

Bordas, M. 1847. "Of the Measurement of the Utility of Public Works." *Annales des Ponts et Chaussées,* 2d ser., vol. XIII. (Translated by Eleanor Evans and edited by R. B. Ekelund, Jr.)

Brady, D. S. 1956. "Family Saving, 1888–1950." In R. W. Goldsmith et. al, *A Study of Saving in the United States,* vol. III, Princeton: Princeton University Press.

Brems, Hans. 1951. *Product Equilibrium Under Monopolistic Competition.* Cambridge: Harvard University Press.

——. 1968. *Quantitative Economic Theory.* New York: Wiley.

Buchanan, J. M. 1958. "Ceteris Paribus: Some Notes on Methodology." *Southern Economic Journal,* vol. XXIV (January).

Buchanan, N. S. 1942. "Advertising Expenditure: A Suggested Treatment." *Journal of Political Economy,* vol. L (August).

Bush, R., and Mostelle, F. 1955. *Stochastic Models for Learning.* New York: Wiley.

Bushaw, D. W., and Clower, R. W. 1957. *Introduction to Mathematical Economics.* Homewood, Ill.: Richard D. Irwin.

Calsoyas, C. D. 1950. "The Mathematical Theory of Monopoly in 1839, Charles Ellet, Jr." *Journal of Political Economy,* vol. LVIII (April).

Chamberlin, Edward H. 1948. *The Theory of Monopolistic Competition.* Cambridge: Harvard University Press, 1948, 1962.

Cheysson, Emile. 1887. "La Statistique géometrique: Ses Applications industrielles et commerciales." *Le Génie Civil,* vol. X (January 29 and February 5). (Translated by Jennifer Hartley and Eleanor Evans, edited by R. F. Hebert. Translation is available in the library of Louisiana State University.)

Chipman, J. S. 1960. "The Foundations of Utility." *Econometrica,* vol. XXVIII (April).

Clark, L. H., ed. 1955. *The Life Cycle and Consumer Behavior.* New York: New York University Press.

Clarkson, G. P. E. 1963. *The Theory of Consumer Demand: A Critical Appraisal.* Englewood Cliffs, N. J.: Prentice-Hall.

Clower, R. W. 1963. "Permanent Income and Transitory Balances: Han's Paradox." *Oxford Economic Papers,* vol. XV (July).

Colson, Clément. 1901. *Cours d'Economie Politique professe a l'Ecole Nationale des Ponts et Chaussées,* vol. I. Paris: Alcon.

Corlett, W. J., and Newman, P. 1953. "A Note on Revealed Preference and the Transitivity Condition." *Review of Economic Studies,* vol. XX (April).

Cournot, Antoine Augustin. 1863. *Principes de la Théorie des Richesses.* Paris: Hachette.

——. 1960. *Researches into the Mathematical Principles of the Theory of Wealth* (1838). Translated by Nathaniel Bacon. New York: Augustus M. Kelley. The translation was originally published in 1897.

Court, L. M. 1941. "Entrepreneurial and Consumer Demand Theories for Commodity Spectra." *Econometrica,* vol. IX (April, July–October).

Davenant, Charles. 1771. *The Political and Commercial Works of Charles D'Avenant, L.L.D.* Collected and revised by Sir Charles Whitworth in five volumes, vol. II. London.

Davidson, D., and Marschak, J. 1959. "Experimental Tests of a Stochastic Decision Theory." In C. W. Churchman and P. Ratoosh, eds., *Measurement: Definitions and Theories.* New York: Wiley.

Davidson, D., and Suppes, P. 1957. *Decision Making: An Experimental Approach.* Stanford: Stanford University Press.

Davis, T. E. 1952. "The Consumption Function as a Tool for Prediction." *Review of Economics and Statistics,* vol. XXXIV (August).

Day, R. H. 1967. "Profits, Learning and the Convergence of Statisficing to Marginalism." *Quarterly Journal of Economics,* vol. LXXXI (May).

Debreu, G. 1954. "Representation of a Preference Ordering by a Numerical Function." In R. M. Thrall et al., eds. *Decision Processes.* New York: Wiley.

———. 1959. *Theory of Value.* New York: Wiley.

Diamond, P. A. 1965. "The Evaluation of Infinite Utility Streams." *Econometrica,* vol. XXXIII (January).

Duesenberry, J. S. 1952. *Income, Saving and the Theory of Consumer Behavior.* Cambridge: Harvard University Press.

Dupuit, Jules. 1844. "On the Measurement of the Utility of Public Works." *Annales des Ponts et Chaussées,* 2nd ser., vol. VII. Translated by R. H. Barback in the *International Economic Papers,* no. 2, London: Macmillan, 1952. Page references are to the translation.

———. 1849. "De l'Influence des Péages sur l'Utilité des Voies de Communication." *Annales des Ponts et Chaussées,* 2nd ser., vol. XVII.

———. 1849. "On Tolls and Transport Charges." *Annales des Ponts et Chaussées,* 2nd ser, vol. XVII. Translated by Elizabeth Henderson in the *International Economic Papers,* no. 11. London: Macmillan, 1962. Page references are to the translation.

———. 1852–1853. "Toll." In *Dictionnaire de l'Economie Politique,* Ch. Coguelin and Guillaumin, eds. Paris: Guillaumin and Co. (Translated by Eleanor Evans and edited by R. B. Ekelund, Jr. Page references are to the translation.)

———. 1853. "On Utility and Its Measure." *Journal des Economistes,* vol. XXXVI (July/September). (Translated by Eleanor Evans and edited by R. B. Ekelund, Jr. Page references are to the translation available in the library of Louisiana State University, Baton Rouge.)

———. 1934. *De l'Utilité et sa Mesure: Ecrits Choisis et Republies.* Edited by Mario de Bernardi. Torino: La Riforma Sociale.

Edgeworth, F. Y. 1881. *Mathematical Physics.* London: C. Kegan Paul and Co.

———. 1923–1926a. "Demand Curves." In H. Higgs, ed. *Palgraves Dictionary of Political Economy.* London: Macmillan.

———. 1923–1926b. "Dupuit." In H. Higgs, ed. *Palgraves Dictionary of Political Economy.* London: Macmillan.

Edwards, W. 1954. "The Theory of Decision Making." *Psychological Bulletin,* vol. LI (September).

Ekelund, Robert B., Jr., and Gramm, William P. 1970. "Early French Contributions to Marshallian Demand Theory." *Southern Economic Journal,* vol. XXXVI (January).

Ellet, Charles, Jr., 1839. *An Essay on the Laws of Trade in Reference to the*

Works of Internal Improvement in the United States. 1st. ed. Richmond: P. D. Bernard, 1839. Reprint ed. New York: Augustus M. Kelley, 1966.

———. 1840. "The Laws of Trade applied to the determination of the most advantageous fare for passengers on Railroads." Edited by Thomas P. Jones, Philadelphia, in *Journal of the Franklin Institute of the State of Pennsylvania,* vol. XXX.

Ellsberg, D. 1954. "Classic and Current Notions of Measurable Utility." *Economic Journal,* vol. LXIV (September).

Encarnacion, J. 1964. "A Note on Lexicographical Preferences." *Econometrica,* vol. XXXII (January–April).

Evans, G. H., Jr. 1967. "The Law of Demand – The Roles of Gregory King and Charles Davenant," *Quarterly Journal of Economics,* vol. LXXXI (August).

Fama, E. F. 1970. "Multiperiod Consumption – Investment Decisions." *American Economic Review,* vol. LX (March).

Fellner, Wm. 1961. "Distortion of Subjective Probabilities as a Reaction to Uncertainty." *Quarterly Journal of Economics,* vol. LXXV (November).

———. 1965. *Competition Among the Few.* New York: Augustus M. Kelley.

Ferber, R. 1954. "The Role of Planning in Consumer Purchases of Durable Goods." *American Economic Review,* vol. XXXXIV (December).

Ferber, R. 1968. "Research On Household Behavior," in *Surveys of Economic Theory,* volume III, New York: St. Martin's Press.

Firestone, O. J. 1967. *The Economic Implications of Advertising.* London: Methuen.

Fisher, J. 1952. "Postwar Changes in Income and Saving Among Consumers in Different Age Groups." *Econometrica,* vol. XX (January).

Foote, N. N., ed. 1961. *Household Decision-Making.* New York: McGraw-Hill.

Friedman, Milton. 1949. "The Marshallian Demand Curve." *Journal of Political Economy,* vol. LVII (December): 463–495. Page references are to reprint in *Essay in Positive Economics.* Chicago: University of Chicago Press, 1953.

———. 1957. *A Theory of the Consumption Function.* Princeton: Princeton University Press.

———. 1962. *Price Theory.* Chicago: Aldine.

Friedman, M., and Savage, L. J. 1948. "The Utility Analysis of Choices Involving Risk." *Journal of Political Economy,* vol. LVI (August).

Friend, I., and Kravis, I. B. 1957. "Consumption Patterns and Permanent Income." *American Economic Review,* vol. XXXXVII (May).

Frisch, R. 1964. "Dynamic Utility." *Econometrica,* vol. XXXII (July).

Fry, Clifford L., and Ekelund, Robert B., Jr. 1971. "Cournot's Demand Theory: A Reassessment." *History of Political Economy,* vol. 3 (Spring).

Furubotn, E. G. 1963. "On Some Applications of the Utility Tree." *Southern Economic Journal,* vol. XXX (October).

———. 1967. "Observed Consumption Patterns and the Utility Function." *Metroeconomica,* vol. XIX (January–April).

———. 1969. "Quality Control, Expected Utility, and Product Equilibrium." *Western Economic Journal*, vol. VII (March).

———. 1970. "A Stock-Flow Model of Monopolistic Competition: The Short-Run Case." *Western Economic Journal,* vol. VIII (March).

Gabor, A., and Granger, C. W. 1966. "Price as an Indicator of Quality: Report on an Enquiry." *Economica,* vol. XXXIII (February).

Gale, D. 1960. "A Note on Revealed Preference." *Economica,* vol. XXVII (November).

Georgescu-Roegen, N. 1936. "The Pure Theory of Consumer's Behavior." *Quarterly Journal of Economics,* vol. L (August).

———. 1954a. "Choice and Revealed Preference." *Southern Economic Journal,* vol. XXI (October).

———. 1954b. "Choice, Expectations and Measurability." *Quarterly Journal of Economics,* vol. LXVIII (November).

———. 1958. "Threshold in Choice and the Theory of Demand." *Econometrica,* vol. XXVI (January).

Gordon, B. J. 1966. "W. F. Lloyd: A Neglected Contribution." *Oxford Economic Papers,* n.s., vol. XVIII (March).

Gorman, W. M. 1957. "Convex Indifference Curves and Diminishing Marginal Utility." *Journal of Political Economy,* vol. LXV (February).

———. 1964. "Professor Friedman's Consumption Function and the Theory of Choice." *Econometrica,* vol. XXXII (January–April).

———. 1967. "Tastes, Habits and Choices." *International Economic Review,* vol. VIII (June).

Graaf, J. De V. 1967. *Theoretical Welfare Economics.* Cambridge: Cambridge University Press.

Gramm, W. P. 1970. "Giffen's Paradox and the Marshallian Demand Curve." *Manchester School,* vol. XXXVIII (March).

Green, H. A. J. 1957. "Some Logical Relations in Revealed Preference Theory." *Economica,* vol. XXIV (November).

———. 1961. "Direct Additivity and Consumer's Behavior." *Oxford Economic Papers,* vol. XIII (June).

———. 1964. *Aggregation in Economic Analysis.* Princeton: Princeton University Press.

———. 1967. "Intertemporal Utility and Consumption." *Oxford Economic Papers,* vol. XIX (March).

Grossack, Irwin M. 1966. "Duopoly, Defensive Strategies, and the Kinked Demand Curve." *Southern Economic Journal,* vol. XXXII (April).

Gutmann, P. M. 1966. "Neoclassical Utility and Intertemporal Consumer Decisions." *Economia Internazionale,* vol. XIX (August).

Hadar, J. 1965. "A Note on Stock-Flow Models of Consumer Behavior." *Quarterly Journal of Economics,* vol. LXXIX (May).

Hadar, J., and Russell, W. 1969. "Rules for Ordering Uncertain Prospects." *American Economic Review,* vol. LIX (March).

Hadley, G. 1964. *Nonlinear and Dynamic Programming.* Reading: Addison-Wesley.

Hakansson, N. H. 1969. "Optimal Investment and Consumption Strategies Under Risk, an Uncertain Lifetime, and Insurance." *International Economic Review,* vol. X (October).

Harwitz, M. 1968. "Indivisibility and Observed Consumer Behavior." *Southern Economic Journal,* vol. XXXIV (January).

Hebert, Robert F. 1970. *A Critical Evaluation of Emile Cheysson's Contributions to Economic Analysis.* Ph.D. dissertation, Louisiana State University, August.

Heertje, A. 1963. "On the Optimum Rate of Savings." *Weltwirschaftliches Archiv,* vol. LXXXX (Jeft.1).

Henderson, J. M., and Quandt, R. E. 1958. *Microeconomic Theory.* New York: McGraw-Hill.

Herstein, I. N., and Milnor, J. 1953. "An Axiomatic Approach to Measurable Utility." *Econometrica,* vol. XXI (April).

Hicks, J. R. 1946. *Value and Capital.* 2nd ed. Oxford: Oxford University Press.

——. 1956. *A Revision of Demand Theory.* Oxford: Oxford University Press.

——. 1958. "The Measurement of Real Income." *Oxford Economic Papers,* vol. X (June).

——. 1965. *Capital and Growth.* Oxford: Oxford University Press.

Hicks, J. R., and Allen, R. G. D. 1934. "A Reconsideration of the Theory of Values." *Economica,* vol. I (February and May).

Hotelling, H. 1932. "Edgeworth's Taxation Paradox and the Nature of Demand and Supply Functions." *Journal of Political Economy,* vol. XL (October).

Houghton, R. W. 1958. "A Note on the Early History of Consumer's Surplus." *Economica,* vol. XXV (February).

Houthakker, H. S. 1950. "Revealed Preference and the Utility Function." *Economica,* vol. XVII (May).

——. 1952. "Compensated Changes in Quantities and Qualities Consumed." *Review of Economic Studies,* vol. XIX, no. 3.

——. 1960a. "Additive Preferences." *Econometrica,* vol. XXVIII (April).

——. 1960b. "The Capacity Method of Quadratic Programming." *Econometrica,* vol. XXVIII (January).

——. 1961. "The Present State of Consumption Theory." *Econometrica,* vol. XXIX (October).

Hoyt, E. E. 1965. "Choice as an Interdisciplinary Area." *Quarterly Journal of Economics,* vol. LXXIX (February).

Huang, D. S. 1964. "Discrete Stock Adjustment: The Case of Demand for Automobiles." *International Economic Review,* vol. V (January).

Jenkin, Fleeming. 1870. "The Graphic Representation of the Laws of Supply and Demand, and their Application to Labour." In *Recess Studies.* Edinburgh, 1870. Reprinted in *The Graphic Representation of the Laws of Supply and Demand, and Other Essays on Political Economy, 1868–1884.* London: London School Reprint, 1931. References are to the reprint.

Jevons, William Stanley. 1957. *The Theory of Political Economy.* New York: Kelley and Millman.

Johnson, Harry G. 1949. "Malthus on the High Price of Provisions." *Canadian Journal of Economics and Political Science,* vol. XV.

Juster, F. T. 1960. "Predictions and Consumer Buying Intentions." *American Economic Review,* vol. L (May).

Katona, G. and Mueller, E. 1953. *Consumer Attitudes and Demand, 1950–52.* Ann Arbor: University of Michigan Survey Research Center.

Kemp, M. C. 1955. "The Efficiency of Competition as an Allocator of Resources:

II. External Economies of Consumption." *Canadian Journal of Economics*, vol. XXI (May).

King, Gregory. 1696. *Natural and Political Observations and Conclusions upon the State and Condition of England.* Reprinted in George E. Barnett, ed. *Two Tracts by Gregory King.* Baltimore: Johns Hopkins Press, 1936.

Knight, Frank H. 1944. "Realism and Relevance in the Theory of Demand." *Journal of Political Economy*, vol. LII (December).

Koopmans, T. C. 1957. *Three Essays on the State of Economic Science.* New York: McGraw-Hill.

Koopmans, T. C., Diamond, P. A., and Williamson, R. E. 1964. "Stationary Utility and Time Perspective." *Econometrica*, vol. XXXII (January–April).

Kotler, P. 1965. "Behavioral Models for Analyzing Buyers." *Journal of Marketing*, vol. XXIX (October).

Kumar, T. K. 1969. "The Existence of an Optimal Economic Policy." *Econometrica*, vol. XXXVII (October).

Lancaster, K. 1963. "An Axiomatic Theory of Consumer Time Preference." *International Economic Review*, vol. IV (May).

———. 1966a. "Change and Innovation in the Technology of Consumption." *American Economic Review*, vol. LVI (May).

———. 1966b. "A New Approach to Consumer Theory." *Journal of Political Economy*, vol. LXXIV (April).

———. 1968. *Mathematical Economics.* New York: Macmillan.

———. 1969. *Introduction to Modern Microeconomics.* Chicago: Rand McNally.

Lardner, Dionysius. 1850. *Railway Economy.* Reprint, New York: Augustus M. Kelley, 1968.

Leibenstein, H. 1950. "Bandwagon, Snob, and Veblen Effects in the Theory of Consumers' Demand." *Quarterly Journal of Economics*, vol. LXIV (May).

Leontief, W. W. 1936. "Composite Commodities and the Problem of Index Numbers." *Econometrica*, vol. IV (January).

———. 1947. "Introduction to a Theory of the Internal Structure of Functional Relationships." *Econometrica*, vol. XV (October).

Lewis, Gene D. 1968. *Charles Ellet, Jr., 1810–1862, The Engineer as Individualist.* Urbana: University of Illinois Press.

Little, I. M. D. 1949. "A Reformulation of the Theory of Consumer's Behavior." *Oxford Economic Papers*, vol. I (January).

———. 1950. *A Critique of Welfare Economics.* Oxford: Oxford University Press.

Liviatan, N. 1966. "Multiperiod Future Consumption as an Aggregate." *American Economic Review*, vol. LVI (September).

Lloyd, C. 1964. "The Real-Balance Effect and the Slutsky Equation." *Journal of Political Economy*, vol. LXXII (June).

———. 1965. "On the Falsifiability of Traditional Demand Theory." *Metroeconomica*, vol. XVII (January–August).

Luce, R. D. 1957. "A Probabilistic Theory of Utility." In R. D. Luce and H. Raiffa, *Games and Decisions.* New York: Wiley.

Majumdar, T. 1961. *The Measurement of Utility.* London: Macmillan.

Malthus, T. R. 1800. *An Investigation of the Cause of the Present High Price of Provisions.* 2d ed. London: J. Johnson.

——. 1836. *Principles of Political Economy Considered with a View of Their Practical Application.* 2d ed. Reprint, New York: Augustus M. Kelley, 1964.

——. 1960. *An Essay on the Principle of Population.* Edited and introduced by Gertrude Himmelfarb. New York: Random House.

Manfra, Modestino Remigio. 1932. *Pietro Verrie i Problemi Economici del Tempo Suo.* Milano: Albrighi, Segati.

March, J. G., and Simon, H. A. 1959. *Organizations.* New York: Wiley.

Markowitz, H. 1952. "The Utility of Wealth." *Journal of Political Economy,* vol. LX (April).

Marschak, J. 1950. "Rational Behavior, Uncertain Prospects and Measurable Utility." *Econometrica,* vol. XVIII (April).

Marshall, Alfred. 1920. *Principles of Economics.* 8th ed. London: Macmillan. 9th ed. edited by Guillebaud, 1961.

Menger, Carl. 1950. *Principles of Economics.* Glencoe, Illinois: Free Press, 1950. Menger's *Principles* was originally published in 1871.

Mill, J. S. 1965. *Principles of Political Economy with Some of their Applications to Social Philosophy.* Edited by Sir W. J. Ashley. New York: Augustus M. Kelley.

Miller, H. L. 1961. "On the Theory of Demand for Consumer Durables." *Southern Economic Journal,* vol. XXVII (April).

Mishan, E. J. 1961. "Theories of Consumers' Behavior: A Cynical View." *Economica,* vol. XXVIII (February).

Modigliani, F., and Ando, A. 1960. "The Permanent Income and the Life Cycle Hypotheses of Saving Behavior: Comparison and Tests." In M. Friedman and R. Jones, eds., *Proceedings of the Conference on Consumption and Saving,* vol. II, Philadelphia.

Modigliani, F., and Brumberg, R. 1954. "Utility Analysis and the Consumption Function." In K. Kurihara, ed., *Post Keynesian Economics.* New Brunswick, N.J.: Rutgers University Press.

Morgan, I. N. 1954. "Factors Relating to Consumer Saving when It Is Defined as a Net Worth Concept." In L. R. Klein, ed., *Contributions of Survey Methods to Economics.* New York: Columbia University Press.

Morgenstern, Oskar. 1948. "Demand Theory Reconsidered." *Quarterly Journal of Economics,* vol. LXII (February).

——. 1964. "Pareto Optimum and Economic Organization." In N. Kloten et al., eds., *Systeme und Methoden in den Wirtschâfts – und Sozialwessenshaften: Erwin von Beckerath zum 75 Geburtstag.* Tübingen: Mohr.

Morishima, M. 1959. "The Problem of Intrinsic Complementarity and Separability of Goods." *Metroeconomica,* vol. XI (December).

——. 1965. "Should Dynamic Utility be Cardinal?" *Econometrica,* vol. XXXIII (October).

Muth, R. F. 1966. "Household Production and Consumer Demand Functions." *Econometrica,* vol. XXXIV (July).

Naylor, T. H., and Vernon, J. M. 1969. *Microeconomics and Decision Models of the Firm.* New York: Harcourt, Brace, and World.

Newman, P. 1955. "The Foundations of Revealed Preference Theory." *Oxford Economic Papers,* vol. VII (June).

———. 1965. *The Theory of Exchange.* Englewood Cliffs, N.J.: Prentice-Hall.

Pantaleoni, Maffeo. 1889. *Pure Economics.* Translated by T. Boston Bruce. New York: Augustus M. Kelley, 1965.

Papandreou, A. G., et al. 1957. "A Test of a Stochastic Theory of Choice." University of California Publications in Economics, 16, no. 1.

Pareto, Vilfredo. 1927. *Manuel d'economie Politique.* Translated from the Italian edition by Alfred Bonnet. Paris: Marcel Siard.

Patinkin, Don. 1949. "The Indeterminancy of Absolute Prices in Classical Economic Theory." *Econometrica,* vol. XVII (January).

———. 1956. *Money, Interest and Prices.* Evanston, Ill: Row, Petersen.

Peston, M. H. 1967. "Changing Utility Functions." In M. Shubik, ed. *Essays in Mathematical Economics.* Princeton: Princeton University Press.

Phlips, L. 1964. "Demand Curves and Product Differentiation." *Kyklos,* vol. XVII (fasc. 3).

Piettre, André. 1961. *Historie de la pensée économique.* Paris: Dalloz.

Pirou, Gaëtan. 1946. *Les théories de L'Equilibre Economique Walras et Pareto.* Paris: Editions Domat Montchrestien, 3rd edition.

Plato. *Republic.* Translated by B. Jowett. New York: Modern Library.

Prest, A. R. 1948. "Notes on the History of the Giffen Paradox: Comment." *Journal of Political Economy,* vol. LVI (February).

Puu, T. 1965. "A Note on the Theory of Consumption for Several Time-Periods with Perfect Foresight." *Swedish Journal of Economics,* vol. LXVII (March).

Quandt, R. E. 1956. "A Probabilistic Theory of Consumer Behavior." *Quarterly Journal of Economics,* vol. LXX (November).

Rader, T. 1963. "The Existence of a Utility Function to Represent Preferences." *Review of Economic Studies,* vol. XXX (October).

Rae, J. 1905. *The Sociological Theory of Capital.* London: Macmillan.

Rambaud, Joseph. 1909. *Historie des Doctrines Economiques.* Lyon: P. Phily.

Ricardo, David. 1951. *Principles of Political Economy and Taxation.* Sraffa Edition. Cambridge: Cambridge University Press.

Richter, M. K. 1966. "Revealed Preference Theory." *Econometrica,* vol. XXXIV (July).

Robertson, Ross M. 1949. "Mathematical Economics Before Cournot." *Journal of Political Economy,* vol. LVII (December).

———. 1951. "Jevons and his Precursors." *Econometrica,* vol. XIX (July).

Rose, A. M. 1957. "A Study of Irrational Judgments." *Journal of Political Economy,* vol. LXV (October).

———. 1963. "Conditions for Irrational Choices." *Social Research,* vol. XXX (July).

Rose, H. 1958. "Consistency of Preference: The Two-Commodity Case." *Review of Economic Studies,* vol. XXV (February).

Rothenberg, J. 1960. "Non-Convexity, Aggregation, and Pareto Optimality." *Journal of Political Economy,* vol. LXVIII (October).

——. 1962. "Consumer's Sovereignty Revisited and the Hospitality of Freedom of Choice." *American Economic Review*, vol. LII (May).

Roy, René. 1933. "Cournot et L'Ecole Mathematique." *Econometrica*, vol. I.

——. 1947. "La Distribution du Revenu entre les Divers Biens." *Econometrica*, vol. XV (January).

——. 1939. L'Oeuvre Economique D'Augustin Cournot." *Econometrica*, vol. VII (April).

Samuelson, P. A. 1938. "A Note on the Pure Theory of Consumer's Behavior." *Economica*, vol. V (February and August).

——. 1942. "Constancy of the Marginal Theory of Income." In O. Lange, F. McIntyre, and T. O. Yntema, eds., *Studies in Mathematical Economics and Econometrics*. Chicago: University of Chicago Press.

——. 1947. *Foundations of Economic Analysis*. Cambridge: Harvard University Press. 2nd edition, 1961.

——. 1956. "Social Indifference Curves." *Quarterly Journal of Economics*, vol. LXX (February).

——. 1963. "Economists and the History of Ideas." *American Economic Review*, vol. LII (March).

——. 1965. "Using Full Duality to Show that Simultaneously Additive Direct and Indirect Utilities Implies Unitary Price Elasticity of Demand." *Econometrica*, vol. XXXIII (October).

Say, Jean-Baptiste. 1803. *A Treatise on Political Economy*. Translated by C. R. Prinsep. Philadelphia: Grey and Elliot, 1836. Page references are to the translation.

——. 1816. *Catechism of Political Economy*. Translated by John Richter. London: Sherwood, Neely and Jones. Page references are to the translation.

Schoeffler, S. 1955. *The Failures of Economics: A Diagnostic Study*. Cambridge: Harvard University Press.

Schultz, H. 1938. *The Theory and Measurement of Demand*. Chicago: University of Chicago Press.

Schumpeter, Joseph A. 1954. *History of Economic Analysis*. New York: Oxford University Press.

Seligman, E. R. A. 1903. "On Some Neglected British Economists." *Economic Journal*, vol. XIII.

Senior, Nassau N. 1836. *An Outline of the Science of Political Economy*. Reprint, New York: Augustus M. Kelley, 1965.

Shaffer, J. D. 1963. "Contributions of Sociologists and Cultural Anthropologists to Analysis of U.S. Demand for Food." *Journal of Farm Economics*, vol. XLV (December).

Shubik, M. 1970. "A Curmudgeon's Guide to Microeconomics." *Journal of Economic Literature*, vol. VIII (June).

Simon, H. A. 1957. *Models of Man*. New York: Wiley.

——. 1968. "Theories of Decision-Making in Economics and Behavioural Science." Reprinted in *Surveys of Economic Theory*, vol. III. New York: St. Martin's.

Slutsky, E. 1915. "On the Theory of the Budget of the Consumer." *Giornale degli economisti*, vol. LI. Page references are to translation reprinted in

American Economic Association, *Readings in Price Theory*. Chicago: Irwin, 1952.

Smith, V. E. 1959. "Linear Programming Models for the Determination of Palatable Human Diets." *Journal of Farm Economics*, vol. XLI (May).

Smith, Victor. 1951. "The Classicists' Use of 'Demand.'" *Journal of Political Economy*, vol. LIX (June).

Sono, M. 1961. "The Effect of Price Changes on the Demand and Supply of Separable Goods." *International Economic Review*, vol. II (September).

Stigler, G. J. 1945. "The Cost of Subsistence." *Journal of Farm Economics*, vol. XLV (May).

———. 1947. "Notes on the History of the Giffen Paradox." *Journal of Political Economy*, vol. LV (April).

———. 1950. "The Development of Utility Theory." *Journal of Political Economy*, vol. LVIII (August, October). Reprinted in G. J. Stigler, *Essays in the History of Economics*. 1965.

———. 1954. "The Early History of Empirical Studies of Consumer Behavior." *Journal of Political Economy*, vol. LXII (April). Reprinted in G. J. Stigler, *Essays in the History of Economics*. 1965.

———. 1965. *Essays in the History of Economics*. Chicago: University of Chicago Press.

Strotz, R. H. 1956. "Myopia and Inconsistency in Dynamic Utility Maximization." *Review of Economic Studies*, vol. XXIII, no. 3.

———. 1957. "The Empirical Implications of a Utility Tree." *Econometrica*, vol. XXV (April).

Suppes, P. 1961. "Behavioristic Foundations of Utility." *Econometrica*, vol. XXIX (April).

Theil, H. 1952. "Qualities, Prices and Budget Enquires." *Review of Economic Studies*, vol. XIX, no. 3.

———. 1965. "The Information Approach to Demand Analysis." *Econometrica*, vol. XXXIII (January).

Theil, H., and Mnookin, R. H. 1966. "The Information Value of Demand Equations and Predictions." *Journal of Political Economy*, vol. LXXIV (February).

Thompson, E. A. 1967. "Intertemporal Utility Functions and the Long-Run Consumption Function." *Econometrica*, vol. XXXV (April).

Thornton, W. T. 1870. *On Labor, Its Wrongful Claims and Rightful Dues*. London: Macmillan.

Tintner, G. 1938. "The Maximization of Utility over Time." *Econometrica*, vol. VI (April).

———. 1946. "A Note on Welfare Economics." *Econometrica*, vol. XIV (January).

Uzawa, H. 1960. "Preference and Rational Choice in the Theory of Consumption," in *Proceedings of a Symposium on Mathematical Methods in the Social Sciences*, Stanford: Stanford University Press.

Veblen, T. B. 1899. *The Theory of the Leisure Class*. London: Macmillan.

Verri, Pietro. 1771. *Meditozioni sull éconumia politica*. Republished in the Custodi collection, Milano, Italy.

Von Neumann, J., and Morgenstern, O. 1947. *Theory of Games and Economic Behavior.* Princeton: Princeton University Press.

Wagner, H. M. 1956. "An Electric Approach to the Pure Theory of Consumer Behavior." *Econometrica,* vol. XXIV (October).

Wald, A. 1936. "Uber einige Gleichungssysteme der mathematischen Okonomie." *Zeitschrift für Nationalökonomie,* vol. VII.

Walras, Léon. 1954. *Elements of Pure Economics.* Translated by William Jaffé. Homewood, Illinois: Richard D. Irwin. Page references are to the translation.

——. 1965. *Correspondence of Léon Walras and Related Papers.* Edited by William Jaffé. Amsterdam: North Holland Publishing Co.

Walsh, V. C. 1970. *Introduction to Contemporary Microeconomics.* New York: McGraw-Hill.

Wan, H. Y. 1966. "Intertemporal Optimization with Systematically Shifting Cost and Revenue Functions." *International Economic Review,* vol. VII (May).

Weinstein, A. A. 1968. "Individual Preference Intransitivity." *Southern Economic Journal,* vol. XXXIV (January).

Weintraub, J. 1942. "The Foundations of the Demand Curve." *American Economic Review,* vol. XXXII (September).

Wold. H., and Jureen, L. 1953. *Demand Analysis.* New York: Wiley.

Wu, D. M. 1965. "An Empirical Analysis of Household Durable Goods Expenditure." *Econometrica,* vol. XXXIII (October).

Wu, S., and Pontney, J. 1967. *An Introduction to Modern Demand Theory.* New York: Random House.

Yaari, M. E. 1964. "On the Existence of an Optimal Plan in a Continuous-Time Allocation Process." *Econometrica,* vol. XXXII (October).

——. 1965. "Uncertain Lifetime, Life Insurance, and the Theory of the Consumer." *Review of Economic Studies,* vol. XXXII (April).

Yeager, L. B. 1960. "Methodenstreit over Demand Curves." *Journal of Political Economy,* vol. LXVIII (February).

Yule, S. Udny. 1915. "Crop Production and Price: A Note on Gregory King's Law." *Journal of the Royal Statistical Society,* vol. LXXVIII (March).

Part II
Early Developments in the Theory of Demand

4 The Classicists' Use of "Demand"

Victor Smith

THE relative lack of attention given to demand by the more influential classical writers was not a consequence of general agreement on proper usage of the term. To be sure, the dominant writers agreed that "demand" meant the quantity demanded; but even within this group there was significant variation. Outside this group, other concepts were contending for supremacy. Indeed, the conflict between demand-and-supply and cost-of-production theories of value developed in part as a conflict between alternative demand usages.

CONCEPTS OF "DEMAND"

Since "demand" has meant many things to many people and often many things to the same person, it will be helpful to have some agreement on terminology. I shall use "demand" without modification to refer either to the term itself or, in a nonspecific manner, to the forces that operate on the buyers' side of a market. When "demand" is used as a quantitative statement of the strength of these forces, it takes on one of four classes of meanings: the quantity demanded; the demand price (these two are the elementary components); their product—the amount spent or to be spent on the commodity; or the demand schedule—the relationship between the demand price and the quantity demanded.[2] "Demand" in the sense of aggregate demand falls into the third class just mentioned—the amount spent or to be spent (on all commodities).

The classic statement of the difficulties involved in using "demand" in explaining the price of a particular commodity is John Stuart Mill's: ". . . if the thing is cheap, there is usually a demand for more of it than when it is dear. The demand, therefore, partly depends on the value. But it was before laid down, that the value depends on the demand. From this contradiction how shall we extricate ourselves?"[3]

Two solutions are in use today. The more common of them defines "demand" as a schedule and distinguishes between movements along the schedule and shifts in the schedule itself. The schedule states the price-quantity relationship. The fact that a larger quantity is demanded when the price is lower is shown by a movement along the schedule but is not termed a change in demand. Demand does not depend on value; value depends on demand. Consistent use of the con-

[1] I should like to express my appreciation to Professor F. S. Deibler, who first directed my attention to Malthus' "intensity of demand," and to Professors Earl J. Hamilton and Milton Friedman, who made many stimulating suggestions.

[2] Another classification will also be useful later on, the distinction between *ex post* and *ex ante* concepts of demand. The demand schedule is always defined as an *ex ante* concept—a list of the quantities that people would like to take (plan to take) if the price were to be each of the various alternative prices indicated. In the cases of the other three meanings of demand, an *ex post* concept is possible: the quantity actually taken, the price actually paid, the quantity of money actually spent. The most important such usage is by Ricardo, as we shall see.

[3] *Principles of Political Economy* (London: John W. Parker, 1848), I, 527.

Reprinted from the *Journal of Political Economy,* Vol. LIX (June, 1951), pp. 242–57, by permission of the publisher and author.

cept of demand as a schedule prohibits speaking of a change in demand occurring in response to a change in the price of the commodity.[4] Demand is price-determining, never price-determined.

The less common solution is to define "demand" as the quantity demanded and to specify that this quantity is a function of the market price. This method is used principally by the mathematically minded, who are not likely to confuse a change in the function itself (the equivalent of a shift in the demand schedule) with a change in the quantity demanded in response to a change in the price.[5] There is no circularity in their solution, for the market price and the quantity actually exchanged are mutually determined as solutions of two simultaneous equations, the demand and supply functions.[6]

When "demand" refers to either the demand price, the quantity demanded, or the amount spent for a commodity, a "change in demand" may be the result either of a shift in the demand schedule or of a movement along the schedule. But a change in the demand schedule is specifically indicated if there is a change in the quantity demanded at a given price, in the demand price at a given quantity, or in the amount spent for the commodity at either a given price or a given quantity. It is conceivable that an author might consistently use demand as a schedule, yet never mention it, defining "demand," instead, as the quantity demanded at a given price.

The writers whom we shall survey as representatives of the dominant classical thought are Smith, Say, Ricardo, and, as a culmination, John Stuart Mill. In addition, we shall look at Lord Lauderdale and James Mill before turning to the other group: Malthus, Longfield, Macleod, and Senior.

ADAM SMITH

Adam Smith was the only major classical economist to use "demand" consistently as price-determining, not price-determined. As is well known, his value theory consisted of a theory of "natural price" (just sufficient to pay the rent of land, the wages of labor, and the profits of stock at their ordinary or average rates)[7] and a theory of market price. The demand for a particular commodity entered directly into his value theory only when the actual or market price was to be explained.

> The market price of every particular commodity is regulated by the proportion between the quantity which is actually brought to market, and the demand of those who are willing to pay the natural price of the commodity. . . . Such people may be called the effectual demanders, and their demand the effectual demand; since it may be sufficient to effectuate the bringing of the commodity to market. . . .
>
> When the quantity . . . brought to market falls short of the effectual demand, all . . . cannot be supplied with the quantity which they want. Rather than want it altogether, some of

[4] Perhaps complete consistency should not be required as evidence that a writer holds the schedule concept. Though Marshall defined an increase in demand as a shift of the schedule, he sometimes spoke of demand's changing in response to a change in price: "For instance, an unexpected and heavy tax upon printing would strike hard upon those engaged in the trade, for if they attempted to raise prices much, demand would fall off quickly" (Alfred Marshall, *Principles of Economics* [8th ed.; London: Macmillan, 1936], p. 414; cf. also p. 98 and, *re* supply, p. 534).

[5] For instance, John R. Hicks, *Value and Capital* (Oxford: Oxford University Press, 1938), p. 62.

[6] Those who use "demand" as a schedule have exactly the same solution for the exchange problem, but they attach the names "demand" and "supply" to the functions themselves rather than to the quantities demanded or supplied.

[7] *An Inquiry into the Nature and Causes of the Wealth of Nations* (New York: Random House, 1937), p. 55.

them will be willing to give more. A competition will immediately begin among them, and the market price will rise.[8]

In modern language Smith's concept of effectual demand was simply the quantity that would be taken at a specific price—the natural price—as can be seen from his practice of comparing the effectual demand with the quantity brought to market. Only quantities are comparable with quantities. Smith's effectual demand was actually that quantity point on the demand schedule which would be a long-run equilibrium point; that is, the natural rates of rent, wages, and profit could be paid from the actual or market price (here equal to the natural price).

Smith dismissed the problem of explaining the relation between market price and the willingness to buy a commodity quite casually. The higher prices that would be paid if there were a shortage of the commodity were attributed to "competition," which varied in strength according to the greatness of the deficiency, the importance of the commodity, and the "wealth and wanton luxury" of the competitors.[9] As there were some who would, if necessary, pay prices above the natural price, so there were some who would buy only at a price below the natural price.

A change in effectual demand must have appeared to Smith as a change in the quantity that people would be willing to take at the natural price rather than as a change in the natural price of a given quantity. The natural price was determined by the cost of production—the size of the "component parts" of price: wages, rent, and profit. The natural rates of the agents yielding these distributive shares were determined for the economy as a whole, not in the market for a single commodity. Hence the natural price could not reflect the demand for the specific commodity, certainly not so long as the quantity produced and the techniques of production were given.

On the assumption of continuity, a change in the quantity demanded at the natural price (a price "given" by the conditions of the economy as a whole) implies a shift in the demand schedule. Such a change in demand is price-determining, not price-determined. Smith's usage was essentially the same as the modern usage of demand as a schedule. Though he never presented the schedule concept explicitly, I have not found a single instance in which a change in demand is other than price-determining or in which demand may not be read as the quantity demanded at a given price.[10] However, he did not try to use his concept of demand to discuss the results of an alteration in the natural price; it would have been an awkward tool for that purpose.

JEAN-BAPTISTE SAY

Jean-Baptiste Say, who did use the concept of demand in analyzing the effects of changes in the natural price, modified Smith by substituting the current price for the natural price, as, in effect, did most classical writers. Thus demand came to mean simply the quantity taken, not necessarily at any given price.[11] Demand ceased to be a composite involving both price and quantity. Note, in the pyramid illustration that follows, that demand is represented by one di-

[8] *Ibid.*, p. 56.

[9] *Ibid.*, p. 56.

[10] For typical examples of his usage see *ibid.*, pp. 59, 60, 80, 116, 218–20, 227, 706.

[11] "The extent of demand . . . [is] the quantity of a good one is disposed to buy" (*Traité d'économie politique* [Paris: Déterville, 1803], II, 68; translations mine). For illustrations of demand changing with changes in the natural price see *ibid.*, pp. 70–71, 90–91, 95.

mension of the pyramid; price by the other: "The consumption of every good resembles a pyramid, of which the width represents the number of consumers or the extent of the demand, and the height the price. The higher the price, the less the width, that is, the demand."[12]

The "law of demand," that the lower the price, the larger the quantity that will be taken, was clearly stated here, substantially in the form of a demand schedule. But recognition that the law of demand exists, or even illustration of it in the form of a demand schedule, does not require that the term "demand" be used to refer to the schedule or that "changes in demand" be confined to price-determining changes.

Say's use of demand and supply in explaining price determination was essentially that of Hicks[13] today:

> Price is determined by the relationship between the quantity of a good that is offered for sale and the quantity people are disposed to buy. The more abundant the good in relation to the demand for it [the greater the excess supply], the more the price must fall; the greater the demand in relation to the supply [the greater the excess demand], the more the price must rise. . . .
>
> A change in the quantities offered and demanded does not change the price as long as the change is equal on both sides. It is the relationship[14] between the two quantities which determines the price; when the relationship is the same, the price remains the same.[15]

Say's usage remained the same throughout his later editions,[16] but his translator, Prinsep, evidently following Malthus,[17] introduced the concept of demand "intensity" into the English edition, although this distorted the sense of the argument.[18] The paragraph likening the consumption of a good to a pyramid was omitted after the first edition, but the same emphasis on the relation between price and quantity demanded is present.[19]

[12] *Ibid.*, p. 72.

[13] *Op. cit.*

[14] Here *rapport* has been translated by "relationship" rather than by "proportion," as in the English phrase that became so common, "the proportion between supply and demand." If *rapport* is read as "proportion," the passage cannot be taken literally. As John Stuart Mill remarked: ". . . the idea of a *ratio*, as between demand and supply, is out of place . . . the proper mathematical analogy is that of an *equation*" (*Principles of Political Economy* [from the 5th London ed.; New York: D. Appleton, 1865], I, 551). Perhaps Say was not very clear that *equality* between the quantity supplied and the quantity demanded was the price-determining condition, else he would have expressed it by something more specific than *rapport*.

[15] Say, *op. cit.*, p. 58. The brackets inclose less literal renditions of the preceding phrases.

[16] Cf. *Traité* (3d ed.; Paris: Déterville, 1817), II, 471; (4th ed.; Paris: Déterville, 1819), II, 10; *A Treatise on Political Economy*, trans. C. R. Prinsep (from the 4th French ed.; London: Longman, Hurst, Rees, Orme & Brown, 1821), II, 10, 42–43.

[17] Thomas Robert Malthus, *Principles of Political Economy Considered with a View to Their Practical Application* (1st ed.; London: J. Murray, 1820), p. 66.

[18] Say had written: "... la demande qui est faite d'un produit ... en embrasse une certaine quantité. La demande du sucre en France s'élève, dit-on, à plus de cinq cent mille quintaux par année. Même pour chaque individu, la demande qui est faite d'un certain produit en particulier peut être plus ou moins forte. Quelle qu'elle soit, appelons cette quantité la *quantité demandée*" (*Traité* [4th ed.; Paris: Déterville, 1819], II, 10).

"Enfin, quelles que soient les causes générales ou particulières qui déterminent la plus ou moins grande quantité de chaque chose qui est offerte ou demandée, c'est cette quantité qui, dans les échanges, influe fondamentalement sur les prix" (*ibid.*, p. 16; this and the preceding passage were omitted from the fifth [final] French edition).

Despite the explicit references to "quantity," Prinsep translated *forte* by "urgent" and the last sentence of the first passage as "whatever be its intensity, it may be called by the general name of demand." In the second passage he simply substituted "intensity" for *quantité* (Say, *A Treatise on Political Economy*, II, 9, 15). Cf. also *Treatise*, II, 42, with *Traité* (5th ed.; Paris: Rapilly, 1826), II, 184; *Treatise* (2d Amer. ed., from the 4th French ed.; Boston: Wells & Lilly, II, 1824), II, 32 n., with *Traité* (1817), II, 24.

[19] See Say, *Traité* (1826), II, 162–63, 165.

Say explained the fact that the quantity taken varied with price by the limitation of people's means,[20] but he did not forget the claims of other commodities. He was careful to point out that one's expenditure on a particular commodity was limited to the amount that was left after providing for other needs.[21] In the fifth edition he added the statement that each individual had to classify his wants in the order of importance. The higher the price, the more "products capable of giving a greater satisfaction for the same price are preferred."[22] As for individual demand, when the price rises, "the individual should be considered as two; one disposed to pay the price asked, the other withdrawing his demand."[23]

LORD LAUDERDALE

Lauderdale stressed the demand for a particular commodity more than did any of the other economists discussed here. He was less consistent than Say, but generally he used "demand" to mean the "quantity demanded."[24] Indeed, he often substituted the phrase the "extension of demand" for "an increase of demand."[25] His deviations from the use of "demand" as "quantity" include instances where "demand" means the amount spent for the commodity[26] and another where it means the price that buyers would pay.[27]

In explaining the relation between price and the quantity demanded, Lauderdale presented a rudimentary demand schedule, the quantities taken being unspecified but diminishing as higher and higher prices exclude more and more families from the market. It may be compared with Malthus' earlier example, which will be presented below, and with Say's "pyramid" illustration in his first edition:[28]

> Thus, the desire for sugar, which either taste or habit may have created, may, in some of these families, make them willing to deprive themselves of a portion of their other enjoyments, equal to the value of twenty shillings, rather than abridge their consumption of sugar. The desire of others for that article may be so great, that . . . they would sacrifice thirty shillings worth of their other enjoyments. And . . . there might exist . . . men willing to sacrifice forty shillings worth of their other enjoyments.[29]

In addition to this explanation of the market "law of demand" by differences in tastes, habits, and preferences, Lauderdale pointed out that individuals might follow a similar law. When confronted by an increase in the price, "some of the consumers of sugar, preferring the enjoyment of the other things to which they were habituated, might be . . . willing to retrench in that article, or perhaps to renounce the use of it altogether."[30]

It would be possible to derive a demand schedule from Lauderdale's illus-

[20] *Traité* (1803), II, 69–73; see also *Treatise* (1821), II, 9–12, and *Traité* (1826), II, 162–63.

[21] *Traité* (1803), II, 70.

[22] *Ibid.* (1826), II, 161–62.

[23] *Ibid.*, II, 164. This position dates back to the first edition (1803), II, 71.

[24] "If . . . the supply continuing at one thousand pounds weight, there should suddenly arise a demand for two thousand pounds weight . . . the demand would be double the quantity for which there existed a supply" (James Maitland, Eighth Earl of Lauderdale, *An Inquiry into the Nature and Origin of Public Wealth* [Edinburgh: Constable & Co., 1804], pp. 73–74; see also pp. 77–78). Demand was not necessarily measured at a given price, for he sometimes spoke of demand's changing in response to a price change (*ibid.*, pp. 65, 70, 289).

[25] *Ibid.*, pp. 75, 78, 95, 109.

[26] *Ibid.*, pp. 83–84, 85, 87–89, 104.

[27] *Ibid.*, pp. 20–21. The phrase "degree of demand" is here used as Malthus later used "intensity." See also p. 107.

[28] See above, p. 245, and below, pp. 249–50.

[29] Lauderdale, *op. cit.*, pp. 62–63.

[30] *Ibid.*, p. 63; see also pp. 65–66, 76, 78–79, 95–97.

trations of the effects of changes in grain production on the price of grain, following Gregory King and others. However, these relationships were not used to explain price determination but to relate changes in the quantity produced to the total expenditures on the commodity. Lauderdale's belief that the elasticity of the demand schedule was less than unity (to use present-day language) was of major importance for his policy conclusions. Because he believed "that the diminution of the quantity has the effect of raising the value for which the total of any commodity sells at the market; and the increase, the effect of diminishing it,"[31] he held that "it may be generally affirmed, that an increase of [private] riches, when arising from alterations in the quantity of commodities, is always a proof of an immediate diminution of [public] wealth."[32]

DAVID RICARDO

Ricardo joins Say and Lauderdale as one of the group whose dominant usage of demand was in the sense of the quantity demanded.[33] The Ricardian distinction was that he chose at times to use what was effectively an *ex post* concept; demand was the quantity actually taken from the market, not the quantity people would be willing to take: "The demand for a commodity cannot be said to increase if no additional quantity of it be purchased or consumed; and yet under such circumstances its money value may rise."[34]

Ricardo's primary concern with demand was to destroy the belief that price depended solely on demand and supply. The quantity actually taken could deviate from the quantity produced only temporarily. If the quantities demanded and supplied changed in the same proportion, as they would between two equilibrium positions, there would be no change in the "proportion of demand to supply." Hence this widely held explanation of price was useless. Of course, since the quantity actually taken, an *ex post* concept, is the result of both demand and supply forces, it cannot be very useful in explaining the effects of demand forces alone on price. It was this interpretation of "demand" by Ricardo that forced Malthus to make explicit his concept of the "intensity of demand."[35]

Ricardo was as varied in his usage as was Lauderdale. At times he used "effective demand" in the sense of Smith's "effectual demand,"[36] and at least twice he seems to have used "demand" in the sense of "demand price," though he usually avoided this.[37] He was aware of the

[31] *Ibid.*, p. 53. Lauderdale cited Gregory King, the *Spectator*, No. 200, and Sir John Dalrymple. Gregory King's estimate was made in 1696; the *Spectator* paper appeared in 1715 (D. R. MacGregor, "Marshall and His Book," *Economica*, IX [new ser.; 1942], 316).

[32] Lauderdale, *op. cit.*, p. 55.

[33] David Ricardo, *The Principles of Political Economy and Taxation* (3d ed.; London: J. M. Dent & Sons, 1911), pp. 199, 264; *On Protection to Agriculture* (4th ed.; London: John Murray, 1822), pp. 17–18. To be sure, most of his references to "demand" do not conclusively indicate the meaning he attached to the word (see *Principles*, pp. 8, 49–50, 175, 180–81, 193–98).

[34] *Principles*, p. 260. The same argument had appeared in his correspondence with Malthus in 1814 (Ricardo, *Letters of David Ricardo to Thomas Robert Malthus*, ed. James Bonar [Oxford: Clarendon Press, 1887], pp. 34–42).

[35] Ricardo occasionally used "demand" as an *ex ante* concept. Two references to supply increasing as a result of an increase in demand show that he sometimes thought of planned as well as of accomplished purchases (*Principles*, p. 262; *Letters of David Ricardo to Hutches Trower and Others, 1811–1823*, ed. James Bonar and Jacob H. Hollander [Oxford: Clarendon Press, 1899], p. 127; see also p. 126).

[36] *Letters to Trower*, pp. 126, 128.

[37] "High profits are the consequence of high price—high price of increased demand—increased

demand-price aspect of the demand relationship but not deeply interested in it; for attention to it interfered with concentration on the long-run, natural values of things. Similarly, he was fully conscious of the law of demand,[38] but the explanation of this phenomenon was of little interest to him.

THE MILLS

The dominance of quantity demanded as the meaning attached to "demand" in the classical period is attested by its adoption by John Stuart Mill:

> Meaning, by the word demand, the quantity demanded, and remembering that this . . . in general varies according to the value, let us suppose that the demand at some particular time exceeds the supply, that is, there are persons ready to buy, at the market value, a greater quantity than is offered for sale. Competition takes place on the side of the buyers, and the value rises . . . [to] the point, whatever it be, which equalizes the demand and the supply. . . .
>
> The proper mathematical analogy is that of an *equation*. Demand and supply, the quantity demanded and the quantity supplied, will be made equal . . . by an adjustment of value.[39]

This was the "true solution" to the paradox that value depended on demand, yet demand depended on value, said Mill, adding that it had previously been given by J.-B. Say.[40] This accords with our reading of Say. The identity between Mill's solution and that of John R. Hicks is even clearer than in the case of Say.

The younger Mill's explanation of the law of demand was rudimentary: "A rise of price . . . may place the article beyond the means, or beyond the inclinations, of purchasers to the full amount."[41] Although he was aware that a fall in value "induces those who were already consumers to make increased purchases,"[42] he did not inquire into the phenomenon.

James Mill, like some others, did not find it necessary to define the term "demand" in order to use it in explaining exchange value. Apparently it sometimes referred to the quantity demanded, for, having said that demand and supply determine the quantities of goods exchanged for one another, he went on to illustrate: "If a great quantity of corn comes to market to be exchanged for cloth, and only a small quantity of

---

demand of an imperfect distribution of capital" (*ibid.*, p. 128). Since he was arguing that an imperfect distribution of capital would be self-correcting, he must have meant that a (relative) shortage of certain commodities would result in a (relatively) high demand price for them. Certainly, such an imperfect distribution of capital could not give rise to an increase in the demand schedule or the quantity demanded.

Again: if a superfine cloth were introduced in limited quantity, "the article would . . . be scarce and therefore in great demand" (*Letters to Malthus*, p. 4 n., quoting speech in Commons, 1822).

He usually avoided such usage by substituting such phrases as those italicized in the following passages: "Commodities which are monopolized . . . rise in proportion to the *eagerness of the buyers* to purchase them (*Principles*, p. 262; italics mine). "If corn rises in price, (though no greater quantity actually be taken) . . . , I should [attribute it to] *a greater competition* (*Letters to Malthus*, p. 42; italics mine).

[38] "The demand for corn . . . must necessarily be limited; and, although it . . . undoubtedly is, true, that when it is . . . cheap, the quantity consumed will be increased, yet it is equally certain, that its aggregate value will be diminished. This is true of all commodities, but of none can it be so certainly asserted as of corn" (*On Protection to Agriculture*, p. 18). See also the *Principles*, pp. 199, 264; *Letters to Trower*, pp. 128–32; *Letters to Malthus*, pp. 3–4 (n.), 5. In the latter (note on pp. 3–4) he stated that the aggregate value of a superfine cloth, newly introduced, would first rise and then fall as it grew in abundance.

[39] *Principles* (1848), pp. 528–30; see also *Principles* (from the 5th London ed.; New York: D. Appleton, 1865), I, 553, 559–60, 588; II, 105, 140, 143.

[40] *Ibid.* (1865), p. 549.

[41] *Ibid.*, p. 550.

[42] *Ibid.*, p. 551.

cloth to be exchanged for corn, a great quantity of corn will be given for a small quantity of cloth."[43] But the term also carried an implication of willingness to pay for a good: "Demand creates, and the loss of demand annihilates, supply. When an increased demand arises . . . an increase of supply . . . follows."[44]

Clarification of the concept became important when he set about to develop the proposition "That Consumption Is Co-extensive with Production."[45] At that point he defined demand as "the will to purchase, and the means of purchasing,"[46] whence he argued that "the equivalent which a man brings is the instrument of demand. The extent of his demand is measured by the extent of his equivalent. . . . The equivalent may be called the demand, and the demand the equivalent. . . . [His] demand, is exactly equal to the amount of what he has produced and does not mean to consume."[47]

From this last definition of demand it followed immediately that demand and supply were always equal and that no general glut was possible.

T. R. MALTHUS

It was Malthus among the classical economists who deliberately chose to measure demand by the demand price rather than by the quantity demanded. However, his first contribution to demand analysis was an approximation to a modern demand schedule, in his second published work, *An Investigation of the Cause of the Present High Price of Provisions*.[48] High corn prices following a short harvest had continued past the next harvest,[49] remaining higher than he thought the degree of scarcity warranted. On a trip through recently famine-stricken areas in Sweden, he had found no evidence of such large price increases as in England, though the dearth had been much worse. The usual explanations —monopoly, speculation, or the increased circulation of bank notes—seemed inadequate. The principal cause, he wrote, was rather the practice of increasing parish allowances in proportion to the rise in corn prices.

> When any commodity is scarce, its natural price is necessarily forgotten, and its actual price is regulated by the excess of the demand above the supply.
>
> Let us suppose a commodity in great request by fifty people, but of which, from some failure in its production, there is only sufficient to supply forty. If the fortieth man from the top have two shillings which he can spend in this commodity, and the thirty-nine above him, more, in various proportions, and the ten below, all less, the actual price of the article, according to the genuine principles of trade, will be two shillings. If more be asked, the whole will not be sold, because there are only forty who have as much as two shillings to spend in the article; and there is no reason for asking less, because the whole may be disposed of at that sum.
>
> Let us suppose, now, that somebody gives the ten poor men, who were excluded, a shilling a-piece. The whole fifty can now offer two shillings, the price which was before asked. According to every genuine principle of fair trading, the commodity must immediately rise. If it do not I would ask, upon what principle are ten, out of the fifty who are all able

[43] *Elements of Political Economy* (London: Baldwin, Cradock & Joy, 1821), p. 66. Malthus spoke of Mill defining demand as the quantity consumed (Malthus, *Definitions in Political Economy* [London: John Murray, 1827], pp. 47–48).

[44] James Mill, *op. cit.*, p. 67.

[45] *Ibid.*, p. 186.

[46] *Ibid.*, p. 188.

[47] *Ibid.*, pp. 188–89.

[48] London: J. Johnson, 1800. Reprinted in Harry G. Johnson, "Malthus on the High Price of Provisions," *Canadian Journal of Economics and Political Science*, XV (1949), 190–202.

[49] In June, 1800, the price of wheat was 134*s.* 5*d.* per quarter, compared with an average price for the year 1794 of 52*s.* 3*d.* The price in the latter year was but little below the high points of the preceding twenty years (Gilbert Slater, *The Growth of Modern England* [Boston: Houghton Mifflin Co., 1933], p. 214, and Diagram I, Appendix).

to offer two shillings, to be rejected? For still, according to the supposition, there is only enough for forty . . . according to every acknowledged principle of commercial dealing, the price must be allowed to rise to that point which will put it beyond the power of ten out of the fifty to purchase. This point will, perhaps, be half-a-crown or more, which will now become the price of the commodity. Let another shilling a-piece be given to the excluded ten: all will now be able to offer half-a-crown. The price must in consequence immediately rise to three shillings or more, and so on *toties quoties*.

The rise in the price of corn, and of other provisions, in this country, has been effected exactly in the same manner . . . and I am firmly convinced, that it never could have reached its present height, but from the system of poor laws and parish allowances, which have operated precisely in the same mode as the donatives of a shilling in the instance I have just adduced.[50]

The technical apparatus used in this argument—an array of the fifty persons' demand prices, each person taking one unit of the good—is clearly a rudimentary market demand schedule, the equivalent of that in Böhm-Bawerk's horse-market example.[51] Each gift of a shilling to each of the excluded participants raises each man's demand price and thus the price of the given quantity of the good. In modern language the part of the schedule that is affected shifts upward (to the right). The shift upward, incidentally, is apparently (correctly) expected to be somewhat less than a shilling at a quantity of forty, for the new prices are assumed to rise by half a shilling "or more" with each increase of one shilling in each man's wealth. This device enabled Malthus to show that, as long as the parish allowances were increased whenever the price of corn rose, every increase in price resulted in an increase of the incomes of the poor, an increase in the market demand schedule at its lower end, and a further rise in price.[52]

Twenty years later, in order to defend the proposition that prices are determined by the proportion between the demand and the supply, Malthus presented his concept of the intensity of demand:

It has been sometimes said that supply is always equal to demand, because no permanent supply of any commodity can take place for which there is not a demand so effective as to take off all that is offered. In one sense of the terms in which demand and supply have been used, this position may be granted. The actual *extent* of the demand compared with the actual *extent* of the supply are always on an average proportioned to each other. . . . It cannot, therefore, be in this sense that a change in the proportion of demand to supply affects prices. . . .

The demand for a commodity has been defined to be, the will combined with the power to purchase it.

The greater is the degree of this will and power with regard to any particular commodity, the greater or more intense may be fairly said to be the demand for it. But . . . as long as . . . sellers . . . bring the quantity wanted to market at a low price, the real intensity of the demand will not show itself.

In fact it may be said, that the giving a greater price for a commodity absolutely and necessarily implies a greater intensity of demand.[53]

[50] *Investigation of the . . . High Price of Provisions* (reprinted in Johnson, *op. cit.*), pp. 194–95 (in the original, pp. 5–7).

[51] Eugen von Böhm-Bawerk, *The Positive Theory of Capital* (New York: G. E. Stechert, 1930), p. 203.

[52] Malthus had used the same general argument, but without the device of the array of demanders, in *An Essay on the Principle of Population*, ed. James Bonar (London: Macmillan & Co., 1926; reprint of 1798 ed.), pp. 74–83. Nor was the array used in the second edition of the *Essay* ([London: J. Johnson, 1803], pp. 396–402). Despite his general disapproval of the poor laws, under the special conditions that gave rise to the *Investigation*, he commended them for the humanitarian reasons that they led to high prices of necessaries, forced "strict economy in all ranks of life," and caused the distress to be shared among larger numbers of people, among other reasons (*Investigation*, pp. 18–20).

[53] Malthus, *Principles* (1820), pp. 65–66.

Here, before James Mill, we have a reinterpretation of the common phrase "the will and power to purchase" to make it mean the "intensity of demand," measured by the demand price. No other economist had based his value theory on such a conception of demand, nor had any other economist recognized explicitly that "demand" might have two measures, extent and intensity. It was demand in the sense of intensity that affected prices, he insisted:

> It is evidently, therefore, not merely the extent of actual demand, nor even the extent of actual demand compared with the extent of the actual supply, which raises prices, but such a change in the relation between demand and supply, as renders necessary the expression of a greater intensity of demand.[54]

What were these changes that rendered necessary the expression of a greater intensity of demand? The causes that raise the price of a commodity[55]

> are an increase in the number or wants of its purchasers, or a deficiency in its supply; and the causes which lower the price are a diminution in the number or wants of its purchasers, or an increased abundance in its supply.
>
> The first class of these causes is obviously calculated to call forth the expression of a greater intensity of demand, and the other of a less.[56]

An increased intensity resulting from an increase in the number, wants, or means of the purchasers is the result of a shift of the demand schedule; an increased intensity resulting from a deficiency in the supply simply represents a movement along a given demand schedule. Malthus' intensity is incapable of distinguishing price-determining from price-determined changes in demand.[57] Probably because it applied to both cases, he could not decide whether the intensity of demand was some latent force, to be called forth as needed, or whether it was simply a quantity susceptible of increase or decrease.[58]

Despite the fact that Malthus' concept of the intensity of demand was unique among the major writers, he insisted that he had not given the term a new meaning but had simply explained the meaning that had always been attached to it when demand was said to raise prices.[59] To be sure, an increase in price did imply an increase in the intensity of demand and in its measure, the demand price; but no other major economist seems to have consciously thought of it in this way.[60] Malthus' use of the

[54] *Principles* (1820), p. 70; see also *Definitions in Political Economy* (London: John Murray, 1827), pp. 44–45.

[55] Evidently following Lauderdale, *op. cit.*, p. 13.

[56] *Principles* (1820), pp. 66–67. Changes in the means of demanders were added to the list in the second edition ([London: William Pickering, 1836], p. 64).

[57] *Ibid.* (1820), pp. 67–70. Malthus showed awareness of the distinctive character of a shift in the schedule in his second edition: "Of course it must often happen that an increased intensity of demand, and an increased extent of demand go together. In fact, an increased intensity of demand, when not occasioned by an increased difficulty of production, is the greatest encouragement to an increase of produce and consumption" (*ibid.* [1836], p. 69 n.).

[58] He used both forms of expression: "call forth" on pp. 66, 67, and 70 of the first edition of the *Principles*, for instance, with "increase" also appearing on p. 67. In the second edition he revised the passage on p. 66 to read "increase" (p. 63), and revised the "increase" on p. 67 to read "exist in such a degree" (p. 64).

[59] *Ibid.* (1820), pp. 71–72. Cf. J. S. Mill's argument that Ricardo meant that profits depend on the cost of labor, though he actually said "wages" (J. S. Mill, *Principles* [1865], p. 512).

[60] Malthus sometimes used "demand" in still other senses. In his earlier writings, of course, he had not clearly formulated his ideas. He once used "effective demand" in the sense of Smith's "effectual demand" when discussing the demand for particular commodities (*Principles* [1820], p. 68); in the *Principles* (1836) the word became "effectual" (p. 65). Beginning in 1824, he sometimes used the total amount spent for a quantity of a commodity as the measure of demand: Value was as "the quantity of service offered divided by the quantity of produce received" ("Essay on Political Economy," *Quarterly Review*, XXX [1824], 318; see also *Definitions*, pp. 247, 258; "Transcript of the Questions on Adam Smith's Wealth of Nations . . . "

intensity of demand enabled him to show that demand considerations were important, even though the quantity taken did not change and even in those cases in which the change in the schedule sense was on the supply side of the market. Thus he was able to defend demand and supply as the determinants of price and to support his general thesis that demand played an active role in determining the prices of particular commodities and of commodities in general.

To be sure, Malthus' resort to the intensity of demand owed its validity not so much to any analytical superiority of intensity, as such, over the quantity-demanded concept as to the fact that his intensity was an *ex ante* concept in contrast with Ricardo's (and his) *ex post* usage of "extent."[61] Say's *ex ante* use of "quantity demanded" was as successful a defense of demand and supply theorizing as was Malthus' *ex ante* use of "intensity."

Having established the concepts of intensity and extent, Malthus was satisfied. He was too practical a person to go deeper than changes in the number, wants, or means of "purchasers" or deficiency or increased abundance in the supply as an explanation of "the causes which either call forth or render unnecessary the expression of the intensity of demand."[62] He emphasized the subjective side of demand in certain respects (intensity is a subjective concept), but he had no interest in analyzing what lay behind the intensity of demand. He stressed the importance of commodities being suited to the tastes of consumers if effective demand were to be maintained,[63] and he insisted that there was a subjective gain from trade[64] and a subjective estimate of the significance of a commodity.[65] At the same time, he cursorily dismissed value in use as a seldom-used concept[66] and argued that "the man who has two pairs of stockings of the same quality instead of one . . . possesses . . . a double portion of the conveniences of life,"[67] though only two pages later he said: "The most useful commodity . . . if it be absolutely in excess, not only loses its exchangeable value, but its power of supplying the wants of society to the extent of its quantity, and part of it therefore loses its quality of wealth."[68]

His lack of analysis of the subjective aspects of demand is not too surprising, when we consider that his propositions about the intensity of demand increasing as the quantity decreased were never explicitly applied to the *individual*. One gets the impression that Malthus thought of the individual as buying either his usual amount or none at all.

[original manuscript in Marshall Library of Economics, Cambridge, England], p. 10; *Principles* [1836], pp. 66 n., 67–68).

[61] On the *ex post* character of Malthus' use of "extent" see the quotation on p. 250 above. The distinction between *ex ante* and *ex post* concepts is not so new as we may think. Compare Malthus' footnote in his second edition: "Sir Edward West seems to think that a demand *in posse* cannot be called demand; but it does not appear to me that there is any impropriety in so applying the term; and it is quite certain that if there were not a greater intensity of demand *in posse* than *in esse*, no failure of supply could raise prices. In reality prices are determined by the demand *in posse* compared with the supply *in esse*" (p. 64).

[62] *Principles* (1820), pp. 66–67; (1836), p. 64.

[63] *Principles* (1836), pp. 301–3.

[64] "Publications on the Depreciation of Paper Currency," *Edinburgh Review*, XVII (1811), 356–57 n.

[65] *Principles* (1820), p. 53; *Definitions*, p. 251.

[66] *Principles* (1820), pp. 51–52.

[67] *Ibid.*, p. 338. In the second edition Malthus remarked that some writers had denied that doubling the quantity doubles the satisfaction, but he maintained his position (p. 300).

[68] *Ibid.*, p. 340.

Malthus was uninterested in the price-quantity relationship for the individual, though he could hardly have been unaware of it. He remarked in the *Investigation of the High Price of Provisions* that high prices led to "strict economy in all ranks of life"[69] and, in the *Essay on Population*, that "the price of corn in a scarcity, will depend much more upon the obstinacy with which the same degree of consumption is persevered in, than on the degree of the actual deficiency."[70] For the problem of the *Investigation* the limitation upon the demand price imposed by the buyers' incomes was the point at issue; he pursued the problem no further. Similarly, in the *Principles*, for the purpose of maintaining his position regarding the intensity of demand for the whole market, it was necessary only to note that the individual might express a greater intensity if necessary in order to obtain the quantity to which he was accustomed; Malthus did not explicitly consider the case of the individual who adjusted the quantity of his consumption in accordance with the price.[71]

[69] Reprinted in Johnson, *op. cit.*, p. 200.

[70] *Essay on Population* (1803), pp. 399–400.

[71] Hla Myint is warranted, with respect to the individual demand schedule, in saying that Malthus "has failed . . . to understand the equilibrium mechanism which adjusts the 'intensity' of demand to price *at the margin* by a simultaneous adjustment of the 'extent' of demand to the given supply" (*Theories of Welfare Economics* [Cambridge: Harvard University Press, 1948], p. 37). I think he errs in applying this observation also to market situations. Malthus thought that for the whole market the normal situation was one in which the extent and the intensity of demand varied together (not necessarily *increased* together). He chose to discuss the limiting cases (horizontal or vertical demand schedules) because he wanted to show that his concept was useful even at the extremes (*Principles* [1820], pp. 67–70). Hla Myint's view that Malthus built his analysis on contradictory assumptions regarding the shape of the demand curve is not convincing (Myint, *op. cit.*, pp. 36–38, 64).

"OBSERVATIONS ON CERTAIN VERBAL DISPUTES"

The anonymous author of *Observations on Certain Verbal Disputes in Political Economy*[72] possessed a sense of the distinction between the price-determined and the price-determining that was unusually strong for his time: "The increase of the intensity of demand must mean (for Mr. Malthus's definition is not exact enough to help us) the existence of a disposition to give more for the quantity actually taken, or to buy more at the same rate."[73] By thus limiting the meaning of the phrase "increase of intensity" to the shift of the schedule, he was able to argue that price increases could occur without corresponding increases in the intensity of demand. Each person might buy half as much at an increased price, though no one would buy his former amount at the old price, he continued, for "half the quantity we use of any article is generally *more* than half as intrinsically desirable, on the whole."[74]

He continued his attack on Malthus' usage with a reference to the case in which a fall in price as the result of a contingent increase of supply was associated with a fall in the intensity of demand: "If the degree of demand can itself be altered by the degree of supply, what information is given us by saying, that something depends on the balance of forces (as it were) between the two?"[75] It is undoubtedly true that the prevalent use of demand in a nonschedule sense,

[72] London: R. Hunter, 1821.

[73] *Ibid.*, p. 65.

[74] *Ibid.* This is one of the earlier statements of diminishing marginal utility, though the "margin" is rather large. Perhaps this is the writer who elicited Malthus' comment given in n. 67 above.

[75] *Ibid.*, pp. 65–66. The reference to Malthus is to *Principles* (1820), p. 69. I have omitted a footnote reference to Say after the word "forces" in the quotation.

by permitting confusion between price-determining and price-determined changes in demand, contributed to the widespread preference for a cost-of-production explanation of price in the classical period.

MOUNTIFORT LONGFIELD

Longfield, like Malthus, recognized both extent and intensity as aspects of demand. Moreover, Longfield was able to utilize both, for he was not under the same compulsion to refute the Ricardian position on demand. Longfield's definition of demand places him in the demand-price group: "the disposition to give something in exchange . . . may be called the demand."[76] This did not prevent him from making extensive use of a modified version of Adam Smith's effectual demand:

> [If] more persons are willing to purchase . . . than the quantity on sale can supply . . . the competition among the buyers will raise the article to such a price that the supply will become equal to the effective demand—that is, the demand of those who are willing to give for it the increased price to which it is raised. This equality is . . . produced . . . by a diminution of the effective demand consequent upon an increase of price.[77]

So far, the only departure from Adam Smith's argument has been to make "effective demand" simply the quantity taken, not requiring that it be the quantity taken at the natural price, as Smith did for his "effectual demand." This change makes the analysis substantially the same as that of Say,[78] but Longfield at a later point developed the demand-price aspect, which he must have obtained from Malthus:[79]

> The measure of the intensity of any person's demand for any commodity is the amount which he would be willing and able to give for it, rather than remain without it. . . . [The] high prices to which provisions rise in time of scarcity, prove the existence of a latent intensity of demand . . . : the intense demand always exists, though it may not be apparent. . . . [The] market price is measured by the demand, which being of the least intensity, yet leads to actual purchases. If the existing supply is more than sufficient to satisfy all the demand equal to or superior to a certain degree of intensity, prices will fall, to accommodate themselves to a less intense demand. . . . [Each] individual contains as it were within himself, a series of demands of successively increasing degrees of intensity . . . the lowest degree of this series which at any time leads to a purchase, is exactly the same for both rich and poor, and is that which regulates the market price.[80]

The analysis is unusually clear. The intensity of demand is measured by the demand price; a different quantity corresponds to each intensity of demand.[81] Moreover, the notion of marginal demand was present: "Now if the price is attempted to be raised . . . the demanders, who by the change will cease to be purchasers, must be those the intensity of whose demand was precisely measured by the former price. . . .[82] Now that portion which any person ceases to consume in consequence of a rise in prices . . . is that for which the in-

[76] Mountifort Longfield, *Lectures on Political Economy* (delivered in 1833) (London: London School of Economics, 1931; reprint of 1834 ed., Dublin: R. Milliken & Son), p. 45.

[77] *Ibid.*, pp. 47–48; see also pp. 46–47, 49, 111.

[78] Cf. Say, *A Treatise on Political Economy*, I, 3–5, and II, 8, with Longfield, *op. cit.*, pp. 27, 47–48.

[79] He cited Malthus on rent (Longfield, *op. cit.*, p. 148), but not in connection with demand analysis. However, Longfield's theory is a development of the intensity of demand, and no writer but Malthus had that concept. Although the English translation of Say's *Traité* refers to intensity, the translator must have adopted the term from Malthus, for it does not appear in the French (see p. 245, above).

[80] Longfield, *op. cit.*, pp. 111–15.

[81] The word "demand" here, when unmodified by "intensity," seems to mean simply the quantity demanded, as in the passage previously quoted.

[82] Longfield, *op. cit.*, p. 113.

tensity of his demand is less than the high price which prevents him from purchasing it. . . ."[83] However, Longfield did not attempt a subjective explanation of the relation between the intensity of demand and the demand (quantity) for the individual.

But Longfield's influence was limited.[84] Theoretical discussions apart from practical problems attracted few,[85] and Francis Horner was probably not the only Englishman who scorned the "rabble of Irish economists."[86]

H. D. MACLEOD

Aside from James Mill, the principal exponent of the amount spent on a commodity as the measure of demand was Macleod. His usage began as the quantity of a particular commodity sold, but it eventually became the quantity of the other commodity given in exchange for that particular commodity. In 1858 he defined demand as the quantity sold[87] and held that "the relation between demand and supply is the sole regulator of value";[88] but his explanation of price utilized a different aspect of demand: "The very same thing may be of far more use at one time than at another, and . . . we may call it a service of greater or lesser intensity."[89] A crust of bread would be a service of great intensity to a starving man.[90] "*Price varies directly as the intensity of the service rendered, and inversely as the power of the seller over the buyer.*"[91]

The concept of the intensity of the service rendered may have been suggested by Malthus' "intensity of demand."[92] A little later Macleod used Malthus' phrase[93] and maintained that "the more intense the desire and the greater the power to purchase, the greater is the Demand."[94] Indeed, "no other Causes influence Value or changes of Value, except Intensity of Demand and Limitation of Supply."[95] He had shifted to the demand-price concept. Although his former concept—the quantity sold—was identical with consumption in Macleod's sense of "purchase,"[96] he now held that demand was not the same as consumption; if the rich crowd into a country town and give higher prices than the poor can, there has been an increase in demand.[97]

However, in the *Elements of Economics* Macleod went further and provided the extreme variant of the demand-

[83] *Ibid.*, p. 114.

[84] Cf. R. D. Black, "Trinity College, Dublin, and the Theory of Value, 1823–63," *Economica*, XII (new ser.; 1945), 140–48.

[85] Edwin R. A. Seligman, "On Some Neglected British Economists," *Economic Journal*, XIII (1903), 534–35.

[86] Leonard Horner (ed.), *Memoirs and Correspondence of Francis Horner* (Boston: Little, Brown, 1853).

[87] Henry Dunning Macleod, *The Elements of Political Economy* (London: Longman, Brown, Green, Longmans & Roberts, 1858), p. 86.

[88] *Ibid.*, p. 111.

[89] *Ibid.*, p. 98.

[90] *Ibid.*, pp. 98–99.

[91] *Ibid.*, p. 100 (italics in the original). The importance of the power of the seller over the buyer was illustrated by the case of a drowning man. To him the intensity of the service rendered by a boatman would be the same whether one or two boatmen were available, but the price would be less if there were two (*ibid.*, pp. 99–100).

[92] That Macleod knew Malthus' *Principles* is attested by his lengthy quotation of Malthus' defense of supply and demand (*The Elements of Economics*, II [1886], Part I, 15–17, quoting *Principles* [1820], pp. 71–73).

[93] *The Theory and Practice of Banking* (3d ed.; London: Longmans, Green, Reader & Dyer, 1875), I, 95: "It is the intensity of Demand which confers such enormous Value on the ground in the heart of London."

[94] *Ibid.*, p. 63.

[95] *The Elements of Economics* (New York: D. Appleton, 1881), I, 259.

[96] *Ibid.*, I, 200.

[97] *The Theory and Practice of Banking*, I, 63.

price usage of the term "demand": "Demand means the Desire and the Power to purchase anything: and so may be used to mean the Quantity of anything which is given in exchange for anything else."[98] He was eager to measure demand (comprising both desire and power) by its manifestation in an act of exchange. Hence he adopted James Mill's suggestion that the quantity of money or anything else given in exchange for a commodity should be called the "demand" for it.[99] He did not explicitly distinguish between the quantity given for a single unit of another commodity (the price or demand price of that commodity) and the quantity given for the whole number of units of that commodity, but he used the term in the latter, inclusive, sense: "Thus each Quantity offered is the Supply of that article, and the Demand is the Value of the other. . . ."[100] In this latter instance Macleod's use of demand as the *value* rather than the *quantity* of the other commodity exchanged involves us in circularity except when we may refer to money, or the *numéraire*, for which the quantity and the value are identical by definition. But Macleod generally referred to demand as the *quantity* of the other commodity given in exchange.[101]

NASSAU SENIOR

Still another meaning of demand was contributed by Senior. If we are to believe his words, his concept was entirely subjective, omitting any requirement of a means of payment, and not in a quantified form. Neither Malthus' two kinds of demand (the quantity purchased and the sacrifice that demanders were willing and able to make) nor Mill's will and power of purchasing conformed to common usage, Senior complained. His own usage would be "as expressing the utility of a commodity; or, what is the same—for we have seen that all utility is relative—the degree in which its possession is desired."[102] The usual meaning of an increase in demand, he added, was an increase in the desire to obtain commodities or their utilities.[103] His illustration had been used in his first Oxford period:

> It must be admitted that the word demand is used in its ordinary sense when we say that a deficient wheat harvest increases the demand for oats and barley. But this proposition is not true in any other sense than as expressing the increased utility of oats and barley; or, in other words, the increased desire of the community to obtain them. The deficiency of wheat would not give to the consumers of oats and barley any increased power of purchasing them, nor would the quantity purchased or consumed be increased. . . . The mode of consumption would be altered . . . the pleasure given or the pain averted by the possession of a given quantity of them (or, in other words, the *utility* of a given quantity of them), would increase.[104]

An increase in demand, in this usage, was clearly price-determining.[105] While this might have been a useful development, his refusal to include the willingness to part with something in exchange as a part of the definition of demand made the term the equivalent of "de-

[98] *The Elements of Economics*, I, 221.

[99] *Ibid.*, pp. 202–3. The reference is evidently to James Mill, *op. cit.*, pp. 188–89.

[100] *The Elements of Economics*, I, 203.

[101] *Ibid.*, pp. 202–3, 221, 225.

[102] Nassau William Senior, *Political Economy* (6th ed.; London: Charles Griffin, 1872), pp. 15–16.

[103] *Ibid.*, p. 15.

[104] *Industrial Efficiency and Social Economy*, ed. S. Leon Levy (New York: Henry Holt & Co., 1928), II, 25, quoting *First Course of Lectures at Oxford, Old Series* (1826–27), pp. 128–31.

[105] However, he sometimes used "demand" in the sense of "quantity taken" (see *Industrial Efficiency*, II, 23, quoting Lecture 7, *Fourth Course of Lectures at Oxford, New Series* [1850–51], pp. 58–63, and p. 239, quoting Lecture 6, *Fifth Course of Lectures at Oxford, New Series* [1851], pp. 7–9).

sire."[106] With no way at hand of expressing desire in quantitative terms, his concept was not very useful. This was no particular burden to him, for he rarely resorted to its use; cost of production was the active force in his theory of value. His definition had the advantage of turning attention toward the subjective aspect and thus was consistent with his statement of the law of variety and of diminishing utility.

CONCLUSIONS

Such diversity of usage as prevailed in the classical period is undoubtedly partially the result of the lack of importance placed on demand as a determinant of value. That controversy continued over this part of their system evidences a lack of complete understanding of the relationships of the various concepts to one another. The classicists' use of "demand" in explaining price changes often relied more on an intuitive or commonsense grasp of the situation than on a precisely stated concept of demand and a strictly logical use of that concept. Either the demand-quantity or the demand-price concept could have been used successfully to explain price determination (as in the quantity-demanded versions of Say and J. S. Mill or the intensity-of-demand version of Longfield. Nor were the two usages mutually exclusive, though Longfield seems to have been the only writer who elaborated both.

But not until Marshall's adoption of the schedule usage did the relationships among these various concepts become generally clear in English economics. The literary economist of today who uses "demand" as the quantity demanded does so with greater success because familiarity with the concept of demand as the schedule has made him sensitive to the distinction between shifts of the schedule and movements along it.

Only two of the classical economists studied here identified an increase in demand with a shift of the schedule—the anonymous author of *Observations on Certain Verbal Disputes* and Adam Smith. The others usually meant by "demand" simply the quantity demanded; but, whether the demand-quantity or the demand-price concept was used, changes in demand were as likely to be price-determined as they were to be price-determining. Hicks's usage is in the classical tradition; the Marshallian use of the schedule is not.

Yet all the classical writers were fully aware of the existence of the law of demand—that more would be taken at lower prices. Several of them (Malthus, Say, Lauderdale, and Longfield, in that order) presented particularly clear illustrations of it that amounted to demand schedules. Of course, recognizing the existence of the schedule relationship does not require one to identify the term "demand" with the schedule and thus limit the meaning of "change in demand" to a price-determining shift of the schedule.

[106] In his later Oxford period he was explicit: "The word *demand* is sometimes used to express desirableness—as when it is said that commodities are valuable directly according to the demand for them, and inversely according to the supply of them. Used in this sense the word demand is a convenient term, and I shall so employ it. And in the future I shall substitute for the word desirableness—the word *utility* . . ." (*Industrial Efficiency*, II, 5, quoting Lecture 6, *Fourth Course of Lectures at Oxford, New Series* [1850–51], pp. 6–16).

5 Cournot's Demand Theory: A Reassessment

C. L. Fry and R. B. Ekelund, Jr.

AUGUSTIN COURNOT'S *loi du débit* (law of sales) has received conflicting interpretations in the literature on demand theory. The empirical nature of Cournot's demand curve has been noted by Leon Walras,[1] Frank Knight,[2] and several other writers.[3] However, these assessments have been eclipsed by the views of a number of other commentators who have identified Cournot's demand curve with Alfred Marshall's utility-based theoretical function. Henry Schultz,[4] J. A. Schumpeter,[5] and others may be placed in this camp.

The purpose of the present paper is twofold: first, to utilize evi-

MR. FRY *and* MR. EKELUND *are Research Assistant in Economics and Associate Professor of Economics, respectively, at Texas A & M University.*

1. *Elements of Pure Economics,* trans. W. Jaffé (Homewood, Ill., 1954), p. 199. Walras did not identify his own theoretically derived function with Cournot's a priori conception, which Walras called an "equation of demand or of sales." Walras reiterated the evaluation of Cournot's demand formulation in letters to Emile Cheysson and Maffeo Pantaleoni; see *Correspondence of Léon Walras and Related Papers,* ed. W. Jaffé, vol. 2 (Amsterdam, 1965), Letter 719, p. 126, and Letter 909, p. 337. Indeed, Walras noted that Cournot's approximate and empirical demand function was the point of departure for his own scientific discoveries; see Léon Walras, "Cournot et l'économie mathématique," *Gazette de Lausanne,* 13 July 1905, fragment reprinted in *Revue d'économie politique* 72, no. 1 (Jan.-Feb. 1962):61–64, esp. p. 62. See also, Jaffé's comments in *Correspondence,* vol. 2, Letter 1593, n. 2, pp. 268–69.

2. See Knight's introduction to Carl Menger, *Principles of Economics* (Glencoe, Ill., 1950), p. 20.

3. For example, see René Roy's "L'Oeuvre économique d'Augustin Cournot," *Econometrica* (1939), esp. pp. 137–39, and F. Bompaire, *Du principe de liberté économique dans l'oeuvre de Cournot et dans celle de l'Ecole de Lausanne* (*Walras, Pareto*) (Paris, 1931).

4. Schultz identifies a "Cournot-Marshall law of demand" in *The Theory and Measurement of Demand* (Chicago, 1938), pp. 6–7. See also Schultz's *Statistical Laws of Demand and Supply* (Chicago, 1928), pp. 14–24.

5. *History of Economic Analysis* (New York, 1954), p. 960. See also, for example, Irving Fisher, "Cournot and Mathematical Economics," *Quarterly Journal of Economics* 12 (Jan. 1898):124.

Reprinted from *The History of Political Economy,* Vol. 3, No. 1, (Spring 1971), pp. 190–197, by permission of the publisher.

dence from Cournot's works[6] in reinforcing the empirical-statistical interpretation of Cournot's demand curve; second, to show that Cournot's demand function, though empirically defined, was a "theory-loaded" concept. By theory-loaded we mean that although there is no explicit derivation of a demand curve in Cournot's writings, Cournot nevertheless had an implicit theoretical conception of demand underlying his empirical definition. It is our contention that Cournot's statements in the *Recherches* (1838) and in the *Principes* (1863) concerning *ceteris paribus* assumptions, the identification problem, and mathematical method in economics lend support to our view of Cournot's demand function as theory-loaded.[7] These statements, taken in conjunction with his subsequent *use* of the demand function, may have led Schultz and Schumpeter to identify Cournot's demand curve with that of Marshall. Hence, a theory-loaded conception of Cournot's demand function contributes to the reconciliation of the conflicting interpretations found in the literature.[8]

Cournot discussed his demand function in chapter 4 of the *Recherches,* immediately preceding the famous chapter on monopoly. The demand function, designated $D = F(P)$, besides being central to Cournot's subsequent analysis of firm behavior, constitutes a pioneering endeavor in the foundation of economic analysis. Thus, an

6. Our quotations are taken from a centennial reproduction of the original *Recherches sur les principes mathématiques de la théorie des richesses,* with introduction by Georges Lutfalla (Paris, 1938). Passages from Cournot's works presented in our article have been translated by us. The corresponding French passages are supplied in footnotes. Two later works by Cournot, *Principes de la théorie des richesses* (Paris, 1863) and *Revue sommaire des doctrines économiques* (Paris, 1877), contain extensions relevant to his earlier formulation of demand.

7. Although Cournot's demand curve was not explicitly derived from earlier assumptions as are demand curves in many current works, some of his discussion of the demand curve could be called theory.

8. A conception of Cournot's demand function similar to the one presented in this paper was introduced by René Roy in his excellent paper, "Cournot et l'école mathématique," *Econometrica* 1 (1933):13–22, esp. pp. 17–19. Roy noted, for example, that "bien que Cournot considère le milieu économique comme constituant un tout, dont les divers éléments réagissent nécessairement les uns sur les autres, il élabore dans sa loi du débit une conception abstraite, telle que la demande d'une marchandise ne soit fonction que d'une seule variable, son prix. Cette manière de voir ne constitue d'ailleurs, pour notre auteur, qu'une approximation, en vertu de laquelle les variations affectant le débit et le prix de tous les autres articles doivent être considérées comme du second ordre, et par conséquent négligeables vis-à-vis de celles qui concernent la marchandise étudiée" (p. 18).

understanding of the reasoning upon which the function rests is crucial in fully appreciating Cournot's contribution to economic theory.

Cournot, unlike his French contemporary Jules Dupuit,[9] clearly eschews utility as a proper foundation for a scientific theory. In the *Recherches,* for example, he notes the confusion which obtained between "the fixed, definite idea of *value in exchange,* and the ideas of utility which everyone estimates in his own way."[10] Opinions concerning utility, he further notes, "are questions of valuation, and not questions resolved by calculation or by logical argument."[11] It is thus apparent that an unqualified identification of Cournot's demand formulation with Marshall's would require a strained reading of Cournot's actual remarks concerning the admissibility of utility into scientific economics.

Cournot, having rejected utility as a foundation for his demand function, presented what was basically an empirical approach to demand. The title of the chapter on demand in the original *Recherches,* "De la loi du débit," or the "law of sales," hints at this empirical approach, and Cournot quite explicitly gave his demand function an empirical definition. He noted: "Sales or demand (for to us these two words are *synonymous* and *we do not see for what account theory need take into consideration a demand which is not followed by a sale*) . . . increase when price decreases."[12] He acknowledges that prices and the "law of demand" could fluctuate in the

9. See Dupuit, "On the Measurement of the Utility of Public Works," trans. R. H. Barback, from the *Annales des ponts et chaussées,* ser. 2, vol. 8 (1844), and "On Tolls and Transport Charges," trans. Elizabeth Henderson, ibid., vol. 17 (1849). Both translations are published in *International Economic Papers* (London, 1952, 1962). For an assessment of Dupuit's role in the development of demand theory see Robert B. Ekelund, Jr., and William P. Gramm, "Early French Contributions to Marshallian Demand Theory," *Southern Economic Journal* 36, no. 3 (Jan. 1970):277–86.

10. ". . . l'idée fixe, déterminée, de valeur échangeable, et les idées d'utilité, que chacun peut apprécier à sa manière." *Recherches,* p. 5.

11. ". . . sont des questions d'appréciation et non des questions résolubles par le calcul ou par l'argumentation logique." *Recherches,* p. 6 n. Cournot adds that "these ideas [on utility] are variable, and by nature indeterminate, and consequently ill suited for the foundation of a scientific theory" (p. 5).

12. "Le débit ou la demande (car pour nous ces deux mots sont *synonymes,* et *nous ne voyons pas sous quel rapport la théorie aurait à tenir compte d'une demande qui n'est pas suivie de débit*) . . . croît en général quand le prix décroît." *Recherches,* p. 48; italics supplied.

period of a year and defines his curve to relate *average* annual price P with $F(P)$, "the quantity sold *annually* in the country or in the market under consideration."[13] Hence, $D = F(P)$ is a curve connecting time series data on sales and the prices at which these sales are realized.

An important problem arising with an empirical function, however—and one of which Cournot was not unaware—was that demand curves, so constructed, need not be negatively sloped. Although Cournot notes the possibility of positively sloping demand functions,[14] he eliminates all possibilities of indeterminacy by asserting that they were *generally* of negative slope. In later chapters, the negatively sloped demand function appears as an assumption, however, along with the assumption that such functions are continuous in character.

Although Cournot draws upon the statistical relations of prices and quantities to explain the law of demand in the *Recherches,* he does so with some theoretically derived organizing principles in the background. Thus, after specifying an empirical relation, Cournot theorizes that the law of demand or of sales depends on "the kind of utility of the article, on the nature of the services it can render or the enjoyments it can procure, on the habits and customs of the people, on the average wealth, and on the scale on which wealth is distributed."[15] Further, in the empirical specification of his time-series demand model, Cournot warned that the law of demand *itself* could

13. ". . . la quantité débitée *annuellement,* dans l'étendue du pays ou du marché que l'on considère." *Recherches,* p. 55.

14. In all of his writings Cournot noted the possibility of demand being related to taste changes, but his discussion of the "Veblen good" is best expressed in the *Principes* (1863). "In general," Cournot points out, "demand for an article must increase when the price falls. There are, however, luxury goods which are sought after only because of their high price, where rarity maintains them. If one could succeed in effecting at little cost the crystallization of carbon and one could produce at one franc a diamond that today sells at one thousand, then it would not be at all surprising if diamonds ceased to serve as jewelry. Since diamonds have few other uses, they would, therefore, scarcely be counted among the objects of commerce. In this case, an enormous lowering of price will nearly annihilate demand. However, articles of this type are so unimportant in the overall economy that they can be safely ignored." *Principes,* p. 95.

15. ". . . du mode d'utilité de la chose, de la nature des services qu'elle peut rendre ou des jouissances qu'elle procure, des habitudes et des moeurs de chaque peuple, de la richesse moyenne et de l'échelle suivant laquelle la richesse est répartie." *Recherches,* p. 50.

vary within the relevant period for data collecting.[16] His solution, already noted, was to use *average* annual price-quantity data, but the caveat attached to the statistical formulation suggests that Cournot had *ceteris paribus* assumptions in mind.

Cournot's discussion of demand in the *Principes de la théorie des richesses* (1863) adds strength to a theory-loaded interpretation of his demand function. Here Cournot explicitly concerned himself with the now familiar identification problem encountered in the construction of empirical demand functions. He noted that the law of demand

> rests essentially on population, on the distribution of wealth, on general well-being, on tastes, on the habits of the consuming population, on the multiplication of markets, on the extension of the market resulting from transport improvements. All these conditions relative to demand remain the same; if we suppose that production conditions change (i.e., that costs rise or fall, that monopolies are restricted or suppressed, that taxes are increased or lightened, that foreign competition is prohibited or allowed) prices will vary and the corresponding variations in demand, provided that prices are actually raised, will serve for the construction of our empirical tables. If, to the contrary, prices change because the law of demand has itself changed, due to a change in causes which no longer influence production but consumption, the construction of our tables will be made impossible, since they must show how demand changes by virtue of a change in price and not by virtue of other causes.[17]

16. *Recherches,* p. 55.

17. ". . . tient essentiellement au chiffre de la population, au mode de répartition de la richesse, à l'aisance, aux goûts, aux habitudes des populations qui consomment, à la multiplication des débouches, à l'extension du marché par suite de la facilité des transports. Toutes ces conditions relatives à la demande restant les mêmes, si nous supposons que les conditions de la production viennent à changer, que les frais s'élèvent ou se réduisent, que des monopoles soient resserrés ou supprimés, que des taxes soient aggravées ou allégées, que la concurrence de l'étranger soit prohibée ou admise, les prix varieront, et les variations correspondantes de la demande, pourvu qu'elles soient bien relevées, pourront servir à la construction de nos tables empiriques. Si, au contraire, les prix changent parce que la loi de la demande a elle-même changé, par suite du changement des causes que influent non plus sur la production, mais sur la

Cournot's remarks listing the *ceteris paribus* assumptions necessary to draw the demand curve, as well as his awareness of the fact that these could not be expected to remain constant through time, clearly suggest an implicit *theoretical* conception of demand (though not one based upon utility). Cournot, in other words, must have had a theoretical conception of demand in order to isolate relevant statistical observations in his empirical "tables."

Two additional arguments may be advanced to support the case for a theory-loaded interpretation of Cournot's demand curve. In the first instance, Cournot does not totally reject a relationship between utility and demand, although he does refuse to base his own conception of demand upon it. He argues, after noting that there is "no fixed standard for the utility of things," that "we do not intend to say that there is neither truth nor error in judgments passed on the utility of things; we only mean that, in general, the truth or the error cannot be demonstrated."[18]

In numerous other passages, both in the *Recherches* and in later works, Cournot carefully notes the influence of "moral causes" which one cannot measure, but which are nevertheless related to the law of demand. It is possible that Cournot's refusal to base his demand function upon the subjective notion of utility rested upon an anticipation of the plethora of problems which Marshall encountered in doing so. But, whatever the reason, Cournot did not deny a *connection* between utility and demand.

Finally, a theory-loaded interpretation of Cournot's demand curve would be wholly consistent with Cournot's views on mathematical analysis in economics. To view Cournot as an ultra-empiricist on the issue of demand, in other words, would require a drastic reinterpretation of his views on the importance of a priori analytical tools. He is most emphatic, for example, in noting that "one of the most

consommation, la construction de nos tables sera rendue impossible, puisqu'elles doivent exprimer comment la demande change en vertu du changement de prix, et non en vertu d'autres causes." *Principes*, p. 100. It is clear that Cournot is identifying the "law of demand" with the modern conception of a demand *function*; likewise his change in "demand" corresponds to the modern usage of a change in "quantity demanded."

18. ". . . nous n'entendons pas dire qu'il n'y ait ni vérité ni erreur dans les jugements portés sur l'utilité des choses; nous voulons dire seulement qu'en général la vérité ou l'erreur ne peuvent être démontrées . . . ." *Recherches*, p. 6.

important functions of [mathematical] analysis consists precisely in assigning determinate relations between quantities to which numerical values and even algebraic forms are absolutely unassignable.''[19]

In a brilliant defense of mathematical investigation, moreover, Cournot's chief criticism of past writers is that ''they imagined that the use of symbols and formulas would have no other end than that of leading to numerical calculations'' and that they did not see that the object of mathematical analysis was to ''find relations between magnitudes which cannot be estimated numerically and between *functions* whose law is not capable of being expressed by algebraic symbols.''[20] This view of method persists in his later works also. ''Science,'' Cournot writes in 1863, ''is not obliged to await empirical laws . . . in order to draw certain and useful consequences from general characteristics which they can supply, or certain relationships which can exist between them and upon which reason, alone, sheds light.''[21] Thus, far from being a blind empiricist, Cournot champions apriorism in establishing economic relations. Cournot's demand function, in all likelihood, constitutes no exception to his strong beliefs on method. Although Cournot appears to ignore these views when he defines his demand function, they are neither inconsistent with his theory-loaded speculations on demand nor with the way in which he later used his demand function. His use of $D = F(P)$ corresponds almost exactly to the manner in which demand is used in the current neoclassical theory of the firm.

Several factors, therefore, lead to the ascription of a theory-loaded demand function to Cournot. It is also probable that Marshall was alive to these nuances in Cournot's treatment of demand and that

19. ''. . . l'une des fonctions les plus importantes de l'analyse consiste précisément à assigner des relations déterminées entre des quantités dont les valeurs numériques et même les formes algébriques sont absolument inassignables.'' *Recherches*, p. 51.

20. ''On s'est figuré que l'emploi des signes et des formules ne pouvait avoir d'autre but que celui de conduire à des calculs numériques; . . . à trouver des relations entre des grandeurs que l'on ne peut évaluer numériquement, entre des *fonctions* dont la loi n'est pas susceptible de s'exprimer par des symboles algébriques.'' *Recherches*, pp. vii–viii.

21. ''. . . la science n'est pas obligée d'attendre . . . lois empiriques . . . pour tirer des conséquences certaines et utiles de quelques caractères généraux qu'elles peuvent offrir, ou de certaines liaisons qui peuvent exister entre elles et que le seul raisonnement met en lumière.'' *Principes*, p. 102.

Marshall's own treatment of the *theory* of demand was at least partially the result of a very careful reading of Cournot. As such, Marshall's debt to Cournot in the area of demand may go beyond that concerning the mathematical concepts of function and continuity. The Schultz-Schumpeter contention that Cournot's and Marshall's demand conceptions are identical is made more understandable in view of the theoretical undertones in Cournot's writings. It is clear nonetheless that statements which identify Cournot's demand formulation with Marshall's are gross misconceptions, for such statements simply fail to account for Cournot's subtle and sophisticated treatment of the issue. It appears that Cournot, in short, was an important progenitor of both empirical and theoretical studies of demand.[22]

22. The authors wish to thank Alfred F. Chalk, Oskar Morgenstern, Patricia A. Fry, William W. Hall, and C. S. Pyun, as well as the editors of this journal, for helpful comments on earlier drafts of this paper. We are in very special debt to an anonymous reviewer who rather thoroughly reoriented the authors' views on Cournot's demand curve in the course of several revisions of this paper. We also wish to thank him for having pointed out discrepancies between the Nathaniel Bacon translation of Cournot's *Researches Into the Mathematical Principles of the Theory of Wealth* (New York: Kelley, 1960; translation originally published in 1897) and the original. Finally, and in spite of our reviewer's excellent direction, we must assume sole responsibility in matters of translation, content, and interpretation. Our appreciation for his suggestions is no less real for his anonymity, however.

6 Early French Contributions to Marshallian Demand Theory

R. B. Ekelund, Jr. and W. P. Gramm

I. INTRODUCTION

It is the purpose of this paper to demonstrate that the Marshallian demand curve [18, 83–137 and App. I–III] is consistent with and in part finds its origin in the writings of Jules Dupuit, an early French engineer and economist.[1] This paper further argues that Marshall's acknowledgments of Dupuit in the *Principles*, although insufficient, were not "in the wrong places," as Professor Schumpeter has suggested [23, 840], but that Marshall's actual references to the works of Dupuit were deliberately well chosen.

It is generally accepted that Marshall used Dupuit's concept of *utilité relative* (which Marshall relabelled consumer's surplus) in the *Principles* [24, 313–314] [16] [1, 297–298]. Unfortunately, writers on the subject have failed to extend this apparent contribution into the realm of Marshall's demand theory—a failure due in part to the fact that English translations of Dupuit's works have only recently become available. More importantly, however, the role of Dupuit in the development of demand theory has been masked by the widely-held belief that Marshall chose to hold *money* income constant when formulating the demand schedule. Thus there has been a general downplay of the importance of Marshall's constant purchasing power of money assumption, and theorists have been disposed to point to Augustin Cournot as Marshall's *maître* in demand theory [23, 839].

II. COURNOT'S CONTRIBUTIONS TO THE MARSHALLIAN DEMAND CURVE

It is generally assumed that the Marshallian demand curve evolved from the work of Cournot. In tracing the origins of the various facets of Marshall's *Principles*, Schumpeter flatly concludes: "the demand and supply curves... are Cournot's" [23, 839]. Schultz expresses the same contention by his analysis of the "Cournot-Marshall law of demand" [22, 6–7]. At the end of Chapter III, Book III of *Principles*, Marshall pays deference to Cournot for having developed a "semi-mathematical language for expressing the relation between small increments of a commodity on the one hand, and on the other hand small increments in the aggregate price that will be paid for it" [18, 101].

In general Cournot's demand formulation is based on empirical observation [3, 47–8], and although it is incomplete, due to the

* We would like to thank Professors Alfred F. Chalk, James P. Payne, Jr., the late David McCord Wright, W. J. Stober, William L. Miller, and Richard H. Timberlake, Jr. for comments and suggestions on various parts and drafts of this manuscript and Jennifer Hartley for technical assistance. We would also like to acknowledge a generous grant from the L.S.U. Foundation of Louisana State University which supported the translation of works of and papers related to Dupuit.

[1] The major economic contributions of Jules Dupuit (1804–1866) are contained in articles appearing in the *Annales des Ponts et Chaussées* and in the *Journal des Économistes* between 1844 and 1866. Only two of these are in published translation, [7] and [10], [10] being translated fragments of [9]. A reprint of Dupuit's major economic works (in French) was published in Italy and edited by Mario de Bernardi [11]. For an excellent biography of Dupuit, written on the occasion of his death, see [14]. Unpublished translations of the works and papers pertinent to Dupuit are available in the library of Louisiana State University at Baton Rouge.

Reprinted from the *Southern Economic Journal,* vol. XXVI (January 1970), pp. 277–286, by permission of the publisher.

lack of assumption of the constancy of the prices of other goods, the Cournot demand curve might be interpreted as falling under the head of the modern constant money income formulation [15, pp. 1–55]. However, the Cournot function *may not be a demand curve at all* in the Marshallian sense in that it appears to represent only a long-run intersection of equilibrium points of supply and demand. As Cournot notes: "The sales or the demand (for to us these two words are synonymous, and we do not see for what reason theory need take account of any demand which does not result in a sale) . . . increases when the price decreases [3, 46].[2]

In the chapter on the theory of value in his *Mathematical Principles* Cournot notes the possible use of a *corrected money* which would allow money to be used as an abstract measure of constant value [3, 18–28]. Though Marshall expanded this analysis into his constant purchasing power of money assumption in demand theory, Cournot did not apply it to his analysis of demand. Thus Schumpeter is not justified in implying that the purchasing power of money is a parameter in Cournot's formulation of the demand curve [23, 981].[3] In his zeal to discredit Marshall as an original contributor to economic theory, Schumpeter read meaning into Cournot's formulation for which there is little justification. Here, as elsewhere, Marshall appears to have taken a facet of Cournot's theory and applied it in expanded form to problems Cournot had not seen fit to analyze.

The most striking dissimilarity between the demand formulations of Marshall and Cournot is the foundation of the demand curve. Cournot refuses to base his demand curve on a utility footing [3, 44]. Despite hints of abstract manipulation Cournot's demand curve is an empirical derivation obtained from a time series of equilibrium points. In contrast Marshall's demand curve, regardless of its interpretation, is a theoretical formulation derivable from the utility function and related directly to a utility measure [18, 92–101]. In short, there is no evidence that Marshall could have derived directly from Cournot's demand analysis more than "semi-mathematical language" for relating changes in price to changes in quantity demanded. While Marshall made use of Cournot's semi-mathematical method and expanded it into areas not analyzed by Cournot, the methodological framework which makes up the Marshallian demand curve is not found in Cournot.[4]

[2] We are grateful to Clifford Fry for pointing out the implications of this passage to us.

[3] It is both interesting and informative to speculate on the origin of the constant purchasing power of money interpretation of the Cournot demand formulation. The most explicit statement of this interpretation and perhaps its source is found in the definition of demand given by J. N. Keynes [20, 539–42]. Keynes interprets Cournot's demand curve as follows:

> But, as is also recognized by Cournot, the conditions of demand rarely do remain the same for any considerable length of time. There are constantly in progress independent changes, such as changes in fashions and habits, in the *purchasing power of money*, in the wealth and circumstances of consumers, and the like, which cause the demand at a given price itself to vary [20, 540] (emphasis added).

Keynes' only reference to the work of Cournot is to his *Principes de la Théorie des Richesses*. Upon translating relevant chapters of the *Principes de la Théorie de Richesses* dealing with the "Law of Demand" and the "Influence of Price on Nominal and Real Value of Revenues," we find not one reference, explicit or implicit, to a constant purchasing power of money assumption [4, 93–105, 293–310]. A similar survey of the relevant portions of Cournot's later *Revue Sommaire des Doctrines Économiques* likewise yields no indication of a constant purchasing power of money assumption as related to the demand schedule [5, 161–70, 187–95]. Thus, J. N. Keynes' assessment of Cournot's demand formulation appears to be unfounded; the assessment, moreover, may have been the source of Schumpeter's misinterpretation.

[4] In Marshall's correspondence with Walras concerning the independence of his work on the doctrine of final utility from the work of Jevons, Marshall states: "I do not claim to have anticipated him [Jevons] as to the doctrine of final utility, but to have learnt what I have learnt from anybody, from Cournot, not from him" [17, 751] (references, following Jaffé's practice, are to letter number). While this passage might seem a contradiction to the above analysis, closer scrutiny re-

III. JULES DUPUIT AND THE THEORY OF DEMAND

Dupuit's role in the development of utility theory and consumer's surplus has received a good deal of attention.[5] Yet this preoccupation with consumer's surplus has hidden an amazing analysis of demand theory, which is inextricably linked with the measurement of a surplus.

In several of his articles Dupuit supplied explicit directions on the construction of a demand schedule, which he called the "curve of consumption." In a contribution to the *Dictionnaire de l'Économie Politique*, for example, his instructions were straightforward:

> If, in a table of two columns, one inserts in the first all the prices, from 0, the one which corresponds to the greatest consumption, up to the price that stops all consumption and in the second, regarding the price, the corresponding quantity consumed, we will have the exact representation of what we call the law of consumption [6, 8].

Dupuit neatly constructed such a demand curve in 1844, six years after Cournot's *Researches,* although their respective formulations appear to have been independent.[6] As Cournot, Dupuit gave the equation for the "curve of consumption" as $y = f(x)$, or alternatively, $Q_d = f(p)$. Additionally, Dupuit placed the independent variable (price) on the x axis and the dependent variable (quantity) on the y axis, as in his construction which is reproduced here as Figure 1.[7] Dupuit described his schedule as follows:

> If . . . along a line *OP* the lengths *Op, Op′, Op″* . . . represent various prices for an article, and the verticals *pn, p′n′, p″n″* . . . represents the number of articles consumed corresponding to these prices, then it is possible to construct a curve *Nn′n″P* which we shall call the curve of consumption. *ON* represents the quantity consumed when the price is zero, and *OP* the price at which consumption falls to zero [7, 106].

The relationship which Dupuit posited between price and quantity was in part derived from observation. It was a "fact of experience," he thought, "which has been verified statistically" [7, 103]. Yet his explanation of demand was far more sophisticated than one derived from simple observation in that it was *explained* with (and not merely juxtaposed with) utility analysis. As Dupuit expressed with reference to Figure 1, "the utility of . . . *np* articles is at least *Op* and . . . for almost all of them the utility is greater than *Op*" [7, 106].

Dupuit's clearest statement of the relationship between demand and utility is to be found in an 1853 contribution to the *Journal des Économistes* entitled "On Utility and Its Measure" [8]. Reviewing principles he had established in 1844, and arguing with the flavor of Carl Menger, who later elaborated on the point [19, 129–30], Dupuit showed that the marginal utility that an individual obtained from a homogeneous stock of goods is determined by the uses

veals that it is not. In this passage Marshall is defending the independence of his marginal utility analysis. Though mathematical notation for maximum conditions is found in Cournot, it is not applied to consumer utility analysis [3, 446]. In that Marshall made use of Cournot's "mathematical notation" to analyze consumer behavior, no contradiction exists between this passage and the above analysis. Further, this paper is concerned with the system of abstraction which is the Marshallian demand curve, not with the question of utility analysis as such. Jevons dismissed the matter of priority in the doctrine of final utility as of little importance in view of earlier works by "Gossen, Cournot, Dupuit, etc." [17, 912, n. 11].

[5] For recent assessments of Dupuit's contributions in the areas of marginal cost pricing and monopoly theory see [12, 462–471] and [13, 257–262].

[6] See F. Y. Edgeworth, "Dupuit," [20, 654] in which Edgeworth found that Dupuit "does not appear to have seen" Cournot's book. Additional corroboration on this point was given by René Roy [21, 143]. Roy cited the neglect of Cournot's works in the nineteenth century, especially in France, and added that he found "une preuve dans le silence manifesté à cet égard par un autre économiste francais, l'Ingénieur des Ponts et Chaussées Jean [sic] Dupuit, qui fut let contemporian de Cournot."

[7] The "hyperbolic" shape of Dupuit's demand curve is the result of his belief that "the increase in consumption due to a price fall will be greater, the lower the initial price" [7, 103].

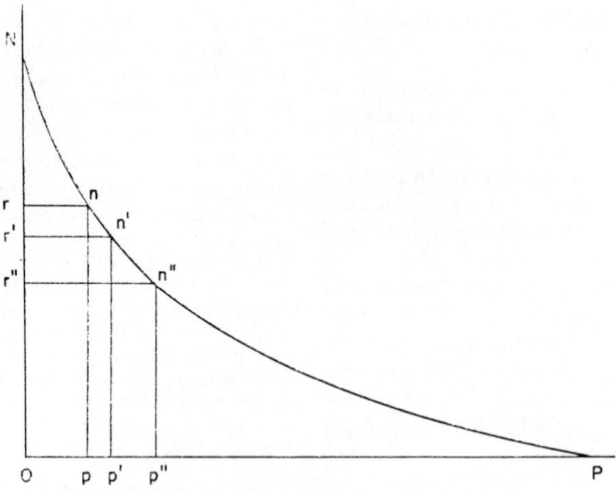

FIGURE 1—Dupuit's "Curve of consumption"

to which the last units of the stock are put. In doing so, he clearly pointed out that the utility of a stock of some particular good diminished with increases in quantity. If one grants his psychological premise that "each consumer himself attaches a different utility to the same object according to the quantity he can consume" [8, 17], his argument followed with ease.

Thus, it is obvious from Dupuit's arguments, graphical analysis [7, 106–10, *et passim*], and numerical examples [8, 42], that he wished to rationalize and explain the demand curve in terms of an analysis of diminishing utility. Further, it is clear that he identified the demand curve with a utility function. Like Marshall, Dupuit acknowledged an "immutable general" principle concerning the demand curve—"... consumption expands when price falls" [7, 103].

An Early Methodenstreit on Consumer's Surplus and Demand: Dupuit and Bordas

Dupuit, of course, developed the demand curve for use in the calculation of the utility (benefit) of public works. Among several utility measures, Dupuit identified *utilité relative* (Marshall's consumer's surplus) which he defined as the "difference between the sacrifice [in money terms] which the purchaser would be willing to make in order to get ... [a product] ... over the purchase price he has to pay in exchange" [7, 90]. Clearly Dupuit intended money to represent a utility measurement and, although he admitted that in the measurement of utility "a rigorous solution is impossible in practice" [7, 105], he did not explicitly indicate that his measurement hinged on an assumption of a constant purchasing power of money. Notably absent in the 1844 formulation, however, is an analysis of the "income effect" which would result from changes in price (taxes, tariffs or tolls). To argue from the absence of a discussion of income effects that real income was held constant in Dupuit's formulation is, of course, wholly inadmissible. The universality of negatively sloping demand curves could be attributed to logical error or to the existence of additive utility functions. However, Dupuit's implicit assumption of constant purchasing power of money in his utility analysis, from which his demand curve is derived, tends to lend weight to the income effect exclusion interpretation.

In 1844, Dupuit's measurement of consumer's surplus contained a myriad of other difficulties. In straightforward fashion he acknowledged the fact that differences in an individual's income would affect maximum offer price. As he put the matter:

> ...it would be difficult to say whose hunger was the greater—the rich man's, who would be willing to give a million [francs] for a kilogramme of bread, or the poor man's who, having nothing else to give, would risk his life for it. But political economy, being concerned only with wealth, can take account of the intensity of wish only through its monetary expression [7, 89].

In a similar vein he assumed away "distribution effects" (which would obtain in the establishment of public projects) with the assumption that, in general, the differential effects of these utility transfers cancel out [7, 98–9].[8] In short, although he admitted in general that there were many difficulties in constructing demand curves and in utility measurement, Dupuit did not present a clear or orderly list of *ceteris paribus* assumptions in his earliest contribution. The tacit identification of demand and utility functions suggest, however, that Dupuit intended to hold the purchasing power of money constant in his demand formulation.

The Bordas Comment—1847

Three years after his first contribution to demand theory, Dupuit encountered a major comment on his work. Bordas, a fellow engineer and apparently an individual of some economic sophistication, wrote a critique entitled "Of the Measure of the Utility of Public Works" with the subtitle "Answer to the Article of the chief Engineer, Mr. Dupuit, inserted in Number 6 of the Annales of 1844" [2] [16]. The comment, in large measure, consisted of a melange of confusions (Bordas') on the meaning of the word utility.

[8] Dupuit thought that "distribution effects," while not in the province of economics, should be the proper concern of the State.

Nonetheless, Bordas brought out some important and relevant points in his assessment of Dupuit's concept of demand and consumer's surplus. Bordas was severe with Dupuit on the issue of the interpersonal comparisons involved when utility was redistributed from taxpayers to users of public projects. Bordas complained that "This connection seems, in effect, very difficult, for the quantities to be matched or compared, although expressed in money, are nonetheless of a different kind" [2, 48]. Dupuit had, however, theoretically avoided this issue with the assumption that "distribution effects" cancel out.

More telling for Dupuit's demand theory was Bordas' criticism that Dupuit had not explicitly stated his *ceteris paribus* assumptions used in drawing up the demand curve. As Bordas stated:

> Let us suppose that it is a matter of appreciating a kilogramme of meat and that a person is asked to state the sacrifice that he is ready to make to procure it. Will it be possible for this person to answer categorically? Evidently not. Indeed, doesn't this sacrifice depend on the means of this person as well as the current price of other alimentary products which are capable of being substituted for the meat? ... Therefore, what theory can one establish on so variable a basis and which depends on the taste as well as the means of each consumer? [2, 41–2].

Here Bordas asked a legitimate question. Should not the price of potatoes be assumed constant in the process of determining the utility for meat in money terms? Bordas implied in these passages that, since the necessary assumption of "other things equal" generally does not obtain in any practical case, Dupuit's demand curve and his measurement of consumer's surplus was practically useless. Bordas could be criticized for not having appreciated the useful convention of holding parameters constant, but he was on the mark when he criticized Dupuit for not having made his parameters explicit.

In what is surely the most interesting passage of the comment, Bordas discovered the income effect which would have permitted the unlinking of demand and utility curves. In the passage Bordas assumed that because of a new process in the manufacture of stockings, the price falls from 6 francs to 3 francs. If the consumer set aside 24 francs a year to buy 4 pair when the price was 6 francs per pair, after the price decrease he will be able to buy 8 pair. But, said Bordas:

> In order to consume as many before, he would have been obliged to set aside a sum of 48 francs for the acquisition of this product, and to subtract 24 francs from his other consumptions. His situation, in relation to the former state of things, is then the same as though he were making an annual gain of 24 francs, or that his *income had been increased by this sum.* If, instead of consuming 8 pair of stockings, he only consumed 7 and used the 3 francs left over to buy other objects of which the price would not have varied, his relative gain would not be more than 21 francs [2, 16] (emphasis supplied).

Bordas discovered that, with a constant money income, a consumer's real income increases with price declines. In the first part of the example the consumer chooses to receive the entire increase in real income in stockings. In the second example Bordas calculates the amount of the gains on stockings at 21 francs, but he points out that some of the real income increase may be realized by directing expenditures in other directions, i.e., on other commodities. Bordas assumed that price declines could take place for many products in the consumer's budget. "Then," he points out, "the increase of the income of the consumer, relative to all of these products would be equal to the sum of the gains relative to each one of them" [2, 16]. Bordas, of course, did not attempt to link changes in real income consequent to price declines with changes in the marginal utility of money. He was, of course, unalterably opposed to the use Dupuit had made of the utility concept. Consequently he did not carry his argument a step further to show that, with variations in real income along the demand curve, Dupuit could not unambiguously identify his demand curve with a welfare measure. But Bordas' intuitive grasp of the income effect could at least be said to have anticipated later theoretical issues in demand theory,[9] and the *Methodenstreit* on the demand curve had begun.

Dupuit's Reply to Bordas—1849

Dupuit took the opportunity to reply to Bordas' comment in his article "The Influence of Tolls on the Utility of Ways of Communication," which appeared in the *Annales des Ponts et Chaussées* of 1849 [9, 170–248]. The article is divided into four sections, the first three sections consisting of the reply, the fourth entitled "On Tolls and Transport Charges" [10].[10] The lion's share of the first three sections consists of an attack on Bordas' confusion over the meaning of the word utility, which is not of direct concern here. The importance of the exchange is that Bordas forced Dupuit to make explicit his determinants of demand, which Dupuit had failed to do in 1844. The contents of Dupuit's *ceteris paribus* assumptions are more clearly brought out in the important passage in which Dupuit directly answered Bordas' questions concerning determinants of the price (or "maximum sacrifice") that an individual would pay for meat:

> Would this price be the same for all persons? Evidently not. Because not only does this price depend on the wealth of that person, as Mr. Bordas observes, but on his taste for meat, on his hunger, on the price of other nourishing commodities, and on a *thousand other circumstances* impossible to enumerate in a complete manner; but all these circumstances do not mean that this price does not exist for each object, for each person and at each instant [9, 184] (emphasis supplied).

[9] Professor Houghton in his brief review of Bordas' comment did not mention the "income effect" passage [16].

[10] Subsequent reference is to the material of the first three sections of [9]. Page references are to the original.

Clearly Dupuit wanted to invoke *ceteris paribus* assumptions when calculating the demand curve and consumer's surplus, and he explicitly notes the following parameters to be held constant: (1) the wealth (or income, if *fortune* is to be interpreted as a flow) of the consumer; (2) the price of other *related* commodities, presumably substitutes; and (3) tastes or intensity of desire. It is not clear which "thousand other circumstances" Dupuit had in mind, but he concluded that such a maximum sacrifice represented by the demand schedule does exist for "each person" and at "each instant." [11]

A weighty argument for a constant purchasing power of money interpretation of Dupuit's demand curve is that he did not bother to discuss Bordas' suggestion that a change in price would affect real income in the reply although he meticulously dissected Bordas' other arguments. It is highly improbable that Dupuit missed the passage; the best explanation is that Dupuit equated the absence of an income effect with his assumption of the constancy of wealth or of the "thousand other circumstances." Dupuit required the constant marginal utility of money assumption to protect his money measure of *utilité relative,* and at the end of the reply he reasserted his original definition of the surplus and proclaimed: "I persist in the consideration on utility that I developed in 1844; I do not wish to change the formula that I gave for the measure of utility" [9, 205].

[11] Dupuit was obsessed with correcting the impression left by Bordas' argument that no theory of demand could be constructed on "so variable a base" as wealth, price of related goods, etc. In a brilliant passage of the reply (which loses its flavor in translation) Dupuit generalized his defense of the use of the scientific method in political economy by showing the parallelism between *ceteris paribus* in Newtonian astronomy and the similar assumption in dealing with economic phenomena. He argued that "...les désirs de l'homme, leur énergie plus ou moins grande pour tel ou tel objet, suivant les circonstances, jouent dans la société le rôle de l'attraction dans le monde matériel. Retranchez de l'astronomie l'immortelle découverte de Newton, ce n'est plus qu'une science d'observation, qui se borne á constater les effets sans remonter aux causes, ce n'est plus une science de raisonnement. Ce n'est donc pas une théorie parteille et restreinte qu'il s'agit d'edifier sur cette base variable, c'est l'économie politique tout entieré" [9, 191–92].

V. CONCLUSION

There is a great deal of parallelism between the demand analyses of Dupuit and Marshall. In general Marshall developed tools to deal with actual market situations. To Marshall the demand curve was a "systematic and organized method of reasoning," and as chief engineer of bridges and highways, Dupuit sensed the need for analytical tools which could give some measure of the desirability of public projects. Dupuit believed that the demand curve was a formulation that made practical economic analysis possible. It is thus evident that both Dupuit and Marshall were one in their conception of the demand curve as a tool used as an engine for discovery and analysis.

Dupuit and Marshall not only based their demand curves on a utility footing, but both used the demand curve as a source for rough measurements of utility. Both wanted to measure the relationship between changes in consumer's surplus and changes in price (the principal problem to which they applied the demand curve). Both stated an "immutable" or "universal" law of demand. Both assumed the constancy of the prices of closely related goods, not all other goods, in the formulation of their demand curves.

The parameters of the demand curve are more complete and rigorous in Marshall's *Principles* than in Dupuit's earlier contributions. Yet all of the principal parameters of the Marshallian demand curve, with the exception of the constancy of the "purchasing power of money," are found explicitly in Dupuit's writings. The assumed constancy of the marginal utility or purchasing power of money is found implicitly throughout Dupuit's works.

Dupuit's consumer's surplus analysis is rigorous only given the assumption of constant marginal utility of money.[12] While Dupuit never explicitly stated this assumption, Rudolph Auspitz and Richard Lieben, in their further development of Dupuit's consumer's surplus (1889), stated explicitly that the marginal utility of money cannot vary as price changes [16, 54].[13] Thus, while their discussion was independent of Marshall's, they were led by Dupuit's analysis to the same explicit assumption of the constancy of the purchasing power of money [16, 55–7].[14] It seems evident, in short, that much of the advancement on Dupuit's analysis—both at the hands of Marshall and others—consisted of making explicit parameters found only implicitly in Dupuit.

Léon Walras had high praise for Dupuit's theory of discriminating monopoly in the *Elements* [25, 435–443], but he criticized him for the tacit identification of utility and demand curves. In Walras' view, Dupuit failed to appreciate the fact that the demand curve depends "on the quantity of the wealth (measured in terms of *numeraire*) which the consumer possesses," and on the utilities of other goods [25, 445] [17, 379, 465]. Not only was Walras partly incorrect (for Dupuit had indeed considered wealth and other parameters), but he used the general equilibrium apparatus to criticize what was essentially (and admittedly) no more than partial equilibrium analysis. In a letter to Maffeo Pantaleoni, Walras himself pointed out that in the analysis of exchange he was considering demand functions containing many independent variables and that this was the basic difference between his concept of demand and those of Dupuit, Marshall and Auspitz and Lieben [17, 913].[15] In this letter and in another to Vilfredo Pareto, Walras identified Marshall's demand formulation with that of Dupuit [17, 1051].[16] Walras viewed his own role as having been the first to have shown the interactions between Cournot's demand apparatus (without utility accoutrements) and Jevon's theory of the final degree of utility [17, 379]. Dupuit and. Marshall were, in Walras' view, illegitimately attempting to explain demand curves in terms of utility curves. Yet, most of these objections to the Dupuit-Marshall demand theory were ill-founded, for in this instance, Walras failed to appreciate the convenience (and useful-

[12] Dupuit disclaimed the feasibility of the calculation of aggregate consumers' surplus. Like Marshall [18, 133], he thought that a rough measure of changes in consumers' surplus in "the neighborhood of the customary changes in price" would be most useful in all areas where a demand curve calculation was applicable. Dupuit said for example, "...that when one cannot know something it is already quite a lot to know the limits of one's ignorance.... One will not know that the utility of the canal will be only 5 million, but one could know that it will not be 6 and it would be enough to give up its construction; one will not know that the utility of a bridge will be 120,000 francs but one could know that it will be more than 80,000 and that is sufficient to show that it will be very useful" [8, 46–47].

[13] In the "Correspondence" section of the *Revue d'Economie Politique* (November-December, 1890), Auspitz and Lieben replied to Walras' charge that they had repeated Dupuit's error of identifying utility and demand curves. Here they defended the legitimacy of *ceteris paribus* assumptions (and, specifically, of assuming the value of money constant for each individual) and found their assumptions superior to Walras'. They believed, moreover, that Walras had himself used the assumption of constancy in declaring that all demand curves were negatively sloped. See Jaffé's comments [17, 990, n. 3].

[14] Houghton believes that Marshall's analysis was in some respects inferior to that of Auspitz and Lieben [16].

[15] To this list Walras added Menger, Wieser, Böhm-Bawerk and Edgeworth in letter 1123 to Pareto.

[16] Walras exempted Jevons and Gossen from his indictment since they did not attempt to deduce demand curves from utility curves. Walras also bitterly noted that Marshall, whom he regarded as "*the great white elephant of political economy*," (emphasis his), and Edgeworth, through "jealousy" and "obstinate stinginess," were attempting to defend Ricardo's and Mill's theory of price [17, 1051].

ness) of the *ceteris paribus* convention in partial equilibrium theory.

Although the parallelism between the demand curve of Dupuit and that of Marshall is obvious, there remains the question of Marshall's indebtedness to Dupuit. It is generally accepted that Marshall's consumer's surplus analysis is derived from Dupuit, but the logical ramifications of this recognition are never explored. Consumer's surplus is based on the disposition of the demand curve. The evaluation of consumer's surplus is mechanical once the demand curve is derived. To admit that Marshall accepted and expanded on Dupuit's consumer's surplus and that both measures are identical is to admit that they are using the same demand curve to measure the surplus. In recognizing Marshall's debt to Dupuit for consumer's surplus, Schumpeter missed Dupuit's real contribution to Marshall's work when he stated that Marshall had neither given adequate footnote recognition to Dupuit nor had he given it in the right places [23, 840]. But Schumpeter believed that Marshall's debt to Dupuit was primarily for consumer's surplus. Marshall, however, recognized a genuine debt to Dupuit at the end of Chapter III, Book III of *Principles* on the theory of demand. Here Marshall acknowledged Dupuit for "first formally describing these small increments of price as measuring corresponding small increments of pleasure" [18, 110]. Equally telling is Marshall's only other reference to Dupuit placed at the end of his chapter on the "Doctrine of Maximum Satisfaction," (in which the famous tax-bounty argument appeared). At this point Marshall noted that "The graphic method has been applied, in a manner somewhat similar to that adopted in the present Chapter, by Dupuit" [18, 476]. Although grossly inadequate, it appears that Marshall's references were in the right places. Dupuit's contribution was to demand theory, for consumer's surplus is but a problem to which the demand curve is applied.

All this is not to imply that Marshall's contributions and additions to the demand curve were not of great importance or that Marshall is not the real progenitor of modern demand theory. Our purpose has been only to demonstrate that it was Dupuit's shoulders, as well as Cournot's, on which Marshall stood in the area of demand.

REFERENCES

1. Blaug, Mark, *Economic Theory in Retrospect.* Homewood: Richard D. Irwin, 1962.
2. Bordas, M., "Of the Measurement of the Utility of Public Works," *Annales des Ponts et Chaussées*, 2nd Ser., XIII (Memoires et Documents), 1847. Translated by E. Evans and edited by R. B. Ekelund, Jr. Baton Rouge: Louisiana State University Library.
3. Cournot, Augustin, *Mathematical Principles of the Theory of Wealth.* Translated by N. T. Bacon. New York: Augustus M. Kelley, 1960.
4. Cournot, Augustin, *Principes de la Théorie des Richesses.* Paris: Hachette, 1863.
5. Cournot, Augustin, *Revue Sommaire des Doctrines Économiques.* Paris: Hachette, 1877.
6. Dupuit, Jules, "Toll," *Dictionnaire de l'Économie Politique.* Paris: Guillaumin, 1853. Translated by E. Evans and edited by R. B. Ekelund, Jr. Baton Rouge: Louisiana State University Library. Page references to the translation.
7. Dupuit, Jules, "On the Measurement of the Utility of Public Works," *Annales des Ponts et Chaussées*, 2nd Ser., VII, 1844. Translated by R. H. Barback. *International Economic Papers*, No. 2, London: Macmillan, 1952.
8. Dupuit, Jules, "On Utility and its Measure," *Journal des Économistes*, 1st Ser., XXXVI, 1853. Translated by E. Evans and edited by R. B. Ekelund, Jr. Baton Rouge: Louisiana State University Library. Page references to the translation.
9. Dupuit, Jules, "De l'Influence des Péages sur l'Utilité des Voies de Communication," *Annales des Ponts et Chaussées*, 2nd Ser., XVII, 1849.
10. Dupuit, Jules, "On Tolls and Transport Charges," *Annales des Ponts et Chaussées*, 2nd Ser., XVII, 1849. Translated by Elizabeth Henderson. *International Economic Papers*, No. 11, London: Macmillan, 1962.
11. Dupuit, Jules, *De l'Utilité et sa Mesure: Écrits Choisis et Republiés.* Edited by Mario de Bernardi. Torino, Italy: La Riforma Sociale, 1933.
12. Ekelund, R. B., Jr., "Jules Dupuit and the Early Theory of Marginal Cost Pricing," *Journal of Political Economy*, May/June 1968.
13. Ekelund, R. B., Jr., "A Note on Jules Dupuit

and Neo-Classical Monopoly Theory," *Southern Economic Journal,* January 1969.

14. Fleury, E. Lamé, "The Life and Works of Mr. Dupuit," *Journal des Économistes,* 3rd Ser., VII, 1867. Translated by Candace Uter and edited by R. B. Ekelund, Jr. Baton Rouge: Louisiana State University Library. Page references to the translation.
15. Hicks, J. R., *Value and Capital.* Oxford: Oxford University Press, 1939.
16. Houghton, R. W., "A Note on the Early History of Consumer's Surplus," *Economica,* February 1958.
17. Jaffé, William, ed., *Correspondence of Léon Walras and Related Papers.* Amsterdam: North-Holland Publishing Company, 1965.
18. Marshall, Alfred, *Principles of Economics,* 8th ed., London: Macmillan, 1920.
19. Menger, Carl, *Principles of Economics.* Translated by James Dingwall. Glencoe: The Free Press, 1950.
20. Palgrave, H. I., *Dictionary of Political Economy.* Edited by H. Higgs. London: Macmillan, 1926.
21. Roy, René, "L'Oeuvre Economique D'Augustin Cournot," *Econometrica,* April 1939.
22. Schultz, Henry, *The Theory and Measurement of Demand.* Chicago: University of Chicago Press, 1938.
23. Schumpeter, J. A., *History of Economic Analysis.* New York: Oxford University Press, 1954.
24. Stigler, G. J., "Development of Utility Theory," *Journal of Political Economy,* August 1950.
25. Walras, Léon, *Elements of Pure Economics.* Translated by W. Jaffé. Homewood: Richard D. Irwin, 1954.

7 Demand Curves

F. Y. Edgeworth

Demand Curves represent the relation between the effective demand for a commodity and the terms on which it can be obtained. The simplest form is where one axis, as OY in the annexed figure, represents price, and the other axis, OX, the quantity of a commodity demanded by a certain individual at that price. Thus at the price O*q* the quantity O*p* is demanded. The curve thus representing the dispositions of a single person may be termed an "individual" demand curve, as contrasted with the "collective" demand curve appertaining to a group of persons such as a market or a nation. The collective curve for a group may be derived from the individual curves of the persons forming the group by adding, for each price, the amounts demanded by all the individuals at that price, and taking this sum as the abscissa of the collective curve; the ordinate as before representing price. The collective curve may be represented by Fig. 7-1, if the scale is altered so that a unit of the abscissa should represent a larger amount of commodity than when the figure stood for an individual demand curve.

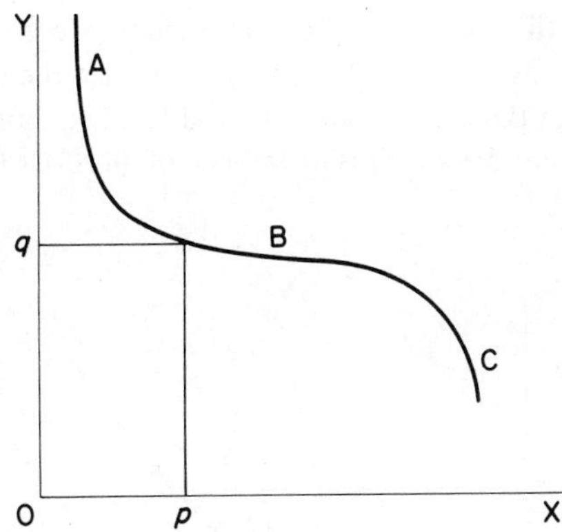

Figure 7-1.

Reprinted from *Dictionary of Political Economy,* edited by H. Inglis Palgrave, London: Macmillan, 1894, pp. 542–544, by permission of the publisher.

This method of representing demand by a curve was introduced by Cournot in his *Principes Mathématiques de la Théorie des Richesses,* 1838. It is remarkable that he began and ended with the collective demand curve, instead of deriving it from the individual curve like many recent writers. Another kind of demand curve is formed by taking one axis as before to represent the quantity of the commodity demanded, while the other axis represents, not as before, the price of each unit of commodity, but the total amount of money (or other article of exchange) corresponding to each amount demanded. Thus in Fig. 7-2 the curve denotes that for the amount of money (or any other specified article, say x) Op, there is demanded the amount of Oq of the article y. This construction was first introduced by Prof. Marshall in a paper read before the Cambridge Philosophical Society, 1873 (to which reference is made in the preface to the first edition of the author's *Principles of Economics.*) The construction is specially suitable to the case where there is a certain symmetry between the conditions of supply and demand, as in international trade. It will be observed that the curve in Fig. 7-2, which has been described as the demand curve with respect to the article y, may also be regarded as the supply curve with respect to the article x; since it represents the amount of the article x which the party or parties under consideration are willing to supply for each amount of y. This kind of demand curve, like that which was first described, may be divided into two species, individual and collective. Another kind of demand curve is used by Prof. Walras in his *Éléments d'Économie Politique Pure.*

The demand curve is a potent aid to abstract theory. It expresses better than ordinary language the relation between price and quantity demanded; of which in general we know only that the quantity varies inversely with the price, but are ignorant what is the law of variation. This ignorance is sometimes not complete; we may know that for the same fall in price the demand increases much more rapidly in the case of one commodity than another; or for the same commodity at different prices. This difference of ELASTICITY is elegantly

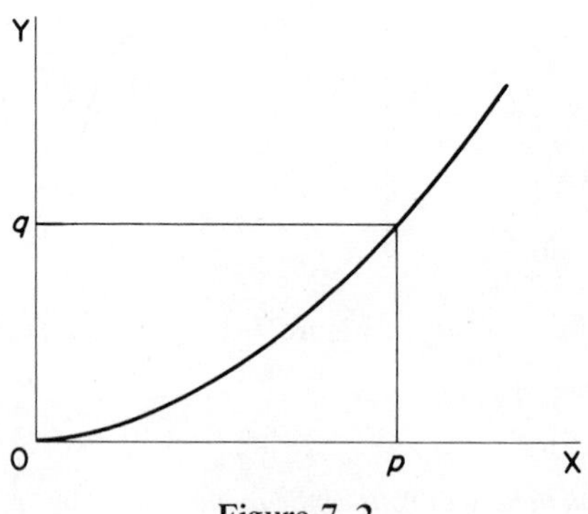

Figure 7-2.

expressed by the shape of the curve. In the case represented by Fig. 7-1 the demand is very elastic in the neighbourhood of B, very inelastic in the neighbourhood of A and C. The case thus represented is a very general one. In Prof. Marshall's words "the elasticity is small when the price of a thing is *very high* relatively to their means [those of the class of purchasers under consideration], and again when it is *very low*; while the elasticity is much greater for prices intermediate between what we may call the high level and the low level." The use of some such device as the demand curve is required for the perfect apprehension of the theory of value. The relation of "individual" to "collective" demand curves best expresses the dependence of the objective fact of price on the subjective dispositions of individual persons. The position of equilibrium towards which the "higgling of the market" tends is best represented by the intersection of a demand with a SUPPLY CURVE (*q.v.*) Ordinary language does not well discriminate the change in price due to a change in the quantity of commodity supplied, the dispositions of the parties remaining the same, from that change which is due to alterations in taste. The latter sort of change is expressed by the shifting of the demand curve from *right* to left (or conversely), so that to every quantity of commodity there corresponds a higher (or lower) price. The demand curve is employed by Prof. Marshall in the proof of several recondite, not to say paradoxical theorems. "If a given aggregate taxation has to be levied ruthlessly from any class, it will cause less loss of CONSUMER'S RENT (*q.v.*) if levied on necessaries than if levied on comforts." (*Principles of Economics*, bk. v. ch. xii. §4, note, 2nd ed., cp. *ibid.* §6). The doctrine that "the maximum satisfaction is generally to be attained by encouraging each individual to spend his own resources in that way which suits him best" is seen by the aid of the demand curve to be inaccurate.

The theory of the demand curve must be received with the following cautions and reservations. First (1) it should be observed that there are "many classes of things the need for which on the part of any individual is inconstant, fitful, and irregular," for instance "wedding cakes, or the services of an expert surgeon" (Marshall, *Principles of Economics*, bk. iii. ch. iii., §5, 2nd ed.) The *individual* demand curve in such a case is discontinuous. But the corresponding *collective* curve will be less irregular. "The fickleness of the individual is merged in the comparatively regular aggregate of the action of a large number of people" (*Ibid.*) Again (2) in comparing the elasticity of demand curves for different commodities care must be taken about the units both of money and commodity. The same dispositions on the part of purchasers will appear more or less "elastic," according as they are expressed in hundredweights or tons, in pounds or shillings. An ingenious method of avoiding this fallacy is given by Prof. Marshall (*Principles of Economics*, bk. iii. ch. iv. §1). Again (3) demand curves as usually understood involve a postulate which is frequently not fulfilled; namely, that while the price of the article under consideration is varied, the prices of all other articles remain constant. This postulate fails in the case of rival commodities such as beef and mutton. The price of one of these cannot be supposed to rise or fall considerably without the price of the other being affected. The same is true of commodities for which there is a "joint demand" as for malt and hops. And in the case of a necessary of life the price cannot be supposed to increase indefinitely without the prices of the other articles falling, owing to the retrenchment of expenditure on articles other than necessaries. The price of clothes has been known to fall during a famine (F. Newman, *Lectures on Political Economy*). It is true indeed that the postulate which has been stated might be dispensed with. But this can only be done at the sacrifice of two of the characteristic advantages which demand curves offer to the theorist. First, unless this postulate is granted, it is hardly conceivable that, when the prices of several articles are disturbed concurrently, the collective demand curve may be predicted by ascertaining the disposition of the individual – a conception which, as employed by Prof. Walras (*Éléments d' Économie Politique,* Art. 50), aids us to apprehend the workings of a market. Secondly, when the prices of all commodities but one are not supposed fixed, there no longer exists that exact correlation between the demand curve and the interest of consumers in low prices which Prof. Marshall has formulated as "consumer's rent." In considering this relation care must be taken to distinguish between demand and desire. The effective demand of the rich and poor man for oatmeal may be the same. But the intensity of desire is not the same, if the one uses the article to feed his horses, the other for his own frugal meal. Again (4) there is an artificial rigidity in demand curves which imperfectly corresponds to the flux character of human desires. One cause of change is the formation of new habits; the disturbance of the demand curve thus caused is well represented by Messrs. Auspitz and Lieben (*Theorie des Preises*). The increased use of petroleum is not to be ascribed simply to the fall in price, the demand curve being supposed constant, but rather to the fact that "petroleum and petroleum lamps have become familiar to all classes of society" (Marshall). One important cause of alteration in demand curves is the increase of the consumer's purchasing power. The case in which that increase is only apparent, being due to a rise in prices (and the converse case), may be specially distinguished. Owing to the variability, it may be doubted whether Jevons's hope of constructing demand curves by statistics is capable of realisation. In the financial year 1890-91, after the reduction of the tax on tea effected by Mr. Goschen, the quantity of tea consumed per head was greater than in the previous year. It is possible to determine whether this change is due to the cheapening of the article – the demand curve being supposed the same – or to an alteration of the demand curve caused partly by a change of taste and partly by an increase in prosperity? Some suggestions for evading these and other difficulties will be found in the third book of Prof. Marshall's *Principles of Economics.*

8 Demand

J. N. Keynes

By "demand" in political economy is meant what may be more distinctively called *effective* demand, that is, not the mere desire for anything, but desire accompanied by the offer of something valuable in exchange. When, therefore, there is a demand for any commodity or service, there must be a supply of some other commodity or service, which is proffered in exchange for it; and when two persons are engaged in exchange, what the one demands the other supplies, and *vice versa*. It follows that demand and supply considered as aggregates are strictly interdependent, and that neither can increase or diminish without necessitating a corresponding increase or diminution of the other. This simple consideration disposes of the fallacy that there may be an over-supply of commodities in general. At the same time, the two different aspects of the phenomenon of exchange are clearly to be distinguished from one another. Demand depends upon men's desires to satisfy their wants by acquiring a command over new goods or services, supply upon their willingness to undergo efforts or part with goods already in their possession. Some of the older economists, *e.g.* Ricardo, tended to concentrate attention upon the conditions determining the supply of commodities, to the comparative neglect of the analysis of demand. This aspect of the problem has, however, been brought into special prominence in recent years by the full discussions of "utility" and "subjective value," which are characteristic of Jevons and the Austrian school. The importance of a full consideration of the side of demand as well as of supply also receives ample recognition in Professor Marshall's *Principles of Economics.*

Assuming the use of a medium of exchange which represents general purchasing power, the question has been raised whether the demand for any commodity should be measured by the quantity of the commodity demanded or by the quantity of purchasing power offered in exchange for it. Cairnes, criticising Mill, considers that on scientific grounds we are bound to select the latter of these alternatives. There is not, however, any fundamental difference between the two when properly interpreted. The quantity of any commodity which people are willing to buy, and the amount of money which they are willing to spend upon it, are, generally speaking, equally indeterminate so long as nothing is said as to the price at which it is to be had. If, then, we measure demand by quantity demanded, it can only be with reference to some particular price

Reprinted from *Dictionary of Political Economy,* edited by H. Inglis Palgrave (London: Macmillan, 1894), pp. 539–542, by permission of the publisher.

or schedule of prices; and hence some specific quantity of purchasing power offered is necessarily implied. But the same is true, *mutatis mutandis,* if we start from the quantity of purchasing power offered. For example, to say that at half-a-crown a pound you will buy six pounds of tea is precisely equivalent to saying that at that price you will spend fifteen shillings on tea. It may sometimes be more convenient to adopt the mode of expression preferred by Cairnes; but usually the other alternative is simpler and less liable to lead to error, since supply and demand can in this case be more directly compared and equated. The *demand* for any commodity at a given price may then be measured by the amount that would be purchased if obtainable at that price; and the *supply* at a given price may be correspondingly measured by the amount that would be offered for sale at that price. If the amount instead of the price is regarded as the independent variable, then the *demand-price* for a given amount of any commodity may be defined as the price just required to attract purchasers for that particular amount; and correspondingly the *supply-price* as the price just required to cause that particular amount to be offered for sale.

It is clear, however, that the circumstances of demand will be very incompletely expressed, if given with reference to some one particular price only or some one particular amount only. We need what Professor Marshall calls a *demand-schedule,* in which the demand at varying prices is recorded. For example, it may be that in the early spring a person will buy one basket of strawberries at ten shillings a basket, two at seven shillings and sixpence, three at six shillings, four at five shillings, and so on. A statement of this kind is said to constitute his demand-schedule for strawberries at the time in question. If the requisite knowledge were forthcoming it would be possible to draw up a schedule of the same kind representing the total demand for any commodity within a given range and over a given period. The variation of demand with price may also be expressed diagrammatically, and the exposition of the general theory of supply and demand may be much facilitated thereby (see Chapter 7).

With improved statistics of consumption, towards which valuable contributions might be afforded by shopkeepers' books and the great co-operative stores, it might be possible to draw up empirical demand-schedules representing approximately the actual variation of demand with price for certain commodities in general use. As Cournot remarks: "If we suppose the conditions of demand to remain the same, but the conditions of production to change, because the expenses of production are raised or lowered, or monopolies put on or suppressed, or taxes increased or diminished, or import duties imposed or removed, then price will vary, and the corresponding variations in demand will give us our empirical tables" (*Principes de la Théorie des Richesses,* §56). But, as is also recognized by Cournot, the conditions of demand rarely do remain the same for any considerable length of time. There are constantly in progress independent changes, such as changes in fashions and habits, in the purchasing power of money, in the wealth and circumstances of consumers, and the like, which cause the demand at a given price itself to vary. Since, therefore, the statistical calculation would have to cover a more or less prolonged period of time, it would always be liable to be vitiated by the effects of such changes as the above, except in so far as these effects could themselves be estimated and allowed for.

For theoretical purposes, however, the inquiry into the variation of demand with price is of the greatest value and importance, independently of any exact empirical constructions. Without elaborate statistics it is possible to determine a *law of demand* to which all demand-schedules will conform, namely, that – other things being equal – a rise in price will be accompanied by a diminished demand and a fall in price by an increased demand. Looked at from the other side, the law may also be expressed by saying that the greater the amount of any commodity offered for sale in a market the lower will be the price at which it will find purchasers.

The above law of demand is a corollary from the law of diminishing utility, namely, that the additional satisfaction which a person derives from an additional increment of any commodity diminishes as the stock of the commodity already in his possession increases. For it clearly follows from this law of diminishing utility that if the general purchasing power of money remains unchanged, then, as the amount of a thing which a person already has increases, the price that he is just willing to give for an additional increment will diminish.

It is an important question how far continuity may be assumed in the variation of demand with price, so that any alteration in the latter, however slight, cannot fail to be accompanied by some alteration in the former. Such an assumption clearly cannot, in general, be justified so far as the demand of individual consumers is concerned. Individual changes in demand will almost always be discontinuous; in other words, there will almost always be more or less wide limits of price within which demand will be constant. The price of coal, for example, might go on rising for some time without leading any given householder to reduce his consumption of coal, although he would probably take steps to economise to a material extent when the rise in price reached a certain point. It is different, however, when we consider the *aggregate* demand for a commodity in general use. Individuals of all degrees of wealth and all varieties of taste will now contribute towards the result, and it becomes a fair assumption that every change in price will affect the demand of certain of them, even if it leaves the demand of others unaffected. It may further be assumed that, as Cournot puts it, "demand does not pass suddenly from one amount to another without passing through the intermediate amounts." The assumption of continuity becomes, for obvious reasons, specially important in the mathematical or diagrammatic treatment of the law of demand.

In speaking of demand as varying with price, it is not of course intended to imply that there is any exact proportion in which the one rises or falls as the other falls or rises. No two commodities are likely exactly to resemble one another in this respect, and even in the case of the same commodity there will be differences at different points. Thus, supposing price to fall fifty per cent, demand might in some cases be increased two or three hundred per cent; it is possible, for instance, that quite a new class of consumers might now be induced to buy the commodity, or it might be worth while to put it to quite a new use. In other cases, the increase in demand might not exceed ten or fifteen per cent, the wants of old purchasers being quickly satiated, and not many new purchasers being attracted. In the former case, demand is said to be very elastic; and in the latter case very inelastic. Professor Marshall gives the following definition: "The *elasticity of demand* in a market is great or small according as the amount demanded increases much or little for a given fall in price, and diminishes much or little for a given rise in price" (*Principles of Economics,* vol. i. 1891, p. 160); and he afterwards lays down, as a general law of variation of the elasticity of demand, the principle that as a rule the elasticity of demand of any given class of consumers for a given commodity is great for medium prices, and small for those which, relatively to the means of the consumers in question, are very high or very low. For so long as price remains very high considerable elasticity is out of the question, while it may, on the other hand, fall so low as to reach what may be called satiety point, consumers already buying as much as they practically care to consume. It is important to recognise that at any given point the demand of one class of consumers may be elastic, while that of other classes is inelastic. In the case of game, for example, the demand of the upper middle class at the present time in England is probably very elastic, while it is much less so on the part of the rich, whose consumption would not appreciably be affected except in the case of very great scarcity, and on the part of the lower middle and working classes, for whom any moderate fall would still leave the price too high.

Unless we confine ourselves to very short periods of time, demand-schedules are themselves liable to modification. For the conditions of demand are constantly changing; and this, as we have already seen, is one of the chief difficulties in the way of obtaining accurate empirical data in regard to the variation of demand with price. A change of fashion, for example, might cause the demand for lace to be greater at every point throughout the list of prices. A spread of teetotalism would, *coeteris paribus,* have a similar effect upon the demand-schedules for certain kinds of drink; and an increase of population upon the demand-schedules for most kinds of food. In all these cases there may be said to be a *rise in the demand-schedule.*

In connection with this point, attention may be called to an ambiguity generally attaching to expressions that relate to variations in demand. The law of demand above laid down is the statement of a variation of demand with price which is manifested in every demand-schedule; and it may perhaps be said to relate to a static condition of things, in which there is supposed to be no change in the number of purchasers or in their circumstances or tastes. But we may pass to the hypothesis of a dynamic condition, in which such changes as these do take place. We then have to recognise, as just pointed out, that the amount of any commodity demanded at a given price is itself subject to variation, or that, in other words, demand-schedules may themselves rise or fall. By an "increase of demand," therefore, may be meant either, first, the extension of demand which results under static conditions from a fall in price, or, secondly, an increase in the quantity demanded at a given price which may occur under dynamic conditions. Professor Sidgwick, who explains this ambiguity very clearly, remarks that it will be convenient to have two unambiguous terms to distinguish the two different kinds of change in demand; and he accordingly proposes to speak of the former kind of increase as an *extension* of demand, and of the latter as a *rise* or *intensification* of demand. For the opposites of "extension" and "rise" respectively, he uses the terms "reduction" and "fall" (*Principles of Political Economy,* 1887, p. 179).

Part III
Demand Theory in Marshall's Tradition

9 The Marshallian Demand Curve

M. Friedman

Alfred Marshall's theory of demand strikingly exemplifies his "impatience with rigid definition and an excessive tendency to let the context explain his meaning."[2] The concept of the demand curve as a functional relation between the quantity and the price of a particular commodity is explained repeatedly and explicitly in the *Principles of Economics:* in words in the text, in plane curves in the footnotes, and in symbolic form in the Mathematical Appendix. A complete definition of the demand curve, including, in particular, a statement of the variables that are to be considered the same for all points on the curve and the variables that are to be allowed to vary, is nowhere given explicitly. The reader is left to infer the contents of *ceteris paribus* from general and vague statements, parenthetical remarks, examples that do not purport to be exhaustive, and concise mathematical notes in the Appendix.

In view of the importance of the demand curve in Marshallian analysis, it is natural that other economists should have constructed a rigorous definition to fill the gap that Marshall left. This occurred at an early date, apparently without controversy about the interpretation to be placed on Marshall's comments. The resulting definition of the demand curve is now so much an intrinsic part of current economic theory and is so widely accepted as Marshall's own that the assertion that Marshall himself gave no explicit rigorous definition may shock most readers.

Yet why this particular interpretation evolved and why it gained such unquestioned acceptance are a mystery that requires explanation. The currently accepted interpretation can be read into Marshall only by a liberal—and, I think, strained—reading of his remarks, and its acceptance implicitly convicts him of log-

[1] I am deeply indebted for helpful criticism and suggestions to A. F. Burns, Aaron Director, C. W. Guillebaud, H. Gregg Lewis, A. R. Prest, D. H. Robertson, G. J. Stigler, and, especially, Jacob Viner, to whose penetrating discussion of the demand curve in his course in economic theory I can trace some of the central ideas and even details of this article. The standard comment that none is to be held responsible for the views expressed herein has particular relevance, since most disagreed with my interpretation of Marshall as presented in an earlier and much briefer draft of this article.

[2] C. W. Guillebaud, "The Evolution of Marshall's *Principles of Economics*," *Economic Journal*, LII (December, 1942), 333.

Reprinted from the *Journal of Political Economy*, Vol. XLVII (December, 1949), pp. 463–495, by permission of the publisher and author.

ical inconsistency and mathematical error at the very foundation of his theory of demand. More important, the alternative interpretation of the demand curve that is yielded by a literal reading of his remarks not only leaves his original work on the theory of demand free from both logical inconsistency and mathematical error but also is more useful for the analysis of most economic problems.

Section I presents the two interpretations of the demand curve and compares them in some detail; Section II argues that a demand curve constructed on my interpretation is the more useful for the analysis of practical problems, whatever may be the verdict about its validity as an interpretation of Marshall; Section III demonstrates that my interpretation is consistent with Marshall's monetary theory and with his work on consumer's surplus; and Section IV presents the textual evidence on the validity of my interpretation. Finally, Section V argues that the change that has occurred in the interpretation of the demand curve reflects a corresponding change in the role assigned to economic theory.

I. ALTERNATIVE INTERPRETATIONS OF MARSHALL'S DEMAND CURVE

The demand curve of a particular group (which may, as a special case, consist of a single individual) for a particular commodity shows the quantity (strictly speaking, the maximum quantity) of the commodity that will be purchased by the group per unit of time at each price. So far, no question arises; this part of the definition is explicit in Marshall and is common to both alternatives to be discussed. The problem of interpretation relates to the phrase, "other things the same," ordinarily attached to this definition.

In the first place, it should be noted that "same" in this phrase does not mean "same over time." The points on a demand curve are alternative possibilities, not temporally ordered combinations of quantity and price. "Same" means "same for all points on the demand curve"; the different points are to differ in quantity and price and are not to differ with respect to "other things."[3] In the second place, "all" other things cannot be supposed to be the same without completely emasculating the concept. For example, if (*a*) total money expenditure on all commodities, (*b*) the price of every commodity other than the one in question, and (*c*) the quantity purchased of every other commodity were supposed to be the same, the amount of money spent on the commodity in question would necessarily be the same at all prices, simply as a matter of arithmetic, and the demand curve would have unit elasticity everywhere.[4] Different specifications of the "other things" will yield different demand curves. For example,

[3] Of course, when correlations among statistical time series are regarded as estimates of demand curves, the hypothesis is that "other things" have been approximately constant over time or that appropriate allowance has been made for changes in them. Similarly, when correlations among cross-section data are regarded as estimates of demand curves, the hypothesis is that "other things" are approximately the same for the units distinguished or that appropriate allowance has been made for differences among them. In both cases the problem of estimation should be clearly distinguished from the theoretical construct to be estimated.

[4] Yet Sidney Weintraub not only suggests that Marshall intended to keep *a*, *b*, and *c* simultaneously the same but goes on to say: "Clearly Marshall's assumption means a unit elasticity of demand in the market reviewed and no ramifications elsewhere; that was why he adopted it" ("The Foundations of the Demand Curve," *American Economic Review*, XXXII [September, 1942], 538–52, quotation from n. 12, p. 541). Weintraub even adds the condition of constant tastes and preferences to *a*, *b*, and *c*, speaking of a change in tastes as shifting the demand curve. Obviously, *a*, *b*, and *c* together leave no room for tastes and preferences or, indeed, for anything except simple arithmetic.

one demand curve will be obtained by excluding *b* from the list of "other things"; another, quite different one, by excluding *c*.

a) THE CURRENT INTERPRETATION

The current interpretation of Marshall's demand curve explicitly includes in the list of "other things" (1) tastes and preferences of the group of purchasers considered; (2) their money income, and (3) the price of every other commodity. The quantities of other commodities are explicitly considered as different at different points on the demand curve, and still other variables are ignored.[5]

On this interpretation, it is clear that, while money income is the same for different points on the demand curve, real income is not. At the lower of two prices for the commodity in question, more of some commodities can be purchased without reducing the amounts purchased of other commodities. The lower the price, therefore, the higher the real income.

[5] Explicit definition of the demand curve in this way by followers of Marshall dates back at least to 1894 (see F. Y. Edgeworth, article on "Demand Curves" in *Palgrave's Dictionary of Political Economy*, edited by Henry Higgs [rev. ed.; London: Macmillan & Co., Ltd., 1926]). Edgeworth's article apparently dates from the first edition, which was published in 1894. While Edgeworth does not explicitly attribute this interpretation to Marshall, it is clear from the context that he is talking about a Marshallian demand curve and that he does not regard his statements as inconsistent in any way with Marshall's *Principles*. Though no explicit listing of "other things" is given by J. R. Hicks, *Value and Capital* (Oxford, 1939), the list given above is implicit throughout chaps. i and ii, which are explicitly devoted to elaborating and extending Marshall's analysis of demand. For statements in modern textbooks on advanced economic theory see G. J. Stigler, *The Theory of Price* (New York: Macmillan Co., 1946), pp. 86–90, and Kenneth E. Boulding, *Economic Analysis* (rev. ed., New York: Harper & Bros., 1948), pp. 134–35.

b) AN ALTERNATIVE INTERPRETATION

It seems to me more faithful to both the letter and the spirit of Marshall's writings to include in the list of "other things" (1) tastes and preferences of the group of purchasers considered, (2) their real income, and (3) the price of every closely related commodity.

Two variants of this interpretation can be distinguished, according to the device adopted for keeping real income the same at different points on the demand curve. One variant, which Marshall employed in the text of the *Principles*, is obtained by replacing "(2) their real income" by (2*a*) their money income and (2*b*) the "purchasing power of money." Constancy of the "purchasing power of money" for different prices of the commodity in question implies compensating variations in the prices of some or all other commodities. These variations will, indeed, be negligible if the commodity in question accounts for a negligible fraction of total expenditures; but they should not be disregarded, both because empirical considerations must be sharply separated from logical considerations and because the demand curve need not be limited in applicability to such commodities. On this variant, all commodities are, in effect, divided into three groups: (*a*) the commodity in question, (*b*) closely related commodities, and (*c*) all other commodities. The absolute price of each commodity in group *b* is supposed to be the same for different points on the demand curve; only the "average" price, or an index number of prices, is considered for group *c;* and it is to be supposed to rise or fall with a fall or rise in the price of group *a*, so as to keep the "purchasing power of money" the same.

The other variant, which Marshall employed in the Mathematical Appendix of the *Principles*, is obtained by retaining "(2) their real income" and adding (4) the average price of all other commodities. Constancy of real income for different prices of the commodity in question then implies compensating variations in money income. As the price of the commodity in question rises or falls, money income is to be supposed to rise or fall so as to keep real income the same.

These two variants are essentially equivalent mathematically,[6] but the assumption of compensating variations in other prices is easier to explain verbally and can be justified as empirically relevant by considerations of monetary theory, which is presumably why Marshall used this variant in his text. On the other hand, the assumption of compensating variations in income is somewhat more convenient mathematically, which is presumably why Marshall used this variant in his Mathematical Appendix.

On my interpretation, Marshall's demand curve is identical with one of the constructions introduced by Slutsky in his famous paper on the theory of choice, namely, the reaction of quantity demanded to a "compensated variation of price," i.e., to a variation in price accompanied by a compensating change in money income.[7] Slutsky expressed the compensating change in money income in terms of observable phenomena, taking it as equal to the change in price *times* the quantity demanded at the initial price. Mosak has shown that, in the

[6] Let x and y be the quantity and price, respectively, of the commodity in question; x' and y' the quantity and price of a composite commodity representing all other commodities; and m, money income. Let

$$x = g(y, y', m, u) \tag{1}$$

be the demand curve for the commodity in question, given a utility function,

$$U = U(x, x', u)\,, \tag{2}$$

where u is a parameter to allow for changes in taste, and subject to the condition

$$xy + x'y' = m\,. \tag{3}$$

From eq. (3) and the usual utility analysis, it follows that eq. (1), like eq. (3), is a homogeneous function of degree zero in y, y', and m; i.e., that

$$g(\lambda y, \lambda y', \lambda m, u) = g(y, y', m, u)\,. \tag{4}$$

On the current interpretation, a two-dimensional demand curve is obtained from eq. (1) directly by giving y' (other prices), m (income), and u (tastes) fixed values. A given value of y then implies a given value of x from eq. (1), a given value of x' from eq. (3), and hence a given value of U (i.e., real income) from eq. (2). The value of U will vary with y, being higher, the lower y is.

On my alternative interpretation, u and U are given fixed values and x' is eliminated from eqs. (2) and (3). This gives a pair of equations,

$$x = g(y, y', m, u_0)\,, \tag{5}$$

$$U_0 = U_0\left(x, \frac{m - xy}{y'}, u_0\right), \tag{6}$$

where the subscript 0 designates fixed values. The two-dimensional variant involving compensating variations in other prices is obtained by eliminating y' from eqs. (5) and (6) and giving m a fixed value; the variant involving compensating variations in income, by eliminating m from eqs. (5) and (6) and giving y' a fixed value.

The homogeneity of eqs. (5) and (6) in y, y', and m means that x is a function only of ratios among them. Thus eqs. (5) and (6) can be written:

$$\left.\begin{aligned} x = g(y, y', m, u_0) &= g\left(\frac{y}{m}, \frac{y'}{m}, 1, u_0\right) \\ &= g\left(\frac{y}{y'}, 1, \frac{m}{y'}, u_0\right), \end{aligned}\right\} \tag{5'}$$

$$\left.\begin{aligned} U_0 = U_0\left(x, \frac{m - xy}{y'}, u_0\right) & \\ = U_0\left(x, \frac{1 - x\frac{y}{m}}{\frac{y'}{m}}, u_0\right) & \\ = U_0\left(x, \frac{m}{y'} - x\frac{y}{y'}, u_0\right). & \end{aligned}\right\} \tag{6'}$$

The choice of price-compensating variations is equivalent to selecting the forms of these two equations in the next to the last terms of eqs. (5′) and (6′); of income-compensating variations, to selecting the forms in the last terms.

[7] Eugenio Slutsky, "Sulla teoria del bilancio del consumatore," *Giornale degli economisti*, LI (1915), 1–26, esp. Sec. 8.

limit, the change in income so computed is identical with the change required to keep the individual on the same level of utility (on the same indifference curve).[8] It follows that a similar statement is valid for compensating changes in other prices. In the limit, the change in other prices required to keep the individual on the same indifference curve when his money income is unchanged but the price of one commodity varies is identical with the change in other prices required to keep unchanged the total cost of the basket of commodities purchased at the initial prices, i.e., to keep unchanged the usual type of cost-of-living index number.

c) COMPARISON OF THE INTERPRETATIONS

The relation between demand curves constructed under the two interpretations is depicted in Figure 1. Curve *Cc* represents a demand curve of an individual consumer for a commodity *X* drawn on the current interpretation. Money income and the prices of other commodities are supposed the same for all points on it; in consequence, real income is lower at *C* than at *P*, since, if the individual sought to buy *OM* of *X* at a price of *OC*, he would be forced to curtail his purchases of something else. As the curve is drawn, of course, he buys none of *X* at a price of *OC*, spending the sum of *OHPM* on other commodities that his action at a price of *OH* shows him to value less highly than he does *OM* units of *X*. The ordinate is described as the ratio of the price of *X* to the price of other commodities. For the demand curve *Cc* this is a question only of the unit of measure, since other prices are supposed to be the same for all points on it.

From the definition of the demand curve *Cc*, *OC* is obviously the maximum price per unit that an individual would be willing to pay for an infinitesimal initial increment of *X* when his money income and the prices of other commodities have the values assumed in drawing *Cc*. Let us suppose him to purchase this amount at a price of *OC*, determine the

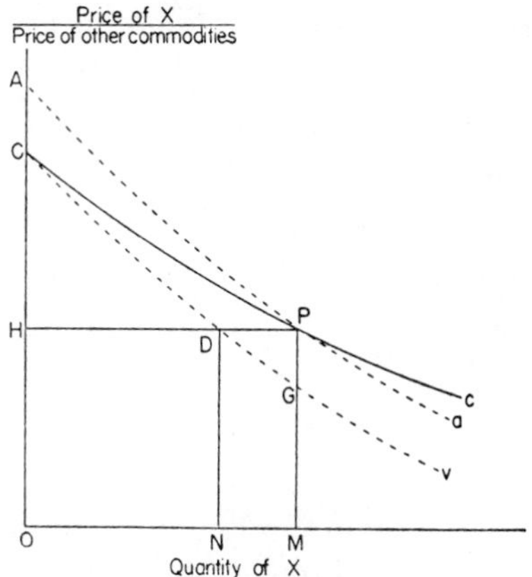

FIG. 1.—Comparison of demand curves constructed under the two interpretations.

maximum price per unit he would be willing to pay for an additional increment, and continue in this fashion, exacting the maximum possible amount for each additional increment. Let these successive maximum prices per unit define the curve *Cv*. The consumer obviously has the same real income at each point on *Cv* as at *C*, since the maximum price has been extracted from him for each successive unit, so that he has gained no utility in the process.

Cv is now a demand curve constructed according to my interpretation of Marshall. If other prices are supposed to be the same, the necessary compensating

[8] Jacob L. Mosak, "On the Interpretation of the Fundamental Equation of Value Theory," in O. Lange, F. McIntyre, and T. O. Yntema, *Studies in Mathematical Economics and Econometrics* (Chicago: University of Chicago Press, 1942), pp. 69–74, esp. n. 5, pp. 73–74, which contains a rigorous proof of this statement by A. Wald.

variations in money income as the price of X falls are given by triangular areas exemplified by HCD for a price of OH: OH is the maximum price per unit that the individual will give for an additional infinitesimal increment of X when he has spent $OCDN$ for ON of X out of his initial income of, say, m; but his situation is exactly the same if, when the price of X is OH, his income is $(m - HCD)$ and he spends $OHDN$ on X; he has the same amount left to spend on all other commodities, their prices are the same, and he has the same amount of X; accordingly, his demand price will be the same, and he will buy ON of X at a price of OH and an income of $(m - HCD)$.[9]

If compensating variations in other prices rather than in money income are used to keep real income the same, the absolute price of neither X nor other commodities can be read directly from Figure 1. For each ratio of the price of X to the price of other commodities, the quantity of X purchased will be that shown on Cv. But the prices of other goods will vary along Cv, rising as the relative price of X falls, so the absolute price of X can no longer be obtained by multiplying the ordinate by a single scale factor.

Figure 1 is drawn on the assumption that X is a "normal" commodity, that is, a commodity the consumption of which is higher, the higher the income. This is the reason Cv is drawn to the left of Cc—at every point on Cv other than C, real income is less than at the corresponding point on Cc; hence less X would be consumed.

Curve Aa represents a demand curve on my interpretation of Marshall for a real income the same as at point P on Cc; it is like Cv but for a higher real income. Real income is higher on Aa than on Cc for prices above OH, lower for prices below OH, which is the reason Aa is to the right of Cc for prices above OH and to the left of Cc for prices below OH.

d) WHY TWO INTERPRETATIONS ARE POSSIBLE

The possibility of interpreting Marshall in these two quite different ways arises in part from the vagueness of Marshall's exposition, from his failure to give precise and rigorous definitions. A more fundamental reason, however, is the existence of inconsistency in the third and later editions of the *Principles*. In that edition Marshall introduced the celebrated passage bearing on the Giffen phenomenon. This passage and a related sentence added at the same time to the

[9] In the notation of n. 6, except that u is omitted for simplicity, the quantities of X and X' that will be purchased for any given values of y and y' and any given real income, U_0, are obtained by solving simultaneously:

$$\frac{U_x}{U_{x'}} = \frac{y}{y'}, \quad (1)$$

and

$$U(x, x') = U_0, \quad (2)$$

where U_x and $U_{x'}$ stand for the partial derivatives of U with respect to x and x', respectively, i.e., for the marginal utility of X and X'. The solution of these equations gives the demand curve on my interpretation of Marshall, using compensating variations in money income.

$U_0(0, m/y')$ is the utility at C in the diagram. For any given amount of X and given value of y', the amount of X' purchased is obtained by solving

$$U(x, x') = U_0\left(0, \frac{m}{y'}\right), \quad (3)$$

which is identical with eq. (2). The amount paid for X (the area under Cv) is

$$m - x'y'. \quad (4)$$

The maximum price that will be paid per unit of X is the derivative of eq. (4), or

$$y = -\frac{dx'}{dx}y' = \frac{U_x}{U_{x'}}y', \quad (5)$$

which is identical with eq. (1). It follows that Cv is a demand curve constructed on my interpretation of Marshall.

Mathematical Appendix fit the current interpretation better than they fit my interpretation. Although these are the only two items that I have been able to find in any edition of the *Principles* of which this is true, they provide some basis for the current interpretation. A hypothesis to explain the introduction of this inconsistency into the *Principles* is offered in Section IV*e* below.

II. THE RELATIVE USEFULNESS OF THE TWO INTERPRETATIONS

The relative usefulness of the two interpretations of the demand curve can be evaluated only in terms of some general conception of the role of economic theory. I shall use the conception that underlies Marshall's work, in which the primary emphasis is on positive economic analysis, on the forging of tools that can be used fairly directly in analyzing practical problems. Economic theory was to him an "engine for the discovery of concrete truth."[10] "Man's powers are limited: almost every one of nature's riddles is complex. He breaks it up, studies one bit at a time, and at last combines his partial solutions with a supreme effort of his whole small strength into some sort of an attempt at a solution of the whole riddle."[11] The underlying justification for the central role of the concepts of demand and supply in Marshall's entire structure of analysis is the empirical generalization that an enumeration of the forces affecting demand in any problem and of the forces affecting supply will yield two lists that contain few items in common. Demand and supply are to him concepts for organizing materials, labels in an "analytical filing box." The "commodity" for which a demand curve is drawn is another label, not a word for a physical or technical entity to be defined once and for all independently of the problem at hand. Marshall writes:

> The question where the lines of division between different commodities should be drawn must be settled by convenience of the particular discussion. For some purposes it may be best to regard Chinese and Indian teas, or even Souchong and Pekoe teas, as different commodities; and to have a separate demand schedule for each of them. While for other purposes it may be best to group together commodities as distinct as beef and mutton, or even as tea and coffee, and to have a single list to represent the demand for the two combined.[12]

a) THE DISTINCTION BETWEEN CLOSELY RELATED AND ALL OTHER COMMODITIES

A demand function containing as separate variables the prices of a rigidly defined and exhaustive list of commodities, all on the same footing, seems largely foreign to this approach. It may be a useful expository device to bring home the mutual interdependence of economic phenomena; it cannot form part of Marshall's "engine for the discovery of concrete truth." The analyst who attacks a concrete problem can take explicit account of only a limited number of factors; he will inevitably separate commodities that are closely related to the one immediately under study from commodities that are more distantly related. He can pay some attention to each closely related commodity. He cannot handle the more distantly related commodities in this way; he will tend either to ignore

[10] Alfred Marshall, "The Present Position of Economics" (1885), reprinted in *Memorials of Alfred Marshall*, ed. A. C. Pigou (London: Macmillan & Co., Ltd., 1925), p. 159.

[11] Alfred Marshall, "Mechanical and Biological Analogies in Economics" (1898), *ibid.*, p. 314.

[12] Marshall, *Principles of Economics* (8th ed.; London: Macmillan & Co., Ltd., 1920), p. 100 n. All subsequent page references to the *Principles*, unless otherwise stated, are to the eighth and final edition.

them or to consider them as a group. The formally more general demand curve will, in actual use, become the kind of demand curve that is yielded by my interpretation of Marshall.

The part of the Marshallian filing box covered by *ceteris paribus* typically includes three quite different kinds of variables, distinguished by their relation to the variable whose adaptation to some change is directly under investigation (e.g., the price of a commodity): (*a*) variables that are expected both to be materially affected by the variable under study and, in turn, to affect it; (*b*) variables that are expected to be little, if at all, affected by the variable under study but to materially affect it; (*c*) the remaining variables, expected neither to affect significantly the variable under study nor to be significantly affected by it.

In demand analysis the prices of closely related commodities are the variables in group *a*. They are put individually into the pound of *ceteris paribus* to pave the way for further analysis. Holding their prices constant is a provisional step. They must inevitably be affected by anything that affects the commodity in question; and this indirect effect can be analyzed most conveniently by first isolating the direct effect, systematically tracing the repercussions of the direct effect on each closely related commodity, and then tracing the subsequent reflex influences on the commodity in question. Indeed, in many ways, the role of the demand curve itself is as much to provide an orderly means of analyzing these indirect effects as to isolate the direct effect on the commodity in question.

The average price of "all other commodities," income and wealth, and tastes and preferences are the variables in group *b*. These variables are likely to be affected only negligibly by factors affecting primarily the commodity in question. On the other hand, any changes in them would have a significant effect on that commodity. They are put into the pound in order to separate problems, to segregate the particular reactions under study. They are put in individually and explicitly because they are so important that account will have to be taken of them in any application of the analysis.

Price changes within the group of "all other commodities" and an indefinitely long list of other variables are contained in group *c*. These variables are to be ignored. They are too numerous and each too unimportant to permit separate account to be taken of them.

In keeping with the spirit of Marshallian analysis this classification of variables is to be taken as illustrative, not definitive. What particular variables are appropriate for each group is to be determined by the problem in hand, the amount of information available, the detail required in results, and the patience and resources of the analyst.

b) CONSTANCY OF REAL INCOME

It has just been argued that any actual analysis of a concrete economic problem with the aid of demand curves will inevitably adopt one feature of my interpretation of Marshall—consideration of a residual list of commodities as a single group. For somewhat subtler reasons this is likely to be true also of the second feature of my interpretation of Marshall—holding real income constant along a demand curve. If an analysis, begun with a demand curve constructed on the current interpretation, is carried through and made internally consistent, it will be found that the demand curve has been subjected to shifts that, in effect, result from failure to keep real income constant along the demand curve.

An example will show how this occurs. Let us suppose that the government grants to producers of commodity X a subsidy of a fixed amount per unit of output, financed by a general income tax, so that money income available for expenditure (i.e., net of tax and gross of subsidy) is unchanged. For simplicity, suppose, first, that no commodities are closely related to X either as rivals or as complements, so that interrelations in consumption between X and particular other commodities can be neglected; second, that the tax is paid by individuals in about the same income class and with about the same consumption pattern as those who benefit from the subsidy, so that complications arising from changes in the distribution of income can be neglected; and, third, that there are no idle resources. Let DD in Figure 2 be a demand curve for commodity X, and SS be the initial supply curve for X, and let the initial position at their intersection, point P, be a position of full equilibrium. The effect of the subsidy is to lower the supply curve to $S'S'$. Since we have ruled out repercussions through consumption relations with other markets and through changes in the level or distribution of money income, it is reasonable to expect that the intersection of this new supply curve and the initial demand curve, point P', will itself be a position of full equilibrium, involving a lower price and larger quantity of X. Yet, if the demand curve is constructed on the current interpretation and if the supply curve is not perfectly inelastic,[13] point P' is not a position of full equilibrium. This can be seen most easily by supposing DD to have unit elasticity, so that the same amount is spent on X at P' as at P. The same amount is then available to spend on all other commodities, and, since their prices are supposed to be the same for all points on DD under the current interpretation, the same quantity of each of them will be demanded. But then where do the resources come from to produce the extra MN units of X? Obviously, our assumptions are not internally consistent. The additional units of X can be produced only by bidding resources away from the production of other commodities, in the process raising their prices and reducing the amount of them produced. The final equilibrium position will therefore involve higher prices and lower quantities of other commodities. But, on the current interpretation, this means a shift in the demand curve for X—say, to $D'D'$—and a final equilibrium position of, say, P''.[14]

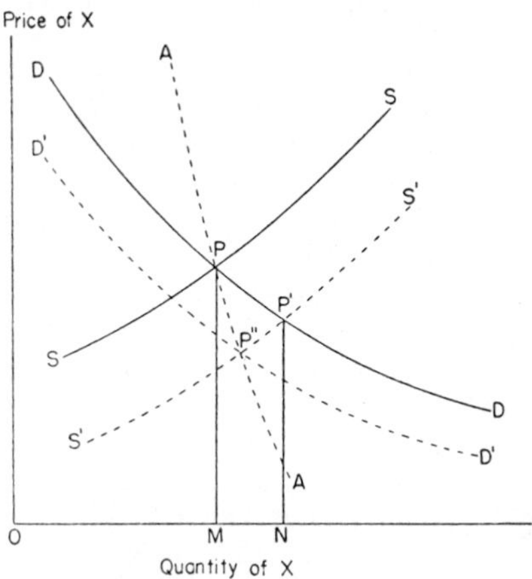

FIG. 2.—Illustrative analysis of effect of subsidy

[13] If it is perfectly inelastic, neither the price nor the quantity of X is changed, so the new position of equilibrium coincides with the old; but the demand curve will pass through the initial position of equilibrium whether constructed on the current interpretation or on mine; hence the two coincide at the one point on them that is relevant.

[14] $D'D'$ will not necessarily be to the left of DD even for a "normal" commodity. The reason is that the ordinate of Fig. 2 measures the absolute price of X, so that ordinates of the same height on DD

The assumption that the elasticity of DD is unity is not, of course, essential for this argument. If the elasticity of DD is less than unity, a larger amount than formerly is available to spend on other commodities; at unchanged prices this means a larger quantity demanded. In consequence, while the additional amount of resources required to produce the increased amount of X demanded is smaller when DD is inelastic than when it has unit elasticity, this is counterbalanced by increased pressure for resources to produce other commodities. Similarly, when DD is elastic, the additional amount of resources required to produce the increased quantity of X demanded is larger than when DD has unit elasticity, but some resources are released in the first instance from the production of other commodities.

No such internal inconsistency as that just outlined arises if the demand curve is constructed by keeping real income the same. Curve AA is such a demand curve. At prices of X less than PM, prices of other commodities are supposed to be sufficiently higher than at P to keep real income the same, which involves the release of just enough resources so that the position of final equilibrium, P'', lies on the demand curve so constructed—at least for small changes in the price of X.[15]

The fundamental principle illustrated by this example can be put more generally. The reason why a demand curve constructed under the current interpretation fails to give the correct solution even when all disturbing influences can be neglected is that each point on it implicitly refers to a different productive capacity of the community. A reduction in the price of the commodity in question is to be regarded as enabling the community, if it so wishes, to consume more of some commodities—this commodity or others—without consuming less of any commodity. But the particular change in supply whose consequences we sought to analyze—that arising from a subsidy—does not make available any additional resources to the community; any increase in the consumption of the commodity in question must be at the expense of other commodities. The conditions for which the demand curve is drawn are therefore

and $D'D'$ represent different ratios of the price of X to the price of other commodities. If the ordinate measured the ratio of the price of X to the price of other commodities, $D'D'$ would always be to the left of DD for "normal" commodities, always to the right for "inferior" commodities.

[15] Let X' be a single composite commodity representing all commodities other than X; x and x', the quantities of X and X'; and y and y', their prices. Let the subscript 1 refer to values at the initial position of equilibrium, P; the subscript 2, to values at the final position, P''. The condition of constant total expenditures means that

$$x_1y_1 + x_1'y_1' = x_2y_2 + x_2'y_2' . \qquad (1)$$

As was pointed out above (Sec. I*b*), in the limit, holding real income constant is equivalent to holding constant the cost of a fixed basket of commodities. Thus, if P'' is considered close to P,

$$x_1y_1 + x_1'y_1' = x_1y_2 + x_1'y_2' . \qquad (2)$$

In the neighborhood of P, y_1 can be regarded as the cost per unit of producing X; y_1', as the cost per unit of producing X'. The condition that sufficient resources be released to permit the production of the requisite additional amount of X is therefore

$$(x_2 - x_1)y_1 = -(x_2' - x_1')y_1' , \qquad (3)$$

which is equivalent to

$$x_1y_1 + x_1'y_1' = x_2y_1 + x_2'y_1' . \qquad (4)$$

But, in the limit, eqs. (1) and (2) imply eq. (4), as can be seen by subtracting eq. (2) from eq. (1) and replacing y_2 and y_2' in the result by $(y_2 - y_1 + y_1)$ and $(y_2' - y_1' + y_1')$, respectively.

More generally, constant real income involves keeping a price index unchanged; constant use of resources involves keeping a quantity index unchanged; and, in the limit, a constant price index and constant total expenditures imply a constant quantity index.

Note that AA need not be steeper than DD in a graph like Fig. 2. The point in question is that commented on in n. 14.

inconsistent with the conditions postulated on the side of supply. On the other hand, if the demand curve is constructed by keeping "real income" the same, no such inconsistency need arise. True, constant "real income" in the sense of "utility" and constant "real income" in the sense of outputs attainable from a fixed total of resources are different concepts, but they converge and can be treated as the same in the neighborhood of a position of equilibrium.

Of course, not all shifts in supply that it is desired to analyze arise in ways that leave the productive capacity of the community unaltered. Many involve a change in productive capacity—for example, changes in supply arising from improvements in technology or the discovery of previously unknown resources. Even in these cases, however, a demand curve constructed on the current interpretation will not serve. There is no reason to expect the differences in productive capacity implicit in constant money income and constant prices of other goods to bear any consistent relation to the change in productive capacity arising on the side of supply.[16] The better plan, in these cases, is to allow separately and directly for the increase in productive capacity by redrawing the demand curves to correspond to an appropriately higher real income and then to use a demand curve on which all points refer to that higher real income.

The main point under discussion can be put still more generally. The opportunities open to a consumer to satisfy his wants depend principally on two factors—the total resources at his disposal and the terms on which he can exchange one commodity for another, that is, on his real income and on relative prices. The form of analysis that is now fashionable distinguishes three effects of changes in his opportunities—the income effect arising from changes in his money income; the income effect arising from changes in the price of a commodity, with unchanged money income and prices of other commodities; and the substitution effect arising from a change in the relative price of a commodity, with unchanged real income.

The distinction between the so-called "substitution" and "income" effects of a change in price is a direct consequence of defining the demand curve according to the current interpretation of Marshall. Its basis is the arithmetic truism that at given prices for all commodities but one, a given money income corresponds to a higher real income, the lower the price of the remaining commodity—at a lower price for it, more of some commodities can be purchased without purchasing less of others. In consequence, a decline in the price of a commodity, all other prices constant, has, it is argued, two effects: first, with an unchanged real income, it would stimulate the substitution of that commodity for others—this is the substitution effect; second, if the money income of the consumers is supposed to be unchanged, the increase in their real income as a result of the decline in price causes a further change in the consumption of that commodity as well as of others—this is the income effect.[17]

[16] Note the difference from the previous case of constant productive capacity. As stated above, there is reason to expect constant real income along a demand curve to bear a consistent relation to constant productive capacity in the neighborhood of equilibrium. The reason, in effect, is provided by one of the conditions of equilibrium: the tangency of consumption and production indifference curves,

[17] See Slutsky, *op. cit.*; Henry Schultz, *The Theory and Measurement of Demand* (Chicago: University of Chicago Press, 1938), pp. 40-46; J. R. Hicks and R. G. D. Allen, "A Reconsideration of the Theory of Value," *Economica*, XIV (1934), 52-76 and 196-219; Hicks, *op. cit.*, Part I.

The two different kinds of income effects distinguished in this analysis—one arising from a change in money income, the other from a change in the price of one commodity—are really the same thing, the effect of a change in real income with given relative prices, arising in different ways. It is hard to see any gain from combining the second income effect with the substitution effect; it seems preferable to combine the two income effects and thereby gain a sharp contrast with the substitution effect.

It has often been stated that Marshall "neglected the income effect."[18] On my interpretation of his demand curve, this statement is invalid. One must then say that Marshall recognized the desirability of separating two quite different effects and constructed his demand curve so that it encompassed solely the effect that he wished to isolate for study, namely, the substitution effect. Instead of neglecting the income effect, he "eliminated" it.

The conclusion to which the argument of this section leads is identical with that reached by Frank H. Knight in a recent article, in which he says:

> We have to choose in analysis between holding the prices of all other goods constant and maintaining constant the "real income" of the hypothetical consumer. . . . The treatment of the Slutzky school adopts the assumption that . . . the prices of all other goods (and the consumer's money income) are constant. Hence, real income must change. Of the two alternatives, this seems to be definitely the wrong choice. . . . The simple and obvious alternative is to draw the demand curves in terms of a change in *relative* prices, i.e., to assume that the value of money is held constant, through compensating changes in the prices of other goods, and not that these other prices are held constant.[19]

III. THE CONSISTENCY OF THE ALTERNATIVE INTERPRETATION WITH OTHER PARTS OF MARSHALL'S WORK

Marshall's demand curve is part of a coherent body of thought; it is designed to fit into the rest of his structure of analysis; and it is used extensively in developing and applying this structure. It would take us too far afield to demonstrate in detail that my interpretation of his demand curve is consistent with the rest of his work. However, two special topics call for some explicit consideration: (1) the relation between the demand curve and Marshall's theory of money, because, in my view, this explains the particular device that he adopted for holding real income constant; and (2) the concept of consumer's surplus, because this is one of the most important applications of the demand curve and certainly the most controversial and because the passages in the later editions of the *Principles* that are inconsistent with my interpretation were introduced into the discussion of consumer's surplus.

a) THE THEORY OF RELATIVE PRICES AND THE THEORY OF MONEY

Granted that real income is to be held constant along the demand curve, why do so by holding money income and the purchasing power of money constant rather than, for example, by holding prices of other goods constant and permitting compensating variations in money income? What reason is there to treat the prices of all other commodities as moving inversely to the price of the commodity in question?

The answer to these questions is given, I think, by one of Marshall's basic or-

[18] Hicks, *op. cit.*, p. 32.

[19] "Realism and Relevance in the Theory of Demand," *Journal of Political Economy*, LII (December, 1944), 289–318, esp. Sec. III, "The Meaning of a Demand Curve," pp. 298–301. Quotation from p. 299.

ganizing principles, namely, the separation of the theory of relative prices from monetary theory, the theory of the level of prices. The *Principles* is devoted to the theory of relative prices under given monetary conditions; *Money, Credit, and Commerce* to the analysis of monetary conditions and their effect on the "purchasing power of money." With *given monetary conditions*, is it possible for the prices of all commodities other than the one in question to remain the same, on the average, while the price of this one rises or falls? Will not a rise or fall in the price of the commodity in question set in motion *monetary* forces affecting other prices? A complete answer requires explicit specification of the content of "given monetary conditions" and perhaps also of the source of the initial price change.

Marshall's selection of a constant purchasing power of money as a means of impounding monetary forces is presumably the end-result of a chain of reasoning about the influence of monetary forces, not the direct content that he gave to "given monetary conditions." The beginning of the chain of reasoning may well be his own version of the quantity theory of money. According to this version, "the value of money is a function of its supply on the one hand, and the demand for it, on the other, as measured by 'the average stock of command over commodities which each person cares to keep in a ready form.' "[20] Given monetary conditions would then imply a given stock of money and a given desired "average stock of command over commodities." A decline in one price alone, all other prices remaining the same, is inconsistent with these "givens." It would increase the real value of a fixed (nominal) stock of money, leave the community with a larger "stock of command over commodities" than previously, and establish an incentive (reflecting "monetary" forces) to increase expenditures and thereby raise prices until the fixed stock of money again represented the same "stock of command over commodities," i.e., until the "purchasing power of money" reached its former level.[21] This argument suggests that not only was constant purchasing power of money a device for separating the theory of relative prices from monetary theory, it was also a bridge between the two. Marshall separated the two theories in his attempt to reduce problems to manageable proportions, but he constructed them in such a way as to make them mutually consistent and thus facilitate ultimate combination.[22]

[20] J. M. Keynes, "Alfred Marshall, 1842–1924," *Memorials*, p. 29.

[21] C. W. Guillebaud has pointed out to me that Marshall typically supposed the desired "stock of command over commodities" to be a given fraction of real income (see *ibid.*) and that the argument in the text might not apply if this fraction were taken as the fundamental given. The monetary effects of a change in one price, other prices given, would then depend on the source of the initial price change. If this involved no change in aggregate real income (e.g., arose from a shift in demand), the argument in the text would remain unchanged. If it did involve a change in aggregate real income (e.g., arose from an invention reducing the cost of producing the commodity in question), no inconsistency need arise, since the desired "stock of command over commodities" would change in proportion to the change in real income. These considerations account for the phrase "perhaps also of the source of the initial price change" at the end of the preceding paragraph of the text.

[22] This interpretation would, of course, be contradicted if Marshall had devised his theory of money after he had substantially completed his theory of relative prices, as might be inferred from the fact that *Money, Credit, and Commerce* was not published until 1923, thirty-three years after the first edition of the *Principles*. But in Marshall's case, the order of publication is a poor guide to the order of construction. Keynes tells us that the essence of his quantity theory of money is contained in a manuscript "written about 1871"; that "by 1871 his progress along" the lines of the material

Marshall was, of course, very much aware of the interaction between real and monetary factors. The 1879 *Economics of Industry* contains an extremely interesting discussion of the trade cycle, part of which Marshall thought sufficiently important to quote at length in 1886 in answering questions circulated by the celebrated Royal Commission on the Depression of Trade and Industry.[23]

Marshall's decision to keep the purchasing power of money the same for different points on a demand curve may not be the device best suited to abstract from monetary factors. It serves, however, to emphasize the necessity of considering explicitly the monetary arrangements under which the forces affecting relative prices are supposed to operate. The best apparatus for tackling problems of relative prices cannot be determined independently of these arrangements and of their mode of operation. Though price theory and monetary theory can be separated, they are not basically independent. From this point of view it is entirely natural that the recent development of alternative monetary theories should have stimulated re-examination of price theory.

b) CONSUMER'S SURPLUS

Marshall's discussion of consumer's surplus constitutes one of the most extensive applications that he made of his demand curve and has probably given rise to more controversy and discussion than any other part of his theory. Recently, consumer's surplus has come in for renewed attention, primarily as a result of J. R. Hick's attempt to rehabilitate and reinterpret the concept.[24] The reason for commenting on it here is not to contribute to the discussion or to evaluate the merits or demerits of the concept but rather to show the relation between Marshall's treatment of consumer's surplus and my interpretation of his demand curve.

Marshall's treatment of consumer's surplus might, offhand, seem inconsistent with my interpretation of his demand curve for either of two different, and almost opposed, reasons. In the first place, consumer's surplus refers to a difference in real income under different situations. But, on my interpretation, all

contained in the *Pure Theory* "was considerably advanced"; that the *Pure Theory* itself was "substantially complete about 1873," though not printed even for private circulation until 1879; that "in 1877 he turned aside to write the *Economics of Industry* with Mrs. Marshall"; and that Mrs. Marshall said "Book III on Demand was largely thought out and written on the roof at Palermo, Nov. 1881—Feb. 1882" (*Memorials*, pp. 28, 21, 23, 39 n.). These dates are extremely suggestive, particularly since the constancy of the purchasing power of money is not explicitly mentioned in the *Pure Theory*, which Marshall was presumably working on at about the same time that he was developing his monetary theory, while it is explicitly mentioned in the 1879 *Economics of Industry*, begun some years later. See also nn. 37 and 38 below.

[23] See Alfred Marshall and Mary Paley Marshall, *Economics of Industry* (London: Macmillan & Co., 1st ed., 1879; 2d ed., 1881), Book III, chap. i, pp. 150–57. This and all later references are to the first edition. "Answers to Questions on the Subject of Currency and Prices Circulated by the Royal Commission on the Depression of Trade and Industry (1886)," *Official Papers by Alfred Marshall* (London: Macmillan & Co., Ltd., 1926), pp. 7–9. See also "Remedies for Fluctuations of General Prices" (1887), *Memorials*, pp. 189–92.

[24] See Hicks, *op. cit.*, pp. 38–41; "The Rehabilitation of Consumers' Surplus," *Review of Economic Studies*, VIII (February, 1941), 108–16; "Consumers' Surplus and Index Numbers," *ibid.* (summer, 1942), 126–37; "The Four Consumer's Surpluses," *ibid.*, XI (winter, 1943), 31–41. See also A. Henderson, "Consumer's Surplus and the Compensating Variation," *Review of Economic Studies*, VIII (February, 1941), 117–21; Knight, *op. cit.*; Kenneth E. Boulding, "The Concept of Economic Surplus," *American Economic Review*, XXXV (December, 1945), 851–69, reprinted in American Economic Association, *Readings in the Theory of Income Distribution* (Philadelphia: Blakiston Co., 1946), pp. 638–59; E. J. Mishan, "Realism and Relevance in Consumer's Surplus," *Review of Economic Studies*, XV (1947–48), 27–33.

points on the demand curve are to be regarded as corresponding to the same real income. A movement along such a demand curve cannot, therefore, involve a change in consumer's surplus. Does this not eliminate the entire notion of consumer's surplus and make Marshall's entire discussion of it pointless? The answer is clearly "No," the reason being that the two situations compared need not correspond to two points on the *same* demand curve, even though a single demand curve is used to *estimate* the difference in real income between the two situations.

In the second place, Marshall regarded his analysis of consumer's surplus as valid only for commodities that account for a small part of total expenditure. He makes this restriction in order to justify neglecting changes in the marginal utility of money. But, if all points on the demand curve correspond to the same real income, does it not then follow that the marginal utility of money is the same everywhere on the demand curve? And does it not also follow that his estimate of consumer's surplus is exact, so that the assumption that a negligible proportion of expenditures is devoted to the commodity in question becomes unnecessary? Again the answer is "No," and for much the same reason. If the two situations compared differ in real income, the fact that real income is the same along the demand curve becomes something of a vice in using it to measure consumer's surplus. The assumption that a negligible proportion of expenditures is devoted to the commodity in question cannot be dispensed with on my interpretation; indeed, if anything, it is even more necessary than on the current interpretation.

To explain and justify these cryptic answers, it will be necessary to examine Marshall's definition of consumer's surplus, his suggested estimate of its magnitude, and the relation of this estimate to the correct value under the two alternative interpretations of the demand curve.

Marshall is more explicit and complete in defining consumer's surplus than was his wont, and his definition admits of little ambiguity: "The excess of the price which he would be willing to pay rather than go without the thing, over that which he actually does pay, is the economic measure of this surplus satisfaction. It may be called *consumer's surplus.*"[25]

Marshall then proceeds to argue that consumer's surplus can be *estimated* by the famous triangle under the demand curve. As Hicks remarks, this "association of Consumer's Surplus with the curvilinear triangle under the demand curve . . . is not a definition; it is a theorem, true under certain restrictive assumptions, but only true if these assumptions are granted."[26] The confusion of the suggested estimate with the definition is perhaps the chief source of misunderstanding on this exceedingly complex subject.

Figure 1, introduced in Section I*c* above to illustrate the relation between demand curves drawn on the current and on my interpretation, can also be used to show the relation between consumer's surplus as defined and estimates of it obtained from demand curves constructed according to the two interpretations. Curve *Cc*, it will be recalled, is a demand curve for the commodity *X* constructed according to the current interpretation. Money income and all other prices are the same for all points on it. *Aa* and *Cv*

[25] *Principles*, p. 124.

[26] "Rehabilitation of Consumers' Surplus," p. 109.

are demand curves constructed according to my interpretation—*Aa* for a real income the same as at *P* on *Cc; Cv* for a real income the same as at *C* on *Cc*. At point *P* on *Aa* and at point *C* on *Cv*, money income and all other prices are the same as on *Cc*. At other points other prices are sufficiently different, or money income is, to compensate for the difference in the price of *X* and thereby keep real income the same.

Now consider the consumer's surplus obtained from this commodity when the consumer is at *P*.[27] This is *defined* as "the excess of the price which he would be willing to pay rather than go without the thing, over that which he actually does pay." "Price" is here to be interpreted as "total amount" rather than "price per unit."[28] Further, it is clear that the sum he would pay rather than go without is to be determined for circumstances otherwise the same as at *P;* in particular, his money income and the other prices are to be the same as at *P*.[29] Now the amount that he actually does pay for *OM* of *X* is given by the rectangle *OHPM* in the figure. By the argument of Section I*c*, the maximum amount that he would be willing to pay for *OM* of *X* rather than go without any of it is given by the area under *Cv* between *O* and *M*, or *OCDGM*. The triangular area *CDH minus* the triangular area *DPG* therefore gives the consumer's surplus. This area is necessarily positive; we know he is willing to pay at least *OHPM* for *OM* of *X;* hence *OCDGM* must be greater than *OHPM*.

Marshall's *estimate* of the maximum sum is the area under the demand curve: *OCPM* if we use the current interpretation, *OAPM* if we use the alternative interpretation. For a "normal" commodity, the case for which the figure is drawn, both are clearly too large. How large the error is depends on the difference between *Aa* and *Cc*, on the one hand, and *Cv*, on the other. Now we have seen (in Sec. I*c*) that these differences arise entirely from differences in the real income associated with the different curves; if real incomes differ little, so will the curves. Here is where Marshall's assumption about the fraction of expenditures devoted to the commodity enters the picture. If this fraction is small, the differences in real income will tend to be small, and both estimates will approach the correct value.[30] Since the error is

[27] For simplicity, the discussion is restricted to the consumer's surplus obtained from the entire amount of *X* consumed; and to facilitate this, the demand curves have been drawn to cut the price axis.

[28] See Mathematical Note II of the *Principles* (p. 838), in which Marshall defines *p* as "the price which he is just willing to pay for an amount *x* of the commodity" and then differentiates *p* with respect to *x* to get the price per unit.

[29] None of the reasons cited earlier for keeping real income the same along the demand curve apply here. The question being asked is purely hypothetical; no other reactions need be allowed for. Further, to keep his real income the same when he has none of *X* as when he has *OM* of *X* would make the entire discussion of consumer's surplus pointless. The whole point of the discussion is to measure the difference in real income between the two situations.

[30] This statement is not rigorous. As the fraction of expenditures devoted to the commodity diminishes, so will aggregate consumer's surplus. It is not enough that the error become small in absolute terms; its ratio to the correct value must become small. This, in general, will occur, as is well known. The chief qualification has to do with the behavior of a demand curve constructed under the current interpretation (e.g., *Cc*) for small quantities of *X*. The crucial question is the difference in real income between *P* and *C*. Expenditure on the commodity might be a small fraction of total expenditure at *P;* yet, if the demand curve constructed under the current interpretation were extremely inelastic, not near *C*. In this case the difference in real income might be large.

This qualification is emphasized by Marshall. For example: "If however an amount *b* of the commodity is necessary for existence, *f*(*z*) [*sic*] [ordinate of the demand curve] will be infinite, or at least indefinitely great, for values of *x* less than *b*. We must therefore take life for granted, and estimate separately the total utility of that part of the supply of

larger for Aa than for Cc, it is clear that Marshall's assumption is, if anything, even more necessary on my interpretation of the demand curve than on the current one.[31]

IV. TEXTUAL EVIDENCE ON WHAT MARSHALL REALLY MEANT

Marshall's writings on demand bear on three different problems: (1) the definition of the demand curve—the problem of form; (2) the shape of the demand curve—the problem of content; and (3) the use of the demand curve—the problem of application. In his usual manner Marshall gives precedence to the problem of content and does not explicitly separate his discussion of content from his discussion of form. His definitions are characteristically given parenthetically and implicitly. He went to extreme lengths to present his tools in the context of concrete problems, so that definitions grew out of the uses to be made of them.[32] His discussion of utility and diminishing utility in the chapter of the *Principles* which introduces the concept of a demand curve (Book III, chap. iii, "Gradations of Consumers' Demand") is part of the discussion of content, even though it precedes his definition. It is the means whereby he rationalizes his "one general *law of demand:*—The greater the amount to be sold, the smaller must be the price at which it is offered in order that it may find purchasers."[33] It is not part of his definition of the demand curve.

Similarly, one of the major applications that Marshall made of the demand curve was his analysis of consumer's surplus. This analysis, too, must be distinguished from his definition of the demand curve. Assumptions made in his

the commodity which is in excess of absolute necessaries" (p. 841). See also pp. 133 and 842. $f(z)$ clearly should be $f(x)$, as it is in the first four editions of the *Principles*. See appendix to this paper.

This discussion of the role of the assumption that the commodity absorbs only a small fraction of income throws some light on an issue about which there has been considerable discussion, namely, whether Marshall assumed the marginal utility of money to be roughly constant with respect to a change in price or a change in income. The above analysis suggests that he assumed constancy with respect to a change in income. This is also Hicks's conclusion (*Value and Capital*, p. 40; "Rehabilitation," p. 109). Samuelson denies this and asserts that he assumed constancy with respect to a change in price (see Paul A. Samuelson, "Constancy of the Marginal Utility of Income," in *Studies in Mathematical Economics and Econometrics*, p. 80).

31 The argument can be easily extended to "inferior" goods. The order of the three curves in Fig. 1 is then reversed; the estimates then become too small, instead of too large; but the error under the alternative interpretation remains larger in absolute value than under the current interpretation.

In the terminology used by Hicks in "The Four Consumers' Surpluses," what I have called the consumer's surplus is what Hicks calls the "quantity-compensating variation." The estimate of consumer's surplus derived from the demand curve constructed under my interpretation (the area APH) Hicks calls the "quantity-equivalent variation." The area CDH in Fig. 1, Hicks calls the "price-compensating variation." Hicks's fourth concept, "price-equivalent variation," is not shown directly in Fig. 1. It is obtained by drawing a horizontal line through C. Designate by E the point at which this line cuts Aa. The "price-equivalent variation" is then equal to the area APH minus AEC. These relations can be checked by noting that curve *mep* in Hicks's Fig. 3 is Aa in our Fig. 1; his curve PCM is Cv in our Fig. 1. Further, in comparing the two figures, the part of Hicks's diagram for quantities less than hN should be neglected. That is, his point P is equivalent to our point C, his p to our P. Our Fig. 1 is also equivalent to Fig. 3B in Boulding, "The Concept of Economic Surplus."

32 Cf. J. M. Keynes, *Memorials*, esp. pp. 33–38; see also Guillebaud, *op. cit.*

33 *Principles*, p. 99. Note that on my interpretation this is truly a *general* law, not subject to the exceptions that have been made in recent literature. It depends for its validity only on (*a*) the postulate that consumers can be treated as if they behaved consistently and attempted to maximize some function of the quantity of commodities consumed; (*b*) the observed fact that consumers choose a higher income in preference to a lower, other things the same; and (*c*) the observed fact that consumers do not spend all their income on one commodity. For proof that a demand curve constructed on my interpretation must slope negatively see Slutsky, *op. cit.*, Sec. 8.

discussion of consumer's surplus cannot, without additional evidence, be supposed to apply equally to other applications of the "demand curve."

a) THE CENTRAL PASSAGES IN THE TEXT OF THE "PRINCIPLES"

The central passages in the text of the eighth and final edition of the *Principles* bearing on the other things to be kept the same seem to me to be three: one governing the entire volume, and two essentially parenthetical comments in his discussion of the demand curve:

> We may throughout this volume neglect possible changes in the general purchasing power of money. Thus the price of anything will be taken as representative of its exchange value relatively to things in general [p. 62].
>
> The larger the amount of a thing that a person has the less, other things being equal (i.e. *the purchasing power of money, and the amount of money at his command being equal*), will be the price which he will pay for a little more of it: or in other words his marginal demand price for it diminishes [p. 95; italics added].
>
> The demand prices in our list are those at which various quantities of a thing can be sold in a market *during a given time and under given conditions*. If the conditions vary in any respect the prices will probably require to be changed; and this has constantly to be done when the desire for anything is materially altered by a *variation of custom, or by a cheapening of the supply of a rival commodity, or by the invention of a new one* [p. 100; second set of italics added].

For our purposes the critical part of the second quotation is the italicized parenthesis and, of the third, the second set of italicized phrases.

Though these quotations are taken from the eighth edition of the *Principles*, their substantive content is contained in Marshall's earliest published work on the theory of demand. All except the constancy of the purchasing power of money is in *The Pure Theory of (Domestic) Values*, printed for private circulation in 1879[34] but, according to Keynes, "substantially complete about 1873";[35] and the constancy of the purchasing power of money is in his and Mrs. Marshall's *The Economics of Industry*, published in 1879.[36] The actual wording of the first and third quotations can be traced back to the first edition of the *Principles* (1890), of the second quotation, to the second edition (1891).[37]

[34] Reprinted, together with the companion paper, *The Pure Theory of Foreign Trade*, by the London School of Economics and Political Science (1930).

[35] *Memorials*, p. 23.

[36] This work should not be confused with the condensation of the *Principles*, published, under the same title but with Alfred Marshall as sole author, in 1892.

[37] In all editions of the *Principles* the statement corresponding to the first quotation is in a subsection dealing with the meaning of the word "value." In the first (1890), second (1891), and third (1895) editions, the subsection on "value" is at the end of Book I, "Preliminary Survey," chap. i, "Introduction," and contains the statement: "Throughout the earlier stages of our work it will be best to speak of the exchange value of a thing at any place and time as measured by its price, that is, the amount of money for which it will exchange then and there, and to assume that there is no change in the general purchasing power of money" (p. 9, all three editions). In the first edition this assumption is repeated at the beginning of the chapter on "The Law of Demand" (Book III, chap. ii): "The purchasing power of this money may vary from time to time; but in these early stages of our work we assume it to be constant" (1st ed., p. 151). This repetition was eliminated in later editions, apparently in the process of introducing into the second edition the chapter on "Wants in Relation to Activities." In the fourth edition (1898), the subsection on "value" was split, part remaining at the end of Book I, chap. i, the remainder, including the material on the purchasing power of money, being transferred to end of Book II, "Some Fundamental Notions," chap. ii, "Wealth." The wording was changed to essentially its final form; the only difference is that the first sentence is in the passive voice, reading: "Throughout this volume possible changes in the general purchasing power of money will be neglected" (4th ed., p. 130). In the fifth edition (1907), the rest of the subsection on "value" was transferred to the end of Book II, chap. ii, and the quotation revised to its present

b) THE BEARING OF THESE PASSAGES ON THE TWO INTERPRETATIONS

The "other things" listed in the three passages cited above are as follows:

1. "Purchasing power of money"
2. "Amount of money at his command"
3. "Custom"
4. Price of "a rival commodity" (to avoid "cheapening of the supply of a rival commodity")

form; even the page number is the same in the fifth and eighth editions (p. 62).

In both editions of *The Economics of Industry*, subsection 4 in Book II, "Normal Value," chap. i, "Definitions. Law of Demand," contains essentially the same material as the subsection on "value" in the *Principles* referred to in the preceding paragraph, including the following statement: "But while examining the theory of Normal value we shall, for convenience, assume that the purchasing power of money remains unchanged. So that a rise or fall in the price of a thing will always mean a rise or fall in its general purchasing power or exchange value" (pp. 68–69). No corresponding statement appears in *The Pure Theory.*

The italicized parenthesis in the second quotation is identical in the second and all later editions of the *Principles*. The remainder of the quotation was worded as follows in the second edition: "An increase in the amount of a thing that a person has will, other things being equal . . . diminish his Marginal Demand-price for it" (p. 152). In the third edition, the words "marginal" and "demand" were not capitalized, and the hyphen was eliminated after "Demand" (p. 170). In the fourth edition the end of the statement was expanded to read, "diminish the price which he will pay for a little more of it: or in other words diminishes his magrinal demand price for it" (pp. 169–70). In the fifth edition the quotation takes its present form, except for the addition of a comma, even the page number being the same as in the eighth edition (p. 95). In all editions from the second on, the indicated quotations are in Book III, chap. iii, the chapter first introducing the demand curve. This chapter is entitled "The Law of Demand" in the second and third editions, "Gradations of Demand" in the fourth, and "Gradations of Consumers' Demand" in the fifth and later editions.

The absence of the statement from the first edition reflects a difference in exposition, not in substance. As noted above, an explicit statement that the purchasing power of money is assumed constant appears in the chapter on "The Law of Demand" in the first edition. In all editions this chapter contains a statement covering the second part of the italicized parenthesis, which is worded as follows in the first edition: "Every increase in his resources increases the price which he is willing to pay for any given pleasure. And in the same way every diminution of his resources increases the marginal utility of money to him, and diminishes the price that he is willing to pay for any pleasure" (p. 156). The only change in this statement in later editions was the substitution of "benefit" for "pleasure" (8th ed., p. 96).

The Economics of Industry also contains a statement anticipating the second part of the italicized parenthesis: "The price which he is willing to pay for a thing depends not only on its utility to him but also on *his means;* that is, the amount of money or general purchasing power at his disposal" (p. 70).

In all editions of the *Principles* the statement corresponding to the third quotation is in the final subsection of the chapter first introducing the demand curve (1st ed., Book III, chap. ii; in later editions, Book III, chap. iii). In the first edition it reads: "It must be remembered that the demand schedule gives the prices at which various quantities of a thing can be sold in a market during a given time and under given conditions. If the conditions vary in any respect the figures of the schedule will probably require to be changed. One condition which it is especially important to watch is the price of rival commodities, that is, of commodities which can be used as substitutes for it" (p. 160). A footnote is attached to the word "rival," the first sentence of which reads: "Or to use Jevons' phrase (*Theory of Political Economy*, Ch. IV), commodities that are nearly 'equivalent' " (1st ed., p. 160, n. 2).

The part of the second sentence of the third quotation following the semicolon assumed its final form in the second edition (p. 157), the footnote reference to Jevons being dropped. The rest of the quotation is the same in the second and third editions as in the first and assumes its final form in the fourth (p. 174). The change made in the second sentence from the first to the second edition argues that the list was not intended to be exhaustive, but illustrative. No change in substance is involved (see 1st ed., p. 155). In all editions the quoted statement is followed by the example of tea and coffee to illustrate the necessity of assuming the prices of rival commodities to be known; in the second edition the example of gas and electricity was added, and in the third edition the example of different varieties of tea. The passage itself, the changes in it, and the examples all indicate that Marshall considered the price of "rival" commodities particularly important. The examples, together with the footnote in the first edition, make it clear that he meant "close" rivals.

For a statement in the *Pure Theory* covering the substance of these quotations, except the constancy of the purchasing power of money, see n. 38, below.

5. Range of rival commodities available (to avoid "invention of a new one")[38]

1. *The current interpretation.*—The current interpretation of Marshall's demand curve treats item 2 as referring to the money income of the group of purchasers to whom the demand curve relates, item 3 to their tastes and preferences, and item 4 to the price of every other commodity rather than of *rival* commodities alone. It ignores entirely items 1 and 5.

Item 2 is not entirely unambiguous. It might be interpreted as referring to the cash balances of the purchasers or to their wealth instead of, or in addition to, their income. On the whole, the most reasonable course seems to be to interpret it as referring to both income and wealth,[39] particularly since wealth qualifies for the list of "other things" by virtue of its possible importance as a factor affecting consumption. This expansion of the current interpretation does not alter it materially; it merely transfers "wealth" from the category of "other things" implicitly supposed to be the same to the list of things mentioned explicitly.

[38] The adequacy of this list as a summary of Marshall's views may be checked by comparing it with two others in Marshall's writings. In *The Pure Theory of (Domestic) Values,* he writes: "The periods with which we are concerned . . . are sufficiently long to eliminate . . . casual disturbances. . . . But they are sufficiently short to exclude fundamental changes in the circumstances of demand and in those of supply. On the side of demand for the ware in question it is requisite that the periods should not include (i) any very great change in the prosperity and purchasing power of the community; (ii) any important changes in the fashions which affect the use of the ware; (iii) the invention or the great cheapening of any other ware which comes to be used largely as a substitute for it; (iv) the deficiency of the supply of any ware for which the ware in question may be used as a substitute, whether this deficiency be occasioned by bad harvests, by war, or by the imposition of customs or excise taxes; (v) a sudden large requirement for the commodity, as e.g. for ropes in the breaking out of a maritime war; (vi) the discovery of new means of utilizing the ware, or the opening up of important markets in which it can be sold" (p. 15).

Item i in this list presumably corresponds with 2 in my list; ii corresponds with 3, and iii and iv with 4 and 5, iii excluding a fall in the price of a rival commodity and iv a rise. Items v and the first part of vi would seem to be contained in 3 and largely redundant with ii. The rest of vi is presumably covered by the restriction of the discussion to a demand curve for a particular market.

The other list is in Marshall's discussion in the *Principles* of the difficulties of the statistical study of demand (Book III, chap. iv), where he writes: "Other things seldom are equal in fact over periods of time sufficiently long for the collection of full and trustworthy statistics. . . . To begin with, [*a*] the purchasing power of money is continually changing. . . . Next come the changes in [*b*] the general prosperity and in the total purchasing power at the disposal of the community at large. . . . Next come the changes due to [*c*] the gradual growth of population and wealth. . . . Next, allowance must be made for changes in [*d*] fashion, and taste and habit, for [*e*] the opening out of new uses of a commodity, for [*f*] the discovery or improvement or cheapening of other things that can be applied to the same uses with it" (*Principles,* pp. 109–10; letters in brackets added). This statement dates from the first edition (pp. 170–71); only trivial editorial changes were made in later editions.

Item *a* in this list corresponds with 1 in my list; *b* with 2; *d* and presumably *e* with 3; and *f* with 4 and 5. Item *c* is presumably in part covered by restriction of the discussion to a demand curve for a particular market; in part it contains an item that may deserve to be added to the list, namely, "wealth." The wording of *f* is ambiguous, since it could refer to substitutes for the good in question, to complements, or to both. The subsequent text and the examples cited make it clear that it refers to substitutes; one example, of petroleum and petroleum lamps, itself ambiguously worded, suggests that it may refer to complements as well.

[39] In the quotations from Book III, chap. iv, in the preceding footnote, "wealth" is mentioned explicitly, though separately from "general prosperity" and "total purchasing power." See also the quotations in the fourth and fifth paragraphs of n. 37. Marshall repeatedly refers to "rich" and "poor" rather than to high- and low-income people (e.g., pp. 19, 95, 98). However, in an illustrative case, a rich man and a poor man are identified by their annual incomes (p. 19). And in Book III, chap. vi, he remarks: "We have throughout this and preceding chapters spoken of the rich, the middle classes and the poor as having respectively large, medium and small incomes—not possessions" (p. 134).

Item 3 requires no discussion, since the only reasonable interpretation of it is that it refers to tastes and preferences.[40]

The important defect of the current interpretation is its treatment of item 4, which is, in turn, responsible for the neglect of items 1 and 5. "Rival commodity" is replaced by, or read to mean, "any other commodity," and hence item 4 is taken to mean that the price of every other commodity is to be supposed the same. For example, Henry Schultz says, as if it were obvious and without citing any statements of Marshall: "Marshall also assumes, in giving definite form to the law of demand for any one commodity, that the prices of all other commodities remain constant."[41] Numerous other statements to the same effect could be cited. It is an amusing commentary on our capacity for self-delusion that the only references to Marshall for support that I have seen are to the page containing the third quotation in Section IV*a* above—the source of the words quoted in item 4.[42] The first set of italicized words in that quotation are the only words on the page even remotely supporting the substitution of "any other" for rival. The specific examples that follow the quotation—tea and coffee, gas and electric lighting, different varieties of tea, beef and mutton—make it clear that Marshall was using the word "rival" in a narrow sense and not in that broad sense in which it may be said that all commodities are "rivals" for the consumer's income.[43] Whatever the merits of the current interpretation, it cannot be found explicitly in Marshall.

The interpretation of item 4 as referring to all other commodities makes item 5 unnecessary and contradicts item 1. Item 5 is unnecessary because the introduction of a new commodity is equivalent to a decline in its price from infinity to a finite amount; hence is ruled out if the price of every other commodity is to be unchanged. Item 1 is contradicted because, if all other prices are unchanged, the purchasing power of money will be lower, the higher the price of the commodity in question. The purchasing power of money cannot, therefore, be the same for all points on the demand curve.

The redundancy of item 5 on this interpretation of item 4 is unimportant; this item is in a list that is illustrative rather than exhaustive, and there is no reason why Marshall should have scru-

[40] See n. 38, above. In discussing the law of diminishing marginal utility, Marshall says: "We do not suppose time to be allowed for any alteration in the character or tastes of the man himself" (p. 94).

[41] *Op. cit.*, p. 53. Immediately after making this statement he quotes from Edgeworth's article on "Demand Curves" cited in n. 5, above, not as evidence for the validity of his interpretation of Marshall but rather as an indication of the difficulties that it raises.

[42] Joan Robinson states without citation: "Marshall instructs us to draw up a demand schedule on the assumption that the prices of all other things are fixed" (*The Economics of Imperfect Competition* [London: Macmillan & Co., Ltd., 1934], p. 20). Paul Samuelson says, also without citation: "All other prices and income are held constant by *ceteris paribus* assumptions" in the "Marshallian partial equilibrium demand functions" (*Foundations of Economic Analysis* [Cambridge: Harvard University Press, 1947], p. 97). In an unpublished exposition of income and substitution effects prepared for class use about 1939, I stated, also without citation: "There is no question but that it [the Marshallian demand curve] was not intended to be . . . interpreted" as "showing the effect of *compensated* variations in price." Similar statements, all citing p. 100 of the *Principles* as authority, are made by Robert Triffin, *Monopolistic Competition and General Equilibrium Theory* (Cambridge: Harvard University Press, 1940), p. 44; Ruby Turner Norris, *The Theory of Consumer's Demand* (New Haven: Yale University Press, 1941), p. 82; and Weintraub, *op. cit.*, p. 539.

[43] If any doubt remains, it is removed by the footnote in the first edition attached to the word "rival" referring to Jevons' phrase "commodities that are nearly 'equivalent'" (see n. 37, above).

pulously avoided overlapping. The logical inconsistency between items 1 and 4 cannot, however, be dismissed so lightly. Retention of the current interpretation requires either that item 1 be eliminated, on the grounds that the quotations on which it is based are exceptional and peripheral, or that Marshall be convicted of logical inconsistency on a fundamental point in his theory of demand.[44] Item 1 cannot, I think, be eliminated. The constancy of the purchasing power of money is clearly fundamental in Marshall's thought, probably more fundamental than any other item on our list.[45]

One excuse for retaining the current interpretation of Marshall, despite the logical inconsistency that it introduces, is to suppose that Marshall intended to restrict the use of his demand curve to commodities that account for only a small fraction of total expenditures. A change in the price of such a commodity would have only a small effect on the purchasing power of money, and it could be argued that Marshall neglected it as a "second-order effect." On this rationalization, item 1 becomes redundant, but, in the limit, not logically inconsistent with an item 4 taken to refer to all other commodities.

I do not believe that Marshall intended to restrict the use of the demand curve to commodities accounting for only a small fraction of total expenditure. He speaks of a demand curve for wheat (p. 106), for houseroom (p. 107), and for other commodities that he cannot have regarded as unimportant. He first explicitly introduces the restriction to unimportant commodities in connection with his discussion of consumer's surplus, which comes well after the initial discussion of the demand curve—in the eighth edition, three chapters later; and the restriction is repeated at most points at which the argument depends on it. At one point the restriction is said to be "generally," not universally, justifiable. This evidence may not be conclusive but it certainly establishes a strong presumption that Marshall did not intend the restriction to carry over to all uses of the demand curve.[46]

[44] The extent to which the current interpretation dominates economic thought could not be more strikingly illustrated than by the fact that so acute an economic theorist as J. R. Hicks can write: "No doubt it [the constancy of the marginal utility of money] was . . . associated in his [Marshall's] mind with the assumption of a constant value of money (constant prices of other consumers' goods than the one, or sometimes ones, in question)" ("The Rehabilitation of Consumers' Surplus," p. 109). Hicks here treats constancy of all other prices as an alternative statement of item 1, when, in fact, it is logically inconsistent with item 1.

[45] See nn. 37 and 38, above. Note also that constancy of the purchasing power of money was a standard assumption of economic theory long before Marshall's day. It was made by Ricardo in his price theory, and Marshall refers to Cournot's discussion of the reasons for making this assumption (see Marshall, *Principles*, pp. ix, 62; Augustin Cournot, *Researches into the Mathematical Principles of the Theory of Wealth* [*1838*], Nathaniel Bacon translation [New York: Macmillan Co., 1897], p. 26).

[46] In connection with the discussion of consumer's surplus and the assumption of a constant marginal utility of money implicit in that discussion, Marshall says: "The assumption . . . underlies our whole reasoning, that the expenditure on any one thing . . . is only a small part of his whole expenditure" (p. 842). The first sentence of the paragraph from which this quotation is taken explicitly limits it to "the discussion of consumers' surplus" (p. 842). The quotation is followed by a cross-reference to the part of Marshall's famous analysis of the process by which equilibrium is reached in a corn-market in which he discusses "the latent assumption, that the dealers' willingness to spend money is nearly constant throughout" (p. 334). "This assumption," he says, "is justifiable with regard to most of the market dealings with which we are practically concerned. When a person buys anything for his own consumption, he generally spends on it a small part of his total resources" (p. 335).

Nowhere in Book III, chap. iii, does Marshall explicitly restrict his discussion to unimportant commodities. The one statement in that chapter that might be regarded as so restricting the dis-

It should be noted that Marshall's explicit introduction of the restriction to unimportant commodities has no bearing on the relative validity of the two interpretations of his demand curve. The restriction is necessary on either of the two interpretations at each point at which Marshall explicitly makes it. So the restriction cannot be regarded as called for by the inconsistency of items 1 and 4 on the current interpretation of 4.

2. *The alternative interpretation.*—My interpretation of the Marshallian demand curve resolves almost all the difficulties that plague the current interpretation, since it accepts at face value the five "other things" listed at the beginning of Section IV*b*. Marshall's words can be taken to mean what they say without uncomfortable stretching, and there is no logical inconsistency in the constancy of both item 1, the purchasing power of money, and item 4, the prices of rival commodities. Item 5, the range of rival commodities available, is still redundant, since, if "rival" has the same meaning in 4 and 5, the invention of a new rival commodity means a change in its price from infinity to a finite value.

My interpretation explains also the precise wording of the second quotation in Section IV*a*, which reads, in part: "The larger the amount of a thing that a person has the less . . . will be the price which he will pay for a little more of it." This is a curious form of phrasing on the current interpretation. Why emphasize the amount of a thing that a person has and the marginal expenditure that he can be induced to make rather than the amount he purchases and the average price he pays? On my interpretation, this phrasing follows directly from the argument of Section I*c* above (and Note II of Marshall's Mathematical Appendix), according to which a demand curve constructed on my interpretation can be viewed as showing the maximum price per unit that a person can be induced to pay for successive increments of the commodity.

One minor puzzle remains on my interpretation. Why does Marshall restrict his attention to "rival" commodities? Why not to "closely related" commodities, whether rivals or complements? His use of the word "rivals" in discussing the demand curve is apparently not a mere verbal accident. He uses the word repeatedly; almost all his examples deal with the effect of, or through, substitutes. I have no very good answer to this puzzle; the only one that seems at all persuasive is that he thought the concept of "joint demand" and the associated analytical apparatus better suited to problems involving complementary goods.[47]

My interpretation follows so directly

cussion is the statement on p. 95 that "the marginal utility of money to him is a fixed quantity." But the context argues and Note II in the Mathematical Appendix demonstrates that this is merely a verbal statement of an identity (if income is unchanged, so is marginal utility of money), and thus is not really relevant to the issue. In the eighth edition, Note II is referred to only at the end of the subsection following the paragraph containing the passage quoted. However, in the first edition, the corresponding note (Note III) is referred to at the end of the paragraph containing the passage quoted, and hence clearly covers it (pp. 155–56, 737–38).

The above quotations are essentially unchanged from the first edition on. The restriction to unimportant commodities is, however, mentioned neither in Marshall and Marshall, *Economics of Industry*, nor in the *Pure Theory*.

[47] In Note VII of the Mathematical Appendix, Marshall qualifies a suggested formula for combining consumer's surplus from different commodities by saying: "if we could find a plan for grouping together in one common demand curve all those things which satisfy the same wants, and are rivals; and also for every group of things of which the services are complementary (see Book V, chap. vi) . . ." (p. 842). Book V, chap. vi, contains the discussion of joint demand. The qualification quoted appears first in the third edition.

from Marshall's words that further defense of it would be unnecessary were it not for the unquestioned dominance of the current interpretation in the economic thinking and writing of the past half-century. This circumstance explains the presentation of additional textual evidence bearing on the validity of the alternative interpretation.

c) COUNTEREVIDENCE FROM THE TEXT OF THE "PRINCIPLES"

I have been able to find only one passage in the text of the eighth edition of the *Principles* that is in any way inconsistent with my interpretation of Marshall. This is the celebrated passage, adverted to above, which deals with the so-called "Giffen phenomenon" and which was first introduced in the third edition:

> For instance, as Sir R. Giffen has pointed out, a rise in the price of bread makes so large a drain on the resources of the *poorer labouring families* and raises so much the marginal utility of money to them, that they are forced to curtail their consumption of meat and the more expensive farinaceous foods: and bread being still the cheapest food which they can get and will take, they consume more, and not less of it [p. 132; italics added].

This passage clearly offsets an income effect against a substitution effect, whereas, on my interpretation of Marshall, real income is the same at all points on the demand curve, so there is no "income effect" (see Sec. II*b*, above). The passage is thus in the spirit of the current interpretation. Yet the words I have italicized indicate that it does not necessarily contradict my interpretation of Marshall. The purchasing power of money and the real income of the community at large may remain constant; yet the real income of a particular group in the community that has a special consumption pattern may be adversely affected by the rise in the price of a particular commodity.[48]

d) THE EVIDENCE OF THE MATHEMATICAL APPENDIX

The Mathematical Appendix to the *Principles* confirms and extends the evidence already presented from the text of the *Principles* and from Marshall's other writings. Note II (III in the first edition) explicitly derives a relation between price and quantity demanded that is identical with a demand curve on my interpretation, in which real income is kept constant by compensating variations in money income. Indeed, my derivation of such a demand curve in Section I*c* above is a verbal paraphrase of Marshall's mathematics. Marshall does not explicitly say that the relation he derives is a demand curve, but Note II is attached to his initial discussion of the demand curve (Book III, chap. iii, in the eighth edition) and is given as the authority for statements made about the demand curve; hence there can be no doubt that it presents the pure theory of his demand curve.

In all editions of the *Principles* Note VI, attached to Marshall's discussion of consumer's surplus, contains a sentence that is definitely wrong on the current interpretation of his demand curve but correct on my interpretation.

Finally, a sentence added to Note VI in the third edition, referred to in the text of the *Principles* in connection with the material added on the Giffen phenomenon, contains an implicit mathematical proposition that is correct on the current interpretation but incorrect on my interpretation. The mathematical point in question is considerably more

[48] See Marshall's explicit discussion of, and emphasis on, this possibility in "Remedies for Fluctuations of General Prices" (1887), *Memorials*, p. 207.

subtle than those referred to in the two preceding paragraphs, so it cannot be given the same weight.

These two notes are examined in some detail in the appendix to this paper, to which the reader is referred for proof of the above statements.

e) A SYNTHESIS OF THE EVIDENCE

There are two differences between the current interpretation of Marshall's demand curve and my interpretation: (1) On the current interpretation, account is taken of the price of each other commodity individually; on my interpretation, only of the average price of all commodities other than the one in question and its close rivals. (2) On the current interpretation, real income varies along the demand curve with the price of the good in question; on my interpretation, real income is constant along the demand curve.

On the first, and less important, point, it is mathematically convenient to consider each other price separately, and this procedure might well have recommended itself to the writer of mathematical Notes XIV and XXI. On the other hand, it is impossible to consider each price separately in a practical analysis; so the use of an average price would clearly have recommended itself to the writer of the text of the *Principles* and is entirely in the spirit of Marshall's explicit methodological statements (see Sec. II*a*, above). Marshall does not discuss this point explicitly; hence the textual evidence is all indirect.

On the second and basic point of difference the evidence leaves little room for doubt: Marshall's theory of demand, in the form in which it is presented in the first edition of the *Principles*, is explicitly based on constancy of real income along the demand curve. This interpretation not only is consistent with both the letter and the spirit of the entire text of the first edition of the *Principles* but is almost conclusively established by the evidence cited above from two notes in the Mathematical Appendix of the first edition. In his determined effort to be persuasive and to make his work accessible to educated laymen, Marshall might well have been vague in his verbal presentation, though even there it seems unlikely that he would have been logically inconsistent. It is hardly credible that he would have been not merely vague but downright wrong on simple mathematical points stated in mathematical language, especially since the mathematical points in question could hardly even have arisen if he had been explicitly using the current interpretation of the demand curve.

I am inclined to believe, however, that by the time Marshall made the revisions incorporated in the third edition of the *Principles*—presumably between 1891, when the second edition appeared, and 1895, when the third edition appeared—he had himself been influenced by the current interpretation, probably without realizing that it was different from his own. This conjecture is based primarily on the two passages cited above as inconsistent with my interpretation: the passage dealing with the Giffen phenomenon and the last sentence of Note VI of the Mathematical Appendix. Both were added in the third edition—and these are the only passages I have been able to find in any edition of the *Principles* that fit the current interpretation better than they fit my interpretation. Further, both show some evidence of confusion about the fine points of his theory of demand (see last paragraph of appendix to this paper).

The hypothesis that Marshall did not

recognize the contradiction between the current interpretation and his earlier work would hardly be tenable if the lapse of time between the work incorporated in the first and the third editions of the *Principles* were as short as between their publication. But, as already noted, this is not the case. The essence of both his theory of demand and his analysis of consumer's surplus is contained in the *Pure Theory of Domestic Values*, which, though not printed until 1879, "must have been substantially complete about 1873."[49] The one important point in the theory of demand that is not in the *Pure Theory*—explicit mention of constancy of the purchasing power of money—is in the 1879 *Economics of Industry*. The only important addition in the *Principles* is the concept of "elasticity of demand"; and even this concept, which is not relevant to the present problem, was worked out in 1881–82.[50] No important substantive changes were made in the theory of demand in successive editions of the *Principles*, though the exposition was amplified and rearranged, the wording changed in detail, and some examples modified. The only important change of substance introduced into the discussion of consumer's surplus (in the third edition) was in connection with a point that has no bearing on the present issue.[51]

Marshall himself writes: "My main position as to the theory of value and distribution was practically completed in the years 1867 to 1870. . . . By this time [from the context, 1874] I had practically completed the whole of the substance of my Mathematical Appendix."[52] Thus Marshall appears to have completed his fundamental work on the theory of demand in the early 1870's and to have made no important substantive changes thereafter. The third edition appeared some twenty or more years later—an ample lapse of time for the precise details of an essentially mathematical analysis to have become vague and their difference from a superficially similar set of details to pass unnoticed. This seems especially plausible in view of the acceptance of the current interpretation by others and the absence of controversy about it.

[49] Keynes, *Memorials*, p. 23.

[50] *Ibid.*, p. 39, n. 3.

[51] This change does not reflect favorably on Marshall's willingness to admit error. The first edition states: "Subject to these corrections then we may regard the aggregate of the money measures of the total utility of wealth as a fair measure of that part of the happiness which is dependent on wealth" (pp. 179–80), the corrections referred to being for "differences in the wealth of different purchasers" (p. 178) and "elements of collective wealth which are apt to be overlooked" (p. 179). A footnote to the first quotation refers to mathematical Note VII, in which he says, subject to the same two qualifications: "if a_1, a_2, a_3 . . . be the amounts consumed of the several commodities of which b_1, b_2, b_3 . . . are necessary for existence, if $y = f_1(x)$, $y = f_2(x)$, $y = f_3(x)$ . . . be the equations to their demand curves . . . , then the total utility of his wealth, subsistence being taken for granted, is represented by

$$\sum \int_b^a f(x)dx\text{"}$$

(1st ed., p. 741).

The eighth edition does not contain the first statement. Instead, the text contains an explicit warning against adding consumer's surpluses for different commodities, and a footnote says: "Some ambiguous phrases in earlier editions appear to have suggested to some readers the opposite opinion" (p. 131). Note VII in the Mathematical Appendix was modified by replacing "his wealth" by "income" and, of more importance, "is represented" by "might be represented" and by adding after the formula the significant qualification, "if we could find a plan for grouping together in one common demand curve all those things which satisfy the same wants, and are rivals; and also for every group of things of which the services are complementary. . . . But we cannot do this; and therefore the formula remains a mere general expression, having no practical application" (p. 842). As noted, these changes date from the third edition.

[52] Letter to J. B. Clark, *Memorials*, p. 416.

Further circumstantial evidence that Marshall did not recognize the contradiction between the current interpretation and his earlier work is provided by the apparent absence of any explicit discussion of the question in the writings of either Marshall or the more prominent of his students or even of any comments that could reasonably be interpreted as implying recognition of the existence of alternative interpretations of the demand curve. Yet, as noted earlier (n. 5), the current interpretation is explicitly given by Edgeworth as early as 1894 in an article on "Demand Curves" in *Palgrave's Dictionary of Political Economy* that Marshall must be presumed to have read. Though the assumption of constant prices of commodities other than the one in question is not explicitly attributed to Marshall, most of the article is based on Marshall; and there is no suggestion that this assumption does not apply to Marshall's demand curve. Further, Walras' definition of the demand curve, which presumably influenced Edgeworth, is identical with the current interpretation of Marshall's demand curve, and Marshall refers to Walras several times in the first edition of the *Principles*, though it seems clear that Marshall developed his theory of demand independently of Walras.[53] So Marshall must have been exposed to a definition of the demand curve corresponding to the current interpretation at a time when he was still making substantial revisions in the *Principles*. If he had recognized that this interpretation was incorrect, would he not have taken the opportunity to clarify his statements in later editions?

[53] *Principles* (1st ed.), pp. xi, xii, 425; Keynes, *Memorials*, pp. 19–24; Marshall's letter to J. B. Clark, *ibid.*, pp. 416–18.

V. ALTERNATIVE CONCEPTIONS OF ECONOMIC THEORY

There remains the mystery how the current interpretation of Marshall's demand curve gained such unquestioned dominance at so early a date and retained it so long, not only as an interpretation of Marshall, but also as "the" definition of "the" demand curve.

One obvious explanation is that mathematical economists were more likely than others to state explicitly and precisely their assumptions about the behavior of other prices; that mathematical economists were likely to be familiar with Walras' independent definition and to take it as a point of departure; and that, in any event, the current interpretation is mathematically more convenient. Other economists, it could be argued, followed the lead of the mathematical economists, and thus the current interpretation was taken for granted and accepted without question.

This explanation seems to me a significant part of the answer; however, I do not believe that it is the entire answer. If, as I have argued above, my interpretation of Marshall is more useful for most practical problems, why has its use been so rarely proposed; why has there been no general feeling of dissatisfaction with the current interpretation? There must, it would seem, be something about the role that has been assigned to economic theory that has made the current interpretation acceptable.

I am inclined to believe that this is, in fact, the case; that, by slow and gradual steps, the role assigned to economic theory has altered in the course of time until today we assign a substantially different role to theory than Marshall did. We curtsy to Marshall, but we walk with Walras.

The distinction commonly drawn between Marshall and Walras is that Marshall dealt with "partial equilibrium," Walras with "general equilibrium." This distinction is, I believe, false and unimportant. Marshall and Walras alike dealt with general equilibrium; partial equilibrium analysis as usually conceived is but a special kind of general equilibrium analysis—unless, indeed, partial equilibrium analysis is taken to mean erroneous general equilibrium analysis. Marshall wrote to J. B. Clark in 1908: "My whole life has been and will be given to presenting in realistic form as much as I can of my Note XXI."[54] Note XXI, essentially unchanged from the first edition of the *Principles* to the last, presents a system of equations of general equilibrium. It ends with the sentence: "Thus, however complex the problem may become, we can see that it is theoretically determinate, because the number of unknowns is always exactly equal to the number of equations which we obtain."[55] The explanation given above why Marshall might have decided to hold the purchasing power of money constant was entirely in terms of constructing the demand curve so that it would be consistent with general equilibrium in those parts of the system not under direct study.

The important distinction between the conceptions of economic theory implicit in Marshall and Walras lies in the purpose for which the theory is constructed and used. To Marshall—to repeat an expression quoted earlier—economic theory is "an engine for the discovery of concrete truth." The "economic organon" introduces "systematic and organized methods of reasoning." Marshall wrote:

> Facts by themselves are silent. . . . The most reckless and treacherous of all theorists is he who professes to let facts and figures speak for themselves, who keeps in the background the part he has played, perhaps unconsciously, in selecting and grouping them, and in suggesting the argument *post hoc ergo propter hoc*. . . . The economist . . . must be suspicious of any direct light that the past is said to throw on problems of the present. He must stand fast by the more laborious plan of interrogating facts in order to learn the manner of action of causes singly and in combination, applying this knowledge to build up the organon of economic theory, and then making use of the aid of the organon in dealing with the economic side of social problems.[56]

Economic theory, in this view, has two intermingled roles: to provide "systematic and organized methods of reasoning" about economic problems; to provide a body of substantive hypotheses, based on factual evidence, about the "manner of action of causes." In both roles the test of the theory is its value in explaining facts, in predicting the consequences of changes in the economic environment. Abstractness, generality, mathematical elegance—these are all secondary, themselves to be judged by the test of application. The counting of equations and unknowns is a check on the completeness of reasoning, the beginning of analysis, not an end in itself.

Doubtless, most modern economic theorists would accept these general statements of the objectives of economic theory. But our work belies our professions. Abstractness, generality, and mathematical elegance have in some measure become ends in themselves, criteria by which to judge economic theory. Facts are to be described, not explained. Theory is to be tested by the accuracy of its "assumptions" as photographic descrip-

54 *Memorials*, p. 417.

55 *Principles*, p. 856. This note was numbered XX in the first edition.

56 The quotations are all taken from Marshall, "The Present Position of Economics" (1885), *Memorials*, pp. 159, 161, 164, 166, 168, 171.

tions of reality, not by the correctness of the predictions that can be derived from it. From this viewpoint the current interpretation of the demand curve is clearly the better. It is more general and elegant to include the price of every commodity in the universe in the demand function rather than the average price of a residual group. Any price may affect any other, so a demand equation including every price is a more accurate photographic description. Of course, it cannot be used in discovering "concrete truth"; it contains no empirical generalization that is capable of being contradicted—but these are Marshallian objections. From the "Walrasian" viewpoint, to take one other example from recent developments in economic theory, it is a gain to eliminate the concept of an "industry," to take the individual firm as the unit of analysis, to treat each firm as a monopoly, to confine all analysis to either the economics of the individual firm or to a general equilibrium analysis of the economy as a whole.[57] From the Marshallian viewpoint this logical terminus of monopolistic competition analysis is a blind alley. Its categories are rigid, determined not by the problem at hand but by mathematical considerations. It yields no predictions, summarizes no empirical generalizations, provides no useful framework of analysis.

Of course, it would be an overstatement to characterize all modern economic theory as "Walrasian" in this sense. For example, Keynes's theory of employment, whatever its merits or demerits on other grounds, is Marshallian in method. It is a general equilibrium theory containing important empirical content and constructed to facilitate meaningful prediction. On the other hand, much recent work based on Keynes's theory of employment is Walrasian.[58]

VI. CONCLUSION

Modern economic theory typically defines the demand curve as showing the relation between the quantity of a commodity demanded and its price for given tastes, money income, and prices of other commodities. This definition has also been uniformly accepted as a correct interpretation of the demand curve defined and used by Alfred Marshall in his *Principles of Economics*. Rarely has the view been expressed that a different definition would be preferable.

Despite its unquestioned acceptance for over half a century, this interpretation of Marshall is, in my view, wrong. Marshall's early writings, the text of the *Principles*, and, even more definitely, the Mathematical Appendix provide almost conclusive proof that Marshall's demand curve differs in two respects from the one commonly used and attributed to him: first, commodities other than the one in question and its close rivals are treated as a group rather than individually, and only their average price is explicitly taken into account; second, and far more important, real income is considered the same at all points on the demand curve, whereas constant money income and other prices imply a higher real income, the lower the price of the commodity in question. Two variants of Marshall's demand curve can be distinguished: one, employed in the text of the *Principles*, uses variations in the prices of other commodities to compensate for variations in the price of the commodity in question and thereby keeps the purchasing power of money constant; the other, employed in the Mathematical

[57] See Triffin, *op. cit.*, pp. 188–89.

[58] O. Lange, *Price Flexibility and Employment* (Bloomington, Ind.: Principia Press, 1944), is perhaps as good an example as any.

Appendix, uses variations in money income to compensate for variations in the price of the commodity in question.

The only textual evidence that conflicts with this interpretation is a passage in the text and a related sentence in the Mathematical Appendix that were added to the third edition of the *Principles*. The inconsistency of these with the rest of the *Principles* can be explained by the hypothesis that Marshall himself was after a point influenced by the current interpretation of the demand curve without recognizing its inconsistency with his earlier work. Some circumstantial evidence also supports this hypothesis.

The alternative interpretation of the demand curve not only is faithful to both the letter and the spirit of Marshall's work but also is more useful for the analysis of concrete problems than is the demand curve commonly employed. The acceptance of a less useful definition seems to me to be a consequence of a changed conception of the role of theory in economic analysis. The current interpretation of the demand curve is Walrasian; and so is current economic theory in general.

APPENDIX ON TWO NOTES IN THE MATHEMATICAL APPENDIX TO THE *PRINCIPLES*

I. NOTE II OF THE EIGHTH EDITION

This note is numbered III in the first edition of the *Principles*, II in the rest. In the first edition the relevant parts are worded as follows (pp. 737–38):

"If m is the amount of money or general purchasing power at a person's disposal at any time, and μ represents its total utility to him, then $d\mu/dm$ represents the marginal utility of money to him.

"If p is the price which he is just willing to pay for an amount x of the commodity which gives him a total pleasure u, then

$$\frac{d\mu}{dm}\Delta p = \Delta u\ ; \quad \text{and} \quad \frac{d\mu}{dm}\frac{dp}{dx} = \frac{du}{dx} \ldots.$$

"Every increase in his means diminishes the marginal utility of money to him; . . . .

"Therefore, du/dx, the marginal utility to him of an amount x of a commodity remaining unchanged, an increase in his means . . . increases dp/dx, that is, the rate at which he is willing to pay for further supplies of it. Treating u as a variable, that is to say, allowing for possible variations in the person's liking for the commodity in question, we may regard dp/dx as a function of m, u, and x. . . ."

The wording in the eighth edition is identical except that "marginal utility of money" is replaced by "marginal degree of utility of money" and that "du/dx" and the words "Treating u . . . in question" are omitted from the last paragraph quoted (pp. 838–39). The changes were first made in the third edition.

In the second sentence of this note, the word "price" is to be interpreted as "total amount" not as "price per unit." This is clear from the context and is demonstrated by the equation that follows and the designation of dp/dx as "the rate at which he is willing to pay for further supplies of it." The words "just willing" in the second sentence and the equations that follow demonstrate that p is the maximum amount he can pay for an amount x and have the same utility as if he had none of the commodity. Thus Marshall is describing a process like that outlined in Section I*c* of this paper, whereby the maximum possible amount is extracted from the individual for each successive increment of the commodity, the individual retaining the same "real income," that is, remaining on the same indifference curve, throughout the process.

The last sentence quoted shows that u is to be regarded as a parameter to allow for changes in tastes. The rest of that sentence simply describes a function like that obtained by eliminating y' from equations (5) and (6) of note 6 of this paper. The parameter m in Marshall's function takes the place of U_o in our footnote, since dp/dx is still to be regarded as the price per unit paid for an additional increment of the commodity rather than as the price per unit at which any amount can be purchased. In consequence, no explicit statement is needed as yet about the compensating variations in income that are implicit in Marshall's analysis.

The word "demand" does not appear in this note. But the note is attached to the chapter in the *Principles* in which Marshall first introduces the demand curve (Book III, chap. ii, in the first edition; Book III, chap. iii, in later editions) and is cited as proof of statements about the demand curve; hence there can be no doubt that the "function" mentioned in the last sentence quoted is the counterpart of Marshall's demand curve.

I have been able to construct no interpretation of this note that would render it consistent with the current interpretation of Marshall's demand curve.

2. NOTE VI

This note has the same number in all editions. In the first edition the relevant parts are worded as follows (p. 740):

"If y be the price at which an amount x of a commodity can find purchasers in a given market, and $y = f(x)$ be the equation to the demand-curve, then the total utility of the commodity is measured by $\int_0^a f(x)\,dx$, where a is the amount consumed.

"If however an amount b of the commodity is necessary for existence, $f(x)$ will be infinite, or at least indefinitely great, for values of x less than b. We must therefore take life for granted, and estimate separately the total utility of that part of the supply of the commodity which is in excess of absolute necessaries: it is of course $\int_b^a f(x)\,dx$ . . . .

"It should be noted that, in the discussion of Consumers' Rent, we assume that the marginal utility of money to the individual purchaser is the same throughout. . . ."

Only trivial changes were made in these sentences in subsequent editions: a typographical error in the fifth edition, which remained uncorrected thereafter, substituted $f(z)$ for $f(x)$ in the second sentence; and "consumers' surplus" replaced "Consumers' Rent." In the third edition the following sentence was added at the end of the note:

"If, for any reason it be desirable to take account of the influence which his expenditure on tea exerts on the value of money to him, it is only necessary to multiply $f(x)$, within the integral given above by that function of $xf(x)$ (i.e. of the amount which he has already spent on tea) which represents the marginal utility to him of money when his stock of it has been diminished by that amount" (3d ed., p. 795). The only subsequent changes were the addition of a comma after "reason" and the deletion of the comma before "within" (8th ed., p. 842).

In its final form Note VI seems internally inconsistent: the second sentence is wrong on the current interpretation of Marshall's demand curve, correct on my interpretation; the final sentence, added in the third edition, seems correct on the current interpretation, wrong on my interpretation.

a) THE SECOND SENTENCE

The second sentence is wrong on the current interpretation, which holds money income and other prices constant along the demand curve, since the ordinate of the demand curve for any quantity x cannot then exceed money income divided by x, and this is not "indefinitely great" for a fixed value of x—say, x_o—whether x_o is greater or less than b. True, $f(x)$ might approach infinity as x approaches zero, but this is not what Marshall says; he says it is "indefinitely great, for values of x less than b," i.e., for any particular value of x less than b—say, $x_o = 0.99b$.

On the variant of my interpretation involving compensating variations in money income—the variant that the note numbered II in the eighth edition leads me to believe Marshall used in the Mathematical Appendix—this sentence is entirely valid. As x declines from a value larger than b, the compensating variation in money income required to keep the individual's real income the same becomes larger and larger, approaching infinity as x approaches b, the minimum amount necessary for existence. This permits the ordinate of the demand curve likewise to approach infinity as x approaches b. On the variant involving compensating variations in other prices—the one Marshall used in the text—the definition of the demand curve breaks down for values of x less than b: for a finite price of the commodity in question, sufficiently high so that the given money income could purchase only a quantity x less than b, there will exist no set of nonnegative prices for the remaining commodities that will keep the purchasing power of money constant in the sense of enabling the same money income to provide the same level of utility; money income and real income cannot both be held constant and at the same time all prices be kept nonnegative. This sentence can therefore be defended as valid on either variant of my interpretation.

One possible ground for dismissing this sentence as evidence against the current interpretation is that the so-called "error" on that interpretation is of my own making, arising from a too subtle and too literal reading of the note. Marshall, it could be argued, was using "demand curve" to mean "utility curve" and $f(x)$ to mean "marginal utility," and therefore he did not consider whether the sentence would be valid if $f(x)$ were to be interpreted literally as the ordinate of the demand curve. A note that Marshall published in 1893 on "Consumer's Surplus" could be cited as evidence for this contention. In this note he quotes part of Note VI as follows: " 'If, however, an amount b of the commodity is necessary for existence, [the utility of the first element] a will be infinite.' "[59] The bracketed expression that Marshall substituted for $f(x)$ would support the notion that he was using "demand curve" and "utility curve" interchangeably.

I do not myself accept this argument; it seems to me to do much less than justice to Marshall. In the first place, I am inclined to give little weight to an incidental, explanatory, phrase inserted by Marshall as late as 1892 or 1893, some twenty years after the fundamental analysis incorporated in Note VI had been completed. I have noted above and shall presently cite evidence that Marshall may have been somewhat confused about the fine points of his own theory of demand by the early 1890's. In the second place, and more important, Marshall clearly distinguishes in the earlier notes in the Mathematical Appendix between a utility curve and a demand curve, repeatedly using the word "utility," and in the first sentence of Note VI says that "the total utility of the commodity is *measured by* $\int_0^a f(x)\,dx$" (1st ed., p. 740; italics added). If he had been using $f(x)$ to stand for marginal utility, the words I have italicized could have been omitted. Finally, Note VI, like most of the rest of the Mathematical Appendix, summarizes a subtle, closely reasoned, and by means obvious, mathematical argument, in which, so far as I know, few errors have ever been found. Is it credible that it would have been worded as loosely and carelessly as the argument being criticized requires; or that, if at one stage it had been, Marshall would have failed to see the simple mathematical error implicit in a literal reading of his words on the current interpretation of the demand curve? It seems to me far more credible that he meant what he said and that the correctness of what he said on my interpretation of his demand curve is strong evidence for that interpretation.

b) THE FINAL SENTENCE

The explanation that follows of the final sentence added to Note VI in the third edition, though not completely satisfactory, is reasonably so, and I have been able to construct no other even remotely satisfactory explanation.

Let U be the utility function of the "individual purchaser" and U_x the marginal utility of x units of tea to him, i.e., the partial derivative of U with respect to x. Now the increase in utility attributable to having a rather than b units of tea—consumer's surplus in utility units—is given by

$$\int_b^a U_x dx\,, \qquad (1)$$

where the integral is computed for constant quantities of other commodities equal to the amounts consumed when a units of tea are consumed and other conditions are those corresponding to the demand curve $y = f(x)$.

At every point along the demand curve,

$$U_x = ny = n\,(x)\,f\,(x)\,, \qquad (2)$$

where n is the marginal utility of money—itself, of course, a function of x along the demand curve. Integrating both sides of equation (2) gives

$$\int_b^a U_x dx = \int_b^a n\,(x)\,f\,(x)\,dx\,. \quad (3)$$

The left-hand side of equation (3) is symbolically identical with equation (1); yet there is an important difference between them. In equation (1), U_x is computed, holding the quantities of other commodities constant as x varies; in equation (3), U_x is computed, holding constant whatever is held constant along the demand curve (money income and other prices on the current interpretation; real income on my interpretation). In general, quantities of other commodities vary along the demand curve (on either interpretation), and U_x may depend on the quantities of other commodities, so the

[59] "Consumer's Surplus," *Annals of the American Academy of Political and Social Science*, III (March, 1893), 618–21 (brackets in original). This note is a reply to some comments by Simon Patten. The letter a after the brackets which appears in the *Annals* note does not appear in the *Principles*, and I can explain it only as a typographical error.

U_x in equation (3) may be numerically different from the U_x in equation (1) for a value of x other than a. This difficulty disappears if U_x is supposed to be independent of the quantities of other commodities—an assumption that Marshall pretty clearly makes as a general rule (e.g., see Nn. I and II of the Mathematical Appendix). On this assumption, then, the right-hand side of equation (3) measures consumer's surplus in utility units.

It is at this point that difficulties of interpretation arise; for the right-hand side of equation (3) is obtained by multiplying "$f(x)$ within the integral given above by that function of" x "which represents the marginal utility . . . of money." Why does Marshall say "that function of $xf(x)$" rather than of x alone? And is it valid to make this substitution? One can argue that to each value of x there corresponds a value of $f(x)$ and hence of $xf(x)$, so that the two forms of statement are equivalent: Marshall has simply made the transformation $z = xf(x)$ and converted $n(x)$ into $n(z)$. This argument is not, however, rigorous. In general, x will not be a single-valued function of z; hence to any given value of z there may correspond more than one value of x and hence more than one value of n. The two forms of statement are equivalent if and only if n is a single-valued function of z, i.e., if $n(x)$ is the same for all values of x for which $xf(x)$ is the same.

Given independence between the marginal utility of tea and the quantity of other commodities, this condition is always satisfied on the current interpretation of the demand curve but not on the alternative interpretation. Let x' stand for the quantity of a composite commodity representing all commodities other than tea, y' for its price, and $U_{x'}$, for its marginal utility. At each point on the demand curve,

$$\frac{U_x}{y} = \frac{U_{x'}}{y'} = n \, .$$

On the current interpretation of the demand curve, money income and the prices of other commodities are the same for all points on the demand curve. It follows that, for all values of x that yield the same value of $xf(x)$, the same amount will be spent on other commodities; so x' is the same (since y' is by definition); so $U_{x'}$ is (since, on the assumption of independence, $U_{x'}$ depends only on x'); and so n is. Marshall's use of $xf(x)$ instead of x is thus valid on the current interpretation of the demand curve.

On my interpretation, either money income varies along the demand curve, so as to keep real income constant, or other prices do; hence the preceding argument is no longer valid. That the two forms of statement are no longer always equivalent can be shown by a counterexample. If other prices are held constant and compensating variations of income are used to keep real income constant, $U = \sqrt{x} + \sqrt{x'}$ is a utility function that gives different values of n for different values of x yielding the same value of $xf(x)$. If money income is held constant and compensating variations of other prices are used to keep real income constant, $U = 3 + x - \frac{1}{10}x^2 + \sqrt{x'}$ is such a utility function. Hence Marshall's use of $xf(x)$ instead of x is invalid on either variant of the alternative interpretation.

This explanation leaves a number of Marshall's verbal statements wrong or ambiguous, whichever interpretation of the demand curve is accepted. (1) The parenthetical explanation of the meaning of $xf(x)$ seems wrong—why the word "already"? If one is thinking of going through the process of extracting as much as possible from the consumer for each successive unit of tea and is supposing the maximum price that he will pay for successive units to be given by the demand curve, then $\int_b^x f(x)dx$ and not $xf(x)$ is the amount he has "already spent on tea." If one is thinking of the amount spent on tea at a given price for tea, then $xf(x)$ is the amount spent when the price is $f(x)$, not the amount "already spent." The explanation offered above accepts the latter rendering of the parenthesis, i.e., supposes the word "already" omitted. (2) The last clause—"when his stock of money has been diminished by that amount"—is ambiguous. To make it consistent with the explanation offered above, one must add "and tea is unavailable, so that the balance is spent solely on other commodities at the prices assumed in drawing the demand curve for tea." The reference to "stock of money" suggests that Marshall was supposing money income constant and so, independently of the rest of the quotation, would tend to rule out compensating variations in money income. It should be noted that there are no such ambiguities in the original version of Note VI, either in the parts quoted above or in the parts not quoted.

UNIVERSITY OF CHICAGO

10 On the Theory of the Budget of the Consumer

E. Slutsky

1. Preliminary Considerations

At first the modern theory of value seemed almost a branch of psychology, and this helped to complicate the question of the applicability of mathematical methods to economic science. For, since the solution of all problems related to the measurableness of psychic phenomena is quite uncertain, a wide field remains subject to controversy. Even aside from the differences of opinion among the followers of the hedonistic school, the very bases of the edifice constructed by this school have been shaken by violent attacks. Thus it is doubtful whether the hedonistic school today still preserves its predominance, although agreement among its opponents is far from universal. Therefore, if we assume the concept of pleasure and pain, or that of desire, as basis of the theory, we remain in a realm open to lively discussions. For the study of such problems we would have to conduct our inquiry in the vast sphere of psychology and of philosophy, without hope of reaching at present, nor in a more or less distant future, results capable of leading to the elimination of today's profound divergence of opinions. From this it follows that, if we wish to place economic science upon a solid basis, we must make it completely independent of psychological assumptions and philosophical hypotheses. On the other hand, since the fundamental concept of modern economics is that of utility, it does not seem opportune to disregard all connections existing between the visible and measurable facts of human conduct and the psychic phenomena by which they seem to be regulated. Utility must therefore be defined in

Reprinted from the translation in the American Economic Association, *Readings in Price Theory,* Chicago: Irwin, 1952, pp. 27–56, by permission of the publisher. Originally published in the *Giornale degli economisti,* Vol. LI (1915).

such a way as to make it logically independent of every disputable hypothesis or concept, without however excluding the possibility of further research regarding the relations between the individual's conduct and his psychic life.

The strictest conception of utility is the one formulated by Pareto. Its purely formal character and its complete independence of all psychological and philosophical hypotheses recommend it as a solid basis for the construction of our own theory. However, Pareto's conception cannot be considered to be well defined. Strictly speaking, it is not composed of only one concept, but of two different ones, which do not seem to us to be closely related. The first is the concept of utility (ophelimity) as that pleasure which an individual receives through an additional quantity of a certain good.[1] This is a purely psychological concept and in no way differs from the usual, rather disputable, hedonistic concept of Gossen, Jevons, and others. In Pareto's theory, however, this first concept is rarely applied. The other concept, that of a function index of utility, is quite a different matter. It is a happy construction, completely strict and abstract in all its aspects. We shall make use of it as the point of departure of our discussion. But it must be noted, that should we limit ourselves to Pareto's definition, *we would not succeed in finding any point of contact whatsoever* between economics and psychology; because from a function determined by empirical data it is impossible to derive Pareto's function uniquely.[2] Nevertheless, we shall start from this concept. We shall see later how it is possible to arrive at another, better defined concept.

2. The Utility Function

Let us start from the following definition: *The utility of a combination of goods is a quantity, which has the property that its value is the greater the more the given combination is desired by the individual whom one considers.*

The more desirable combination must be understood to be the one the individual chooses in preference to another when he has the possibility of choice between the two. Only if an individual, possessing combination A, does not pass over to com-

[1] Pareto, *Manuel d'économie politique* (1909), pp. 158–159.

[2] *Ibid.*, pp. 539–557.

bination B, and vice versa, possessing B, does not pass over to A, must the utility of the two combinations be considered of equal value.

The analysis of the definition of utility leads us to the following conclusions. First of all, it is clear that the subject always tends to relinquish one combination to pass on to another of greater utility. This proposition, an obvious deduction from the definition, can be regarded as a theory without exceptions. It is clear, besides, that the one possible state in which an individual's budget could remain unchanged, even for a short time, is that whose present utility is equal to or greater than that of all states immediately proximate. Such a state can be called a state of equilibrium. It is *stable* if any divergence from it tends to diminish utility, *unstable* in the contrary case. But in practice, every individual's budget being subject to innumerable influences incessantly perturbing its equilibrium, it is evident that there can in actuality exist *only stable budgets.* Therefore, the discovery of the conditions of stability is a problem of the greatest importance in the theory of consumer budgets.

As to the utility function, we must remember that it can be regarded as empirically given, even though the experiments by means of which it should be construed cannot be carried out in practice. Only after the theory of the consumer's budget will have been completely developed, will one be able to face and solve the problem of the determination of the utility function by means that are practicably attainable, such as the variations of demand as a function of income and of prices.

Whatever be the data used for constructing the function of utility, there are cases (and they are the most frequent ones) in which it cannot be unequivocally determined. The question has been studied by Pareto, and we do not intend proceeding to a complete revision of his conclusions; we shall attempt only to establish the conditions of the second derivatives of the utility function in order that it be uniquely determined. As we shall see, this problem is intimately connected with that of the possibility of an agreement between the formal and the psychological aspects of the problem of utility.

Let us now formulate the hypotheses upon which the theory of the budget is constructed:

(1) The hypothesis of the continuity of the utility function and of its derivatives of at least the first two orders.

(2) The hypothesis that the character of the utility function undergoes no variation during the period considered.

(Both hypotheses would probably find approximate confirmation in experience, if, instead of considering a single individual, we were to consider a group, applying statistical methods in the investigation.)

(3) The hypothesis that the increment of utility obtained in passing from one combination of goods to another does not depend upon the mode of passage. In mathematical language this leads to the condition:

$$\frac{\delta^2 U}{\delta x_1 \delta x_2} = \frac{\delta^2 U}{\delta x_2 \delta x_1}$$

We shall see later how this can be verified empirically.

Since we intend to treat the problem in the most general manner, the utility function should not be subjected to further restrictions. If we put

$$U = \Psi(x_1, x_2, \cdots, x_n),$$

($x_1, x_2, \ldots, x_n$ being the quantities of the various goods bought by the subject in a given interval of time, and U the utility gained by the subject by means of that combination of goods), the marginal utility of a good, for example of the good i, is represented by the partial derivative,

$$u_i = \frac{\delta \Psi}{\delta x_i} \cdot$$

We can regard it as always positive, if, as in this study, we limit ourselves to the budgets of consumers, and hence consider only goods which are positively desirable. By desirability of a good we mean the fact that the individual would rather have the good itself or one of its increments, than not have it.

The second derivatives of the same function indicate the dependence of the marginal utilities of a good upon the quantity of this good or other goods:

$$u_{ii} = \frac{\delta^2 \Psi}{\delta x_i^2}; \qquad u_{ij} = \frac{\delta^2 \Psi}{\delta x_i \delta x_j} \cdot$$

As to Gossen's law of the satiability of needs, we must regard it simply as an empirical generalization, which as yet lacks rigorous demonstration. On that account, we will disregard it and consider two kinds of goods: those whose marginal utility decreases with the increase of their quantity ($u_{ii} < 0$), which we shall call *satiating* goods, and those whose marginal utility increases in the same situation ($u_{ii} > 0$), which we shall call *non-satiating* goods.

3. On the Stability of the Equilibrium of the Consumer Budget

Let s be the income of an individual, $p_1, p_2, \ldots, p_n$ the prices of n goods which he buys, $x_1, x_2, \ldots, x_n$ the quantities bought. We have then

$$(1) \qquad p_1x_1 + p_2x_2 + \cdots + p_nx_n = s.$$

We have seen that in order for the budget to be stable, the utility function must have a maximum value; evidently we are concerned with a maximum consistent with equation (1). It is known, however, that this condition resolves itself into:

1. the equations:

$$(2) \qquad \frac{u_1}{p_1} = \frac{u_2}{p_2} = \cdots = \frac{u_n}{p_n} = u',$$

where u′ is the marginal utility of money;

2. the inequality:

$$(3) \quad d^2U = u_{11}dx_1^2 + u_{22}dx_2^2 + \cdots + 2u_{12}dx_1dx_2 + \cdots < 0.$$

If we put

$$(4) \qquad dx_i = c_{i1}d\xi_1 + c_{i2}d\xi_2 + \cdots + c_{in}d\xi_n,$$

where

$$(5) \qquad \begin{aligned} c_{ik} &= 0 \quad \text{if } i > k \\ c_{ik} &= 1 \quad \text{if } i = k, \end{aligned}$$

and substitute these values in (4) and in (3), the coefficients c_{ik} can be determined in such a way as to render the coefficients of all the products equal to 0. In this manner we shall obtain:

$$(6) \qquad d^2U = A_1\, d\xi_1^2 + A_2\, d\xi_2^2 + \cdots + A_n\, d\xi_n^2,$$

where the values, $d\xi_1, d\xi_2, \cdots, d\xi_n$ are related by the linear equation:

$$(7) \qquad B_1\, d\xi_1 + B_2\, d\xi_2 + \cdots + B_n\, d\xi_n = 0.$$

In order to determine the coefficients $B_1, B_2, \ldots, B_n$, as functions of c_{ik}, let us differentiate equation (1) and substitute for dx_1, dx_2, . . . the expressions for them resulting from (4).

Taking account of the conditions (5) we obtain:

$$(8)\quad \begin{cases} B_1 = p_1 \\ B_2 = p_1c_{12} + p_2 \\ B_3 = p_1c_{13} + p_2c_{23} + p_3 \\ \dots\dots\dots\dots\dots\dots \\ B_n = p_1c_{1n} + p_2c_{2n} + \cdots + p_{n-1}c_{n-1n} + p_n. \end{cases}$$

The determination of c_{ik} will be indicated in the following paragraph. From the analysis of equation (6) one can easily draw the following conclusions:

1. *If all the values $A_1, A_2, \dots, A_n$ are negative, d^2U is negative definite.*

2. *If two or more quantities among $A_1, A_2, \dots, A_n$ are positive, d^2U cannot be negative for all the values of $d\xi_1, d\xi_2, \dots, d\xi_n$.*

3. *Further investigation is necessary for the case in which only one of the quantities $A_1, A_2, \dots, A_n$ is positive.*

Let us suppose:

$A_i > 0, A_1 < 0, A_2 < 0, \cdots, A_{i-1} < 0, A_{i+1} < 0, \cdots, A_n < 0.$ If $d\xi_i = 0$, $d^2U < 0$; and therefore there remains to be considered only the case in which $d\xi_i$ is different from zero.

The expressions (6) and (7) can now be divided, respectively, by $d\xi_i^2$ and by $d\xi_i$, and we obtain:

$$(9)\quad d^2U = d\xi_i^2(A_1\eta_1^2 + A_2\eta_2^2 + \cdots + A_{i-1}\eta_{i-1}^2 + A_i + A_{i+1}\eta_{i+1}^2 + \cdots + A_n\eta_n^2) < 0,$$

and

$$(10)\quad B_1\eta_1 + B_2\eta_2 + \cdots + B_{i-1}\eta_{i-1} + B_i + B_{i+1}\eta_{i+1} + \cdots + B_n\eta_n = 0,$$

where

$$\eta_k = \frac{d\xi_k}{d\xi_i}.$$

We deduce from (9) that d^2U can always remain negative only if the maximum value of the quantity

$$(11)\quad A_1\eta_1^2 + A_2\eta_2^2 + \cdots + A_{i-1}\eta_{i-1}^2 + A_i + A_{i+1}\eta_{i+1}^2 + \cdots + A_n\eta_n^2$$

is negative. Indicating for brevity's sake this quantity by the letter Y, and differentiating the auxiliary expression:

$$Z = Y - 2\lambda(B_1\eta_1 + B_2\eta_2 + \cdot\cdot\cdot + B_{i-1}\eta_{i-1} + B_i + B_{i+1}\eta_{i+1} + \cdot\cdot\cdot + B_n\eta_n),$$

we obtain:

$$\frac{1}{2}\frac{dZ}{d\eta_1} = A_1\eta_1 - \lambda B_1 = 0,$$

$$\frac{1}{2}\frac{dZ}{d\eta_2} = A_2\eta_2 - \lambda B_2 = 0, \text{ etc.};$$

and hence:

$$(12) \qquad \eta_1 = \lambda\frac{B_1}{A_1}, \quad \eta_2 = \lambda\frac{B_2}{A_2}, \cdot\cdot\cdot, \quad \eta_{i-1} = \lambda\frac{B_{i-1}}{A_{i-1}}, \quad \eta_{i+1} = \lambda\frac{B_{i+1}}{A_{i+1}}, \cdot\cdot\cdot, \eta_n = \lambda\frac{B_n}{A_n}.$$

Substituting these values into (10), we find λ:

$$(13) \quad \lambda = -\frac{B_i}{\frac{B_1^2}{A_1} + \frac{B_2^2}{A_2} + \cdot\cdot\cdot + \frac{B_{i-1}^2}{A_{i-1}} + \frac{B_{i+1}^2}{A_{i+1}} + \cdot\cdot\cdot + \frac{B_n^2}{A_n}}.$$

Substituting (12) and (13) in (11), the maximum value of Y is given by:

$$(14) \qquad Y_{max.} = A_i + \lambda^2\left(\frac{B_1^2}{A_1} + \frac{B_2^2}{A_2} + \cdot\cdot\cdot + \frac{B_{i-1}^2}{A_{i-1}} + \frac{B_{i+1}^2}{A_{i+1}} + \cdot\cdot\cdot + \frac{B_n^2}{A_n}\right)$$

$$= A_i \frac{\frac{B_1^2}{A_1} + \frac{B_2^2}{A_2} + \cdot\cdot\cdot\cdot\cdot\cdot\cdot\cdot\cdot\cdot\cdot\cdot\cdot\cdot\cdot + \frac{B_n^2}{A_n}}{\frac{B_1^2}{A_1} + \frac{B_2^2}{A_2} + \cdot\cdot\cdot + \frac{B_{i-1}^2}{A_{i-1}} + \frac{B_{i+1}}{A_{i+1}} + \cdot\cdot\cdot + \frac{B_n^2}{A_n}}.$$

It can easily be seen that, A_i being positive, $Y_{max.}$ can be negative only if:

$$(15) \qquad \Omega = \frac{B_1^2}{A_1} + \frac{B_2^2}{A_2} + \cdot\cdot\cdot\cdot + \frac{B_n^2}{A_n} > 0.$$

We have thus determined all the conditions for the stability of a budget. I propose to call a budget *normal* if all the A_i are < 0. It is always stable if the first condition of equilibrium (2) is verified and $\Omega < 0$.

On the contrary I call a budget *abnormal* if only one of the quantities A_i is positive. The conditions for its stability are furnished by (2) and (15), that is by the first condition of equilibrium and by the inequality $\Omega > 0$.

Finally, if two or more of the quantities A_i are positive the budget can in no case be stable.

4. Determination of the Values c_{ik}, A_i, and B_i

From (4) it follows that:

$$dx_i^2 = \sum_k (c_{ik}^2 d\xi_k^2) + \sum_k \sum_{\substack{l \\ k \neq l}} (c_{ik} c_{il} d\xi_k d\xi_l),$$

$$dx_i dx_j = \sum_k (c_{ik} c_{jk} d\xi_k^2) + \sum_k \sum_{\substack{l \\ k \neq l}} (c_{ik} c_{jl} d\xi_k d\xi_l) \cdot$$

Substituting these expressions in (3), we obtain the coefficient of $d\xi_i^2$:

$$(16) \quad \begin{aligned} A_i = {} & c_{1i}(u_{11}c_{1i} + u_{12}c_{2i} + \cdots + u_{1n}c_{ni}) \\ & + c_{2i}(u_{21}c_{1i} + u_{22}c_{2i} + \cdots + u_{2n}c_{ni}) \\ & + \cdots\cdots\cdots\cdots \\ & + c_{ni}(u_{ni}c_{1i} + u_{n2}c_{2i} + \cdots + u_{nn}c_{ni}), \end{aligned}$$

and half of the coefficient of $d\xi_i d\xi_j$:

$$(17) \quad \begin{aligned} A_{ij} = {} & c_{1i}(u_{11}c_{1j} + u_{12}c_{2j} + \cdots + u_{1n}c_{nj}) \\ & + c_{2i}(u_{21}c_{1j} + u_{22}c_{2j} + \cdots + u_{2n}c_{nj}) \\ & + \cdots\cdots\cdots\cdots \\ & + c_{ni}(u_{n1}c_{1j} + u_{n2}c_{2j} + \cdots + u_{nn}c_{nj}) = 0. \end{aligned}$$

Remembering conditions (5), we obtain from (17) the following system of $\frac{n(n-1)}{2}$ equations:

$$(18) \quad \begin{cases} u_{11}c_{12} + u_{12} = 0 & \text{from } A_{12} = 0 \\ u_{11}c_{13} + u_{12}c_{23} + u_{13} = 0 & \text{from } A_{13} = 0 \\ \cdots\cdots\cdots\cdots & \cdots\cdots \\ u_{11}c_{1n} + u_{12}c_{2n} + u_{13}c_{3n} + \cdots + u_{1n} = 0 & \text{from } A_{1n} = 0 \end{cases}$$

$$
\begin{array}{ll}
(18) & \left\{\begin{array}{ll}
u_{21}c_{13} + u_{22}c_{23} + u_{23} = 0 & \text{from } A_{23} = 0 \\
u_{21}c_{14} + u_{22}c_{24} + u_{23}c_{34} + u_{24} = 0 & \text{from } A_{24} = 0 \\
\cdots\cdots\cdots\cdots & \cdots\cdots \\
u_{21}c_{1n} + u_{22}c_{2n} + u_{23}c_{3n} + \cdots + u_{2n} = 0 & \text{from } A_{2n} = 0
\end{array}\right. \\
(Cont.) &
\end{array}
$$

$$\cdots\cdots\cdots\cdots\cdots\cdots\cdots\cdots\cdots\cdots$$

$$
\left\{\begin{array}{ll}
u_{n-2,1}c_{1,n-1} + u_{n-2,2}c_{2,n-1} + \cdots & \\
\quad + u_{n-2,n-2}c_{n-2,n-1} + u_{n-2,n-1} = 0 & \text{from } A_{n-2,n-1} = 0 \\
u_{n-2,1}c_{1,n} + u_{n-2,2}c_{2n} + \cdots & \\
\quad + u_{n-2,n-1}c_{n-1,n} + u_{n-2,n} = 0 & \text{from } A_{n-2,n} = 0 \\
u_{n-1,1}c_{1n} + u_{n-1,2}c_{2n} + \cdots & \\
\quad + u_{n-1,n-1}c_{n-1,n} + u_{n-1,n} = 0 & \text{from } A_{n-1,n} = 0
\end{array}\right.
$$

This system is formed by various independent linear systems (I, $A_{12} = 0$; II, $A_{13} = 0$, $A_{23} = 0$; III, $A_{14} = 0$, $A_{24} = 0$, $A_{34} = 0$; etc.), which could easily be solved.

Let:

$$
(19) \qquad R_i = \begin{vmatrix} u_{11} & u_{12} & \cdots & u_{1i} \\ u_{21} & u_{22} & \cdots & u_{2i} \\ \cdots & \cdots & \cdots & \cdots \\ u_{i1} & u_{i2} & \cdots & u_{ii} \end{vmatrix}
$$

where $u_{kl} = u_{lk}$; and $R_{i(kl)} = R_{i(lk)}$ are the cofactors of R_i. From (18) we obtain:

$$
(20) \qquad c_{ij} = \frac{R_{j(ij)}}{R_{j(jj)}} = \frac{R_{j(ij)}}{R_{j-1}} .
$$

Returning to (16), we observe that in consequence of conditions (5), the lines from $(i + 1)$ to n cancel, and in consequence of (18) the lines from 1 to $(i - 1)$ also cancel. Hence we have

$$
(21) \qquad \begin{aligned} A_i &= u_{i1}c_{1i} + u_{i2}c_{2i} + \cdots + u_{ii} \\ &= \frac{1}{R_{i-1}} (u_{i1}R_{i(i1)} + u_{i2}R_{i(i2)} + \cdots + u_{ii}R_{i(ii)}) \\ &= \frac{R_i}{R_{i-1}} . \end{aligned}
$$

If now we put

$$
(22) \quad H_{i(j)} = \begin{vmatrix} u_{11} & u_{12} & \cdots & u_{1,j-1} & p_1 & u_{1,j+1} & \cdots & u_{1i} \\ u_{21} & u_{22} & \cdots & u_{2,j-1} & p_2 & u_{2,j+1} & \cdots & u_{2i} \\ \cdots & \cdots & \cdots & \cdots & \cdots & \cdots & \cdots & \cdots \\ u_{i1} & u_{i2} & \cdots & u_{i,j-1} & p_i & u_{i,j+1} & \cdots & u_{ii} \end{vmatrix} = p_1R_{i(1j)} + p_2R_{i(2j)} + \cdots + p_iR_{i(ij)},
$$

we find, by means of (8):

$$(23)\quad B_i = \frac{1}{R_{i-1}}\left(p_1R_{i(1i)} + p_2R_{i(2i)} + \cdots + p_iR_{i(ii)}\right) = \frac{H_{i(i)}}{R_{i-1}}.$$

The formulas (21) and (23) can be considered absolutely general if we put $1 = R_o$; in this case (as also results directly from (8) and (16)), $A_1 = \frac{R_1}{R_0} = u_{11}$ and $B_1 = \frac{H_{1(1)}}{R_0} = p_1$.

5. Determination of the Value of Ω

Substituting expressions (21) and (23) into (15), we obtain:

$$(24)\qquad \Omega = \frac{H^2_{1(1)}}{R_0R_1} + \frac{H^2_{2(2)}}{R_1R_2} + \cdots + \frac{H^2_{n(n)}}{R_{n-1}R_n}.$$

Indicating the same quantity by the symbol Ω_n, we shall show that it can be reduced to a more symmetrical form. Let us begin by putting:

$$(25)\quad M_i = \begin{vmatrix} o & p_1 & p_2 & \cdots & p_i \\ p_1 & u_{11} & u_{12} & \cdots & u_{1i} \\ p_2 & u_{21} & u_{22} & \cdots & u_{2i} \\ \cdot & \cdot & \cdot & \cdots & \cdot \\ p_i & u_{i1} & u_{i2} & \cdots & u_{ii} \end{vmatrix} = (p_1H_{i(1)} + p_2H_{i(2)} + \cdots + p_iH_{i(i)}).$$

We now have

$$(26)\qquad \Omega_2 = \frac{H^2_{1(1)}}{R_oR_1} + \frac{H^2_{2(2)}}{R_1R_2} = \frac{p_1^2}{u_{11}} + \frac{(p_2\,u_{11} - p_1u_{12})^2}{u_{11}(u_{11}u_{22} - u_{12}^2)}$$

$$= \frac{p_1^2u_{22} + p_2^2u_{11} - 2p_1p_2u_{12}}{u_{11}u_{22} - u_{12}^2} = -\frac{M_2}{R_2}.$$

The foregoing result can be generalized. For this purpose it suffices to demonstrate that if it is valid for Ω_i, it is also valid for Ω_{i+1}; or that

$$(27)\quad \Omega_{i+1} = \frac{H^2_{1(1)}}{R_0R_1} + \frac{H^2_{2(2)}}{R_1R_2} + \cdots + \frac{H^2_{i(i)}}{R_{i-1}R_i} + \frac{H^2_{i+1(i+1)}}{R_iR_{i+1}}$$

$$= -\frac{M_i}{R_i} + \frac{H^2_{i+1(i+1)}}{R_iR_{i+1}} = -\frac{M_iR_{i+1} - H^2_{i+1(i+1)}}{R_iR_{i+1}}$$

To reduce the numerator to a different form we shall make use of the well-known formula of the theory of determinants:

$$\Delta_{ij}\,\Delta_{kl} - \Delta_{ik}\,\Delta_{jl} = \Delta\Delta_{(ij)\,(kl)}, \tag{28}$$

where the quantities of the first member are cofactors of the first order of the determinant Δ (the first index corresponds to the suppressed row and the second to the suppressed column); and $\Delta_{(ij)\,(kl)}$ is the cofactor of the second order obtained by suppressing rows i and k and columns j and l.

Let us indicate, then, by $M_{i(kk)}$ and by $M_{i(kl)}$ the cofactors of M_i corresponding respectively to the elements u_{kk} and u_{kl}; and by $M_{i(00)}, M_{i(01)}, M_{i(02)}, \ldots$, and $M_{i(00)}, M_{i(10)}, M_{i(20)}, \ldots$ the cofactors of the first row and the first column.

We have:

$$\begin{cases} M_i = M_{i+1\ (i+1\ i+1)} \\ R_i = M_{i(00)} = M_{i+1\ (i+1\ i+1)\ (00)} \\ H_{i+1(i+1)} = -M_{i+1(0\ i+1)} = -M_{i+1(i+1\ 0)}. \end{cases} \tag{29}$$

Using this notation, and remembering (28), we easily find:

$$\begin{aligned} &M_iR_{i+1} - H^2_{i+1(i+1)} = M_{i+1(i+1\ i+1)}\,M_{i+1(00)} \\ &-M_{i+1(i+1\ 0)}\,M_{i+1(i+1\ 0)} = M_{i+1}M_{i+1(i+1\ i+1)(00)} \\ &= M_{i+1}R_i; \end{aligned} \tag{30}$$

and hence, substituting into (27) the preceding value:

$$\Omega_{i+1} = -\frac{M_{i+1}}{R_{i+1}}. \tag{31}$$

We have seen that this formula is valid for Ω_2; therefore its general validity is demonstrated. Hence:

$$\Omega_n = -\frac{M_n}{R_n}, \tag{32}$$

or, more simply:

$$\Omega = -\frac{M}{R}. \tag{32'}$$

6. Variations of the Individual's Demand as a Function of Income

It follows from (2) that:

$$u_1 = p_1u',\ u_2 = p_2u',\ \cdots,\ u_n = p_nu'. \tag{33}$$

Differentiating with respect to s, we obtain:

$$
(34)\quad \begin{cases} u_{11}\dfrac{\delta x_1}{\delta s} + u_{12}\dfrac{\delta x_2}{\delta s} + \cdots\cdots + u_{1n}\dfrac{\delta x_n}{\delta s} = p_1\dfrac{\delta u'}{\delta s} \\ u_{21}\dfrac{\delta x_1}{\delta s} + u_{22}\dfrac{\delta x_2}{\delta s} + \cdots\cdots + u_{2n}\dfrac{\delta x_n}{\delta s} = p_2\dfrac{\delta u'}{\delta s} \\ \cdots\cdots\cdots\cdots\cdots\cdots\cdots\cdots\cdots\cdots \\ u_{n1}\dfrac{\delta x_1}{\delta s} + u_{n2}\dfrac{\delta x_2}{\delta s} + \cdots\cdots + u_{nn}\dfrac{\delta x_n}{\delta s} = p_n\dfrac{\delta u'}{\delta s} \end{cases}
$$

Solving this system, we may write:

$$
(35)\qquad \frac{\delta x_i}{\delta s} = \frac{H_{n(i)}}{R_n}\frac{\delta u'}{\delta s}
$$

Differentiating now the equation (1) with respect to s, we have:

$$
(36)\qquad p_1\frac{\delta x_1}{\delta s} + p_2\frac{\delta x_2}{\delta s} + \cdots\cdots + p_n\frac{\delta x_n}{\delta s} = 1;
$$

and hence substituting for $\frac{\delta x_1}{\delta s}$, $\frac{\delta x_2}{\delta s}$, etc., their expressions taken from (35):

(37)

$$
\frac{\delta u'}{\delta s} = \frac{R_n}{p_1H_{n(1)} + p_2H_{n(2)} + \cdots + p_nH_{n(n)}} = -\frac{R_n}{M_n} = \frac{1}{\Omega}.
$$

Making use of this, we have:

$$
(38)\qquad \frac{\delta x_i}{\delta s} = -\frac{H_{n(i)}}{M_n} = \frac{M_{n(0i)}}{M_n}
$$

It is impossible to formulate any one specific proposition, true in all cases, about the sign of this expression. We only know that the value of $\frac{\delta x_i}{\delta s}$ can be positive as well as negative; and observation confirms the fact that both cases actually occur. It is therefore necessary to proceed to a classification of goods: those whose quantity increases with the increase of income can be said to be *relatively indispensable;* those whose quantity diminishes with the increase of income, *relatively dispensable.*

For example, suppose that a poor family in consequence of a slight increase of income consumes more meat, more sugar, more tea, and less bread and potatoes. The first victuals should then be considered relatively indispensable, the others relatively dispensable, for the family.

Keeping in mind formula (37), and remembering the discussion of the problem of stability, we immediately deduce that in the case of a normal budget the marginal utility of money should decrease with the increase of income and increase with its decrease. In the case of an abnormal budget the contrary occurs.

7. Variations of Demand as a Function of Price

Differentiating equations (33) with respect to p_i, we obtain:

$$(39)\quad \begin{cases} u_{11}\dfrac{\delta x_1}{\delta p_i} + u_{12}\dfrac{\delta x_2}{\delta p_i} + \cdots + u_{1n}\dfrac{\delta x_n}{\delta p_i} = p_1\dfrac{\delta u'}{\delta p_i} \\ u_{21}\dfrac{\delta x_1}{\delta p_i} + u_{22}\dfrac{\delta x_2}{\delta p_i} + \cdots + u_{2n}\dfrac{\delta x_n}{\delta p_i} = p_2\dfrac{\delta u'}{\delta p_i} \\ \cdots\cdots\cdots\cdots\cdots\cdots\cdots\cdots \\ u_{i1}\dfrac{\delta x_1}{\delta p_i} + u_{i2}\dfrac{\delta x_2}{\delta p_i} + \cdots + u_{in}\dfrac{\delta x_n}{\delta p_i} = p_i\dfrac{\delta u'}{\delta p_i} + u \\ \cdots\cdots\cdots\cdots\cdots\cdots\cdots\cdots \\ u_{n1}\dfrac{\delta x_1}{\delta p_i} + u_{n2}\dfrac{\delta x_2}{\delta p_i} + \cdots + u_{nn}\dfrac{\delta x_n}{\delta p_i} = p_n\dfrac{\delta u'}{\delta p_i}, \end{cases}$$

and hence:

$$(40)\quad \begin{cases} R_n\dfrac{\delta x_i}{\delta p_i} = H_{n(i)}\dfrac{\delta u'}{\delta p_i} + u'R_{n(ii)} \\ R_n\dfrac{\delta x_j}{\delta p_i} = H_{n(j)}\dfrac{\delta u'}{\delta p_i} + u'R_{n(ij)}\,. \end{cases}$$

Then, differentiating (1) with respect to p_i, we have:

$$(41)\quad p_1\frac{\delta x_1}{\delta p_i} + p_2\frac{\delta x_2}{\delta p_i} + \cdots + p_n\frac{\delta x_n}{\delta p_i} = -\,x_i\,;$$

and substituting (40) into (41), and writing $-\,M_{n(0i)}$ instead of $H_{n(i)}$, we obtain:

$$(42)\quad \frac{\delta u'}{\delta p_i} = \frac{-\,u'\,M_{n(0i)} + x_i\,R_n}{M_n}.$$

Now, substituting the preceding expression in (40), we obtain:[3]

$$(43)\quad \frac{\delta x_i}{\delta p_i} = u'\,\frac{R_{n(ii)}\,M_n + M^2_{n(0i)}}{R_nM_n} - x_i\,\frac{M_{n(0i)}}{M_n}\,;$$

[3] The formulas in the text were deduced by Pareto, and published in this *Giornale,* August 1892 (see also the *Manuel d' économie politique,* 1909, p. 581). The differences in notation and form between our formulas and Pareto's are so unimportant that they can be considered identical.

Our attempt at developing the formulas aims only at putting them in more convenient form for mathematical analysis.

$$(44)\qquad \frac{\delta x_j}{\delta p_i} = u'\,\frac{R_{n(ij)}M_n + M_{n(0i)}M_{n(0j)}}{R_nM_n} - x_i\,\frac{M_{n(0j)}}{M_n}\,.$$

By a procedure analogous to that employed in Section 5, we can simplify these expressions considerably. In fact:

$$R_{n(ii)}M_n + M^2_{n(0i)} = M_{n(00)(ii)}M_n + M_{n(0i)}M_{n(0i)}$$
$$= M_{n(00)}M_{n(ii)} = R_nM_{n(ii)},$$
$$R_{n(ij)}M_n + M_{n(0i)}M_{n(0j)} = M_{n(00)(ij)}M_n + M_{n(0i)}M_{n(0j)}$$
$$= M_{n(00)}M_{n(ij)} = R_nM_{n(ij)},$$

whence we obtain from (43) and (44):[4]

$$(45)\qquad \begin{cases} \dfrac{\delta x_i}{\delta p_i} = u'\,\dfrac{M_{ii}}{M} - x_i\,\dfrac{M_{0i}}{M}\,, \\[2ex] \dfrac{\delta x_j}{\delta p_i} = u'\,\dfrac{M_{ij}}{M} - x_i\,\dfrac{M_{0j}}{M}\,. \end{cases}$$

Or, using (38):

$$(46)\qquad \frac{\delta x_i}{\delta p_i} = u'\,\frac{M_{ii}}{M} - x_i\,\frac{\delta x_i}{\delta s}\,;$$

$$(47)\qquad \frac{\delta x_j}{\delta p_i} = u'\,\frac{M_{ij}}{M} - x_i\,\frac{\delta x_j}{\delta s}\,.$$

8. Dependence of the Demand for a Good on its Price

Let us now study formula (46); and let us begin by demonstrating that there always exists the inequality:

$$(48)\qquad \frac{M_{ii}}{M} < 0\,.$$

For this purpose we must analyze the two cases of normal and abnormal budgets separately.

I. Normal Budgets. Using the notation of Section 5, we have:

$$\frac{\Omega_{n-1}}{\Omega_n} = \frac{M_{n-1}}{M_n}\ \frac{R_n}{R_{n-1}} = \frac{M_{n-1}}{M_n}A_n\,.$$

All the A_i being negative, Ω_{n-1} and Ω_n are also negative and hence:

$$\frac{M_{n-1}}{M_n} < 0\,.$$

---

[4] Here and in the following differentiations the index n in $M_{n(ii)}$, $M_{n(ij)}$, $M_{n(0i)}$, etc., is omitted in each case where the omission does not lead to misunderstanding.

II. ABNORMAL BUDGETS. We distinguish two cases:

(α) If $A_n > 0$, then $\Omega_{n-1} < 0$, $\Omega_n > 0$; and hence $\dfrac{M_{n-1}}{M_n} < 0$.

(β) If $A_n < 0$, then $\Omega_{n-1} > 0$, $\Omega_n > 0$; and hence $\dfrac{M_{n-1}}{M_n} < 0$.

It is clear that the order in which the goods are considered is indifferent; the i-th good can hence be put after the n-th. We now have:

$$\begin{aligned} M_n &= (0, u_{11}, u_{22}, \cdots, u_{nn}) \\ &= (0, u_{11}, \cdots, u_{i-1\ i-1}, u_{i+1\ i+1}, \cdots u_{nn}, u_{ii}) \\ M_{n(ii)} &= (0, u_{11}, u_{22}, \cdots, u_{i-1\ i-1}, u_{i+1\ i+1}, \cdots, u_{nn}); \end{aligned}$$

for the value which, in the new arrangement of the system, takes the place of M_{n-1}. Therefore $\dfrac{M_{ii}}{M} < 0$.

We can now easily deduce from (46) the following *laws of demand:*

I. *The demand for a relatively indispensable good* $\left(\dfrac{x\delta_i}{\delta s} > 0\right)$ *is necessarily always normal, that is, it diminishes if its price increases, and increases if its price decreases.*

II. *The demand for a relatively dispensable good* $\left(\dfrac{\delta x_i}{\delta s} < 0\right)$ *can be abnormal in certain cases, that is, it can increase with the increase of price and diminish with the decrease of price.*

We now put:

$$k_{ii} = u' \frac{M_{ii}}{M} = \frac{\delta x_i}{\delta p_i} + x_i \frac{\delta x_i}{\delta s}, \tag{49}$$

$$k_{ij} = u' \frac{M_{ij}}{M} = \frac{\delta x_j}{\delta p_i} + x_i \frac{\delta x_j}{\delta s}. \tag{50}$$

We can demonstrate that the inequality (48) has a well-defined economic significance. In fact, if price increases by dp_i, the value $x_i dp_i$ can be said to be an *apparent loss*, since, in order to make possible the purchase of the same quantities of all the goods that had formerly been bought, the income should have to increase by $ds = x_i dp_i$. But the individual, though having the possibility of preserving unchanged the preceding budget, will no longer consider it preferable to any other, and there will take place some kind of *residual variations* of demand:

$$(51)\quad \begin{cases} dx_i = \dfrac{\delta x_i}{\delta p_i} dp_i + \dfrac{\delta x_i}{\delta s} ds = \left(u' \dfrac{M_{ii}}{M} - x_i \dfrac{\delta x_i}{\delta s}\right) dp_i \\ \quad + \dfrac{\delta x_i}{\delta s}(x_i dp_i) = u' \dfrac{M_{ii}}{M} dp_i = k_{ii} dp_i; \\ dx_j = \dfrac{\delta x_j}{\delta p_i} dp_i + \dfrac{\delta x_j}{\delta s} ds = \left(u' \dfrac{M_{ij}}{M} - x_i \dfrac{\delta x_i}{\delta s}\right) dp_i \\ \quad + \dfrac{\delta x_i}{\delta s}(x_i dp_i) = u' \dfrac{M_{ij}}{M} dp_i = k_{ij} dp_i. \end{cases}$$

The increment dp_i of price, accompanied by an increment of income equal to the apparent loss, can be said to be the *compensated variation* of price. In such a case k_{ii} and k_{ij} can be regarded as residual variations of the demand for each unit of the compensated increment of price, and can be called the *residual variability* of x_i and x_j respectively.

Using this terminology, the inequality (48) can be expressed thus:

III. *The residual variability of a good in the case of a compensated variation of its price, is always negative.* Or:

$$(52)\qquad k_{ii} = u' \frac{M_{ii}}{M} = \frac{\delta x_i}{\delta p_i} + x_i \frac{\delta x_i}{\delta s} < 0.$$

For example, if after an increase of the price of bread, wages increase only by the amount of the apparent loss, the demand for bread on the part of the wage-earners will not be maintained at the original level; on the contrary, it will fall.

Concluding, we note that if $\dfrac{\delta x_i}{\delta p_i}$ and $\dfrac{\delta x_i}{\delta s}$ are of opposite sign, the formula (52) resolves itself into the following inequalities between the numerical values of the derivatives:

Case I

$$\frac{\delta x_i}{\delta s} > 0, \frac{\delta x_i}{\delta p_i} < 0;$$

$$(53)\qquad \frac{\left|\dfrac{\delta x_i}{\delta p_i}\right|}{\left|\dfrac{\delta x_i}{\delta s}\right|} > x_i;$$

Case II

$$\frac{\delta x_i}{\delta s} < 0, \frac{\delta x_i}{\delta p_i} > 0.$$

$$(54)\qquad \frac{\left|\dfrac{\delta x_i}{\delta p_i}\right|}{\left|\dfrac{\delta x_i}{\delta s}\right|} < x_i.$$

The foregoing formulas belong to the category of relations which to date have never been the object of research in social science; that is, they belong to relations quantitatively defined between empirical, measurable facts; therefore they can be *verified* by means of observation of real budgets.

9. Dependence of the Demand for One Good on the Price of Another

It follows from (47) that:

$$\frac{\delta x_j}{\delta p_i} = u' \frac{M_{ij}}{M} - x_i \frac{\delta x_j}{\delta s}\,; \quad \frac{\delta x_i}{\delta p_j} = u' \frac{M_{ji}}{M} - x_j \frac{\delta x_i}{\delta s}\,.$$

M_{ij} being equal to M_{ji}, and so $k_{ij} = k_{ji}$; or

$$\frac{\delta x_j}{\delta p_i} + x_i \frac{\delta x_j}{\delta s} = \frac{\delta x_i}{\delta p_j} + x_j \frac{\delta x_i}{\delta s}\,. \tag{55}$$

This important relation can be called the *law of reversibility* of residual variations, and expressed thus:

The residual variability of the j-th good in the case of a compensated variation of the price p_i is equal to the residual variability of the i-th good in the case of a compensated variation of the price p_j.

Equation (55) belongs to the previously mentioned category of quantitatively defined relations between observable quantities. Empirical confirmation is highly desirable, inasmuch as it would demonstrate the correspondence to the truth, or at least the plausibility, of the hypothesis that the increments of utility do not depend upon the mode of variation. It is clear, in fact, that if this hypothesis were not to correspond to the real phenomena of budgets, u_{ij} would not be equal to u_{ji} nor M_{ij} to M_{ji}, and the law of reversibility would not have been verified.

Continuing, we write:

$$\frac{\delta x_i}{\delta p_1} = u' \frac{M_{1i}}{M} - x_1 \frac{\delta x_i}{\delta s}$$

$$\frac{\delta x_i}{\delta p_2} = u' \frac{M_{2i}}{M} - x_2 \frac{\delta x_i}{\delta s}$$

$$\cdots\cdots\cdots\cdots\cdots\cdots$$

$$\frac{\delta x_i}{\delta p_n} = u' \frac{M_{ni}}{M} - x_n \frac{\delta x_i}{\delta s}.$$

Multiplying the foregoing equalities by $p_1, p_2, \ldots, p_n$, respectively, and adding them, we have:

$$p_1 \frac{\delta x_i}{\delta p_1} + p_2 \frac{\delta x_i}{\delta p_2} + \cdots + p_n \frac{\delta x_i}{\delta p_n} = \frac{u'}{M}(p_1 M_{1i} + p_2 M_{2i} + \cdots + p_n M_{ni}) - (p_1 x_1 + p_2 x_2 + \cdots + p_n x_n)\frac{\delta x_i}{\delta s}$$

Adding $0\ M_{0i}$ to the polynomial in the first parentheses, we obtain the sum of the cofactors of the determinant M corresponding to the elements of column (i), multiplied by the elements of column (0). The sum is therefore zero; and we have the interesting relation:

$$(56)\quad p_1 \frac{\delta x_i}{\delta p_1} + p_2 \frac{\delta x_i}{\delta p_2} + \cdots\cdots\cdots + p_n \frac{\delta x_i}{\delta p_n} = -s\frac{\delta x_i}{\delta s}$$

We write, then, on the basis of (55):

$$\frac{\delta x_i}{\delta p_j} - \frac{\delta x_j}{\delta p_i} = x_i \frac{\delta x_j}{\delta s} - x_j \frac{\delta x_i}{\delta s};$$

$$\frac{\delta x_i}{\delta p_k} - \frac{\delta x_k}{\delta p_i} = x_i \frac{\delta x_k}{\delta s} - x_k \frac{\delta x_i}{\delta s}$$

Multiplying the first equation by x_k and the second by x_j, and subtracting the second product from the first, we obtain:

$$x_k\left(\frac{\delta x_i}{\delta p_j} - \frac{\delta x_j}{\delta p_i}\right) - x_j\left(\frac{\delta x_i}{\delta p_k} - \frac{\delta x_k}{\delta p_i}\right) = x_i\left(x_k \frac{\delta x_j}{\delta s} - x_j \frac{\delta x_k}{\delta s}\right) = x_i\left(\frac{\delta x_k}{\delta p_j} - \frac{\delta x_j}{\delta p_k}\right);$$

from which we have:

$$(57\quad \frac{1}{x_i x_j}\frac{\delta x_i}{\delta p_j} + \frac{1}{x_j x_k}\frac{\delta x_j}{\delta p_k} + \frac{1}{x_k x_i}\frac{\delta x_k}{\delta p_i} = \frac{1}{x_i x_k}\frac{\delta x_i}{\delta p_k} + \frac{1}{x_k x_j}\frac{\delta x_k}{\delta p_j} + \frac{1}{x_j x_i}\frac{\delta x_j}{\delta p_i}.$$

This *cyclic relation* can be extended to the general case of any number of goods. Putting, in fact, $\xi_{ij} = \dfrac{\frac{\delta x_i}{\delta p_j}}{x_i x_j}$; and writing:

$$\xi_{12} + \xi_{23} + \xi_{31} = \xi_{13} + \xi_{32} + \xi_{21}$$
$$\xi_{13} + \xi_{34} + \xi_{41} = \xi_{14} + \xi_{43} + \xi_{31}$$
$$\cdots\cdots\cdots\cdots\cdots\cdots\cdots\cdots\cdots\cdots\cdots\cdots$$
$$\xi_{1\,n-1} + \xi_{n-1\,n} + \xi_{n1} = \xi_{1n} + \xi_{n\,n-1} + \xi_{n-1\,1},$$

by adding the preceding equalities we find:

$$\xi_{12} + \xi_{23} + \xi_{34} + \cdots + \xi_{n-1\,n} + \xi_{n1} = \xi_{1n} + \xi_{n\,n-1} + \cdots + \xi_{32} + \xi_{21}\,. \tag{58}$$

10. Theory of the Budget in the Case in Which the Marginal Utility of Any One Good Is a Function Only of Its Quantity

This particular case has special importance in the history of economic science, having furnished the first basis for the theory of marginal utility. None of the authors who elaborated the theory of the budget, because they regarded it necessary to accept the so-called law of satiability of needs (Gossen's law), could reach results of general validity. Gossen's law itself remains what it always was, that is, an empirical proposition, not a rigorously demonstrated truth; and several authors have had occasion to express doubts on its general validity.[5]

It is common opinion that if there are exceptions to this law, they are rare; but one can point out that natural laws, if they admit of exceptions, become things but slightly different from the rules of grammar. Speaking from the logical viewpoint, one cannot call *law* any rule which admits of exceptions—it matters not whether they are few or many—in *unknown* conditions or circumstances. In our case, moreover, it is doubtful whether the exceptions are indeed so few as one is wont to believe, since the question was never tested on the basis of scientifically arranged, empirical observations. And we hold that specialized research,

[5] Gossen himself was the first to express doubts in that respect. See *Entwickelung der Gesetze des menschlichen Verkehrs* (N. Augs., 1889), pp. 47–48. See also: Edgeworth, *Mathematical Psychics* (1881), pp. 34–35; Pantaleoni, *Principii di economia pura* (1889), pp. 40, 87; Pareto, *Proprietà fondamentale dei gradi finali d'utilità* (in this *Giornale* [1893], Vol. I, pp. 1, 2) and *Manuel d'économie politique* (1909), p. 266; Marshall, *Principles of Economics* (1895), p. 169, n. 2; von Schubert-Soldern, *Das menschliche Glück und die soziale Frage, Tueb. Zeitschr.* (1896), Vol. I, p. 68, Vol. III, p. 512; Cuhel, *Zur Lehre von den Bedürfnissen* (1907), pp. 238–239.

directed above all toward the life and labor of the poorer classes, will be rewarded by unexpected results.[6]

To carry out such research one needs as a basis a theory which to this day has been almost completely lacking. As far as we know, only one author has studied the theory of demand of a non-satiating good: Umberto Ricci.[7] Using mathematical analysis, he has reached the conclusion that the demand for a non-satiating good increases with the increase of its price, if:

$$\frac{p_1^2}{u_{11}} + \frac{p_2^2}{u_{22}} + \cdots\cdots\cdots + \frac{p_n^2}{u_{nn}} < 0 .$$

But since, as we shall see, the first member of the preceding inequality is nothing but our criterion of stability, it is obvious how unstable Ricci's budget is. Hence in consequence of the increase of price and of the disturbance of equilibrium, it will not tend to approach the displaced point of minimum [maximum] utility, but to move away from it. It follows from the theory of equilibrium that Ricci's result, which refers to a case which cannot occur in reality, does not correspond to the truth.

Having developed the general theory, we will now easily obtain the theory for the case under examination. From the fundamental form of the condition of stability:

$$d^2U = u_{11}dx_1^2 + u_{22}dx_2^2 + \cdots\cdots + u_{nn}dx_n^2 < 0 ,$$

it follows that:

I. The budget is stable if all the u_{ii} are negative.

II. If only one of the u_{ii} is positive, the budget is stable if $\Omega > 0$, unstable if $\Omega < 0$.

III. The budget can never be stable if more than one of the u_{ii} is positive.

Let us apply the method of Section 5 to the determination of Ω; the deduction of the general formula will be facilitated here by remembering the fact that all the $u_{ij} = 0$. We have, hence:

$$M = \begin{vmatrix} 0 & p_1 & p_2 & \cdots & p_n \\ p_1 & u_{11} & 0 & \cdots & 0 \\ p_2 & 0 & u_{22} & \cdots & 0 \\ \cdots & \cdots & \cdots & \cdots & \cdots \\ p_n & 0 & 0 & \cdots & u_{nn} \end{vmatrix} = u_{11}u_{22}\cdots u_{nn}\left(\frac{p_1^2}{u_{11}} + \frac{p_2^2}{u_{22}} + \cdots + \frac{p_n^2}{u_{nn}}\right)$$

[6] Marshall, *op. cit.*, p. 208.

[7] *Curve crescenti di ofelimità e di domanda* (in this *Giornale* [1904, August], pp. 112–138).

$$R = \begin{vmatrix} u_{11} & 0 & 0 & \cdots & 0 \\ 0 & u_{22} & 0 & \cdots & 0 \\ 0 & 0 & u_{33} & \cdots & 0 \\ \cdots & \cdots & \cdots & \cdots & \cdots \\ 0 & 0 & 0 & \cdots & u_{nn} \end{vmatrix} = u_{11}u_{22} \cdots u_{nn}$$

and consequently:

$$\Omega = \frac{M}{R} = \frac{p_1^2}{u_{11}} + \frac{p_2^2}{u_{22}} + \cdots\cdots + \frac{p_n^2}{u_{nn}} . \tag{59}$$

Similarly we obtain:

$$H_i = -M_{0i} = u_{11}u_{22} \cdots u_{nn} \frac{p_i}{u_{ii}}$$

$$M_{ii} = -u_{11}u_{22} \cdots u_{nn} \frac{\Omega - \dfrac{p_i^2}{u_{ii}}}{u_{ii}}$$

$$M_{ij} = u_{11}u_{22} \cdots u_{nn} \frac{p_1p_2}{u_{ii}u_{jj}}$$

and hence:

$$\left\{ \begin{aligned} \frac{\delta x_i}{\delta s} &= \frac{p_i}{u_{ii}\Omega} \\ \frac{\delta x_i}{\delta p_i} &= \frac{u'\left(\Omega - \dfrac{p_i^2}{u_{ii}}\right) - p_i x_i}{u_{ii}\,\Omega} \\ \frac{\delta x_j}{\delta p_i} &= -\frac{p_j(u_i + x_i u_{ii})}{u_{ii}u_{jj}\,\Omega} . \end{aligned} \right. \tag{60}$$

The analysis of the preceding formulas leads to the following conclusions:

If the budget is *normal*, the demand for any one good increases with the increase of the income and diminishes with the increase of the price of that good. If the budget is *abnormal*, the increase of income causes an increase in the demand for the non-satiating goods, and a decrease in that for the satiating goods. Moreover, with the increase of price of a non-satiating good, its demand should always decrease; the contrary can happen only in the case of a satiating good. The satiating goods being, in the case considered, relatively dispensable, the result is in accord with the previously deduced laws of demand.

11. Determination (Possibly by Means of Empirical, Quantitative Data) of the Second Derivatives of the Utility Function

The values of $\frac{\delta x_1}{\delta s}, \frac{\delta x_2}{\delta s}, \ldots\ldots\ldots, \frac{\delta x_n}{\delta s}$ and of all the quantities of the type $\frac{\delta x_i}{\delta p_i}$ and $\frac{\delta x_i}{\delta p_j}$ can be determined by virtue of the observation of real budgets; on that account we shall consider them as empirically measurable data and we shall make use of them to determine u_{ii} and u_{ij}. Using the usual notation, and remembering the formulas (38), (49), and (50), we find:

$$(61)\qquad \begin{cases} M_{0i} = M\,\dfrac{\delta x_i}{\delta s} \\ M_{ii} = k_{ii}\,\dfrac{M}{u'} \\ M_{ij} = k_{ij}\,\dfrac{M}{u'}. \end{cases}$$

Indicating then by Δ the determinant formed by means of the cofactors of M, we obtain from the well-known formulas of the theory of determinants:

$$(62)\qquad \Delta = \begin{vmatrix} R & M_{01} & M_{02} & \cdots & M_{0n} \\ M_{10} & M_{11} & M_{12} & \cdots & M_{1n} \\ \cdots & \cdots & \cdots & \cdots & \cdots \\ M_{n0} & M_{n1} & M_{n2} & \cdots & M_{nn} \end{vmatrix} = M^n$$

and

$$(63)\qquad 0 = \frac{\Delta_{00}}{M^{n-1}},\ p_i = \frac{\Delta_{0i}}{M^{n-1}},\ u_{ii} = \frac{\Delta_{ii}}{M^{n-1}},\ u_{ij} = \frac{\Delta_{ij}}{M^{n-1}}.$$

Let us substitute in Δ the expressions for the cofactors obtained in (61):

$$(64)\qquad \Delta = \begin{vmatrix} R & M\dfrac{\delta x_1}{\delta s} & M\dfrac{\delta x_2}{\delta s} & \cdots\cdots & M\dfrac{\delta x_n}{\delta s} \\ M\dfrac{\delta x_1}{\delta s} & \dfrac{M}{u'}k_{11} & \dfrac{M}{u'}k_{12} & \cdots\cdots & \dfrac{M}{u'}k_{1n} \\ \cdots & \cdots & \cdots & \cdots & \cdots \\ M\dfrac{\delta x_n}{\delta s} & \dfrac{M}{u'}k_{n1} & \dfrac{M}{u'}k_{n2} & \cdots\cdots & \dfrac{M}{u'}k_{nn} \end{vmatrix}$$

$$= \frac{M^{n+1}}{u'^{n-1}} \begin{vmatrix} \frac{R}{u'M} & \frac{\delta x_1}{\delta s} & \frac{\delta x_2}{\delta s} & \cdots\cdots & \frac{\delta x_n}{\delta s} \\ \frac{\delta x_1}{\delta s} & k_{11} & k_{12} & \cdots\cdots & k_{1n} \\ \cdots & \cdots & \cdots & \cdots & \cdots \\ \frac{\delta x_n}{\delta s} & k_{n1} & k_{n2} & \cdots\cdots & k_{nn} \end{vmatrix}$$

Putting for brevity's sake:

(65) $$\theta = \frac{R}{u'M} = \frac{1}{u'\Omega},$$

(66) $$N = \begin{vmatrix} \theta & \frac{\delta x_1}{\delta s} & \frac{\delta x_2}{\delta s} & \cdots\cdots & \frac{\delta x_n}{\delta s} \\ \frac{\delta x_1}{\delta s} & k_{11} & k_{12} & \cdots\cdots & k_{1n} \\ \cdots & \cdots & \cdots & \cdots & \cdots \\ \frac{\delta x_n}{\delta s} & k_{n1} & k_{n2} & \cdots\cdots & k_{nn} \end{vmatrix}$$

we obtain from (62) and (64):

$$\Delta = \frac{M^{n+1}}{u'^{n-1}} N = M^n ;$$

and hence:

(67) $$M = \frac{u'^{n-1}}{N} .$$

Applying the same procedure to the cofactors of Δ, we find:

$$\Delta_{00} = \frac{M^n}{u'^n} N_{00} , \ \Delta_{0i} = \frac{M^n}{u'^{n-1}} N_{0i} ,$$

$$\Delta_{ii} = \frac{M^n}{u'^{n-2}} N_{ii} , \ \Delta_{ij} = \frac{M^n}{u'^{n-2}} N_{ij} .$$

Substituting these values in (63), and taking account of (67), we have:

(68) $$0 = \frac{N_{00}}{u'N} , \ p_i = \frac{N_{0i}}{N} , \ u_{ii} = u' \frac{N_{ii}}{N} , \ u_{ij} = u' \frac{N_{ij}}{N} .$$

Let us introduce the quantities:

$$(69)\quad P = \begin{vmatrix} 0 & \frac{\delta x_1}{\delta s} & \frac{\delta x_2}{\delta s} & \cdots\cdots & \frac{\delta x_n}{\delta s} \\ \frac{\delta x_1}{\delta s} & k_{11} & k_{12} & \cdots\cdots & k_{1n} \\ \cdots & \cdots & \cdots & \cdots & \cdots \\ \frac{\delta x_n}{\delta s} & k_{n1} & k_{n2} & \cdots\cdots & k_{nn} \end{vmatrix} \quad \text{and } Q = \begin{vmatrix} k_{11} & k_{12} & \cdots\cdots & k_{1n} \\ k_{21} & k_{22} & \cdots\cdots & k_{2n} \\ \cdots & \cdots & \cdots & \cdots \\ k_{n1} & k_{n2} & \cdots\cdots & k_{nn} \end{vmatrix}$$

which can be expressed entirely by means of empirical data. If $Q = N_{00} = 0$, as appears from (68), we find the following definitive formulas:

$$(70)\qquad u_{ii} = u'\left(\frac{P_{ii}}{P} - \theta\,\frac{Q_{ii}}{P}\right),$$

$$(71)\qquad u_{ij} = u'\left(\frac{P_{ij}}{P} - \theta\,\frac{Q_{ij}}{P}\right).$$

To demonstrate that this solution is definitive, we must prove the impossibility of obtaining θ as a function of empirical data.

For this purpose, let us begin by supposing the contrary thesis is true. Then the second derivatives of the utility function could be expressed as functions of u' and of the quantities of goods $x_1,x_2, \ldots\ldots, x_n$; and we would have:

$$u_{i1} = u'\ \varphi_1(x_1,x_2,\cdots\cdots,x_n)$$
$$u_{i2} = u'\ \varphi_2(x_1,x_2,\cdots\cdots,x_n)$$
$$\cdots\cdots\cdots\cdots\cdots\cdots\cdots\cdots$$
$$u_{in} = u'\ \varphi_n(x_1,x_2,\cdots\cdots,x_n)\,.$$

Moreover, it being always possible (at least in principle) to find the individual demand functions, the prices could be expressed as empirical functions of the quantities $x_1,x_2, \ldots\ldots, x_n$. And we could write:

$$(72)\qquad u_i = u'p_i = u'f(x_1,x_2,\cdots\cdots\cdots,x_n)\ \cdot$$

Indicating, then, by ψ_k the quotient $\dfrac{\varphi_k(x_1,x_2,\cdots\cdots\cdots,x_n)}{f(x_1,x_2,\cdots\cdots\cdots,x_n)}$, we will obtain:

$$(73)\quad \begin{cases} \dfrac{u_{i1}}{u_i} = \dfrac{\dfrac{\delta u_i}{\delta x_1}}{u_i} = \dfrac{\delta(\log u_i)}{\delta x_1} = \psi_1 \\ \dfrac{u_{i2}}{u_i} = \dfrac{\dfrac{\delta u_i}{\delta x_2}}{u_i} = \dfrac{\delta(\log u_i)}{\delta x_2} = \psi_2 \\ \dots\dots\dots\dots\dots\dots\dots\dots \\ \dfrac{u_{in}}{u_i} = \dfrac{\dfrac{\delta u_i}{\delta x_n}}{u_i} = \dfrac{\delta(\log u_i)}{\delta x_n} = \psi_n. \end{cases}$$

If our hypothesis that the utility is independent of the mode of variation corresponds to the truth, it is easy to demonstrate that there should exist equalities of the type, $\frac{\delta\psi_1}{\delta x_2} = \frac{\delta\psi_2}{\delta x_1}$, etc.; and the function log u_1 can be determined by the well-known procedure of integrating the total differential:

$$d(\log u_i) = \psi_1 dx_1 + \psi_2 dx_2 + \dots\dots + \psi_n dx_n.$$

We thus have: $\log u_i = \Psi(x_1, x_2, \dots\dots\dots, x_n) + \log C$;

$$(74)\qquad u_i = C\,e^{\Psi},$$

C being a constant of integration independent of $x_1, x_2, \dots\dots, x_n$.

If we take as our unit of measure the marginal utility of money, corresponding to a certain state of the budget, for example to that in which $x_1 = a_1$, $x_2 = a_2$, ..., $x_n = a_n$; and if we put:

$$\Psi_0 = \Psi(a_1, a_2, \cdots\cdots, a_n), \qquad f_0 = f(a_1, a_2, \cdots\cdots, a_n),$$

we shall have:

$$u' = \frac{u_i}{p_i} = \frac{C\,e^{\Psi_0}}{f_0} = 1;$$

and hence $C = f_0 e^{-\Psi_0}$. We thus obtain the solution:

$$(75)\qquad u_i = f_0\,e^{\Psi - \Psi_0}$$

Knowing, besides, all the marginal utilities as functions of

$x_1, x_2, \ldots\ldots, x_n$, it would be possible to find the total utility by the application of the same method to the equations:

$$\frac{\delta U}{\delta x_1} = u_1, \; \frac{\delta U}{\delta x_2} = u_2, \; \cdots\cdots\cdots, \; \frac{\delta U}{\delta x_n} = u_n \, .$$

The constant of integration would be given by the equation:

$$U_0 = \Phi(0,0, \cdots\cdots ,0) = 0 \, .$$

We see therefore that, if θ is known, all the marginal utilities and the utility function itself can be unequivocally determined as functions of the empirical data. But, the question having been completely clarified by V. Pareto's researches,[8] we know that when all the marginal utilities are assumed to be functions of the quantities of all the goods, unequivocal determination becomes impossible. We conclude, therefore, that θ also is not determinable, and that it should be considered an entirely arbitrary function of $x_1, x_2, \ldots\ldots, x_n$.

12. On the Concept of Utility

The definition of utility given in Section 2, being governed by a completely empirical concept, can serve as basis for the entire theory of the budget. But since the values of the marginal utilities and their variations connected with variations in the quantities of goods remain undetermined, obviously an irreconcilable conflict exists between the two aspects of the problem of utility. The value of θ being, in fact, arbitrary, we can explain observable and measurable facts of human conduct by attributing to the quantity

$$u_{ij} = \frac{P_{ij}}{P} - \theta \, \frac{Q_{ij}}{P} \, ,$$

or to the quantity:

$$u_{ii} = \frac{P_{ii}}{P} - \theta \, \frac{Q_{ii}}{P} \, ,$$

any value whatsoever: great or small, positive or negative, at our pleasure. It will be permissible, therefore, to attribute all the facts of my economic conduct to any hypotheses whatsoever on dependence, for example, between the quantity of apples I consume and the marginal utility of the paper upon which I am writing; and to suppose that with the consuming of one apple more per month the utility of a sheet of paper becomes 1000 times greater or 1000

[8] *Manuel d'économie politique* (1909), pp. 539–557.

times smaller. Both hypotheses would attribute determinate values to all the quantities u_{ii}, u_{ij}, and no contradiction need exist between either of the two modes of *explanation* and the real facts of my conduct.

Nor will a contradiction exist between the psychological concept of utility and the results at which we have arrived, it being clear that our definition of utility (the *index of ophelimity* of Pareto) is completely foreign to psychology. Nevertheless, the conclusion is not satisfactory; because, even though attaching great importance to the absolute logical independence of the methods of economic science from those of psychology, we could not ignore the existence of a very complicated interdependence between the *facts* studied by the two sciences.

We therefore consider it necessary to complete the formal concept of utility in such a manner as to put the economic aspect of the problem of utility in close relation with the psychological one. Specifically, we propose to investigate whether the following definition is admissible:

The utility of a combination of goods is a quantity which possesses the following properties: it is greater the more the combination is desired by the individual; and *its variations are immediately perceptible by the subject.*

For our present purpose a more profound investigation with respect to the character of the manifestations of utility in the consciousness of the individual is superfluous; therefore, we leave the task to future studies. On the basis of the preceding definition it can be said that, if after an increment in the quantity of good α has occurred, an individual does not observe any modification in his subjective relations with the good β, the marginal utility of the latter has not noticeably changed and there exists the approximate equality:

$$u_{\alpha\beta} = 0.$$

By "lack of modification in the subjective relations with the good" we mean to indicate all possible psychic phenomena: pleasure obtained by means of consumption, pain through loss, intensity of desire for possession, etc. Only if it could be verified that there exist no modifications of this kind, would it be permissible to assert the complete independence of the marginal utility of one good from the quantity of another.

The foregoing addition to the definition of utility notably modifies this definition from the mathematical point of view; because it determines all the values in question. In fact, solving the equation $u_{\alpha\beta} = 0$ for θ, and substituting this value in the expressions for all the other second derivatives, we find, by the method of the preceding section, the marginal utility and the utility function.

It is doubtful, however, whether the proposed definition is admissible. For, if one assumes that an individual observes no dependence, not only between the good α and the good β, but also between the goods γ and δ, ϵ and ζ, etc., we have:

$$(76)\qquad \begin{cases} u_{\alpha\beta} = \dfrac{u'}{P}\left(P_{\alpha\beta} - \theta\, Q_{\alpha\beta}\right) = 0 \\[2ex] u_{\gamma\delta} = \dfrac{u'}{P}\left(P_{\gamma\delta} - \theta\, Q_{\gamma\delta}\right) = 0 \\[2ex] u_{\epsilon\zeta} = \dfrac{u'}{P}\left(P_{\epsilon\zeta} - \theta\, Q_{\epsilon\zeta}\right) = 0 \end{cases}$$

whence it follows:

$$\theta = \frac{P_{\alpha\beta}}{Q_{\alpha\beta}} = \frac{P_{\gamma\delta}}{Q_{\gamma\delta}} = \frac{P_{\epsilon\zeta}}{Q_{\epsilon\zeta}} = \cdots.$$

But will experience confirm these relations? That is the problem.

13. On the Consciousness of Economic Conduct

Let us try to penetrate into the meaning of the question. All the economists who discussed it have thought it possible to consider marginal utilities (at least in the greater number of instances) as obeying Gossen's law as much in the case of dependence on, as in the case of independence of, the quantities of other goods; and they have classified the cases of dependence by distinguishing complementary and competing goods. This whole edifice falls if one remains loyal to the formal definition of utility, for it is impossible to deduce from the facts of conduct the character (that is, the sign) of the second derivatives of utility.

If, instead, we are convinced that the marginal utility of any one good decreases with an increase of its quantity; that, moreover, for example, sugar and tea, salt and meat, etc., are complementary, while pork and mutton are normally competing, etc., it is obvious that this conviction can be founded only upon some sort of *inter-*

nal evidence, not on facts of economic conduct. The generality of this conviction authorizes us to call it *faith in the consciousness of economic conduct.* It is in fact common opinion that the motives by which we are guided, or at least factors parallel to these, manifest themselves, more or less clearly, in our consciousness, so as to enable us to perceive the increase and decrease in their intensity.

If we admit, by way of hypothesis, such a proposition as true, our formulas permit the derivation of the following laws:

I. *If an individual does not perceive any modification in his subjective relation with the good* α *when the quantity of the good* β *varies, nor in that with* γ *when the quantity of* δ *varies, nor in that with* ϵ *when the quantity of* ζ *varies, etc., the following equalities must exist:*

$$\frac{P_{\alpha\beta}}{Q_{\alpha\beta}} = \frac{P_{\gamma\delta}}{Q_{\gamma\delta}} = \frac{P_{\epsilon\zeta}}{Q_{\epsilon\zeta}} = \cdots .$$

II. If this proposition is true, one can calculate θ and substitute its value in the formulas for u_{ii} and u_{ij}. Then, *in the case of goods which on the basis of internal evidence must be considered satiating, the following relations must hold:*

$$\frac{P_{ii}}{P} - \theta\frac{Q_{ii}}{P} < 0, \text{ or } \qquad \frac{P_{jj}}{P} - \theta\frac{Q_{jj}}{P} > 0.$$

III. *In the case of two goods which on the basis of internal evidence are regarded as complementary or competing, there must be, respectively:*

$$\frac{P_{ij}}{P} - \theta\frac{Q_{ij}}{P} > 0, \text{ or } \qquad \frac{P_{kl}}{P} - \theta\frac{Q_{kl}}{P} < 0.$$

Since the foregoing propositions can be treated empirically, we find ourselves again compelled to insist upon the urgent necessity for passing from abstract schemes to positive research, in the field embraced by the theory of the budget. Only thus could certain problems be solved, only thus certain formulas verified. But as to other problems (like those to which the propositions last propounded refer) it cannot be hoped that the empirical data required for their solution will be obtained. The calculation of the value of the determinants P and Q and of their cofactors would be possible only if we knew the quantities of *all* goods consumed by the individual and *all* the variations in the demand of *any one* good due to changes in income and in the prices of *all* goods.

It is evidently impossible to obtain all these values by observation of existing budgets; therefore, the only way that remains open is that of *experiment,* by means of which a totality of conditions similar to the budget could be created, and hence, the laws we have propounded could be confirmed or confuted.

It is worth the effort to attempt the enterprise, because if the experimental results were to lead to a confirmation of the laws, we shall have obtained in addition to this direct advantage also the ability to proceed further in investigations of the psychological aspect of utility. If, instead, the laws were not to find experimental verification, we would come to very important conclusions, not so much for the economic as for the psychic and moral sciences, for it would have been demonstrated that the variations in the value of utility were not perceptible by the subject, so the motives which govern human conduct not only by their nature escape from our consciousness but do not even indirectly become manifest to it.

These problems are much too complicated for us to attempt here not only to solve but even to present in an adequate manner. But we hope to have succeeded in bringing to light how they are connected with the theory of the budget, and in demonstrating the necessity for developing this theory further by employing the procedures proper to experimental science.

11 A Reconsideration of the Theory of Value

J. R. Hicks and R. G. D. Allen

Part I

By J. R. Hicks

THE pure theory of exchange value, after a period of intensive study by economists of the generation of Jevons and Marshall, has received comparatively little attention from their successors in the twentieth century. Apart from some very interesting inquiries into what may be called the dynamics of the subject, due to contemporary writers of the school of Vienna,[1] there has been only one major achievement in this field since 1900. That achievement was the work of Pareto, whose *Manuel* (and particularly its mathematical appendix) contains the most complete static theory of value which economic science has hitherto been able to produce.

Of all Pareto's contributions there is probably none that exceeds in importance his demonstration of the immeasurability of utility. To most earlier writers, to Marshall, to Walras, to Edgeworth, utility had been a quantity theoretically measurable; that is to say, a quantity which would be measurable if we had enough facts. Pareto definitely abandoned this, and replaced the concept of utility by the concept of a scale of preferences. It is not always observed that this change in concepts was not merely a change of view, a pure matter of methodology; it rested on a positive demonstration that the facts of observable conduct make a scale of preferences capable of theoretical construction (in the same sense as above) but they do not enable us to proceed from the scale of preference to a particular utility function.

The first signs of a break-down of the old conception of

[1] Schönfeld, *Grenznutzen und Wirtschaftsrechnung*; Hans Mayer, *Der Erkenntniswert der funktionellen Preistheorien* (*Wirtschaftstheorie der Gegenwart II*); Rosenstein-Rodan, "La Complementarità" (*Riforma Sociale*, May 1933).

Reprinted from *Economica*, Vol. 1, Parts 1 & 2, (February, 1934), pp. 52–76; and (May, 1934), pp. 196–219, by permission of the publisher and authors.

utility had already made their appearance in Irving Fisher's *Mathematical Investigations into the Theory of Prices.* Fisher had pointed out (1) that the whole theory of equilibrium in a market depends on the assumption of directions of indifference, and does not involve anything more; (2) that with three or more commodities the directions of indifference may not be integrable, so that it is impossible to deduce any utility function from a knowledge of these directions.[1] This latter point also makes its appearance in Pareto; it led him to his celebrated but mysterious theory of " open cycles "; however, it is *not* with that point that we are at present concerned. It is with Pareto's more general and economically more significant contention, that even if it is possible to deduce a utility function from the directions of indifference, that utility function is to a very large extent indeterminate.

Though Pareto states this conclusion in the text of the *Manuel*,[2] he does not prove it there, and this has no doubt been responsible for the failure of many readers to see its significance. But a proof is given in the mathematical appendix;[3] it is not a difficult proof, and its sense can be set out in words quite easily.

Suppose, for the moment, that we have a utility function given; that is to say, we know, for the individual in question, how much utility he would derive from any given set of quantities of the goods on the market. Then we can deduce from this function (assuming always that he will prefer a higher to a lower utility) a scale of preferences; we can say, of any two sets, whether he will prefer one to the other, or whether they will be indifferent to him. If there are only two sorts of goods, this scale of preferences can be represented by a diagram of indifference curves.

It is thus possible to proceed from a utility function to a scale of preferences; but is it possible to proceed in the reverse direction? The answer is no; for the function with which we started is not the only function which will determine the scale in question. It is not only that there may be an indeterminate constant (this would not matter very much); but we can take as an " index " of utility any variable which has the same value all along an indifference curve, and which increases as we proceed from one indifference curve to a higher one. Thus we might take the function with which we started; or we might take double that function (but this would only mean a change in units); however, we might also take its

[1] *Mathematical Investigations*, p. 88. [2] *Manuel*, p. 159. [3] *Ibid.*, pp. 540-2.

square, or any variable having a more complex relation with the first, so long as the essential condition of increasing in preferred positions is preserved.

To take an arithmetical illustration : Successive positions might be numbered 1, 2, 3, 4, 5; or 1, 4, 9, 16, 25; or 1, 2, 4, 5, 7; or any increasing series we like to take. So far as the actual behaviour of any individual can possibly show, any such series would do absolutely as well as any other.

The methodological implications of this " ordinal " conception of utility have been discussed elsewhere;[1] they are very far-reaching indeed. By transforming the subjective theory of value into a general logic of choice, they extend its applicability over wide fields of human conduct. Two opportunities for the exercise of this new freedom seem of particular importance for the future of economics. One is the economic theory of the state, where the shackles of utilitarianism have always galled; the other is the theory of risk, where the application of the same logic seems fundamental to any progress in economic dynamics.

The present paper, however, is not concerned with these wide questions. Its task is the more pedestrian one of examining what adjustments in the statement of the marginal theory of value are made necessary by Pareto's discovery. As it happens, this task was not by any means completely carried through by Pareto himself. Much of his theory had already been constructed before he realised the immeasurability of utility, and he never really undertook the labour of reconstruction which his discovery had made necessary.

There are, however, two later writers whose work goes some way towards supplying this deficiency; they are W. E. Johnson and R. G. D. Allen. Johnson's work[2] does not appear to spring directly from Pareto; it is based rather upon Edgeworth; but it is much less dependent upon a " cardinal "

[1] Cf. Zawadski, *Les Mathématiques appliquées à l'économie politique*, ch. iii; Schönfeld, *Grenznutzen und Wirtschaftsrechnung*, Part I ; Wicksteed, *Common Sense of Political Economy*, ch. v ; Robbins, *Nature and Significance of Economic Science*, ch. vi.

Reference should also be made to Edgeworth's interesting remarks on Pareto's doctrine (*Papers*, vol. ii, pp. 472-6). It has become increasingly hard to accept Edgeworth's contention that the existence of theories of Public Finance and Industrial Conciliation depending on the measurability of utility ought to be regarded as an argument in favour of maintaining that assumption. For its abandonment need not imply the abandonment of these undoubtedly valuable doctrines ; it serves instead as a stimulus to the construction of new theories of wider validity, into which the traditional teaching can subsequently be fitted as a special case, depending on the introduction of a particular ethical postulate.

[2] "The Pure Theory of Utility Curves," ECONOMIC JOURNAL, 1913.

conception of utility than any of theirs. It was further developed by Mr. Allen in a pair of articles written before our collaboration began;[1] the present paper is the result, first, of my own reflections about Mr. Allen's work, and secondly, of our collaboration in working out the details of a theory which shall be free of the inconsistencies detected in Pareto.[2]

What has now to be done is to take in turn a number of the main concepts which have been evolved by the subjective theory; to examine which of them are affected by the immeasurability of utility; and of those which have to be abandoned, to enquire what, if anything, can be put in their place. It is hoped in this way to assist in the construction of a theory of value in which all concepts that pretend to quantitative exactitude, can be rigidly and exactly defined.

I

1. *Marginal utility.* If total utility is not quantitatively definable, neither is marginal utility. But the theory of value does not need any precise definition of marginal utility. What it does need is only this; that when an individual's system of wants is given, and he possesses any given set of goods, *X*, *Y*, *Z*, . . . we should know his *marginal rate of substitution* between any two goods. The marginal rate of substitution of any good *Y* for any other good *X* is defined as the quantity of good *Y* which would just compensate him for the loss of a marginal unit of *X*. If he got less than this quantity of *Y*, he would be worse off than before the substitution took place; if he got more he would be better off; there must be some quantity which would leave him exactly as well off as before.

It will be evident to the reader that this *marginal rate of substitution* is nothing else than what we have been in the habit of calling the ratio of the marginal utility of *X* to that of *Y*; we might have called it the "relative marginal utility."

[1] "Nachfragefunktionen für Güter mit korreliertem Nutzen" (*Zeitschrift für Nationalökonomie*, Mar. 1934); "A Comparison between different definitions of complementary and competitive goods" (to appear in *Econometrica*).

[2] Our co-operation has been so close that it has been completely impossible to separate out his results from mine in any orderly presentation. It has therefore seemed best that I should present our whole theory in a non-mathematical form, while Mr. Allen follows it with a mathematical version. But this division does not of course correspond in any way to the actual process by which the theory was constructed. Mathematics and economics went hand in hand; nor would the reader find it easy to identify our respective shares by a consideration of the technique necessary to reach particular points.

My reasons for suggesting what is certain to be a rather tiresome change in terminology are these. If once we introduce marginal utilities, then, with the best will in the world, it is extraordinarily difficult to keep these two marginal utilities together; they have an almost irresistible tendency to wander apart. It would be possible to work out the whole of the following theory, using as our basic concept the ratio of the marginal utility of *X* to that of *Y*, the quantities possessed (or consumed) of all commodities being given; but we should have to keep a strong hold on ourselves, or we should soon be finding some indirect way of talking about one marginal utility by itself— or, what is equally indefensible, talking about the ratio of the marginal utility of *X* (when one set of quantities is possessed) to the marginal utility of *Y* (when the quantity possessed is in some way different).

A second reason may perhaps become clear in what follows. There does seem to be some advantage to be gained from concentrating our attention at this early stage on the essentially substitutional character of the concept.

If an individual is to be in equilibrium with respect to a system of market prices, his marginal rate of substitution between any two goods must equal the ratio of their prices. Otherwise he would clearly find an advantage in substituting some quantity of one for an equal value (at the market rate) of the other. This is the form in which we now have to write the law of proportionality between marginal utilities and prices.

When quantities of *X* and *Y* are represented on an indifference-diagram (quantities of all other goods possessed being therefore supposed given), the marginal rate of substitution between *X* and *Y* is measured by the slope of the indifference-curve which passes through the point at which the individual is situated. This depends simply upon the system of indifference-curves; given the indifference-map, we can read off directly the slope at any point; given the slopes at all points within a region, we can reconstruct the indifference-map for that region.[1]

[1] For more than two commodities the corresponding proposition is not necessarily true. For n goods, we have n-1 independent marginal rates of substitution (those of *X* and *Y*, *X* and *Z*, *X* and *W*, etc.; the rest can be deduced from these). But from these n-1 marginal rates of substitution it is only possible to construct an indifference-diagram (or what corresponds to an indifference-diagram in n-dimensional space) if some further conditions are satisfied (the integrability conditions). This proposition, which exercises a great fascination over the minds of mathematical economists, remains of doubtful economic significance. Some conclusions which are only valid if the integrability conditions are satisfied, will be given below.

2. *Diminishing marginal utility*. The principle of diminishing marginal utility must similarly give place to *increasing marginal rate of substitution*. Starting with given quantities of all the goods *X*, *Y*, *Z*, . . .; if we first replace a marginal unit of *X* by that quantity of *Y* which just makes up for it; and then replace a second marginal unit of *X* by that quantity of *Y* which just makes up for this second unit: the second quantity of *Y* must be greater than the first. In other words, the more we substitute *Y* for *X*, the greater will be the marginal rate of substitution of *Y* for *X*.

This condition is expressed on the indifference diagram by drawing the indifference-curves convex towards the axes. (The curves must of course always slope downwards if the goods are both positively desired.)

The replacement of *diminishing marginal utility* by this principle of *increasing marginal rate of substitution* is something more than a mere change in terminology. When we seek to translate the principle of *diminishing marginal utility* into definable terms, it does not appear at first sight evident that this is the condition we must use. And it is an interesting historical fact that when Pareto found himself confronted with this question, he first of all gave the condition that the indifference-curves must be convex to the origin, and then went on to add a further condition: that the marginal rate of substitution will increase, not only when *Y* is substituted for *X*, but also when the supply of *Y* is increased without any reduction in the supply of *X*. This condition looks as good a translation of *diminishing marginal utility* as the other, but (as Pareto ultimately realised[1]) it stands on an altogether different footing. Cases which do not satisfy this latter principle undoubtedly exist in plenty, and there is no particular difficulty in fitting them into a general theory.[2] Exceptions to the true principle of increasing marginal rate of substitution would be much more serious.

For it is certain that for a position to be one of stable equilibrium at given prices, the marginal rate of substitution *at that point* must be increasing. If it is not, then, even if the marginal rate of substitution equals the price ratio, so that the sale of one marginal unit of *X* would not give any appreciable advantage, nevertheless the sale of a larger quantity would be advantageous. Equilibrium would be unstable—the individual would be at a point of minimum, not maximum, satisfaction.

[1] *Manuel* (French edition), p. 573-4; cf. the earlier Italian edition, pp. 502-3 (of the 1919 reprint).

[2] See below, sec. ii, 1, of this paper.

The assumption that the principle of increasing marginal rate of substitution is universally true, thus means simply that any point, throughout the region we are considering, might be a point of equilibrium with appropriate prices. There must be some points at which it is true, or we could get no equilibrium at all. To assume it true universally is a serious assumption, but one which seems justifiable until significant facts are adduced which make it necessary for us to pay careful attention to exceptions.[1]

3. *Elasticity of substitution.* The replacement of *diminishing marginal utility* by *increasing marginal rate of substitution* has this further advantage: it becomes significant and useful to ask: " Increasing how rapidly ? " Economists whose theory was based on diminishing marginal utility have rarely had the courage to ask a corresponding question; and when they have done so they have not derived much advantage from it. But our conception is strictly quantitative; and the rate of increase of the marginal rate of substitution may be expected to play an important part in the development of theory.

It is obvious that the two main conditions under which indifference lines are drawn—(1) downward slope, since an increase in either commodity leads to a preferred position; (2) convexity to the origin, from the principle of *increasing marginal rate of substitution*—leave open a wide variety of different shapes which may be taken by the curves. They may vary from the one extreme of straight lines at an oblique angle to the axes (the case of perfect substitutes) to the other of pairs of perpendicular straight lines parallel to the axes (the case of goods which must be used in fixed proportions). Between these extremes any degree of curvature is possible.

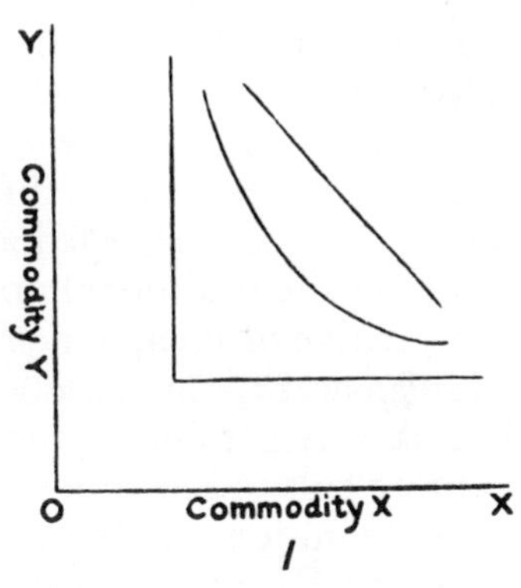

I

The curvature of the indifference-curve describes the same property as the " rate of increase of the marginal rate of substi-

[1] Exceptions would presumably take the form of " blind spots " on the indifference diagram—regions within which no stable equilibrium would be possible. These would also involve the possibility of cases of " Buridan's ass "; the consumer with given income, confronted with given prices, would still be unable to decide between a number of different distributions of expenditure.

tution." But to take either as our measure without correction for units would be impossible—the result would have as little significance as the uncorrected *slope* of a demand curve. A measure free from this objection fortunately now lies ready to our hand. It is the *elasticity of substitution*, when defined in a a way analogous to that used by Mrs. Robinson and Mr. Lerner.[1]
Applied to this problem it becomes

$$\frac{\text{relative increase in the proportion possessed of the two commodities } (Y/X)}{\text{relative increase in the marginal rate of substitution of } Y \text{ for } X}$$

when a small amount of Y is substituted for X, in such a way as to compensate the consumer for his loss. (That is to say, it is taken along the indifference-curve.)

One of the advantages of this particular measure is that it is symmetrical; if we write X for Y, and Y for X, in the above, the result is unchanged. It is therefore a general measure of substitutibility; when the commodities are perfect substitutes, (so that the rate of increase of the marginal rate of substitution is zero), the elasticity of substitution becomes infinite; when they have to be used in fixed proportions (the other extreme) the elasticity of substitution is zero. Negative elasticities of substitution are, of course, ruled out by the principle of increasing marginal rate of substitution.

4. *Complementarity.* If (as appears from the above) any two goods are to be regarded as more or less substitutes, what becomes of the traditional doctrine that two goods may be either competitive or complementary? It will not be possible to give a full answer to this question until much later in this paper, but it is already possible to indicate why the traditional conception entirely fails to accommodate itself to our present construction. The definition of complementary (and competitive) goods given by Pareto and Edgeworth[2] (these seem to be the only major economists who have given an exact definition in terms of the general theory of wants) is completely dependent on the

[1] Robinson, *Economics of Imperfect Competition*, p. 256; Lerner, "Elasticity of Substitution" (*Review of Economic Studies*, Oct. 1933, pp. 68-70). The definition given in my *Theory of Wages*, though appropriate, under certain assumptions, to the theory of production, is not valid here.

[2] Pareto, *Manuel*, p. 268; Edgeworth, *Papers*, vol. i, p. 117.

notion of utility as a determinate function. On their view, complementary goods are such that an increase in the supply of one will increase the marginal utility of the other; competitive goods are such that the marginal utility of the other will be lowered. This test cannot be translated into terms of marginal rates of substitution; it becomes definitely ambiguous when account is taken of the immeasurability of utility. In the vast majority of cases, the goods will be complementary or competitive, *on this definition*, according to the particular arbitrary measure of utility we choose to take.[1]

For the moment, then, let us put complementarity aside.

[1] If the utility function could be uniquely defined as $\phi(x,y)$, then the Paretian test would be given by the sign of ϕ_{xy}. But if we adopt his own doctrine that any other function of ϕ, $F(\phi)$, could equally well be taken as the utility function, this test breaks down. For

$$\frac{\partial^2}{\partial x \partial y} F(\phi) = F'(\phi) . \ \phi_{xy} + F''(\phi) . \ \phi_x \phi_y$$

and in general there is no reason why this should have the same sign as ϕ_{xy}, even though $F'(\phi)$ should be taken as positive.

II

1. *The expenditure curve.* We have in the elasticity of substitution one of the fundamental concepts on which our further enquiries will be based; but it is not by itself an adequate foundation for a theory of value. For the elasticity of substitution refers only to one possible kind of change: that which takes place if one commodity is substituted for another, if, that is to say, the individual moves from one position to another on the same indifference-curve. But this kind of movement is not the only one of which we have to take account. When the conditions of the market change, the individual does not usually move along the same indifference-curve; he is usually made better off or worse off by the change, so that he moves from one indifference-line to another. We, therefore, need information, not only about the shapes of particular curves, but about the mutual relations of the curves.

Take any point P on a given indifference-map, and draw the tangent at P to the indifference-curve that passes through P. Now draw a series of straight lines parallel to that first tangent, and mark off on each line the point where it touches a curve of the system. (By the principle of increasing marginal rate of substitution there can for each line be only one such point.) Now join these points. The curve so formed I shall call an *expenditure-curve*. It follows from the same principle of increasing marginal rate of substitution, that this expenditure-curve can cut any indifference-curve in one point only, and that there can be only one expenditure-curve through any point. But through any point an expenditure-curve can be drawn.[1]

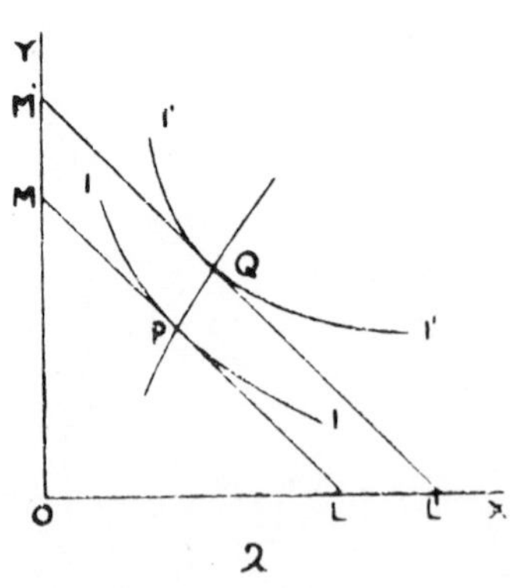

The significance of this construction should be clear. The point P is a position of equilibrium (income being spent wholly upon commodities X and Y), when the relative prices of X and

[1] The reason why these further elaborations are not necessary in the theory of production—at least in its elementary stages—is that the assumption of a homogeneous production function implies that all "expenditure-curves" are straight lines through the origin.

E

Y are as OM/OL, and when the income of the individual is OL (measured in terms of X) or OM (measured in terms of Y). The point Q is a position of equilibrium when the relative prices are the same (since the tangents are parallel) but income has increased (from OL to OL', or OM to OM'). The expenditure-curve thus describes the way in which the consumption of the two commodities varies, when prices remain unchanged, but there is a change in total expenditure.

What is the relation between the expenditure-curve through P (or rather its slope at P) and the elasticity of substitution at P? Strictly, they describe different things, for while the latter is a characteristic of a single indifference-curve, the former describes the relationship of one indifference-curve to others. Expenditure-curves of all sorts of slopes are compatible with elasticities of substitution of all sorts of magnitudes.

There is, however, one limitation on this. Since no expenditure-curve can cut an indifference-curve more than once, the variety of possible slopes the expenditure-curve can show is a little more restricted when the elasticity of substitution is low than when it is high. For finite changes, at any rate, an expenditure-curve through P which slopes very much to the left, or very much downwards, becomes distinctly more probable the flatter the expenditure-curve at P is, though this probability is reduced if there are stretches of greater curvature

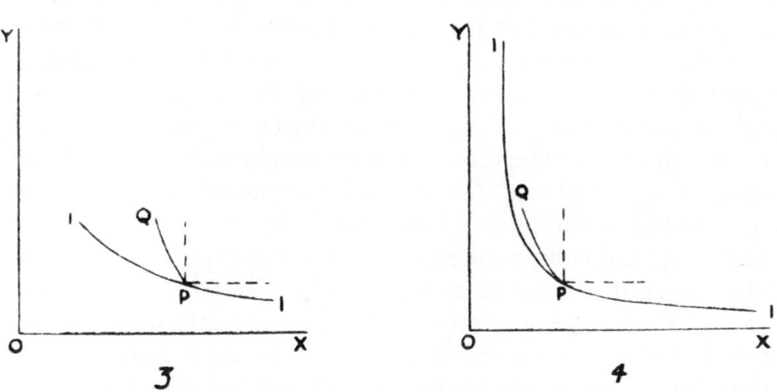

(or lower elasticity of substitution) in the neighbourhood of P.[1] In the case of fixed proportions (elasticity of substitution

[1] Very abnormal expenditure-curves (downward or backward sloping) are undoubtedly most likely at the extremities of the indifference-curves; for most indifference-curves become fairly flat as they approach the axes.

zero) the expenditure-curve must of course slope to the right and upwards.

Now if the expenditure-curve is positively inclined, this means that an increase in income will increase the consumption of both commodities (*X* and *Y*). If the expenditure-curve is downward-sloping, an increase in income will increase the consumption of *X* but diminish that of *Y*; if it is backward-sloping, *X* will be diminished and *Y* increased. These latter cases may arise whether or not the goods are easily capable of substitution, but they are distinctly less likely when the elasticity of substitution is low.

It is these cases which are ruled out by Pareto's condition, which we quoted above as a possible interpretation of *diminishing marginal utility*—the interpretation which we discarded. If, for example, the expenditure-curve is backward-sloping, this means that the point *Q* (where the higher indifference-curve has the same slope as the lower curve at *P*) lies to the left of *P*; and since (by *our* principle of increasing marginal rate of substitution) the slope of any indifference-curve must increase from right to left, or diminish from left to right, the higher indifference-curve must have a smaller slope at the point vertically above *P* than the lower indifference-curve has at *P*. The marginal rate of substitution therefore diminishes when *Y* is increased and *X* is left unchanged.

Pareto's condition would thus limit us to positively-inclined expenditure-curves; but there is no particular reason why we should limit ourselves to cases which satisfy this condition.[1] Negatively-inclined expenditure-curves do occur; they are found whenever one of the commodities is an "inferior" good, which is most largely consumed at relatively low levels of income, being replaced (or partially replaced) by goods of higher quality when income increases.

The most convenient measure for that property expressed by the expenditure-curve is simply the elasticity of demand for *X* (or *Y*) *in terms of income*. (The two are interdependent.) We shall find it convenient in this paper to use the conception of elasticity of demand in several senses additional to that given it by Marshall. Strictly speaking, the individual's demand for any commodity depends, not only on the price of that commodity, but also on the prices of all other commodities purchased, *and on his income*. A change in any one of these

[1] A theory limited by this condition (and by this alone), would not be appreciably simpler than a more general theory; and it would certainly fail to cover all the facts.

variables may affect the demand for X; and we can measure the dependence of demand on any of these variables by an elasticity. (Of course, many of these elasticities will usually be negligible.)[1]

The income-elasticity of demand for X therefore

$$= \frac{\text{relative increase in demand for } X}{\text{relative increase in income}}$$

when income is increased by a small amount, but the prices of all goods remain the same.

If there are only two goods purchased (the case to which our expenditure-curve directly refers), then a negative income-elasticity of demand for X means that the expenditure-curve is backward-sloping. A zero elasticity gives a vertical expenditure-curve. An elasticity of unity indicates that the consumption of each good increases in the same proportion as income, so that the slope of the expenditure-curve becomes the same as that of the line OP. If the expenditure-curve is downward-sloping, the income-elasticity of Y must be negative, and consequently the income-elasticity of X must be greater than $\frac{1}{k}$, where k_x is the proportion of income initially spent on X.[2]

The conception of income-elasticity of demand is obviously applicable, however many are the goods on which income is spent.

2. *Constant marginal utility.* A simple application of the preceding argument is the translation of Marshall's " constant marginal utility " into exactly definable terms. If the marginal utility of commodity Y is constant, the marginal rate of substitution between X and Y must depend on X only. If the quantity of X is given, the marginal rate of substitution (or the slope of the indifference-curve) is given, too; the tangents to the indifference-curves at all points with the same abscissa must be parallel.

Since the expenditure-curve is drawn through points of

[1] Cf. Lange, " Die allgemeine Interdependenz der Wirtschaftsgrössen und die Isolierungsmethode " (*Zeitschrift für Nationalökonomie* 1932).

[2] This latter proposition follows at once from the condition that k_x × income-elasticity of demand for X + k_y × income-elasticity of demand for $Y = 1$; for the small increase in income is supposed to be spent wholly upon X and Y. A similar proposition holds for any number of commodities.

parallel tangency, the expenditure-curve must be vertical, and the income-elasticity of demand for X must be zero. This property is again capable of extension to any number of goods. If the marginal utility of any one commodity out of many is constant, the income-elasticities of all the rest will be zero.[1]

III

1. *The demand-curve.* The two indices we have now developed, the elasticity of substitution and the income-elasticity of demand, describe the two most important characteristics of the individual's scale of preferences in the immediate neighbourhood of the position where he happens to find himself. They are the analytical tools which we may now proceed to apply; and the first object of analysis must inevitably be the ordinary demand-curve.

Here we may conveniently begin with a geometrical treatment, concentrating in consequence on the case where income is spent on two goods only—the case most amenable to the geometrical method.

Income is now to be taken as fixed, and the price of Y as fixed: but the price of X is variable. The possibilities of expenditure open to him are thus given by straight lines joining M (OM = income measured in terms of Y) to points on OX which vary as the price changes. Each price of X will determine a line LM (OL increasing as the price falls); and the point of equilibrium corresponding to each price will be given by the point where the line LM touches an indifference-curve. Joining these points, we get a demand-curve.[2]

Now it is obvious (again from the convexity of the indifference-curves) that any single indifference-curve must be touched by a line through M at a point to the right

[1] When restated in accordance with this, the argument of Marshall V. 2. (that notable incursion into the dynamic theory of value) remains of course perfectly valid. If the article on which interest is concentrated is only one among many, only a small part of the increase in income due to an early favourable bargain is likely to be spent on that particular article; so that the demand curve for further units is unlikely to be much affected by such market aberrations. That is essentially all Marshall's argument comes to.

[2] Strictly speaking, demand-and-supply curve reversed. Supposing the individual to start with a given amount OM of Y, we might subtract each ordinate of the above curve from OM, and get a demand-and-supply (or offer) curve of the ordinary type.

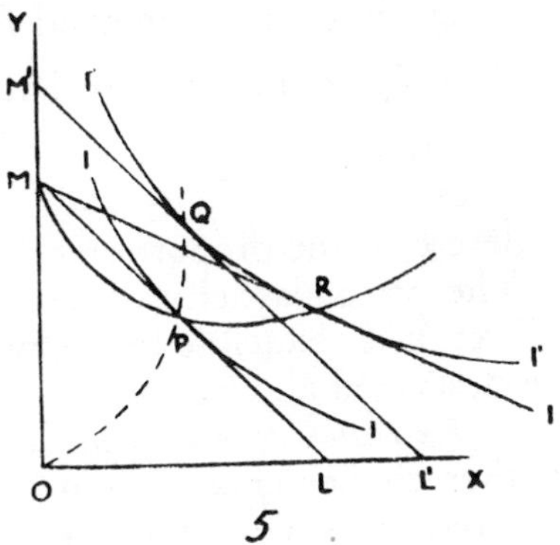

of that where it is touched by a line parallel to LM and above it. Therefore, as we move on to higher indifference curves, the demand-curve through P must lie to the right of the expenditure-curve through P; that is to say, the slope of the demand-curve must be less than the slope of the expenditure-curve.

Further, it is fairly evident from the diagram that the difference between these slopes—the extent to which R will be pushed to the right of Q—will depend upon the curvature of the indifference-curves, that is to say, upon the elasticity of substitution. The greater the elasticity of substitution—the flatter, therefore, the indifference-curves—the greater will be the divergence between the expenditure-curve and the demand-curve.

The increase in demand for a commodity X, which results from a fall in its price, depends therefore partly upon the income-elasticity of demand for X, and partly upon the elasticity of substitution between X and Y. We can in fact look upon the increase in demand as consisting of two parts, one of which is due to the increase in real income which a fall in the price of X entails, the other to the opportunity of substituting X for other goods which results from the fall in the *relative* price of X.

The relative importance of these two components depends fairly obviously upon the proportion of income initially spent on X. The larger that proportion, the greater will be the increase in real income resulting from a given fall in the price of X; and this will increase the importance of the income-elasticity relatively to the elasticity of substitution.

These geometrical and verbal reasonings hardly enable us to proceed to a formula for the elasticity of demand for X (in the ordinary sense, elasticity with respect to the price of X). But they are exactly corroborated by the algebraic analysis which will be given by Mr. Allen.[1] It is there rigorously proved that with two commodities:

[1] See Part II of this article, sect. I, 3 (*b*).

Price-elasticity of demand for X

$$= k_x \times \text{income-elasticity of demand for } X + (1 - k_x) \times \text{elasticity of substitution between } X \text{ and } Y$$

(where k_x is the proportion of income spent upon X).

The price-elasticity of demand is thus not an independent index; it is reducible to the two primary characteristics which we described above.

2. *Extension to more than two goods.* Our formula has this further convenience, that it is capable of extension, with the slightest possible amendment, to the much more important case where more than two goods are consumed. We have only to write, instead of " elasticity of substitution between X and Y," " elasticity of substitution between X and all the other goods taken together." For the rest, the formula remains unchanged.[1]

The sense of this extension can be interpreted as follows: Since it is only the price of X which varies, while the prices of Y, Z . . . remain unchanged, these latter goods remain freely substitutible for each other at fixed ratios given by their relative prices. They behave, therefore, just like perfect substitutes, and a collection of perfect substitutes can be regarded as a single commodity. But the single composite " commodity," which is thus formed by Y, Z, . . . taken together must be regarded as similar to a commodity with a wide variety of *uses*; the substitution among themselves of Y, Z, . . . is of precisely the same character as the reshuffling of quantities of the second commodity among different uses which might very well take place, even if there were only two commodities altogether.

Now it is fairly clear that with two commodities only, the elasticity of substitution between X and Y is likely to be greater, other things being equal, if Y has a wide variety of uses than it will be if Y is very specialised—this is evidently one of the main influences affecting the elasticity of substitution. Applying this to the " many commodities " case, it follows that the elasticity of substitution between X and the " composite commodity " is likely to be greater the more various the components of the latter are, i.e. the smaller are their mutual elasticities of substitution.[2]

[1] See Part II, sect. II, 4 (*b*).

[2] The elasticity of substitution between X and YZ thus varies inversely with the elasticity of substitution between Y and Z.

Consequently, the elasticity of demand for any commodity is likely to be greater the more various are the objects of consumption with which it is in competition.

3. *The " rising " demand-curve.* Our analysis has now provided us with an exact definition of the conditions on which the elasticity of an individual's demand for a particular commodity X must depend. Since, of the two terms of which our formula is composed, the second must be positive, but the first is not restricted in sign, a highly inelastic demand is possible either (1) if both terms are positive and very small, or (2) if the first term is negative. Now, as we have seen, when X is only one good among several, it is unlikely that the elasticity of substitution between X and the other goods together will be very small, so that a highly inelastic demand is less probable in case (1) than in case (2). In that second case, where X is an inferior good, the elasticity of demand will clearly be smaller, the higher the proportion of income spent on X.

When the income-elasticity is negative, there is no absolute reason why we should be limited to positive price-elasticities of demand, i.e. to downward-sloping demand-curves. If X is a good very decidedly " inferior," so that its income-elasticity is negative and fairly large; if k_x is also large, so that a large proportion of income is spent on X; if, finally, the elasticity of substitution between X and other goods is moderately small; then the first (negative) term in our formula may outweigh the second (positive) one.

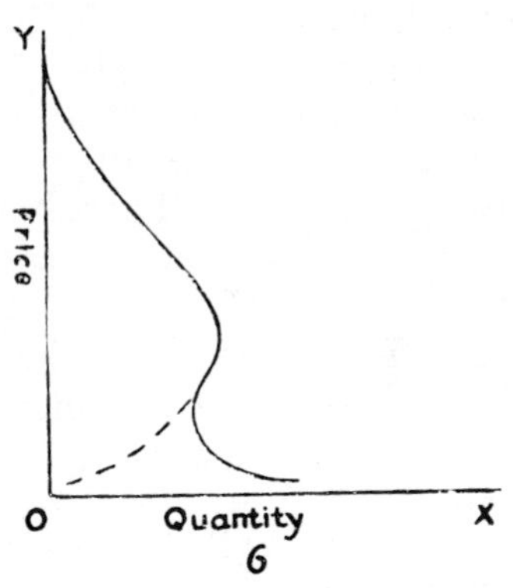

6

This possibility can easily be recognised as the celebrated Giffen case referred to by Marshall,[1] when the consumption of bread may actually be reduced by a fall in its price. Our analysis shows that it is perfectly consistent with the principle of *increasing marginal rate of substitution*; but it is only possible at low levels of income, when a large proportion of expenditure is devoted to this "inferior" commodity, and when, among the small number of other objects consumed, there are none that are at all easily substitutible for the first. As the standard of living rises, and

[1] Marshall, *Principles*, 8th edition, p. 132.

expenditure becomes increasingly diversified it is a situation which becomes increasingly improbable.[1]

IV

Complementarity

1. It is perfectly consistent with the theory we have so far elaborated, to suppose that all goods are more or less related in consumption; yet we have made no use of the conception of *complementary and competitive goods*. We have not used it, because we had no need to use it; we had not yet come to the problem where it is relevant.

Substitution, indeed, comes into the theory of value from the start. Any two goods are substitutes—more or less. But complementarity, in the strict sense in which we shall define it, is not a possible property of two goods; it only has sense when the goods in question are at least three.

We have already examined the reaction of a fall in the price of one good on the quantity demanded of that good; and we have discovered that our analysis was applicable, however many other goods are simultaneously consumed. We have now to enquire how such a fall in price reacts on the demand for one particular good out of these other goods.

The same principle which we have previously applied will obviously hold here. The change in the demand for Y resulting from a fall in the price of X will again consist of two parts. (1) There will be the change in demand for Y resulting from the increase in real income; (2) there will be the change in demand resulting from the substitution of X for the rest, owing to the fall in its relative price.

Of these two components, the first will normally be positive, but will be negative if Y is an " inferior " good. The second will depend on how far the substitution in favour of X takes place at the expense of Y rather than of the other goods (Z). If Y and Z are more or less on the same footing in the scale of wants, so that they are sacrificed fairly equally, then the second

[1] The demand curve on our diagram (p. 21) must first descend from M as the price of X falls (its elasticity > 1). After a time it may rise again (become inelastic); and then—only then—it may curl back towards the Y-axis.

On a price-quantity diagram the resultant curve would look like Fig. 6, page 68. But it might conceivably continue to curve back to the price-axis (dotted line).

component will evidently be negative; and such negativeness we clearly ought to regard as the normal case. When the second component is negative, we shall say that *Y is competitive with X against Z.*

On the other hand, it is possible that the substitution in favour of X may not, as in this case, take place partly at the expense of Y, partly at the expense of Z. It may carry with it a simultaneous substitution of Y for Z; so that the whole effect of the substitution in favour of X is that the consumption of *X and Y* is increased, but that of Z is diminished—of course, more than in the preceding case. If this is so, we shall say that *Y is complementary with X against Z*; and here the *second component* of the preceding paragraphs will be positive.

For three goods, we may thus distinguish three possible cases; either Y and Z are both competitive with X (against Z and Y respectively); or Y is complementary and Z competitive; or Z is complementary and Y competitive. It is impossible for both Y and Z to be complementary with X, since this would infringe the principle of increasing marginal rate of substitution.

For more than three goods, the possibilities are obviously extended; but it remains impossible for all of the other n-1 goods to be complementary with any one good. It is possible, however, for all the remaining n-1 goods to be competitive with the first.

2. The definition of complementarity just given, although it indicates the most important property of complementary (or competitive) goods, is, as a definition, not altogether satisfactory. For there is implied in it the assumption that when X is substituted for Y and Z, the ratio of the prices of Y and Z remains unchanged, and it is only the price of X relatively to these prices which varies. (Any change in the YZ price-ratio would of course affect the quantities substituted.) Since there is implicit in our definition this assumption about price-ratios, we have not succeeded in defining complementarity (as we ought to do) purely in terms of the individual's preference-scale; we are making a reference to the market which is better avoided.

Since there is an indefinite number of ways in which two goods Y and Z can be substituted for a marginal unit of X, it is best to concentrate our attention on that case which is the watershed between competitiveness and complementarity—the case when substitution in favour of X tends to leave the amount consumed of *Y* unchanged. Suppose then that *X* is substituted for *Z*, but *Y* remains unchanged. This simple substitution will affect not only the marginal rate of substitution between *X* and *Z* (in the way previously analysed), it will also affect the marginal rate of substitution between *Y* and *Z*. Since the quantity of *Z* is being diminished, the " normal " effect will be to shift the marginal rate of substitution between *Y* and *Z* in favour of *Z*, or against *Y*[1]; *Y* is then competitive with *X* against *Z*. But if (as is possible) the marginal rate of substitution is shifted in the opposite direction (in favour of *Y*), then *Y* is complementary with *X*.

This second definition is really nothing more than a re-statement of the first, and their equivalence is readily shown. If the marginal rate of substitution is shifted against *Y*, then (if the price ratio between *Y* and *Z* remains unchanged), there will be a tendency to substitute *Z* for *Y*, i.e. some *Y* will be sacrificed. If the marginal rate of substitution is shifted in favour of *Y*, then not only is *X* substituted for *Z* (as we are already supposing to be the case), but *Y* increases at the expense of *Z* as well.[2]

3. The test of complementarity or competitiveness is thus established: the change in the marginal rate of substitution between *Y* and *Z* which follows on a marginal substitution of *X* for *Z*. Not only does the direction of this change indicate *whether* the goods are complementary or competitive, but also the degree of change (when properly adjusted) can be used as a *measure* of complementarity. But the definition of this "elasticity of complementarity," and the detailed analysis which it makes possible, are so complex, that we must content ourselves here with a mere statement of results, whose proof must be left over to Mr. Allen's mathematical version.[3]

It is there shown that:

(*a*) the elasticity of demand for *Y* relatively to the price of *X*

$= k_x \times$ (Income-elasticity of demand for *Y* + Elasticity of complementarity of *Y* with *X* against *Z*).

(The elasticity of complementarity is, of course, positive or negative, according as the goods are complementary or competitive.)

[1] That is to say, it will increase the amount of *Y* needed to replace a marginal unit of *Z*. [2] See Part II, sect. II, 4, 5. [3] See Part II, sect. II and sect III, 1, 2.

(*b*) If the integrability conditions are satisfied (and as a general rule we may probably take it that they are), so that *a* utility function could be formed, though not one utility function only; then it is true that the elasticity of complementarity of *Y* with *X* against *Z* *equals* the elasticity of complementarity of *X* with *Y* against *Z*. In general, therefore, it is quite correct to talk about *X* and *Y* being complementary (or competitive) with respect to *Z*, without having recourse to the more elaborate terminology we have hitherto employed.[1]

(*c*) From this it can be shown in precisely what way complementarity will be reflected in demand relations. For the elasticity of demand for *X* relatively to the price of *Y* $= k_y \times$ (Income-elasticity of demand for *X* + elasticity of complementarity of *XY* against *Z*).

Whether or not this will have the same sign as the elasticity of demand for *Y* relatively to the price of *X* thus depends on the difference between the income-elasticities of the two commodities. If this difference is small, the two cross-elasticities of demand will generally have the same sign; but they may not if the difference between the income-elasticities is considerable. If, for example, one of the income-elasticities is positive and the other negative, then we may get reactions of price on demand which go in completely opposite directions—unless the goods are sufficiently complementary (or sufficiently competitive) for this variation to be swamped by the complementarity term.[2]

(*d*) Since the elasticity of complementarity of *Y* with *X* against *Z* measures the extent to which a substitution of *X* for *YZ* takes place at the expense of *Y* (when the relative prices of *Y* and *Z* are unchanged); and since the elasticity of complementarity of *Z* with *X* against *Y* measures the extent to which the same substitution takes place at the expense of *Z*; there must be a relation between these two elasticities and the elasticity of substitution of *X* with *YZ* taken to-

[1] Subject to the same condition, it follows that of three goods, *X*, *Y*, *Z*, only one pair at most can be complementary.

[2] The valuable investigation into this problem by Professor Henry Schultz ("Interrelations of Demand," *Journal of Political Economy*, August 1933) is limited by the assumption of "constant marginal utility of money" (i.e. of our third good *Z*). This comes to the same thing as neglecting the income-elasticities of demand, which the present analysis shows to be highly significant for the problem, as they may easily be of comparable magnitude with the (symmetrical) complementarity term.

gether. In the general case, where there are six elasticities of complementarity and three elasticities of substitution (*X* for *YZ*, etc.) we get three equations connecting them, and could thus write the elasticities of substitution in terms of the elasticities of complementarity.

But when the integrability conditions are satisfied, and the six elasticities of complementarity therefore reduced to three, we can also use these three equations to give us the elasticities of complementarity in terms of the elasticities of substitution.[1] Hence we can derive the following propositions:

(1) *XY* are more likely to be complementary with regard to *Z*, the lower is the elasticity of substitution between *X* and *Y*, relatively to those between *X* and *Z*, and *Y* and *Z*.

(2) *XY* are more likely to be complementary with respect to *Z*, the larger is the proportion of total income spent upon *Z*, and therefore the smaller the proportion spent on *X* and *Y* together.

(3) If the elasticity of substitution between *X* and *Y* is zero, they must be complementary with respect to any third good less closely related ; if the elasticity of substitution between them is infinite, they must be competitive.[2] If the elasticities are equal, they must be competitive.

[1]See Part II, sect. III, 2.

[2] In this sense, therefore, and in this sense alone, is it possible to say that competitive goods are easily substitutible ; complementary goods not easily substitutible. This statement, so agreeable to common sense, turns out to be correct—so long as we speak in relative, not absolute, terms.

V

Independence

1. According to the Edgeworth-Pareto definition of complementarity (based on the reaction of the marginal utility of one commodity to a change in the quantity of the other), it was natural to regard the case intermediate between complementarity and competitiveness (where the effect on the marginal utility is zero) as a case of " independent goods." This definition must be abandoned for the same reason as we have abandoned their definition of complementarity.[1]

Nor is it in any way appropriate to regard the watershed between complementarity and competitiveness (on our definition)[2] as a case of independence. For, if, as would happen at our watershed, the marginal rate of substitution between Y and Z is unaffected by compensating changes of X and Z, this does not mean that the goods are in any useful sense " independent "—there subsists a very complex relation between them.

But there does exist another property to which the term *independence* can much more usefully be applied. If the marginal rate of substitution between Y and Z is unaffected by the quantity of X possessed, then we may say that YZ is *independent* of X.[3] If this condition holds, then it is clear that a substitution of X for Z can exert an influence on the marginal rate of substitution between Y and Z in only one way. The increase in X has no influence at all; it is only the decrease in Z which is effective. But that decrease in Z may still affect the marginal rate of substitution between Y and Z in either direction. For although the normal effect will undoubtedly be to move the marginal rate in favour of Z, nevertheless, if the relationship between Y and Z is such that, were they to be consumed in isolation, Y would be an *inferior* good, then the marginal rate of substitution would be shifted in favour of Y.[4]

It is therefore possible for YZ to be independent of X, and at the same time XY may be either competitive or complementary against Z.

[1] It was a feeling of disquiet about this definition in the mind of Dr. Rosenstein-Rodan which first led me to a consideration of the whole problem of this paper.

[2] When the elasticity of complementarity is zero.

[3] Similarly, for more than three goods, if the marginal rate of substitution between any pair depends on the quantities of these goods alone, it may be said to be " independent."

[4] See above, sect. II, 1

2. To say that *YZ* is independent of *X*, is a very different matter from saying that *X*, *Y*, *Z*, are independent goods. Can we give any meaning to the latter statement?

There is only this. If *YZ* is independent of *X*, and *XZ* is independent of *Y*, then *XY* may also be independent of *Z*.[1] If this is the case, then *X*, *Y*, *Z* are clearly independent in a wider sense, which approximates more closely to the older definition.[2] (This can be extended to any number of goods, which will be independent if the marginal rate of substitution between any pair of them depends on the amounts of those goods alone.)

Independent goods may be either complementary or competitive; but it follows from the preceding section that *X* and *Y* can only be complementary if *Y* is an *inferior* good. Further, since the integrability conditions must always be satisfied for independent goods, a substitution of *Y* for *Z* must also move the marginal rate of substitution between *X* and *Z* in favour of *X*, i.e. *X* must be an *inferior* good too. There are thus two possible cases of independent goods:

(1) where all pairs are competitive, and all the income-elasticities positive.

(2) where one pair is complementary, and two income-elasticities negative.

It will be shown in the mathematical analysis that this relation between complementarity and income-elasticity (in the case of independent goods) refers not only to sign, but to magnitude as well. If three goods are independent, then their income-elasticities depend on their complementarities.[3] It would not be difficult to demonstrate this on a three-dimensional indifference-diagram, where it would emerge in the following form: that in this case, given one indifference-surface, all the other indifference-surfaces of the system could be deduced.

This property, however, does not reproduce itself in the case of two commodities. The independence condition[4] is not then sufficient to enable us to deduce other indifference-curves from one curve alone. And so, in the two-commodity

[1] It will be if the integrability condition is satisfied.

[2] The marginal rate of substitution between any pair *XY* must then be of the form $f(x)/g(y)$, where x, y, are the quantities possessed (This can be used as a definition of independence in the case of two goods.) In cases of complementarity and inferiority, $f'(x)$ or $g'(y)$ may be positive, i.e. we must avoid being entrapped again in the law of diminishing marginal utility!

[3] See Part II, sect. III, 3.

[4] See note 2.

case, but only in this case, it is always possible, however the goods are in fact related, to find a pair of independent utility functions which will give us an indifference-map, closely approximating, over a small region, to the true map. This suggests a method of mathematical economic analysis which is much simpler than the quite general analysis followed in this paper, and which will, for small variations, give a close approximation to correct results.

Substantially, that method is the method of Marshall; it is one which has rendered great services to economics, even when *rationale* was not fully understood. But it is a method which is applicable, in strictness, only to the case of two commodities; for more than two commodities it loses its generality altogether.[1]

[1] The second part of this article, by Mr. R. G. D. Allen, will be published in ECONOMICA, No. 2 (May, 1934).

Part II.—A Mathematical Theory of Individual Demand Functions

By R. G. D. Allen

The established definition of the way in which a pair of goods can be related in an individual's scale of preferences is due, in its precise form, to Edgeworth and Pareto. The definition assumes the existence of a utility function giving the utility to the individual of any combination of the set of consumers' goods, $X, Y, Z, \ldots\ldots$, which enter into the individual's budget. Denoting the function by $u=\phi(x,y,z, \ldots\ldots)$, the Edgeworth-Pareto definition of the relation between any pair of goods, X and Y, depends on the sign of $\frac{\partial^2 u}{\partial x \partial y}$. The goods are *complementary* or *competitive* according as $\frac{\partial^2 u}{\partial x \partial y}$ is positive or negative. If the individual possesses an increased amount of one good, the marginal utility of the other good increases in the complementary case and decreases in the competitive case.

This definition ignores one fundamental fact. Even if the utility function exists at all, it is by no means unique and it can serve only as an *index*, and not as a *measure*, of individual utility. Pareto himself established this fact, but failed to deduce the logical corollary that the derivative $\frac{\partial^2 u}{\partial x \partial y}$ is also indeterminate both in sign and in magnitude. To prove this corollary we proceed as follows. The utility function index is the integral of the " indifference " differential equation:

$$\phi_x dx+\phi_y dy+\phi_z dz+ \ldots\ldots=0,$$

where ϕ_x, ϕ_y, ϕ_z, ... are the marginal utility functions, determinate only as to their ratios. If $u=\phi(x,y,z,\ldots\ldots)$ is *one* form of the integral, and if $\phi_x, \phi_y, \phi_z, \ldots\ldots$ are arranged to be the partial derivatives of this function, then the general utility function index is :

$$u=F\ \{\phi(x,y,z,\ldots\ldots)\}$$

where F is an arbitrary function with a positive derivative.[1]

The partial derivatives of the function index are

$$\frac{\partial u}{\partial x}=F'(\phi).\phi_x;\ \frac{\partial u}{\partial y}=F'(\phi).\phi_y;\ \frac{\partial u}{\partial z}=F'(\phi).\phi_z;\ldots\ldots$$

The signs of these derivatives are the signs of $\phi_x, \phi_y, \phi_z, \ldots\ldots$ respectively and their ratios are determinate (as required). On the other hand, the sign of the second-order derivative

$$\frac{\partial^2 u}{\partial x \partial y}=F'(\phi).\phi_{xy}+F''(\phi).\phi_x.\phi_y$$

cannot be taken as determinate and it depends entirely on the form adopted for the arbitrary function.[2] The above definition of complementary and competitive goods is thus indefinite; for a given combination $(x,y,z,\ldots\ldots)$, the same pair of goods can be sometimes complementary and sometimes competitive according to the form taken for the utility function index. The Edgeworth-Pareto definition is not adequate for the distinction of relations between a pair of goods and it must be rejected in any precise theory of individual choice. The development which follows will decide, amongst other things, what can be put in its place.

I. INDIVIDUAL DEMAND IN THE CASE OF TWO GOODS

1. In the present section we shall consider the case where only two goods, X and Y, enter into the budget of a given individual. The case can be interpreted in two ways. *Either* all goods other than the pair XY are possessed by the individual in known amounts, and he considers his expenditure on X and Y independently, *or* the pair XY represent two broad classes of goods (e.g. food and other items) which together make up the individual's complete budget. In either case, it is seen that the theory of demand for two goods is subject to severe limitations in possible applications.

[1] The positive derivative is only necessary to ensure that u is a genuine index of utility in the sense that all its forms increase or decrease together.

[2] The only case in which $\frac{\partial^2 u}{\partial x \partial y}$ is definite in sign is when either ϕ_x or ϕ_y is zero, i.e. when the marginal utility ratio $\phi_x : \phi_y$ is zero or infinite and the individual is "saturated" with one of the goods. This possibility does not concern us in our consideration of the individual under market conditions.

F

2. *The individual's scale of preferences.*—The individual possesses the combination (x,y) of amounts of the two goods X and Y.[1] The fundamental postulate of the theory is that there exists a unique " indifference direction " for variations from the combination (x,y) defined by a differential equation:

$$dx + R_x^y dy = 0 \qquad \ldots\ldots\ldots\ldots\ldots\ldots\ldots\ldots(1).$$

The equation expresses a relation between increments dx and dy (one positive and one negative) which just compensate each other as far as the individual is concerned. The expression $R_x^y = -dx/dy$ is the (limiting) ratio of compensating increments in x and y,[2] i.e. R_x^y is *the marginal rate of substitution of X for Y*. As the combination (x,y) varies, so does the individual's indifference direction and the value of R_x^y. In fact, R_x^y is a function of x and y, and its values for various combinations (x,y) describes *the scale of preferences* of the individual. Only the function R_x^y is needed, since the marginal rate of substitution of Y for X is $R_y^x = 1/R_x^y$.

Three assumptions are made about the scale of preferences:

(1) R_x^y is a continuous function of x and y.

(2) R_x^y is positive at all points (x,y).

(3) For the variation of the indifference direction from any point, the expression $dx + R_x^y dy$ always decreases: $d(dx + R_x^y dy) < 0$ subject to $dx + R_x^y dy = 0$,

i.e. $$\begin{vmatrix} 1 & R_x^y \\ \frac{\partial}{\partial x} R_x^y & \frac{\partial}{\partial y} R_x^y \end{vmatrix} = \frac{\partial}{\partial y} R_x^y - R_x^y \frac{\partial}{\partial x} R_x^y < 0 \quad \ldots\ldots(2).$$

The differential equation (1) is always integrable, and from it is obtained a system of *indifference curves* in the OXY plane. The tangent to the indifference curve at any point has gradient $(-R_x^y)$ referred to OY, or gradient $(-R_y^x)$ referred to OX. The first two assumptions imply that each indifference curve has a continuously variable tangent which is always downward sloping. The third assumption implies that the indifference curves are everywhere convex to O. The numerical value of the tangent gradient referred to OY (or to OX) increases as

[1] The problem is a completely static one and the time element is abstracted by taking x and y as amounts that come into the possession of the individual (to be disposed of by him) per unit of time.

[2] The " preference direction " of the individual (i.e. his most preferred direction of acquisition of the goods) is at right angles to the " indifference direction." Hence, $R_x^y = dy/dx$ along the preference direction. There is thus a second interpretation of R_x^y, the marginal rate of increase of y with respect to x for a change in the preference direction.

we move along an indifference curve away from OY (or away from OX). The marginal rate of substitution of X for Y increases as we continue to substitute X for Y. This is *the principle of increasing marginal rate of substitution.*[1]

There are three characteristics or *indices of the individual's scale of preferences* which are sufficient to describe the complete form of the scale or of the indifference curve system. All the indices are expressed in terms of first-order variations of R^y_x; they refer only to the scale of preferences itself and not to market conditions. It will be found, further, that the indices are sufficient for the description of the individual's reaction to market conditions.

The first index refers to a single indifference curve only. *The elasticity of substitution* between X and Y is defined as

$$\sigma = \frac{d\left(\frac{x}{y}\right)}{\frac{x}{y}} \bigg/ \frac{dR^y_x}{R^y_x} = \frac{d\left(\frac{y}{x}\right)}{\frac{y}{x}} \bigg/ \frac{dR^x_y}{R^x_y}$$

taken along the indifference direction at (x,y). Hence:

$$\sigma = -\frac{R^y_x}{xy} \frac{x + R^y_x y}{\frac{\partial}{\partial y} R^y_x - R^y_x \frac{\partial}{\partial x} R^y_x} > 0$$

from the condition (2). The elasticity of substitution is independent of units and is symmetrical with respect to x and y. It is a measure of the curvature of the indifference curve at (x,y), varying in value from zero when the curve is in the form of a right angle at (x,y) to very large values when the curve is flat.

The other two indices refer to the relation of one indifference curve to another and adjacent curve, and they can be called the *coefficients of income-variation*:

$$\rho_x = -\frac{y}{R^y_x}\frac{\partial}{\partial y} R^y_x \text{ and } \rho_y = \frac{x}{R^y_x}\frac{\partial}{\partial x} R^y_x.$$

Both coefficients are expressed in " elasticity " form and are

[1] Of the three assumptions made here, the first is introduced simply for mathematical convenience, but, apart from this, there is no reason to assume away discontinuities in the indifference curve system. The other two assumptions are on a different footing, but they are not *necessarily* satisfied. They must certainly be relaxed when the individual possesses so much of one (or more) of the goods that he would pay to get rid of it. Further, it is not contended that they apply to a position on the preference scale where the individual finds himself below the " subsistence level." It *is* maintained, however, that the assumptions serve to describe all positions in which the individual is likely to find himself under market conditions.

independent of units. It follows from (2) that ρ_x and ρ_y cannot both be negative; they are both positive in the " normal " case and one is positive and the other negative in the " exceptional " case.

3. *The individual demand functions.*—If the individual spends a given money income μ on the two goods X and Y at given uniform market prices p_x and p_y, then his equilibrium purchases are given by the following conditions for equilibrium:

$$xp_x + yp_y = \mu \text{ and } \frac{1}{p_x} = \frac{R_x^y}{p_y} \quad \ldots\ldots\ldots\ldots(3).$$

In diagrammatic terms, the equations correspond to the fact that the purchases of the individual in equilibrium are represented by the co-ordinates of the point in XY space where the given price line (i.e. $xp_x+yp_y=\mu$) touches an indifference curve. The solution of the equations (3) gives x and y as functions of μ, p_x and p_y—the individual *demand functions*. By the assumption of increasing marginal rate of substitution (indifference curve system convex to the origin), a single equilibrium position exists for each set of μ, p_x and p_y, and the demand functions are single-valued.[1]

Let the proportions of total income spent on X and on Y be denoted by $\kappa_x = \frac{xp_x}{\mu}$ and $\kappa_y = \frac{yp_y}{\mu}$ (where $\kappa_x+\kappa_y=1$). From the equations (3) the values of the three indices of the scale of preferences in the equilibrium position are:

$$\sigma = -\frac{\frac{\mu}{xy}\frac{p_y}{p_x}}{p_x\frac{\partial}{\partial y}R_x^y - p_y\frac{\partial}{\partial x}R_x^y}\ ; \quad \rho_x = -\frac{yp_x}{p_y}\frac{\partial}{\partial y}R_x^y\ ;$$

$$\rho_y = \frac{xp_x}{p_y}\frac{\partial}{\partial x}R_x^y.$$

The problem is to trace the variation of the equilibrium position and of the demand functions as income or prices vary.

(*a*) *Income-elasticities of demand.*—Let μ vary while p_x and p_y are kept fixed, and denote the income-elasticities of the demand functions by

$$E_\mu(x) = \frac{\mu}{x}\frac{\partial x}{\partial \mu} \text{ and } E_\mu(y) = \frac{\mu}{y}\frac{\partial y}{\partial \mu}.$$

[1] The relaxing of the third assumption made above leads to multiple positions of equilibrium and to multi-valued demand functions. The introduction of this complication is not necessary unless, and until, the simpler theory, based on the third assumption, fails to describe the phenomena of the market.

Differentiate (3) partially with respect to μ:

$$\left.\begin{aligned} xp_x\, E_\mu(x) \quad &+ \quad yp_y\, E_\mu(y) &= \mu \\ x\frac{\partial}{\partial x} R^y_x\, E_\mu(x) &+ y\frac{\partial}{\partial y} R^y_x\, E_\mu(y) &= 0 \end{aligned}\right\} \qquad \ldots\ldots\ldots\ldots(4).$$

The solution of the equations (4), making use of the equilibrium values of σ, ρ_x and ρ_y, appears quite easily in the form:

$$E_\mu(x) = \sigma\,.\,\rho_x \text{ and } E_\mu(y) = \sigma\,.\,\rho_y \qquad \ldots\ldots\ldots\ldots\ldots\ldots(5).$$

From the first equation of (4), it follows at once that

$$\kappa_x E_\mu(x) + \kappa_y E_\mu(y) = 1.$$

and hence that $\kappa_x\rho_x + \kappa_y\rho_y = \dfrac{1}{\sigma}$.

It is not possible for both $E_\mu(x)$ and $E_\mu(y)$ to be negative: in the "normal" case both are positive and the demands for X and Y increase with increasing income. In the "exceptional" case, on the other hand, one income-elasticity is negative and the demand for this good decreases with increasing income. If the income-elasticity of demand for a good is negative, this good is said to be *inferior* to the other good.

Notice that $E_\mu(x)$ is a positive multiple (σ) of the second index of the individual's preference scale and that $E_\mu(y)$ is the same multiple of the third index. The income-elasticities of demand can thus be used instead of these two indices.

(*b*) *Price-elasticities of demand.*—Let p_x vary while μ and p_y are kept fixed, and denote the p_x-elasticities of demand by

$$E_{px}(x) = -\frac{p_x}{x}\frac{\partial x}{\partial p_x} \text{ and } E_{px}(y) = -\frac{p_x}{y}\frac{\partial y}{\partial p_x}$$

Differentiate (3) partially with respect to p_x:

$$\left.\begin{aligned} xp_x\, E_{px}(x) \quad &+ \quad yp_y\, E_{px}(y) &= xp_x \\ x\frac{\partial}{\partial x} R^y_x\, E_{px}(x) &+ y\frac{\partial}{\partial y} R^y_x\, E_{px}(y) &= \frac{p_y}{p_x} \end{aligned}\right\} \qquad \ldots\ldots(6).$$

$$\text{So } \frac{xE_{px}(x)}{xp_x\frac{\partial}{\partial y}R^y_x - \frac{p_y^2}{p_x}} = \frac{yE_{px}(y)}{xp_x\frac{\partial}{\partial x}R^y_x - p_y} = \frac{1}{p_x\frac{\partial}{\partial y}R^y_x - p_y\frac{\partial}{\partial x}R^y_x}.$$

$$\text{Hence } E_{px}(x) = \frac{yp_x}{\mu p_y}\,\sigma\left(\frac{xp_y}{y}\rho_x + \frac{p_y^2}{p_x}\right) = \kappa_x E_\mu(x) + (1-\kappa_x)\,\sigma$$

$$\text{and } \quad E_{px}(y) = \frac{xp_x}{\mu p_y}\,\sigma\,(p_y\rho_y - p_y) = \kappa_x E_\mu(y) - \kappa_x\sigma,$$

using the results (5) and the equilibrium values of σ, ρ_x and ρ_y

Similar results hold for the p_y-elasticities of demand. Hence:

$$\left.\begin{aligned} E_{px}(x) &= \kappa_x E_\mu(x) + (1-\kappa_x)\,\sigma \\ E_{px}(y) &= \kappa_x E_\mu(y) - \kappa_x\,\sigma \\ E_{py}(x) &= \kappa_y E_\mu(x) - \kappa_y\,\sigma \\ E_{py}(y) &= \kappa_y E_\mu(y) + (1-\kappa_y)\,\sigma \end{aligned}\right\} \quad \ldots\ldots\ldots\ldots\ldots\ldots(7).$$

Two relations exist between the four price-elasticities of demand given by (7). From the first equation of (6)

$$\kappa_x E_{px}(x) + \kappa_y E_{px}(y) = \kappa_x.$$

Similarly $\qquad \kappa_x E_{py}(x) + \kappa_y E_{py}(y) = \kappa_y.$

The conclusions that can be derived from the equations (7) are set out fully by Dr. Hicks.[1] There is, however, one point that cannot be over-emphasised. The substitution term in $E_{py}(x)$ and in $E_{px}(y)$ is always negative, and a fall in the price of one good causes a substitution of this good for the other. Hence, two goods must always be regarded as substitutes, or as "competitive," when they stand by themselves; complementarity is a characteristic which does not appear until at least three goods are considered.[2] Further, if the elasticity of substitution is a more important (i.e. numerically larger) quantity than the income-elasticities, then both the "cross" price-elasticities $E_{px}(y)$ and $E_{py}(x)$ are negative, i.e. both $\frac{\partial y}{\partial p_x}$ and $\frac{\partial x}{\partial p_y}$ are positive. This is the traditional characteristic of substitute or "competitive" goods in a general sense. But, if the income-elasticities are at least as important in magnitude as the elasticity of substitution, then the derivatives $\frac{\partial y}{\partial p_x}$ and $\frac{\partial x}{\partial p_y}$ can be of either sign, and their signs need not agree.

II. INDIVIDUAL DEMAND IN THE CASE OF THREE OR MORE GOODS

1. We turn now to the general case where any number of inter-related goods enter into the individual's budget. In order to simplify the mathematical analysis, only the case of three goods is considered in detail. It is a difficult step from the case of two goods to that of three goods, but no additional difficul-

[1] Hicks, ECONOMICA, February 1934, pp. 65 *et seq.* This is the first part of the present joint article.

[2] The coefficient of κ_x or κ_y in the second term of $E_{px}(y)$ or $E_{py}(x)$ is what corresponds to the "elasticity of complementarity" in the general case considered in the following section. Here the coefficient is equal in magnitude but opposite in sign to the elasticity of substitution.

ties or complications are encountered in the generalisation of the latter to the case of n goods.

2. *The individual's complex of preferences.*—The fundamental postulate is that, for variations from any combination (x,y,z) of amounts of three goods, X, Y and Z, possessed by the individual, there exist certain definite "indifference directions" defined by the differential equation:

$$dx + R_x^y dy + R_x^z dz = 0 \quad \ldots\ldots(8),$$

where the increments dx, dy and dz can take any values that compensate for each other as far as the individual is concerned. The expression $R_x^y = -dx/dy$ (z constant) is *the marginal rate of substitution of X for Y*, and $R_x^z = -dx/dz$ (y constant) is *the marginal rate of substitution of X for Z*. Both R_x^y and R_x^z are functions of x, y and z, and together their values make up the individual's *complex of preferences*.[1] Other marginal rates of substitution exist but can be obtained from the two written above:

$$R_y^x = 1/R_x^y;\ R_z^x = 1/R_x^z;\ R_y^z = R_x^z . R_y^x;\ R_z^y = R_x^y . R_z^x = 1/R_y^z.$$

Three assumptions[2] are made about the individual's complex of preferences:

(1) R_x^y and R_x^z are continuous functions of x, y and z.

(2) R_x^y and R_x^z are positive at all points (x,y,z).

(3) For a variation in any indifference direction from any point, the expression $dx + R_x^y dy + R_x^z dz$ decreases:

$d(dx + R_x^y dy + R_x^z dz) < 0$ subject to $dx + R_x^y dy + R_x^z dz = 0$,

i.e. $\begin{vmatrix} 1 & R_x^y \\ \frac{\partial}{\partial x} R_x^y & \frac{\partial}{\partial y} R_x^y \end{vmatrix}$ and similar determinants are *negative*

and $\begin{vmatrix} 1 & R_x^y & R_x^z \\ \frac{\partial}{\partial x} R_x^y & \frac{\partial}{\partial y} R_x^y & \frac{\partial}{\partial z} R_x^y \\ \frac{\partial}{\partial x} R_x^z & \frac{\partial}{\partial y} R_x^z & \frac{\partial}{\partial z} R_x^z \end{vmatrix}$ is *positive* ....(9).

[1] The term "complex" of preferences is a better description of this idea in the general case than the term "scale" of preferences which suffices in the simpler two goods case. In the general case (without the integrability condition) it is not possible to "integrate" the preferences of an individual into anything like a complete and ordered scale. The "preference direction" (the most preferred direction) of the individual is still unique, and it is at right angles to each of the indifference directions. It is given by

$$\frac{dx}{1} = \frac{dy}{R_x^y} = \frac{dz}{R_x^z}.$$

Hence, $R_x^y = dy/dx$ and $R_x^z = dz/dx$ for a change in the preference direction.

[2] As before, the assumptions are not *necessarily* satisfied but serve to describe all situations in which the individual is likely to find himself under market conditions.

If the differential equation (8) is integrable (which is not always, or even usually, the case), then a complete indifference surface system exists in XYZ space. The first two assumptions imply that each indifference surface has a continuously variable tangent plane which is always downward sloping both in the OX direction and in the OY direction. The third assumption implies that the indifference surfaces are everywhere convex to O. In particular, the second-order determinants with negative values in (9) give the principle of increasing marginal rate of substitution—the marginal rate of substitution of one good for another increases as we continue to substitute these goods, the third good remaining fixed in amount.

The following notations are required:

$$\sigma = \frac{R^y_x R^z_x}{xyz} \frac{x + R^y_x y + R^z_x z}{\begin{vmatrix} 1 & R^y_x & R^z_x \\ \dfrac{\partial}{\partial x} R^y_x & \dfrac{\partial}{\partial y} R^y_x & \dfrac{\partial}{\partial z} R^y_x \\ \dfrac{\partial}{\partial x} R^z_x & \dfrac{\partial}{\partial y} R^z_x & \dfrac{\partial}{\partial z} R^z_x \end{vmatrix}}$$

The coefficient σ is positive from the condition (9); it is independent of units and symmetrical with respect to x, y and z. Further, it denotes the mutual substitutability of the three goods and, if the indifference surface system exists, it measures the curvature of the surface passing through any point.

Consider now one good, say X, apart from the other two. The elasticity of substitution between Y and Z is

$$\frac{d\left(\dfrac{y}{z}\right)}{\dfrac{y}{z}} \quad \text{divided by} \quad \frac{dR^z_y}{R^z_y},$$

where the differential can be taken along any one of the three perpendicular indifference directions at the point (x,y,z). There are thus three elasticities of substitution between Y and Z which we can denote by ${}_{yz}\sigma_{yz}$, ${}_{xz}\sigma_{yz}$ and ${}_{xy}\sigma_{yz}$, according as it is taken along the YZ indifference direction (X constant), along the XZ indifference direction (Y constant), or along the XY indifference direction (Z constant). Evaluating:

$$ {}_{yz}\sigma_{yz} = -\frac{R_y^z}{yz} \frac{y + R_y^z z}{\begin{vmatrix} 1 & R_y^z \\ \frac{\partial}{\partial y} R_y^z & \frac{\partial}{\partial z} R_y^z \end{vmatrix}} \quad \text{which is } positive, $$

$$ {}_{xz}\sigma_{yz} = \frac{R_y^z}{z \begin{vmatrix} 1 & R_x^z \\ \frac{\partial}{\partial x} R_y^z & \frac{\partial}{\partial z} R_y^z \end{vmatrix}} \quad \text{and} \quad {}_{xy}\sigma_{yz} = \frac{-R_y^z}{y \begin{vmatrix} 1 & R_x^y \\ \frac{\partial}{\partial x} R_y^z & \frac{\partial}{\partial y} R_y^z \end{vmatrix}} $$

All these elasticities are independent of units. The first ${}_{yz}\sigma_{yz}$ is symmetrical with respect to y and z and measures the ordinary elasticity of substitution between Y and Z (X being now fixed in amount). The other two elasticities are new and can be positive or negative; ${}_{xz}\sigma_{yz}$ measures the elasticity of substitution between Y and Z when the relation between these goods varies on account of a substitution of X for Z, Y remaining fixed in amount, and similarly for ${}_{xy}\sigma_{yz}$. There are three similar elasticities when Y is considered apart from XZ and three more when Z is considered apart from XY.

3. The form of the individual's complex of preferences is described by twelve indices, all of which are expressed in terms of first-order variations of R_x^y and R_x^z. The indices refer only to the complex of preferences and not to market conditions. The twelve *indices of the complex of preferences* can be divided into three sets:

(1) *The elasticity of substitution between X and the pair YZ*

$$ = \frac{\sigma}{{}_{yz}\sigma_{yz}} $$

and two similar elasticities $\frac{\sigma}{{}_{xz}\sigma_{xz}}$ and $\frac{\sigma}{{}_{xy}\sigma_{xy}}$ All three elasticities are positive. In general terms, $\frac{\sigma}{{}_{yz}\sigma_{yz}}$ is the mutual elasticity of the triad X, Y and Z reduced by the elasticity of substitution of Y and Z between themselves. The elasticity can be large, therefore, if the triad is a highly substitutable one (σ large) or if Y and Z themselves are hardly substitutable at all (${}_{yz}\sigma_{yz}$ small).

(2) *The elasticity of complementarity of Y with X against Z*

$$ = \frac{\sigma}{{}_{xz}\sigma_{yz}} $$

and *the elasticity of complementarity of Z with X against Y*

$$= \frac{\sigma}{{}_{xy}\sigma_{yz}}.$$

In these elasticities σ is again reduced by one of the elasticities of substitution between Y and Z—the new ones in this case. The signs of the elasticities of complementarity can be positive or negative, and these will be interpreted later in terms of the competitive and complementary nature of the relations between X, Y and Z. There are four other and similar elasticities of complementarity:

$$\frac{\sigma}{{}_{yz}\sigma_{xz}}\;;\;\frac{\sigma}{{}_{xy}\sigma_{xz}}\;;\;\frac{\sigma}{{}_{yz}\sigma_{xy}}\;;\text{ and }\frac{\sigma}{{}_{xz}\sigma_{xy}}.$$

(3) *The coefficients of income-variation*:

$$\rho_x = \frac{yz}{R_x^y R_x^z}\begin{vmatrix} \frac{\partial}{\partial y}R_x^y & \frac{\partial}{\partial z}R_x^y \\ \frac{\partial}{\partial y}R_x^z & \frac{\partial}{\partial z}R_x^z \end{vmatrix}\;;\;\rho_y = -\frac{xz}{R_x^y R_x^z}\begin{vmatrix} \frac{\partial}{\partial x}R_x^y & \frac{\partial}{\partial z}R_x^y \\ \frac{\partial}{\partial x}R_x^z & \frac{\partial}{\partial z}R_x^z \end{vmatrix}$$

and
$$\rho_z = \frac{xy}{R_x^y R_x^z}\begin{vmatrix} \frac{\partial}{\partial x}R_x^y & \frac{\partial}{\partial y}R_x^y \\ \frac{\partial}{\partial x}R_x^z & \frac{\partial}{\partial y}R_x^z \end{vmatrix}.$$

These coefficients are the co-factors (adjusted to be independent of units) of the first row of the positive third-order determinant given in (9). It follows that they cannot be all negative; they are all positive in the " normal " case, and either one or two of them are negative in the " exceptional " cases.

The three indices of (1) and the six indices of (2) refer only to the indifference directions at the point (x,y,z), i.e. to a single indifference surface (if the system exists). The three indices of (3) refer to variations from one set of indifference directions to another and adjacent set, or from one indifference surface to another and adjacent surface.

4. *The individual demand functions.*—If the individual spends a given money income μ on the three goods X, Y and Z at given uniform market prices p_x, p_y and p_z, then his purchases in equilibrium are given by the conditions:

$$xp_x + yp_y + zp_z = \mu \text{ and } \frac{1}{p_x} = \frac{R_x^y}{p_y} = \frac{R_x^z}{p_z} \quad \ldots\ldots\ldots(10).$$

If the indifference surface system exists, these equations

correspond to the diagrammatic condition that the individual's equilibrium purchases are the co-ordinates of the point in XYZ space where the given price plane $(xp_x + yp_y + zp_z = \mu)$ touches an indifference surface. The equations (10) suffice to determine x, y and z as functions of μ, p_x, p_y and p_z—the individual *demand functions*. These functions are single-valued since the assumption (9) implies that a unique equilibrium position exists for any set of μ, p_x, p_y and p_z.

Let $\kappa_x = \frac{xp_x}{\mu}$, $\kappa_y = \frac{yp_y}{\mu}$ and $\kappa_z = \frac{zp_z}{\mu}$ denote the proportions of total income spent on X, Y and Z respectively $(\kappa_x + \kappa_y + \kappa_z = 1)$. For convenience, denote

$$D = \begin{vmatrix} p_x & p_y & p_z \\ \frac{\partial}{\partial x} R_x^y & \frac{\partial}{\partial y} R_x^y & \frac{\partial}{\partial z} R_x^y \\ \frac{\partial}{\partial x} R_x^z & \frac{\partial}{\partial y} R_x^z & \frac{\partial}{\partial z} R_x^z \end{vmatrix}$$

The values, in the equilibrium position, of the various elasticities and coefficients defined above are:

$$\left.\begin{aligned}
\sigma &= \frac{\mu}{xyz}\frac{p_y p_z}{p_x^2}\frac{1}{D}\,; \quad {}_{yz}\sigma_{yz} = \frac{-\dfrac{\mu(1-\kappa_x)}{yz}\dfrac{p_z}{p_y}}{\begin{vmatrix} p_y & p_z \\ \frac{\partial}{\partial y} R_y^z & \frac{\partial}{\partial z} R_y^z \end{vmatrix}} \quad \text{etc.} \\
{}_{xy}\sigma_{yz} &= \frac{\dfrac{\mu\kappa_x}{xz}\dfrac{p_z}{p_y}}{\begin{vmatrix} p_x & p_z \\ \frac{\partial}{\partial x} R_y^z & \frac{\partial}{\partial z} R_y^z \end{vmatrix}}\,; \quad {}_{xz}\sigma_{yz} = \frac{-\dfrac{\mu\kappa_x}{xy}\dfrac{p_z}{p_y}}{\begin{vmatrix} p_x & p_y \\ \frac{\partial}{\partial x} R_y^z & \frac{\partial}{\partial y} R_y^z \end{vmatrix}} \quad \text{etc.} \\
\rho_x &= \frac{yzp_x^2}{p_y p_z} D_x\,; \quad \rho_y = \frac{xzp_x^2}{p_y p_z} D_y\,; \quad \rho_z = \frac{xyp_x^2}{p_y p_z} D_z
\end{aligned}\right\} \quad \ldots(11),$$

where D_x, D_y and D_z are the co-factors of the first row of D. The problem of the variation of the demand functions, as income or as prices vary, is treated by the method adopted in the two-goods case.

(*a*) *Income-elasticities of demand*.—Denoting the three income-elasticities of demand by

$$E_\mu(x) = \frac{\mu}{x}\frac{\partial x}{\partial \mu}\,; \quad E_\mu(y) = \frac{\mu}{y}\frac{\partial y}{\partial \mu}\,; \quad E_\mu(z) = \frac{\mu}{z}\frac{\partial z}{\partial \mu}\,,$$

differentiate (10) partially with respect to μ:

$$\left.\begin{aligned} xp_x E_\mu(x) \quad + yp_y E_\mu(y) \quad + zp_z E_\mu(z) &= \mu \\ x\frac{\partial}{\partial x} R^y_x E_\mu(x) + y\frac{\partial}{\partial y} R^y_x E_\mu(y) + z\frac{\partial}{\partial z} R^y_x E_\mu(z) &= 0 \\ x\frac{\partial}{\partial x} R^z_x E_\mu(x) + y\frac{\partial}{\partial y} R^z_x E_\mu(y) + z\frac{\partial}{\partial z} R^z_x E_\mu(z) &= 0 \end{aligned}\right\}\ldots(12).$$

Solving the equations (12) in determinant form,

$$\frac{xE_\mu(x)}{D_x} = \frac{yE_\mu(y)}{D_y} = \frac{zE_\mu(z)}{D_z} = \frac{\mu}{D}.$$

Substituting the values of the various expressions given by (11),

$$E_\mu(x) = \sigma . \rho_x ; E_\mu(y) = \sigma . \rho_y ; E_\mu(z) = \sigma . \rho_z \ldots\ldots\ldots\ldots(13).$$

From the first equation of (12) we have a relation between the income-elasticities and hence between ρ_x, ρ_y and ρ_z:

$$\left.\begin{aligned} \kappa_x E_\mu(x) + \kappa_y E_\mu(y) + \kappa_z E_\mu(z) &= 1 \\ \kappa_x \rho_x + \kappa_y \rho_y + \kappa_z \rho_z &= \frac{1}{\sigma} \end{aligned}\right\}\ldots\ldots\ldots\ldots(14).$$

It follows that all three income-elasticities cannot be negative. In the " normal " case they are all positive and each demand increases with increasing income. In the " exceptional " cases one (or two) of the income-elasticities is negative and the demand for one (or two) of the goods decreases with increasing income. A good is said to be *inferior* if its demand decreases with increasing income, and it is possible, therefore, for one or two of a set of three goods to be inferior in this sense.

Since the income-elasticities of demand are positive multiples of the third set of indices, they can be used instead of the latter to characterise the individual's complex of preferences.

(*b*) *Price-elasticities of demand.* Denoting the p_x-elasticities of demand by

$$E_{px}(x) = -\frac{p_x}{x}\frac{\partial x}{\partial p_x};\ E_{px}(y) = -\frac{p_x}{y}\frac{\partial y}{\partial p_x};\ E_{px}(z) = -\frac{p_x}{z}\frac{\partial z}{\partial p_x},$$

differentiate (10) partially with respect to p_x:

$$\left.\begin{aligned} xp_x E_{px}(x) \ + yp_y E_{px}(y) \quad + zp_z E_{px}(z) &= xp_x \\ x\frac{\partial}{\partial x} R^y_x E_{px}(x) + y\frac{\partial}{\partial y} R^y_x E_{px}(y) + z\frac{\partial}{\partial z} R^y_x E_{px}(z) &= \frac{p_y}{p_x} \\ x\frac{\partial}{\partial x} R^z_x E_{px}(x) + y\frac{\partial}{\partial y} R^z_x E_{px}(y) + z\frac{\partial}{\partial z} R^z_x E_{px}(z) &= \frac{p_z}{p_x} \end{aligned}\right\}\ldots(15).$$

Solving the equations (15) in determinant form:

$$\frac{x\,E_{px}(x)}{\begin{vmatrix} xp_x & p_y & p_z \\ \frac{p_y}{p_x} & \frac{\partial}{\partial y}R^y_x & \frac{\partial}{\partial z}R^y_x \\ \frac{p_z}{p_x} & \frac{\partial}{\partial y}R^z_x & \frac{\partial}{\partial z}R^z_x \end{vmatrix}} = \frac{y\,E_{px}(y)}{\begin{vmatrix} p_x & xp_x & p_z \\ \frac{\partial}{\partial x}R^y_x & \frac{p_y}{p_x} & \frac{\partial}{\partial z}R^y_x \\ \frac{\partial}{\partial x}R^z_x & \frac{p_z}{p_x} & \frac{\partial}{\partial z}R^z_x \end{vmatrix}} = \frac{z\,E_{px}(z)}{\begin{vmatrix} p_x & p_y & xp_x \\ \frac{\partial}{\partial x}R^y_x & \frac{\partial}{\partial y}R^y_x & \frac{p_y}{p_x} \\ \frac{\partial}{\partial x}R^z_x & \frac{\partial}{\partial y}R^z_x & \frac{p_z}{p_x} \end{vmatrix}} = \frac{1}{D},$$

$$\text{i.e. } E_{px}(x) = \frac{yz}{\mu}\frac{p_x^2}{p_y p_z}\,\sigma\left[xp_x D_x + \frac{p_y}{p_x}\left\{p_z\frac{\partial}{\partial y}R^z_x - p_y\frac{\partial}{\partial z}R^z_x\right\} + \frac{p_z}{p_x}\left\{p_y\frac{\partial}{\partial z}R^y_x - p_z\frac{\partial}{\partial y}R^y_x\right\}\right]$$

$$= \kappa_x\,\sigma\,.\,\rho_x - \frac{yz}{\mu}\frac{p_y}{p_z}\,\sigma\left(p_y\frac{\partial}{\partial z}R^z_y - p_z\frac{\partial}{\partial y}R^z_y\right),$$

using the expressions (11) and making the transformation $R^z_x = R^z_y . R^y_x$ together with the equilibrium equations (10). Hence, from (11) and (13),

$$E_{px}(x) = \kappa_x E_\mu(x) + (1 - \kappa_x)\frac{\sigma}{{}_{yz}\sigma_{yz}}.$$

By an exactly similar procedure, we obtain

$$E_{px}(y) = \kappa_x E_\mu(y) + \kappa_x\frac{\sigma}{{}_{xz}\sigma_{yz}} \text{ and } E_{px}(z) = \kappa_x E_\mu(z) + \kappa_x\frac{\sigma}{{}_{xy}\sigma_{yz}}.$$

Similar sets of results can be obtained for the p_y-elasticities and for the p_z-elasticities of demand. Hence:

$$\left.\begin{aligned} E_{px}(x) &= \kappa_x E_\mu(x) + (1 - \kappa_x)\frac{\sigma}{{}_{yz}\sigma_{yz}} \\ E_{px}(y) &= \kappa_x E_\mu(y) + \kappa_x\frac{\sigma}{{}_{xz}\sigma_{yz}} \\ E_{px}(z) &= \kappa_x E_\mu(z) + \kappa_x\frac{\sigma}{{}_{xy}\sigma_{yz}} \\ &\text{and two similar sets of three equations} \end{aligned}\right\} \quad \ldots\ldots\ldots\ldots\ldots(16).$$

Each price-elasticity of demand thus consists of two terms, the first term being a multiple of the third set of indices of the complex of preferences (the coefficients of income-variation) and the second term being a multiple of the first and second set of indices (the elasticities of substitution and complementarity).

One relation can be found between each of the three sets of

price-elasticities of demand. From the first equation of (15),

$$\left.\begin{array}{c}\kappa_x E_{px}(x) + \kappa_y E_{px}(y) + \kappa_z E_{px}(z) = \kappa_x \\ \text{and two similar relations} \\ \text{Hence, } (1 - \kappa_x)\dfrac{\sigma}{{}_{yz}\sigma_{yz}} + \kappa_y \dfrac{\sigma}{{}_{xz}\sigma_{yz}} + \kappa_z \dfrac{\sigma}{{}_{xy}\sigma_{yz}} = 0 \\ \text{and two similar relations}\end{array}\right\} \quad \ldots\ldots(17).$$

The three relations of the type (17) between the indices of the first and second sets imply, amongst other things, that the elasticities of substitution can be obtained in terms of the elasticities of complementarity. Further, since $\dfrac{\sigma}{{}_{yz}\sigma_{yz}} > 0$, both $\dfrac{\sigma}{{}_{xz}\sigma_{yz}}$ and $\dfrac{\sigma}{{}_{xy}\sigma_{yz}}$ cannot be positive. There are, therefore, only two possibilities. *Either* both elasticities of complementarity of Y and Z with X are negative *or* one elasticity is negative and the other positive.

5. A number of important conclusions can be derived from the results (16).[1] The increases and decreases in the various demands that follow a change in any one price are made up of two separate changes, the first due to the change in real income and the second to the substitutions made possible by the change in the relative prices.

The effect of a change in the price of a good on the demand for the *same* good is clear. The change is measured by an elasticity of the form $E_{px}(x)$ and this is positive in almost all cases. The demand for a good is thus increased by a fall in its price. It is possible, however, that this result is reversed in very exceptional cases. A price-elasticity of the form $E_{px}(x)$ can be negative and the demand for a good can increase with a *rise* in its price, provided that the income-elasticity of demand for the good is negative and large relative to the substitution effect. Hence, the demand curve for a good X can be rising, in the Giffen-Marshall sense, provided that X is an inferior good and that a large proportion of total income is spent on X for which no ready substitutes are available.

The effect of a change in the price of a good on the demands for other goods is more involved, and it is here that we must look for observable evidence of the " competitive " or " complementary " nature of the relations between the three goods.

[1] For a complete account of these conclusions, see the first part of this article by Dr. Hicks, ECONOMICA, February 1934, p. 67 and pp. 69 *et seq.*

Consider the three-way substitution made possible by the *relative* price changes apart from the effect of the change in the level of real income. The second terms of the results (16) indicate this substitution effect. The effect of substitution following a fall in the price of X is to increase or decrease the demand for Y according as the elasticity of complementarity of Y with X against Z is positive or negative. *A negative elasticity of complementarity implies that Y competes with X against Z and a positive elasticity that Y complements X against Z.* The signs of the elasticities of complementarity determine the competitive and complementary nature of the relations between the three goods and their magnitudes indicate the extent of the relations.[1] Since both elasticities of complementarity of Y and Z with X cannot be positive, it is impossible that both Y and Z complement X. There must be an element of competition between one good and the other pair. In conclusion, it is important to notice that these competitive and complementary relations depend only on the indices of the individual's complex of preferences, and not on market prices or conditions.

III. THE INTEGRABILITY CASE

1. The development of the previous section was perfectly general and, in particular, it was independent of the existence of an integral of the fundamental differential equation (8). The results to be set out in the present section, on the other hand, hold only in cases where the equation (8) is integrable.

The mathematical condition for integrability imposes a restriction on the form of R_x^y and R_x^z.[2] Assuming that the condition is satisfied, there exists a function index of utility

$$u = F\{\phi(x,y,z)\}$$

where $\phi(x,y,z)$ is any one integral of (8) and F denotes the arbitrary function involved in the general integral. Writing the partial derivatives of $\phi(x,y,z)$ by ϕ_x, ϕ_y and ϕ_z, we have

$$R_x^y = \frac{\phi_y}{\phi_x} \text{ and } R_x^z = \frac{\phi_z}{\phi_x}.$$

[1] In the complementary case the demands for both X and Y increase at the expense of the demand for Z (apart from the effect of the change in real income). This is why only competitive goods are possible in the two-goods case; there is no third good to absorb the loss that must occur in substitution.

[2] The condition is $\frac{\partial}{\partial z} R_x^y - \frac{\partial}{\partial y} R_x^z + R_x^y \frac{\partial}{\partial x} R_x^z - R_x^z \frac{\partial}{\partial x} R_x^y = 0$.

The analysis can now be expressed in terms of the function $\phi(x,y,z)$ and its partial derivatives of the first and second orders, remembering that only the ratios of ϕ_x, ϕ_y and ϕ_z are definite. All the results given below, however, can be shown to involve only these ratios or the derivatives of the ratios, and not the functions themselves.

2. *Simplification of the competitive and complementary relations.*—In the integrability case the values of the six elasticities of complementarity are

$$\frac{\sigma}{{}_{xz}\sigma_{yz}} = \frac{x\phi_x + y\phi_y + z\phi_z}{xy}\,\frac{\Phi_{xy}}{\Phi} = \frac{\sigma}{{}_{yz}\sigma_{xz}}$$

$$\frac{\sigma}{{}_{xy}\sigma_{xz}} = \frac{x\phi_x + y\phi_y + z\phi_z}{yz}\,\frac{\Phi_{yz}}{\Phi} = \frac{\sigma}{{}_{xz}\sigma_{xy}}$$

$$\frac{\sigma}{{}_{yz}\sigma_{xy}} = \frac{x\phi_x + y\phi_y + z\phi_z}{xz}\,\frac{\Phi_{xz}}{\Phi} = \frac{\sigma}{{}_{xy}\sigma_{yz}},$$

where $-\Phi$ stands for the negative and symmetrical determinant

$$\begin{vmatrix} \phi_{xx} & \phi_{xy} & \phi_{xz} & \phi_x \\ \phi_{xy} & \phi_{yy} & \phi_{yz} & \phi_y \\ \phi_{xz} & \phi_{yz} & \phi_{zz} & \phi_z \\ \phi_x & \phi_y & \phi_z & 0 \end{vmatrix}$$

and Φ_{xy}, Φ_{yz} and Φ_{xz} are the co-factors of ϕ_{xy}, ϕ_{yz} and ϕ_{xz} in the determinant.

Symmetry is, therefore, introduced into the relations between the three goods when the integrability condition is satisfied. For the relation between any pair of goods X and Y (with respect to the third good Z), the elasticity of complementarity of Y with X against Z is equal to the elasticity of complementarity of X with Y against Z. It is now possible to speak of the elasticity of complementarity of the pair XY (against Z):

$$\sigma_{xy} = \frac{\sigma}{{}_{xz}\sigma_{yz}} = \frac{\sigma}{{}_{yz}\sigma_{xz}},$$

and there are only three of these elasticities, σ_{xy}, σ_{yz} and σ_{xz}, instead of the full set of six.[1] The signs of σ_{xy}, σ_{yz} and σ_{xz} determine the competitive and complementary relations of the whole set of three goods. If σ_{xy} is negative X and Y are competitive, if positive X and Y are complementary (with respect to Z in each case). Similar criteria apply to the relation between the other pairs.

[1] The integrability condition is clearly *sufficient* for this symmetry ; it also appears to be a *necessary* condition.

The equations (17) now take the form:

$$(1-\kappa_x)\frac{\sigma}{_{yz}\sigma_{yz}}+\kappa_y\sigma_{xy}+\kappa_z\sigma_{xz}=0.$$

and two similar relations

Hence, at least two of σ_{xy}, σ_{yz} and σ_{xz} are negative, and it is not possible for more than one pair of the three goods to be complementary. Further, the equations can be solved either to give the elasticities of substitution of the goods in pairs ($_{yz}\sigma_{yz}$, $_{xz}\sigma_{xz}$ and $_{xy}\sigma_{xy}$) in terms of the elasticities of complementarity of the goods in pairs (σ_{xy}, σ_{yz} and σ_{xz}), or conversely. The latter is the more interesting solution. We obtain:

$$\sigma_{xy}=\tfrac{1}{2}\sigma\left\{\frac{1}{_{xy}\sigma_{xy}}\left(\frac{\kappa_z}{\kappa_x}+\frac{\kappa_z}{\kappa_y}\right)-\frac{1}{_{yz}\sigma_{yz}}\frac{1-\kappa_x}{\kappa_y}-\frac{1}{_{xz}\sigma_{xz}}\frac{1-\kappa_y}{\kappa_x}\right\}\quad\ldots(18).$$

and two similar expressions

Hence, the goods X and Y can only be markedly complementary if the term $\frac{1}{_{xy}\sigma_{xy}}\left(\frac{\kappa_z}{\kappa_x}+\frac{\kappa_z}{\kappa_y}\right)$ is large compared with the other two terms of the expression (18), i.e. if the elasticity of substitution of the pair XY is small compared with the two similar elasticities, or if κ_z is large compared with κ_x and κ_y, or both. The results stated by Dr. Hicks on this point follow at once.[1]

Consider, finally, the two actual variations in demand:

$$\frac{\partial x}{\partial p_y}=-\frac{xy}{\mu}\{E_\mu(x)+\sigma_{xy}\}\text{ and }\frac{\partial y}{\partial p_x}=-\frac{xy}{\mu}\{E_\mu(y)+\sigma_{xy}\}.$$

Both $\frac{\partial x}{\partial p_y}$ and $\frac{\partial y}{\partial p_x}$ are independent of units and can be compared directly. The two variations are equal only if $E_\mu(x)=E_\mu(y)$, i.e. if an increase in income has the same proportional effect on the demands for the two goods. This may approximate to the actual state of affairs in many cases, but it is certainly not exactly true in general. Further, the two variations are in the same direction (without necessarily being of equal magnitude) either if both income-elasticities are small or if they are large but differ by a small amount.[2] It is, how-

[1] Hicks, ECONOMICA, February 1934, p. 73.

[2] It is worth while distinguishing the two alternatives. It is only in the first alternative, where $E_\mu(x)$ and $E_\mu(y)$ are small, that we can say that the common sign of $\frac{\partial x}{\partial p_y}$ and $\frac{\partial y}{\partial p_x}$ is determined by the sign of σ_{xy}. In this case the two variations are positive if

G

ever, quite possible that $\frac{\partial x}{\partial p_y}$ and $\frac{\partial y}{\partial p_x}$ are different, not only in magnitude, but also in sign. The symmetry of the system does not necessarily extend to these two changes in demand.

3. *The case of independent goods.*—The three goods form an independent system if the marginal rate of substitution of one good for another depends only on the amounts possessed by the individual of these two goods, i.e. if R_x^y is a function of x and y, R_y^z a function of y and z and R_z^x a function of x and z. It follows at once that each marginal rate of substitution can be expressed as a product of two functions of a single variable, and that we can write:

$$\frac{1}{\phi_x(x)} = \frac{R_x^y}{\phi_y(y)} = \frac{R_x^z}{\phi_z(z)}.$$

The differential equation (8) is

$$\phi_x(x)dx + \phi_y(y)dy + \phi_z(z)dz = 0$$

and this is always integrable. The function index of utility is

$$u = F\{\Phi_x(x) + \Phi_y(y) + \Phi_z(z)\},$$

the general integral of the equation, where

$$\Phi_x(x) = \int \phi_x(x)dx;\ \Phi_y(y) = \int \phi_y(y)dy;\ \Phi_z(z) = \int \phi_z(z)dz.$$

The utility index is, in all its forms, a function of the sum of three functions of a single variable, and the goods X, Y and Z make independent contributions to the utility index. The case of independent goods is thus at least mathematically significant.

It is only in the independent goods case that we can derive anything corresponding to the marginal utility functions and curves of the traditional analysis. The marginal rate of substitution of Y for X is $R_y^x = \phi_x(x) : \phi_y(y)$, and this is a constant times $\phi_x(x)$ when only x varies. The same is true of the marginal rate of substitution of Z for X. There is, therefore, a single-variable function $\phi_x(x)$ which represents the marginal rate of substitution of any good for X for various amounts of X. It is only necessary to multiply the function by a constant depending on which good is substituted for X and on the (fixed) amount of this good possessed by the individual.

Let $E_x(\phi_x) = \frac{x}{\phi_x}\frac{d}{dx}\phi_x$ represent the elasticity of the function

X and Y are competitive and negative if X and Y are complementary. In the second alternative, though the variations are in the same direction, the direction does not necessarily correspond to the competitive or complementary relation between the pair of goods XY.

$\phi_x(x)$, i.e. the elasticity of the marginal rate of substitution of any good for X taken for variations in the amount possessed of X. In the same way we can obtain two other elasticities, $E_y(\phi_y)$ and $E_z(\phi_z)$. Each of these three elasticities is perfectly definite, being independent of units, of which good is substituted for the one named and of the amount of the substituted good that happens to be possessed. The elasticities correspond to the elasticities of the marginal utility functions or curves of Pareto's theory of value. If the signs of all $E_x(\phi_x)$, $E_y(\phi_y)$ and $E_z(\phi_z)$ are negative we have the case of " decreasing marginal utility " in Pareto's sense. It is, however, not necessary that this case should obtain for all sets of independent goods.

In the case of independent goods the following equilibrium values of the fundamental coefficients are obtained:

$$\sigma = \frac{1}{E_x E_y E_z}\frac{1}{K};\ {}_{yz}\sigma_{yz} = -\frac{1-\kappa_x}{E_y E_z}\frac{1}{K-\dfrac{\kappa_x}{E_x}} \text{ etc.};$$

$$ {}_{xz}\sigma_{yz} = {}_{yz}\sigma_{xz} = \frac{1}{E_z} \text{ etc.};\ \rho_x = E_y E_z \text{ etc.},$$

where $K = \dfrac{\kappa_x}{E_x} + \dfrac{\kappa_y}{E_y} + \dfrac{\kappa_z}{E_z}$ and E_x stands for $E_x(\phi_x)$, and so on.

The equilibrium values of the twelve indices of the individual's complex of preferences are:

(1) the elasticities of substitution are

$$\frac{\sigma}{{}_{yz}\sigma_{yz}} = -\frac{1}{1-\kappa_x}\frac{1}{E_x}\left(1-\frac{\kappa_x}{E_x}\frac{1}{K}\right).$$

and two similar expressions, all being positive

(2) the elasticities of complementarity are

$$\sigma_{xy} = \frac{1}{E_x E_y}\frac{1}{K} = \sigma E_z.$$

and two similar expressions

(3) the coefficients of income-variation are

$$\rho_x = E_y E_z;\ \rho_y = E_x E_z \text{ and } \rho_z = E_x E_y,$$

and so $\quad E_\mu(x) = \sigma E_y E_z$; $E_\mu(y) = \sigma E_x E_z$ and $E_\mu(z) = \sigma E_x E_y$.

The indices are all determined by the three elasticities E_x, E_y and E_z. There must, therefore, be a number of relations between them. As in the general integrability case the elasticities of substitution can be expressed in terms of the elasticities of complementarity, or conversely, by means of equations (18). In the independent goods case, however, there is a further set of relations between the indices. The coefficients of income-variation, and hence the income-elasticities of demand, can be expressed in terms of the elasticities of complementarity also. We have:

$$E_\mu(x) = \frac{\sigma_{xy}\sigma_{xz}}{\sigma}\ ;\ E_\mu(y) = \frac{\sigma_{xy}\sigma_{yz}}{\sigma}\ \text{and}\ E_\mu(z) = \frac{\sigma_{xz}\sigma_{yz}}{\sigma}\ \ldots(19).$$

As in the integrability case at least two of σ_{xy}, σ_{yz} and σ_{xz} must be negative. Since $\sigma_{xy} = \sigma E_z$, $\sigma_{yz} = \sigma E_x$ and $\sigma_{xz} = \sigma E_y$ (σ being positive), at least two of E_x, E_y and E_z must also be negative. There are thus only two possibilities; *either* all E_x, E_y and E_z are negative, *or* one of them is positive and the other two negative.

(1) When E_x, E_y and E_z are all negative we have the case of " decreasing marginal utility." From the expressions above all the elasticities of substitution are positive, all the elasticities of complementarity are negative, and all the coefficients of income-variation are positive. It follows that all the income-elasticities of demand are positive. Further, from the results (16), $E_{px}(x)$, $E_{py}(y)$ and $E_{pz}(z)$, i.e. the demand elasticities with respect to the price of the good concerned, are also all positive. The three goods compete with each other in pairs and there is no possibility of " exceptional " behaviour of any kind.

(2) When E_x is positive and E_y and E_z are negative we have the case where one good has " increasing marginal utility." Since σ must be positive there is one restriction in this case:

$$\frac{\kappa_x}{E_x} > \frac{\kappa_y}{-E_y} + \frac{\kappa_z}{-E_z}.$$

The elasticity of complementarity of the pair YZ is now positive, and the other two elasticities are negative. Of the income-elasticities of demand only $E_\mu(x)$ is positive and the other two are negative. In this case both Y and Z are inferior to X, and they complement each other while competing separately with X. The p_x-elasticities of demand are all definite in sign from (16), $E_{px}(x)$ being positive and the other two negative. A fall in the price of the superior good X increases the demand for the good at the expense of a decrease in the demand for each of the inferior goods. The other price-elasticities can be of either sign and, in particular, rising demand curves for Y and Z are possible.

The independent goods case includes a case of perfectly "normal" relationship between X, Y and Z. But it also includes a case where a pair of goods is inferior to, and complement each other against, the third good. It is, therefore, not sufficient to take the goods as an independent set if it is desired to give a simple analytical treatment (as a first approximation) of the case of three goods "normally" related. One additional condition is necessary for this, the condition that the elasticities of the marginal rates of substitution are all negative.[1]

To return to the case of two goods for a moment, the only definition of two independent goods that can be given is that the marginal rate of substitution divides into two functions of a single variable : $R_x^y = \frac{\phi_y(y)}{\phi_x(x)}$. There are again two possibilities. *Either* $E_x(\phi_x)$ and $E_y(\phi_y)$ are both negative, in which case the income-elasticities of demand are both positive. *Or* $E_x(\phi_x)$ and $E_y(\phi_y)$ are of opposite signs, in which case the income-elasticities of demand are also of opposite signs. But these two possibilities cover all the cases that *can* arise when there are only two goods. The case of two independent goods is thus no more restricted (in general terms) than the complete case, and any relationship between two goods can be represented, at least approximately for small variations, by the independent relationship. The two-goods case can be treated perfectly well by assuming independence from the beginning.[2] This is not

[1] Only *one* condition is required here since two of the three elasticities are negative in any case.

[2] See Hicks, ECONOMICA, February 1934, pp. 75-6. In the case of two independent goods X and Y, the two fundamental elasticities are $E_x(\phi_x)$ and $E_y(\phi_y)$. The former is the elasticity (X variable) of the marginal rate of substitution of Y for X, or (broadly) the elasticity of the marginal utility of X. The other elasticity is similarly interpreted. All demand elasticities are expressed in terms of E_x and E_y ; in particular

$$E_\mu(x) = -\sigma E_y \text{ and } E_\mu(y) = -\sigma E_x,$$

where $\sigma = -\frac{1}{E_x E_y} \frac{1}{\frac{\kappa_x}{E_x} + \frac{\kappa_y}{E_y}}$, the elasticity of substitution between X and Y.

These remarks throw some light upon the meaning of Professor Frisch's "money flexibility" (*New Methods of Measuring Marginal Utility*, 1932). Professor Frisch, in effect, takes X as one particular commodity (say sugar) and Y as the group of all other commodities. Then E_y is the elasticity of the marginal rate of substitution of sugar for all other commodities when the expenditure on the latter varies. This is the elasticity of the marginal utility of all other commodities, i.e. of money income. Hence, Professor Frisch's money flexibility is E_y. It follows, for example, that income-elasticity of demand for sugar is the product of the elasticity of substitution between sugar and all other commodities and the numerical value of money flexibility. The question arises whether the value of E_y is independent of the choice of X. If this is the case, as Professor

true in the case of more than two goods, and here the case of independence is definitely more restricted than the general case (even if integrability is assumed), and must be treated as such.

4. *Notes on the " degrees of freedom " of the system.*—Three cases of the relationship between three or more goods have been considered:

(*a*) The general case.
(*b*) The case where the integrability condition is satisfied and a utility function index exists.
(*c*) The case of independent goods.

It is proposed to add a number of concluding remarks on the way in which the number of " degrees of freedom " of the system is decreased as we proceed from the general to the more particular cases. The meaning of the term " degrees of freedom " will be apparent from the nature of these remarks.

(*a*) In the general case it is found that three relations (17) exist between the elasticities of substitution and of complementarity and one relation (14) between the coefficients of income-variation. The restrictions (9) are only inequalities and do not affect the independence of the indices. There are thus *eight independent indices of the individual's complex of preferences* and these can be taken as the six elasticities of complementarity and two of the coefficients of income-variation.

The variation of individual demand for changes in income or in the market prices is described by twelve income and price-elasticities of demand. By the relations (14) and (17) one income-elasticity and three price-elasticities depend on the others. There are thus eight independent elasticities of demand and the eight independent indices account for these. The general case, therefore, has eight degrees of freedom.

(*b*) The integrability case introduces symmetry into the system. The six elasticities of complementarity are reduced to three, and there are now only *five independent indices of the individual's complex of preferences.* These can be taken, for example, as the three elasticities of complementarity and two coefficients of income-variation. There is a reduction of three in the number of degrees of freedom in the system. On the demand side this must be paralleled by three relations between the eight independent elasticities of demand. These relations

Frisch claims, the income-elasticity of demand for any commodity is a constant multiple of the elasticity of substitution between this and all other commodities.

are provided by the symmetry of the system and are, from the equations (16),

$$\frac{1}{\kappa_x} E_{px}(y) - \frac{1}{\kappa_y} E_{py}(x) = E_\mu(y) - E_\mu(x)$$

and two similar relations. As we found, these relations provide a means of comparing $E_{px}(y)$ and $E_{py}(x)$, and so on.

The fact that there are five degrees of freedom in the system is also shown by the number of second-order derivatives of $\phi(x,y,z)$. There are six of these derivatives and one is not independent since the integrability condition must be satisfied. The remaining five are independent and describe the system.

(*c*) The further particular case of a set of three independent goods introduces two further restrictions. From the equations (19), it follows that the two independent coefficients of income-variation are expressible in terms σ_{xy}, σ_{yz} and σ_{xz}, and are no longer independent. There are now only *three independent indices of the individual's complex of preferences*. These can be taken as σ_{xy}, σ_{yz} and σ_{xz}. Alternatively, since all indices can be expressed in terms of the definite elasticities $E_x(\phi_x)$, $E_y(\phi_y)$ and $E_z(\phi_z)$, these can be taken to represent the three independent indices. There are thus three degrees of freedom in the system.

On the demand side, in addition to the relations of the integrability case, there are two relations connecting the income-elasticities and the price-elasticities. Hence, of the elasticities of demand, only three are independent (e.g. the p_x-elasticities), and these are accounted for by the three independent indices. This is checked by the fact that there are only three non-zero second-order derivatives of the function $\phi(x,y,z) = \Phi_x(x) + \Phi_y(y) + \Phi_z(z)$.

Finally, the independent goods case with one additional condition can be used to describe a case of three goods related in a perfectly " normal " way. Since the additional condition takes the form of an inequality there is no further reduction in the number of degrees of freedom. The case of independent goods " normally " related is still described by three independent indices and still displays three degrees of freedom.

12 Realism and Relevance in the Theory of Demand

F. H. Knight

THE treatment of demand is the branch of economic theory in which methodological problems are most important and most difficult. This is because it is here that behavior facts are most inseparably bound up with motivation and that objective data call most imperatively for interpretation by subjective facts and meanings.[1] The objective in this paper is largely negative—to criticize certain recent innovations in the treatment of demand which have been generally hailed as representing an advance but which, in the writer's opinion, constitute a movement in a backward direction. The particular reference is to the treatment of demand and utility by J. R. Hicks, pioneered by E. Slutzky, and also followed, and more or less independently worked out, by Henry Schultz and many others.[2] The essential features of the theory are a new psychology of consumption and a distinctive treatment of the demand curve based upon the former. The new interpretation of consumption is more relativistic than the conventional view, specifically that of Marshall, and is adopted for the sake of greater objectivity. It has two aspects. The first is replacement of the conception of "absolute" diminishing incremental utility (of a single good) with a diminishing "coefficient of substitution" of one good for another, assumed to be a purely behavioristic principle, or at least purely relative. The second aspect is a distinctive view of the relation between change in income and change in the psychic state of the subject—his economic well-being. In this second connection the thinkers criticized have not been willing to follow through with a behavioristic complete rejection of subjective

[1] In the pure theory, or ultimate analysis, of economic behavior, production is for consumption and does not involve any motivation other than that which is derived or imputed from the consumer interest. Production and consumption should be defined in such a way as to make this distinction clear. Immediate preferences between productive activities will then be treated as situations in which a certain amount of consumption is simultaneous with production, and the two are inseparable. And saving—net production of capital—will be viewed in the usual (only partly realistic) way as provision for future consumption. The sweeping limitation of such assumptions, in contrast with the inclusive facts of motivation, can be given only incidental notice in this paper.

[2] Hicks, *Value and Capital* (Oxford, 1939), chap. i; Schultz, *The Theory and Measurement of Demand* (Chicago, 1938); see also the contributions of Mosak and Samuelson to *Studies in Mathematical Economics and Econometrics, in Memory of Henry Schultz*, edited by O. Lange, F. McIntyre, and T. O. Yntema (Chicago, 1942).

Reprinted from the *Journal of Political Economy*, Vol. LII (December 1944), pp. 289–318, by permission of the publisher and author.

magnitudes—or their reduction to the role of a "force" impelling men to buy and consume and to compare and choose. They still think of the individual as controlling his consumption with a view to securing more rather than less of something called "utility"—a subjective magnitude which is maximized when the consumer's behavior conforms to the economic ideal. They merely insist that this something-maximized need not, and therefore should not, be treated as a quantity in the ordinary "cardinal" meaning, but as only "ordinal," that is, utilities are subject to ranking but not to real quantification, which is identified with measurement.[3]

[3] In the course of this discussion we shall distinguish sharply between quantification and measurement, stressing quantification by estimation without measurement, and will use the terms "quantity" and "ordinal magnitude" to designate the two main concepts which are to be contrasted.

This article will not be encumbered with references to the literature—even that which is known to the writer and which, in view of his mathematical limitations, he feels competent to judge. This applies especially to recent work (including articles by Hicks) based on the assumption of absolute money prices and relative utility, which it is the main purpose of the article to criticize. Earlier references may be found in the books of Schultz and Hicks cited above in n. 2. The aim here is to clarify issues and state a position in nonmathematical and the simplest possible terms. To venture into detailed criticism of the history of doctrine would both extend the paper far beyond allowable compass and make its perusal laborious and confusing. The writer may note, however, that he was first jolted out of complacency and led to rethink the problem by reading a short article by Oscar Lange, "The Determinateness of the Utility Function," *Review of Economic Studies*, I (1934), 218–25. Also that in the discussion which followed the publication of this article and of articles by Schultz and Hicks and Allen in 1934 and 1935, and their independent rediscovery of Slutzky's paper of 1915, Harro Bernardelli stands out as a thinker, and particularly one of mathematical competence, who has "kept his feet on the ground" and not been swept away by the romantic glamour of revolution and the temptation to indulge in logical ingenuity presented by the "new" form of analysis. Cf. "Notes on the Determinateness of the Utility Function," *Review of Economic Studies*, II (1934–35), 69–77. It goes without saying that we recognize the high intellectual quality of the work which has gone into the development of the "new approach" and its value in contributing to the clarification of the issues, and also that choice between fundamental assumptions is, to some extent, a matter of taste and may depend on the purpose in view in a particular exposition.

In the way of construction we shall attempt to clarify the relationship between the subjective and the objective aspects of the economic values of different consumption goods—more accurately, services—under given conditions correctly defined and the relation between levels of objective consumption, or real income, and economic well-being. On the basis of this analysis we shall outline a realistic theory of the demand curve. Part IV of the paper will take up the problem of measurement in connection with economic well-being and motivation; Part V will offer a brief re-examination of the problem of consumer's surplus. In the first three parts, it will be assumed that the reader has a general knowledge of recent controversial discussion, and our treatment will be confined to a brief statement of essentials, without elaboration in detail.

I. THE THEORY OF INDIFFERENCE—VARIOUS METHODS OF EXPOSITION

For a clear, sound, and useful theory of demand, or the demand curve, the first essential is a sharp separation between the comparative economic values of different goods in relation to a given level of "economic well-being" of the individual consumer and a theory of the relation between changes in the level of well-being and changes in consumption. In the absence of any better terminology, we may refer to the first as the "theory of comparative value" (relative in the sense of comparing different goods) and to the second as the "theory of dynamic valuation." It is to be understood that the term "value" is used in the strictly economic sense, without any implication of "objectivity," as in ethics or aesthetics, where valuations may be "right" or "wrong" or be affected with a quality of imperative or "oughtness." As in all economic discussion, we take the consumer's individual evaluations as final. We also exclude the factor of "error" in its more intellectual meanings; we assume that what the consumer wants is what he gets, and describe his behavior under the condition that he "correctly" solves his "economic" problem, actually maximizing whatever it is that he tries to maximize in the choices which direct his behavior as a consumer.

We first consider different methods of graphing in the simple case of a two-commodity system. In order to make the most useful approximation to the conditions of real life, we assume that an individual A is given a total income (over a short interval of time dt) in the form of a definite amount y, of commodity Y, measured along a vertical axis and that he is confronted with the opportunity of exchanging successive increments of Y for increments of another commodity, X, measured along a horizontal axis (see Fig. 1). The conditions are such that A "buys" successive infinitesimal increments of X, seriatim, paying for the first the maximum amount of Y which he is willing to pay, for the second the maximum amount he is willing to pay after having bought the first, and so on. Thus we picture the "generation" of a curve IC_1, the simplest form of indifference curve; for the purpose of distinction we shall call it the "indifference-combinations" curve. The ordinate on this curve at any point on the X-axis measures the amount of Y which A will have left out of his original supply (per unit of time) after carrying the process to any point, while the abscissa of the same point measures the amount of X he will have secured. (The total amount of Y given up is measured downward from y.) Every point on the curve represents a different combination of amounts of X and Y such that to the given subject A (with initial income y) exchange or choice between any two combinations is a matter of indifference. The ratio or price at which the last exchange is made (or the next one will be made) is measured by the slope of the curve at any

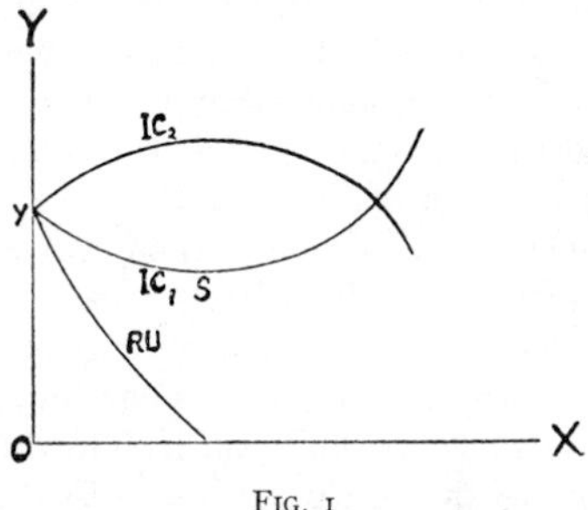

Fig. 1

point—with a negative sign, if, as is usual, we think of the price of X in terms of Y, the price of the good secured in terms of that given up.

If we continue such a curve to the right over a sufficient interval, it will take the general form shown in Figure 1. The facts here are not in dispute, especially as far as the descending section of the curve is concerned. The curve will descend over some interval, with a decreasing (negative) slope, to a point at which it becomes horizontal; and then, if the experiment is continued, it will ascend at an increasing (positive) slope. The lowest point S on the curve (the point at which it is horizontal) corresponds to complete satiety with good X; the price of X here is zero, and no further amount of Y will be voluntarily given up for any further amount of X. Under the conditions of a two-commodity system, this point should ordinarily have the same X value, regardless of the subject's initial income, if X and Y are "independent," i.e., noncomplementary but different goods.

Along the ascending leg of the curve the increasing slope shows that it would be necessary to give back to A increasing amounts of Y, previously given up, to "hire" him to consume each successive increment of X. (We assume consumption, compulsory if necessary, ignoring the possibility that later increments of X might be simply ignored or might be disposed of in some other way.) Over the interval between S and y corresponding to the initial supply of Y, the curve will have dual Y values; there will be two equivalent combinations of each quantity of Y with different quantities of X, one corresponding to a deficiency, the other to a superfluity, of X. The ascending part of the curve is unrealistic under ordinary conditions where the subject has freedom of choice; but the hypothetical procedure is useful for depicting the psychology of demand. The curve IC_1 may be extended upward beyond y, giving A more Y than his initial income, to a point at which it would become vertical, indicating that no more of X could be consumed without making him absolutely worse off (or more than would be voluntarily consumed) no matter how much Y were given him at the same time. The facts shown by the indifference curve may also be presented by a curve drawn upward initially and then downward (curve IC_2 in Fig. 1). This has some advantages, particularly that the amounts of Y given up are indicated in positive instead of negative terms in the significant part. But points on the curves will not then represent "indifference combinations" of X and Y, on the same axes.

Exactly the same facts may again be portrayed by a curve of relative incremental (marginal) utility, as shown in curve RU, which may be called a "curve of indifference-prices" or a "price-indifference curve." On this second curve the vertical axis is a scale of exchange ratios or prices (Y/X or Y per unit of X, at the margin, i.e., dY/dX, in the previous notation); that is, the price at any point is measured by the ordinate instead of by the slope. Hence the ordinate of RU measures the slope of curves IC_1 and IC_2 at any point on X, or it is the "derivative" of either of these except for algebraic sign in case of the former. Curves IC_1 and IC_2 may be viewed as curves of total expenditure drawn under the condition that a consumer buys from a monopolist who exacts the maximum total amount (or maximum price per unit) the buyer is willing to pay for each amount of X. The radical difference between RU, the derivative curve, and a demand curve, showing amounts purchased at given prices with the buyer free to choose the amount he will take at each price, will come into consideration repeatedly as the argument proceeds. Curve RU will intersect the X-axis at the point at which the indifference curve as previously drawn (in either form) becomes horizontal, and beyond that point the indifference-price will become increasingly negative.

The hypothesis of a two-commodity system is, of course, unrealistic and should be used with great caution. Details of the curves would depend on necessarily arbitrary assumptions as to the character of the two goods and the relations between them. To make the discussion more realistic, we should first take the vertical axis as a scale in terms of "money" representing a complex of alternative commodities, at prices which vary together, but inversely with the price of *X*, so that the money has constant total purchasing-power. This change in the facts represented will not change the general form of any of our curves. This is still true if any of the commodities in the complex *Y* are interrelated among themselves or with *X* by any degree of complementarity or similarity. And it is immaterial for the general argument just what price changes occur within the alternative complex, among the infinitude of possibilities, to offset the changing price of *X* and keep the value of money constant. The indifference-combinations-curve method of graphing (for *X* and money) has a great advantage over the indifference-price method, in that the former shows money income directly on a plane diagram and so makes it possible to represent a whole "system" of curves, corresponding to different levels of income. But its use is limited because it does not correspond with market quotations and everyday ways of thinking, which necessarily run in terms of price and quantity.[4]

II. CONSUMER'S VALUATION AS A "DYNAMIC" PROBLEM

We turn to the psychological problem of the interpretive explanation of the curves considered in Part I or of the facts which they represent. The curves are taken as portraying objective facts of consumer behavior (though under idealized conditions), with only incidental reference to any subjective state as "indifference." But it is necessary to decide whether they are to be allowed to stand as purely empirical or are to bring the behavior facts into some intelligible relation to facts of subjective experience.[5] The second position is the one to be defended in this paper as a whole. The more philosophical aspect of the argument for considering motives, and not merely the facts of choice, will be developed in Part IV. In the present section we shall merely explore certain psychological relations. Further than this, we need only remark here that such terms as "willingly" and "voluntarily" occur in the earlier exposition and suggest that it would not be easy to eliminate them and make the discussion seem to "talk sense."

The main concrete issue directly raised is whether we should think of the "utility" of a single good—the property which causes it to be consumed and

[4] We more commonly meet with the indifference-combinations curve for two goods as generated by changes in opposite directions from an intermediate starting-point, as roughly suggested in the accompanying figure. Only a part of the negatively inclined portion of the curve is usually drawn, the continuous line in the figure. If the curve is projected in

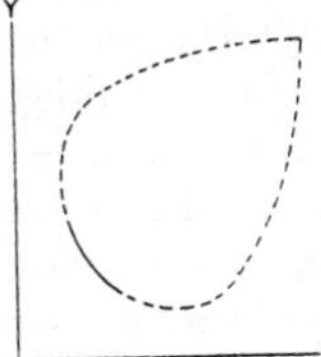

realistic form in both directions, it will have the general shape indicated by the dotted portions. Details would largely depend on the goods in question, their absolute and relative importance, relations of complementarity and substitution, etc. Single commodities that are actually "necessary" hardly occur, and this and other special cases need not be considered. In both directions the curve will ordinarily become parallel, first, with the neighboring axis and then with the other axis. This second event might occur before reaching a point of intersection with the other branch, preventing completion of the closed figure shown. In any event the situation represented by the parts of the curve beyond zero marginal utility for either commodity is unrealistic and need not be discussed.

[5] The former procedure was followed by Cournot in a pure-theory treatment and is the point of view of statistical investigators of demand.

chosen for consumption in preference to other goods—as an independent variable, or as inherently and solely a comparison between the particular good and other goods. In other words, should we view the essence of (final) economic value as purely a comparison or think of relative value as a comparison between the values of different goods? Investigation of the question will take the form of an inquiry into the dynamic problem of the quantitative relation between uncompensated variation in the consumption of individual goods or combinations of goods and variations in desirable experience or state of being in the consumer, i.e., in his "mind." In terms of the established principles used in the analysis of demand, prior to this new controversy, the issue will be found to center in the principle of diminishing utility in connection with an individual good. As pointed out earlier, the Slutzky school deny this principle; they replace it by a combination of two devices, the principle of a decreasing ratio of substitution of one good for another—at a constant level of well-being expressed through "free" choice—and a ranking without "measurement" (or quantification) of states of total well-being, as an individual passes from one indifference level to another.

Our first step will be to inquire into the reality of the principle of diminishing utility for a single good. The investigation may take the form of reflecting upon a series of simple imaginary experiments. To make the analysis accurate and the conditions realistic, in contrast with the vague and misleading assumptions usually met with, we must begin by carefully stating the *ceteris paribus* conditions. We postulate an individual who is consuming a "reasonable" list or budget of commodities, not including the one involved in the experiments, and who continues throughout to consume these in unvarying amount. The first experiment consists in adding to the individual's consumption of these items successive equal small (infinitesimal) increments (per unit of time) of the particular commodity or good X, not before consumed, and having him report upon his experience of "satisfaction." These conditions allow full play for all relations of complementarity and similarity ("substitutability") among all the commodities, including the one which is varied in the experiment.

In the interest of precision and clarity, other conditions of the experiment need to be carefully stated and some terms defined. We must sharply separate consumer behavior from all productive activity, and especially from saving and investment, and must be clear about the dimensionality of the magnitudes with which we are dealing. To touch first on the second point, consumption (like production and all "activity") has the dimensionality of a flow or "flux." But the correct physical analogy is not the flow of a material such as water, which exists and can be measured when it is not flowing. Light is perhaps the best physical analogue in this respect. The rate of flow of water is realistically viewed as a composite magnitude—quantity divided by time. With light the relation is the opposite. Only the intensity can be measured directly (though the unit may be defined in terms of other dimensions); quantity is the composite and derivative magnitude, an arithmetical product of intensity *times* time—candle-power-hours. It is a mere concept, essentially fictitious.

The same relation holds for consumption, whether thought of as a subjective or as an objective magnitude. What is consumed is always a *service* (of some agent, human or "physical"). The result, which is the end or purpose and which gives consumption quantitative meaning, may be called "want-satisfaction," or simply "satisfaction"; but "subjective service" is a less objectionable designation. Any more concrete definition will commit the economist on psychological or moral issues with which he has nothing to do. It is simply the common quality underlying all direct economic comparison and choice—"that which" the consumer strives to maximize and does maximize when his behavior is "economic." It must be a homogeneous magnitude if we are to speak of quantitative change; and, since there is no physical attribute which is common to all sources of satisfaction, the end of consumption must be a single variable state or condition of the individual. We assume that what is desired is identical with what is realized and experienced; that is, we abstract from error—connected with the fact that consumption may be treated as a means to welfare as the real end—and from the fact that novelty, surprise, and gratification of curiosity are elements in real enjoyment and in the motivation of choice. This assumption is largely implied by ideal stationary conditions, in which desire and satisfaction, production and consumption, are strictly simultaneous. ("Utility" is the attribute of an agent by virtue of which it yields subjective service, and the two terms are not always interchangeable.) Correspondingly, the primary meaning of production is "objective service" or the use of any agent to render subjective service.

The main source of confusion in relation to consumption is the fact that production in this primary meaning is not necessarily equal to consumption over any interval of time. Production may exceed consumption, the difference being (axiomatically) added to "capital"; i.e., it may consist in the production of (additional) capital and not of "satisfaction." And, conversely, consumption may exceed production, the difference representing a decrease of capital. (Production of what is consumed includes maintenance of capital.) Since the production of any amount of capital (saving and investment) represents the sacrifice of a given amount of consumption and results in future consumption, it seems natural to think of a quantity of capital as a quantity of consumption stored up in a stock. But this is invalid, for two reasons. The quantity of capital accumulated in any finite interval is not the amount of consumption sacrificed—intensity *times* time—but contains an additional element, a return on investment, continuously compounded at a certain "rate." (This is usually referred to as the rate of interest, but it has no connection with the lending of money—or of anything else—and would have exactly the same meaning in a Crusoe economy as in a pecuniary society.) On the other hand, a quantity of capital does not represent any determinate quantity of future consumption. Until and unless the capital itself is consumed, the total yield grows without limit; and in any case it also is affected by the rate of return or interest. Analysis requires treatment of the production of capital during any interval and its subsequent use to yield consumption-service (or further investment) as distinct acts or processes of production.[6]

[6] It should go without saying that the "production of capital" means here "net production" or "growth," distinguished from the maintenance of capital already existing, including all replacements, even by a different type of concrete agent (and that "capital" consumption means "net" consumption). In real life the bulk of investment is "presumptively permanent"; only the yield is expected to be con-

Elimination of all investment and disinvestment in effect reduces exchange to the purchase and sale of services, without any transfer of "goods" (all of which are "capital"), and imposes stationary conditions. It also eliminates all lending of money; for, under ideal conditions, such a loan is indistinguishable from a lease for a rental. Similarly excluded are all "contracts" for the purchase and sale of services, involving any commitment for the future. It is most convenient to think of the consumer as not owning any productive capacity, and particularly any money.[7]

Returning to our imaginary experiment, we are to think of our subject as having no alternatives of choice; he is simply given increasing amounts (per time unit) of a particular objective service, which we shall now call os_i. We submit that beyond any possibility of doubt he will report decreasing increments in the intensity of subjective service ss_i from equal increments of os_i (added to his original budget). That is, the variation in his additional satisfaction will show progressive satiation up to a point of complete satiety, and then run into supersatiation with increasing increments of negative satisfaction. It will be represented by a curve of the shape of a round arch or inverted U (preferably measured upward from a false base line). It is to be stressed that the increments of subjective service are not quantified (on "measurement" see below) by comparison with any other kind of satisfaction. Each increment of satisfaction is compared only with the increments of the same kind which precede it in the sequence. The total real income of the subject increases by equal steps, as defined and measured in physical units by an ideal index number, while, in subjective terms, it behaves in the manner described. Thus the curve and its derivative are very different in meaning from IC_2 of Figure 1.

The experiment is, next, to be modified in two steps. First, we give the subject increasing amounts, in fixed proportions, of all the items in any fixed budget or list of services. The resulting variation in total satisfaction will certainly take the same form as before. Next we give him "money" in increasing amounts (increasing by equal increments), restricted to the purchase of a given list of items at fixed (absolute) money prices, with freedom to reapportion his expenditure among them at will. The reported result will again be of the same kind—total satisfaction increasing by decreasing steps and then decreasing.

If introspection leaves any room for doubt as to the declining (arithmetic) rate of increase, it is proved by the unquestionable fact that if the money income of an individual increases, under realistic conditions (i.e., if he has freedom of choice) he will not merely buy more of the services previously consumed but, in addition to buying more of these, will spend part of his increased income for services not previously consumed.

---

sumed, or not all of that, apart from some emergency—but, of course, there are important exceptions. We cannot go into the special difficulties of investment in human beings or their capacities (and its maintenance) in "free" society, beyond noting that in essential respects these are much like any other capital. This fact and its practical limitation will be evident if one compares conditions in a slave economy with those of free individualism (see also n. 7 below).

[7] This assumption again raises the difficulty of the individual's ownership and use of himself as a productive agent. It is really necessary to assume only that all ownership, of things or capacities or money, is held constant. Consumption must be separated from such changes, particularly in the holding of money, in order to isolate the special problems connected with that cause. One important desideratum in economic analysis is to bring out explicitly the unrealistic assumptions necessary to generality at every point.

This is wholly inexplicable and would not happen, except for the fact that the whole list previously consumed is subject to diminishing incremental utility. Mere growth of total income cannot increase the utility of items not previously consumed and cannot increase their relative marginal utility or coefficient of substitution, in comparison with earlier items, unless increased consumption absolutely reduces the marginal utility of the earlier budget items. We cannot realistically interpret the decline in the marginal utility of one good increased in supply relative to others not consumed, hence its decreasing coefficient of substitution for the latter, without taking into account its decreasing absolute marginal utility as its consumption increases, *ceteris paribus*. Further, the negative price elasticity of demand for a good cannot be dissociated from declining positive income elasticity, all prices being constant and with the consumer free to add new items. And decreasing income elasticity can result only from decreasing marginal utility of any whole list of goods or of money to be spent for them at given prices.[8]

The propositions (*a*) that utility and satisfaction are purely relative and (*b*) that the total is merely an ordinal magnitude are impossible even under the assumption that demand curves are to be studied exclusively with reference to a given list of commodities. If absolute marginal utility did not decrease, no determinate apportionment of income would be made. If we think of the consumer's income beginning at zero and gradually increasing, the first increment would be spent on the service yielding the most satisfaction for the initial unit, or one chosen at random. And if increasing consumption of this item carried increasing or constant incremental satisfaction, no other items would ever be added but all further additions to income would be spent for the same good. (With incremental change constant, adding new items would either involve loss or be a matter of indifference.) It is logically admissible to think that the marginal utility of a particular good may increase with increasing consumption over a narrow initial interval; and this might even be true of total income, under special conditions. But the rational consumer will never stop using

[8] There is actually no reasonable ground for doubt that money income of constant objective purchasing-power decreases in marginal utility (and utility per unit) as its amount increases, even if expenditure is not restricted to the purchase of the same goods. This restriction only makes the conclusion more obvious and the decline more rapid than if the individual is free to add new items to his budget. The rate of decline might be reduced by a high degree of complementarity between items previously consumed and new items; but the general effect of this will be merely a greater variety in consumption at all income levels. It is a judgment of common sense, on a level of self-evidence virtually that of the simpler mathematical axioms that, other things being equal, the addition or subtraction of a dollar per week or month from his income means less to the recipient of a larger income than to one whose income is smaller. Apart from this principle, no one would defend or suggest the justice of progressive income taxation. Equality of sacrifice of "final value" to the subject (however this is interpreted) would then call for absolutely equal taxation, not even equality in the fractional levy, to say nothing of progression. (The statement assumes that consumption is the only significance of income, ignoring such factors as security, prestige, power, justice, etc., which may make equality a consideration for other reasons or on its own account.)

As far as the present discussion is concerned, we need not dispute the usual assumption that the desire for income is insatiable, that its marginal utility would never fall to zero or become negative, if it can be used to satisfy additional wants. However, the proposition is doubtful if wants are strictly defined in terms of consumption, excluding social emulation, prestige, and power. And it is surely false if we go on and exclude special costs of change desired purely for the sake of change. However, this factor bulks large in want-satisfaction even at low income levels and introduces an element of unreality into a mechanical or function-and-variable theory of demand.

freely apportionable income to purchase any quantity of a good within an interval of increasing marginal utility but will proceed at least to the point of maximum utility per unit of expenditure; and (with proportions freely variable) no budget items will be added in the interval of increasing utility of money income. The situation is parallel with that of productive services, where the operations are limited to the range of diminishing physical returns. All facts of complementarity and similarity are essentially the same in the two cases. Subjective service is not physically measurable, but its quantitative variation is factually indubitable; and even if it were possible to explain the facts of demand without it, the procedure would be interesting only as an intellectual "stunt."

We must hasten to take account of a realistic difficulty in reasoning from the addition of new items to a budget, with increasing income in money of constant purchasing-power. In this situation an individual will not usually increase his consumption of all previous items but, besides adding new items, will to some extent *replace* commodities previously consumed with new ones, decreasing his purchase of some of the former, or even dropping them altogether. In a familiar illustration, if he has been eating chiefly bread, at a higher income he may not only add some meat but consume less bread. Moreover, he may also replace a lower "grade" of bread with a higher grade. As we classify commodities more "finely," even to correspond with market facts in a high civilization, displacement of items may predominate over increased consumption.

The phenomenon of replacement of "inferior" by "superior" goods or the reverse, as income changes, has received much attention in recent discussion. The correct view is that they are different goods. Even the "same" good bought from a dealer of a different class is really a different thing—certainly, if a different price is paid, whatever the reason. The underlying fact is that any commodity, as named and sold in the market, yields a "bundle" of diverse subjective services, which are to be had only (or more economically) in combination rather than separately. Things regarded as differing only in grade are usually named with reference to some predominant useful quality which they have in common, along with different assortments of other qualities. At the most general level of analysis it should be assumed that each single good (objective service) as purchased yields a single type of satisfaction. This might still be allowed to vary in degree in accord with the price for the ordinary market unit, "quality" differing in that sense. Under this assumption, displacement obviously will not occur in consequence of income change.

III. THE MEANING OF A DEMAND CURVE

We must now briefly consider the demand curve in terms of its expository meaning rather than its psychological or philosophical interpretation. Here we are concerned with an aspect of the Slutzky view which has little logical connection with the methodological conceptions with which we find it associated. The demand curve in the tradition of modern economic theory shows the functional relation between price and quantity taken (or sold) for a particular good, "all other things being equal." It is always assumed that the buyer confronts a set price at which he is free to purchase as much or as little of the good as he may choose—a fact which differentiates the curve sharply from any of those we have previously considered. Until quite recently few, if any, writers were at all careful to say what they meant by this *ceteris paribus* condition; and in general it probably did not occur to them that price is ambiguous or that it is not possible for all other things to be equal. The money price and sale of a particular good cannot change while all other variables in an economic system are constant. We have to choose in analysis between holding the prices of all other goods constant and maintaining constant the "real income" of the hypothetical consumer. For, obviously, if the price of a single good, X, increases, while the prices of other goods are unchanged (along with the money income of the individual), the "value of money" to the subject will have decreased—in objective and in subjective terms—and vice versa. The strict *ceteris paribus* assumption can be valid only when there is no finite change, i.e., for the partial derivative of a total-consumption function at a single point.

The treatment of the Slutzky school adopts the assumption that the price of X varies under the condition that the prices of all other goods (and the consumer's money income) are constant. Hence, real income must change. Of the two alternatives, this seems to be definitely the wrong choice. It throws together two distinct effects upon consumption, the "price effect" and the "income effect." The treatment then proceeds to separate these by means of an ingenious analysis. The cleverness of it all must be conceded. But it is called for only because of an initial confusion in the statement of the problem, which is wholly unnecessary and should clearly be avoided. The simple and obvious alternative is to draw the demand curve in terms of a change in *relative* prices, i.e., to assume that the value of money is held constant, through compensating changes in the prices of other goods, and not that these other prices are held constant. The "income effect" of Slutzky *et al.* is merely a particular case or mode of change in the purchasing-power of money, or the price level; and it is this problem as a whole that should be isolated and reserved for separate treatment.[9]

As to reality, important price changes generally approximate one or the other of two patterns. Either the price of a particular good changes, relative to the prices of other goods—reflecting some change in tastes or productive conditions—without a significant change in the general price level, or all prices change more or less simultaneously, in consequence of monetary changes. In so far as change is general and uniform, the whole phenomenon is purely arithmetical, particularly since incomes change in the same ratio as the prices of consumption goods. Of course, the two types of change occur together, to some extent; and especially the relative prices of consumption goods and of various indirect goods and productive services (and the present values of contracts and other commitments) are differentially changed over substantial periods by changes which originate in the field of money and ultimately lead chiefly to a movement of the general price level. Boom and depression are incidents of such temporary changes. Real, practical price problems arise only in connection with changes in relative prices, and it is exclusively the connection of general changes with such relative changes that gives the general price

[9] The conception of price changes as relative is, of course, the view which was made classical by the treatment of J. S. Mill and is perhaps the position generally adopted in textbooks—when the authors state their assumptions or make it possible to discern any consistent position.

level any practical importance. Consequently, the separation of price changes due to monetary causes from those due to other causes is one of the main tasks of price analysis as a whole. An approach to any particular price problem which "jumbles" effects of change in the purchasing-power of money (however caused) with effects of change in its relative value for purchasing different things is mere gratuitous confusion. And it is easy to avoid, specifically in the theory of demand. In fact, this confusing procedure is much more complex and difficult than one based on formulating the problem in more realistic terms to begin with, in the manner already indicated. That is: in drawing the demand curve, the utility and the objective purchasing-power of money are the factors which should be held constant ("impounded in *ceteris paribus*," in Marshall's familiar phrase) and not the prices of other consumption goods. This procedure has the further great advantage of eliminating the spurious "Giffen paradox" (see below) and making the theory of consumption logically parallel with the theory of production, which is in accord with the essential facts.[10]

It is a fairly simple matter to explain the general shape—the descending slope—of the demand curve (of an individual for a particular good) in terms of its (independent) diminishing incremental utility in comparison with that of other goods. Quantity purchased decreases as the relative price increases (*ceteris paribus*) because at the higher price the same amount of money buys less of the particular good, while there is a small converse effect on the complex of other goods, which fall in price. Consequently, if the consumer's marginal "dollar" bought equal increments of total satisfaction in terms of all services before the change, it will, after the change, buy less satisfaction if spent for the particular service, os_i, than if spent for competing services; and enough of os_i will be replaced in the individual's budget by other goods to restore the equality. The total expenditure upon os_i may increase or decrease or remain constant, according as the elasticity of demand (determined by all the factors which enter into the demand

[10] We may digress to point out that the general point of view and habit of mind reflected in the Hicks-Slutzky analysis has wide ramifications in recent literature and has led to utter confusion in the whole body of economic thought. We refer, of course, to the huge corpus of discussion beginning with Keynes's *General Theory* and following the lead of that work. J. R. Hicks's book, *Value and Capital*, is especially interesting as a general treatise which combines the theory of Keynes's treatment of unemployment and money with the Slutzky analysis of demand and theory of utility. It should be kept in mind that there is no logical connection between the confusion of price changes due to monetary causes and those due to other causes with either the use of indifference curves or their distinctive psychological-philosophical interpretation.

This whole episode may be viewed as a reaction against the neglect of monetary changes and their extremely important effects (boom and depression) in the main line of treatises of classical economic theory, including Marshall. Mill and other classical writers paid some incidental attention to monetary or trade crises but strangely neglected the more important and longer-range repercussions upon production, as well as the converse causal relation between productive maladjustments—especially in the field of investment—and price disorganization. Failure to deal somewhere with these phenomena is doubtless a valid criticism of the classical economic theory as a whole. But it does not follow at all that the omission is to be corrected by jumbling other maladjustments, real and pecuniary, in with the general theory of economic equilibrium. The valid remedy for the defect represents much less of a departure from tradition. It consists simply in adding what has been lacking, i.e., adding a theory of monetary perturbations to the theory of general equilibrium. We need not here enter upon this task, but we may note that, since all the important phenomena could well occur without either commercial banking or any lending of money, the perturbations of the interest rate (or rates) and their causes and effects are a relatively minor topic in the inquiry as a whole.

situation) is below, above, or equal to unity.[11]

IV. SATISFACTION AS A QUANTITY

We come to the crucial methodological, or philosophical, issue in the interpretation of economic choice, and specifically in the theory of demand. The question raised by the new school of thought has two forms or aspects. The question is whether "total satisfaction" is a cardinal magnitude, a "quantity," or is merely ordinal. This is the variable which the "economic man" strives to maximize in his choices as a consumer with a given income and as a producer with given productive resources, and strives to increase by increasing his income through saving and investment. The question is identical with that as to the reality of the diminishing marginal or incremental utility of a particular good or group of goods, as increasing amounts are consumed by an individual, *ceteris paribus*. The Slutzky analysis of demand, as developed by Hicks and others (after it was suggested by Pareto), sharply separates movement along an indifference curve (with a fixed real income) from movement from a lower to a higher indifference curve with increasing real income. We assume here that the analysis is correctly set up, with the money income of the individual increasing while all prices are constant, and that the indifference curves start from an axis of money.

The "new" analysis admits that the individual moving outward from the origin across his indifference curves is really moving "up hill" along a third perpendicular axis of total satisfaction or well-being, that the indifference curves are projections downward of contour lines on a surface. But it denies the need of assigning any vertical scale of magnitude to change in this direction. It is held that the upward movement can be represented by an index function, all other properties of which are immaterial except that it is increasing. Since that is all we need to know about it, no other information should be used in analysis.[12] This view eliminates diminishing marginal (incremental) utility of increasing total income, in whatever manner the increase is effected, in terms of actual goods. As we have pointed out, recognition of diminishing utility is another way of saying that we can draw a curve of total satisfaction in a vertical plane

[11] If we consider the whole range of price variation, the elasticity of demand will normally have a high value at the highest price at which consumption begins, and will fall to zero as price declines to some point at which consumption no longer increases appreciably with its further decline. Elasticity must, of course, be measured at a position of equilibrium. It will ordinarily be low if determined in relation to sudden changes; and the fact that these afford practically the only possibility of determining it inductively largely vitiates statistical measurements; for if a change is slow, other things cannot be assumed equal, and we cannot distinguish empirically between a movement along the curve and a movement of the curve as a whole. The elasticity of demand depends on the availability of substitutes; but freedom of substitution is only in part a matter of physical similarity between goods or even between the types of satisfaction which they yield.

It must be emphasized that the demand curve, showing the relation between price and quantity taken, under the condition that the subject is free to buy as much or as little as he pleases of os_i at a uniform price (other things being equal in other respects), is a very different thing from any form of indifference curve. A demand curve cannot be drawn from an indifference curve, nor from a system of indifference curves in the form in which these usually appear. A curve of the Hicks-Slutzky type can be drawn from an indifference map only if objective money or commodity values are given for the curves; a true demand curve could presumably (in theory) be computed from a complete "map" in n dimensions (in algebraic form) and a given income and given pattern of compensating price changes.

[12] In the absence of experimental determination of a satisfaction-function we actually work with the supposed essential properties of such functions.

through any straight line in the base plane, cutting all the indifference curves, as an X-axis and that it will ascend at a decreasing slope. This decrease in slope is a fact additional to that of ascent and can be present only if a linear scale is assigned to the perpendicular axis.

For convenience we consider movement along the axis of money, observing that the curves are spaced at equal intervals along that axis (but nowhere else) and that money has constant objective purchasing-power. For the purpose of the moment this may be given the simplest meaning—constancy of all prices. For convenience we may take this Y-axis or money axis as a new X-axis and treat the vertical third axis as a Y-axis and ask what variable it may be assumed to measure and what will be its mode of variation. There are obviously four possibilities of interpretation. The first is that the Y-axis measures merely quantity of consumption, in units of some ideal index number. The curve would be a straight line diverging from the X-axis itself only because of a different unit than money price for measuring income. Anything that may be happening to the individual internally, in his mind, is ignored if not denied. This would be the rigorously objective or behavioristic view. It is appropriate in statistical economics; but even statistics implicitly assumes comparison and direction of choice by a principle of maximizing something. Second, this view might be modified, or restated without any change in substance, by interpreting the economic tendency or urge (to consume and to proportion expenditures in one way rather than another) in terms of a "force" on the analogy of mechanics, without assuming that any conscious experience or "conation" is involved.

At the opposite extreme (third) is interpretation in terms of the theory of diminishing incremental utility, in more or less the orthodox form. This is the view advocated in this paper. It includes two statements: (*a*) that the subject becomes economically better off, in terms of conscious (or "subconscious") experience, i.e., that he enjoys an increasing "quantity" (meaning intensity) of satisfaction or subjective service; and (*b*) that he can, and will, say that the increasing conscious well-being experienced in passing from a particular indifference curve I_j to the next higher one I_k is less than the increase experienced in passing from the next lower curve I_i to curve I_j. Hence the change in his well-being can be shown by a curve of decreasing upward slope. Fourth, this third position may be modified by dropping the second statement, leaving only the first. This last is the Slutzky position, which is attacked in this paper. It admits and uses comparison between levels of satisfaction but denies or ignores all comparison of differences between different levels—all judgment by the subject as to "how much" better off he becomes through any addition to income. This view is defended by appeal to the principle that entities or fundamental concepts are not to be multiplied unnecessarily—the principle known as "Occam's Razor"; its advocates hold that the statement dropped is superfluous and, if not false, is at least irrelevant. The position has to be judged with reference to the psychological reality of decreasing increments and to its usefulness in interpreting the phenomena scientifically and for practical purposes.

The validity of the decreasing additions to satisfaction or subjective service derived from equal additions to consumption of measurable objective service, regardless of kind, has already been demonstrated in our discussion of hypothetical experiments, and little remains to be said directly on that point. It is obvious to introspection that the successive equal "doses" of the service os_i or of money could be replaced with increasing doses, experimentally so adjusted that the subject would report equal, instead of decreasing, increments of satisfaction intensity. It should go without saying that we assume psychological stability in the subject and the economic or rational character of his thinking and motivation. The increments of satisfaction received from increments of a single good os_i might be experimentally quantified, and in a sense measured, by ascertaining how much of any good, or of the whole collection of goods previously consumed, represented by money, the subject would be willing to give up to secure an additional increment of the particular good at any point in the experimental variation of the latter. This could not be done for money or income as a whole, for total satisfaction can be measured only in units of itself.

There may be no harm in saying that the experiments we have described constitute "measurement," in terms of money, of the added satisfaction derived from successive increments of os_i, provided there is a clear understanding of the conditions and of the meaning of measurement in this connection. The satisfaction derived from os_i, or its "capacity" to yield satisfaction, ordinarily has no clear and direct relation to any physical attribute of the service consumed. Further, as the service enters into a budget, it cannot be said to yield a particular kind of satisfaction or a complex of particular kinds, but simply added total satisfaction. Most physical services actually yield an unanalyzable and varying complex of kinds of satisfaction, involving manifold complementary relations with other goods. We are dealing with a unique universe of subjective comparison. To investigate this new problem we must consider the relations between objective measurement, subjective experience, and estimation.

The measurement of any physical magnitude (any that is directly perceptible to the senses) is a technical procedure for improving upon the accuracy of a subjective judgment or estimate. The operation does not measure or change in any way the estimate itself as a quantitative experience; and, to whatever degree of refinement measurement is carried, there always remains an element of comparison by subjective estimation. This source of inaccuracy is much reduced, but not eliminated, by the use of the "zero method," whereby the judgment is one of equality rather than of what multiple one magnitude is of another. (The theory of demand and of all forms of indifference curves runs in terms of the zero method; at any chosen position the subject judges that a small shift in his expenditure makes no difference in his level of satisfaction.)

Physical mechanics is built around the three primary magnitudes of space, mass (or force [see below, pp. 305 ff.]), and time; and in physics as a whole the units for measuring other magnitudes are viewed as derived from these three elementary "dimensions." (Here we need think only of the classical or Newtonian conceptual system.) Of the three, space is measured in a primary and direct sense, which is not true of the other two or of any other magnitude whatever. It is only space—and, practically speaking, only length, not even area and volume—that we can cut into equal pieces, compare the pieces for equality by superposition, and count their number. The role of estimation in this process is obvious, and the relation between measurement of distance (whether by the crude yardstick method or by one which is in any degree more refined) and its outright estimation need not be discussed. All other magnitudes, including time and mass (or force), are measured indirectly through the measurement of length, by the use of some apparatus based on a theory which brings the magnitude to be measured into correlation with a scale of length. (Usually the correlation is linear—the scale divisions on the instrument are equal—but this is a detail.)

Some aspects of the relation between subjective and objective magnitudes can be brought out by the example of thermometry. Here, again, a length—familiarly, the height of a column of mercury —is assumed to measure temperature as a physical magnitude, defined by dynamic theory, which corresponds *in a general way* with our sensations of warmth and cold. If the correspondence were exact in all cases, we should hardly need thermometers; and if there were no correspondence at all, it is idle to speculate as to what might have been the development of our concept of temperature as a measurable quantity. But the quantitative changes in sensation are none the less real, whether the correspondence with the thermometer follows some nonlinear function (such as the logarithmic relation of the Weber-Fechner law, roughly valid for some magnitudes within some limits) or whether there is no simple functional relation. In the nature of the case there can be no physical measurement of the feeling of temperature (or of the estimate of length); this is a matter of direct experience and of verbal reporting. Yet either judgment—that the temperature as felt shows a linear correspondence with that measured, that they are related by any other function, or that they are not related—proves with equal and complete conclusiveness that temperature as felt is quantitative (in the cardinal sense). The subject "knows" approximately—he can estimate—whether a second change in his feeling is equal to or greater or less than a preceding one, and experimental changes could be adjusted to seem equal; and there would literally be no sense in saying that any such judgment is wrong. We hold it to be self-evident that what has been said of temperature is true of every subjective variable, regardless of its nature or relation to a measurable physical variable as a cause—or in what sense, if at all, we attribute the experience to such a cause. Whenever our minds judge one experience to be greater, more intense, than another, it is always possible to distinguish between (approximately) equal and unequal degrees of change.

An illustration which seems made to order for expository purposes (and has been used) is the grading of examination papers, in any subject from arithmetic to any branch of aesthetics, or grading human performance of any kind. Of course, the effort to grade is an effort to quantify a magnitude which is assumed to be objective in some sense, in contrast with the mere subjective experience or feeling of the grader; estimation of merit must be distinguished from mere liking. But this fact is immaterial for the argument, as long as there is no conceivable possibility of physically measuring the "real" merit of the object or performance or of describing it in terms of physical qualities. We need not go into the special problem of the objectivity of values as magnitudes or inquire as to how far "real" values enter into economic desire and satisfaction or investigate the relation between the aesthetic merit and the economic (money) value of the same objects. What is essential is only the fact that grading is done, and on a linear numerical scale; this is conclusive for the fact of quantification and removes the main question from the sphere of argument. Manifestly, the activity is one of estimation, not of measurement, in any proper use of the word. The word "measure" ought to be used very cautiously in connection with distinctively human data, i.e., with respect to any but the simplest physical capacities of man, such as speed in running, the lifting of weights, and the like, and the ability to estimate measurable physical quantities. Averaging estimates or guesses is not measuring and should not be so called, though the notion of "reliability" implies objectivity of some kind.

Experiment shows that if the same person holds one hand for a brief interval in very warm water and the other in cold and then places both hands in water at an intermediate temperature, the latter will at the same time feel cold to one hand and warm to the other. But even such a fact has nothing to do with the quantitative character of the feeling of warmth or coldness in either hand or with the validity of its quantitative estimation by the subject. Where measurement is impossible, our confidence in the validity of estimates of magnitude or rank can itself only be estimated. It may well be true that the reliability of ranking is greater than that of estimation of differences in degree, as tested by repetition by the same or a different estimator. The essential fact here is that wherever it is possible to say of three "experienced data" of any kind, *A*, *B*, and *C*, that *C* is "greater" than *B* and *B* is greater than *A*, it is also possible to compare the differences, i.e., to judge (though perhaps with less accuracy) whether *C* is greater than *B* by an amount—a difference—greater or less than that by which *B* is greater than *A*. We certainly make such estimates in economic choice.[13]

We turn now to the relation between the first and second of our four possible views of the theory of choice—a purely behavioristic interpretation and one which runs in terms of "force." Early in the history of modern physics objection was raised to use of the concept of force, on the double ground that it is never open to direct observation and that it is not objective but animistic or anthropomorphic. It was (and is) pointed out that we observe or measure only the effects of forces and contended that it would be simpler and more candid to talk only about effects, i.e., equations of motion, in relation to observed and measured antecedents or conditions. The place of motive in economic choice presents a closely parallel problem. In mechanics the issue arises at the very beginning, in the question as to what it is that is measured in the second of the three primary units—grams or pounds. Those who repudiate the notion of force contend that the gram (or pound) is a unit of mass and that the word "force" is simply a shorter designation of the de-

[13] The writer knows of only one case of quantitative variation in a physical quality where it is possible to rank but impossible to space the ranks along a linear or numerical scale. This is the case of the hardness of solids as determined exclusively by the scratching test. In this case, and in any case where magnitudes are ranked and only the rank is given, no valid numerical correlation with any other series can be computed. Correlation between ranked series, or of such a series with any measured variable, rests on an arbitrary assumption that all the ranks are equally spaced along a scale.

Estimates of differences are fairly definite only within the range of direct observation. In this fact also there is a difference of degree from the comparison of primary magnitudes.

fining relationship, the product of mass by acceleration. The expression $f = ma$ should then be treated as a definition and not as an equality.

This reasoning is plausible, but any effort to follow the procedure advocated runs at once into insuperable difficulty; for, in fact, mass is not measured and not experienced directly, but only as force. In practice, the unit is a unit of weight and is measured with the balance or by elastic deformation (of a steel spring or the like). Theoretically, mass should be measured by comparing the accelerations of two masses when these "interact." But, unfortunately for the theory, interaction itself is never directly observed, or even inferred, without the mediation of some force. It has, of course, long been known that impact is no exception to this statement, that literal impact between rigid solids is both unreal and theoretically impossible, since it would involve infinite acceleration. (In modern theory mass would be infinite at a relative velocity equal to that of light.) The empirical phenomenon of impact involves either elastic or permanent deformation, and neither can be interpretively conceived without using the idea of force as an elementary datum. The palpable fact is that the most elementary mechanical phenomena cannot be thought of in purely empirical terms, in the meaning which our minds seem to crave, namely, *visual* observation. The impossibility of such a "behavioristic" view should be evident to reflection and has been pointed out by theoretical physicists.[14]

It may be admitted that the notion of force "seems" more anthropomorphic and subjective than other qualities of objects which seem to be more directly perceived. When we see, or picture in thought an interaction between two bodies, such as the familiar impact of billiard balls, we think we observe (see, literally or in imagination) the change in motion and only infer the operation of force. And the inference seems to involve "reading into" the physical process something from an imagined experience of our own—either tactile pressure or muscular effort. However, reflection makes it a serious question whether we do not observe force at least as truly and "primarily" as we observe anything, specifically, when we see objects. We certainly feel both weight and inertia in our own bodily members and in objects which exert pressure upon us or offer resistance to our efforts to change their state of rest or motion. It is noteworthy that the qualities early distinguished as "primary" are those perceived in this way, in contrast with visual properties as secondary; and it is an accepted doctrine of psychology that the visual recognition of physical objects in their external three-dimensional reality is learned through the education of the eyes by tactile sensation, pressure, and movement or muscular kinesthesis. In fact, no one has ever proposed a distinction acceptable to critical common sense between what we perceive and what we infer. We think we see objects, but if in thinking we go back of immediate (adult)

[14] See, e.g., a review article by H. Poincaré, "Les Idées de Hertz sur la mécanique," *Revue générale des sciences pures et appliquées*, VIII, No. 16 (August 30, 1897), 734–43.

Of course, all real, observable, terrestrial, physical phenomena also involve friction and loss of energy. This concept is even more metaphysical than that of force, specifically since it involves the notion of potential energy. The problem of friction and its analogue in economic phenomena will be touched upon later. We need not go into the modern replacement of the force concept by field-theory, beyond noting that hyperspace raises equal difficulty for common sense.

experience, what we really perceive is light waves or some physicochemical change in eye or nerve or brain. The difference between the cognition of force and perception by sight (and perhaps hearing) seems to be that one perceives a force only when it is acting directly on his own body, while vision (and in a sense hearing and smell, but not taste) "report" on objects at a distance. However, we usually do not see anything unless we voluntarily look at it (in contrast with hearing and smell); but we believe things "visibly" exist whether we momentarily see them or not, and the apparent anthropomorphism of force rests on an unwillingness to assume that they similarly exert force.

In human, and specifically in economic, behavior, motive—i.e., desire for things or their services or for experiences of "satisfaction"—is the analogue of force in mechanics. Objects of choice may be thought of as exerting a "pull" upon the subject and so causing a response in behavior. (Repulsions can always be interpreted in positive terms, and we need not inquire into the ground of the occasional negative quality of the feeling.) But in the field of conduct, the a fortiori argument for the reality of the force (motive) is irresistibly conclusive. If interpretive thinking cannot do without the notion of force as a reality in physical nature, it becomes arbitrary in the *n*th degree to rule motive out of our conception of the conduct of human beings, where everyone is directly aware of it in his own experience and has the most certain knowledge of its reality in others. Our knowledge of what is in other minds is more certain than that which we have of the reality of the physical world, and prior to the latter. All our common-sense knowledge of the world of objects and especially all of our scientific knowledge manifestly depend on valid intercommunication with other minds, since no observation is regarded as valid unless it is or can be confirmed through other observers.

Our thinking about conduct must conform to common-sense introspection and intelligible intercommunication, which always run in terms of "reasons" for action or choice, meaning ends or motives. In the discussion of conduct we cannot separate description from teleological interpretation—the "what" from the "why" in this sense—what is done from what is achieved or expected to be achieved. Motive in relation to conduct—as a form of answer to the question "Why?"—is an intermediate and ambiguous category, much like force in relation to motion. Under critical scrutiny motive tends to "go over" one way or the other, giving place either to a purely empirical (perceptual but not really physical) view of behavior as taking place in accord with scientific laws or to an idealistic, subjectivistic world view. But in the one direction lies naïve materialism and in the other "solipsism"—equally impossible positions.[15]

[15] To the earlier distinction between primary and secondary qualities—the former supposed really to exist in things, the latter only in the mind of the observer—a nineteenth-century school of thought added "tertiary" qualities to take care of values. Apart from the dubious character of the distinctions as drawn, this scheme still fails to take account of another distinction which is even more important for both theoretical and practical thinking. That is the difference between the mere fact of being desired and having "value" in some objective meaning. It is a distinction which everyone constantly makes, and cannot help making, though many will "argue" that value is "really" nothing but desiredness. The truth is rather that all perception or cognition of fact rests on value judgments, in the weighing of evidence, not different in kind from those of aesthetics or morals. This "reducing" process may go further; it is also familiar in pseudo-scientific argument that desire itself becomes merely a "tendency to react." Here "tendency" apparently has the meaning of a force,

There is a special reason (motive!) against admitting motive into the interpretation of economic choice, in that choices do not seem to correspond accurately with motives. This is true with respect to other persons, and also of one's own choices, viewed with detachment or from a later point in time. This discrepancy is partly a matter of error in choice itself and partly one of error in the assignment of motives, including one's own. Probably everyone makes choices "really knowing" at the time that he will be sorry afterward—or will feel sorry—rightly or wrongly! In physical causality the fact that we know a force only by inference from its effects means that discrepancy between the two is impossible. When any force known to be operating does not fully and accurately account for an observed effect, we confidently impute the difference to some other force, known or unknown. Why we do not spontaneously and finally do the same in the case of human responses raises the ultimate problem of *freedom*. With respect to freedom or will the essential fact is that we "know too much" about human motivation to consider it exhaustively interpretable in terms of antecedent physical conditions as causes. Especially, we know indubitably the complex fact of *error*. We have to assume that the behavior of inert objects is not affected by *effort* or by thinking which is *aimed* at *solving problems* and so is not like human choice, inherently subject to error. This also means that freedom in choice involves more than mere contingency or chance or caprice, and ordinarily more than "arbitrary" thought and action.

The philosophical question of whether the comparison of satisfactions (utilities) should be thought of as a comparison between magnitudes which exist separately and are quantified separately or whether the recognition of utility inherently involves a comparison has a certain parallel in the case of force. We are apparently unable to think of any force as existing and acting entirely apart from some other force, or a "resistance" of some sort (Newton's third law of motion). It is also evident that the idea of economic value, or utility, always arises out of the necessity of choosing between alternative "goods," more or less different in kind. The giving-up of an alternative good is the meaning of cost. The relativity of desires is more intimate than that of forces. But in mechanics forces are dealt with one at a time, and the same is true of desires in economics; any one desire or attraction is a distinct factor and the associated satisfaction an independent variable under any actual conditions of choice. (However, discussion of the psychological effect of variation in the consumption of a single good, under the condition that it is the only one consumed by the individual, in place of reasonable *ceteris paribus* conditions, is one of the "classical errors" from which theory needs to free itself.) Desire for a particular service might, of course, be viewed as a mutual attraction between the human being and the good, as in the case of masses, electric charges, or magnetic poles; but the economist should doubtless follow the common-sense procedure of locating the attraction in the "mind" of the human being. In fact, even physicists speak of the magnet one-sidedly attracting its armature, the earth

---

or force component, if it has any meaning at all. In scientific economics, of course, we are concerned only with the quality of desiredness, without regard to any basis it may have in valuation in the higher sense or even to the "satisfaction" which may actually follow upon choice and action.

the apple, etc., where theory makes the attraction mutual.[16]

One or two observations on the use of physical analogy in economic analysis should be added, by way of warning, particularly with reference to the concepts of statics and dynamics and to units and dimensions. We have pointed out that the fundamental economic magnitudes have the nature and dimensionality of flow or flux, not of existent masses. In an economic system the forces and their equilibrium relate to rates of flow, i.e., the distribution of a current among alternative paths, under a (difference of) pressure or potential of some sort. There is no direct analogy with equilibrium between objects stationary in a field of force. The true physical analogy would require an elaborate construction hardly undertaken so far in the literature, to the writer's knowledge. It is not to be undertaken here, but one or two points call for mention.

Of the three elementary dimensions in (Newtonian) mechanics, only time carries over into economics with at all the same meaning.[17] As to space, economists speak of direction and velocity of change; but it seems impossible either to bring these notions into any intelligible relation with the three-dimensional field of Euclidean space or to formulate any usable conception of economic hyperspace. The analogy of mass, in relation to force, presents even greater difficulties; and we probably cannot formulate any usable analogy for physical friction, involving energy loss. The best "model" for an economic system would seem to be one based on the phenomena of electric current, generated by a large number of interconnected sources and distributing itself through a complex network of circuits. One should, of course, begin with the case of a single generator feeding a number of circuits, as the analogue for a Crusoe economy. At the outset the role of inertia would be ignored, as electromagnetic induction is ignored in Ohm's law stating the relations for electricity. The relation between potential, resistance, and flow—maximizing satisfaction under diminishing utility—will be less simple than Ohm's formula, because electrical resistance is invariant with respect to current; but it is quite manageable mathematically. Another serious difficulty lies in the fact that in the human case the treatment of the "source" itself, the human being, as either simple or constant involves heroic abstraction, even if we could think of our Robinson Crusoe as using only his own "person" in the satisfaction of his economic wants, ignoring all other instrumentalities. The difficulty centers in the concept of capital (the whole complex "source" itself) and its maintenance and/or growth or decline. (Capital theory is the central difficulty in any attempt at rigorous formu-

[16] For many problems in price theory, it is convenient and admissible to treat money as an absolute measure of value, hence to view both price and utility changes as entirely relative to money. This assumption gives rise to serious problems in accounting practice. The economist must have in mind, wherever it is relevant, that the value of money does change, in terms both of objective purchasing-power and of subjective utility. The ultimate practical concern of the economist (as of all scientists) is with "welfare"; but to deal with this he must first have a sound scientific theory of utility, both in relative and in absolute terms, on the analogy of a force causing and explaining choice but consciously known to the choosing subject. Ultimately, "satisfaction" must be conceived, for the purpose of economic analysis, as only one ingredient or factor in human well-being; others may, in fact, have greater practical importance.

[17] Professor Sorokin in his recent work, *Socio-Cultural Causality, Space, Time* (Durham, N.C., 1943), advocates developing a special conception of time for use in social theory.

lation of economic relationships and processes.)

Turning from theoretical to practical difficulties, it is actually quite unrealistic to think of the functional (cause-and-effect) relations between economic variables as remaining unchanged through a real change in any independent variable.[18] There is always a significant "lag" in time; and in the meantime other things will not remain "equal." The demand curve (our special topic in this paper) affords an excellent illustration, being undoubtedly the most solidly real of all the functional relations dealt with in economic theory. The individual curve for a particular good describes a theoretical position of equilibrium in the relation between price and quantity taken. In reality, any change in the price, unless infinitely gradual, will carry the rate of consumption to a point off the curve, and it will "tend" to return to the curve at a new point. But conceptual interpretation of the lag of consumption change behind price change involves a causal sequence bearing some analogy to the action of a force against a resistance in which inertia is combined with friction (opposing the redistribution of a flow among alternate paths). The result to be expected under stationary conditions would be "damped oscillations," settling down at a new point on the curve. The nature of the concepts required for interpreting such phenomena calls loudly for investigation, particularly with respect to the possibility of finding any magnitude which can be assumed to remain constant, on the analogy of the conservation principles of mechanics (with or without allowance for energy loss). This line of argument suggests a basis for a pure theory of economic fluctuations. But the realism of such theorizing would be severely limited because the heart of the phenomena in the human case is uncertainty, error, and speculation (with some analogy to mental inertia!) in the thinking by which economic behavior is controlled, and these are not considered to be present in mechanical processes.

For numerous and important reasons, economic theory cannot approach the analytical realism of mechanics—remote from the empirical facts and the conditions of practical problems as are the assumptions of the latter science. Motives are not analogous to forces, i.e., merely concepts for interpreting conduct, which could be left out, to yield an empirical description of the causal sequence in physical or behavioristic terms. As already observed, we "know too much"; we have direct knowledge, not only that motives are present but that they do *not* correspond with hypothetical forces connecting behavior with its antecedent conditions. Their operation disrupts the uniformity of sequence. In the first place, action rarely leads to exactly the intended result, because it is always affected by error, which also is of several kinds. And, beyond this fact, ends are never really given. Actual desires are partly a matter of curiosity—the urge to explore—giving rise to the paradox

[18] This is a convenient place for the important observation that price theory must explain a change in any dependent variable by a change in a really independent one, i.e., as the effect of some force impinging on the price system from without and to be explained or treated by some other science. No price change can be validly treated as a cause, except for changes in the situation of some individual or limited sector of the economy, where the price change is due to some cause entirely outside the area considered. Error in this regard is frequently met with, especially in the work of the earlier writers. Much of Ricardo's reasoning is nonsensical on this account. Of course, it is also vital to avoid the blunder of making incompatible assumptions as to the classification and interrelations of dependent and independent variables.

of expected surprise as an important element in motivation. A different matter is the problem-solving interest, the quest of the "right" answer to some question, which it is a sheer contradiction to treat as an end given in advance. Well-being is largely of this nature, the answer to an unsolved problem, to be sought through "intelligent" experiment.

Finally, the practical significance of economic theory is in the field of social action, not of individual conduct. Particularly in a democratic society the instrumental pattern of means and end hardly fits this problem at all. It would have some application, though even then a very limited one, if we could think of the social problem as that of an absolute dictator, entirely outside of society and viewing his "subjects" merely as passive instruments for his own purposes. (They would have to be "lower" than any real slaves or even beasts of burden.) In free society the primary objective is agreement on terms of association, and the secondary objective is agreement on "right" terms and on the "best" ends and procedures. Actually, association itself has only to a limited extent the purpose assumed in economic analysis—co-operation for the achievement of any ends, of individuals or of groups. To a very large extent it is a matter of formulating the rules of a game, in which individuals do indeed pursue ends, but ends symbolic in character, set up to make activity interesting, instrumental to this purpose, and in large part effective because of their conflicting or competitive nature. The intelligence involved in playing games is a very different kind of faculty from either technical-instrumental rationality or the thinking used in apportioning means. Incidentally, the ability to invent games or improve the rules is much less common in the human species than these other capacities—which still do not exhaust the ambiguity of the word "intelligence."

V. CONSUMER'S SURPLUS

The consumer's surplus idea was doubtless first adumbrated by Dupuit; but the term and the classical treatment come from Marshall, and the general observations to be offered here will be oriented primarily to his treatment. It has extremely little practical significance, but a correct exposition is useful in bringing out the relations between the individual demand curve and indifference curves, with which it is much confused. It may also be useful for the pure theory of monopoly, in connection with perfectly classified monopoly price.

Marshall defines the concept as the excess of the price which a person would be willing to pay rather than go without the thing, over that which he actually does pay (*Principles* [8th ed.], p.124). We shall see that this definition is incorrect as well as loosely stated. The amount by which a person's total expenditure for a good under demand conditions (buying freely at a given price) is less than he would be willing to pay for the same amount rather than do without it altogether does not correspond with the value to him of having the good available at the price rather than unavailable—other conditions being the same[19] —and the latter is the essential idea.

There can be no question of the "theoretical reality" of the concept of con-

[19] For simplicity we assume that all the individual's income is spent for consumption (no saving) and also, of course, that we are comparing an initial with a final state of equilibrium in the individual's use of his income. We need not consider here the highly problematical use of the concept in connection with collections of commodities and/or groups of persons, as in the theory of foreign trade.

sumer's surplus, as defined, and it would need to be considered by a rational individual in the situation used by Marshall as an illustration. That (as will be recalled) is the case of a man choosing between living in a modern city and in a primitive community (central Africa) where the products available are assumed to have the same prices but where the same money income purchases less "value" because some products are not to be had. (To make the comparison valid, we must assume that there are no compensating advantages in other uses of income and that the choice is permanent and the income the same, so as to exclude temporary residence in the primitive community and saving for later expenditure in the higher civilization.) The problem is to find an unambiguous measure or expression for the advantage, in terms of money.

One difficulty in connection with Marshall's theory is that of forming any clear and defensible conception of what is meant by neglecting the change in the marginal utility of money. In the main argument, based on the purchase of tea for domestic consumption, which is introduced "in order to give definiteness to our notions" (*Principles*, pp. 125–27), the object seems to be to set up the assumption that there is no difference between a demand curve for tea (under the conditions of free purchase) and a marginal utility curve or an indifference curve in the price form. This is also clearly implied in the discussion of the diagram in his footnote on page 128. But the whole argument is economically nonsensical; to make the various curves identical or to give meaning to the area under the demand curve, we must practically assume that all the curves are horizontal; and this assumption not only defies the facts but eliminates consumer's surplus altogether.

A second interpretation of the Marshallian assumption is adopted in a brief and ingenious discussion by A. Henderson. It is that "the marginal rate of substitution between *X* and money is independent of income."[20] This view seems to be neither a reasonable interpretation of Marshall's position nor economically defensible. It would make the demand curve and the indifference curves independent of the individual's income, and, as argued above, this would also make the consumption independent of the price. The most plausible view would again treat the indifference-combinations curves as straight lines, the other curves as horizontal and coincident. (It is geometrically possible to introduce, respectively, curvature and declining slope, as Henderson does.) The assumption that the demand has neither income nor price elasticity is not impossible, as an approximation, for an unimportant commodity over a limited range. That is, within this range, the consumer may buy approximately the amount of *X* he would consume if it were a free good, while at a lower income or a higher price he will not buy it at all. If the assumption is generalized, it means that the consumer's only response to price or income change will be to add fixed amounts of different goods to his budget or to drop them, as the case may be.

A third possibility is to take Marshall as meaning quite literally what he seems to say, most explicitly in his mathematical note (p. 842), namely, that "the mar-

[20] See "Consumer's Surplus and the Compensating Variation," *Review of Economic Studies*, VIII (1940–41), 117–21, esp. 119, n. 1. Professor Lange called my attention to this paper. I have found it helpful, in spite of inability to accept some of the author's conclusions, for reasons which will presently be indicated in part.

ginal utility of money to the individual purchaser is the same throughout." That is, money is assumed to have an "absolute" marginal utility in the consumer's equilibrium position from which we start (with or without the opportunity to purchase X freely at a fixed price), and this magnitude is assumed to be invariant with respect to the amount of income spent for X, as the price of X varies from zero to infinity.[21] Whether

[21] This assumption seems to be implied by the statement that "in mathematical language the neglected elements would generally belong to the second order of small quantities" (*Principles of Economics*, p. 132, n. 1). Marshall goes on to chide Professor Nicholson for not recognizing "the legitimacy of the familiar scientific method by which they are neglected." In spite of diffidence in challenging Marshall—and Pigou (*Economics of Welfare* [1st ed.], p. 935)—on such a matter, the present writer must suggest that this mathematical argument is invalid. The theory of orders of infinitesimals does not seem to be applicable unless total utility is assumed to be represented by an algebraic expression of a fairly simple type, and this clearly cannot be done. The question of what can be neglected, and in comparison with what, is purely one of fact; and the facts are magnitudes which are a matter of estimation only, and their importance, absolute or relative, varies indefinitely with the particular good in question and depends on many other conditions.

(This matter of what magnitudes are practically negligible is of great importance for other problems in economic theory where unknown functions are involved, notably the conception of perfect competition among producers. It is hard to give much meaning to elaborate curves of total and marginal cost for a firm assumed to be of negligible size, which means that the whole diagram reduces to the area of a point!)

In sec. 4 (pp. 132–33) Marshall discusses as an exception the effect of a rise in the price of X, specifically in connection with the "Giffen paradox." Here, as the price of X increases, an increased quantity of X is purchased—the consumption of bread by very poor families being used as an illustration. As our previous argument has shown, what this case really illustrates is the confusion which results from drawing a demand curve on the assumption that all other prices are constant. What happens in such cases is a consequence of a disastrous fall in the value of money to the buyers affected, though not necessarily connected with a change in its value in the social economy, as measured by any general index number. From the standpoint of the theory of demand, it is the spurious problem of the "income effect."

the change so neglected would really be negligible or not manifestly depends on the importance of X in the consumer's budget. This, in turn, is partly a matter of the total number of commodities consumed, partly one of the intrinsic qualities of X, and partly of its complementarity relations with other goods. Marshall explicitly makes an exception for "commodities some supply of which is necessary for life" (p. 133, n. 1). He apparently fails to recognize that necessity is entirely a matter of degree or that no particular commodity as bought in the market under ordinary conditions is necessary; finally, in assuming that we can know the individual's utility (satisfaction) function for money, he fails to see that income as a whole is in a sense necessary, but not in any definable amount. His suggestion, that we take the necessary supply for granted and estimate the total utility of the excess over this amount, must be applied to money, not to a particular commodity, and must be interpreted to mean an income which would actually yield zero satisfaction.

The problem of consumer's surplus is that of finding a monetary measure or expression for an increment of total satisfaction which accrues to a consumer through having the opportunity to purchase a freely chosen amount of a particular good at a particular price, in comparison with a situation in which the good is not available and all other conditions are the same. In the second situation he will spend the same amount of money on other goods at the same prices (but not necessarily quite the same list of other goods), freely distributing his expenditure among these. The problem lies in the field of value dynamics, surveyed in Section II above, not in that of price-quantity relations under given conditions. To begin with, it is impossible literally to measure in money a change in the total utility of an income which itself is expressed in money. The only problem which can be pictured as real is that which is indicated by the third assumption we have been considering. We must measure a change in total satisfaction in units of the absolute satisfaction yielded by an increment of money income under some given conditions, assuming that this magnitude is not changed by the actual change in the use of the increment of income in question.

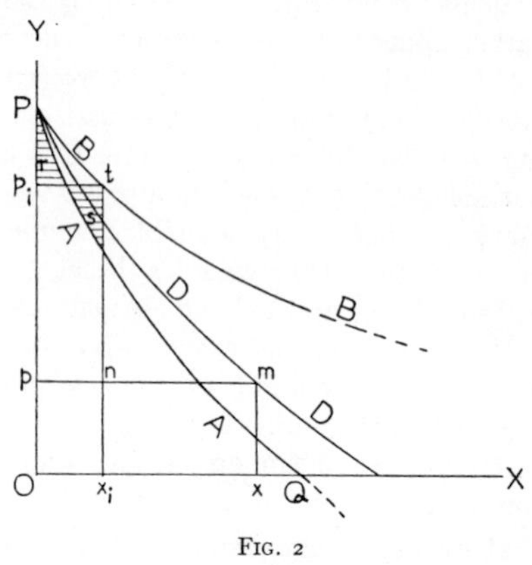

FIG. 2

Of course, it would be changed, more or less. If the change is substantial, the result is merely that our measurement still runs in terms of the original value; it will not become relative to the actual new value.

To handle this problem analytically, it will be useful to have in mind three curves, as shown in Figure 2. Curve *A* shows the variation in the relative marginal utility of good (service) *X*, measured by money. It is really an indifference curve, being drawn under the condition that the subject actually purchases each successive small unit of *X* at the maximum price he is willing to pay, after buying the earlier units seriatim on these terms. Curve *B* shows the same facts but with prices averaged out. It is so drawn in relation to *A* that any three-cornered area, *r*, is equal to the area, *s*, for any point, p_i (see shaded areas). That is, the ordinates of *B* show the highest price at which any quantity of *X* can be sold to the consumer, if he is free only to take or leave the whole amount. (We do not go into the meaning of curves *A* or *B* beyond the point *Q*, where *A* intersects the X-axis.) *D* is a demand curve. We cannot draw this curve from the data of the other two. We know only that it will run between *A* and *B* except for the terminal point *P* on the vertical axis. This means that at any positive (relative) price at which the consumer buys good *X* at all, he will buy less of it if free to choose the amount than he can be made to buy if he must take all or none at a maximum average price (or the price he will pay for any amount is less than he could be made to pay under the more restricted terms of choice). But the amount he will freely buy is greater than that which would have the same marginal utility in terms of money at his stopping-point if he bought all the earlier units seriatim at the maximum price for each in turn (or bought the whole block at his maximum total or average price). This is because under the demand condition he will have money left after reaching the terminal point of the second condition and will spend some of this for *X* (if all goods are "simple"). This last fact is a consequence of the existence of diminishing utility and of consumer's surplus.

The consumer's surplus obviously is *not* measured by the three-cornered area bounded by the price axis, the demand curve, and the upper boundary of the expenditure rectangle *Opmx*, *Ox* being the amount purchased at price *p* under demand conditions. In fact, *the area under a demand curve has no economic meaning whatever.* Consumer's surplus as a subjective magnitude is the difference between the total satisfaction yielded by the quantity of a particular good freely purchased at any price and that which would be secured by freely spending the *same amount of money* for other goods at (just below) the actual uniform margin. In terms of money it must be the money value of this difference. The second alternative is, of course, identical with spending the same money for good X under indifference conditions (however represented graphically), which by definition makes it a matter of indifference what quantity of X is purchased, including zero amount. The surplus should not be measured by the difference between two different money expenditures for the same quantity of X, since this result differs from the value determined by the other comparison.[22]

To obtain (on this form of diagram) the money measure of the difference—the surplus—we must first locate the point t on curve B, which subtends with the two axes a rectangle of the same area as the expenditure rectangle under the demand curve for the given demand price p. The magnitude sought is, then, the area of the rectangle cut off from this total-expenditure rectangle by the ordinate of this point, i.e., at x_i. It is the area of the rectangle $x_i nmx$. The "indifference expenditure rectangle," $Op_i tx_i$, has, of course, the same area as that under curve A between the price axis and the ordinate at x_i.[23]

Since, as repeatedly emphasized, the curve of marginal utility relative to money, or the indifference curve in any form, cannot be drawn from demand data, all this procedure is purely formal and without practical meaning. Its only use is to clarify certain analytical concepts and to prevent making certain errors. The primary error in Marshall's analysis, and in the textbooks which have commonly followed the same procedure, is that of identifying or confusing the demand curve with the curve of marginal utility in terms of money and of treating the area under the demand curve as the measure of total satisfaction.

A theoretical measure of consumer's surplus could be derived more simply in graphic terms by using a series of indifference-combinations curves for quantities of money and of good X. It must be emphasized that the procedure would still be purely hypothetical, since market data do not provide the facts required for drawing indifference curves. These

[22] See Hicks, *op. cit.*, pp. 38–40; also Henderson, *op. cit.*, p. 118. It is rather strange that Henderson slips into this error after making the statement in italics on the first page of his article. A minor slip in Henderson's argument is the statement (p. 118) that the consumer's surplus, defined as the difference in two expenditures for the same quantity of X, is "the maximum increase in return which the seller could obtain through negotiating all-or-none bargains with [the] consumer." It is the maximum increase *for the same amount of X*. The maximum without this unjustifiable condition would depend on the cost curve of the seller and on special conditions of bargaining (see below, p. 316).

[23] We might have proceeded by locating hypothetically the one appropriate point on curve A and drawing a horizontal line $p_i t$ of the right length to yield the equivalent equal-expenditure rectangle without drawing the whole curve B. If the marginal utility under indifference conditions is assumed identical with the marginal utility under demand conditions, for the same quantities, curves A, B, and D will all coincide, and consumer's surplus will disappear.

Professor Viner has pointed out the fallacy of confusing the demand curve with the equivalent of an indifference-combinations curve (see *Studies in the Theory of International Trade* [New York, 1937], pp. 573–74). In classroom lectures he also presents a graphic measure of consumer's surplus, showing the difference.

might be had only from actual experimentation with strictly classified monopoly price. But it would also be necessary to establish conditions under which the buyer would not know or suspect the nature of his situation or in which purchasers are, in fact, so numerous that any one is negligible to the seller, while, at the same time, purchase for resale is somehow excluded. Otherwise the situation will be one of bargaining and "bluffing," between a monopoly and a monopsony, and the price will be indeterminate within a range depending on the details of the two curves. However, for the purpose of clarifying analytical procedure (as before) we may impose the arbitrary conditions called for and proceed.

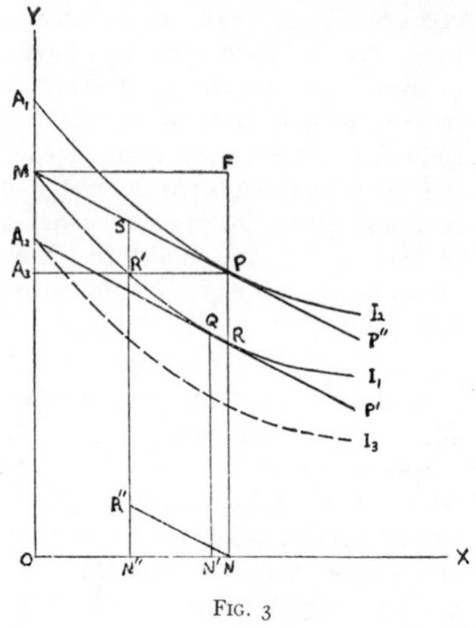

FIG. 3

Our figure embodies the same basic diagram and notation employed by Henderson, and before him (in an incomplete form) by Hicks (Fig. 3). The point M on the vertical axis shows the money income of the individual. The line MP'' is a line of slope p, where p is the price of X. It is tangent to some indifference curve I_2 at P, which point marks the position of equilibrium for the consumer under market-demand conditions, where ON measures the amount of X bought. (For clarity the diagram is drawn off-scale, with vertical distances greatly exaggerated.) Curve I_1 is the indifference-combinations curve of the individual for X and money, corresponding to income M. The vertical distance PR is, indeed, the excess amount of money the individual would pay for ON of X offered as an indivisible block, over the amount FP which he does pay in the free market. But it is not the consumer's surplus. Henderson is correct in saying that "if the individual had spent FR in buying ON of X he would have been just as well off as if the commodity had not been available, whereas in fact he only had to spend FP on it." But he overlooks the fact that the individual would also have been just as well off at any other point (than R) on indifference curve I_1 (and as well off at any other point than P on I_2). Yet he recognizes that the money measure of the difference in situation represented by the two curves is not the same at any two points on either—unless the curves are arbitrarily drawn in an admittedly indefensible way. The correct comparison with free purchase is clearly the point at which he spends the same amount of money for less X and not where he spends more money for the same amount of X (in both cases paying a higher average price but not the same price in these two cases); for, if X had not been available he would have spent the same amount on other things.

To find the money measure of consumer's surplus, defined as we have defined it, we draw the horizontal line PA_3, cutting the indifference curve I_1 at R'. Spending the same amount of money FP under the indifference conditions, the individual would buy A_3R' (or ON'') of X instead of ON; i.e., he would buy $N''N$ less than if he bought under market conditions. The money value of this difference at the given price is $N''R''$ (NR'' being drawn parallel to the original price line), or it is $R'S$. This is less than PR even if the curves are drawn according to Henderson's interpretation of Marshall's assumption, i.e., so as to have the same slope for the same X value, hence a uniform vertical distance between them.

A still more defensible money measure of the difference in satisfaction represented by two indifference-combinations curves is afforded by the notion of a "compensating variation." The term was introduced by Hicks as the best way of looking at consumer's surplus but was mistakenly identified by him with his graphic measure of the surplus, the line segment PR. As Henderson shows, the magnitude has two values, both different from that of the consumer's surplus as defined by Hicks and Henderson and also different from our "correct" definition. The measurement calls for a system of indifference-combinations curves beginning or terminating on the Y-axis or money axis, and it derives its superiority from this feature. (Hicks drew only one of these curves in this way, the one at point M.)

Expressed in words, the compensating variation might, in fact, take any of four different forms. First, we may consider the position of an individual with an income M and without the privilege of buying X freely at a certain market price and may ask either (I-a) what is the maximum amount of income he would be willing to give up in exchange for the privilege, or (I-b) what is the minimum additional income he would accept as an equivalent to getting it. Second, we may consider the position of an individual who has an income M and also has the privilege in question and may ask (II-a) how much additional income he would demand to give it up, or (II-b) how much of his actual income he would be willing to give up as an alternative to parting with the privilege. There are actually but two magnitudes, since I-a and II-b are identical, as are I-b and II-a. Henderson works out, first, I-a (equals MA_2) and then II-a (equals A_1M), which he strangely says is also the Marshallian consumer's surplus. It should be noted that two of the four different magnitudes—i.e., Henderson's *second* form of the compensating variation (II-a or A_1M) and the Hicks-Henderson consumer's surplus (PR)—will be identical if (and only if) the indifference curves are straight lines identical with the price line or are otherwise so drawn that the vertical distance between them is the same for all values of X. The other two magnitudes will be different from both, as well as between themselves, unless still more implausible conditions are imposed.

The two compensating variations are different because an individual buying X freely at the same price at different income levels will buy different amounts (if it is a "simple" good or one of any probable utility composition). The two values of the compensating variation involve the two intervals between three successive indifference curves. For an individual to be on I_1 with the privilege of buying X freely at price p is equivalent to being on I_2 without the privilege; and being on I_1 without it is equivalent to being on a lower curve I_3 passing through A_2 with the privilege open. But movement from M to A_1 represents a greater monetary difference on the Y-axis than movement from M to A_2, because more X will be bought out of a higher income at the same price, because, in turn, the marginal utility of money is lower compared with that of a given supply of any single good.

The vertical or monetary distance between two indifference curves, or the order of two such distances, at other points cannot be inferred from the magnitudes along the axis of money. This is true whether or not a linear scale is assigned to the suppressed third axis (of utility or satisfaction). The indifference curves are projections upon the base plane of contour lines on a surface, defined either by a utility function or by some index function with the properties considered essential. In either case the shape of the curves depends on the character of the good X and its relationships with other goods available for purchase. We can draw curves spaced equally, or in any other way, along the money axis; but their vertical spacing anywhere else obviously depends on their shape. About this we know in general only three facts. They always have a negative slope (within the significant range), they do not intersect (or meet), and they *cannot* have a uniform slope and vertical spacing for different values of X. This third feature would involve zero income elasticity of demand for X; and this, as we have seen, is conceivable only for a good with a complex utility so arranged that displacement of other goods would exactly offset the diminishing utility of the various component types of satisfaction which it yields.[24]

The utility value of a difference in money income is still another matter. This would be measured along a third axis perpendicular to the plane of a diagram of the type here discussed.

University of Chicago

[24] We should note, finally, that the notion of maximizing consumer's surplus cannot be entertained (as so often assumed) as a description of rational consumer behavior. Any aggregation of distinct consumer's surpluses is without meaning—though conditions might justify or require treating some complex of goods as a unit.

To pursue the analysis further would lead into a discussion of the familiar "antinomies of value" of Wieser *et al.* The suggestion that total satisfaction be increased by taxing goods of inelastic demand and subsidizing consumption of those of the opposite character would justify the taxation of free goods so as to make the consumer pay for them. It is hard to deny that this might actually increase total conscious satisfaction, but it would hardly increase real well-being to have one's total consumption cut down to famine conditions. In the ordinary course of events, one must agree with the position of Nicholson (see Marshall, *Principles*, p. 127, n. 1), that the consumer is not conscious of receiving the "free satisfaction" described by the theory of consumer's surplus. It is a real antinomy of economic psychology, but an indubitable fact, that our feelings of satisfaction depend more on *changes* in income (or particular prices) than on the absolute level—and surprise, in relation to established expectations, is also vitally important, irrespective of the accustomed standard.

13 The Marshallian Demand Curve[1]

M. Bailey

In an article with the above title, Professor Friedman[2] has urged that a constant-real-income demand curve is a more satisfactory tool for economic analysis than the customary constant-other-prices-and-money-incomes demand curve and that, at least in the first two editions of the *Principles*, this was the type of demand curve which Marshall really had in mind. On the latter, historical question nothing will be said here; but on the former, analytical question I shall contend that Friedman did not make the best choice of a curve as an improvement on the conventional one and that the constant-real-income curve, strictly interpreted, does not on balance possess the superiority he claims for it. Of the various interesting alternative types of demand curve which can be defined, one at least possesses most, if not all, of the advantages which Friedman can claim for any type of constant-real-income demand curve and none of its disadvantages.

In his argument in support of the constant-real-income demand curve Friedman demonstrated that the use of an ordinary demand curve in a demand-supply diagram to show the effects of a subsidy on a given commodity fails to take account of the necessary withdrawal of resources from other uses; on the other hand, the constant-real-income demand curve, which in the limit is an approximation of what the community can actually have, allows for this withdrawal of resources and therefore presents a better picture of the final outcome.[3] While Friedman's analysis does not contain any errors, it is liable to serious misinterpretation if its assumptions and their relevance are overlooked; on the other hand, with a different type of demand curve which I shall propose the pitfalls can be avoided, and an analytically superior tool can be had in the bargain.

DEMAND CURVES AND PRODUCTION POSSIBILITIES

Suppose, for simplicity of arrangement, that a fully employed community has the production possibilities between its two competitively produced commodities X and Y as shown by the opportunity-cost curve ST in Figure 1A. Money, different from either commodity, is used as a unit of account only; money incomes are assumed to be spent in full, and the absolute price level to be determined arbitrarily.[4]

From the community indifference curves (for the moment assumed to be defined unambiguously) shown in Figure 1A, we may derive the two demand curves mentioned so far (the constant-real-income and the other-things-equal demand curves) in the customary manner. DD in Figure 1B is defined by the price-consumption line PC in Figure 1A, and RR is obtained from the equilibrium

[1] I wish to thank Mr. Amotz Morag and Professors Arnold C. Harberger and Carl F. Christ for their helpful advice and criticisms of early drafts of this note; and I wish to thank Professor Milton Friedman for his advice and criticism at a later stage. Specific acknowledgments to Professor Friedman appear at appropriate points in the text of this note. Responsibility for such errors as remain is, of course, my own.

[2] Milton Friedman, "The Marshallian Demand Curve," *Journal of Political Economy*, LVII (1949), 463–95.

[3] *Ibid.*, pp. 467–74.

[4] Friedman's assumption of a fixed supply of factor services is retained here, since its retention does not cause any loss of generality in the argument.

Reprinted from the *Journal of Political Economy,* Vol. LXII (June, 1954), pp. 255–261, by permission of the publisher and author.

indifference curve I_1 by noting the quantity of X at which I_1 has any given slope (i.e., marginal rate of substitution, interpreted as a price ratio, P_x/P_y).

Suppose now that the government pays a subsidy on production of X; the apparent effect after production adjusts itself to the new conditions will be to lower the price of X by some fraction of the amount of the subsidy, changing the price line from $S'T'$ to $S'L$ in Figure 1A, and to leave the price of Y and money income unchanged. Given this apparent opportunity, the community would like to consume to the point C in Figure 1A, that is, to the point W in Figure 1B. However, as Friedman pointed out, this is clearly impossible. Physical supplies are not available, and corresponding to this lack there is an inflationary gap equal to the going amount of the subsidy; also the relative price of Y must fall owing to the shift of production toward more X.

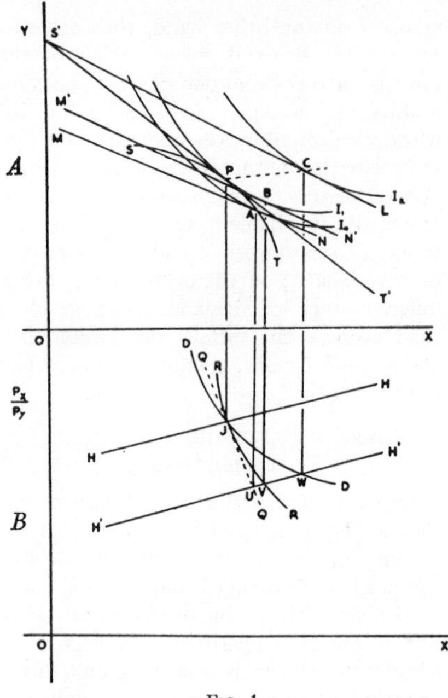

Fig. 1

Hence we must further suppose that the government imposes an income tax always equal to the subsidy. The final equilibrium point is found where a price line which is tangent to an indifference curve where it crosses the production frontier differs in slope from the slope of the production frontier at that point by an amount corresponding to the subsidy. $S'L$ will "shift" to MN, where it is tangent to the indifference curve I_0, lower than I_1, at A. This equilibrium point is only slightly distant from B, the point at which $M'N'$ is tangent to I_1. ($S'L$, $M'N'$, and MN have it in common that each one's slope differs by the rate of subsidy from the slope of the production frontier beneath the point where each one is tangent to an indifference curve.)

It can be seen from this result that neither DD nor RR, in Figure 1B, shows the final outcome correctly. The correct outcome could be obtained only from another type of demand curve, the "production-frontier" demand curve, which would show, for each amount of X, the marginal rate of substitution of the indifference curve which crosses the production frontier at the point where that amount of X is produced. This demand curve is shown as QQ in Figure 1B; if X is not an inferior good, QQ must lie to the left of both RR and DD below J and must lie between them above J (where J in Fig. 1B corresponds to P in Fig. 1A). Its intersection with $H'H'$ at U, corresponding to A in Figure 1A, shows the true outcome as the result of the imposition of the combination subsidy and income tax.

The production-frontier demand curve is clearly the one hypothetically most desirable for use in the comparative statics of demand analysis, since it shows what in fact the community will take when the repercussions on the production of other commodities are taken into account. Its weakness is that it is defined only for given production conditions. Presumably tastes are relatively constant, whereas real or apparent production conditions are always changing because of fluctuations in weather and crops, changes in government policy, and other factors. Data on market behavior may, to the extent that this is true, be supposed to tell us something about consumer preferences but to tell us little about production conditions. At any moment of time, however, production conditions are in some sense fixed; and for economic analysis it would be desirable to take these conditions into account in analyzing demand. Lacking knowledge of these conditions of the moment, we must adopt some more or less arbitrary method of approximating the effects of a change in policy or the like.

Friedman argues in effect that *RR* (in Fig. 1*B*) is a better approximation to *QQ* than is *DD*, since I_1 is tangent to *ST* at *P* and so approximates it in the limit, whereas *PC* has no such limiting property. That is to say, *RR* is tangent to *QQ*, but *DD* is not. This is correct, as long as the community preference field (the function represented by the indifference map) is innocent of any discontinuities in the first and all higher derivatives. Though I suppose there is no reason to doubt its innocence for practical purposes, this qualification should be recognized as relevant. But other arguments developed below substantially weaken the case for the constant-real-income demand curve.

THE CONSTANT-REAL-INCOME CONCEPT

The argument so far has been greatly aided by the use of unexplained community indifference curves. It is now necessary to investigate the meaning of these curves of constant community real income and of the idea of a constant-real-income demand curve. The construction of community indifference curves will not be repeated here; suffice it to say that constant community real income means constant real income for *every individual* in the community.[5] The relevant construction necessarily implies the existence of different distributions of money incomes at different points along a given community indifference curve; the reason for this will become clear in the following discussion.

Consider, in Figure 2, the indifference curves of two individuals whose money incomes are equal.[6] When the two indifference maps are superimposed on one another, their opportunity lines will coincide, as, for example, in *AB*. The individual *I* will be in equilibrium at *P*, and the individual *J* will be in equilibrium at *Q*, given the opportunity line *AB*. Now for an arbitrary change in the price of, say, commodity *Y*, what price change of *X* will keep both individuals on the same levels of real income *J* and *I*? It is at once apparent that there need not be *any* price change of *X* which will do the trick. If the price of *Y* should rise until the given money income of each individual could purchase only *OC* of *Y*, then a price of *X* corresponding to the opportunity line *CD* would do it, since *CD* happens to be

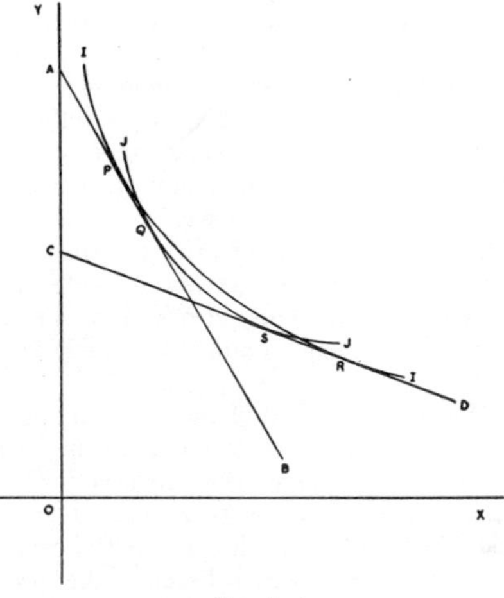

FIG. 2

[5] William J. Baumol, "The Community Indifference Map: A Construction," *Review of Economic Studies*, XVII (1949–50), 189–97; and E. J. Mishan, "The Principle of Compensation Reconsidered," *Journal of Political Economy*, LX (1952), 514–17.

[6] For persons with different money incomes, the scales of *X* and *Y* quantities for the person with the larger income may be compressed (in the same proportion) until the two opportunity lines coincide when the indifference maps are superimposed. The argument in the text then applies without change to this case.

tangent to both I and J at R and S, respectively. But the set of points C through which a line can be drawn tangent to both indifference curves is in general a finite set (the principal exception being the case where the two indifference curves coincide) and may be empty, aside from the point A. A price compensating constant-real-income demand function for the two individuals must remain undefined except at points such as C—that is, we cannot, in general, have a constant-real-income demand "curve" at all, as long as money incomes are held constant.

On the other hand, if money income changes are used—in general, a different change for each individual—then it will always be possible to find an income change for each individual that will just offset any price change (or set of price changes) and permit him to achieve the same indifference curve as before. This, in effect, is what is done in defining community indifference curves.

But if the method of compensating price changes is used, there is no such thing as a constant-real-income demand curve for two individuals taken together. Such a curve can be defined for each one, but the curves cannot be aggregated because the price changes of Y offsetting a given price change of X would be different for the two individuals. This would be true a fortiori for a larger community; and it would continue to be true whatever the number of commodities.

It should be clear, then, that a constant-real-income demand curve for a community cannot be defined in terms solely of offsetting price movements for all possible price changes of a given commodity unless everybody's tastes are, in effect, identical. In fact, identity of tastes is not sufficient when money incomes are different. What is required is that the indifference curve on which each individual finds himself in equilibrium must be an exact projection of the corresponding indifference curve of every other individual. Unless all indifference systems were homogeneous, identity of tastes would guarantee this coincidence only for an equal distribution of income.

TWO APPROXIMATIONS: CONSTANT APPARENT REAL INCOME AND CONSTANT APPARENT PRODUCTION

The objections against a constant-real-income demand curve, as I have so far defined it, are for any practical purpose overwhelming; recourse may be had, however, to an approximating concept which avoids these objections.[7] This concept is that of the constant-*apparent*-real-income demand curve, which can be defined for constant-money incomes all around and with no particular knowledge of individual consumer preferences. In Figure 3A the point P represents, as before, the initial equilibrium point, and $S'T'$ is the equilibrium price line. If the price of X is lowered, the consumers' real income will "apparently" be the same if the price of Y is raised to the point where the consumers are just able to buy the same bill of goods they bought before; that is, the new price line $M''N''$ should pass through P. This, to a first order of approximation, cancels out the income effect to consumers in the aggregate[8] but allows them a small gain

[7] In his text Friedman uses the constant-apparent-real-income demand curve (*op. cit.*, pp. 466–67).

[8] If individual incomes are not adjusted, then "income effects" are not removed by this procedure even to a first order of approximation for individuals, since no individual need be consuming the two commodities in the same proportions as they are consumed by the whole community.

However, this consideration may be ignored for the constant-apparent-real-income demand curve, if we like, whereas in the nature of the case it cannot be ignored for the "true" constant-real-income demand curve. Furthermore, if we choose not to ignore it, we need only to know the original quantities bought by each consumer in order to define the constant-apparent-real-income demand curve, whereas for the constant-real-income demand curve one must know the shape and position of each consumer's relevant indifference curve. Similar remarks apply to the constant-apparent-production demand curve discussed below in the text,

So far as I can see, the production-frontier demand curve has the disadvantage that there is no logical way to define it for each individual in the community—it is a purely aggregate function, and any relative income distribution is consistent with

in "real income" by substituting X for Y; the new bill of goods they would choose if they had this opportunity would be B', on the community indifference curve I_3, higher than I_1.

The demand curve derived in this way is not the same thing as the true constant-real-income demand curve as previously defined (which depended on the shape of I_1 only), but it can be proved to be a first-order approximation of it,[9] just as the true constant-real-income demand curve is a first-order approximation of the production-frontier demand curve. It follows that the constant-apparent-real-income demand curve is a first-order approximation of the production-frontier demand curve. Furthermore, it does not suffer from the difficulties of definition of the other curve, since it can unambiguously be defined in terms of constant-money incomes for every individual.

In practice, something in the nature of a constant-apparent-real-income demand curve could be derived statistically from ordinary total market data; whereas a true constant-real-income demand curve could not but would require data on every individual. With a statistically derived demand curve in our hands, we would not know what values of the price variables (if any) would give every consumer the same real income (for a constant-money income) as some other set of values of the price variables. However, it would be a simple matter to choose a set of price variables giving the same *apparent* real income (as here defined) to the community as some other set; all that has to be done is to choose a set of prices which keeps a base-weights price index unchanged in value.[10]

However, the possibilities for better practical approximation of the production-frontier demand curve are not yet exhausted. We may with comparable simplicity define a constant-apparent-*production* demand curve; and this will be the best approximation of the lot. In Figure 3*B* the line $S'T'$ represents the equilibrium price line as before, and, being tangent to the production frontier ST at P, it represents a local approximation of ST, just as does I_1. A useful demand concept is defined by moving along $S'T'$: for any given price ratio for X and Y, we obtain from the community indifference map that bill of goods among those along $S'T'$ which the community would prefer; that is, we find the community indifference curve I_4, which at its point of crossing of $S'T'$ has the same slope as the given price line, $M'''N'''$.

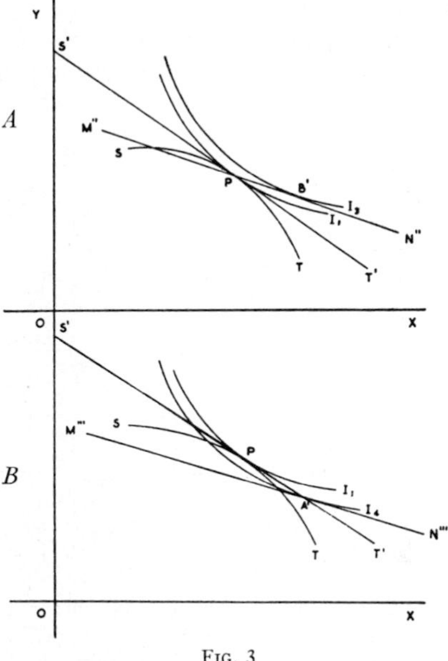

FIG. 3

We may now compare the different con-

its definition. This disadvantage is the antithesis of the disadvantage of the constant-real-income demand curve, which in effect is defined only for the individual.

My earlier omission of the points in this footnote was brought to my attention by Friedman.

[9] See Jacob L. Mosak, "On the interpretation of the Fundamental Equation of Value Theory," in O. Lange *et al.* (eds.), *Studies in Mathematical Economics and Econometrics* (Chicago: University of Chicago Press, 1942), p. 73 n.

[10] Friedman, *op. cit.*, p. 467.

ceptions of demand set forth here; the curves are illustrated in Figure 4, which is derived from Figures 1*A*, 3*A*, and 3*B* in the same manner as Figure 1*B* is derived from Figure 1*A*. The curves *DD*, *RR*, and *QQ* in Figure 4 are the same as in Figure 1*A*; the new curves *R'R'* and *Q'Q'* are the approximations—constant *apparent* real income and production, respectively—discussed in this section.

The curves *R'R'*, *RR*, and *Q'Q'* are all tangent to *QQ* at *J*, a condition which will hold provided the necessary continuity ob-

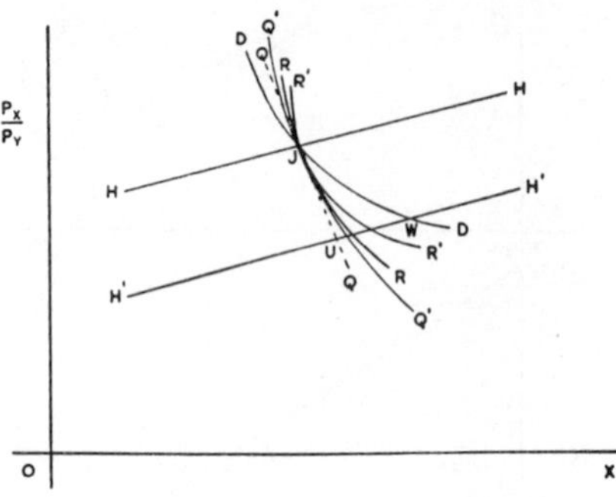

FIG. 4

tains in preference and production; and it can also be seen that *R'R'*, *RR*, and *Q'Q'* are successively better approximations in that order to *QQ*, which represents the demand derived from what the community can actually have. (The relative positions of the various curves depend on the assumption that commodity *X* is not inferior.) No importance should be attached to the absolute curvatures of the different curves, which depend on the conditions of preference and production; but under the assumed conditions it is necessarily true that *QQ*, *Q'Q'*, *RR*, and *R'R'* are successively more concave upward and that *Q'Q'* is the best approximation to the shape of *QQ*.

The constant-apparent-production demand curve can, like the constant-apparent-real-income demand curve, be derived from market data on quantities sold and prices. Just as the constant-apparent-real-income demand curve is obtained from the knowledge of the original equilibrium quantities and of the relevant part of the consumer preference field as revealed in market data, so the constant-apparent-production curve is obtained from a knowledge of the original equilibrium *prices* and of the relevant part of the consumer preference field. The first involves keeping a base-weights price index constant; the second involves keeping a base-weights quantity index constant. Such awkwardness of definition as exists in the constant-apparent-production demand curve disappears if the Continental procedure of expressing prices as a function of quantity is adopted.[11]

The constant-apparent-production curve has the advantage, however, that it represents the true possibilities closer than does the constant-real-income demand curve. *It utilizes information which the latter curve does not use, namely, that the equilibrium price ratio is itself an approximation of the alternative bills of goods which the community can in fact have.*

There is one other point on which the suggested "improvement" of the conventional demand curve might be rejected: the conventional demand curve is unambiguous about how "other prices" behave, whereas none of the other demand curves is. If there are several commodities, a given change in the price of commodity *X* may be offset by price changes in other goods in any of a number of different ways still meeting the specifications of the other four types of demand curves. It may make a good deal of difference to the demand for *X* whether the prices of closely competing or complementary goods are changed a little or a lot to compensate for the change in the price of *X*. If any demand curve other than the all-other-prices-and-incomes-equal demand curve is used, some arbitrary specification must be made as to how other prices are to change to offset changes in the price of *X*, such as that all other prices change in the

[11] I am indebted to Friedman for this point.

same proportion. It should be recognized that such a solution *is* arbitrary, since whatever choice is made does not necessarily have any connection with the way these prices would really change if, say, a subsidy were imposed on commodity X. The conventional demand curve solves this problem (also arbitrarily, of course) by assuming that other prices do not change at all.

FINAL COMMENT

The conclusion of the above remarks finds me substantially in agreement with Friedman's argument in favor of revising the conventional notion of a demand curve when we desire to analyze the effects of an excise tax or subsidy, although I have come out in favor of even greater revision than he suggested. In the policy problem in question, the community's production opportunities are unaffected, but *apparent* supply conditions are changed. Therefore, it is simplest to use a demand curve along which true supply conditions are (exactly or approximately) unchanged. The conventional demand curve does not meet this specification; consequently, in the problem under consideration one must show a shift in such a demand curve, as well as in the apparent supply curve, as the effect of the policy action.[12] If market data are sufficiently informative, both demand and supply conditions are hypothetically ascertainable, and the production-frontier demand curve may be used. If not, the approximations discussed here may be used, the better of which is the constant-apparent-production demand curve.

The situation is not the same if the problem under consideration involves changes in actual supply conditions such as (*a*) changes in technique, (*b*) crop variations and the like, and (*c*) changes in government activity, altering the availabilities to the private sector of the economy. In any such case the relevant demand curve would change, that is, would "shift." This is true of the production-frontier demand curve and of all three of its approximations. It is possible that, by coincidence, the new equilibrium might be on the old price-consumption line (*PC* in Fig. 1*A*); and in this case the conventional demand curve would give the true result without shifting. No such coincidence is possible for the other four demand curves if the new production frontier lies entirely above or below the old one. Beyond this, however, nothing can be said as to whether the outcome of a change in conditions can or cannot be approximated with any single demand curve defined here.

It is therefore evident that the choice of a demand curve for purposes of analysis should depend on the problem in hand; and for some problems no demand curve will perform with the simplicity we might desire. It should therefore also be evident that the use of general equilibrium diagrams such as Figure 1*A* is an important supplement to clear and accurate analysis. With such diagrams it is still necessary to state the relevant qualifications regarding income distribution, but subject to this the interrelationships between different types of changes in conditions can be shown.

[12] Friedman, *op. cit.*

14 A Reply

M. Friedman

Both my own earlier discussion of the definition of the demand curve and Bailey's interesting comments are phrased in terms of the variables that it is appropriate to hold constant along a demand curve viewed as a two-dimensional relation between quantity and price. It may help in bringing out the issues involved in this choice to present the problem in rather different terms.

Reprinted from the *Journal of Political Economy,* Vol. LXII (June, 1954), pp. 261–266, by permission of the publisher and author.

Let us consider the simple case analyzed by Bailey in which there are only two commodities, X and Y, sold at money prices p_x and p_y to an individual with money income I. Given his tastes, we can regard the quantity of X that he wants to buy (x) as depending on p_x, p_y, and I:

$$x = f(p_x, p_y, I) . \qquad (1)$$

This is a demand function in which x appears to depend on three different variables. But in the nonmonetary context in which we generally use such a demand function, this view is clearly misleading. If p_x, p_y and I are doubled, or multiplied by some other common factor, x will be unaffected, as is clear from Bailey's Figure 1*A*. The demand function (1) is homogeneous of zero degree; the quantity demanded depends not on three independent variables but only on the ratios among them, and thus only on two independent variables.

This view accords fully with those informalized judgments we label "common sense" (when we agree with them): the quantity of a good demanded by an individual is determined by two basic factors—the terms on which he can exchange this good for other goods (relative prices) and the volume of goods in general that he can command (real income). The appearance of three variables in (1) is occasioned by the inclusion of what from this point of view is a scale factor—the absolute level of prices.

Up to this point there is, I think, no disagreement, not only between Bailey and me, but among economists in general. Disagreement arises about the precise way of collapsing the three variables, p_x, p_y, and I, into two, which in turn reduces to the precise definition of "real income." In place of (1), we want to write

$$x = g\left(\frac{p_x}{p_y}, \xi\right), \qquad (2)$$

where ξ stands for some as yet unspecified concept of real income. The usual two-dimensional demand curve is obtained from (2) by giving ξ some constant value, which is why the question how to define ξ is the same as the question what to hold constant along a demand curve. Similarly, a two-dimensional curve is obtained by giving p_x/p_y some constant value. This is the quantity-income relation or Engel curve.

The usual procedure of treating money income and other money prices as constant along a demand curve is equivalent to defining real income as

$$\xi = \frac{I}{p_y}, \qquad (3)$$

that is, as the maximum quantity of Y that the individual's money income can buy. This definition yields the demand curves labeled *DD* in Bailey's figures. The objection to this definition is that it does not in general provide a satisfactory counterpart to the qualitative distinction between changes in terms of exchange and in command over resources. For an individual who consumes goods other than Y, the same quantity of Y means a different command over goods in general, depending on the relative price of Y and other goods. One consequence of the use of this definition of income has accordingly been the subdivision of the effect of a change in price into substitution and income effects—a somewhat backhanded recognition that I/p_y may be a misleading definition of income, since, even if it is constant, there are effects that need to be attributed to a change in income.

It should perhaps be emphasized that this definition is not "wrong"; it is a formally valid way to convert (1) into (2). The objection is that it is not likely to be the most *useful* way to collapse the three variables into two; that it is likely to lead to confusion in analysis because it more or less arbitrarily classifies the same effect under two different headings. At the same time there doubtless are special problems for which it is peculiarly well adapted. For example, suppose that Y stands for the output of a country engaging in international trade and X for the goods it imports and that this country's trade is small relative to total world trade in X and Y. For an analysis of the effect on this country alone of external changes in the supply of X, the ratio of I to p_y may well be the most useful concept of income; constancy of this ratio corresponds to constancy in internal conditions of production.[1] A corresponding statement will not, of course, hold for the world as a whole.

An alternative definition of real income for an individual, and the one that is most directly suggested by the usual theory of consumer choice, is

$$\xi = U \, , \tag{4}$$

where U is level of utility or the index of a consumption indifference curve, so that movement from one indifference curve to another means a change in income. This yields the demand curves labeled RR on Bailey's figures. Though intuitively appealing, this definition has the defect that it introduces a variable into the demand function that is not directly observable on the market. We are after all interested in the demand curve of the individual not so much for its own sake as for the aid it can give us in analyzing market phenomena. For that purpose we want it to be expressed in terms of prices and quantities, not individual utility levels.

One escape from this difficulty is to accept an approximation to the utility definition which is in terms of observable magnitudes but is valid only locally in the neighborhood of any arbitrary initial point. One such definition is

$$\xi = \frac{I}{(x_o p_x + y_o p_y) \,/\, (x_o p_{xo} + y_o p_{yo})} \tag{5}$$

where x_o and y_o are the quantities of X and Y demanded, and p_{xo} and p_{yo}, the prices of X and Y, at some initial point, at which the individual is in equilibrium. This involves defining income as the number of initial baskets the individual can buy and yields the demand curves labeled $R'R'$ on Bailey's figures.[2] This is the definition that I attributed to Marshall and described in terms of holding money income and the purchasing power of money constant along the demand curve.

Another definition that has the same approximative property in the neighborhood of an initial equilibrium position is

$$\xi = \frac{I}{(x p_x + y p_y) \,/\, (x p_{xo} + y p_{yo})} \, , \tag{6}$$

where x and y are the quantities of X and Y purchased at the new prices. This involves defining real income as the number of ultimate baskets the individual can buy and yields the demand curves labeled $Q'Q'$ on Bailey's figures. Bailey describes this demand curve as one that keeps a quantity index constant or, on the community level, as an approximation to a constant-production-frontier demand curve; but it is clear from his analysis and figures, as from my own earlier article (especially n. 14 and associated text), that it is equally an approximation to what he calls a constant-real-income demand curve.[3] Indeed, as is shown most clearly by his Figure 4, his $R'R'$ and $Q'Q'$ curves are on opposite sides of RR and so furnish limits to it. Their relation to RR is precisely the same as, and is a particular instance of, the relation of the Laspeyres

[1] I am indebted to Lloyd A. Metzler for first suggesting this example to me.

[2] The requirement imposed in computing $R'R'$ is that the budget line for the new prices pass through the initial equilibrium point, or

$$I = x_o p_x + y_o p_y \, . \tag{a}$$

This is clearly equivalent to keeping ξ as defined by (5) constant, as can be seen most readily by dividing (a) by

$$I_o = x_o p_{xo} + y_o p_{yo} \, . \tag{b}$$

[3] The requirement imposed in computing $Q'Q'$is that the equilibrium position for the new prices be on the initial budget line, or

$$I_o = x p_{xo} + y p_{yo} \, , \tag{c}$$

which corresponds to describing $Q'Q'$ as keeping a quantity index constant. But it is also equivalent to keeping ξ, as defined by (6), constant, as can be seen most readily by dividing (c) by

$$I = x p_x + y p_y \, . \tag{d}$$

and Paasche cost-of-living index numbers to the "true" cost-of-living index number.[4]

Equation (2) and the alternative definitions of real income are all for the individual consumer unit. We can aggregate such equations for the different units in the community, whom we may suppose to number m, and construct a community demand function. If we take the relative price of the two products to be the same for all individuals, the function so obtained will, in our simple example, express the aggregate quantity demanded as a function of $m + 1$ variables: relative price and the real income, however defined, of each of the m members of the community. Clearly, such a demand curve is not very useful in positive analysis; one cannot pay more than lip service to variables that are specific to individual consumers. If the demand curve is to be useful, it must be reasonable to neglect detailed differences in the behavior of individual incomes on the grounds either that they cancel out or that individuals can be treated as homogeneous. The most that can be done is to use as variables aggregate income and perhaps one or a few other general parameters describing the distribution of income.

Bailey's emphasis on the transition from the individual to the aggregate demand curve is called for by my own failure to deal explicitly with this problem. He himself regards the transition as raising especially acute difficulties for definition (4), which equates income with level of utility for the individual, and especially for the variant of the associated demand curve which holds money income constant and uses changes in the price of Y to compensate for any effect on the utility level that might otherwise result from a change in the price of X. I do not believe that this is so; the difficulty only takes a somewhat different form. In principle, we can conceive of an aggregate demand curve that keeps each individual separately on the same indifference curve by means of price compensations, the differential price compensations required for different individuals because of differences in tastes and resources being produced by a system of excise taxes or subsidies varying from one individual to another. There is no substantial difference between this device and the system of special income taxes or subsidies required on the income-compensating variant. Indeed, the required excise and income taxes are simply the same taxes under different aliases. In both cases, we can make effective use of the aggregate demand curve only if we can neglect, or handle in some crude way, the differences among individuals in the required price or income compensations. And, as already implied, precisely the same problem arises for the other definitions of real income and the demand curves associated with them. In the usual demand curve, we must neglect detailed changes in the amount of Y commanded by particular individuals; in the approximations to the constant utility demand curve, the differences among individuals in the appropriate weights for one or the other cost-of-living index number used to deflate money income.[5] The basic difference between definition (4) and the others is not the difficulty of passing from the individual to the aggregate, given the price or income compensation required for the individual, but the difficulty of expressing the condition imposed on the individual in terms of prices and quantities directly observable on the market.

On the aggregate level another definition of real income is

$$\xi = Q\,, \qquad (7)$$

where Q is the level of "production," or the index of a production indifference curve, so

[4] When the initial and terminal positions are on approximately the same indifference curve, here assured by definition.

[5] The problem at issue is one that plagues computers and interpreters of cost-of-living index numbers and has been extensively discussed in that connection. To speak of "the" change in the cost of living for a community is clearly an approximation. The use of this language implies that differences between individuals can be neglected, either because they are regarded as averaging out in some relevant sense or because the individuals can be regarded as essentially alike for the purpose at hand.

that keeping income constant means staying on the same production indifference curve. The production indifference curve refers to the total possible output of the community as a whole for given resources, and so can be defined strictly only for the community. But the use of this definition of income does not avoid the problem of reconciling the aggregate and the individual demand functions; the problem simply comes up in reverse form. Consider a point on a production indifference curve. Is knowledge of this point sufficient to determine a unique price ratio at which consumers would clear the market? Clearly not, at least if consumers differ in taste and resources. In principle, the precise price ratio depends on the distribution of resources among individuals of different taste, so again, for this demand curve to be useful, it must be possible to neglect or handle in some crude way detailed differences among individuals.[6]

The production-frontier demand curve associated with definition (7) may be particularly well suited for some problems.[7] However, it seems to me that it will not be for most. (i) Definition (7) shares with (4) the defect that it introduces a variable that is not directly observable on the market. (ii) The concept of "level of production" implicit in this procedure, if we are to use it to generate a family of demand curves for different values of ξ, does not play the role in current economic theory that individual utility levels do. No one way of generating the required family of production indifference curves seems especially meaningful. (iii) Definition (7) seems to me to import supply considerations too directly into the demand function. We want demand functions precisely in order to analyze the effect of changes in supply; and they can be useful for this purpose only if the factors affecting demand can be regarded as largely independent of the factors affecting supply. We want demand analysis to be so constructed as to fit together and be consistent with supply analysis; yet we also want the two to be largely independent. From this point of view, it is an important ancillary advantage of definition (4) that under certain conditions the interpretation of "constant real income" as "on the same consumption indifference curve" yields the same results, to first-order effects, as if it were interpreted to mean "on the same production indifference curve," and it is this that my tax-and-subsidy example was designed to show. At the same time this is not a reason for using the latter interpretation directly in analyzing demand.

In large measure these objections are directed against a straw man. Bailey recognizes that defect (i) is critical, and, in consequence, the two demand curves whose relative merits he mainly contrasts are two approximations: one, based on definition (6), that he regards as an approximation to a constant-production-frontier demand curve; the other, based on definition (5), that he regards as an approximation to a constant-utility demand curve. But, as my earlier comments make clear, this contrast too is a straw man. Both (5) and (6) can with equal validity be regarded as yielding approximations to a constant-utility demand curve, the only difference being that one uses a base-weighted index number to measure purchasing power, the other a terminal-weighted index number. Equally, both can be regarded as yielding approximations to a constant-production-frontier demand curve, at least up to effects of the first order. In

[6] One frequent device, at least in theoretical analyses, is to regard all individuals as having identical resources, so that a production indifference curve can be defined for the individual which is a small-scale replica of the community curve. This is the device, for example, that I use in "The 'Welfare' Effects of an Income Tax and an Excise Tax," *Journal of Political Economy*, LX (February, 1952), 25–33; reprinted in corrected form in my *Essays in Positive Economics* (Chicago: University of Chicago Press, 1953), pp. 100–113, esp. 106–13.

[7] The production-frontier demand curve is used by I. F. Pearce, "Total Demand Curves and General Equilibrium," *Review of Economic Studies*, XX (1952-53), 216–27. However, the problem he uses it for seems to me largely artificial, arising from attaching importance and significance to the scale factor, the elimination of which is the very purpose of collapsing the three variables into two.

consequence, I see little to choose between (5) and (6) and less need to do so. In practice, (5) will probably be the more convenient form if the problem is one in which it is appropriate to regard relative prices as the independent variables from the point of view of the consumers, and quantities as the variables they adjust. On the other hand, (6) will probably be the more convenient if it is appropriate to regard quantities as the independent variables, as, for example, in a problem concerned with the effects on prices of limiting the physical supplies available to individual consumers.

The only question that remains is how to interpret demand curves based on (5) and (6) when one or the other is used. In order to interpret them as approximations to a constant-utility demand curve in the neighborhood of an initial position, it is necessary, first, that differences among individuals can be largely neglected or regarded as averaging out; second, that, at the initial position, the budget line can be regarded as tangent to an indifference curve. The second condition in turn generally requires that the consumer can be treated as if he were maximizing utility and were free to buy all he wants at the specified prices (i.e., no effective rationing other than by the purse and no monopsony). The first condition, about individual differences, is equally necessary in order to interpret these demand curves as approximations to a constant-production-frontier demand curve in the neighborhood of an initial position. In addition, it is necessary to suppose that, at that position, money prices can be regarded as proportional to the relevant marginal costs for all goods (i.e., that there are no differential degrees of monopoly, taxes, or subsidies, and no differential external technical economies or diseconomies, or that these offset one another). There is no need to decide in advance what interpretation to use and no need to use only one. Both can be simultaneously valid, as indeed they are in my tax-and-subsidy example.

15 *Methodenstreit* Over Demand Curves[1]

L. Yeager

I. RIVAL DEMAND CURVES

THIS paper seeks to clarify some points raised in the literature that has grown up around Milton Friedman's Marshallian demand curve.[2] It examines some methodological precepts set forth in this literature: its insistence on a particular conception of empirical falsifiability and concrete applicability of theories and its insistence that theories deal only with actually or conceptually attainable positions of equilibrium. Published appraisal of this point of view has so far been remarkably scant.

First, it is necessary to summarize the proposed innovations in demand theory. Friedman objects to the currently prevalent conception of the demand curve (the "Hicksian" or, as Knight says, the "Slutzky-school" conception). For a particular commodity, this curve shows the alternative quantities per time period that the buyers would want to buy at various alternative prices, assuming no change in their tastes and so forth, in their *money* incomes, and in the prices of goods and services other than the particular one in question. A change in the commodity's own price will affect quantity demanded through the familiar "income effect" and "substitution effect." Friedman wants to work, instead, with what he calls a "Marshallian"[3] demand curve. Such a curve would show the alternative quantities of a particular commodity demanded at alternative prices on the condition of constancy in the buyers' tastes and so forth, in their *real* incomes, and in the prices of all close substitutes for and complements of the commodity considered. A change in the one particular price would be accompanied by a change in the average level of prices of substantially unrelated goods in such a way as to freeze the general purchasing power of money and thus the real income corresponding to the given money income. In principle, the offsetting changes in the other prices would be such as to keep buyers at the same utility levels as before.[4] These price changes cannot be exactly specified in practice because the necessary detailed knowledge of utility functions cannot be obtained and because of other complications. As an approximation, Friedman proposes adjustments to make the unchanged money income just barely adequate to buy the same assortment of goods in the new price situation as in the old situation.[5] Bailey proposes an alterna-

[1] I am indebted to Professor James M. Buchanan for the title of this article and for lengthy, patient, and exceedingly helpful, though not necessarily concurring, written comments on earlier drafts.

[2] Milton Friedman, "The Marshallian Demand Curve," *Journal of Political Economy*, LVII (December, 1949), 463–95, reprinted in *Essays in Positive Economics* (Chicago: University of Chicago Press, 1953), pp. 47–99; as Friedman points out, his argument is an extension of that presented by Frank H. Knight in "Realism and Relevance in the Theory of Demand," *Journal of Political Economy*, LII (December, 1944), 289–318. Further writings in the same tradition include Martin J. Bailey, "The Marshallian Demand Curve," *Journal of Political Economy*, LXII (June, 1954), 255–61; Milton Friedman, "A Reply," *Journal of Political Economy*, LXII (June, 1954), 261–66; Martin J. Bailey, "Saving and the Rate of Interest," *Journal of Political Economy*, LXV (August, 1957), 279–305; James M. Buchanan, "Saving and the Rate of Interest: A Comment," *Journal of Political Economy*, LXVII (February, 1959), 79–82; James M. Buchanan, "*Ceteris Paribus:* Some Notes on Methodology," *Southern Economic Journal*, XXIV (January, 1958), 259–70.

[3] The present paper ignores the question of "what Marshall really meant." The merits of Friedman's approach and methodological precepts can be examined separately from matters of textual interpretation.

[4] Friedman, *Essays*, esp. pp. 51–54.

[5] Cf. Friedman's summary statement in *Journal of Political Economy*, June, 1954, p. 263.

Reprinted from the *Journal of Political Economy,* Vol. LXVIII (February, 1960), pp. 53–64, by permission of the publisher and author.

tive constant-real-income demand curve corresponding to the fixity of the community's production-possibility frontier; his approximation would keep constant a quantity index weighted by base prices.[6]

There is no need here to explore the relative merits of the Friedman and Bailey constructions; they both exemplify the same methodological approach.[7] Whatever the details may be, this approach is supposed to have advantages in comparison with the conventional Hicksian demand curve. It isolates the substitution effect of a price change for study, with the income effect being "eliminated," or removed from consideration.[8] A Friedman-Marshall demand curve *must* slope negatively: under the conditions presupposed in its very construction, a cut in the price of the commodity will without exception increase quantity demanded (or, in the limit, leave it unchanged). The theorist need not hedge his predictions to allow for the possibility of a strong inferior-good income effect outweighing a normal substitution effect. Friedman-Marshall predictions are meaningful because refutable if wrong.[9] The Hicksian demand curve, by contrast, "contains no empirical generalization that is capable of being contradicted. . . ."

In general, the Friedman approach is said to be more "useful" than its rival for dealing with practical problems.[10] This apparently means that the Hicksian approach, in regarding all prices as kept constant except the price of the particular commodity to which the demand curve refers, reflects the Walrasian notion that the quantity demanded of any particular commodity depends on *all* prices in the economic system. Such a striving for generality, elegance, and photographic accuracy in assumptions sabotages the treatment of practical problems and the search for the "concrete truth" stressed by Marshall. The more modest Friedman-Marshall approach does not try to take account of all prices in the system, not even by keeping them constant. Instead, it fixes the prices only of obvious substitutes and complements and concerns itself further only with the behavior of an average of all other prices rather than with those other prices individually. Because it has more modest aims than rival approaches, the rough-and-ready Friedman demand curve is a more practical and usable tool.

Setting aside until later the question of just what might be meant by the practical "usefulness" of a demand curve, we may now consider the implied claim that Friedman's concept has an advantageous rough-and-ready simplicity. Actually, if we are going to find fault with the Hicksian demand curve for the complexity of in principle taking account of all prices in the system in order to keep all but one of them constant, we are even more entitled to question Friedman's concept on similar grounds. (Friedman and Bailey themselves have already noted most of what follows here, though apparently without taking it enough to heart. The only reason for repeating it is to lay the basis for considering their methodological precepts.) First of all, a great am-

[6] *Journal of Political Economy*, June, 1954, esp. 259–60.

[7] Constant real income in the utility sense and constant real income in the sense of outputs obtainable from a fixed total of resources converge in the neighborhood of equilibrium. Friedman, *Essays*, p. 63.

[8] Friedman, *Essays*, pp. 64–65.

[9] This claim is admittedly not made perfectly explicit—in print. It may be inferred from statements such as the one quoted in the next sentence of the text (from Friedman, *Essays*, p. 91). Furthermore, Knight (*Journal of Political Economy*, December, 1944, p. 300) recommends drawing the demand curve with "utility and the objective purchasing-power of money . . . held constant," since "This procedure has the further great advantage of eliminating the spurious 'Giffen paradox'. . . ." Bailey's attempt in his 1957 article (already cited) to settle the question whether a rise in the rate of interest can be expected to increase or decrease saving bears an obvious though loose analogy to attempts to exclude the possibility of the Giffen paradox in the demand for an ordinary commodity.

[10] For remarks about usefulness, see Friedman, *Essays*, pp. 48, 56–57, 89, 93; Friedman, *Journal of Political Economy*, June, 1954, p. 263.

biguity surrounds the "Chicago"[11] demand curves as to just *which* other prices in the system are conceived to vary, and by how much, to offset the income effect of the change in the price of the particular commodity considered. Any specified set of price changes must be arbitrary, since the changes are not necessarily those that would occur in the real world in response to the change in underlying conditions that also caused the change in the price of the particular commodity. The Hicksian approach is also arbitrary in specifying no change in the other prices, but at least it is not ambiguous.[12] A related ambiguity in the Chicago approach concerns the starting price considered for the commodity, since the level of buyers' real income to be kept constant by offsetting price variations is different for different starting prices.

The Friedman method of offsetting price changes is not only an approximation to what would leave each individual on the same utility level as before; it is also a mere approximation to what would leave each individual just able to afford his original assortment of goods. For the individuals will in fact have been buying different original assortments, and any actually specified set of price changes will affect different individuals in different ways and will somewhat redistribute effective purchasing power. Friedman's construction is a mere approximation to an approximation to keeping each individual on the same utility level as before.[13] Bailey's construction, on the other hand, is incapable of being defined logically for each individual in the community; it can aim to keep approximately constant only the production possibilities available to the community as a whole.[14]

We see that neither Friedman's nor Bailey's construction can analyze how a particular price change affects quantity demanded under the assumptions both of an unchanged distribution of real income and of a constant level of real income or of production opportunities. Any price change or set of price changes is bound to benefit some and harm other members of the community; a rise or fall in some particular price is almost certain to reduce or increase the real opportunities available to those who happen to be actual or potential buyers of the commodity in question. In reality, then, the income effect is as inherent a part of the influences determining consumer behavior as is the substitution effect. Yet Friedman wishes to "eliminate" the income effect and consider only the substitution effect; he wishes to keep real income unchanged not merely for the community as a whole but even for the group of purchasers of the particular commodity in question.[15] This seems illegitimate: to abstract from the way a price change in the real world *does* affect the real income of a particular group of buyers and potential buyers is to abstract from a possibly important part of the reason why the price change will affect quantity de-

[11] Labels such as this are merely a convenient shorthand. As is clear from the context, they have a restricted meaning and imply no monolithic unity among all "Chicagoans."

[12] Bailey, *Journal of Political Economy*, June, 1954, pp. 260–61.

[13] Cf. *ibid.*, pp. 257–59. Friedman himself (*Journal of Political Economy*, June, 1954, p. 264) acknowledges his own earlier failure to deal explicitly with the problem of transition from the demand curve of the individual to the demand curve of the community.

[14] Bailey, *Journal of Political Economy*, June, 1954, pp. 258–59, crediting Friedman for the point.

[15] He makes this explicit on pp. 50–51 of his *Essays*. Furthermore, in considering a price change due to subsidizing a particular commodity, Friedman postulates that the revenue to pay for the subsidy is raised from broadly the same group of individuals as those who benefit from it, "so that complications arising from changes in the distribution of income can be neglected . . ." (pp. 59–60). On p. 84, however, where he is seeking to reconcile the Giffen Paradox with his interpretation of Marshall, Friedman envisages constancy in the real income of the community at large but not of the particular consumer group. In *Journal of Political Economy*, June, 1954, pp. 262–63, in connection with an international-trade example suggested by Lloyd Metzler, Friedman does recognize that there are special problems for which the Hicksian demand analysis is appropriate.

manded. These are perhaps the considerations that James Buchanan (a champion of the Friedman methodology) had in mind when he recognized that there is some justification for the widespread acceptance and use of the uncompensated or Hicksian demand curve in analyzing the behavior of one individual or some one group of individuals smaller than the whole community.[16] What remains to be emphasized is that, in contemplating a demand curve, we *always are* analyzing the behavior of a group smaller than the whole community: not everyone is a buyer of a particular commodity. (Or, to be precise, even if every member of the community does buy at least some small amount of the commodity in question, not all members are buyers to the same extent; some members count importantly and others only trivially as buyers of the commodity.)

In developing his objection that a reduction in price along a Hicksian demand curve illegitimately implies a change in the productive capacity of the community, Friedman considers an excise subsidy that lowers the effective supply curve of commodity X. The new intersection with the Hicksian demand curve is MN units to the right of the old intersection. "But then," asks Friedman, "where do the resources come from to produce the extra MN units of X? Obviously, our assumptions are not internally consistent. The additional units of X can be produced only by bidding resources away from the production of other commodities, in the process raising their prices and reducing the amount of them produced." A Hicksian demand curve "fails to give the correct solution even when all disturbing influences can be neglected" because "each point on it implicitly refers to a different productive capacity of the community."[17] It is noteworthy that Friedman refers to the community rather than to buyers and potential buyers of the particular commodity. Even supposing the productive opportunities open to the community to remain unchanged, it is perfectly easy to conceive of an improvement of the supply opportunities open to particular buyer groups. Perhaps, for instance, the ingredients used in making a product have become cheaper because of a shift in tastes away from other products made from these same ingredients.

On a more general plane, what is the objection, after all, to considering changes in the supply opportunities open not merely to particular groups but even to the community as a whole? Perhaps the product has been cheapened by advances in technology. What is illegitimate about asking how this price reduction will affect quantity demanded? And why must we somehow compensate out of the analysis the increase in people's real incomes that this cheapening does imply?[18]

Part of the explanation is that the Chicagoans are not typically concerned with examples involving changes in resources or technology; they deal with price changes brought about by excise taxes and subsidies.[19] They are quite right in insisting that, with unchanged resources and technology,

[16] *Southern Economic Journal*, January, 1958, p. 262.

[17] *Essays*, pp. 61–62.

[18] Friedman, *Essays*, p. 63, does take note of this question; and he suggests redrawing a demand curve of his type to correspond to the appropriately higher but again constant level of real income. Bailey, *Journal of Political Economy*, June, 1954, p. 261, also recognizes that a change in actual supply conditions would cause a compensated demand curve of his type to shift; from this he concludes that the choice of a demand curve should depend on the problem in hand. We should bear these remarks in mind when we later turn to consider the claim that the Chicago approach best fits in with the ideal of keeping demand factors and supply factors as separate and independent as possible. It appears that the Chicagoans mingle supply and demand factors together despite their own precept . Furthermore, if the proper conception of the demand curve does admittedly depend, after all, on each particular problem in hand, one wonders just what is left of the general methodological insights ostensibly connected with the Chicago curve.

[19] For example, see Friedman, *Essays*, pp. 59–62; Bailey, *Journal of Political Economy*, June, 1954, pp. 255, 261; Bailey, *Journal of Political Economy*, August, 1957, pp. 283–84, 288; Friedman, "Leon Walras and His Economic System," *American Economic Review*, XLV (December, 1955), middle of p. 904.

the tax or subsidy is necessarily accompanied by a revenue-disposal or revenue-raising aspect whose neglect may involve serious analytical error. If this other aspect impinges to any important extent on the same persons directly affected by the tax or subsidy, it may be necessary to take account of this effect on their real income by redrawing their demand curve accordingly. Perhaps this is a clumsy expedient, but no more so than to shift the demand curve when supply shifts because of changed resources or technology (see n. 18). In cases like this, shifting the curves seems a more straightforward and more generally applicable approach than trying to rig given demand curves in advance to take account of possible supply changes affecting real income. Even if a tax or subsidy is the cause of the supply and price change, there still is not much justification for trying to draw a given demand curve that gets rid of income effects, for the demanders of the particular taxed or subsidized commodity may very well have their real incomes changed. If the Chicagoans object that others in the community will necessarily have their real incomes changed in the opposite direction and that repercussions even onto the first market will occur, they are just pointing out the fact of general interdependence and the fact that partial analysis is only an approximation.

II. WAYS OF ALLOWING FOR GENERAL ECONOMIC INTERDEPENDENCE

Any demand curve drawn on a two-dimensional diagram is a piece of partial-equilibrium analysis and is incapable of reflecting, in itself, the full interdependence of all aspects of the economic system. Any demand curve is a way of contemplating how buyers would react to a change in supply price; but, in general, the particular price in question cannot change apart from other changes in the economic system. Sometimes, as Buchanan has persuasively shown,[20] theorists fail to take this incomplete character of partial-equilibrium analysis adequately into account and arrive at seriously wrong conclusions about the general-equilibrium aspects of the economy. But a warning against illegitimate use of *ceteris paribus* and against illegitimate neglect of general-equilibrium considerations, however necessary and persuasive, makes no conclusive case against the Hicksian demand curve. Objections to the Hicksian curve are essentially objections to any attempt to use partial-equilibrium tools, however supplemented, in an approach to the complexities of reality; as such, these objections lose their force.

Two expressions recur in the Chicago discussions of methodology: the question "How can *one* price change?" and the insistence on "genuinely attainable alternatives."[21] The question refers to the interdependence of all aspects of the economy: one item cannot change all by itself, devoid of all repercussions. This is of course true. Yet there is no harm in contemplating, for example, what would happen if government price-controllers tried to decree a change in one single price. There is no harm in considering how demanders would want to respond to various prices *if* they somehow could prevail. Part of the purpose of such an analysis might be to show the inconsistency among the plans of various members of the community at disequilibrium prices and to analyze the processes of groping toward equilibrium.

Relating to the same set of problems is the insistence that demand curves represent only "genuinely attainable alternatives" or "conceptually attainable alternatives"; "each point on a demand curve must represent an attainable equilibrium between demand and supply."[22] What this apparently means is that it is legitimate to ask ourselves what quantities of some product

[20] *Southern Economic Journal*, January, 1958.

[21] The question is attributed to Frank Knight, *op. cit.*, p. 261, where the other expression also occurs on, e.g., p. 264. A less epigrammatic version of the "one-price" remark appears in Knight's 1944 article, p. 299.

[22] Buchanan, *Southern Economic Journal*, January, 1958, p. 264. Compare Friedman's worry (*Essays*, p. 63) that the conditions for which the Hicksian demand curve is drawn are inconsistent with the conditions postulated on the side of supply.

would be demanded only at prices which in fact can represent points of intersection between the demand curve and various supply curves under the supply possibilities open to the economy. (We can conceive of the effective supply curve being shifted about by one of the tax or subsidy schemes of which the Chicago theorists are so fond.) The insistence on attainable alternatives apparently forbids us to consider what quantities of the product people would want to buy at prices which cannot in fact prevail (at least not as equilibrium prices) under given supply conditions. This insistence on attainable price-quantity situations right along the demand curve itself is an example of the half-recognized inclination, mentioned previously, to build general-equilibrium considerations, and in particular supply considerations, right into the demand curve itself.[23]

Buchanan remarks that "in general, demand curves are useful only because they allow some predictions to be made regarding the effects of changes in supply."[24] In short, demand curves are useful only for the purpose of comparative statics, only to enable us to specify the new price-quantity equilibrium corresponding to changed supply conditions. Actually, there are several uses of supply-and-demand analysis other than to make comparative-static predictions. There can be good reason for studying disequilibrium situations—for studying what demanders and suppliers would be wanting to do at a price at which their plans cannot in fact mesh. Precisely one of the characteristics of a disequilibrium situation, and one of the reasons why it cannot endure, is that real incomes appear different to people from what they can actually be. We conceive of disequilibrium situations precisely in order to show that they are *not* genuinely attainable in the sense that the plans of various persons can be carried out and can mesh. We can study how the failure of plans to mesh would unleash competitive processes tending to establish a price or a set of prices at which plans finally would mesh. (In teaching the Law of Supply and Demand to beginning students, for instance, it is not enough to draw two curves on the blackboard and point to their intersection. It is necessary to show the competitive pressures that *would be* at work at prices "too low" or "too high" to be "genuinely attainable.") Consideration of disequilibrium and of equilibrating processes is further useful in helping us understand the consequences of interferences with these processes, such as price ceilings and wage floors.

The Chicagoans' insistence on attainable alternatives and comparative-static predictions suggests a reluctance to consider questions of disequilibrium, of equilibrating processes, and of the stability or instability of equilibrium. Perhaps this attitude stems from a feeling that such questions lead into talk about obscure "forces" and about things not observable in the market place. Yet in order to qualify as meaningful rather than metaphysical, propositions need not be falsifiable by direct observation, understood in the narrow behaviorist sense. Introspection and what people say may be counted among the numerous legitimate sources of empirical fact.[25]

[23] It is interesting that Friedman (*Journal of Political Economy*, June, 1954, p. 265) should have criticized Bailey's construction as seeming "to import supply considerations too directly into the demand function."

[24] *Southern Economic Journal*, January, 1958, p. 264.

[25] Unfortunately, the arguments supporting this remark would strike some readers as long-exploded fallacies, while others would find them correct but too banal to bear repetition. These, like certain other propositions in economics, have met the paradoxical fate of becoming too hackneyed for continued attention even before a reasoned consensus on their truth or falsity has been reached. I can only urge readers to take the existing literature seriously. I especially commend to the Chicagoans some perceptive remarks by their own mentor: Frank Knight in *Journal of Political Economy*, December, 1944, p. 307. For an introduction to the literature on the use in economics of information on anticipations and plans, such as is obtainable from surveys, and for an explanation of the "realization-function" approach to using such information in combination with facts of a more obviously "objective" nature, see Franco Modigliani and Kalman J. Cohen, "The Significance and Uses of Ex Ante Data," in Mary Jean Bowman

III. INDIVIDUAL-EXPERIMENTS AND MARKET-EXPERIMENTS

The Chicago insistence on genuinely attainable alternatives seems, further, to overlook Patinkin's illuminating distinction between individual-experiments and market-experiments.[26] An individual-experiment involves discovering, at least conceptually, the desired behavior of an individual person, of a small or large group of individuals, or even of all individuals in the community, acting in certain capacities, under certain specified circumstances. Whether these circumstances are compatible with other economic conditions and whether they can in fact prevail (whether they are genuinely or even conceptually attainable, to use the Chicago terminology) is beside the point: it is not the purpose of an individual-experiment, by itself, to describe the economic equilibrium that will tend to emerge. A demand curve is the standard example of the result of a set of (conceptual) individual-experiments; it shows the desired purchases of the buyers and potential buyers of a particular commodity under various specified circumstances, which include, notably, various alternative prices of the commodity. It is true that facts about the economic system other than those (the circumstances and attitudes of the demanders) reflected in the demand curve rule out many and perhaps all but one of these prices as genuine possibilities. But this does not invalidate drawing the demand curve in the way described. For the demand curve, by itself, is not meant to describe the prices that can in fact prevail. This description is possible only by an analysis that takes all of the relevant circumstances into account, including the results of other conceptual individual-experiments reflecting the circumstances and attitudes of groups other than the buyers and potential buyers of the commodity in question. This other type of analysis, which pulls together the results of various individual-experiments, examines the conditions under which the plans of various persons would and would not mesh, describes the processes at work when plans fail to mesh, and describes the equilibrium position, is what Patinkin means by market-experiments.

The anxiety to have even each demand curve by itself reflect attainable alternative positions for the whole economy is an attempt to build market-experiment considerations right into the conduct of individual-experiments. While this procedure strikes me as a source of confusion, it might perhaps be defended as a way of guarding against the worse confusion caused by misapplication of partial analysis to a description of aspects of the general equilibrium of the whole system; that this latter kind of confusion is widespread and serious can hardly be doubted by anyone who has studied Buchanan's lucid article on *ceteris paribus*. The errors so deftly examined by Buchanan may be interpreted as a confusion between individual-experiments and market-experiments in one particular direction: individual-experiment or partial notions have carelessly been carried over into analysis of market or general equilibrium. The Friedman-Buchanan school wants to move in the other direction, carrying market-experiment considerations directly into individual-experiments. It sees people so badly confusing individual- and market-experiments as to neglect relevant market considerations and reach wrong market conclusions on the basis of individual-experiment considerations inadequately supplemented. To prevent this error, the school insists (if I correctly interpret it) on building market-experiment considerations directly into the individual-experiments. I, on the other hand, do not believe that mistakes can so easily be prevented. Neither with the Chicago conception of demand curves nor with any other ready-made approaches can ingenious theorists mechanically guard their less perceptive or methodo-

(ed.), *Expectations, Uncertainty, and Business Behavior* (New York: Social Science Research Council, 1958), pp. 151–64.

[26] Don Patinkin, *Money, Interest, and Prices* (Evanston, Ill.: Row, Peterson & Co., 1956), pp. 15, 275–81. Patinkin, though a Chicago Ph.D., is not included among the "Chicagoans" as I am using the term here.

logically less alert colleagues against error. There is no easy way out: each theorist must himself grasp certain distinctions and must himself remain clearly aware of what he is doing. And the Chicago approach, blurring the distinctions between desired behavior and realizable behavior and between individual-experiments and market-experiments, seems not to contribute to the necessary clarity. Confusion in one direction can hardly be remedied by insisting on its counterpart in the opposite direction. Of course, this judgment may be a matter of personal opinion or taste: what seems simple to one person may be confusing to another, and vice versa. But if the issue does boil down to matters of personal opinion and preference and convenience, then the methodological precepts connected with the Friedman demand curve lose their force—which is precisely my argument.

IV. THE EXAMPLE OF THE DEMAND FOR MONEY

The demand-curve issue may be sharpened up and summarized by considering both Patinkin's demand curve for cash balances and a powerful objection recently made to it. Patinkin re-examined the question whether the demand for money is of unitary elasticity with respect to the purchasing-power of the money unit, as traditionally supposed.[27] Is it true, in other words, that a postulated doubling or halving of the general price level would make people want to hold precisely twice or half as many dollars as before (in order to keep the real value of their cash balances unchanged)? Patinkin says no. A doubling of the price level would mean a halving of the real purchasing power of existing cash balances and a corresponding real impoverishment of their holders. Being poorer than before, people would have to economize on various uses of their incomes or wealth; in particular, they would somewhat cut down on their planned holdings of real cash balances. The total of nominal cash balances demanded would thus rise somewhat *less* than in full proportion to the assumed rise in the price level; the elasticity of demand for cash balances would prove to be less than unity.[28]

Speaking from the methodological standpoint of the Friedman-Marshall demand curve, Buchanan takes issue with Patinkin. For one thing, he says, the purchasing power of money cannot in fact be supposed to double or halve in the context of an unchanged money supply; the corresponding points on the Patinkin demand curve are not genuinely or conceptually attainable alternatives. Admittedly they are not; and precisely one of the reasons for contemplating them, anyway, is to show that they are not attainable because of the incompatibilities among the plans of various persons that they would imply and thus to show both the

[27] Patinkin, *op. cit.*, pp. 28–30, 103–4, 388–89, 408–9. Buchanan's critique of Patinkin's position appears in the article already cited, *Southern Economic Journal*, January, 1958, pp. 262–64, 266–67.

[28] Patinkin's less-than-unitary elasticity depends on the fact that a change in the price level, postulated in an individual-experiment, implies a one-shot change in the real wealth of persons already holding cash balances. This one-shot change becomes negligible, however, in comparison with total real income considered over the fulness of time. The long-run-full-equilibrium amount of real balances demanded thus depends entirely on tastes and on the flow of real income (and on the costs of holding cash) and to only a vanishingly small extent on the one-shot change in wealth associated with the price-level change. With reference to long-run full equilibrium and to a population of immortal beings, then, the demand for cash balances does, after all, have the traditional unit elasticity. Patinkin's inelasticity relates only to mortals operating in less-than-infinite time periods. Substantially this point is made in G. C. Archibald and R. G. Lipsey, "Monetary and Value Theory: A Critique of Lange and Patinkin," *Review of Economic Studies*, XXVI (1), No. 69 (October, 1958), 1–22, esp. p. 9. This point seems to me to be less a refutation of Patinkin's argument than a spelling-out of something already implicit in it. Patinkin's emphasis is not on the degree of departure from unit elasticity (which may quickly become very slight) but on the distinction between an individual-experiment (portrayed in the demand curve for cash balances) and a market-experiment (portrayed in what he calls the "market-equilibrium curve"). Patinkin's discussion also helps show that the assumptions necessary to the quantity theory are less rigorous than traditionally supposed.

equilibrating process that would be touched off and the necessity and stability of the equilibrium price level. Incidentally, one of the further uses of contemplating the aggregate demand for cash balances at a disequilibrium price level is to understand the consequences of a government attempt to decree a disequilibrium price level, such as an attempt to decree a "roll-back" of an accomplished price inflation.

Another objection raised by Buchanan is that Patinkin's demand curve for money presupposes some definite existing supply of money. Supply influences demand. This fact not only is apparent from Patinkin's explanation of the less-than-unitary elasticity but also is explicitly stated by Patinkin. A doubling of the money supply would imply that the holders of the increased cash balances would feel richer than before at a not-yet-changed price level, and their demand curves not only for ordinary commodities but also for cash balances would shift to the right. The equilibrium supply-and-demand intersection would lie not only on a new money-supply curve but also on a new money-demand curve, indicating that the original demand curve was not a set of possible intersections with alternative supply curves. Patinkin gets into this alleged trouble because he draws an uncompensated demand curve, along which changes in the purchasing power of the money unit have wealth effects analogous to the income effects of price changes along an ordinary uncompensated Hicksian commodity demand curve. What Patinkin supposedly should have done instead is to devise some sort of compensated money demand curve, analogous to the Friedman-Marshall commodity demand curve, such that all points on it corresponded to a constant level of real wealth. This curve would consist of a set of conceivable intersections with various money supply curves and would, under traditional assumptions, have unit elasticity. Patinkin is of course aware of the uncompensated nature of his demand curve and is also aware of another type of curve that, under assumptions spelled out in admirable detail, would have the traditional unit elasticity. This other curve, which he calls the "market-equilibrium curve," expresses the comparative-static proposition that the equilibrium value of the purchasing power of the money unit is inversely proportional to the total money supply.

Patinkin makes perfectly clear what he is doing and, as Buchanan recognizes, cannot justly be accused of actual error. At worst he can be accused of an inexpedient approach conducive to error in the hands of persons less careful than himself. But this is a fuzzy charge—that a certain approach is not really erroneous, but conducive to error. Furthermore, an uncompensated money demand curve *is* useful: it is useful, for instance, in understanding the consequences of an attempt to "roll back" prices by decree. Precisely one of the difficulties is the fact that at a rolled-back price level, total real wealth (including the purchasing power of cash balances) would appear to the members of the community to be larger than it in fact could be under the objectively existing supply conditions. In understanding why disequilibrium price levels are untenable, we also understand the necessity of the equilibrium price level. There is more to economics than comparative statics: there is also the matter of equilibrating processes.

The question of expediency must be considered with special reference to Patinkin's listing of the supply of money among the factors affecting the demand for money. As the Chicagoans insist, it is admittedly desirable to apportion demand factors and supply factors into categories as separate and distinct as possible.[29] But what is to be done when the nature of the real world makes complete separation impossible? The only demand curve that never shifts is a curve—

[29] "We want demand functions precisely in order to analyze the effect of changes in supply; and they can be useful for this purpose only if the factors affecting demand can be regarded as largely independent of the factors affecting supply. We want demand analysis to be so constructed as to fit together and be consistent with supply analysis; yet we also want the two to be largely independent." Friedman, *Journal of Political Economy*, June, 1954, p. 265.

or hypersurface, rather—taking account of everything imaginable among the determinants of quantity demanded. A standard two-dimensional price-quantity demand curve is conceptually obtained by taking a cross-section or slice through a multidimensional hyperspace. To seek a curve that stays put on a two-dimensional price-quantity slice despite shifts in supply is to chase a will o' the wisp; the reason is the hard fact of reality that everything does depend on everything else. Shifts in price-quantity curves are an expedient necessary for dealing on flat sheets of paper with matters involving general interdependence. Of course, when this interdependence is negligible, as when we are dealing with a commodity without significant substitutes or complements and on which buyers spend only a small fraction of their incomes, then the shifts of the demand curve on a two-dimensional diagram are too small to worry about; and for practical purposes we can regard the demand curve as staying fixed in the face of supply changes. When interdependence is important, however, and when demand factors and supply factors cannot be kept substantially separate, the most straightforward way of dealing with this fact of reality is to follow Patinkin in recognizing that supply itself influences the position of the demand curve. The rival Chicago approach seems at least as awkward and at least as bedeviled with concepts of questionable operational meaning.

It is ironic, incidentally, that the criticism of Patinkin for allowing supply to affect demand should come from the very methodological camp which itself insists on building supply considerations directly into the demand curve. For this is what the Chicagoans are doing when they insist on constant-real-income or constant-production-possibility demand curves and criticize a Hicksian demand curve on the grounds that a fall in price along it implies an increase in real income which is incompatible with supply conditions.[30]

V. USEFULNESS AND OPERATIONALITY CONCLUSION

One further aspect of the Chicago methodology remains to be considered. The Chicagoans repeatedly purport to compare the practical "usefulness" of different varieties of demand curve.[31] Though the present paper has so far uncritically adopted such references to "usefulness," I must now confess that, except perhaps in special contexts, I honestly do not know what it means to make practical "use" of one demand curve rather than of another. Sometimes Friedman seems to be claiming practical usefulness for his demand concept only in comparison with a Walrasian function into which, in principle, all prices individually enter. For the analysis of concrete real-world situations, it is of course impossible to draw up actual Walrasian demand functions; any demand curve for practical employment must be a partial curve. But as far as the choice between a Friedman demand curve and an ordinary Hicksian demand curve is concerned, it is hard to see what is meant by employing one rather than the other. Suppose a railroad hires a consulting economist to predict how the volume of railroad travel would respond to a cut in fares. Just what would it mean to tell this economist that the Friedman-Marshall demand curve is more "useful" and that he should

[30] So convinced is Friedman of the necessity for keeping real income constant along the demand curve that in one passage he interprets even the Hicksian construction as attempting to do this, though unsuccessfully. The real issue between rival concepts of the demand curve centers, he says, on the definition of the real income to be kept constant. The Hicksian construction goes astray by inappropriately defining real income as purchasing power over all goods except the particular one for which the demand curve is drawn. *Journal of Political Economy*, June, 1954, p. 262. This is certainly a strained reinterpretation of the forthright Hicksian specification that *money* income and all prices but one, and *not* real income, are to be supposed constant (in the individual-experiment sense, of course).

[31] Friedman concedes, for example, that the Hicksian approach is not actually "wrong." Though "formally valid," it is open to the objection of not being the most "useful" approach. *Ibid.*

work with it rather than with a Hicksian curve? Can the economist really bother with deciding whether or not to suppose that the fare cut is accompanied by rises in other prices so as to keep constant the real incomes of passengers and potential passengers?

Similarly, what would it mean to claim greater operationality for the Friedman-Marshall demand curve on the grounds that it unequivocally predicts an inverse price-quantity relation, whereas the Hicksian demand theorists hedge this prediction with reference to the Giffen Paradox?[32] The Chicagoans, correspondingly, could always explain away the failure of one of their own predictions on the grounds that real income had not been kept constant as it should have been. And, of course, anyone venturing a prediction could always take refuge in postulated changes in tastes, expectations, and so forth.

If a demand curve is to be conceived of as a set of predictions of the various price-quantity equilibria that would actually be established and observed under various supply situations, then it is appropriate to doubt whether opportunities to keep real incomes constant by compensating price variations can be created and whether the techniques of econometrics will ever develop to the point where it makes sense to draw a distinction between actual predictions by means of a Hicksian demand curve and actual predictions by means of a Friedman-Marshall demand curve. The overwhelming econometric difficulties in the way of actually drawing up one or both curves are not the main issue. More fundamentally, there is no such thing as *the* Hicksian or *the* Friedman-Marshall relation between price and quantity demanded of a given commodity. The amount per time period that buyers would demand at any given price depends on how long a time period buyers are conceived of as having to adjust to a newly established price, on the price history of the commodity, and on innumerable other circumstances.

So far, this paper has uncritically tolerated the notion of the demand curve. Usually there is no reason to stress something that most economists are no doubt aware of anyway: that the real world never contains an actual entity corresponding to *the* demand curve for a commodity. Here, however, the point is relevant. Rather than as a set of numerical predictions, a demand curve might better be regarded as a pedagogical device for helping students grasp the inverse price-quantity relation asserted by the Law of Demand. A demand curve is an aid to straight thinking (helping avoid confusion, for example, between changes in demand and in quantity demanded). The demand curve—or rather the Law of Demand which it portrays, together with the Law of Supply—helps us understand why a free market tends to clear itself (and seeing this depends on seeing what forces would be at work in a disequilibrium situation in which buyers' and sellers' plans did *not* mesh). The generalizations portrayed by demand and supply curves enter into explanations of the rationing and production-motivating functions of price. They help us understand how prices act as signals transmitting relevant information to decision-makers and how an economy without central planning can nevertheless be a co-ordinated economy. They help us understand, qualitatively and without numerical precision, what would happen to price and quantity when tastes or technology or taxes underwent specified changes. They help us understand the consequences of price ceilings and floors. We can go a long way in economic theory with a mere knowledge of the signs of partial derivatives. Of course, it is all the better, in definite histori-

[32] Actually, I do not regard mention of the Giffen Paradox as a mere empty hedge. While I never expect to hear of an adequately documented real-world instance of it, the phenomenon could conceivably occur; and in being able to explain a range of potential phenomena to this extent broader than the range explainable by the Chicago demand theory, the Hicksian construction is superior. The assertion that an observed positive association between price and quantity demanded is an instance of the Giffen Paradox need not be a metaphysical proposition. It can be meaningful: evidence can be obtained by questioning the persons involved. The legitimacy of this kind of evidence has already been alluded to.

cal situations, to have a pretty good idea of the magnitudes as well; the consulting economist for the railroad would certainly think so. But even this last consideration does not justify regarding demand curves as objectively existing things.

The Chicagoans sometimes appear to fall into just the non-operational metaphysics against which they warn other economists. In particular, their worries about which is the correct or most useful conception of the demand curve seem to imply that a substantive issue is involved and that a demand curve is something which objectively exists and whose properties should be rightly rather than wrongly perceived. To suppose so is to verge on the fallacy of "conceptual realism," the "reification" of concepts. Of course, Friedman implicitly disavows reification and implicitly recognizes that theoretical concepts, far from corresponding to actual things are but tools employed in the gathering and systematization of data.[33] In practice, however, the Chicagoans sometimes seem to forget this.

The foregoing survey of Chicago demand methodology provides new support for a familiar proposition that K. Klappholz and J. Agassi have recently restated with eloquence. They deplore "the illusion that there can exist in any science methodological rules the mere adoption of which will hasten its progress" and warn against the impatient "belief that, if only economists adopted this or that methodological rule, the road ahead would at least be cleared (and possibly the traffic would move briskly along it)." They recognize that methodological dogmas can even retard progress. This is particularly true, I might add, of methodological taboos. As the Chicagoans themselves have impressively illustrated in their work apart from propounding methodological advice, it is far more constructive to show the actual application of particular methods to particular problems: success speaks for itself. On the other hand, there is no warrant for *exclusive* insistence on particular methods, successful though they may have been in answering particular questions. Klappholz and Agassi will heed only the general "exhortation to be critical and always ready to subject one's hypotheses to critical scrutiny." Additional rules to reinforce this general maxim are "likely to be futile and possibly harmful."[34]

[33] Cf., e.g., *Essays*, p. 57.

[34] "Methodological Prescriptions in Economics," *Economica*, XXVI (new ser.; February, 1959), 60, 74.

Part IV
The State of Contemporary Demand Theory

16 Theories of Consumers Behaviour: A Cynical View[1]

E. J. Mishan

Since the popularization in the Eighteen Seventies of the concept of marginal utility, theories of consumer's behaviour have come to occupy one of the central positions in that corpus of economic analysis which, before the war at any rate, was customarily referred to as the theory of value. It is surely a tribute to the influence of a powerful tradition raised on the authority of such names as Jevons, Marshall and Edgeworth, and, more recently, Hicks and Samuelson, to mention only those in the English-speaking assemblage, that although frequently questioned and sometimes challenged, theories of consumer's behaviour continue to form a necessary part of the syllabus of all students specializing in economics. And if with the older techniques, marginal utility and indifference-preference fields, the interest in such theories eventually appeared to languish, the invention of revealed preference has revived our spirits wonderfully by providing us with a rather impressive technique in which to express familiar theorems and in which to carry on the staple controversies of old.

I must, therefore, reconcile myself to being regarded as something of a killjoy when I propose that we abandon all this; that we seek to dislodge such theorems from their hold on our imagination and to face the fact that though fascinating in themselves they form an unnecessary adornment on the apparatus of economic analysis. Recognizing the strong intellectual vested interest in the current doctrines I cannot, of course, expect the reader to fall in with these proposals unless cogent reasons are adduced for them. To that extent this paper constitutes an essay in persuasion. My aim is to convince the reader that, after all the display of technical virtuosity associated with such theorems, there is nothing the practising economist can take away with him to help him come to grips with the complexity of the real world. Indeed, he would be no worse off if he remained ignorant of all theories of consumer's behaviour, accepting the obviously indispensable " Law of Demand " on trust[2].

[1] I am deeply indebted to W. J. Corlett for pointing out several errors in a first draft of this paper.

[2] It is well known that Gustav Cassell rejected the current marginal utility theory of Marshall on the grounds, among other things, that it was quite superfluous in economic science. See his *Theory of Social Economy*, Vol. I (London, 1932), pp. 80 *et seq*.

Reprinted from *Economica,* Vol. XXVIII (February, 1961), pp. 1–11, by permission of the publisher and author.

I

As a matter of chronological order and convenience we shall examine the propositions arising from Hicks' indifference -preference hypothesis[1] and from Samuelson's revealed preference hypothesis in that order.

The explicit assumptions in *Value and Capital* are (i) that utility is any monotonic increasing function of all goods —measurement is ordinal, not cardinal—and (ii) that the individual maximizes satisfaction subject to his budget constraint. Tacit assumptions are (iii) transitivity, and (iv) convexity of the indifference surfaces.[2] The chief propositions which, in their more general formulation, may be derived mathematically from this set of assumptions are to be found in a few pages of the appendix to that work.[3] They are (a) that the substitution effect on the quantity of good x of a change in its price is always negative; (*b*) the rate of substitution of a good x in response to a change in the price of y is equal to the rate of substitution of a good y in response to a change in the price of x; (c) in response to a rise in the price of x alone, the sum of the substitution effects on all goods other than x, weighted by their corresponding prices, is equal and opposite to the substitution effect on x weighted by its price; (d) if we divide the number of goods into two groups, the sum of the rates of substitution of all goods in the first group, each with respect to a change in the price of every good belonging to the second group, is always positive, provided that each such effect is weighted by the product of the corresponding pair of prices, and (e) the sum of the changes in all prices times

[1] Several of the propositions to be found in *Value & Capital* have been re-stated in Hicks' *Revision of Demand Theory* using the new language of price-quantity data. With my present aim in mind there is nothing to be gained by making any appraisal of Hicks' second thoughts on this subject or in trying to gauge his present position. I shall take the version given in *Value & Capital* as fully representative of the indifference-preference hypothesis as originally proposed by Allen and Hicks in *Economica*, February, 1934, (and anticipated, as it transpired, by Slutsky in 1915).

[2] In the appendix to his *Value & Capital*, Hicks derives what he calls the Fundamental Equation of Value Theory:

$$\frac{\partial x_s}{\partial p_r} = -X_r \frac{\partial x_s}{\partial Y} + \mu \frac{U_{rs}}{U}$$

In the special case of the response of the good x_r to the price p_r, the last term in the equation becomes U_{rr}/U which, it has been shown, is always negative. This negative term carries the interpretation that the response of the consumer's demand for x_r to a change in the price of x_r, all other prices remaining constant, is always negative in so far as substitution alone is concerned.

Since a negative U_{rr}/U is in this appendix, a corollary of the sufficient conditions for a (local) maximum, it was inferred that these conditions—referred to by Hicks as " the stability conditions " of the consumer's equilibrium—ensured the negative substitution effect and that, therefore, convexity of the indifference surfaces was not an independent postulate but in fact could be inferred from the " stability conditions ". This, however, is not the case. The adoption of the calculus, which does not lend itself to corner solutions of a constrained extremum, is to be interpreted as a clear *assumption* that the solution is at a point of tangency; in economic terms, that the individual purchases, in general, some of all the goods. Since the condition of a tangency solution to the constrained maximum in question is convexity of the indifference surfaces, the latter must be considered as an independent assumption of the hypothesis. The negative substitution effect is, then, *not* inferred; it is a postulate of the model.

[3] *Value and Capital* (2nd Edition), pp. 305-311.

the corresponding change in their substitution effects is always negative—the general statement of the negative substitution effect.[1]

We do well to notice from the start that all these implications involve substitution terms only and hold only for small movements about the individual's " equilibrium ". If there are income effects—and they can hardly be avoided in any real situation—the resultant direction of response in any of the above propositions is no longer certain. For this reason, if for no other, such implications are difficult to put to the test. This difficulty increases if, as is usual, our test draws upon aggregative data, for a good which is observed to have a zero income effect for the whole population may not have a zero effect for each individual. And, if we are to be strict in our test, it is the latter condition which must be met if we are to measure unadulterated substitution effects.

However, if such propositions as these are difficult to test it is not likely that the practising economist suffers much frustration on this account. Other than (a), which forms the basis of the demand curve and which we examine later, such propositions do not provide the kind of knowledge that the economist interested in prognostication is likely to be seeking.[2] Inasmuch as he is interested in the consequences which stem from changes in one or two variables on one or two other variables, such propositions—even if he sees fit to ignore the impact of income effects—are of little use to him. In (c), (d), and (e), for instance, he cannot predict the substitution effect on a chosen good given its change of price unless he already has knowledge of the substitution effects on all other goods with respect to the prices that have changed: to predict anything he must have discovered almost everything to begin with. It is not surprising that there is no evidence of any attempts to make practical use of such propositions.

Another group of implications in terms of elasticities, though of comparable peculiarity, can also be derived from the same hypothesis, and in particular from the assumption that the individual's total expenditure is equal to his income and from the implication that, for the individual, demand functions are homogeneous of degree zero in prices and income. Some of these describe the relationships between individual elasticities and those of the market; e.g., that the income elasticity of the *market* demand for a good is the averages of the elasticities of the *individuals*, each such elasticity weighted by the income of

[1] Using Hicks' notation in the appendix to *Value and Capital*, *loc. cit.*, where in general x_{rs} is the consumer's substitution of a good s in response to a change in the price of a good r, these propositions may be represented as:
(a) $x_{rr} < O$,
(b) $x_{rs} = x_{sr}$, (c) $\sum_{s=1}^{n} p_s x_{rs} = O$, (d) $\sum_{s=1}^{m} \sum_{s=m+1}^{n} p_r p_s x_{rs} > O$, and (e) $\sum_{r=1}^{n} dx_r \, dp_r < O$.

[2] (*b*) might be thought fairly simple to test. The idea is simple enough, but we must remember that we want pure substitution effects for two goods whose prices change when all others remain and that, moreover, the theorem holds for the consistent individual whose tastes remain unchanged, and not for the market.

the corresponding individual. This is obvious, perhaps, but of little use to the economist who wishes to obtain a measure of the market elasticity. Other such propositions trace a relationship for the individual between price elasticities, between income elasticities, or between both. Typical are propositions such as (a) the sum of the income elasticities of demand for each good in the individual's budget, weighted by the fraction of total expenditure on it, sums to unity, or (b) that the sum of the elasticities of demand for a good x with respect to the price of each good in question is equal, and opposite in sign, to the income elasticity of demand for x.[1]

The comments on the previous group of propositions apply with equal force to this group. It may be urged that such relationships serve as a rough check on the statistical estimation of elasticities. But the number of other elasticities required in order to check the one reduces the practical value of such a check to something approaching zero. Even if we play down the problem of the probable errors in the estimation of a host of elasticities, the cost in time and effort of calculating the relevant elasticities for each good, or for each group of goods, in the economy would be incomparably greater than the cost of direct applications of any statistical refinements.

II

Since the term revealed preference was introduced into economics by Samuelson in 1938, there has been a proliferation of papers making use of its basic technique. One may legitimately surmise that it was the fascination of the relational algebra which inspired most of the contributions rather than an inherent interest in economic theory. At all events, the economic content of such contributions has, in the main, been slight. Indeed, in so far as the subject matter of economics is taken to be a study of market behaviour, revealed preference has yielded no more useful empirical implications than the indifference-preference hypothesis that preceded it.

The term, revealed preference, is not altogether satisfactory since the basic notion is merely that of consistent choice. If an individual chooses a batch of goods Q_2 rather than the batch Q_1 in circumstances in which both batches are available, provided his tastes remain unaltered consistency demands that in such circumstances he never chooses Q_1. This somewhat tautological statement is translated into an index number theorem—a theorem couched in terms of prices and quantities, since these are the only data we observe directly. According to this theorem, if we observe that $\Sigma P_2Q_2 \geq \Sigma P_2Q_1$, where Q_1 and Q_2 are the batches of goods chosen in the I and II situations in which respectively the price sets P_1 and P_2 prevail we can infer from our observation that if both batches of goods were available

[1] For a fairly exhaustive account of elasticity relationships, see H. Wold's *Synthesis of Pure Demand Analysis*, especially pp. 90-108.

he would choose Q_2. In other words, since he would not choose Q_1, $\Sigma P_1 Q_1 \geqq \Sigma P_1 Q_2$. That is, we should also observe $\Sigma P_1 Q_1 < \Sigma P_1 Q_2$

The idea of consistent choice[1] and the index number theorem derived therefrom are what we start with. How far do they take us?

Developments have in fact branched off in three directions. Two appear to lead nowhere in particular though the traffic along these routes is still heavy. The third development leads directly to a demand theorem of sorts but, alas, not one of much use to the economist.

Of the two developments which I have suggested are blind alleys, the first constitutes an endeavour to derive from the basic idea of consistent choice in alternative budget situations, a set of indifference surfaces for the individual having the familiar properties of ordinal ranking, convexity, and non-intersection. This has been accomplished by Little, by Samuelson, and by Houthakker, in each case in a slightly different way from the others.[2] The question of integrability arose as, indeed, it did in the indifference-preference hypothesis, for unless the integrability conditions are satisfied there is, apparently, no assurance that the individual might not contradict himself. In the event, and after some bewilderment, Houthakker, adopting an axiom of " semi-transitivity "—an axiom which asserts that if batch I is revealed preferred to batch 2, batch 2 revealed preferred to batch 3, and so on down to batch *n*-1 revealed preferred to batch *n*, then batch *n* cannot be revealed preferred to batch 1—deduces transitivity, and therefore integrability, for the indifference surfaces which he generates.

That this integrability issue should have arisen at all, points to a prepossession with mathematical problems rather than with economic ones. After all, if the real concern in our model is that economic man does not contradict himself, why should we not demand this attribute of him from the outset? What argument can there be to prevent our requiring of all the economic men we shall have occasion to deal with that their choices be transitive (and, therefore, consistent)? If we can go along with Houthakker and slip in semi-transitivity to help us along, on what methodological grounds are we inhibited from introducing the axiom of full transitivity? Whether or not there is a convincing answer to this question[3] this issue—apart from some

[1] Unless we seek to ' rationalize ' the individual's behaviour, the mere fact of choosing Q_2 rather than Q_1 does not oblige us to interpret this choice as revealing a preference for Q_2. Indeed, this recklessly non-operational interpretation has long been abandoned by those concerned to preserve their methodological chastity. In deference to established custom, however, the term revealed preference continues to be used rather than a more accurate form of designation such as revealed choice.

[2] I. M. D. Little, " A Reformulation of the Theory of Consumer's Behaviour," *Oxford Economic Papers*, January 1949.

P. A. Samuelson, " Consumption Theory in Terms of Revealed Preference," *Economica*, November 1948.

H. S. Houthakker, " Revealed Preference and the Utility Function," *Economica*, May 1950.

[3] It is surely paring things too fine with Occam's razor to save on an axiom—or, rather, half an axiom, since Houthakker starts off with the axiom of " semi-transitivity "—at a cost of several pages of close reasoning when, in the end, the implications for consumer's behaviour, slight enough as we shall see, are no different.

bickering on the side lines as to how well Houthakker managed the proof[1]—appears to be at an end. Assuming for the time being that an indifference map is a desirable construct, was it ever necessary?

The advantages of constructing an indifference map from the axioms of revealed preference rather than from those of the indifference-preference hypothesis of consumer's behaviour, or from a direct description of the properties of such a map, has been argued most lengthily by Little.[2] He demonstrates a method of constructing what is, in effect, a system of indifference curves from hypothetical observations of price-quantity data using only four assumptions—fewer, he alleges, than are required in the Hicksian model.[3] He is emphatic, however, in calling the curve he generates a " behaviour line "—a boundary above which all batches are preferred to some given batch, say Q_1, and below which all batches are rejected for Q_1—since the concept of an indifference curve is rejected by him as non-operational. Indifferent behaviour, he states, is not observed in the market.[4]

Now it is true, at least for single choice situations to which we confine ourselves in the theory of demand, that we cannot observe indifferent behaviour. But then we are not required to observe it. In the implications for market behaviour—which behaviour we *do* observe—indifference certainly does not feature. After all, the implications we seek to observe from the indifference-preference hypothesis are always of a price-quantity nature, in principle observable enough, and in any case no different from the implications which are derivable from the model constructed by Little. However, since we can generate a consistent set of indifference surfaces using the axioms of revealed preference, it follows that all those implications which flow from the indifference-preference analysis, and which I have suggested are rather sterile, may be said to flow also from the revealed preference hypothesis.

[1] See, for instance, H. A. John Green, " Some Logical Relations in Revealed Preference Theory," *Economica*, November 1957, and Peter Newman, " A Further Note on Revealed Preference," *Economica*, May 1959.

[2] *Loc. Cit.*

[3] Little's assumptions are (i) the individual never chooses a smaller collection if a larger one is available; (ii) all collections which are available are chosen in some price-income situation; (iii) if the individual chooses collection A to B, he will always choose A to B; (iv) transitivity of choices. Presumably (iii) can be subsumed under (iv), and, as for (ii), his argument seems to call rather for an axiom which asserts that in any price-income situation one, and only one, collection of goods is chosen, which is more restrictive than (ii).

Hicks' explicit assumptions are (i) that utility is any monotonic increasing function of all goods, and (ii) that the individual maximizes subject to his budget constraint. Tacit assumptions are (iii) transitivity, and (iv) convexity.

The demonstrations of both Hicks and Little also require the assumption of differentiability of the utility function of the first and second order.

On the test of counting axioms, then, Little appears to win by a nose, having one axiom the fewer. It is difficult to be impressed by this.

[4] Little further alleges that the index number criterion of revealed preference is " fundamental," indifference curves being derivable therefrom. The derivation of indifference curves from index number data does not, however, suffice to bear out this contention. In any event, Hicks, in his " Valuation of the Social Income " (*Economica*, May 1940) shows how the index number theorem may be derived from the logic of indifference curve analysis.

III

The second branch of development of the revealed preference technique has forked off into welfare economics. Since I wish to limit the scope of my arguments to positive economics, little will be said here about this development. On the one hand, there have been attempts to state anew propositions which have been known for more than half a century, but in terms of consistent choice,[1] or else to attire in a panoply of symbolism contributions of little more than footnote stature.[2] On the other hand, since hypothetical price-quantity data is employed directly in this technique, it is not surprising that we have witnessed attempts to use index numbers as indicators of change in the welfare of the community.[3] From the trend of recent contributions, however, it seems fairly clear that the revealed preference technique adds nothing new to welfare economics. It provides only alternative formulations of familiar welfare propositions.

IV

Finally, revealed preference opens up a direct route to the demand curve, the original *raison d'être* of theories of consumer's behaviour. The best known theorem is that of Samuelson[4] which builds on the axioms (i) that the individual behaves consistently, (ii) that he chooses

[1] For a recent instance, see Kelvin Lancaster, " Welfare Propositions in Terms of Consistency and Expanded Choice," *Economic Journal*, September 1958.

[2] As an example, the proposition that a system of taxes which causes the ratio of the commodity prices to deviate yet further from the individual's no-tax optimum, further reduces his welfare. For an attempted rigorous proof of this proposition see McManus, " A Theorem on Undercompensated Price Changes", *Economica*, November 1959. That this theorem has no application to the community at large, even within the familiar static analysis, may be gathered from my paper, " A Reconsideration of the Principles of Resource Allocation ", *Economica*, November 1957.

[3] Unless such index numbers propositions can be generalized successfully so as to encompass the community at large they are, however, of little use to economists. Yet the only serious attempt to face up to the difficulties of making the transition from the individual to society was made by Hicks in his " Valuation of Social Income " paper (*loc. cit.*). It was a gallant and ingenious attempt but, for all that, it failed. Let us recall, briefly, why.

If the index numbers revealed that $\Sigma P_2Q_2 \geq \Sigma P_2Q_1$ then, according to Hicks, the welfare situation in Q_2 was to be regarded as an improvement for the community compared with Q_1. For with the P_2 prices—the prices ruling in the Q_2 situation—each person in the community can be made worse off with the Q_1 collection of goods than he would be in the Q_2 situation. However, after the controversy which flared up eight years later in *Economica*, in which Kuznets, Hicks, and Little took part (and which controversy was to some extent summarized in Samuelson's " Evaluation of Real Income ", *Oxford Economic Papers*, January 1950), it transpired that this criterion was no less vulnerable than the original Kaldor-Hicks compensation test of which, indeed, it was but a variant. Thus, owing to the intimate connection between welfare distribution and the relative valuation of goods, data which revealed the simultaneous existence of $\Sigma P_2Q_2 \geq \Sigma P_2Q_1$ and of $\Sigma P_1Q_1 \geq \Sigma P_1Q_2$ pointed to no inconsistency in the behaviour of individuals in the community. In consequence, however, no unambiguous index of an improvement in welfare emerged either.

This matter is further explained and illustrated in my " Survey of Welfare Economics, 1939-1959 ", *Economic Journal*, June 1960, p. 231, n. 2.

[4] " Consumption Theorems in Terms of Overcompensation rather than Indifference Comparisons ", *Economica*, February 1953.

only one collection in every budget situation, and (iii) that he prefers more goods to less. It states that if an individual buys more of a good when his income rises he will buy less of it when the price of that good rises. The diagrammatic exposition is straightforward enough and will suffice for the purpose in view. In Fig. 1, the individual is purchasing

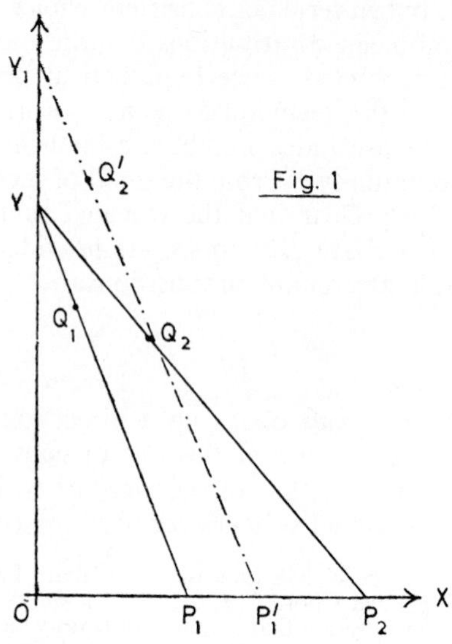

a batch of goods Q_2 along his budget line YP_2. The price of X rises to P_1, the new budget line facing him being YP_1. We are to show that Q_1, that batch of goods chosen in this new situation, is to the left of Q_2.

First, " overcompensate " the individual for the rise in price of X by giving him just enough additional income, Y_1Y, to enable him to continue purchasing Q_2 if he wishes. His opportunities can therefore be represented by Y_1P_1', parallel to YP_1, which passes through Q_2.

Since Q_2 was chosen to all other points in the area YOP_2, he cannot forgo Q_2 for a point along Q_2P_1'. He either stays at Q_2 or else takes up a position along Q_2Y_1. Suppose he does the latter and chooses the batch Q_2'. We now subtract the original compensation Y_1Y, so that he is faced with YP_1 again, the original position with the price of X raised. His income effect on X being assumed positive, he reduces his consumption of X and therefore chooses a position Q_1, along YP_1, that is to the left of Q_2'.

Since the amount of X in Q_1 is, by assumption, less than that in Q_2', and the amount of X in Q_2' is, by consistent behaviour, less than or equal to that in Q_2, the amount of X in Q_1 is less than that in Q_2. *Q.E.D.*

We may, in passing, compare this theorem with an analogous one derivable from the individual's indifference map. An exact income compensation now being possible, the form it takes is somewhat less restrictive: if the price of a good rises less of it will be bought by the individual if its income effect is *non-negative.*[1]

V

We cannot fail to notice that such demand theorems are conditional theorems, not universal ones. If the income effect is not positive—

[1] In his review article, " Revising Demand Theory ", *Economica*, November 1957, Lancaster has suggested that this kind of theorem can be derived from the consideration of consistency alone and offers a similar proof which omits Samuelson's axiom (iii), above, the so-called non-saturation axiom, in this way allowing for the possibility that the individual may choose a collection of goods *inside* the budget frontier. His argument can be depicted graphically in much the same way as Samuelson's argument, which procedure it follows.

We start the individual with a budget line YP_1 in Fig. 2, but, since we have discarded the non-saturation axiom, we have him choose q_1 *inside* his budget frontier. The price of X now falls to p_2. We must show that the new collection of goods he buys, q_2, contains more of X; i.e., q_2 is to the right of q_1.

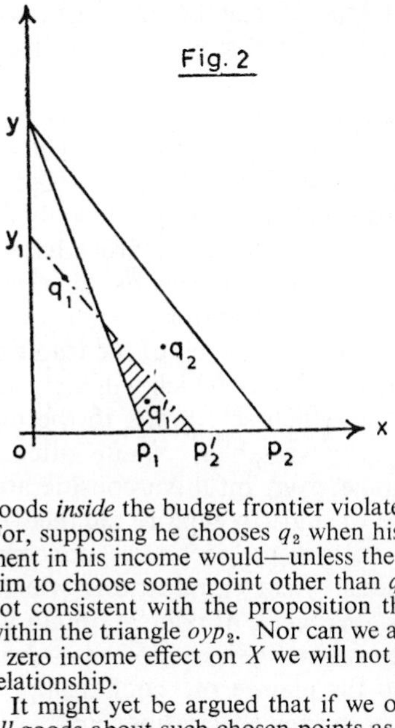

Fig. 2

We subtract from his income an amount equal to yy_1 so that he can just continue to buy q_1 if he wishes. y_1p_2' is, therefore, drawn parallel to yp_2 and passes through q_1. Consistency of choice requires that the individual either remain at q_1 or choose a point q_1' within the shaded triangle. Suppose he chooses q_1'. We now restore yy_1 of income. Since we assume observation of a positive income effect for X, he chooses some batch of goods, q_2 outside the shaded triangle and to the right of q_1'.

Since q_2 is to the right of q_1' which itself is equal to or to the right of q_1, q_2 must be to the right of q_1.

However, on reflection it can be appreciated that the choice of a collection of goods *inside* the budget frontier violates the axiom of consistency in such a theorem. For, supposing he chooses q_2 when his budget frontier is yp_2, a small enough increment in his income would—unless the income effect were zero on all goods—impel him to choose some point other than q_2 inside the frontier yp_2. But this behaviour is not consistent with the proposition that he chooses q_2 above all other collections within the triangle oyp_2. Nor can we allow a zero effect on all goods, for if we allow a zero income effect on X we will not be able to generate the inverse price-quantity relationship.

It might yet be argued that if we observe *discontinuities* in the income effect on *all* goods about such chosen points as q_1 and q_2, we might yet reconcile consistency with a choice of goods within the budget frontier. Whether so peculiarly contingent a theorem is worth any attention is a moot point. For, although consistency might be preserved if such comprehensive discontinuities were in fact observed, we now have to put up with the implication that *not all reductions* in the price of X lead to an increase in the quantity purchased.

If, however, as all empirical evidence suggests, we can ignore the suggestion of discontinuities in the income effects on all goods, we are left with an inconsistency in choice when we drop the non-saturation axiom. Apparently then, the requirement of consistency in this theorem relegates non-saturation from an axiom to an implication—unless, that is, the individual does choose a collection of goods along his budget frontier he is not behaving consistently.

or, in the one derivable from the indifference map, the income effect is negative—we can say nothing of the response of the individual to a change in the price of a single good.

More important yet, such theorems have reference only to the individual. Even if we managed to derive downward-sloping demand curves for X for each individual in the economy, it does not follow that the market demand curve for X slopes downward. True, the frequently invoked clause of *ceteris paribus* lays it down that for the market demand curve all other prices remain unchanged. But while no exception need be taken to this procedure in so far as the demand curve of the individual is concerned, it cannot in general be maintained for a market demand curve without violating logical necessity. If the price of X falls on the market, we cannot hold all other prices constant unless the supply curves of all other goods are infinitely elastic. In general, then, product prices alter. So also do factor prices; which is to say that the distribution of real income in the community is altered. Though each individual have a downward-sloping demand curve for this good X, redistributions of real income can be envisaged which issue, for some range of prices, in an upward-sloping demand curve for the market.

We may be justified in believing that this contingency is highly unlikely; that market demand curves are always, or almost always, downward-sloping. However, we are constrained to acknowledge that this supposition in no way derives from our theorizing, but only from intuition and observation. In consequence, then, we are advised to join hands with Gustav Cassel and begin our analysis of the demand side, in the theory of value, with the " law of demand ".

This sort of disappointment is not unusual in much of the traditional theory of value. We begin by aiming at a theory which will yield some transparently modest implication—one which sets limits to the direction of change in the price or quantity variables. Quite often, we already suspect the direction of change from intuitive considerations or from casual observation. Yet once we start to explore the theory we discover, to our chagrin, that the customary postulates concerning behaviour, technology and institutions, yield implications which in fact cover all the logical possibilities. We may, of course, obtain what we are looking for by imposing more restrictive assumptions—though recourse to this treatment is open to the charge of ' cooking up ' the theory to account for the observed or suspected relationships. Alternatively, we can escape this impasse by explicit use of the taxonomic method which in effect makes our theorems conditional upon the prior fulfilment of one or more particular provisions, a procedure which, though frequently necessary, obviously limits the applicability of economic theory and increases the difficulty of testing it.

In the last resort we might think to justify theories of consumer's behaviour as useful exercises in economic thinking, in which case even manifestly false theories might qualify in our syllabus. A less exceptionable argument might be that when all is said and done the indifference-preference hypothesis does provide us with some very fruitful suggestions. The distinction between substitution and wealth effects, for instance, runs right through price economics. It helps to organize our thinking on complex questions.

I have sympathy with this view, but it cannot be decisive. For until we have tested the implications of those theorems which utilize this distinction we cannot legitimately vouch for the advantages of having our thoughts organized in this particular way.

The London School of Economics.

17

Observed Consumption Patterns and the Utility Function

E. G. Furubotn

I. Introduction: Nonnegative Consumption and Equilibrium.

In the standard exposition of the theory of choice, the ordinal utility function is specified in highly general form as:

$$U = \Phi (q_1 , q_2 , ..., q_r) . \tag{1}$$

We understand from (1) that an individual's satisfaction (U) depends on the amounts of the different commodities ($q_1 , q_2 . ,, q_r$) he consumes per period, but, beyond this, the equation conveys relatively little concrete information. While there is broad agreement that the utility function is non-additive (1), its precise functional form is left open. Indeed, if the ordinal property is to be preserved, (1) cannot be unique; any increasing monotonic transformation of the original function must constitute an acceptable utility index. What prevents equation (1) from being completely neutral and devoid of empirical content is the assumption of strict convexity (2).

This last characteristic, of course, plays a key role in the analysis of consumer demand. The basic formal problem is to maximize (1) subject to the budget constraint:

$$y^0 - \sum_{i=1}^{r} p_i q_i = 0 . \tag{2}$$

(1) The basic position here is well known. However, there has been increasing interest in additive functions over the last decade. See: G. J. STIGLER, « The Development of Utility Theory. II », *Journal of Political Economy*, LVIII, Oct. 1950, 373-96. G. W. NUTTER, « On the Independence of Utility of Product Groups », *Review of Economics and Statistics*, XXXVIII, Nov. 1956, 484-86. R. H. STROTZ, « The Empirical Implications of a Utility Tree », *Econometrica*, 25, April 1957, 269-80. W. M. GORMAN, « Separable Utility and Aggregation », *Econometrica*, 27, July 1959, 469-81. H. S. HOUTHAKKER, « Additive Preferences », *Econometrica*, 28, April 1960, 244-57. H. A. GREEN, « Direct Additivity and Consumers' Behavior », *Oxford Economic Papers*, 13, June 1961, 132-36. A. P. BARTEN, « Consumer Demand Functions under Conditions of Almost Additive Preferences », *Econometrica*, 32, Jan.-April 1964, 1-38.

(2) This is the usual assumption and its presence makes possible the derivation of single-valued demand functions. Other less stringent assumptions can be employed; indeed the empirical justification for strict convexity is not assured. See: W. M. GORMAN, « Convex Indifference Curves and Diminishing Marginal Utility », *Journal of Political Economy*, LXV, Feb. 1957, 40-50. J. ROTHENBERG, « Non-Convexity, Aggregation, and Pareto Optimality », *Journal of Political Economy*, LXVIII, Oct. 1960, 435-68.

Reprinted from *Metroeconomica*, Vol. XIX (January–April, 1967), pp. 42–61, by permission of the publisher.

Strict convexity of the utility function insures that the second-order conditions for the maximum will hold. Then, provided the first-order conditions are also met, an equilibrium solution for the consumer can be found. However, the methods of the calculus do not necessarily lead to an economically meaningful solution; some of the « optimal » quantities may be negative [3]). To secure useful results (while viewing the consumer as a buyer), a series of additional restrictions have to be imposed:

$$q_i \geq 0 \,, \qquad i = 1\,, 2, \ldots, r\,. \tag{3}$$

The commodity set which satisfies both the first- and second-order conditions *and* (3) is the one usually discussed by traditional theory; the consumer's choice of such a set is viewed as the normal outcome of the optimization process.

The equilibrium just described is familiar enough, but one if its implications deserves notice. If things are as stated, the consumer must be expected to purchase positive quantities of *each* of the r commodities shown in (1). For, other than in one special and unlikely case, ([4]) particular commodities can never be consumed at zero rates so long as the first-order conditions for the maximum are met (i. e., corner solutions are ruled out).

Now, to say that an individual or household will buy units of each commodity period after period may seem reasonable at first thought; particularly so if analysis is conducted in terms of just two goods. In effect, the idea emphasized is that the typical consumer does not specialize in the consumption of one item but seeks to enjoy a « wide » range of goods. Since even the most casual observation of actual consumption expenditures supports the general thesis of non-specialization, the conventional utility formulation has some justification. However, the theory goes too far and overstates the case for equation (1). It is one thing to recognize that consumers choose num-

---

([3]) See H. S. HOUTHAKKER, « The Present State of Consumption Theory », *Econometrica*, 29, Oct. 1961, 722-24.

([4]) Given a particular type of utility function and just the correct price structure, it is possible for equilibrium to be reached at a position where certain items are consumed at zero rates. For example, in a two commodity world, the budget curve can be tangent to an indifference curve at a point on one of the axes ($q_1 = 0$, $q_2 = q^0$); then, the first- and second-order conditions and (3) will all be satisfied simultaneously. However, this case is of little pratical significance. The outcome turns on the existence of a special pattern of prices (and particular budget level). But when there are many commodities in the model, the chances are small that the prices (budget) will all be of the appropriate magnitudes so that zero consumption can always appear as an equilibrium solution rather than a corner solution. In general, then, the analytical system based on calculus maximization will not be able to reflect a position of consumer equilibrium consistent with zero consumption of many products.

Moreover, as Houthakker points out, the solution must involve positive quantities of commodities if the more interesting conclusions of the theory are to hold. See: H. S. HOUTHAKKER, « Compensated Changes in Quantities and Qualities Consumed », *Review* of *Economic Studies*, XIX, n. 3 1952, 155.

bers of different products, it is quite another to suggest that consumers buy positive amounts of *all* products in existence, or that they never alter the commodity compositions of their budgets (5).

Although generalizations about consumption are dangerous, at least one statement can be made with confidence. We know an individual living in a modern economy will have direct experience with only a small fraction of the numerous types of goods available but that, despite this, he will shift from one subset of goods to another as changes in income and prices take place. Normally, substitues abound; and particular physical or social needs can be satisfied by any of a large number of similar commodities. (6) These alternative commodities may be in the same general price class or, as Professor Duesenberry has stressed, (7) in different classes. But, whatever the absolute qualities of the goods involved, the essential idea is that the consumer, operating subject to a given budget constraint like (2), will tend to select only one or a few variants from among the alternative commodities which can be used for a specific consumption purpose. Further, the commodity composition of the equilibrium mix will tend to vary systematically with changes in the economic conditions reflected in the constraint.

The facts here are clear and there is no need to belabor the obvious. Nevertheless, the behavior noted is significant because it underlines a serious deficiency in the structure of the orthodox theory. (8) If consumers do act in the manner just described, their actions should be accounted for by the theory. Yet, as has been explai-

---

(5) If the n commodities shown in (1) represent the total number of goods in the economy, the implication is that the consumer buys positive amounts of all goods; if the n items are interpreted as some subset of the universe of commodities, it follows that the consumer must buy the same types of goods regardless of price and income shifts.

(6) H. Theil, « Qualities, Prices and Budget Enquiries », *Review of Economic Studies*, 19, no. 3 1952, 129-47. H. S. Houthakker, op. cit., pp. 155-64.

(7) Conventional demand theory focuses attention on how many units of given commodities are purchased and neglects questions of how new or different goods are introduced into the consumption plan. As Professor Duesenberry states: ... But (these theories) lead one to think of differences in consumption patterns in terms of differences in the amounts of the same specific goods rather than in terms of the qualities of goods consumed. But it seems clear that psychologically an improvement in the living standard consists in satisfying one's needs in a better way. This may sometimes involve consuming more of something but it very often consists in consuming something different. J. S. Duesenberry, *Income, Saving and the Theory of Consumer Behavior*, (Cambridge: Harvard Univ. Press, 1952), p. 22.

(8) Professor Houthakker has summarized the case in this way: The validity of this (orthodox) approach is therefore restricted to changes in income and prices which do not cause anything to be introduced into or disappear from the list of items that are actually bought (apart from certain exceptional cases). Consequently, it does not apply to the complete replacement of one variety of an item of consumption by another, and as it is well known that such replacements (known as quality variations) occur frequently and fairly systematically an extension of the theory appears to be indicated. H. S. Houthakker, op. cit. pp. 155-56.

ned, conventional utility analysis conveys no such insight. Because the first-order conditions are usually inconsistent with zero consumption rates, the indication is that, at equilibrium, all of the goods specified in the utility function (1) will be demanded. True, non-consumption situations can show up' as corner solutions. But this possibility offers small comfort. To accept corner solutions is to admit that useful marginal rules cannot be stated and, thus, to give up the traditional equilibrium approach. Further, insofar as the usual rules are violated, the impression may easily be created that non-consumption of certain of the r commodities constitutes an extraordinary outcome. Of course, nothing could be more misleading; far from being an extraordinary act, selective rejection of products is a central feature of the economic system being studied. A modern theory of consumption must be as much at home in explaining situations where particular commodities are rejected as it is in explaining those where commodities are accepted.

From a technical standpoint, there is another important reason for dissatisfaction with the corner solution as an answer to the problems besetting consumption theory. Ideally, the orthodox model has to be extended and given sufficient flexibility to show that any number of goods can be chosen — from one to the total r. However, there is considerable difficulty in finding a single continuous equation which can meet the mathematical requirements for a utility function and also yield corner solutions covering the range one to r. This is not to say that no suitable functions are available, but those that qualify represent a restricted class of functions. Thus, reliance on corner solutions reduces ultimately to reliance on specialized preference fields; in effect, limitations are placed on the possible reactions of the consumer to commodities. The latter condition is clearly unacceptable and the need for a different line of attack is indicated.

Granting that relatively few types of goods are chosen by any one consumer and that the corner solution approach is defective, the question is where to go for an adequate theory. Two general strategies seem to exist. On the one hand, it is possible to introduce a radically different set of assumptions about consumption activity and attempt to build up utility theory from an entirely new base — as Lancaster has done with his discussion of the intrinsic technical properties possessed by commodities. This kind of procedure has real interest; yet gains tend to be made only in proportion to the willingness of writers to commit themselves to bold and detailed assertions concerning the nature of the economic universe. In any event, the problem of consumer equilibrium can be handled by following a different and easier course. An alternate model can be formulated which gives a persuasive explanation of observed consumption patterns *while still remaining very close to the conventional theory of choice.*

All that has to be added to the minimal assumptions of the standard presentation is a mild condition on functional separability. Specifically, we must assume the r commodities constituting the set of independent variables in (1) can be partitioned into *m* subsets (which need not be mutually exclusive). The principle of separation used is simple. We say that certain commodities are related and form a group if the consumer thinks the respective items all contribute to the same general consumption purpose and yield a given type of satisfaction. For example, there are grounds for believing different kinds and qualities of foods contribute to the complex of satisfactions which arise from the act of eating. It should be emphasized that the subsets considered here are not necessarily independent of one another; only weak separability conditions are invoked and so the ultimate level of utility the consumer derives depends non-additively on the *m* different types of satisfaction generated by the elements in the *m* commodity subsets. The last point is significant because it is difficult to accept an additive utility function as a valid representation of behavior even when the variables added are branch utilities based on numbers of commodities. In general, then, the objective is to avoid extreme assumptions and make the revised consumption model as flexible as possible consistent with the need to rationalize actual phenomena.

As would be expected, the utility function which emerges from the system sketched above bears a strong resemblance to the orthodox function. However, the structure of the new construct is more elaborate and involves a series of separate equations or utility sub-functions. With the aid of these equations, it becomes feasible to treat all consumption situations in the same way. In other words, the equilibrium approach comes back into prominence and the marginal rules regain *universal* applicability. This result is useful in itself, but the analysis points up another interesting condition. In the context of the new model, a conventional utility function like (1) is seen to be nothing more than a special and rather improbable case.

II. The Basic Model.

The task which follows will be made more straightforward if the independent variables of the utility function are taken as the set of all commodities in the economy. The set is assumed to be finite, but commodities are defined narrowly so that, in principle, the total number of variables can be very large. Similar items of different quality are considered as distinct elements and, therefore, we should expect only a fraction of the existing goods to be chosen by any one consumer. As explained, the objective is to establish a model which preserves the familiar marginal approach but which emphasizes the fact that the consumer normally foregoes consumption of many types of commodities. Perhaps the simplest way of accomplishing the desired revision is to set up the utility function as a multi-equation construct. (9)

(9) The general problem of nonnegative equilibrium has not attracted a great deal of attention in the literature of economics. The articles of Houthakker and Theil cited earlier attack the quality question by introducing qualities

Specifically, the proposal is to replace equation (1) by a set of equations (or utility sub-functions) which indicate, broadly, the manner in which the various commodities can contribute to consumer satisfaction. The multi-equation structure is important because it enables us to see that consumer choices have a « mutually exclusive » character; the options existing in any given utility sub-function may yield definite satisfaction, but may still be rejected totally because other alternatives in other sub-functions are relatively more attractive. The precise nature of the new utility scheme is best explained in terms of a formal model, and this follows below.

To begin the argument, we can consider an elementary system involving only four distinct commodities: $q_1, \ldots, q_4$. Assume the first two goods (q_1 and q_2) have generally comparable properties and that it is possible to use either one in meeting a certain class of social and/or physical needs. Let us say, further, that the particular satisfaction arising from this kind of consumption is identifiable and can be represented by the variable S_1. In other words, we are following the organizational pattern of a utility tree; [10] but, in the present case, each branch (pertaining to a specific area of consumption) has two possible forms because of the presumed tendency of the consumer to employ one or the other of the available commodities. Thus, the alternate branch utility functions [11] for the first area of consumption are:

$$(4) \qquad S_{1j} = {}_jf\,(q_j)\,, \qquad j = 1\,,2\,.$$

---

as separate variables in the utility function and, then, assuming that the quality variables will be determined by the consumer along with quantities. Appropriate signs are assured for the commodity variables (and values for the quality variables) by establishing sensible boundary conditions and confining the analysis to movements around a point where these conditions are met.

Houthakker seems to believe that a truly satisfactory solution to the basic problem here will be reached only if the standard calculus approach is abandoned and new mathematical techniques are adopted. Along these lines, he experiments with a quadratic programming method. Using this device, the formal problem is to maximize a quadratic utility function subject to a number of linear constraints which, inter alia, rule out negative commodity quantities. See: H. S. Houthakker, « The Capacity Method of Quadratic Programming », *Econometrica*, 28, Jan. 1960, 62-87.

(10) R. H. Strotz, op. cit. R. H. Strotz, « The Utility Tree-A Correction and Further Appraisal », *Econometrica*, 27, July 1959, 482-88. H. A. J. Green, *Aggregation in Economic Analysis* (Princeton: Princeton Univ. Press, 1964), chaps. 2-4.

(11) Presumably, the branch functions are so constituted that any satisfaction index S is a monotonically increasing function of the relevant commodity q, $(\partial S/\partial q > 0)$. However, this does not imply that the item q cannot become a discommodity-i. e., $\dfrac{\partial U}{\partial q} = \dfrac{\partial U}{\partial S}\,\dfrac{\partial S}{\partial q} > 0$. See E. G. Furubotn, « On Some Applications of the Utility Tree », *Southern Economic Journal*, XXX, Oct. 1963, 128-143.

Similarly, commodity q_3 or q_4 can be used to meet a second type of consumption need, and the branch functions for this area are:

(5) $$S_{2k} = {}_k f\,(q_k)\,, \qquad k = 3, 4\,.$$

As noted, the basic idea here is that the individual will tend to select only one, not both, of the commodities in a given consumption area. As a first approximation to observed behavior, this assertion seems reasonable. Typically, consumers do not buy, e. g., clothing of all existing quality levels, or furniture of all possible designs, etc. In any event, the assumption appears much less inhibiting and mechanical when the analysis is extended to consider many commodities.

The two types of satisfaction, provided by the different forms of consumption activity, are, of course, not ends in themselves. Rather, to be consistent with the structure of the utility tree, it is clear that the ultimate satisfaction (U) derived by the consumer must be a function of these intermediate variables. And since there is no reason to believe S_1 and S_2 contribute to the consumer's total satisfaction in a strictly independent (or additive) manner, we can assume any pattern of interaction consistent with strict convexity. ([12])

(6) $$U_i = {}_i F\,(S_{1j}\,,\ S_{2k}) \qquad \begin{array}{l} i = 1\,, \ldots, 4 \\ j = 1\,,\ 2 \\ k = 3\,,\ 4\,. \end{array}$$

The implication here is that the level of U finally produced depends not only on the magnitudes of the intermediate variables but on the particular interdependence relationship which holds. Various forms of interdependence are conceivable between S_1 and S_2; however, the main focus of interest is on the different combinations of variables found in (6).

We see four possible arrangements have to be assessed. ([13]) This is so because S_1 can be generated in either of two ways and can combine with an S_2 which has been produced with the aid of either q_3 or q_4.

([12]) In the present simplified example, where each branch utility function contains only one element, an additive arrangement would imply a utility function having the general form: $U_i = aq_j + bq_k$. Since this type of equation yields straight line indifference curves, it does not appear a very promising model to follow.

([13]) On strictly logical grounds, the four commodity system considered here can lead to a total of 15 separate utility indexes. That is, the branch utility functions in the two sectors of consumption can be based on the commodity sets: $(q_1\,,\ q_2)\,,\ (q_1)\,,\ (q_2)\,,\ (0)$ and $(q_3\,,\ q_4)\,,\ (q_3)\,,\ (q_4)\,,\ (0)$, respectively. From these sets, 16 possible $(S_1\,,\ S_2)$ combinations emerge. However, if positive amounts of at least one good must be consumed to validate an index, 15 possibilities hold. In the present example, the total is further reduced by the assumption that positive consumption is always undertaken in both sectors, and that the consumer concentrates on one or the other of the commodities in the food and shelter categories. As a result of these conditions, there are but two branch functions in each sector and four different combinations (utility indexes).

By establishing the system of equations in the way shown, allowance is made for all the basic variations in consumer taste that are possible within the framework of mutually exclusive choice. For example, if the two consumption areas relate to food and shelter, and if the alternative products are, respectively, white bread (q_1) or rye bread (q_2) and modern (q_3) or traditional (q_4) housing, the range of option is obvious. The consumer has choice of the basic combinations: white bread and modern housing, white bread and traditional housing, etc. The either-or choices are a bit strained here, but need not be in *a* more refined model where each branch utility function involves more than one commodity element and the system, in general, admits of much greater variety in consumption. In any case, the rationale for (6) should be apparent.

When alternate means exist for satisfying an individual's food (q_1 or q_2) and shelter (q_3 or q_4) requirements, it seems inevitable that some means will be preferred to others. Thus, for the simple example given above, white bread and homes of modern design might represent the desired commodities. In other words, if equivalent physical quantities are considered, the consumer will assign higher utility numbers to options from the former group than to alternatives involving the less attractive rye bread and traditional houses. However, tradeoffs are possible in all directions and since, e. g., a traditional house is not a discommodity, it can easily be chosen in some price situations to the exclusion of the modern house. In effect, the consumer can jump from one sub-function in (6) to another; indeed, he must take into account the possibilities shown in all four equations if he is to maximize utility (U).

Just as he can substitute q_1 for q_2 or q_3 for q_4, the consumer is also able to decide what the indifference system is with respect to any pair of items representing food and shelter (e. g., q_1 vs. q_3). Specifically, a separate indifference map is associated with each sub-function of (6). Each such map has properties similar to the one described by the conventional theory of choice and is interpreted in essentially the same way. We should expect that satisfactions from the two areas of consumption will normally be desired and, thus, the indifference curves for any given sub-function are drawn so as to indicate that items of both food and shelter will be taken. This is the only real limitation envisioned. In general, the consumer is considered free to establish whatever pattern of substitution he will between commodities from the different areas (as q_1 and q_3).

III. Geometric Exposition of the Model.

The discussion, so far, has been tied to a relatively trivial case so as to make possible a geometric exposition of the theory. Thus, the next task of the paper must be to illustrate a position of consumer equilibrium consistent with a simple utility function like (6). We begin by assuming a particular income for the consumer (y^0) and a set of prices for the goods in the system $(p_1, ..., p_4)$. Four budget constraints can now be written which match the series of utility sub-functions in (6).

(7)
$$
\begin{aligned}
y^0 - p_1 q_1 - p_3 q_3 &= 0 \\
y^0 - p_1 q_1 - p_4 q_4 &= 0 \\
y^0 - p_2 q_2 - p_3 q_3 &= 0 \\
y^0 - p_2 q_2 - p_4 q_4 &= 0
\end{aligned}
$$

These constraints appear as straight lines in the respective quadrants of figure (1).

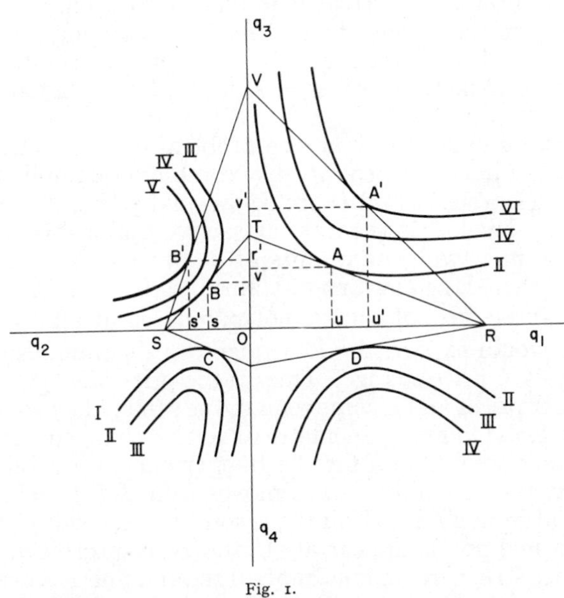

Fig. 1.

As usual, the consumer's basic objective is to select a combination of goods which he is able to purchase with the income y^0 and which provides maximum utility (U). However, in the context of the present analytical system, the maximization process can be conceived as taking place in two steps. First, a set of sub-optimal positions is determined by considering, in turn, each of the « rival » utility functions defined in (6). For example, the first quadrant of figure (1) deals with the equation: [14]

(8)
$$U_1 = {}_1F(q_1, q_3).$$

---

[14] In the simple case studied, we know that $U_1 = {}_1F(S_{11}, S_{23})$. However, since $S_{11} = {}_1f(q_1)$ and $S_{23} = {}_3f(q_3)$, it follows that U_1 depends on the two commodities q_1 and q_3.

This expression must be maximized subject to the corresponding budget constraint found in (7). The solution represents the most satisfying mix the consumer is able to buy if he spends his *entire* income on the goods q_1 and q_3. Relative to figure (1), the equilibrium point discussed is at A; and, following similar procedure, analogous points B, C and D can be established for the other subfunctions.

The separate solutions $A , ..., D$ are important because the consumer's ultimate resting place, the optimum optimorum, is at one of these points. According to what has been said, not all of the commodities $q_1 , ..., q_4$ will actually be consumed. Consequently, the points $A , ..., D$ are alternate or rival possibilities, and only the best one will be chosen in the second stage of the maximization process. Discovery of the final solution requires a systematic comparison to be made of the satisfaction levels [15] $U^0{}_1 , ..., U^0{}_4$ obtainable from the alternatives $A , ..., D$.

The diagram suggests how the problem can be worked out. At the initial set of prices, the commodity combination implied by point B is the most desirable; A and D are equally satisfying [16] but represent a lesser utility level, C is the least attractive option. It follows, then, that the consumer will buy s units of q_2 and r units of q_3, and as a result of the choice the consumer attains indifference. Level III. Commodities q_1 and q_4 are, of course, not purchased at all.

As one would expect, the four quadrant diagram also lends itself to the analysis of price change. Thus, if the price of, e. g., q_3 is reduced while all other prices and income remain the same, the new equilibrium position is easily found. Geometrically, the changed conditions are reflected in different slopes for the budget curves involving p_3. We observe that the constraint curve moves from RT to RV in the first quadrant and from ST to SV in the second. As a result of these shifts, new sub-optimal points appear at A' and B' respectively. Naturally, since the price structures in quadrants three and four have not changed, the equilibrium points C and D continue to be effective. In general, then, the possible operating points are A', B', C and D.

Again, the problem is to select the commodity combination which promises the highest level of satisfaction (U). Figure (1) shows that, under the new set of prices, the alternatives can be ranked as follows: $A' > B' > D > C$. Thus, the optimum optimorum position is at A'; and the consumer must choose u' units of commodity q_1 and v' units of q_3. In constrast to the first case, where q_1 and q_4 were the rejected products, q_2 and q_4 are now the ones consumed at zero rates. The situation is of particular interest because the variation in p_3 has led

(15) Since only one individual is involved in the choice process, it is valid to compare the « readings » of the separate indifference sub-systems.

(16) If a non-unique solution should appear as the optimum optimorum, the consumer could select either one of the commodity mixes indicated using some arbitrary procedure.

to a dramatic change in the use of q_2; its consumption has fallen from s units per period to zero in response to the decrease in p_3. Cross elasticity with respect to the complementary good q_3 is obviously quite high.

Enough has been said to suggest how figure (1) or its mathematical counterpart, equations (6) and (7), can be manipulated to yield demand schedules for the various commodities, Engel curves, etc. Constructs derived from the new system generally parallel those of the conventional theory, but individual curves will tend to show sudden discontinuities. To the extent the « either-or » utility scheme provides a more accurate reflection of consumer behavior, the present model should yield a superior explanation of demand phenomena. However, detailed consideration of these matters is beyond the scope of the paper.

IV. Some Possible Objections.

The mechanics of the model introduced in Section III are straightforward, yet questions may still exist concerning some of the basic conceptions on which it rests. Perhaps the most serious doubt arises because of the « either-or » behavioral pattern assumed for the decision maker. Specifically, one can ask why an individual might not find it advantageous, in some circumstances, to split his income among more than two of the existing commodities. Conceivably, the consumer could operate within, rather than on, several of the budget curves in figure (1) — with the hope of reaching a higher level of total utility by this action. Or, alternately, the utility function could be formulated as a single equation having all variables represented. Then, with something akin to the conventional maximizing procedure undertaken, the solution might show the desirability of consuming many different goods simultaneously ([17]).

However, the justification for the structure of the present model becomes clear when the special properties assumed for the branch utility functions (4) and (5) are considered. The situation is this. We assert that the consumer is able to rank the alternate ways of meeting any social'or consumption need in order of their desirability and effectiveness. Knowledge of (4) allows us to associate a utility number with any stipulated quantity of q_1 or q_2, but if consumption of q_1 represents the *preferred* way of providing for, e. g., food requirements, a unit by unit comparison must show that S_{11} is everywhere greater than S_{12}. Since, by definition, S_{11} and S_{12} refer to the *same* general type of satisfaction, straightforward ordinal contrasts are legitimate. This means that, in the case described, the consumer will always choose q_1 and not q_2; specialization generates the greatest S_1 and, hence, is consistent with maximizing the ultimate utility index (U).

To this point, no mention has been made of commodity prices.

([17]) The programming approach used by Houthakker is an example of this technique. See: H. S. Houthakker, op. cit.

Yet, once prices are introduced, it is apparent that the important consideration is not S_1 per commodity unit, but S_1 per dollar. Given a set of prices (p_1, p_2), the effectiveness of a dollar's expenditure on q_1 and q_2 respectively can be defined in terms of the relative satisfaction produced (S_{11} vs. S_{12}). However, depending on the actual magnitudes of the prices, either q_1 or q_2 can seem preferable; price may overcome innate preference so no commodity need be ruled out as a possible choice. In any event, if, after accounting for prices, it is still true that S_{11} is everywhere greater than S_{12}, the consumer should not be interested in good q_2. As long as the initial conditions hold, dollars devoted to q_1 will yield a greater payoff in the satisfaction S_1 than the same dollars spent on q_2 (i. e., $S_{11} > S_{12}$). Of course, a similar result must obtain for the other area of consumption involving S_2, and the either-or pattern emerges as universal.

While the foregoing argument may make the formal case for rejecting q_2, a fundamental question remains. Why should one of the branch indexes, as S_{11}, be consistently greater than the other over the entire range of possible consumption levels? In terms of the earlier example, why should consumer preferences be so ordered that white bread (q_1) is always preferred to rye bread (q_2) as a means of satisfying food needs? To ascribe such choice to peculiarities of taste does not seem entirely appropriate because, then, no provision is made for variety in diet or for complementary food items. However, this last problem is more apparent than real; it exists only because of the small number of commodities used in the geometric model.

To gain some impression of how the consumer might react in a more normal environment of many commodities, we can assume another food option in the form of wholewheat bread (q_0), and desire on the consumer's part for different kinds of foodstuffs. In principle, an individual could attain variety in food consumption by purchasing positive amounts of all three goods (q_0, q_1, q_2). But, thinking of actual behavior, this strategy seems unlikely. Observation suggests that no one person buys all of the food items in existence, or, for that matter, all the available items in any consumption area. Presumably, the range of products is so wide in each area that sufficient variety can be found within a sub-set of certain *preferred* commodities.

For example, if q_2 is quite unappealing relative to q_1 and q_0, any comparable combination of the latter group (q_0, q_1) may well be preferable to a combination drawn from the other existing sets: (q_1, q_2), (q_0, q_2) or (q_0, q_1, q_2). In other words, according to our assumptions, a given monetary expenditure on q_0 and q_1 will generate a higher level of satisfaction S_1 than an equivalent expenditure on combinations from the rival commodity sets: (q_1, q_2), etc. The desire for variety (or complements) is tempered by a simultaneous desire to avoid relatively unattractive goods; in the case at hand, adequate variety is provided by the subset (q_0, q_1), while the more extensive set (q_0, q_1, q_2) is rejected because of the presence of q_2.

Of course, price structure must influence the outcome here and, as long as q_2 is not regarded as a discommodity, conditions may arise which permit commodity sets incorporating q_2 to be taken. For this reason, then, the sub-functions:

$$
\begin{aligned}
S_{1\cdot 01} &= {}_{01}f(q_0, q_1) \\
S_{1\cdot 02} &= {}_{02}f(q_0, q_2) \\
S_{1\cdot 12} &= {}_{12}f(q_1, q_2) \\
S_{1\cdot 012} &= {}_{012}f(q_0, q_1, q_2),
\end{aligned} \tag{9}
$$

are legitimately part of the formal utility scheme ([18]); ultimately, *all* possible combinations have to be considered if the most general model of consumer equilibrium is to be established. However, it should be re-emphasized that the alternative sub-functions of (9) do not have equal probabilities of use. Prices must be just right for the intrinsically unattractive products to be chosen; moreover, the last equation ($S_{1\cdot 012}$) is quite special because it implies the desire for variety is so great that all commodities, including the less desirable items, are demanded.

In effect, this limiting case ($S_{1\cdot 012}$) is the one assumed by the conventional theory, the one the new utility function (6) is designed to counter. What the issue reduces to is a question of coverage; we must decide how general a formulation is desired for the utility function. ([19]) If all *logical* possibilities are to be covered, the complete array of utility sub-functios must be established. That is, we require equations based on commodity subsets involving one element, two elements, three elements, ... and so on up to a set containing all the commodities existing in a given consumption area. ([20]) Systems (4) and (9) together with the branch function: $S_{1\cdot 0} = {}_0f(q_0)$ indicate this comprehensive pattern. On the other hand, if the objective is merely to suggest the range of commodity combinations the consumer is likely to show interest in, the number of sub-functions specified can be much smaller. The use of the simple geometric model of fi-

([18]) If variety in consumption is unimportant, or unattainable because of the budget constraint, additional sub-functions are required for completeness. These are:

$$
\begin{aligned}
S_{1\cdot 0} &= {}_0f(q_0) \\
S_{1\cdot 1} &= {}_1f(q_1) \\
S_{1\cdot 2} &= {}_2f(q_2).
\end{aligned}
$$

Further, as noted in section II, the consumption pattern might be such that no commodities from this area are taken.

([19]) See section V below.

([20]) With the complete set of sub-functions present, it is possible to represent all shades of consumer preference with respect to the range of products wanted. For example, at one extreme, the consumer may have such an overwhelming preference for one kind of food item (or may be so insistent on economy in this area) that neither variety nor complementary foods are needed. Then, one of the one element sub-functions will be germane. At the other extreme, the desire for variety is very strong and a commodity mix including units of all foods becomes essential. As noted, this case is the one emphasized by conventional theory.

gure (1) rests on such understanding and, on balance, the approach seems justified.

Even when the special characteristics of the branch utility functions are accepted, a further question can be brought up relative to the procedure followed in determining the consumer's final equilibrium position. From the explanation given earlier, we know the ideal commodity mix is decided by a comparison of the separate utility indexes $U^0_1, \ldots, U^0_4$. However, it is also apparent that no formal mechanism has been introduced to make a choice among the alternatives in (6). Presumably, the consumer just scans the array $U^0_1, \ldots, U^0_4$ and selects the mix associated with the highest utility number. This action is simple enough when only four possibilities exist, but, under more realistic conditions, where both the number of different consumption sectors and the number of branch functions in each sector are large, the scanning process can become formidable. The problem is, then, whether it is reasonable to assume the individual can sift through the numerous sub-optimum solutions without special help and range in on the optimum optimorum position.

It is certainly difficult to conceive of the consumer functioning with computer-like precision and consistency. Thus, any practical realization of a rigorous scanning procedure is doubtful. Nevertheless, this is not a truly valid objection to the model based on (6) and (7) because essentially the same criticism can be made of all utility theory. If the consumer is able to catalogue myriad consumption possibilities to generate indifference hyper-surfaces, he is quite capable of scanning an array like U^0_1, $U^0_2, \ldots, U^0_n$ to determine the optimum optimorum. After all, discovery of the best commodity combination is never a straightforward problem in applied mathematics. What traditional choice models provide is merely a rationalization of consumer behavior under certain idealized conditions. And judged against this standard, the model of section II seems reasonable; it assumes no more than other constructs, but gives somewhat greater insight into the nature of the choice process.

V. Generalization to Many Commodities.

Although the essential features of the proposed utility scheme have been explained in the sections above, there is still something to be gained by considering a general model involving a large number of commodities. The extended system has some interest in itself, but, beyond this, it serves both to emphasize the great variety that is possible in consumer choice patterns and to illustrate the applicability of the basic theory to these diverse situations. Any attitude of the consumer with respect to the particular types of goods desired can be rationalized. Using a common analytical framework, it is possible to deal with all conceivable equilibria — from the case where each of the r commodities in the system is consumed, to the opposite extreme where only one commodity is selected.

In what follows, both the notation employed and the interpretations made of the variables are consistent with the usage of section II. Thus, by analogy with (4) and (5), we can write:

$$
\begin{aligned}
S_{11} &= {}_{11}G\,(q_{11}\,,\ q_{12}\,,\ \ldots,\ q_{1a}) \\
&\ \ \vdots \\
S_{1j} &= {}_{1j}G\,(q_{11}\,,\ \ldots,\ q_{1u})\quad ,\ a > u \\
&\ \ \vdots \\
S_{1A} &= {}_{1A}G\,(q_{1a}) \\
S_{21} &= {}_{21}G\,(q_{21}\,,\ q_{22}\,,\ \ldots\ q_{2b}) \\
&\ \ \vdots \\
S_{2k} &= {}_{2k}G\,(q_{21}\,,\ \ldots,\ q_{2v})\quad ,\ b > v \\
&\ \ \vdots \\
S_{2B} &= {}_{2B}G\,(q_{2b}) \\
&\ \ \vdots \\
S_{m1} &= {}_{m1}G\,(q_{m1}\,,\ q_{m2}\,,\ \ldots,\ q_{mz}) \\
&\ \ \vdots \\
S_{ms} &= {}_{ms}G\,(q_{m1}\,,\ \ldots,\ q_{mw})\quad ,\ z > w \\
&\ \ \vdots \\
S_{mZ} &= {}_{mZ}G\,(q_{mz})\ .
\end{aligned}
\tag{10}
$$

Collectively, the system of $A + B + \ldots + Z$ equations in (10) represents the array of alternative branch utility functions. As things are organized, r separate types of goods exist in the economy and these are partitioned into various subsets associated with m distinct consumption areas. [21] For example, the first group of A equations,

[21] The elements within the m commodity subsets need not be mutually exclusive and, thus, the sum of $a + b + \ldots + z$ is not necessarily equal to the total number of commodities r. However, if the subsets do intersect, there must be two or more sources of demand for the common commodity. For example, if gasoline is used for transportation and for housing (via a power lawnmower),

based on commodities q_{11}, q_{12}, ..., q_{1a}, might relate to food needs; the second group, based on q_{21}, q_{22}, ..., q_{2b}, to shelter, etc. However, from the composition of the respective subsets shown in (10), it is clear that not all of the items falling into a given consumption category need appear as the independent variables of a branch function. [22] Merely the first equation in each group (S_1, S_2, ..., S_m) allows for *all* the related commodities. Thus, just the function $_{11}G$ considers all possible food items, $_{21}G$ all possible forms of shelter, etc. This last arrangement enables us to deal with the very unlikely case of a consumer who wishes to secure, at equilibrium, units of every commodity extant in a particular consumption area. A more normal outcome is, presumably, for the consumer to want only certain items in any category (like a limited range of foods). Often, by concentrating expenditure on a lesser number of desired commodities, an individual is able to secure greater satisfaction than by spreading the same outlay over an extensive range of different types of goods. To account for the more selective pattern of choice, then, branch functions containing less than the total number of commodities in a given sector must appear — as $_{1j}G$, $_{2k}G$, ..., $_{ms}G$.

The trouble is, of course, that, once consideration of the smaller commodity subsets is begun, a great many possibilities spring to view. It is necessary to specify branch functions for all conceivable combinations of the variables; thus, in the case of foodstuffs, we require all combinations of the commodities q_{11}, q_{12}, ..., q_{1a} taking them a-1 at a time, a-2 at a time, and so on down to one commodity at a time. The result of such manipulations is a set of A equations, and similar sets (B, C, ..., Z) are obtainable for each of the other m-1 areas of consumption. All the equations are assembled in (10) and appear as a series of inverted pyramids.

From an a priori standpoint, not one of the equations just discussed can be dismissed as impossible. Each is a valid alternative in the sense that the consumer may believe the commodities stipulated by the function represent the most desirable avenues of expenditure open. Even a branch function like $_{1A}G$ is feasible; it suggests that conditions can arise which make spending the equilibrium food budget on the single good q_{1a} generate the largest possible satisfaction S_1.

The ultimate utility level achieved by the consumer depends upon the intermediate variables S_{11}, ..., S_{mZ}. However, it is important to recognize that there is not just one utility index but many alternative forms based on particular combinations of the intermediate variables (or branch functions). Every variant index (U_i) involves no more than one branch function from each of the different consumption

the optimal quantities determined for the respective sectors would have to be added to secure the individual's total demand for this commodity.

[22] By assumption, the indifference manifolds produced by any branch function are strictly convex. The idea here is that the various commodities within a branch are linked by some type of complementary relationship.

areas 1, 2, ..., m. Since all possible combinations of these S elements are relevant, the total number of independent utility indexes is large and must be given by the product of A times B times C, ..., times Z. [23] The parameters refer, of course, to the number of equations in each of the m areas of consumption. For convenience, we can say there are n alternate indexes in all.

$$(11) \qquad U_i = {}_i\Phi\,(S_{1\alpha}\,,\ S_{2\beta}\,,\ \dots,\ S_{m\Omega}) \qquad \begin{array}{l} i = 1\,,\ 2\,,\ \dots,\ n \\ \alpha = 1\,,\ \dots,\ j\,,\ \dots,\ A \\ \beta = 1\,,\ \dots,\ k\,,\ \dots,\ B \\ \cdot \qquad\quad \cdot \qquad\quad \cdot \\ \cdot \qquad\quad \cdot \qquad\quad \cdot \\ \cdot \qquad\quad \cdot \qquad\quad \cdot \\ \Omega = 1\,,\ \dots,\ s\,,\ \dots,\ Z\,. \end{array}$$

This elaborate schema may be cumbersome, but it is essential if the complete range of choices open to the consumer is to be reflected. The structure of (11) is arranged so that each possible configuration of consumer preferences, no matter how peculiar, can be represented. For example, our consumer may choose to concentrate on a single food product (S_{1A}) while simultaneously insisting on the entire set of shelter items (S_{21}), a moderate number of recreation items (S_{ms}), etc. In general, any number of commodities, from zero to the total available, may be selected from each of the m consumption sectors.

It is instructive to compare a conventional utility function like (1) with the new formulation shown in (11). From what has been said, the relationship between the two is easily understood; in effect, (1) is a special case of (11). If an individual insists on consuming the complete range of commodities existing in each of the m consumption sectors, all r commodities will be selected *at equilibrium* and the orthodox solution emerges. The index:

$$(12) \qquad U_1 = {}_1\Phi\,(S_{11}\,,\ S_{21}\,,\ \dots,\ S_{m1})$$

is essentially the same as (1), but (12) is just one of the n possibilities represented in (11). Seen in this light, the deficiencies of (1) or (12) become glaringly apparent. The conventional function presupposes the most extraordinary behavior on the part of the consumer and, thus, (1) *is not only a special case but an extremely unlikely one.* Although the behavioral pattern suggested by (1) cannot be rejected as impossible, it is so very improbable that, if we were limited to the

---

(23) To take account of the fact that no commodities may be chosen from some of the m consumption sectors, we can add one dummy equation (representing non-consumption) to each subset of branch utility functions in (10). Then, the total number of alternate utility indexes will be equal to the product of $(A + 1)$ times $(B + 1)$, ..., times $(Z + 1)$ minus one. The minus one term arises because of the assumption that at least one commodity will be consumed from among the r in existence. Of course, the parameter n noted below must be understood to be larger or smaller depending on the conventions followed.

choice of a single utility index, almost any other of the n sub-functions in (11) would constitute a better, or more plausible, alternative.

Moreover, there is no real escape from this line of criticism. It is true that when the first-order equilibrium condition are abandoned and corner solutions are admitted, a single equation utility function does not have to yield outcomes where all r commodities are consumed each period. Indeed, many or few types of goods may be indicated as desirable in these circumstances; and, on the surface, the corner solution would seem to provide for necessary flexibility. However, a fundamental difficulty exists. A utility function based on a single equation is not equivalent to (11); *in general, a continuous function like* (1) *is unable to duplicate the preference ordering which can be specified by system* (11). Thus, an impasse is reached. To use (1) is to impose an implicit set of restrictions on the form of the utility function or, more basically, on the possible shape of consumer preferences. But since mathematical requirements cannot be allowed to distort the content of theory, the only acceptable course is to adopt the general formulation of (11). By drawing on n alternate (and independent) indexes, we are freed of constraints and all conceivable variations of consumer attitude can be reflected.

A few words should be said about the mathematical properties of the individual indexes in (11). As suggested earlier, each ${}_i\Phi$ can be expected to have convex indifference manifolds with respect to the intermediate variables $S_1, S_2 \ldots, S_m$. However, because not all of the latter variables need be greater than zero in every case, the various utility sub-functions may well have additive segments. [24] To recognize this feature is not to imply that each index must have a generally additive form like:

$$(13) \qquad U_i = {}_i\Phi\,(S_{1\alpha} + S_{2\beta} + \ldots + S_{m\Omega})\,.$$

The normal assumption is that the commodity set associated with ${}_i\Phi$ is separable into m subsets of related commodities — but only the weak separability conditions are stipulated. In other words, the general requirement is merely that the marginal rate of substitution between any two commodities in the same subset (as q_{tu} and q_{tv}) must be independent of the use of any commodity in some other subset (as q_{sw}).

$$(14) \qquad \partial\left(\frac{\partial S_t/\partial q_{tu}}{\partial S_t/\partial q_{tv}}\right)/\partial q_{sw} = 0\,.$$

By establishing the relationships in this way, allowance is made for interdependence among some or all of the m intermediate variables in

(24) The situation might approximate that considered by Dr. Barten. See: A. P. Barten, op. cit.

the generation of utility. And while an equation like (13) is possible, it is not a necessary outcome.

Determination of the consumer's final equilibrium position proceeds as before. A series of n budget constraints similar to (7) is specified and, then, the relative maxima relating to the alternate utility indexes are found. Since the utility sub-functions of (11) are based on commodity sets containing anywhere from one to all r commodities, these functions must reflect all possible options open to the consumer and the optimum optimorum must lie among the relative maxima obtained. In short, comparison of $U^0{}_1$, $U^0{}_2$, ..., $U^0{}_n$ should show one index to be greater than the others; the commodity mix associated with this solution constitutes the ideal combination and, presumably, will be the one purchased. If two or more different sets of commodities lead to the same level of satisfaction ($U^0{}_i = U^0{}_j$), choice is less critical, but some (arbitrary) decision would still have to be made. In any event, the probability of such a non-unique outcome seems small.

The foregoing paragraphs merely sketch in the main outlines of the general model; they are not designed to make a rigorous presentation of the case. However, the fact is that intensive discussion is unnecessary. Once the basic ideas concerning the special structure of (10) and (11) are understood, everything travels along well worn tracks and the conventional theory of consumer choice can be applied without much change. To be sure, the concept of the utility tree represents a somewhat less familiar area. Yet, use is made of only the most elementary and uncontroversial aspects of this doctrine; it is neither daring nor implausible to say that a group of commodities may be related because they all contribute to some common consumption purpose. Thus, to establish non-additive branch functions on such basis seems entirely reasonable.

If the proposed utility model can be accepted as logically sound, the approach appears to offer a number of advantages.

(1) Because of its simplicity, the model is highly flexible and has general applicability; by contrast with other methods, it avoids commitment to a specific mathematical form for the utility function.

(2) The model is able to explain how consumer equilibrium can be reached with many commodities consumed at zero rates, and why shifts may be made from one type of product to another as changes in prices and income occur. Further, the basic technique is easily extended to consider the case where new products are introduced into the system. Unlike function (1), (11) does not have to be replaced by a wholely different function each time a new commodity appears.

(3) By emphasizing the "either-or" character of the utility function, the analysis is able to preserve the traditional marginal rules and the general mathematical procedures on which the rules rest.

(4) The formulation in terms of a utility tree implies that (11) has greater empirical content than the conventional utility function (1).

Hence, there are somewhat improved chances for developing testable hypotheses about consumer behavior.

(5) The model's close logical connections with the marginal analysis make it possible to employ familiar geometric techniques.

For these reasons, then, the new construct seems worthy of attention.

18 Revealed Preference and the Utility Function

H. S. Houthakker

Professor Samuelson's "revealed preference" approach[1] has proved to be a useful basis for deriving a considerable part of the static theory of consumer's choice. Its existing versions are not sufficient, however, to determine whether or not consumer's preferences can be described by a utility function of the customary type (the problem of integrability),[2] except in the unrealistic case of two commodities. In this note Samuelson's "fundamental hypothesis" will be generalised so as to imply integrability while continuing to satisfy the methodological requirements of the revealed preference approach and without losing its plausibility. An attempt will be made to stress the logical, as distinct from the technically mathematical, aspects of the subtle problem of integrability, and to assess its importance.

It may be convenient to start with a brief discussion of the revealed preference approach. Though originally intended "to develop the theory of consumer's behaviour freed from any vestigial traces of the utility concept",[3] i.e., as a substitute for the "utility function" and related formulations, it has since tended to become complementary to the latter; in his *Foundations* Professor Samuelson uses it to express the empirical meaning of utility analysis, to which he apparently no longer objects.

[1] P. A. Samuelson, "A Note on the Pure Theory of Consumer's Behaviour", *Economica*, 1938, pp. 61–71, 353–354; "The Empirical Implications of Utility Analysis", *Econometrica*, 1938, pp. 344–356; *Foundations of Economic Analysis* (Cambridge, Mass., 1947), Ch. V-VI; "Consumption Theory in Terms of Revealed Preference", *Economica*, 1948, pp. 243–253. Cf. also I. M. D. Little, "A Reformulation of the Theory of Consumer's Behaviour", *Oxford Economic Papers*, 1949, No. 1, pp. 90–99.

[2] Samuelson, *Foundations*, p. 111, note 14. For integrability in general, cf. R. G. D. Allen, *Mathematical Analysis for Economists* (London, 1938), pp. 422–423, 513–517; H. T. Davis, *The Theory of Econometrics* (Bloomington, Ind., 1947), pp. 77–81.

[3] Samuelson, "Pure Theory", *Economica*, 1938, p. 71.

Reprinted from *Economica*, Vol. XVII (May, 1950), pp. 159–174, by permission of the publisher and author.

Its fundamental concept is the relation which exists between a batch of goods X^a, bought by a consumer at prices P^a and income P^aX^a, and another batch X^b that might have been bought at the same income P^aX^a and prices P^a, its cost P^aX^b being smaller than or equal to this income, but was not in fact bought. This relation is described by the formula $P^aX^b \leqq P^aX^a$ and may be interpreted to mean that the consumer prefers X^a to X^b. Hence, by this comparison of value sums, X^b is "revealed to be inferior to" X^a, and X^a is "revealed to be superior to" X^b. The expressions between quotation marks, the first of which is fundamental, can be described under the name "revealed preference". In order to erect a theory on the basis of this relation a rule must be introduced for drawing conclusions from it. For this purpose Professor Samuelson remarks that if the inequality stated really reveals the inferiority of X^b to X^a, then X^a must not also be revealed to be inferior to X^b, as would be the case if $P^bX^a \leqq P^bX^b$. Therefore, $P^aX^b \leqq P^aX^a$ must imply $P^bX^b < P^bX^a$; this also means that at the income and prices at which X^b is bought, X^a must be too expensive, else it would have been bought instead. In the terminology of formal logic this implication (Samuelson's "fundamental hypothesis") declares revealed preference to be "asymmetric"; it will be further discussed below.

Another characteristic of this approach which should be noticed is the preponderant use of finite differences; it is felt that differential expressions should be avoided because they do not directly correspond to real phenomena.[1] This, together with the use of value sums, makes for a formulation of consumption theory in immediately observable quantities.

In what follows individual prices will be designated by p_i^t and quantities of goods by x_i^t; subscripts refer to the kind of good and superscripts to the price-income situation. For briefness the subscripts will be dropped whenever possible, price-sets being denoted by P^t and goods-combinations by X^t; value sums obtained by pricing a batch of goods will be written $P^sX^t = \sum_i p_i^s x_i^t$. The number of different goods (called n) is arbitrary. Two price-sets or batches of goods

[1] Samuelson, *Foundations*, p. 46.

will be said to be different if at least one of the components p_i (or x_i) is different in them.

In this notation a batch X^b is revealed to be inferior to another batch X^a if $P^aX^b \leqq P^aX^a$, and Samuelson's " fundamental hypothesis "[1] which states that the relation of revealed preference is asymmetric, reads :

$$\textit{If } X^a \neq X^b \textit{ and } P^aX^b \leqq P^aX^a, \textit{ then } P^bX^b < P^bX^a$$

It may be remarked that the use of this axiom implicitly assumes that to each batch X^t corresponds at least one price-set P^t ; it can therefore be valid only in the " optimum region "[2] the class of all goods-combinations which are bought in *some* price-income situation. It need not be supposed (nor can it be deduced from the axiom) that there is only one price-set corresponding to each batch in the optimum region ; this subject will require more attention as we proceed.

The main object of our investigation is to find a proposition which, apart from continuity assumptions, summarises the entire theory of the standard case of consumer's behaviour (no indivisible goods or choices between probabilities ; all income spent). Such a proposition should imply and be derivable from utility analysis ; in other words, it should be a necessary and sufficient condition for the existence of ordinal utility. Samuelson's hypothesis does not satisfy this criterion, being only a necessary condition and not a sufficient one, for although it can be derived from utility considerations it does not entail integrability, which is an essential property of utility functions. Consequently it is not " the ultimate generalisation of the law of demand ".[3]

The reason for this deficiency appears to be that Samuelson's hypothesis relates only to two price-sets and, unlike utility analysis, throws no light on cases of three or more price-sets, except under special conditions. If we know, e.g., that $P^aX^b \leqq P^aX^a$ and that $P^bX^c \leqq P^bX^b$, we still cannot determine whether $P^cX^a \lesseqqgtr P^cX^c$; this means that if X^b is revealed to be inferior to X^a and X^c is revealed to be inferior to X^b, then the hypothesis does not rule out the possibility that X^a is revealed to be inferior to X^c. This paradox,

[1] *Foundations*, pp. 110, 116.

[2] H. Wold, " A Synthesis of Pure Demand Analysis II ", *Skandinavisk Aktuarietidskrift*, 1943, pp. 227–228. To this penetrating exposition the present note owes much.

[3] J. R. Hicks, *Value and Capital* (2nd edition, Oxford, 1946), p. 51. This quotation refers to a proposition still more restricted than Samuelson's hypothesis.

which is borne out by numerical examples, proves that Samuelson's hypothesis does not tell everything about revealed preference.

The general proposition we are looking for should prevent such anomalies; this can be achieved as follows. We consider a sequence of batches of goods X^t ($t = 0, 1, 2, \ldots T$; T arbitrary but finite) each of which is bought at prices P^t and an income P^tX^t. First we assume that each batch X^t is different from and revealed to be inferior to its predecessor in the sequence X^{t-1}. The sequence is then described by the formula $P^{t-1}X^t \leqq P^{t-1}X^{t-1}$; t now runs from 1 to T. If a utility function exists, and the utility of X^t is called $U(X^t)$, then the revealed inferiority we assumed implies that $U(X^0) > U(X^1) > U(X^2) > \ldots > U(X^T)$; consequently X^0 is superior to X^T. We cannot demand that in these circumstances X^T must be revealed to be inferior to X^0, for a batch may be inferior to another batch without being "revealed to be inferior"; but our axiom should exclude the case that X^0 is revealed to be inferior to X^T. It must therefore state that for the sequence under consideration $P^TX^T < P^TX^0$, for otherwise we should find $U(X^0) < U(X^T)$.

A further generalisation is possible and useful for later developments. We postulated that two successive commodity-combinations in the sequence are always different, but this condition may be weakened; it is sufficient that there is at least one pair of successive and different batches. To explain this we suppose that X^s and X^t are identical; then it is evidently true that $P^tX^s \leqq P^tX^t$, and the statement $U(X^s) \leqq U(X^t)$ is equally unobjectionable and uninformative. Now, as an example, in the sequence previously considered we take $T = 3$ and we assume that X^1 and X^2 are different, whereas the other successive batches may or may not be different; as before, the formula $P^{t-1}X^t \leqq P^{t-1}X^{t-1}$ holds throughout. Then utility analysis tells us that $U(X^0) \geqq U(X^1) > U(X^2) \geqq U(X^3)$ so that X^3 is still inferior to X^0. It is clear that this example is of general application; consequently the axiom should still state, as required above, that X^0 is not revealed to be inferior to X^3. We can even improve on the condition that there exists at least one pair of successive different batches, for if we know that any two batches in the sequence are different, then there must necessarily be somewhere a batch which differs from its predecessor.

To sum up, the new axiom reads:

If $X^0, X^1, X^2 \ldots X^T$ *is a sequence of batches of goods such that each batch is bought at prices* $P^0, P^1, P^2 \ldots P^T$ *respectively, and if at least two of these batches are different, and if the cost* $P^{t-1}X^t$ *of each batch* X^t *at prices* P^{t-1} *is not greater than the cost* $P^{t-1}X^{t-1}$ *of the preceding batch in the sequence* X^{t-1} *at the same prices, then the cost* P^TX^T *of the last batch* X^T *at prices* P^T *is less than the cost* P^TX^0 *of the first batch* X^0 *at the same prices.*

or more shortly:

If for every finite t and T $(t = 1, 2, \ldots, T)$ *the inequality* $P^{t-1}X^t \leqq P^{t-1}X^{t-1}$ *holds, and if there are numbers i and j such that* $0 \leqq i < j \leqq T$ *and* $X^i \neq X^j$, *then* $P^TX^T < P^TX^0$.

As to the significance of this axiom, like Samuelson's "fundamental hypothesis" it serves to substantiate the revealed preference relation, but in a more exhaustive way. The revealed preference relation, it will be remembered, exists between a batch X^a actually bought and another batch X^b which might have been bought but was not (for a given price-income situation); this was interpreted to mean that X^b is inferior to X^a. Now Samuelson's hypothesis states that this interpretation is not contradicted if X^b is actually bought (in another price-income situation), for then X^a must be too expensive. The extended axiom says essentially the same, but it also takes into account information provided by intermediate revealed preferences.

From a logical point of view it will be noticed that the above axiom is a statement about the relation between the first and last elements of a chain when something is known about the intermediate links in the chain. The property of the relation of revealed preference it postulates is therefore akin to transitivity, though weaker than transitivity itself; it might be called "semi-transitivity".[1] This is not the place for an investigation of the difference between transitivity and semi-transitivity, but it may be in order to point out that a transitivity postulate need involve only three elements, while the above axiom involves $T + 1$ elements, where T is any finite number.

[1] Compare the concept of "acyclicity" discussed by J. von Neumann and O. Morgenstern, *Theory of Games and Economic Behaviour* (2nd edition, Princeton, 1947), p. 591 ff. Cf. also Samuelson, *Foundations*, pp. 151–152.

We have now seen that the new axiom is a necessary condition for the existence of ordinal utility; our next task is to prove that it is also a sufficient condition; i.e., we must reconstruct the concept of ordinal utility on the basis of the semi-transitivity of revealed preference.

To begin with, Samuelson's hypothesis will be derived as a theorem. This is extremely simple, for we need only take $T = 1$ to find that if $X^0 \neq X^1$, then $P^0X^1 = P^0X^0$

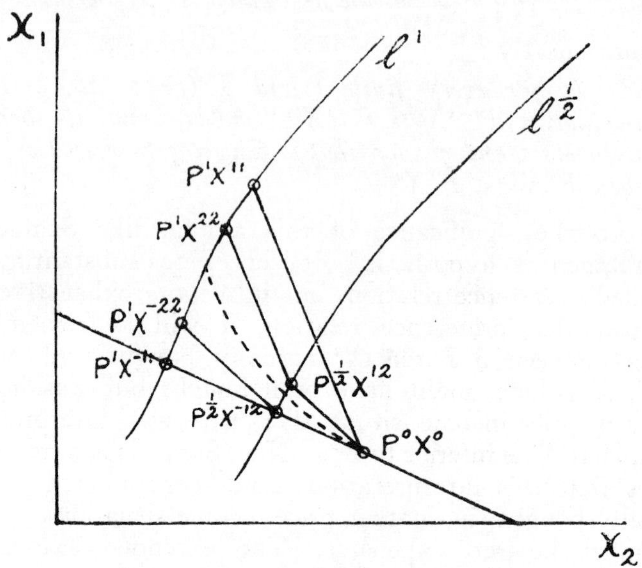

FIG. 1.

l^1 is the locus of all batches bought at prices P^1 for varying income; similarly for $l^{\frac{1}{2}}$. The straight line through P^0X^0 and P^1X^{-11} has a slope P^0; the lines going to the south-east from P^1X^{11} and P^1X^{22} have a slope P^1; and those going to the south-east from $P^{\frac{1}{2}}X^{12}$ and from P^1X^{-22} have a slope $P^{\frac{1}{2}}$. The dotted curve is the limiting line.

implies $P^1X^1 < P^1X^0$. Because of this theorem several well-known results become available at once. Two properties in particular will be needed[1]: that each set of prices and income uniquely determines one collection of goods bought, and that quantities bought remain the same if all prices and income change in the same proportion.

The proposed construction of indifference surfaces (i.e., of ordinal utility) will be carried out by a method the outlines of which were first suggested in the *Foundations* (pages

[1] Samuelson, *Foundations*, pp. 111–112.

147–153) and which has since been considered in more detail by Mr. Little (*loc. cit.*) and by Professor Samuelson himself (*Economica*, 1948), though only for the case of two goods. I shall restate this procedure in somewhat different terms and without restricting the number of goods. The exposition will deal with a gradually extended sequence of price-sets, to be defined later on. As a preliminary a convention will be introduced in order to avoid irrelevant complications due to mutually proportional price-sets (in view of the homogeneity of demand-functions): in each price-set P^t one of the individual prices, viz., p_1^t, will be put equal to unity. Furthermore, it will have to be assumed that demand-functions have continuous derivatives with respect to prices and income.

After these preparations we can start building up indifference-surfaces; in other words, we shall try to find all the batches "equivalent" to a given batch. (A two-dimensional illustration is given in Fig. 1. The argument depends neither on this graph nor on the following ones.) We consider a batch of goods X^0, which is bought at prices P^0, and a price-set P^1 at which X^0 is not bought.[1] The batch bought at prices P^1 and income P^1X^0 will be called X^{11}; this batch is obviously different from X^0 and it is also revealed to be superior to it, as $P^1X^{11} = P^1X^0$. We shall regard P^1 as an element in a sequence of price-sets which will be increased to infinity by the following procedure. Between P^0 and P^1 we take an "intermediate" price-set $P^{\frac{1}{2}}$, by which is meant a price-set whose components satisfy the condition:

$$p_i^{\frac{1}{2}} = \tfrac{1}{2}(p_i^0 + p_i^1)$$
$$(i = 2, 3, \ldots, n)$$

The collection of goods X^{12} which is bought at prices $P^{\frac{1}{2}}$ and income $P^{\frac{1}{2}}X^{12} = P^{\frac{1}{2}}X^0$, is either equal to X^0 (a case we cannot exclude) or revealed to be superior to it. We also define a batch X^{22}, bought at prices P^1 and income $P^1X^{22} = P^1X^{12}$; this is either equal to X^{12} or revealed to be superior to it; but if X^{22} is identical with X^{12}, then X^{12}

[1] This implies that P^0 and P^1 are different (for identical price-sets determine identical batches), but this condition is not enough, as different price-sets cannot be proven to determine different batches. The latter property is introduced by Samuelson (*Economica*, 1948, p. 273) as an extra assumption, but it unnecessarily impairs the significance of revealed preference theory, for Wold (*loc. cit.*, III, *Skandinavisk Aktuarietidskrift*, 1944, pp. 78–88) has shown that this assumption by itself implies the existence of ordinal utility, which would make revealed preference considerations superfluous. After the above was written Professor Samuelson informed me that he does not accept Wold's theorem.

is not identical with X^0, and vice versa, for we have postulated that X^0 is not bought at prices P^1 and so all batches bought at prices P^1 must be different from X^0.

We go on by taking a price-set $P^{\frac{1}{4}}$ intermediate between P^0 and $P^{\frac{1}{2}}$, which together with an income $P^{\frac{1}{4}}X^{14} = P^{\frac{1}{4}}X^0$ determines a batch X^{14} that is again either equal or revealed to be superior to its predecessor X^0. After having considered X^{24}, bought at prices $P^{\frac{1}{2}}$ and income $P^{\frac{1}{2}}X^{24} = P^{\frac{1}{2}}X^{14}$, we proceed to the price-set $P^{\frac{3}{4}}$, intermediate between $P^{\frac{1}{2}}$ and P^1. By now the process will have become clear; ever more intermediate price-sets are introduced and batches and incomes are determined accordingly. For every given number S of price-sets between P^0 and P^1 we obtain a sequence of incomes (called the *superior income-sequence* of length S) each of which determines a batch that is either equal or revealed to be superior to the batch determined by the preceding income; and the last batch thus determined (i.e., X^{SS}) is always different from the original batch X^0.

As counterparts to the superior income-sequences we shall construct *inferior income-sequences* for various lengths of S, which are also based on the sequence of price-sets we have just considered. The process of finding intermediate price-sets need not be repeated and we shall assume for simplicity that $S = 4$, which means that we shall fit an inferior income-sequence to the prices P^0, $P^{\frac{1}{4}}$, $P^{\frac{1}{2}}$, $P^{\frac{3}{4}}$ and P^1. As before, X^0 is taken as given, and X^{-14} is to be a price-set bought at prices $P^{\frac{1}{4}}$ and satisfying $P^0X^{-14} = P^0X^0$, i.e., X^{-14} is either equal or revealed to be inferior to X^0.[1] In the same way, $P^{\frac{1}{2}}X^{-24}$ is defined to determine a batch X^{-24} which at prices $P^{\frac{1}{4}}$ costs as much as X^{-14}, $P^{\frac{3}{4}}X^{-34}$ is implicitly described by the equation $P^{\frac{1}{2}}X^{-34} = P^{\frac{1}{2}}X^{-24}$, and the terminal element in this inferior income-sequence of length 4 is chosen to make true $P^{\frac{3}{4}}X^{-44} = P^{\frac{3}{4}}X^{-34}$.

Now we shall prove that for any finite S the superior terminal income P^1X^{SS} is higher than the inferior terminal income P^1X^{-SS}. For this purpose we shall observe a sequence of goods-batches which starts at X^{SS}, then proceeds along the superior income-sequence (but in the inverse direction) to X^0, and thence along the inferior income-sequence (in the original direction) to X^{-SS}. From the

[1] If there is more than one batch satisfying this condition we should take the one that gives the highest value of $P^{\frac{1}{4}}X^{-14}$.

definitions of the two income-sequences it is clear that the formula $P^{t-1}X^{t} = P^{t-1}X^{t-1}$ holds throughout (i.e., each batch is either equal or revealed to be inferior to its predecessor), while X^{-ss} and X^{0} are known to be different (cf. above), so our axiom may be applied for $T = 2S$ and we see that $P^{1}X^{-ss} < P^{1}X^{ss}$.[1] It should be evident that this inequality is valid also for intermediate incomes (i.e., incomes belonging to intermediate price-sets), provided they determine batches different from X^{0}. Consequently for any finite S the incomes belonging to the superior income-sequence are all higher than their counterparts in the inferior income-sequence.

What happens if S approaches infinity? Because of the process by which intermediate price-sets were selected the differences between individual prices in succeeding price-sets become steadily smaller as the number of price-sets increases; for the value of each newly-introduced individual price lies between the values of the two adjacent prices. In the limit prices will vary continuously between P^{0} and P^{1}.

To observe the consequences for the income-sequences we take an arbitrary intermediate price-set P^{a}, which will be kept fixed, and another intermediate price-set P^{b} which is varied as to the successor of P^{a} for any S; we abandon the previous notation which has served its purpose. For the superior income-sequence we have by definition (whether X^{+a} and X^{+b} are different or not) $P^{b}X^{+b} = P^{b}X^{+a}$. If we denote $P^{b}X^{+b} - P^{a}X^{+a}$ by $\triangle M^{+}$, and $p_i^b - p_i^a$ by $\triangle p_i$, we can write $\triangle M^{+} = \sum_i x_i^a \triangle p_i$. If P^{b} approaches P^{a} indefinitely we can replace " $\triangle$ "s by " d "s (remembering the assumed differentiability) and put $dM^{+} = \sum_i x_i^a dp_i$. This is a differential equation for the " superior income-line ", the envelope of the superior income-sequence of length S when S tends to infinity.

According to the definition of the inferior income-sequence $P^{a}X^{-b} = P^{a}X^{-a}$, and therefore with an obvious extension of our notation, we write $\triangle M^{-} = \sum_i x_i^b \triangle p_i = \sum_i x_i^a \triangle p_i - \sum_i \triangle x_i \triangle p_i$. In the limit the last term becomes of the second order of smallness and may therefore be neglected (again remembering our continuity assumptions), so we obtain $dM^{-} = \sum_i x_i^a dp_i$ as the differential equation of the " inferior income-line ".

[1] This theorem can also be derived from Samuelson's (unextended) hypothesis.

It will be noticed that the superior and inferior income-lines satisfy the same differential equation

$$dM - \sum_i x_i \frac{\partial p_i}{\partial t} dt = 0$$

where x_i is a function of prices and income, while prices are constrained by belonging to the price-sequence described. Therefore prices can be represented as functions of one parameter t, and the differential equation itself contains only two variables. The point X^0 is known to satisfy this equation, which gives M as a function of t (i.e., of prices) if the so-called Lipschitz conditions[1] are fulfilled:

$$| \sum_i x_i(t, M^1) - \sum_i x_i(t, M^2) | < K | M^1 - M^2 |$$

where M^1 and M^2 are any two possible values of M for given prices and K is a constant. Clearly these conditions follow from our continuity assumptions. Therefore the differential equation defines just one curve, which means that the superior and inferior income-lines coincide.

Having found that the superior and inferior income-sequences have one common limit, which can be approached as closely as wanted by taking a sufficient number of intermediate price-sets, we must now consider the incomes belonging to this limit. To every price-set between and including P^0 and P^1 there is precisely one such income, which belongs neither to a superior nor to an inferior income-sequence of any finite length. It is therefore the only income (for a given price-set) to determine a batch about which no direct or indirect indications as to its inferiority or superiority with respect to X^0 are available.[2] Does this mean that this batch is "equivalent" to X^0? No doubt this is a reasonable guess, but in connection with the elusive problem of integrability nothing should be taken for granted. We shall find, in fact, that at this stage of our analysis Samuelson's hypothesis is no longer adequate and our axiom of semi-transitivity must be invoked.

Since P^1 was chosen arbitrarily (except for the condition that X^0 is not bought at these prices) we may now allow it to vary among all price-sets satisfying the latter condition.

[1] Cf. E. L. Ince, *Ordinary Differential Equations* (New York, 1944), pp. 62–63.

[2] Incomes higher than those belonging to some superior income-sequence are evidently revealed to be superior to the latter. A similar remark can be made for the inferior income-sequence.

For each price-set we then have one income with the unique property mentioned above, which may less precisely be described to be that all higher incomes are connected with X^0 by a chain of goods-batches of descending superiority and all lower incomes by a chain of batches of ascending superiority. Now if this unique property is an equivalence between X^0 and the terminal batches thus determined, it must be reflexive (X^0 must be equivalent to itself), symmetric (if X^0 is equivalent to X^1, then X^1 is equivalent to X^0) and transitive (if X^0 is equivalent to X^1 and X^1 is equivalent to X^2, then X^0 is equivalent to X^2).[1] These characteristics of relations are indispensable for the construction of indifference surfaces, i.e., of classes of equivalent batches.

We shall start by proving that this presumed equivalence is symmetric, which is another consequence of the argument used previously to show that the superior and inferior income-sequences coincide in the limit. Let P^1X^1 be the income at prices P^1 which separates the inferior and superior income-sequences of ever-increasing length which start at X^0; then X^1 is presumed to be equivalent to X^0. By a similar process P^0X^{00} has been found such that X^{00} is presumed to be equivalent to X^1. For presumed equivalence to be a symmetric relation X^0 and X^{00} must coincide, and that this is in fact true, can be seen as follows: The differential equation of the common limit (of superior and inferior income-sequences) between X^0 and X^1 is $dM = \sum_i x_i dp_i$, as we found above, but this equation also holds for the common limit between X^1 and X^{00}. Since the two limits coincide at X^1 they coincide everywhere, and so X^0 and X^{00} are identical.

Transitivity cannot be proved in this way, and here for the first time we must make full use of our axiom, which postulates the semi-transitivity of revealed preference. We suppose that, because of the construction described, X^1 is presumed to be equivalent to X^0, and X^2 is presumed to be equivalent to X^1. Furthermore, there is a direct link of this kind between X^{22} (also bought at prices P^2) and X^0.[2] If this presumed equivalence is transitive X^{22} and X^2 cannot be distinct, and this we shall proceed to prove. (cf. Fig. 2). Let us assume, in fact, that $P^2X^{22} > P^2X^2$

[1] Cf. e.g., A. Tarski, *Introduction to Logic* (2nd edition, New York, 1946), p. 96 ff.
[2] X^2 is not bought at prices P^0 or P^1, and X^1 is not bought at prices P^0.

and that $P^2X^{22} - P^2X^2 = 4D$ (say). We know that, by selecting a suitable number of intermediate price-sets, we can make our inferior and superior income-sequences end as near as we wish to their common limit. Now we take a superior income-sequence starting at P^0X^0 and ending at an income $P^1X^1 + D$ (for prices P^1), and another superior income-sequence starting at $P^1X^1 + D$ and ending at

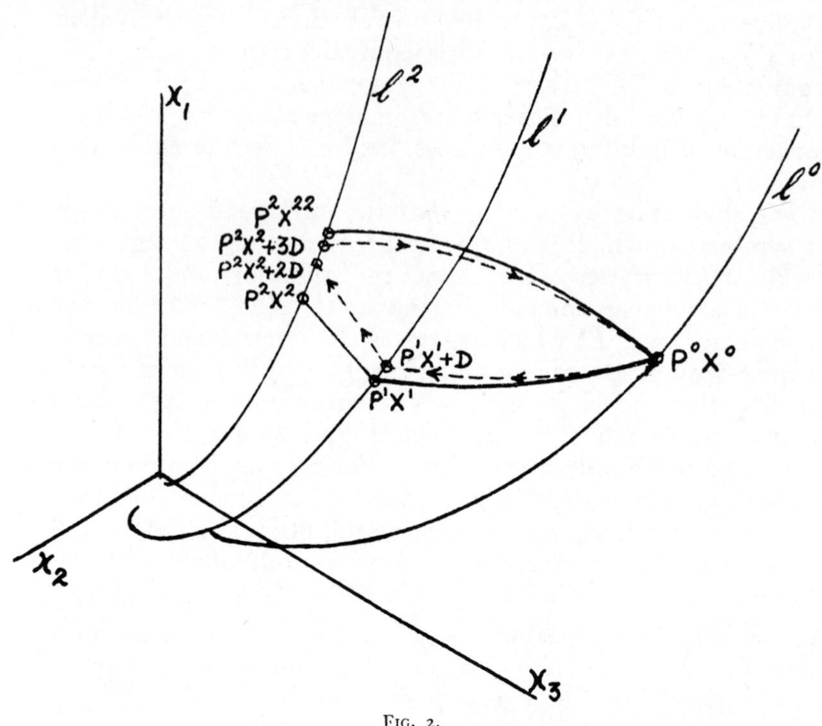

FIG. 2.

l^0, l^1 and l^2 have a similar meaning as in Fig. 1. The arrows on the dotted curve point from inferior to superior batches.

$P^2X^2 + 2D$, i.e., halfway between P^2X^2 and P^2X^{22}. We also construct an inferior income-sequence starting at P^0X^0 and ending at an amount D below P^2X^{22}, i.e., at $P^2X^2 + 3D$. Then we apply the axiom of semi-transitivity to the whole of the three sequences. We start at $P^2X^2 + 2D$ and proceed to P^0X^0 (by way of $P^1X^1 + D$) along the originally superior income-sequences, which are now looked at in the inverse direction, so that each consecutive batch is either equal or revealed to be inferior to its predecessor.

From P^0X^0 we continue along the original inferior income-sequence (in the original direction) to $P^2X^{22} - D = P^2X^2 + 3D$.

If $P^2X^{22} > P^2X^2$ the above construction is always possible (and so is a similar one for the case $P^2X^{22} < P^2X^2$), but it leads to a contradiction of the axiom. For $P^2X^2 + 2D$ is linked to $P^2X^2 + 3D$ by a chain of batches of which each is equal or revealed to be inferior to its predecessor, and at least two of these batches are different,[1] and then the axiom tells us that the first income is higher than the last one. But $P^2X^2 + 2D < P^2X^2 + 3D$ (since $D > 0$), so $P^2X^{22} > P^2X^2$ is not true. The reader will have no difficulty in applying this argument to $P^2X^{22} < P^2X^2$. Consequently $P^2X^{22} = P^2X^2$, and the relation of presumed equivalence is transitive.[2]

It remains to show that it is reflexive, i.e., that every batch is equivalent to itself. If we denote presumed equivalence by R, we have now demonstrated that X^0RX^1 implies X^1RX^0 (symmetry) and that X^0RX^1 and X^1RX^2 imply X^0RX^2. Our proof of transitivity can easily be extended to the case where X^0 and X^2 are identical which yields X^0RX^0.

These results enable us to drop the word presumed and simply speak of " equivalence ". It is true we have shown only that the relation defined by the limiting lines of ever longer inferior and superior income-sequences is an equivalence in the sense of formal logic, but previously we had remarked that it meant the absence of both superiority and inferiority. We also saw that to every price-set there is just one collection of goods equivalent to a fixed collection X^0. The class of all equivalent batches can be identified with the indifference surface through X^0. The existence of indifference surfaces implies the existence of a utility function, for to each class of equivalent batches we can assign a number (the " utility " of that class), giving higher numbers to preferred classes. As is well known, this can be done in infinitely many ways, since only ordinal properties are involved.

[1] Because of the assumptions in note 2 on p. 169.

[2] In Pareto's language this means that a " cycle ouvert " is impossible. Cf. V. Pareto, *Manuel d'Economie Politique* (2nd edition, Paris, 1927, p. 556). This proof also shows that the method of selecting " intermediate " price-sets does not influence the result.

For the benefit of mathematicians it may be pointed out that this part of the proof amounts to showing that the line integral (of the difference in utility between equivalent batches) is zero along a closed curve and therefore independent of the path. This is a well-known integrability condition ; cf. R. Courant, *Differential and Integral Calculus II* (London and Glasgow, 1936), p. 351.

Before turning to some more general questions it may be useful to point out why the problem of integrability does not arise in the case of two commodities, which was investigated by Mr. Little and Professor Samuelson (*loc. cit.*).

The process by which inferior and superior income-sequences were made to coincide in the limit (cf. above) consisted in allowing prices to vary continuously between two given price-sets P^a and P^b. We also introduced a

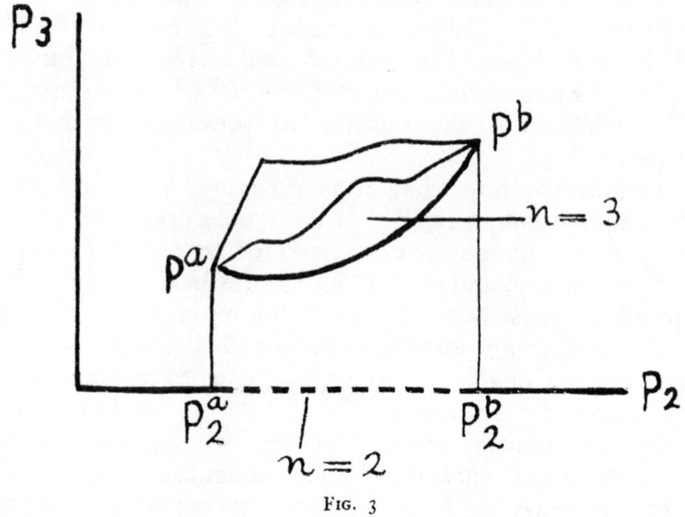

FIG. 3

convention, with a view to proportionality complications, by which the first price in every price-set was put equal to unity. If there are only two goods this implies that there is but one price (i.e., p_2) which is different between P^a and P^b, and there is but one way of changing it continuously between p_2^a and p_2^b in the way described. Consequently there can be no question of P^b being reached from P^a in more than one way, which means that there is no need to prove that " presumed equivalence " is transitive. Since, in the general case of n goods, this was the only place where our extended axiom was indispensable, no appeal to this axiom need be made if there are only two goods ; then Samuelson's original hypothesis is enough.

If there are three or more goods, and therefore two or more varying prices, there are several paths from P^a or P^b, as can be seen from Fig. 3. If $n = 2$ the relevant price p_2 can change only along its axis, but if $n = 3$ there are two prices which can vary through the plane, and similarly if $n > 3$. Integrability means that the relation between two points does not depend on the path followed from the one to the other.

As a conclusion some comments on the significance of our results will be made.

We have shown that a theory based on semi-transitive revealed preference entails the existence of ordinal utility, while the property of semi-transitivity itself was derived from utility considerations. The "revealed preference" and "utility function" (or "indifference surface") approaches to the theory of consumer's behaviour are therefore formally the same.[1]

This solves the problem suggested by Professor Samuelson,[2] viz., to deduce integrability from a generalisation of his "fundamental hypothesis". He also required an expression for the integrability conditions in finite form, i.e., "conceivably refutable by a finite number of point observations",[3] instead of by statistically smoothed curves. Our axiom of semi-transitivity is precisely this; it is not a property of curves, but of relations between a finite number of batches. Nevertheless, the practical importance of integrability can more clearly be seen from the well-known Slutsky conditions:

$$x_j \frac{\partial x_i}{\partial M} + \frac{\partial x_i}{\partial p_j} = x_i \frac{\partial x_j}{\partial M} + \frac{\partial x_j}{\partial p_i}$$

a set of reciprocal relations between cross-derivatives of demand.

The difference between the unextended hypothesis and our generalisation is merely that the latter takes into account information provided by the choices at other prices than the two price-sets which figure in Samuelson's axiom. This suggests that the problem of integrability arises only because of an incomplete statement of assumptions; no real generality is lost by supposing revealed preference to be semi-transitive instead of only asymmetric. The reasons for assuming asymmetry are no different from those for assuming semi-transitivity, as can be seen from our motivation of the extended axiom.

[1] The same result was proved by essentially analogous methods for the "marginal substitution" approach by Professor Wold, loc. cit., Part I, *Skandinavisk Aktuarietidskrift*, 1943, pp. 103–117.

[2] *Foundations*, p. 111, *n.* 19; p. 139, *n.* 17. Cf. also *Economica*, 1948, p. 251, *n.* 2.

[3] *Foundations*, p. 107, *n.* 13.

Integrability therefore appears to be essentially a spurious problem, a " will o' the wisp " as Professor Hicks has called it.[1] It might be used as a test for the completeness of any set of axioms for the static theory of consumer's behaviour, at least if saturation phenomena are excluded.[2]

University of Cambridge.

[1] *Value and Capital*, p. 19, note 1. This is borne out by the result mentioned in note 1 on previous page.

[2] The connection between non-integrability and saturation has been investigated by N. Georgescu-Roegen, " The Pure Theory of Consumer's Behaviour ", *Q.J.E.*, 1936, pp. 545–593.

19 A Probabilistic Theory of Consumer Behavior*

R. E. Quandt

I. The State of Affairs

Recent years have witnessed a great deal of controversy concerning the theory of the consumer. This controversy has revolved essentially around the problem of the measurability of utility. The initial approach to utility theory was the cardinalist approach of Jevons, Walras, Marshall, etc. The consumer was considered capable of assigning numerical utilities to the commodities he consumed; in addition, utilities could be added or subtracted and differences between various levels of utility could be compared. It was shown by Hicks and Allen that measurability assumptions were not necessary to explain the consumer's behavior.[1] For some years economists were content with ordinal preference maps until von Neumann and Morgenstern reconsidered the issue of measurability.[2] Since then the formerly discredited concept of cardinal utility has, in a new guise, regained a good deal of lost ground.

Both the ordinalists and cardinalists depend on the Complete Ordering Axiom which states that for any pair of commodities A and B, exactly one of the following is true: A is preferred to B or A is indifferent to B or B is preferred to A. Symbolically, $A\ P\ B$, $A\ I\ B$, or $B\ P\ A$. Furthermore, the axiom states that $A\ P\ B$ and $B\ P\ C$ together imply $A\ P\ C$. Without this axiom one can construct neither an ordinal preference map nor a cardinal utility index.[3] The first

* I am indebted to Professors Wassily W. Leontief and James S. Duesenberry and Messrs. Richard E. Caves and Thomas J. Finn who have read and criticized the manuscript. Of course, I alone am responsible for errors.

1. Cf. R. G. D. Allen, "The Nature of Indifference Curves," *Review of Economic Studies*, I (1934), 111; J. R. Hicks and R. G. D. Allen, "A Reconsideration of the Theory of Value," *Economica*, N. S. Nos. 1 and 2 (1934), especially pp. 52–60; J. R. Hicks, *Value and Capital*, 2d ed., Part I.

2. J. von Neumann and O. Morgenstern, *Theory of Games and Economic Behavior*, 2d ed., pp. 15–31.

3. Without complete ordering it is meaningless to speak of indifference curves and without transitivity indifference curves could intersect. Similarly,

Reprinted from the *Quarterly Journal of Economics*, Vol. LXX (November, 1956), pp. 507–536, by permission of the publisher and author.

part of the axiom states that the consumer can compare and evaluate alternatives. The second part of the axiom implies that the consumer's reaction to the various alternatives is consistent.[4] The purpose of this article is to question the universal applicability of this axiom and to suggest a modification of present theory.

II. The Deficiency of the Complete Ordering Axiom

The assumption of knowledge and of the comparability of alternatives is widespread in economics. The assumption of knowledge is composed of two distinct assumptions. First, it is assumed that the consumer knows the available alternatives. Secondly, it is assumed that he is familiar with the methods of finding a set of strategies which will maximize his chances of attaining his goals.

Consider a two-person zero-sum game and the problem of finding an optimal strategy or set of strategies with the optimal probabilities. In order to find an optimal strategy or an optimal probability distribution of strategies one must make two assumptions: (a) that every element of the pay-off matrix is known (or at least that the mathematical expectation of every element of the pay-off matrix is known) and (b) that the players know what they mean by "optimum strategy." For example, consider a person about to make a choice between two brands of soap. He plays a game in which he has two strategies: to buy soap *A* or soap *B*. (For simplicity's sake we assume that there are no other brands of soap and that the potential buyer cannot do without some soap.) Nature, consisting of the producers of soaps *A* and *B*, has the following, say, four strategies: *A* can advertise truthfully and *B* can advertise falsely; *A* can advertise falsely and *B* can advertise truthfully; both can advertise truthfully, both can advertise falsely. Then the consumer must know the utility he is going to

cardinalist theory is inconceivable without the Complete Ordering Axiom. For example, cf. A. A. Alchian, "The Meaning of Utility Measurement," *American Economic Review*, XLIII (1953), 36; J. Marschak, "Rational Behavior, Uncertain Prospects and Measurable Utility," *Econometrica*, XVIII (1950). As will be shown later, the assumption of probabilistic preferences allows the consumer to act inconsistently in the sense of "intransitively." Mr. Ellsberg seems to be in error when he attempts to minimize the importance of empirical evidence of inconsistent behavior by raising the possibility of defining preference "stochastically" while apparently keeping the remainder of the traditional framework intact. Cf. D. Ellsberg, "Notions of Measurable Utility," *Economic Journal*, LXIV (1954), 540 fn.

4. This point is somewhat delicate, as "*A P B*, *B P C* implies *A P C*" could also be taken to be a definition of consistency or rationality. Traditionally, "transitive behavior" and "optimizing behavior" are considered to be equivalent definitions of "rational behavior."

derive from each of the two brands if they live up to expectations, and he must also know the disutility of being deceived.

The problem is more basic than merely having or not having a cardinal measure of utility. It is even doubtful whether the consumer will be able to order his preferences, i.e., whether he will be able to say that, if all advertisements are truthful, he prefers a certain quantity of brand A (which is a somewhat better detergent) to a certain quantity of brand B (which has a somewhat better fragrance).

An additional unrealistic feature of traditional theory is the assumption that the consumer has a neat, easily manageable criterion for selecting his optimum strategy or strategies, that he can choose between, say, the minimax criterion and the Hurwicz criterion, that he knows what his optimism coefficient is, etc.[5] Introspection may be sufficient to show that in at least a sizeable portion of cases these assumptions are false. In most cases we probably know only that certain disasters are definitely to be avoided. Apart from this we might have a vague feeling of optimism or pessimism at best.

Surely, we shall not go to the extreme of arguing that the consumer is ignorant of his preference between three meals a day and an extended trip to the Antarctic. But it *is* argued that (a) although the consumer may know his preferences with respect to decisions in the large, he will seldom know his preferences with respect to decisions in the small, (b) frequently the consumer may not even know his preferences in the large and (c) the consumer will, in more cases than not, be unaware of the existence of any rational calculus for the selection of an optimal strategy.[6] Of course, the consumer will hardly be in a state of ignorance with respect to all commodities. The average amount of ignorance concerning a particular commodity depends on the nature of the commodity itself and on the extent to which the consumer can experiment with substitutes and thus acquire information, perhaps through conscious randomization of strategies. The applicability of the analysis to various types of commodities will be

5. For various criteria of optimization see, for example, R. Radner and J. Marschak, "Note on some Proposed Decision Criteria," *Decision Processes*, ed. R. M. Thrall, C. H. Coombs and R. L. Davis (New York: John Wiley & Sons, 1954), pp. 61–63; J. Milnor, "Games against Nature," *ibid.*, pp. 49 *et seq.*

6. It has to be emphasized that the present assertion of the consumer's ignorance does not imply that the consumer is indifferent between the relevant alternatives. By "ignorance" we mean that the consumer is incapable of stating whether he prefers A to B or B to A or whether he is indifferent between them. Good empirical evidence concerning the lack of circumspection in buying can be found in L. H. Clark, et al., *Consumer Behavior*, Vol. I (New York University Press, 1954).

briefly discussed at a later point. However, these considerations make it necessary to revise the theory of preference and consumer's choice.

III. Redefinition of Preference and the Choice Mechanism

The consumer may be ignorant of his preferences and of his criterion of optimization and yet he continues to make choices. These choices, however, do not conform to what traditional theory would lead us to expect. When the consumer is said to prefer *A* to *B*, traditional theory means that if he were given the choice of having either *A* or *B* he would elect to have *A*.[7] One might notice, however, that if the consumer is presented with several choices between *A* and *B* over a period of time, he will not necessarily make the same choice on every occasion. Of course, this is not surprising. If the consumer faces unsure prospects, i.e., if in a game he knows only the probability distribution of his opponent's strategies, his optimal behavior will consist of using a probability mix of his own strategies according to the appropriate probability distribution.

In ordinal theory, dealing with sure prospects, one would say that the consumer's tastes had changed. This is, however, inadequate for the following reasons: (a) the desire for variety may well be part of the consumer's "tastes"; (b) the statement that "tastes have changed" is the customary subterfuge of consumer theory whenever it is unable to explain a phenomenon; (c) "changes of taste" may occur with such frequency (and perhaps with such regularity) as to render timeless utility functions and a timeless definition of "tastes" meaningless.

It is not obvious how this problem could be handled by defining the utility function over time and incorporating into it "variety" in some explicit form. For example, if we notice that during the time period for which the utility function is defined the consumer's ice-cream purchases consist of 60 per cent vanilla and 40 per cent strawberry ice cream, we might introduce a commodity bundle consisting of the above kinds of ice cream in the stated proportions. However, this device would not explain why at some time during the period the consumer "prefers" vanilla to strawberry and at some other time strawberry to vanilla. All this device can accomplish is to state that before the horizon is reached the consumer will buy a certain number of bundles of vanilla and strawberry ice cream in every income period.

7. This is merely a result of the underlying postulate of utility maximization. If *A* has more utility for the consumer than *B*, he will "prefer" *A* to *B*.

The consumer is often ignorant of the exact state of his preferences and he is frequently insensitive to small changes or differences in stimuli.[8] As a result, a small movement in any direction from any initial position may leave the consumer as well off as before. It might be suggested that we deal with this problem by considering an indifference map consisting not of indifference curves but of indifference

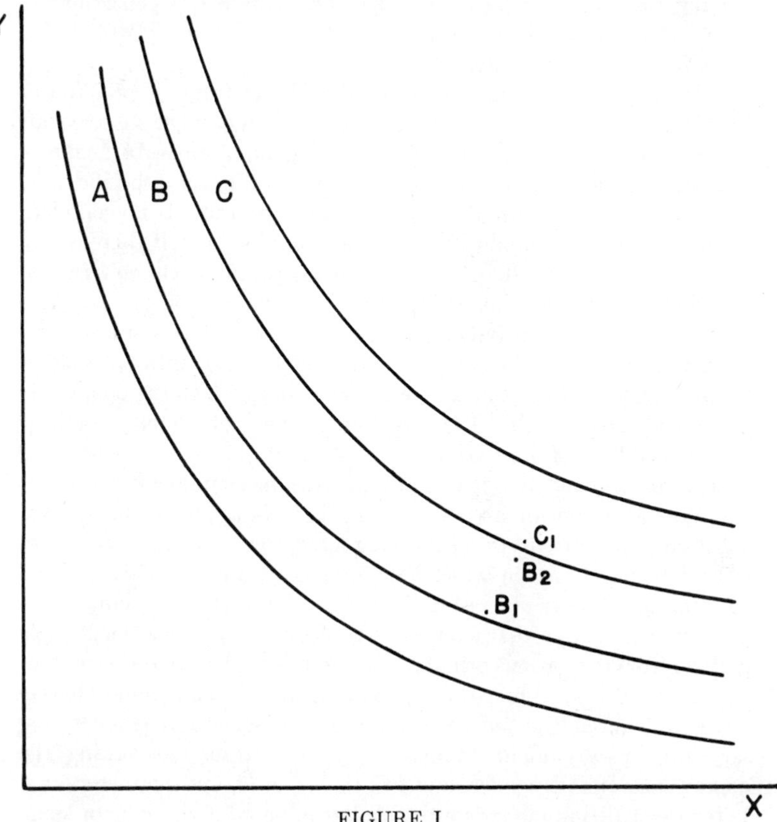

FIGURE I

bands as in the diagram above.

An indifference band, such as A, would be defined as a set of points closed toward the origin and open toward the positive orthant between any two of which the consumer had no preferences. This is

8. Consider the problem of the "threshold" of sensations. Cf. N. Georgescu-Roegen, "The Pure Theory of Consumer Behavior," this *Journal*, L (1936), 570.

clearly an unsatisfactory way of solving the problem. First, the utility surface corresponding to such an indifference map would clearly be discontinuous. Secondly, a small change may have a larger effect on the consumer than a large one. For instance, the addition of small quantities of x and y in the initial position B_2 and moving the consumer to C_1 would increase his utility. Taking B_1 as the initial position, much larger additions of x and y would still leave the consumer indifferent.

It becomes necessary to reconsider the concept of preference. Each commodity can be regarded as a collection of what we may call *primitive characteristics*. Such primitive (or nondecomposable) characteristics are size, weight, color, quantity, suitability for a specific task, etc. It has been stated before that, in general, there is no complete ordering among commodities in the traditional sense. If there is any complete ordering at all, it is, at best, among primitive characteristics. We shall make the weak assumption that there exists a complete ordering among primitive characteristics. Thus it is assumed that the consumer knows that he prefers the detergent qualities of soap A to those of soap B but that he prefers the odor of B to the odor of A. A particular commodity A is regarded as being completely described and defined by its primitive characteristics $(a_1, a_2, \ldots, a_n)$ where the a's may or may not be capable of numerical measurement.

When the consumer is about to make a choice, he must evaluate and compare various primitive characteristics. He is assumed to have a utility function which tells him the utility he derives from consuming a particular commodity with a certain amount of a particular primitive characteristic. It also tells him how the utilities derived from the various primitive characteristics have to be weighted, i.e., it tells the consumer the utility derived from compound characteristics (combinations of primitive characteristics). It is not necessary for the argument to make any assumption concerning the dependence or independence of utilities of primitive characteristics. Later we shall assume independence but merely for the sake of keeping the notation simple.

The utility function is assumed to have the following properties:

(a) U is continuous

(b) $U(a_j) = 0$, $a_j \neq 0$ means that a_j is an irrelevant characteristic

(c) $U(a_j + \Delta a_j) \geq U(a_j)$

(d) Any monotonic transformation of U is a utility function.[9]

9. Notice that we do not assume measurability in the von Neumann-Morgenstern sense, since we have not assumed that only linear transformations of U are also utility functions. By not assuming additivity of utilities, we do not have Jevons-Marshall type measurability either.

Not all primitive characteristics are equally important. In fact, there will be some characteristics which the consumer will take into consideration every time he is presented with the alternative of choosing the commodity in question. For example, if the consumer is about to buy a house, he might always consider the location of the buildings which appeal to him. On the other hand, there will be some primitive characteristics which will not always be taken into consideration. Whether or not these factors will be taken into consideration depends mainly on external factors and the circumstances surrounding the choice situation. For instance, a certain man purchasing wine by himself may not pay the slightest attention to vintage; but in the presence of a critical friend he may pay a great deal of attention to it.

It is, then, not very meaningful to say that the consumer prefers A to B or that his utility index for A is 16.7 "utils." All one can really say is that at the time of choice the consumer preferred A to B. Since the consumer may base his evaluation of commodities on more or less different sets of primitive characteristics as time passes and external circumstances change, his preferences between A and B may change without any change in underlying tastes.[1]

The consumer lives in a certain environment and makes his choices in that environment. Experience may show, for example, that the primitive characteristic a_i is considered in p per cent of the cases in which the consumer has to choose between A and some other commodity. There is a certain probability that in a particular (randomly selected) choice situation the consumer will consider primitive characteristic a_i. Similarly, there is a certain probability that the consumer will consider the compound characteristic consisting of the primitive characteristics a_i, a_j, a_k. In exactly analogous fashion there is a certain probability that in a randomly selected choice situation concerning commodities A and B, particular a_i's and b_j's will be evaluated by the consumer.

Let A have n and B have m primitive characteristics. Let the first r a's and the first s b's be those characteristics which are always taken into consideration.[2] At any particular time, one or two or three or perhaps all $n - r$ nonessential characteristics may be taken into consideration. Since the nonessential primitive characteristics may be considered by the consumer in various combinations, we consider

1. I.e., there is no change in the function U. A "change in taste" in traditional consumer theory corresponds to a change in the function U.

2. Call these "essential" characteristics and let the rest be "nonessential" characteristics.

instead of the $n - r$ nonessential primitive characteristics the 2^{n-r} compound characteristics which can be formed by the $n - r$ primitive characteristics.[3] Each of these compound characteristics has a certain probability of being considered.[4] In order to simplify notation, we now assume the measurability, independence, and additivity of utilities. The utility index for commodity A at a particular time can be written as

$$\sum_{i=1}^{r} w_i U(a_i) + w_j U(a_j)$$

for some single $j = r + 1, \ldots, r + 2^{n-r}$, where the w's are weights such that $\sum_{j=1}^{2^{n-r}+r} w_j = 1$. Notice that a_j, $j \geqq r + 1$, denotes the compound characteristics which can be formed out of the last $n - r$ (nonessential) primitive characteristics. Similarly, the utility index for B is

$$\sum_{i=1}^{s} v_i U(b_i) + v_k U(b_k)$$

for some single $k = s + 1, \ldots, s + 2^{m-s}$. Then, assuming that the consumer desires to maximize utility, A will be chosen over B (or A will be preferred to B) in a particular choice situation if

$$\sum_{i=1}^{r} w_j U(a_i) + w_j U(a_j) > \sum_{i=1}^{s} v_i U(b_i) + v_k U(b_k)$$

for some single j and k.

It should be noted that it would be meaningless to define preference in terms of the *expectation* of the second terms of the above

3. We may consider no nonessential characteristic at all. We can consider one nonessential characteristic in $\binom{n-r}{1}$ ways, two in $\binom{n-r}{2}$ ways, etc. The total number of ways of considering zero or one or two, etc., out of $n - r$ nonessential primitive characteristics is $\binom{n-r}{0} + \binom{n-r}{1} + \ldots + \binom{n-r}{n-r-1} + \binom{n-r}{n-r} = 2^{n-r}$.

4. If the probabilities of the primitive characteristics are independent, the probability of the compound characteristics is the product of the probabilities of the primitive characteristics. If these probabilities are not independent, i.e., if considering one primitive characteristic enhances the probability of considering a certain other primitive characteristic, we have to use conditional probabilities. The set of compound characteristics contains only mutually exclusive members; i.e., the joint probability of any two is zero.

expressions for the utility index; i.e., it would be meaningless to say that A is preferred to B if

$$\sum_{i=1}^{r} w_i U(a_i) + E[w_j U(a_j)] > \sum_{i=1}^{s} v_i U(b_i) + E[v_k U(b_k)]$$

because the expectation carries no implication concerning either a particular choice or the frequency of choices in the long run. For simplicity's sake let the utility of the essential primitive characteristics of both A and B be the same. Then we consider only the nonessentials. Let these be a_1, a_2, a_3 and b_1, b_2, b_3 with the following utilities and probabilities:

	Utility	Probability		Utility	Probability
a_1	16	.9990	b_1	15	1/3
a_2	100	.0005	b_2	15	1/3
a_3	116	.0005	b_3	30	1/3

$E(A) = 16.092$ and $E(B) = 20.000$. The expectation of B is greater than the expectation of A, yet in the long run A will be preferred to B (chosen over B) in well over half the cases.

We have temporarily used the term "preference" to refer to the relative magnitude of utility indices at a particular moment. Since the magnitude of the utility index changes randomly,[5] sometimes A will be "preferred" to B and sometimes B to A. We now define preference as follows: A is preferred to B if, in the long run, A is chosen over B more than 50 per cent of the time, i.e., if A's utility index exceeds B's utility index in more than half the cases in which the consumer has to choose between them. The utilities of the various primitive and compound characteristics and the probabilities that certain characteristics will be taken into consideration by the consumer allow us to calculate the probability that A will be preferred to B, i.e., the relative frequency with which A will be chosen over B in the long run. To summarize: *at a particular moment A is preferred to B* if at that moment the utility index of A is greater than the utility index of B.[6] *A is preferred to B* if the probability of A being chosen over B at a particular randomly selected moment is greater than .5. Similarly, A is indifferent to B if that probability

5. Of course, this assumes that external circumstances change randomly.

6. This is virtually tautological. It amounts to asserting that (a) the consumer tries to maximize his utility and (b) that he "prefers" what he actually chooses.

is equal to .5 and B is preferred to A if that probability is less than .5.[7]

It may be noted that the consumer is assumed to act *as if* he were facing sure prospects. It is clear that his prospects are sure only if he takes all their characteristics into consideration, because otherwise his expectations may not be fulfilled. If his expectations are not fulfilled, error has been committed either by faulty evaluation of characteristics or by failing to evaluate all characteristics. If the consumer realizes that the outcome of his strategies is uncertain, it is plausible that his behavior will be probabilistic, since he will randomize his strategies in order to behave optimally. It has been shown that the consumer may act in a probabilistic manner even though he acts as if the outcome of his strategies were objectively certain.

Previously we have considered only the case in which the consumer acts in a probabilistic manner as a result of incomplete scanning of characteristics[8] but bases his decision on error-free evaluation

7. Cf. N. Georgescu-Roegen, "The Pure Theory of Consumer Behavior," *op. cit.*, 545–94; *idem*, "The Theory of Consumer's Choice and the Constancy of Economic Laws," this *Journal*, LXIV (1950), 130. It should be noted that the present definitions are different from the ones employed by Georgescu-Roegen. In his analysis A is preferred to B if $p[\phi\ (A,B,t_a,t_b)] = 1$ where p denotes probability, ϕ is the preference function of A over B and t_a and t_b are the lengths of time during which the consumer had experimented with A and B in the past. Similarly, B is preferred to A if $p = 0$ and A and B are indifferent if $0 < p < 1$ (or in the limit, as $t_a, t_b \rightarrow \infty$, $p = \frac{1}{2}$). This is a reasonable way of defining preference and indifference if the consumer experiences doubt at the moment of choice such that he does not really know what he wants. In our case this would occur only if the two sets of characteristics evaluated by the consumer had the same utility for him. In that case, the consumer would presumably flip a coin or resort to some similar method of conscious randomization and the probability of A being preferred to B would be $\frac{1}{2}$. This is a situation of indifference in Georgescu-Roegen's analysis, but it is the sole situation of indifference as a limiting case only.

In a recent article, Georgescu-Roegen concludes that indifference does not exist. He argues that the list of criteria or characteristics by which alternatives can be compared is inexhaustible such that if the consumer is indifferent between the first n pairs of corresponding characteristics of commodities A and B, there always exists an $(n + 1)$st characteristic which will cause the consumer to prefer A to B or vice versa. See "Choice, Expectations and Measurability," this *Journal*, LXVIII (1954), 518–21.

8. H. A. Simon, "A Behavioral Model of Rational Choice," this *Journal*, LXIX (1955), 110–11. Simon suggests a plausible reason why the scanning of alternatives (characteristics in this case) should be incomplete. Alternatives or characteristics are examined in a sequence and the moment one is found which is above the *aspiration level*, the process of scanning is discontinued. In Simon's example, the chess player contents himself with finding *one* way of checkmating the opponent; as soon as one way has been found, the process of examining alternatives stops. Similarly, when the consumer scans nonessential characteristics,

of characteristics. If one now assumes the opposite extreme; i.e., that all characteristics are taken into consideration but subject to error, it can be shown that the consumer will again tend to behave in a manner customarily considered inconsistent. If the consumer's judgment is subject to error but he acts as if his prospects were certain, he will eventually make a mistake and his judgment will have been proved wrong. Error may be due to one or both of the following two factors: (a) the consumer estimates correctly the quantity, degree, etc., of each characteristic present in the commodity but errs in his judgment that a particular ranking or numerical utility is appropriate in view of these characteristics; (b) he may attach rankings or utilities to characteristics correctly (i.e., consistently with the satisfaction which he actually derives from the commodity at the time of actual consumption), but errs in attributing particular quantities and degrees of characteristics to the commodity.

After error has occurred, it becomes clear which of these two factors was responsible. If the former, the consumer will revise the function or mechanism by which rankings or numerical utilities are assigned to commodities. If the latter, the consumer's successive evaluation of a commodity may change even without a change in tastes and he may behave in an apparently inconsistent manner; i.e., prefer A to B, then prefer B to A, then, if new errors have occurred, A to B again, etc. However, if the consumer *learns* from his mistakes, the probability of successive errors is diminished and the probability that A will be preferred to B approaches either 1 or 0 with time. It must be emphasized that the assumption of learning is necessary for the assertion that successive errors decrease. If learning does not take place, the consumer's probabilistic behavior will depend on the probability distribution of errors.

It is not asserted that the consumer acts probabilistically (or, from the point of view of traditional theory, inconsistently) with respect to all commodities. The consumer's action has both a systematic and a random component.[9] Which one of these components is the dominant one is surely a function of the nature of the com-

he may stop as soon as he comes upon a satisfactory one (one above a certain aspiration level), provided that the previously considered characteristics of the commodity in question are not sufficiently noxious to put the commodity *hors de combat.* At any rate, the more satisfactory characteristics the consumer has found, the likelier it may be that he will discontinue the process of scanning.

9. Note that the random component may be the result of two distinct factors: (a) conscious randomization as in Section II, (b) random behavior not involving conscious randomization as in the present section.

modity. The final answer to the question whether the consumer does or does not act randomly with respect to a particular commodity is essentially a matter of degree. For example, in the case of consumers' durables like houses, television sets, etc., the consumer customarily equips himself with a great deal of information about the market and in most cases choice occurs only after extensive deliberation. Neither conscious nor unconscious randomization is likely to play a large role. In the case of daily necessities which are sufficiently low priced so that they account for a small percentage of the consumer's budget, experimentation with various brands has virtually no cost and the consumer will soon obtain all the information he needs. If, at the beginning of his career as a consumer, he is totally ignorant, he will experiment and perhaps behave randomly for a while until learning has taken place.[1] Both types of random behavior are most likely to occur in the intermediate category of semidurables or minor durable goods: commodities which are sufficiently durable so that experimentation cannot be exhaustive (clothing, rented apartments, fountain pens, etc.) yet are sufficiently nondurable or inexpensive so that error is not too heavily penalized. There is some empirical evidence in support of these hypotheses.[2] In the sample used in the study cited below it was found that a sizeable portion of durable goods purchases (about one-third) was unplanned, the proportion being noticeably higher for the intermediate, semidurable category. Impulse buying (unplanned purchases which could have been postponed) account for almost one-fifth of consumers' durables purchases with somewhat higher incidence in the intermediate category.

IV. Intransitivity

According to the present definition, preferences are not generally transitive. This is contrary to the postulates of traditional consumer theory. Even though most people would admit that in reality there exist at least some cases of irrational behavior, one instinctively rebels against expressly incorporating into theory the concept of irrationality.[3] But it is clear that (a) intransitive and irrational

1. This tendency may be counteracted if the aspiration level for the commodity is sufficiently low so that the real cost of acquiring the commodity does not correspond to the satisfaction derived from it. An example of this was suggested by Professor Duesenberry: in supermarkets people seem to have a tendency to buy brands located on the top shelves rather than on bottom shelves.

2. R. Ferber, "Factors Influencing Durable Goods Purchases," *Consumer Behavior*, Vol. II, ed. L. H. Clark, *op. cit.*, pp. 80–83, 101–2.

3. Of course, intransitive behavior is merely one aspect of irrational behavior. A person consciously attempting to minimize utility would also be called irra-

behavior in the traditional sense may be reasonable in the present analysis, (b) even if one found human behavior irrational by all known standards, there could be no presumption against explicitly incorporating such irrationality into theory.

One does not have to look far for examples of irrational or inconsistent behavior. The causes of such behavior are numerous: indolence, inertia, habit, superstition, supra-economic values, the threshold of sensations, etc.[4] The present analysis attempts to introduce some further causes of possibly irrational behavior and to systematize the treatment of such behavior. It has been shown above that errors and incomplete analysis of choice situations result in probabilistic behavior by the consumer. It now has to be shown that such behavior may be irrational in the traditional sense.

To show the possibility of intransitive behavior in the present analysis we shall resort to some numerical examples. We shall consider three commodities A, B, and C each of which has three primitive and one compound characteristic. The first primitive characteristic is an irrelevant one; the compound characteristic consists of a combination of the relevant ones. All are assumed to be nonessential. Assume that the utilities associated with each of the characteristics of the three commodities are as in Table I:

$U(a_1) = 0$	$U(b_1) = 0$	$U(c_1) = 0$
$U(a_2) = 1$	$U(b_2) = .5$	$U(c_2) = .6$
$U(a_3) = 2$	$U(b_3) = 2.6$	$U(c_3) = 2.3$
$U(a_4) = 3$	$U(b_4) = 3.1$	$U(c_4) = 2.9$

TABLE I

tional. So would an entrepreneur who failed to maximize profits, with the exception of certain obvious modifications of the profit maximizing principle. See for example T. Scitovszky, "A Note on Profit Maximization and Its Implications," *Review of Economic Studies*, XI (1943), 57–60; F. and V. Lutz, *The Theory of Investment of the Firm* (Princeton University Press, 1950), pp. 70–75 and 190–92.

4. Cf. L. Baudin, "Irrationality in Economics," this *Journal*, LXVIII (1954), 487–502. Baudin defines rationality as "conscious and logical adaptation of means to coherent ends." By this definition our consumers are no longer rational, since, in the absence of full information, they lack the "conscious and logical adaptation of means to coherent ends."

In artificial choice situations inconsistent behavior was found by F. Mosteller and P. Nogee, "An Experimental Measurement of Utility," *Journal of Political Economy*, LIX (1951), 371–404. The choice situations in which the experimental subjects were tested appear to have been much simpler than the situations which the average consumer faces. For instance, the subjects were provided with a description of the odds of winning or losing in particular gambling experiments. Increase in the complexity of choice situations seemed to be favorable to inconsistent behavior.

For example, A might be a particular fountain pen with which the consumer is confronted. For this particular consumer the first or irrelevant characteristic, a_1, is color, i.e., he derives no utility from the fact that this particular pen is, say, grey. The other characteristics are relevant. These are the fineness of the point (a_2) and the pen's capacity to hold ink (a_3). These characteristics can be considered either singly or jointly. When the consumer considers both the fineness of the point and the pen's capacity to hold ink we say that he considers the compound characteristic a_4 which denotes the simultaneous consideration of both a_2 and a_3. In this example it is assumed that the consumer expects to derive one unit of satisfaction (1 "util") from the quality of the point and 2 "utils" from the pen's ink capacity. If at the moment of choice, he considers both of these characteristics, he will expect to derive from them the amount of satisfaction which is the sum of the satisfactions derived from the individual characteristics.[5] Therefore the utility derived from a_4 is $1 + 2 = 3$ "utils." The alternative commodity B can be either a commodity of essentially the same type as A, i.e., another fountain pen or something quite different, say, an alarm clock. In the latter case the characteristics of B which the consumer considers may also be of radically different types. For example, in the case of the alarm clock the irrelevant characteristic b_1 might be the shape of the clock (round or square), b_2 is, say, the accuracy of the clock, and b_3 the loudness of its ring.

First, we shall describe the joint probability distribution of pairs of sets of characteristics[6] on the assumption that no two sets of characteristics are independently distributed (Tables II). If the joint distribution of A and B (or rather of their characteristics) is $F(A,B)$, A is preferred to B if $\int_{U(A) > U(B)} dF(A,B) > .5$ and similarly for the pairs (B,C) and (A,C). A particular number in Tables IIa and IIIa represents the probability of evaluating the relative desirability of the two commodities in question on the basis of the characteristic of A shown on the left for the row in question, and of the characteristic of B shown at the top of the same column. These characteristics may be primitive or compound, as the case may be. The probabilities are postulated here without reference to empirical

5. As can be seen, additivity of utilities has been assumed. This assumption is not necessary.

6. By a set of characteristics I mean all the characteristics of a particular commodity.

knowledge. They will generally depend on the external circumstances surrounding the choice situation, such as the type of advertising, the arrangement of commodities in showrooms, the consumer's past experience, etc. As above, let us assume that A represents a particular fountain pen and B a particular alarm clock. When the consumer considers only the accuracy of the alarm clock (b_2) as the criterion by which he judges its desirability, there might be a certain probability, say, .05 that he will base his evaluation of the fountain pen on the characteristic a_1 (color), the probability .10 that he will consider a_2 (fineness of the point), etc.[7] These probabilities of considering particular A characteristics may or may not depend on the particular B characteristic which is being considered. For example, in Table IIa the relative magnitude of the probabilities of

	b_1	b_2	b_3	b_4
a_1	0	.05	.02	.01
a_2	*.10*	*.10*	.02	.01
a_3	*.10*	*.10*	.02	.01
a_4	*.30*	*.10*	*.05*	.01

TABLE IIa

	c_1	c_2	c_3	c_4
b_1	0	0	0	0
b_2	*.025*	.025	.025	.025
b_3	*.025*	*.025*	*.025*	*.025*
b_4	*.200*	*.200*	*.200*	*.200*

TABLE IIb

	c_1	c_2	c_3	c_4
a_1	0	.1	.1	.2
a_2	*0*	*0*	.2	.2
a_3	*0*	*0*	0	.2
a_4	*0*	*0*	*0*	*0*

TABLE IIc

considering various A characteristics depends on which B characteristic is being considered. This means that the particular characteristic of the alarm clock which the consumer considers has some influence on which characteristics of the fountain pen will be taken into account with high probability. This kind of relationship is not assumed to hold in the hypothetical example in Tables III. If A and B are essentially similar (say, different brands of the same commodity), it seems likely that if there is a high probability of considering a particular characteristic of A, say, capacity to hold ink, there will also be a high probability of considering the same characteristic in B. In every table the sum of the probabilities of considering some characteristic of A and some of B is by definition equal to one.

7. See Table IIa.

In any particular situation the consumer will choose A over B if the A characteristic considered gives him more satisfaction or utility than the B characteristic which he evaluates. A is preferred to B (in the present sense of the word "preferred") if the sum of the probabilities of considering pairs of characteristics for which the A characteristic has higher utility is greater than .5. This information can be obtained by combining the information in Table I with Tables II and III. The probabilities of those situations in which A will be chosen over B (and also for the pairs (B,C) and (A,C)) are italicized in Tables II and III. For instance, in Table IIa the entry in the second row and the second column (.10) is italicized. This entry represents the probability of basing one's choice between the fountain pen and the alarm clock on the satisfaction derived from the fineness of the point and the accuracy of the clock. From Table I it can be seen that the consumer derives 1 "util" from the former and only .5 "utils" from the latter. Hence in this situation A will be chosen, as indicated by italicizing the entry. The total probability of choosing A over B or $\int_{U(A) > U(B)} dF(A,B)$ is given by the sum of the italicized entries in Table IIa and similarly for the other distributions in Tables IIb and IIc. The sum of the italicized entries in Table IIa is .85 which is greater than .5. Hence by the present definition A is preferred to B. In Table IIb this sum is .925, which again is greater than .5. Therefore B is preferred to C. In Table IIc this sum is zero. This means that A is not preferred to C, or C is preferred to A.

Assuming that the probability distributions of the characteristics of A, B, and C are independent, we might have the following hypothetical joint distributions:

	b_1	b_2	b_3	b_4
a_1	.040635	.180600	.225750	.004515
a_2	*.002979*	*.013240*	.016550	.000331
a_3	*.002979*	*.013240*	.016550	.000331
a_4	*.043407*	*.192920*	*.241150*	.004823

TABLE IIIa

	c_1	c_2	c_3	c_4
b_1	.0045	.0045	.0810	0
b_2	*.0200*	.0200	.3600	0
b_3	*.0250*	*.0250*	*.4500*	*0*
b_4	*.0005*	*.0005*	*.0090*	*0*

TABLE IIIb

	c_1	c_2	c_3	c_4
a_1	.022575	.022575	.406350	0
a_2	*.001655*	*.001655*	.029790	0
a_3	*.001655*	*.001655*	.029790	0
a_4	*.024115*	*.024115*	*.434070*	*0*

TABLE IIIc

In this case the marginal distributions are as follows:[8]

$p(a_1) = .4515$	$p(b_1) = .09$	$p(c_1) = .05$
$p(a_2) = .0331$	$p(b_2) = .40$	$p(c_2) = .05$
$p(a_3) = .0331$	$p(b_3) = .50$	$p(c_3) = .90$
$p(a_4) = .4823$	$p(b_4) = .01$	$p(c_4) = .00$

According to the marginal distributions, the three commodities A, B, and C can be characterized as follows. In the case of A it is very likely that either no relevant characteristic or both relevant characteristics will be taken into consideration. In the case of B it is very likely that one or the other (but not both or neither) relevant characteristic will be considered. In the case of C it is most likely that one particular relevant characteristic will be taken into account. It may be possible to find real commodities which fit the implications of the above marginal distributions. A might be a television set. It is either bought irrespective of its relevant features (there is a high probability of considering only an irrelevant characteristic) or the consumer considers both relevant characteristics, namely the clearness of the picture (a_2) and the clearness of the sound (a_3). This is shown by the fact that the probability of the compound characteristic a_4 is high whereas $p(a_2)$ and $p(a_3)$ are both small. In other words, if the consumer considers one of the relevant characteristics, he will most likely also consider the other one, since the television set is worthless unless both of these features are satisfactory. B might be the latest edition of the *Encyclopedia Britannica.* It may be characterized by the fact that the consumer will almost certainly consider only one of its two relevant characteristics. Let these characteristics be suitability for providing information (b_2) and capacity to fill up empty library shelves (b_3). The consumer will rarely consider both characteristics, because if he is interested in information he might not care about improving the looks of his library by filling empty shelves, and vice versa. C might be any commodity for which only one relevant characteristic will be considered with high probability. For example, in the case of a washing machine

8. The marginal distributions are obtained from the joint distributions in Tables III in the following manner. Take as an example Table IIIa. Add the probabilities shown in the first row. This sum is .4515. This means that the probability of considering a_1 *irrespective* of what characteristics of B the consumer considers, is .4515. This addition is performed for each row of Table IIIa (or IIIc) and the resulting probabilities are the marginal distribution of the characteristics of A. Performing this for the columns of Table IIIa (or the rows of Table IIIb) gives the marginal distribution for B and analogously for C.

the salesman might seldom emphasize any characteristic other than the machine's efficiency in washing clothes (c_3). These examples are admittedly somewhat artificial. At any rate, B comes closest to our analogy to the Simon example of not considering all possible characteristics; A comes closest to Georgescu-Roegen's latest contention that all relevant characteristics are considered.[9]

It is plausible to assert that the probabilities of basing choice on a particular combination of characteristics change over time. Past decisions and choices probably influence the frequency with which particular characteristics will be chosen in the present and in the future.[1] The consumer learns partly by past successful choice and partly by past unsuccessful choice. Thus if the consumer makes a particular choice on the basis of a particular set of characteristics, and the results of the choice do not make him wish he had chosen differently, he is likely to base his next decision concerning the same commodity on the same characteristics. Hence the probability of those characteristics being considered is increased. If his choice is unsuccessful, the opposite may happen.

When the consumer considers a particular compound characteristic one should think of him as choosing a particular strategy. This strategy has a certain probability of being successful. In certain cases the consideration of a particular compound characteristic will always lead to the purchase of the commodity in question and this purchase will always be considered optimal by the consumer ex post facto. This is the case of a commodity which has absolute superiority, both actual and imputed, over all its rivals. In this case the consumer should always consider the compound characteristic a_j the consideration of which invariably leads to the purchase of the commodity, if he is to behave optimally. One can say that the optimal probability of considering the characteristic a_j is unity. If learning takes place, and the initial probability of considering a_j (denoted by $p(a_j)$) was less than one, the consumer's behavior will alter with time and his $p(a_j)$ will approach unity. The optimal $p(a_j)$, however, is not necessarily one. First, the consideration of the same characteristics does not always lead to the purchase of the possibly always optimal commodity (if changes in the advertising

9. It has been conjectured, however, that transitivity will hold in empirically verified cases. See A. J. Papandreou, "An Experimental Test of a Proposition in the Theory of Choice," *Consumer Behavior, op. cit.*, I, 90–91.

1. N. Georgescu-Roegen, "The Theory of Consumer's Choice and the Constancy of Economic Laws," *op. cit.*, 129–31; J. S. Duesenberry, *Income, Saving and the Theory of Consumer Behavior* (Harvard University Press, 1952), Chap. III.

techniques of the producers of inferior rival commodities temporarily obscure the issue). Secondly, the consideration of the same characteristics may always lead to the purchase of a commodity which is not always optimal as a result of the appearance on the market of new and better substitutes. In either case, the optimal probability with which a_j should be considered is less than one. Empirical evidence has shown that there is an approach to the true probability but it appears that this approach is less satisfactory in the case in which the true probability is less than one.[2] In fact, the consumer can be expected to vacillate between certain not too wide limits around the true probability. It is clear from the present analysis that his behavior will continue to be probabilistic and his preferences may be intransitive even in the long run.

In one of the numerical examples it was assumed that the various sets of characteristics are independently distributed; in the other example they were assumed to be dependent. It appears likely that these variables are not independently distributed. For example, the characteristics considered by a potential buyer of wine may depend on whether the alternative is cider or champagne.[3]

Assume now that the consumer's learning process is such that all bivariate distributions collapse to a point with probability one as time approaches infinity; i.e., after a long time the consumer will almost certainly consider the same characteristics every time. Then it is clear that in the limit the preference relation is intransitive only if the probability distributions of the characteristics of the various commodities involved are not independent.

V. Expected Behavior under Price and Income Changes

It is clear that the customary indifference map cannot be used in the present analysis. In order to allow for intransitivity, we would have to allow indifference curves to intersect. To interpret an indifference curve as a line along which the consumer prefers one

2. W. K. Estes, "Individual Behavior in Uncertain Situations: An Interpretation in Terms of Statistical Association Theory," *Decision Processes*, pp. 127–38.

3. The primitive characteristics of a particular commodity (instead of the two sets of characteristics of a pair of commodities) may themselves be either independently or not independently distributed. If the former, the probabilities of particular compound characteristics are the products of the probabilities of the component primitive characteristics. This is not true in the latter case. Which of these two cases will obtain is difficult to say a priori; in certain cases the consideration of one primitive characteristic will enhance the probability of another being considered, in certain others it may not. Cf. note 4, p. 514.

batch of commodities to any other batch exactly 50 per cent of the time is not very meaningful. The deterministic conclusion of traditional theory that the consumer *will* buy certain quantities, given prices and his income, is no longer admissible except as a limiting case. All one can now say is that there is a high probability or a low probability that the consumer will act in a certain way.

We shall make the following simplifying assumptions: (a) there are only two commodities, x and y, (b) these commodities can be bought only in certain combinations, namely in A-units consisting of 1 x and 2 y's and in B units consisting of 2 x's and 1 y. This assumption is made in order to render the present analysis more easily comparable with the traditional theory of the consumer.[4] Realism would be enhanced by considering all practical combinations in which x and y can be bought: thus the combinations 0 x and 1 y, 0 x and 2 y, . . . , 1 x and 0 y, 1 x and 1 y, 1 x and 2 y, etc. This would unfortunately make the model unwieldy for the present purpose, just as it would be too cumbersome in the customary geometric analysis to consider more than two commodities.[5]

Let us plot along the horizontal axes quantities of the combinations A and B, and let us plot vertically the probability that the consumer will prefer the A-batch in a particular situation in which he has to choose between certain quantities of A-batches and B-batches represented by a point in the horizontal plane. Then the probability surface showing the probability of an A-batch being preferred to a B-batch for all possible combinations of A and B batches may appear as in the diagram on the following page.

The reason for the shape of the surface, as drawn, is the following: starting at 0, move to the right along OM. The probability of choosing any positive quantity of A instead of a zero quantity of B must be unity. Hence the probability surface above OM is RS. If now, at M, we start increasing the quantity of alternative B-batches

4. In traditional theory the consumer always buys a batch of commodities except when they are perfect substitutes and the price ratio is not equal to the slope of the indifference curves. Then a corner solution results and one of the commodities is not bought at all.

5. The present analysis does suffer from the fact that in any geometrically manageable case one has to restrict oneself to dealing with various quantities of only two types of batches of x and y, whereas in the usual theory of the consumer the proportions of x and y are continuously variable even in two-dimensional geometric analysis. Therefore, the present analysis can only deal with the direction of the change in the composition of the consumer's purchases; i.e., will the consumer's purchases become more x-intensive or more y-intensive as some parameter changes?

along MN, the probability of A being preferred declines along ST. If at N we decrease the quantity of A along NP, the probability of A being chosen declines along TP. This outlines the surface as shown in Figure II.[6] We can now intersect this three-dimensional surface by horizontal planes corresponding to different probabilities of A being preferred to B. Projecting the resulting intersections on the base plane we obtain a set of contour lines or iso-probability curves. Along each of these lines the probability of A being preferred to B is the same. One possible iso-probability map is shown in Figure III.[7]

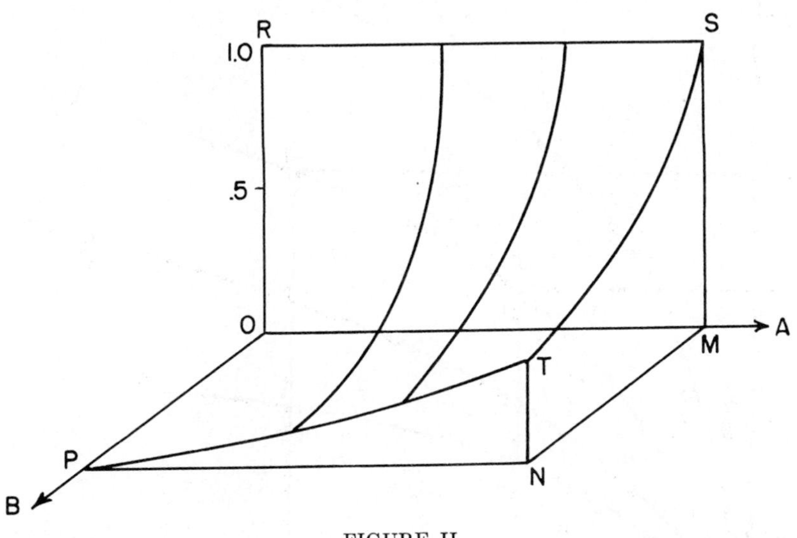

FIGURE II

The iso-probability curve corresponding to the probability .5 is of crucial importance as we shall see below. It is the curve along which the consumer is indifferent between having either the A-batch shown by the vertical co-ordinates of points on that curve or the B-batch shown by the horizontal co-ordinates of points on it. It must be remembered that the interpretation of these curves is

6. This is only one of several shapes that the probability surface could assume and could be termed the "normal" case.

7. In the "normal" case the iso-probability curves go through the origin and may be straight lines or may be concave upwards or downwards (or may consist of a combination of these elements). If they are concave downwards, the relative desirability of B decreases as the quantities of A and B offered increase. If they are concave upwards, the opposite is true.

different from customary indifference curves. For example, along OI the consumer is not indifferent between points P and Q, but he is indifferent between OM of B and ON of A or OT of B and OV of A.

Let the consumer's income and the prices of the commodities x and y (and hence of the combined batches A and B) be given such

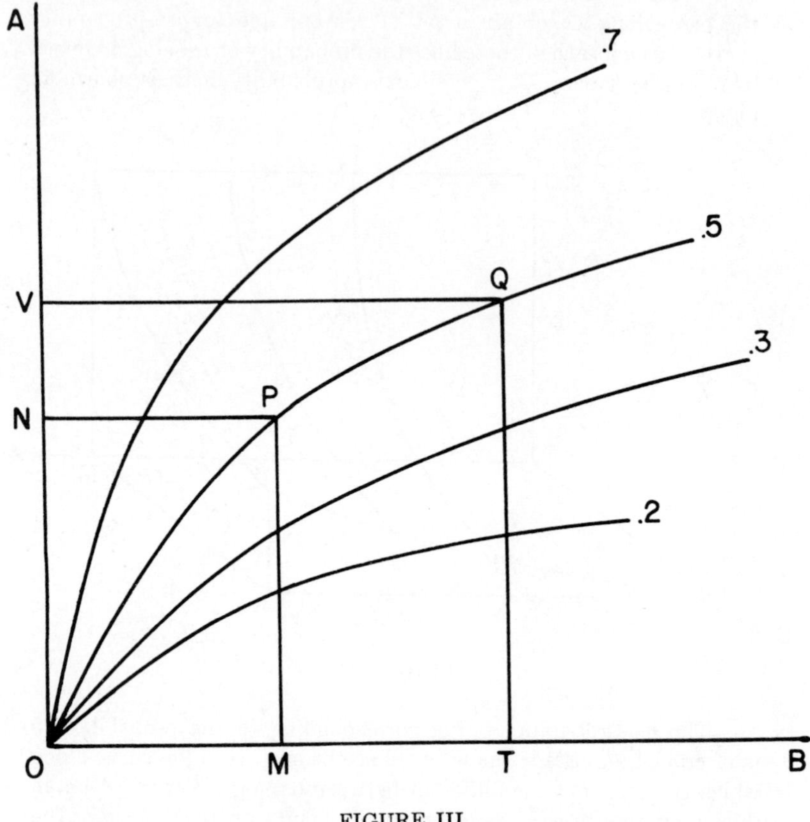

FIGURE III

that the consumer can either purchase ON of A or OM of B (Figure IV). The consumer will probably purchase (can be expected to purchase) ON of A for the following reason. Suppose he wanted to buy OM of B. Then we could ask the consumer how much of A he would require to be offered to him as an alternative so that he would be indifferent between A and B.[8] He would require OT of A. On the other hand, if he chose ON of A, he would require OV of B to be offered as an alternative before he would be indifferent. But OV of B is more than the consumer can afford to buy with his given income. Therefore, the quantity of B that would be necessary to tempt him away from A is more than he can buy. Alternatively, the iso-probability curve OW which goes through the point P repre-

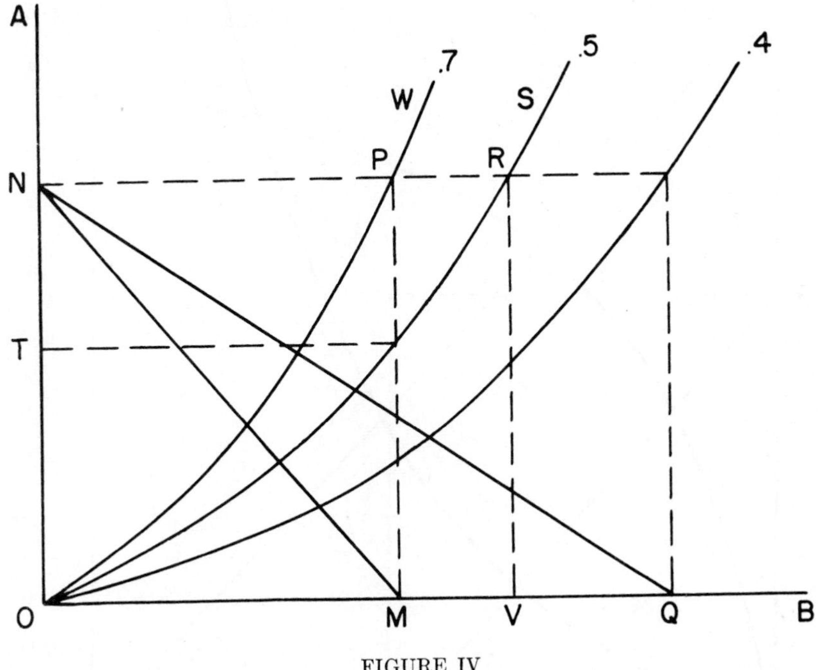

FIGURE IV

senting the consumer's alternatives indicates that with those alternatives the probability of spending on A is higher than the probability of spending on B. Hence, the expectation is that A will be bought.

Assume now that the price of B falls and the price of A remains constant.[9] The price ratio is now OQ/ON instead of OM/ON. By a similar argument, the consumer will tend to purchase B. Thus a

8. In other words, how much A would we have to offer the consumer as an alternative such that he would choose the specified quantities of A and B with equal frequencies.

9. This implies that the price of x falls and the price of y rises. It could be assumed just as easily that only the price of x falls. There is no essential differ-

relative fall in the price of x increases the probability of more x being purchased relative to y.

An increase or decrease in the consumer's income can be analyzed in analogous fashion. A parallel shift of the budget line from RM to SN will increase, leave unchanged, or decrease the prob-

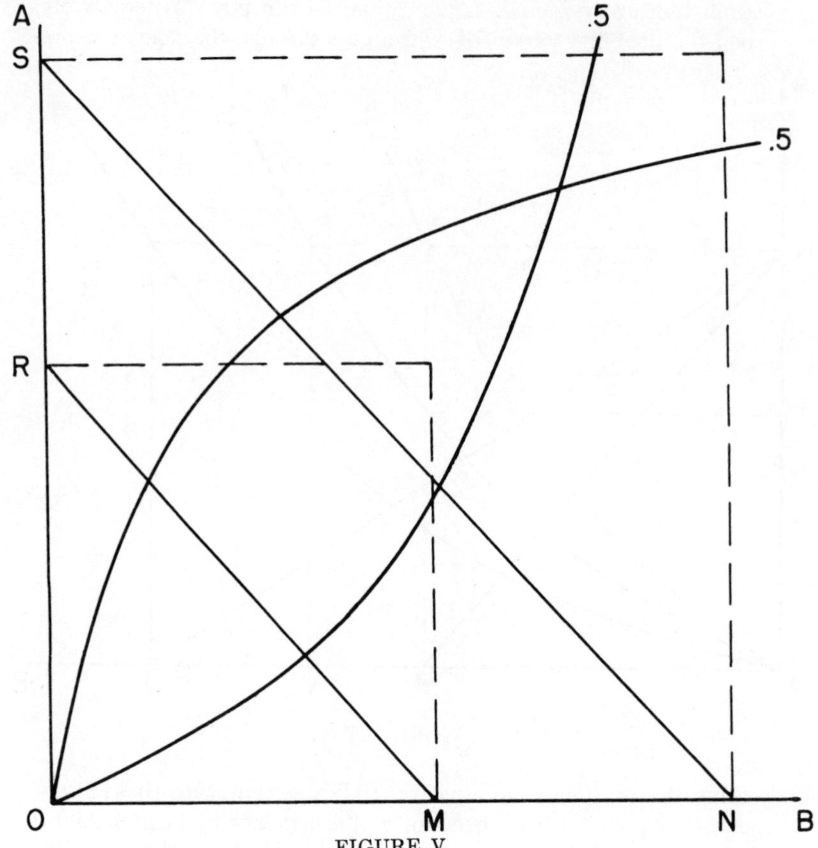

FIGURE V

ability of purchasing A according as the iso-probability curves are concave from below, are straight, or concave from above. Corresponding to the two-fold definition of inferior commodities in tradi-

ence in the final outcome and no generality is lost by the present procedure. The present assumption simplifies the diagrammatic treatment.

tional theory,[1] we may define a commodity as inferior if (a) an increase in income decreases the probability of its being bought or (b) a decrease in its price decreases the probability of its being bought. The latter is the stronger condition and implies the former as can be seen from Figures VI and VII. In Figure VI an increase in income

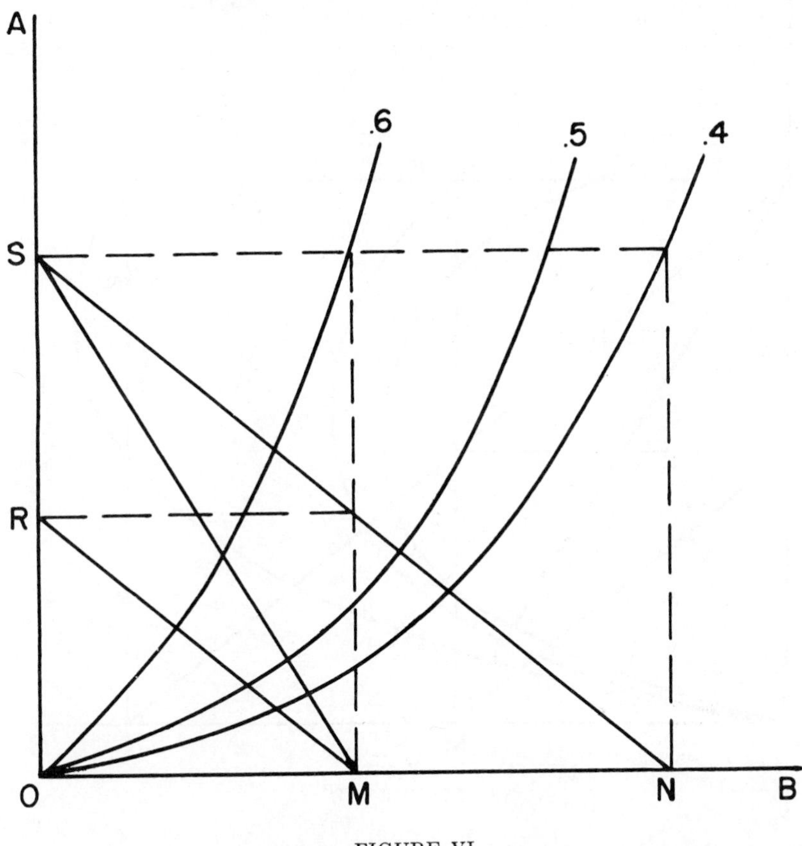

FIGURE VI

causes the probability of A being bought to decrease, whereas a fall in the price of A increases this probability. In Figure VII the decrease

1. A commodity is inferior if its purchases decline either with a decrease in its price or an increase in the consumer's income. The former is the stronger condition and implies the latter.

in the price of A lowers the probability of A being purchased. When income rises, this probability drops a fortiori.[2] These definitions in terms of A and B can be extended readily to x and y.

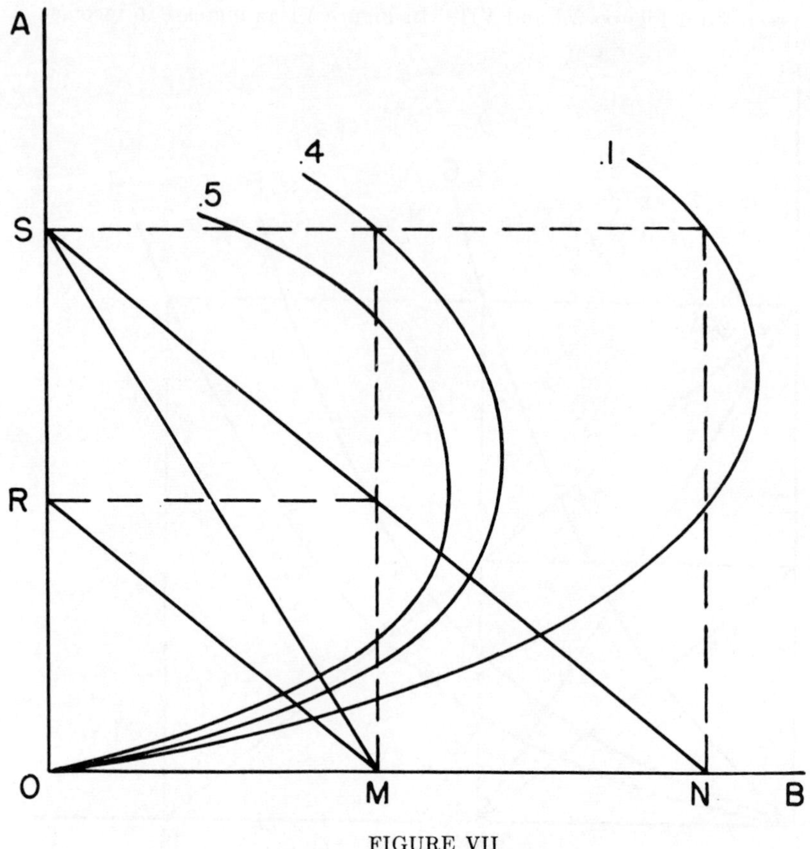

FIGURE VII

From the iso-probability curves we can derive a demand curve which differs from the ordinary demand curve only by being the consumer's "expected" demand curve. This demand curve will show for each price the quantities that the consumer may be expected

2. Note that the probability map in Figure VII represents the interesting case of two commodities of which one (B) is "normal," whereas the other gradually becomes a nuisance as its quantity increases. Thus A might be a perishable commodity, one with high storage costs, or one dangerous to store (combustibility).

to desire. It is possible to derive demand curves for the combined commodities A and B as well as for x and y. In order to derive the individual's demand curve for, say, x, we let y stand for all other commodities and observe his probable behavior at various prices with respect to A-batches consisting of 1 x and 2 y's and B-batches consisting of 2 x's and 1 y.

Let P_y be the price of y and let it be a constant and equal to unity. Then the price of A is $P_x + 2$ and the price of B is $2P_x + 1$. Hence, for each price of x there will be a unique price ratio for A and B. Let P_A and P_B be the prices of A and B, Q_A and Q_B the quantities of A and B which are alternatives at the various prices, Q_{xA} and Q_{xB} the quantities of x which are contained in alternative A and B-batches, $P(A)$ and $P(B)$ the probabilities of choosing A or B (where $P(A) = 1 - P(B)$) and $E(Q_x)$ the expected quantity of x bought at each price of x. Furthermore, we define $E(Q_x^2)$ as the second moment of the quantities of x, $E^2(Q_x)$ as the square of the expectation and hence $E(Q_x^2) - E^2(Q_x)$ as the variance of the quantities demanded.

Assuming certain prices of x, quantities of A and B which are alternatives at those prices given the consumer's income, and probabilities, we can set up a schedule of expected demand in the following manner:

P_x	P_A	P_B	Q_A	Q_B	Q_{xA}	Q_{xB}	$P(A)$	$P(B)$	$E(Q_x)$	σ
6	8	13	2	2	2	4	.1	.9	3.8	.60
5	7	11	4	3	4	6	.2	.8	5.6	.80
4	6	9	6	4	6	8	.3	.7	7.4	.91
3	5	7	8	5	8	10	.4	.6	9.2	.98
2	4	5	10	6	10	12	.5	.5	11.0	1.00
1	3	3	12	7	12	14	.6	.4	12.8	.98

TABLE IV

The demand curve has the usual negative slope but differs from the customary demand curve of the individual consumer in the sense that it is an *expected* demand curve. For each price there exists a probability density of demand for the individual consumer. From the last column in Table IV it is clear that the standard deviation of demand is the greater the closer the consumer is to a situation of indifference. It is also clear that an increase in $P(A)$ will decrease the expected quantity of x demanded.

The present analysis leads to the conclusion that the long-run elasticity of demand is smaller than the short-run elasticity. When the consumer is introduced to a pair of alternative commodities for the first time, he is more likely to be in a state of ignorance concerning those commodities than after using them for some time. If he is in a state of total ignorance, he chooses only by means of a random process like tossing a coin. In this case the probability of preferring one commodity to another is .5. If he is in a state of partial ignorance, his threshold of sensitivity to changes will probably be high with the result that he will not be able to distinguish adequately between (being offered) the alternatives 3 A and 5 B on the one hand, and, say, 3 A and 6 B on the other. This implies that the probability of preferring A changes only slightly as we substitute the second set of alternatives for the first. As the consumer acquires information and becomes more familiar with the commodities in question through use, the threshold will be lowered and his sensitivity to small changes will increase. Therefore, if we start at any arbitrary point on the iso-probability map and move in the direction of less A while keeping the quantity of alternative B constant, the probability of A being preferred will tend to fall faster than it does at the time when the consumer is still unfamiliar with the commodity. Similarly, moving in the direction of more A will tend to increase the probability of A being preferred relative to the consumer's initial iso-probability map.[3] Analogous statements hold with respect to changes in $P(A)$ and $P(B)$ when the quantity of A is held constant and the quantity of B is varied. These facts cause the demand curve for x to become steeper. Considering the probabilities in Table IV to be relevant after the "familiarization" with commodity x, we could consider alternative probabilities to have been relevant before the familiarization. If before familiarization the $P(A)$'s are given by, say, .30, .35, .40, .45, .50, .55, the corresponding $E(Q_x)$'s will be 3.4, 5.3, 7.2, 9.1, 11.0 and 12.9. The demand curve has become steeper after familiarization and, in fact, more inelastic. This is contrary to the customary hypothesis that in the long run the demand curve tends to become more elastic. The traditional hypothesis is based on the assumption that in the long run the consumer becomes aware of substitutes. This would tend to increase the elasticity of demand. The present analysis implies that in the long run commodities tend to become necessities; hence a decrease in the elasticity of demand. This conclusion is in marked agreement with Duesenberry's analysis.[4]

3. Similar statements can be made with respect to the probability of B being preferred.

4. The implication seems to be that familiarization causes the demand curve to rotate around a fixed point on the demand curve. This is not necessarily true.

In conclusion we shall briefly consider an interesting property of the present model. An aggregate expected demand curve can be obtained from individual expected demand curves by summing the latter horizontally. Assuming that consumers' demands (i.e., preferences) are independent, the aggregate demand curve is the sum of independently distributed random variables. Under certain simple conditions the distribution of aggregate demand will be asymptotically normal by the Central Limit Theorem.[5] If the assumption of independence is unwarranted, i.e., if there is a demonstration effect as Duesenberry's analysis indicates, a Central Limit Theorem of a certain type may still hold if consumers can be arranged in m-dependent sequences such that the preferences of certain sets of m adjacent consumers in the sequence are dependent but the preferences of consumers in any such set are independent of the preferences of consumers outside the set.[6]

This is an important conclusion from the point of view of the

The demand curve may move towards the origin or away from it throughout its length, depending on the particular behavior of the probability of A being preferred.

The demand curve is also a function of the consumer's income. It can be shown that there is at least one income for which increasing familiarity with the commodity in question does rotate the demand curve around one of its points and makes it steeper and thus certainly decreases the elasticity of demand at each point on the price axis. To show this we make the plausible assumption that the iso-probability curves constitute a bounded, closed set of points. Then the process of familiarization can be thought of as a mapping of this set into itself. Hence Brouwer's Fixed Point Theorem applies and the iso-probability map has at least one point fixed under such a mapping. Cf. S. Lefschetz, *Introduction to Topology* (Princeton University Press, 1949), pp. 117–19. Every point of the iso-probability map can become a point of choice for some income and some combination of prices. Since the fixed point may be on any one of the boundaries, we have to assume that these points are also accessible. For this to be true we have to assume that the prices of the combined commodities A and B can become zero. (This implies that the price of x and the price of y can become negative). Under these circumstances there necessarily exists an income such that the fixed point in the iso-probability map is relevant for the demand curve corresponding to that income. By virtue of its nature, this point will correspond after the familiarization to the same probability of A being preferred as before the familiarization. Hence one point of the demand curve is fixed and familiarization decreases the elasticity of demand at every price.

5. H. Cramer, *Mathematical Methods of Statistics* (Princeton University Press, 1951), pp. 215–18.

6. Cf. for example, S. Bernstein, "Sur l'extension du théorème limite du calcul des probabilités aux sommes de quantités dépendentes," *Mathematische Annalen*, XCVII (1927), 1–59 and more recently G. Marsaglia, "Iterated Limits and the Central Limit Theorem for Dependent Variables," *Proceedings of the American Mathematical Society*, V (1954), 987–92.

The word "adjacent" could, of course, be given a geographical as well as a social connotation.

statistical estimation of aggregate demand curves. Employing the method of least squares and minimizing the sum of squares in the quantity direction (thus taking price as independent variable) we may safely make the customary but not necessary assumption of regression models that the dependent variable is normally distributed around the regression line.[7] However, the assumption of homoscedasticity will not generally be true because the variance around the regression line (i.e., around the expected demand curve) will vary with the expected quantity demanded, unless the probability surface is a horizontal plane, i.e., unless the consumer's preference for A over B does not change with changes in the quantities of alternative A's and B's.

VI. Conclusion

The model presented in this article does not replace the traditional theory of the consumer but rather completes it with respect to one of its shortcomings. In fact, traditional theory is a limiting case of the present model in a meaningful sense.

In the foregoing sections we have tried to establish that (1) the Complete Ordering Axiom is not generally true, (2) the deficiency of the Complete Ordering Axiom necessitates a revision of the concepts of preference and indifference, (3) it is meaningful to define preference and indifference in a probabilistic sense, (4) on the basis of such a definition the prevailing notion of rationality has to be eliminated, (5) the probabilistic definition of preference and indifference allows the construction of a model which predicts the consumer's behavior probabilistically but does not contradict the conclusions of traditional theory concerning the direction of changes in behavior resulting from some change in parameters, and (6) the model provides a rationale for some assumptions of a statistical nature.

Richard E. Quandt

Princeton University

7. The same assumption is employed by the method of maximum likelihood.

20 The Meaning of Utility Measurement

A. A. Alchian*

Economists struggling to keep abreast of current developments may well be exasperated by the resurgence of measurability of utility. After all, the indifference curve analysis was popularized little over ten years ago amidst the contradictory proclamations that it eliminated, modified, and strengthened the rôle of utility. Even yet there is confusion, induced partly by careless reading and exposition of the indifference curve analysis and partly by misunderstandings of the purposes and implications of utility measurement. This paper attempts to clarify the rôle and meaning of the recent revival of measurement of utility in economic theory and of the meaning of certain concepts and operations commonly used in utility theory.

Measurement in its broadest sense is the assignment of numbers to entities. The process of measurement has three aspects which should be distinguished at the outset. First is the purpose of measurement, second is the process by which one measures something, *i.e.*, assigns numerical values to some aspect of an entity, and the third is the arbitrariness, or uniqueness, of the set of numerical values inherent in the purpose and process. In the first part of this paper we briefly explore the idea of arbitrariness or uniqueness of numbers assigned by a measurement process. In Part II we state some purposes of utility measurement. In Part III we examine a method of measuring utility, the purpose of the measurement and the extent to which the measurement is unique. In Part IV we look at some implications of the earlier discussion.[1]

* The author is associate professor of economics at the University of California, Los Angeles. He wishes to acknowledge gratefully the aid of Norman Dalkey and Harry Markowitz, both of The RAND Corporation. The patient explanations of Dalkey in answering innumerable questions overcame early impulses to abandon the attempt to understand recent utility literature. Markowitz detected several ambiguities and errors in earlier drafts of this exposition. Since neither has seen the final draft they must be relieved of responsibility for remaining errors and ambiguities.

[1] The explanation assumes no mathematical background and is on an elementary level. This paper is not original in any of its ideas, nor is it a general review of utility and demand theory. It is merely a statement of some propositions that may help the reader separate the chaff from the wheat. It may even make clear to the reader, as it did to the writer, one meaning of utility. Most of the material presented here is contained in J. Marschak, "Rational Behavior, Uncertain Prospects and Measurable Utility," *Econometrica* (April 1950), XVIII, 111-41, an article written for the mathematically mature.

Reprinted from the *American Economic Review,* Vol. XLIII (March, 1953), pp. 26–50, by permission of the publisher and author.

I. *Degree of Measurability*

The columns of Table I are sequences of numbers illustrating the concept of the "degree of measurability." The entities, some aspect of which we wish to measure, are denoted by letters. Later we shall discuss the meaning of these entities. Our first task is to explain the difference between monotone transformations and linear transformations.

TABLE I.—ILLUSTRATION OF TYPES OF MEASUREMENT

Entities	Alternative Measures of "Utility"								
	1	2	3	4	5	6	7	8	9
A	1	2	6	11	2	6	5	6	3
B	2	4	7	12	4	12	7	10	7
C	3	5	8	13	6	18	9	14	13
D	4	8	9	14	8	24	11	18	21
E	5	11	10	15	10	30	13	22	31
F	7	14	12	17	14	42	17	30	43
G	11	22	16	21	22	66	25	46	57
H	14	28	19	24	28	84	31	58	73
I	16	33	21	26	32	96	35	66	91
J	17	34	22	27	34	102	37	70	111

We shall begin with monotone transformations and then come to linear transformations via two of its special cases, additive and multiplicative constants.

Monotone Transformations

Let there be assigned a numerical magnitude (measure) to each entity concerned. For example in Table I, for the ten entities, A-J, listed in the extreme left-hand column, nine different sets of numbers are utilized to assign nine different numbers to each of the entities. If two sets of numbers (measures) result in the same ranking or ordering of the entities (according to the numbers assigned), then the two sets are *monotone transformations* of each other. In Table I it will be seen that all nine measures give the same ranking, thus all nine measures are monotone transformations of each other. If this property holds true over the entire class of entities concerned, then the two measures are monotone transformations of each other for that class of entities. The possible set of monotone transformations obviously is very large.

A bibliography is included, to which those who might wish to read more deeply should refer. Excellent starting points are M. Friedman and L. J. Savage, "The Utility Analysis of Choices Involving Risk," *Jour. Pol. Econ.* (Aug. 1948), LVI, 279-304, and J. Marschak, "Why 'Should' Statisticians and Businessmen Maximize 'Moral Expectation'?", *Proceedings of the Second Berkeley Symposium on Mathematical Statistics and Probability* (Berkeley, University of California Press, 1951), pp. 493-506.

Linear Transformations: Additive Constants

We shall approach the linear transformation by considering two special forms. Look at the numbers in column 3. They are the same as those in 1 except that a constant has been added, in this case 5, *i.e.*, they are the *same "up to"* (except for) an *additive constant*. The measure in column 4 is equivalent to that in column 1 with 10 added. Columns 1, 3 and 4 are *transforms* of each other "up to" (by means of) *additive constants*. This can also be expressed by saying they are equivalent except for an additive constant. The term "up to" implies that we may go through some simpler types. For example, all the transforms up to an additive constant are also contained in the larger, less restricted class of possible transforms known as monotone transforms. An additive constant is a quite strong restriction, even though it may not seem so at first since there is an unlimited number of available constants. But relative to the range of possibilities in the general linear transformations this is very restrictive indeed.

Linear Transformations: Multiplicative Constants

Now look at column 5. It is equivalent to column 1 except for multiplication by a constant, in this case, 2. Column 5 is a monotone transform of column 1, and it is also a "multiplicative by a constant" transform of column 1. Column 6 is column 1 multiplied by 6. Thus, while columns 1, 5 and 6 are monotone transforms of each other, they are also a more particular type of transform. They are transforms up to a multiplicative constant. These are special cases of linear transformations which we shall now discuss.

General Linear Transformations

The numbers of column 7 are equivalent to column 1 except for multiplication by 2 and addition of 3. Letting y denote the numbers or "measures" in column 7 and x those of column 1, we have $y = 2x + 3$. Column 8 is derived similarly from column 1; the multiplier is 4 and the added constant is 2. Column 8 is given by $4x + 2$, but a little inspection will show that column 8 can be derived from column 7 by the same process of multiplying and adding. In this case column 8 is obtained from column 7 by multiplying by 2 and adding -4. Columns 1, 7 and 8 are thus "linear transforms" of each other. This is also expressed by saying that they are the same measures "up to a linear transformation"; that is, any one of these measures can be obtained from any other one by simply selecting appropriate constants for multiplication and addition.

There is a particular property of the linear transformation that has historical significance in economics. Look at the way the numbers change as one moves from entity to entity. For example, consider columns 1 and 7. The numerical change from entity E to entity F has a value of 2 in the measure of column 1, while in the measure of column 7, it has a numerical value of 4. From F to G the change is 4 in measure 1, and in measure 7 it is 8. If the increment is positive, it will be positive in all sequences which are linear transforms of this particular sequence. But this is true also for all monotone transformations—a much broader class of transformations or measures. Of greater significance, however, is the following attribute of linear transforms: if the differences between the numbers in one of the sequences increases (or decreases) from entity to entity, then the differences between the numbers of these same entities in all of its *linear* transformations will also be increasing (or decreasing). In general, the property of increasing or decreasing increments is not affected by switching from one sequence of numbers to any linear transformation of that given sequence. In mathematical terms, the sign of the second differences of a sequence of numbers is invariant to linear transformations of that sequence.[2] The significance of invariance will be discussed later, but we should note that this property of increasing (or decreasing) differences between the numbers assigned to pairs of entities is nothing but increasing marginal utility—if one christens the assigned numbers "utilities."

II. *Purpose of Measurement*

Order

In the nine columns of Table I are nine "different" measures of some particular aspect of the entities denoted A, B, C, . . . J. How different are they? We have already answered this. Which is the "right" one? This depends upon what one wants to do with the entities and the numbers. It would be more useful to ask which one is a *satisfactory* measure, for then it is clear that we must make explicit for what it is to be satisfactory.[3] For example, if my sole concern were to predict which of the entities would be the heaviest, the next heaviest, etc., I could, by successively comparing pairs in a balancing scale, completely order the entities. [Having done so, I could then assign the numbers in *any* one of columns 1 through 9] so long as I assign the biggest number to the heaviest, and so on down. This means that for the purpose of indicating *order,* any one of the monotone transforms is acceptable.

[2] In monotonic transformations the sign of the *first* differences only are necessarily left undisturbed.

[3] A pause to reflect will reveal that there is a second problem besides that of deciding what "satisfactory" means. This second problem, which we have so far begged, is: "How does one assign numbers to entities?" It is deferred to the following section.

The remaining task is to determine whether the order is "correctly" stated; the fact that the order is the same, no matter which one of the above transforms is used, does not imply that the order is correct. What do we mean by "correctly"? We mean that our stated or predicted order is matched by the order revealed by some other observable ordering process. You could put the entities on some new weighing scales (the new scales are the "test"), and then a matching of the order derived from the new scales with our stated order is a verification of the correctness (predictive validity) of our first ordering. Any monotone transform of one valid ordering number sequence is *for the purpose* in this illustration *completely equivalent* to the numbers actually used. That is, any one of the possible monotone transformations is just as good as any other.

We may summarize by saying that, given a method for validly ordering entities, any monotone transformation of the particular numerical values assigned in the ordering process will be equally satisfactory. We may be technical and say that "all measures of order are equivalent up to (except for being) monotone transformations." Or, in other words, a method of validly denoting *order* only, is not capable of uniquely identifying a particular set of numbers as *the* correct one. Any monotonic transformation will do exactly as well. The degree of uniqueness of an ordering can also be described by saying it is only as unique as the set of monotone transformations. Thus, we often see the expression that "ordering is unique up to a monotone transformation."

Ordering Groups of Entities

But suppose our purpose were different. Suppose we want to be able to order *groups* of entities according to their weights. More precisely, suppose we want to assign numbers to each of the component objects so that when we combine the objects into sets or bundles we can order the weights of the composite bundles, knowing only the individually valid numbers assigned to each component, by *merely adding* together the numbers assigned to each component. And we want to be able to do this for any possible combination of the objects. Fortunately, man has discerned a way to do this for weights. The numbers which are assigned by this discovered process are arbitrary up to a multiplicative constant (of proportionality), so that the numbers could express either pounds, ounces, tons or grams. That is, we can arbitrarily multiply all the numbers assigned to the various components by any constant we please, without destroying the validity of our resulting numbers for this particular purpose. But we can not use any monotone transformation as we could in the preceding case where our purpose was different.

If we were to add an arbitrary constant to each component's individually valid numerical (weight) value we would not be able to add the resulting numbers of each component in order to get a number which would rank the composite bundles. Thus, the numbers we can assign are rather severely constrained. We can not use any linear transformation, but we can use a multiplicative constant, which is a special type of linear transformation. And if we were to "measure" lengths of items so as to be able simply to "add" the numbers to get the lengths of the items laid end to end, we would again find ourselves confined to sequences (measures) with a multiplicative constant as the one available degree of arbitrariness.

Utility and Ordering of Choices

The reader has merely to substitute for the concept of weight, in the earlier example about weight orders, the idea of "preference" and he is in the theory of choice or demand. Economics goes a step further and gives the name "utility" to the numbers. Can we assign a set of numbers (measures) to the various entities and predict that the entity with the largest assigned number (measure) will be chosen? If so, we could christen this measure "utility" and then assert that choices are made so as to maximize utility. It is an easy step to the statement that "you are maximizing your utility," which says no more than that your choice is predictable according to the size of some assigned numbers.[4] For analytical convenience it is customary to postulate that an individual seeks to maximize something subject to some constraints. The thing—or numerical measure of the "thing"—which he seeks to maximize is called "utility." Whether or not utility is some kind of glow or warmth, or happiness, is here irrelevant; all that counts is that we can assign numbers to entities or conditions which a person can strive to realize. Then we say the individual seeks to maximize some function of those numbers. Unfortunately, the term "utility" has by now acquired so many connotations, that it is difficult to realize that for present purposes utility has no more meaning than this. The analysis of individual demand behavior is mathematically describable as the process of maximizing some quantitive measures, or numbers, and we assume that the individual seeks to obtain that combination with the highest choice number, given the purchasing power at his disposal. It might be harmless to call this "utility theory."[5]

[4] The difficult (impossible?) psychological, philosophical step of relating this kind of utility to some *quantity* of *satisfaction, happiness, goodness* or *welfare* is not attempted here.

[5] The author, having so far kept his opinions submerged, is unable to avoid remarking that it would seem "better" to confine utility "theory" to attempts to explain or discern why a person chooses one thing rather than another—at equal price.

Three Types of Choice Predictions

Sure Prospects. Before proceeding further it is necessary to indicate clearly the types of choice that will concern us. The first type of choice is that of selecting among a set of alternative "riskless" choices. A riskless choice, hereafter called a sure prospect, is one such that the chooser knows exactly what he will surely get with each possible choice. To be able to predict the preferred choice means we can assign numbers to the various entities such that the entity with the largest assigned number is the most preferred, the one with the second largest number is the next most preferred, etc. As said earlier, it is customary to christen this numerical magnitude with the name "utility."

An understanding of what is meant by "entity" is essential. An entity denotes any specifiable object, action, event, or set or pattern of such items or actions. It may be an orange, a television set, a glass of milk, a trip to Europe, a particular time profile of income or consumption (*e.g.*, steak every night, or ham every night, or steak and ham on alternate nights), getting married, etc. Identifying an entity exclusively with one single event or action would lead to unnecessary restrictions on the scope of the applicability of the theorem to be presented later.[6]

Groups of Sure Prospects. A second problem of choice prediction would be that of ordering (predicting) choices among riskless *groups* of entities. A riskless group consists of several entities all of which will be surely obtained if that group is chosen. The problem now is to predict the choice among riskless groups knowing only the utilities assigned to the individual entities which have been aggregated into groups. Thus if in Table I we were to assemble the entities A through J into various groups, could we predict the choice among these groups of entities knowing only the utility numbers that were assigned to the component entities for the purpose of the preceding choice problem? Of course we ask this question only on the assumption that the utilities previously assigned to the component entities were valid predictors of choice among the single sure prospects.[7]

Uncertain Prospects. A third type of problem is that of ordering choices among risky choices, or what have been called uncertain prospects. An uncertain prospect is a group of entities, only one entity of

[6] For example, see H. Wold, "Ordinal Preferences or Cardinal Utility? (With Additional Notes by G. L. S. Shackle, L. J. Savage, and H. Wold)"; A. S. Manne, "The Strong Independence Assumption-Gasoline Blends and Probability Mixtures. (with Additional Notes by A. Charnes)"; P. Samuelson, "Probability, Utility, and the Independence Axiom"; E. Malinvaud, "Note on Neumann-Morgenstern's Strong Independence Axiom," *Econometrica* (Oct. 1952), XX, 661-79.

[7] For an illustration of this problem of rating a composite bundle by means of the ratings of the ratings of the components, see A. S. Manne, *op. cit.*

which will be realized if that group is chosen. For example, an uncertain prospect might consist of a fountain pen, a radio and an automobile. If that uncertain prospect is chosen, the chooser will surely get one of the three entities, but which one he will actually get is not known in advance. He is not completely ignorant about what will be realized, for it is assumed that he knows the probabilities of realization attached to each of the component entities in an uncertain prospect. For example, the probabilities might have been .5 for the fountain pen, .4 for the radio and .1 for the automobile. These probabilities sum to

TABLE II.—EXAMPLES OF UNCERTAIN PROSPECTS

Uncertain Prospect	Probabilities of getting		
	Pen	Radio	Automobile
1	.5	.4	.1
2	.58	.30	.12
3	.85	.0	.15
4	.0	.99	.01

1.0; one and only one of these entities will be realized. An uncertain prospect is very much like a ticket in a lottery. If there is but one prize, then the uncertain prospect consists of two entities, the prize or the loss of the stake. If there are several prizes, the uncertain prospect consists of several entities—the various prizes and, of course, the loss of the stake (being a loser).

But there is another requirement that we want our prediction process to satisfy. Not only must we be able to predict the choices, but we want to do it in a very simple way. Specifically, we want to be able to look at each component separately, and then from utility measures assigned to the elements, as if they were sure prospects, we want to be able to aggregate the component utility measures into a group utility measure predicting choices among the uncertain prospects. For example, suppose the uncertain prospects consisted of a pen, a radio and an automobile as listed in Table II.

Are there utilities which can be assigned to the pen, the radio and the automobile, so that for the purpose of comparing these four uncertain prospects the same numbers could be used in arriving at utility numbers to be assigned to the uncertain prospects? In particular, can we assign to the pen, the radio and the automobile numbers such that when multiplied by the associated probabilities in each uncertain prospect they will yield a sum (expected utility) for each uncertain prospect, and such that these "expected utilities" would indicate preference?

Before answering we shall briefly indicate why choices among uncertain prospects constitute an important class of situations. Upon reflection it will be seen to be the practically universal problem of choice. Can the reader think of many cases in which he *knows* when making a choice, the outcome of that choice with absolute certainty? In other words, are there many choices—or actions—in life in which the *consequences* can be predicted with absolute certainty? Even the act of purchasing a loaf of bread has an element of uncertainty in its consequences; even the act of paying one's taxes has an element of uncertainty in the consequences involved; even the decision to sit down has an element of uncertainty in the consequence. But to leave the trivial, consider the choice of occupation, purchase of an automobile, house, durable goods, business investment, marriage, having children, insurance, gambling, etc. ad infinitum. Clearly choices among uncertain prospects constitute an extremely large and important class of choices.

III. *Method of Measurement*

So far we have discussed the meaning and purpose of measurement. We turn to the method of measurement recognizing that for each type of choice prediction the method of measurement must have a rationale as well as a purpose. For a moment we can concentrate on the rationale which is properly stated in the form of axioms defining rational behavior.

Sure Prospects

Let us start with a rationale for the first type of choice. We postulate that an individual behaves consistently, *i.e.*, he has a consistent set of preferences; that these preferences are transitive, *i.e.*, if B is preferred to A, and C to B, then C is preferred to A; and that these preferences can be completely described merely by attaching a numerical value to each. An implication of these postulates is that for such individuals we can predict their choices by a numerical variable (utility). Asking the individual to make pairwise comparisons we assign numbers to the sure prospects such that the choice order will be revealed by the size of the numbers attached. The number of pairwise comparisons that the individual must make depends upon how fortunate we are in selecting the pairs for his comparison. If we are so lucky as first to present him a series of pairs of alternatives of sure prospects exactly matching his preference order, the complete ordering of his preferences will be obtained with the minimal amount of pairwise comparisons. Any numbering sequence which gives the most preferred sure prospect the highest number, the second preferred sure prospect the second highest number, etc., will predict his choices according to "utility maximization." But any other sequence of numbers could be used so long as it is a *monotone transformation* of the first sequence. And this is exactly the meaning of the statement that utility is *ordinal* and not cardinal. The transitivity postulate enables this pairwise comparison to reveal the complete order of preferences, and the consistency postulate means he would make his choices according to the prediction. Thus if he were to be presented with any two of ten sure prospects, we would predict his taking the one with the higher utility number. If our prediction failed, then one of our postulates would have been denied, and our prediction method would not be valid. A hidden postulate is that the preferences, if transitive and consistent, are stable for the interval involved.[8] Utility for this purpose and by this method is measurable up to a monotonic transformation, *i.e.*, it is ordinal only.

Groups of Sure Prospects

The second type of choice, among *groups* of sure prospects, can be predicted using the same postulates only if we treat each group of sure prospects as a sure prospect. Then by presenting pairs of "groups of sure prospects" we can proceed as in the preceding problem. But the interesting problem here is that of predicting choice among groups of sure prospects (entities) only by knowing valid utility measures for choices among the component sure prospects. Can these utility numbers of the component entities of the group of sure prospects, which are valid for the entities by themselves, be aggregated to obtain a number predicting choice among the groups of sure prospects? In general the answer is "no." Hence, although utility was measurable for the purpose of the kind of prediction in the preceding problem, it is not measurable in the sense that these component measures can be aggregated or combined in any known way to predict choices among *groups* of sure prospects. Utility is "measurable" for one purpose but not for the other.[9]

[8] Some problems involved in this assumption and in its relaxation are discussed by N. Geogescu-Roegen, "The Theory of Choice and the Constancy of Economic Laws," *Quart. Jour. Econ.* (Feb. 1950), LXIV, 125-38.

[9] It is notable that the usual indifference curve analysis is contained in this case. Any *group* of sure prospects (point in the xy plane of an indifference curve diagram) which has more of each element in it than there is in another group of two sure prospects, will be preferred to the latter. And further, if one group of sure prospects has more of one commodity than does the other group of sure prospects, the two groups can be made indifferent by sufficiently increasing the amount of the second commodity in the other group of sure prospects. The indifference curve (utility isoquant) approach does not assign numbers representing utility to the various sure prospects lying along either the horizontal or the vertical axis and then from these numerical values somehow obtain a number which would order choices among the groups of prospects inside the quadrant enclosed by the axes.

Uncertain Prospects

We want to predict choices among uncertain prospects. And we want to make these predictions solely on the basis of the utilities and probabilities attached to the elements of the uncertain prospects.

Without going into too many details an intuitive idea of the content of the axioms used in deriving this kind of measurability will now be given.[10] For expository convenience the statement that the two entities A and B are equally desirable or indifferent will be expressed by A = B; if however A is either preferred to or indifferent to B, the expression will be A $\geq$ B.

(1) For the chooser there is a transitive, complete ordering of all the alternative possible choices so far as his preferences are concerned. That is if C $\geq$ B and B $\geq$ A, then C $\geq$ A.

(2) If among three entities, A, B, and C, C $\geq$ B, and B $\geq$ A, then there is some probability value p, for which B is just as desirable as the uncertain prospect consisting of A and C, where A is realizable with probability p, and C with probability -p. In our notation: if C $\geq$ B and B $\geq$ A, then there is some p for which B = (A, C; p), where (A, C; p) is the expression for the uncertain prospect in which A will be realized with probability p, and otherwise, C will be realized.

(3) Suppose B $\geqq$ A, and let C be any entity. Then (B, C; p) $\geqq$ (A, C; p) for any p. In particular, if A = B, then the prospect comprising A and C, with probability p for A and 1-p for C, will be just as desirable as the uncertain prospect comprised of B and C, with the same probability p for B, and 1-p for C.

(4) In the uncertain prospect comprising A and B with probability p for A, it makes no difference what the process is for determining whether A or B is received, just so long as the value of p is not changed. Notationally, (A, B; p_1), B; p_2) = (A, B; $p_1\, p_2$).

To help understand what these axioms signify we give an example of behavior or situation that is inconsistent with each, except that I can think of no totally unreasonable behavior inconsistent with the first axiom. Behavior inconsistent with the second axiom would be the following: Suppose C is two bars of candy, B is one bar of candy, and A is being shot in the head. Form an uncertain prospect of C and A with probability p for C. If there is no p, however small or close to zero, which could possibly make one indifferent between the uncertain

[10] This is the method developed by J. von Neumann and P. Morgenstern, *The Theory of Games and Economic Behavior* (Princeton University Press, 1944). A very closely analogous method was suggested in 1926 by F. Ramsey, *The Foundations of Mathematics and Other Logical Essays* (The Humanities Press, N. Y., 1950), pp. 166-90. The neatest, but still very difficult, exposition is by J. Marschak, *op. cit.* Still another statement of essentially the same set of axioms is in Friedman and Savage, *op. cit.*

prospect and B, the one bar of candy, he is rejecting axiom (2). Are such situations purely hypothetical?

The third axiom, sometimes called the "strong independence assumption," has provoked the most vigorous attack and defense. So far no really damaging criticism has been seen. It takes its name from the implication that whatever may be the entity, C, it has no effect on the ranking of the uncertain prospects comprised of A or C and B or C. This kind of independence has nothing whatever to do with independence or complementarity among groups of commodities. Here one does not receive both A and C, or B and C. He gets either A or C in one uncertain prospect, or he gets either B or C in the other. Even if A and C were complements and B and C were substitutes, the ordering would not be affected—this is what the postulate asserts.[11]

Axiom (3) is inconsistent with a situation in which the utility of the act of winning itself depends upon the probability of winning, or more generally if probability itself has utility. For example, at Christmas time, one does not want to know what gift his wife is going to give him; he prefers ignorance to any hints or certainty as to what his gift will be. This is a type of love for gambling. Conversely, one may be indifferent to whether he gets roast beef or ham for dinner, but he does want to know which it will be purely for the sake of knowing, not because it will affect any prior or subsequent choices.

Axiom (4) is inconsistent with a concern or difference in feeling about different ways of determining which entity in an uncertain prospect is actually received even though the various systems all have the same probability. For example, suppose an uncertain prospect had a probability of .25 for one of the entities. It should make no difference whether the probability is based on the toss of two successive coins with heads required on both, or whether it is based on the draw of one white ball from an urn containing one white and three black. But consider the case of the slot machine. Why are there three wheels with many items on each wheel? Why not one big wheel, and why are the spinning wheels in sight? One could instead have a machine with covered wheels. Simply insert a coin, pull the handle and then wait and see what comes out of the machine. Does seeing the wheels go around or seeing how close one came to nearly winning affect the desirability? If observation or knowledge of the number of steps through which the mechanism must pass before reaching the final decision makes any difference, even if the fundamental probability is not subjectively or objectively affected, then axiom (4) is denied.

Implied in the stated axioms is a method for assigning numerical

[11] See the literature listed in footnote 6.

utility values to the various component entities. The method is perhaps explained best by an illustration of the method using the entities of Table I. Take one entity, A, and one other, say B, as the two base entities. Between these two entities you choose B as preferable to A. Now I *arbitrarily* assign (*i.e.*, choose any numbers I wish so long as the number for B exceeds that for A) the number 2 to B and some smaller number, say 1, to A. You then consider entity C, which you assert you prefer to A and to B. The next step is rather involved; I now form an uncertain prospect consisting of C and A. You are now offered a choice between B, a sure prospect, and the uncertain prospect comprised of "A or C", where you get A or C depending upon the outcome of a random draw in which the probability of A is p, otherwise you get C.

You are asked to, and you do, select a value of p which when contained in the uncertain prospect leaves you indifferent between B and the uncertain prospect, "A or C."[12] If p were set at nearly zero, you would choose the uncertain prospect, since C is assumed here to be preferred to A; choosing the uncertain prospect would mean that you would almost surely get C. The converse would be the outcome if p were set at nearly 1. Therefore, some place in between there is a value of p which would leave you indifferent between B and the uncertain prospect of "A or C." After you indicate that value of p, I assign to the uncertain prospect the same number, 2, I did to B since they are equally preferred by you.

Now we may determine a number for C by the following procedure. Treat the probability p, and its complement $1\text{-}p$, as weights to be assigned to the numbers for A and C such that the weighted sum is equal to the number 2, which has been assigned to the uncertain prospect. If, for example, you were indifferent when p was equal to .6, then we have the following definitional equation, where we let U(A) stand for the number assigned to A, U(B) for the number assigned to B, and U(C) for the number assigned to C:

$$U(B) = p \cdot U(A) + (1\text{-}p) \cdot U(C)$$

$$\frac{U(B) - p \cdot U(A)}{(1\text{-}p)} = U(C) = 3.5.$$

Using this convenient formula we can assign numbers to the entities D, E, F by appropriately forming uncertain prospects and letting you determine that value of p which produced indifference. These revealed

[12] It is important to notice that the sure prospect must not be preferred to both of the components of the uncertain prospects, for in that event no probability value would induce indifference.

numbers will completely order the entities. If E has a larger number than G, E will be preferred over G. This assignment of numerical value is made without ever comparing E and G directly. Each has been compared with a base entity. A brief pause to reflect will reveal that in this paragraph we have been specifying a convenient method for manipulating, or combining the "utilities" or "choice indicator numbers" as well as specifying a process of attaching numbers (utilities) to the entities.

It happens that if we insist on using the simple formula above, rather than some more complicated one, the numerical magnitudes assigned by this process are unique up to a linear transformation. For example, suppose that by our process of assigning numbers we obtained the set of numbers in column 3 of Table I for entities A to J. Now, instead of assigning 7 and 6 to B and A, had we decided in the first place to assign a value of 7 to entity B and a value of 5 to entity A, we could have obtained instead the sequence in column 7. Column 7 is a linear transformation of column 3. In other words, we may arbitrarily, at our complete discretion, assign numbers to *two* of the entities; once that has been done, our method will determine the remaining unique numbers to be assigned. But all the various *sets* of numbers (utilities) that could have been obtained, depending upon the two initial numerical values, are linear transformations of each other. Thus, our measurement process is unique "up to" a linear transformation.

If the preceding method of assigning numbers does predict correctly the choice a person actually makes among uncertain prospects, then we have successfully assigned numbers as indicators of choice preferences. We have successfully measured utility and have done it with the convenient computational formula above. Furthermore, every linear transformation of our predicting numbers, "utilities," would be equally valid—or invalid.

In summary, (1) we have found a *way* to assign numbers; (2) for the way suggested, it so happens that the assigned numbers are unique up to linear transformations; (3) the numbers are convenient to manipulate. All this was implicit in our set of postulates. Before asking whether the numbers predict actual behavior, we shall discuss some side issues.

Diminishing or Increasing Marginal Utility

Recalling our earlier exposition of the mathematical properties of linear transformations, we see that in all of the columns (except 2 and 9 which are not linear transformations of the others) the pattern of *increments* between the numbers assigned to entities is similar. For example, between pair H and I on scale 7 the increment is 4 and between pair I and J it is 2. Moving from H through I to J we have a diminishing increment in the numerical magnitudes assigned. In more familiar terminology we have diminishing marginal utility among H, I and J.[13] Similarly, all the linear transforms of scale 7 will retain this diminishing marginal utility over the range of entities H, I and J. And the suggested way of assigning numbers to the component entities assigns numbers (utilities) which are equivalent up to a linear transformation; that is, any one of the linear transformations will be just as good—for our purposes—as any other of them. By implication we can determine whether there is diminishing or increasing marginal utility.

Maximization of Expected Utility

By this method of assigning utilities we have ordered all the entities. However, our purpose was more than this; otherwise the uniqueness of the numbers up to a linear transformation would have been an unnecessary restriction. As we know, any monotonic transformation would leave order unaffected. The linear transformation restriction is imposed by our desire to predict choices among uncertain prospects from the utilities and probabilities of the component entities and to do it in a convenient form, *viz.*, according to maximization of expected utility.[14]

Implied in our set of postulates is not only the preceding method of assigning numbers for utilities but also (in fact the two are merely two aspects of the same implication) a method for combining the utilities of the component entities into a utility number for the uncertain prospect.

This method is based on the implication that a person who behaves according to the axioms will choose among uncertain prospects according to expected utility. Expected utility is merely the sum of the weighted utilities of the components of the uncertain prospects where the weights are the probabilities associated with each component. In symbolic form

$$U(A \text{ or } B, p) = p\, U(A) + (1-p)\, U(B)$$

where the expression $U(A \text{ or } B, p)$ denotes the utility of the uncertain prospect of entities A and B in which A will be received with probability p, and B otherwise. For example, we could from any one of our measures in Table I (except columns 2 and 9) predict what one would do when faced with the following choice: he is presented first with an

[13] More strictly we should also have some scale for measuring the amount of H, I and J, either in weight or volume, etc. While the process for assigning these scales also is a complex one, we may pass over it in order to concentrate upon the "utility" measure.

[14] It is not dictated by any nostalgia for diminishing marginal utility.

uncertain prospect containing entities B and C. If he chooses this prospect, his probability of getting B is one-half; otherwise, he will get C. The other uncertain prospect which he is offered contains entities A and E, and if he chooses this prospect his probability of getting *F* is one-fourth—otherwise, he gets A. Our individual will choose the first prospect, no matter which of our acceptable measures we use. We obtain this prediction by multiplying (weighting) the "utility" measures of each entity in each prospect by the probability of that entity. If we use the utility measure of column 8, we have for the first prospect $(\frac{1}{2} \times 14) + (\frac{1}{2} \times 10) = 12$, and for the second prospect, $(\frac{3}{4} \times 6) + (\frac{1}{4} \times 22) = 10$. The first prospect has the larger expected "utility" and will be chosen.[15] How can we justify this procedure of adding the products of probabilities and "measures of utilities" of entities in an uncertain prospect and calling the result "the utility" of the uncertain prospect? The axioms of human behavior on which it is based are those which earlier gave us the procedure for "measuring utility" up to a linear transformation.[16]

Another way to express this implication that a rational person chooses among uncertain prospects so as to maximize expected utility is in terms of the implied shapes of indifference curves in the plane of *probabilities* of the various components of the uncertain prospects.

Suppose that I am indifferent between receiving a watch and receiving $30.00. In Figure 1a, the horizontal scale measures the probability with which I will get $30.00 and the vertical axis measures the probability with which I will get the watch. The origin represents the point at which I am sure to get nothing. The point W on the vertical axis presents the situation in which I am sure to get the watch and not get the $30.00. The point M on the horizontal axis represents the situation in which I am sure to get the money and am sure not to get the watch. A straight line drawn from W to M represents all the various uncertain prospects in which I might get the watch or I might get the money, where the probabilities are given by the horizontal distance for

[15] If column 9 had been used, the chooser would have been declared indifferent, *i.e.*, the two combinations have equal utility. This is inconsistent with the utility value and predictions derived from the measures in the other columns.

[16] If our task is merely to order choice among the uncertain prospects, we could, after obtaining the expected utility of the prospect, obviously perform any monotonic transformation on it without upsetting the order of choices among the uncertain prospects. However, there seems little point in doing so, and there is good reason not to do so. In particular one might wish to predict choices among groups of uncertain prospects where, in each group of prospects, the entities are themselves uncertain prospects. This combination of several uncertain prospects into one resultant uncertain prospect is a consistent operation under the preceding postulates, and the utility measures attached to it will have an implied validity if the utility measures attached to the component prospects, derived in the manner indicated earlier, are valid.

the money and the vertical distance for the watch. Thus, the point P represents the prospect in which I will get the watch with probability ⅔ or otherwise the money (with probability ⅓). The preceding axioms imply that this straight line is an indifference line or utility isoquant. In other words, the utility isoquant is a *straight* line in the space of probabilities, in this case a straight line from one sure prospect (the watch with certainty) to the other equally sure prospect (the $30.00 with certainty).

The straight line utility isoquants need not go from sure prospect to sure prospect, as can be seen from a second example. Suppose that I am

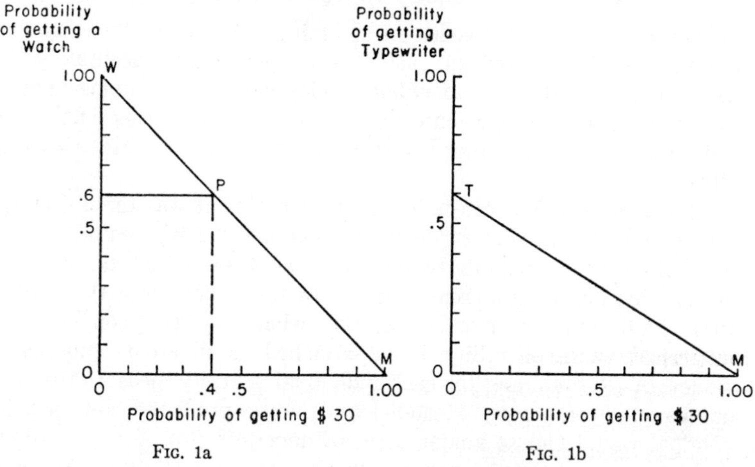

Fig. 1a

Fig. 1b

indifferent between receiving $30.00 with certainty (sure prospect of $30.00) and the uncertain prospect in which I will get a particular typewriter with probability .6 and nothing with probability .4. In Figure 1b, this latter uncertain prospect is T on the vertical axis. Since I am indifferent between this uncertain prospect T and the $30.00 with certainty (point M) a straight line, TM, is a utility isoquant, and all prospects represented by the points on that line are indifferent to me—have the same utility. In summary, in any such figure, a straight line through any two equally preferred prospects will also contain all prospects (certain and uncertain) that are equally preferred to the first two. This can be generalized into three and more dimensions in which case the straight line becomes a plane surface in three or more dimensions.

The additivity of the simple weighted (by probabilities of the components of the entities) "utilities" enables us to call this composite utility function a linear utility function. This means that the measure of "utility" of uncertain prospects (in a probability sense) of entities is the sum of the "expectation" of the "utilities" of the component entities; it does not mean that our numerical numbers (measuring utility) assigned to the entities are linear functions of the physical amounts (*e.g.*, weights or counts) of the magnitude entities. Here linearity means that the utility of the uncertain prospects is a linear function of the utility of the component entities; incidentally the utility function is also a linear function of the probabilities of the entities.

IV. *Validity of Measurement*

Has anyone ever succeeded in assigning numbers in this way and did the sequence based on past observations predict accurately the preferences revealed by an *actual* choice among new and genuinely available prospects? The only test of the validity of this whole procedure, of which the author is aware, was performed by Mosteller and Nogee.[17]

The essence of the Mosteller-Nogee experiment was to subject approximately 20 Harvard students and National Guardsmen to the type of choices (indicated above on pages 37-39) required to obtain a utility measure for different entities. In the experiment, the entities were small amounts of money, so that what was being sought was a numerical value of utility to be attached to different amounts of money. After obtaining for each individual a utility measure for various amounts of money, Mosteller and Nogee predicted how each individual would choose among a set of uncertain prospects, where the entities were amounts of money with associated probabilities. Although some predictions were incorrect, a sufficiently large majority of correct predictions led Mosteller and Nogee to conclude that the subjects did choose among uncertain prospects on the basis of the utilities of the amounts of money involved and the probabilities associated with each, *i.e.*, according to maximized expected utility. Perhaps the most important lesson of the experiment was the extreme difficulty of making a really good test of the validity of the implications of the axioms about behavior.

Whether this process will predict choice in any other situation is still unverified. But we can expect it to fail where there are pleasures of gambling and risk-taking, possibly a large class of situations. Pleasures of gambling refers not to the advantages that incur from the possibility of receiving large gains, but rather to the pleasure of the act of gambling or act of taking on extra risk itself. There may be an

[17] F. Mosteller and P. Nogee, "An Experimental Measurement of Utility," *Jour. Pol. Econ.* (Oct. 1951), LIX, 371-404.

exhilaration accompanying sheer chance-taking or winning per se as distinct from the utility of the amount won. Even worse, the preference pattern may change with experience.

V. *Utility of Income*

We can conclude our general exposition with the observation that although the preceding discussion has referred to "entities" we could have always been thinking of different amounts of income or wealth. The reason we did not was that we wanted to emphasize the generality of the choice problem and to emphasize that utility measures are essentially nothing but choice indicators. However, it is useful to consider the utility of income. How do the numerical values (utilities) assigned by the preceding method vary as income varies? Now this apparently sensible question is ambiguous, even after our preceding discussion which we presume to have eliminated confusion about the meaning of "measurability of utility." For the question still remains as to whether the utility measure assumes (1) a utility curve that stays put and along which one can move up and down as income varies; or, (2) a utility curve whose shape is definable only on the basis of the current income as a reference point for change in levels of income. The former interpretation emphasizes dependence of utility on levels of income, while the latter emphasizes the dependence of utility on the changes in income around one's present position.

The most common type of utility curve has been one whose shape and position is independent of the particular income actually being realized at the time the curve of utility of income is constructed. For example, Friedman and Savage draw a utility curve dependent primarily upon levels of income rather than upon changes in income, and it is presumed that individuals choose as if they were moving along that curve.[18] The generic shape of the curve postulated by Friedman and Savage is shown in Figure 2.[19] This shape is supposed to explain the presence of both gambling and insurance. How does it do this?

Reference back to our method of predicting choices among uncertain prospects reminds us that choices will be made so as to maximize expected utility. A graphic interpretation is very simple. In Figure 2, let the income position now existing be A; let the individual be faced with a choice of staying where he is, or of choosing the uncertain prospect of moving to income position B with probability .999 or of moving to income position C with probability .001. Position A represents paying fire insurance, while positions C and B form the uncertain prospect where C is the position if a fire occurs with no insurance and B is the position if no fire occurs with no insurance.

[18] *Op. cit.*

[19] The utility curve is unique up to a linear transformation.

Will he choose the uncertain prospect or the sure position A? The basis for the choice as implied in our postulates can be described graphically as follows: From point B′ draw a straight line to point C′. This straight line gives the expected utility of all uncertain prospects of the incomes B and C as the probability attached to C varies from zero to one. The point on this straight line yielding the expected utility of our uncertain prospect can be found by computing the expected *income,* D, and then rising vertically to point D′ on the straight line

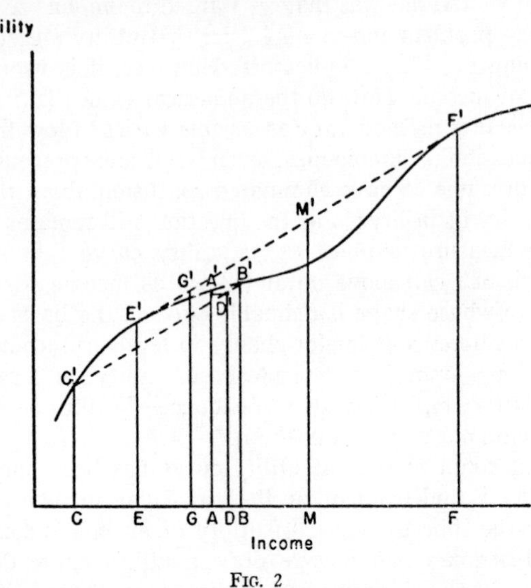

FIG. 2

B′C′. The ordinate DD′ is the expected utility of the uncertain prospect. If the length of DD′ is less than AA′, as it is in our example, where AA′ denotes the utility of the income after taking insurance, then the person will choose the insurance and conversely.

It is apparent that if the utility curve were always convex as in the first and last part of the curve in Figure 2, a person would never choose an uncertain prospect whose expected income was no greater than the insured income position. And if the curve were concave, a person would always choose the uncertain prospect where the expected income was at least equal to the present insured position.

If the curve has the shape postulated by Friedman and Savage, it is possible to explain why a person will take out insurance and will at the same time engage in a gamble. To see how the latter is possible, suppose a person were at position A. At the same time that he might be willing to take out insurance he may also be willing to gamble by choosing an uncertain prospect of ending up at E or F, despite its lower expected income at G, because the expected utility GG′ of the uncertain prospect is larger than the utility AA′ of position A. Friedman and Savage tentatively attempt to lend some plausibility to this shape of utility curve by conjuring that economic society may be divisible into two general income level classes, the lower one being characterized by the first convex part of the curve and the higher one by the upper convex section. An intermediate group is in the concave section.

H. Markowitz has pointed out certain unusual implications of the Friedman-Savage hypothesis.[20] A person at the point M would take a fair bet with a chance to get to F. This seems unlikely to be verified by actual behavior. Secondly, if a person is at a position a little below F, he will not want insurance against small probabilities of large losses. Further, any person with income greater than F will never engage in any fair bet. But wealthy people do gamble. Is it solely the love of risk taking? To overcome these objections, Markowitz postulates that utility is related to *changes* in the level of income and that "the utility function has three inflection points. The middle one is at the person's "customary" income level, which except in cases of recent windfall gains and losses is the present income. The income interval between the inflection points is a nondecreasing function of income. The curve is monotonically increasing but bounded; it is at first concave, then convex, then concave, and finally convex.

Markowitz's hypothesis is consistent with the existence of both "fair" (or slightly "unfair") insurance and lotteries. The same individual will both insure and gamble. The hypothesis implies the same behavior whether one is poor or rich.

Markowitz recognizes that until an unambiguous procedure is discovered for determining when and to what extent current income deviates from customary income, the hypothesis will remain essentially nonverifiable because it is not capable of denying any observed behavior. The Markowitz hypothesis reveals perhaps more forcefully than the Friedman-Savage hypothesis, that utility has no meaning as an indicator of a level of utility. Utility has meaning only for changes in situations. Thus while I might choose to receive an increase in income rather than no increase, there is no implication that after I have received it for a while I remain on a higher utility base—however interpreted—than formerly. It may be the getting or losing, the rising or the falling that counts rather than the actual realized position. In any event Markowitz's hypothesis contains no implications about anything other than changes in income.

Our survey is now completed. We started with developments after

[20] H. Markowitz, "The Utility of Wealth," *Jour. Pol. Econ.* (April 1952), LX, 151-58.

the Slutsky, Hicks, Allen utility position in which utility is measured up to monotone transformations only. This meant exactly no more and no less than that utility is ordinal. In other words, the numerical size of the increments in the numbers in any one measure (column of numbers in Table I) is without meaning. Only their signs have significance. Utility translation: marginal utility has meaning only in being positive or negative, but the numerical value is meaningless, *i.e.*, *diminishing* or *increasing* marginal utility is completely arbitrary since one can get either by using the appropriate column.[21]

The first postwar development was the Neumann and Morgenstern axioms which implied measurable utility up to a linear transformation, thus reintroducing diminishing or increasing marginal utility,[22] and which also implied a hypothesis or maxim about rational behavior. This was followed by the Friedman and Savage article and Marschak's paper. These papers are essentially identical in their postulates and propositions although the presentation and exposition are so different that each contributes to an understanding of the other. The Friedman and Savage paper however contains an added element: they attempt to prophesy the shape of the curve of utility of income that would be most commonly revealed by this measurement process. Mosteller and Nogee then made a unique contribution in really trying to verify the validity and applicability of the postulates. Most recently, Markowitz criticized the Friedman and Savage conjecture about the shape of utility of income curve, with his own conjecture about its dependence upon income changes. And that is about where matters stand now.

A moral of our survey is that to say simply that something is, or is not, measurable is to say nothing. The relevant problems are: (1) can numerical values be associated with entities and then be combined according to some rules so as to predict choices in stipulated types of situations, and (2) what are the transformations that can be made upon the initially assigned set of numerical values without losing their predictive powers (validity)? As we have seen, the currently proposed axioms imply measurability up to a linear transformation. Choices among uncertain prospects are predicted by a simple probability-weighted sum of the utilities assigned to the components of the uncertain prospect, specifically from the "expected utility."

And now to provide emotional zest to the reader's intellectual activity the following test is offered. Imagine that today is your birth-

[21] It is a simple task—here left to the reader—to find current textbooks and articles—which will be left unnamed—stating that the indifference curve analysis dispenses with the concept of utility or marginal utility. Actually it dispenses only with *diminishing* or *increasing* marginal utility.

[22] Incidentally, the *Theory of Games* of Neumann and Morgenstern is completely independent of their utility discussion.

day; a friend presents you with a choice among three lotteries. Lottery A consists of a barrel of 2000 tickets of which 2 are marked $1000 and the rest are blanks. Lottery B consists of another barrel of 2000 tickets of which 20 are marked $100 and the rest are blanks. Lottery C consists of a barrel of 2000 tickets of which 1 is marked $1000 and 10 are marked $100. From the chosen barrel one ticket will be drawn at random and you will win the amount printed on the ticket. Which barrel would you choose? Remember there is no cost to you, this is a free gift opportunity. In barrel A the win of $1000 has probability .001 and the probability of getting nothing is .999; in barrel B the probability of winning $100 is .01 and getting nothing has probability .99; in barrel C $1000 has probability .0005, $100 has probability .005 and winning nothing has probability .9945. For each barrel the mathematical expectation is $1.00. The reader is urged to seriously consider and to make a choice. Only after making his choice should he read the footnote.[23]

Conclusion

1. Some readers may be jumping to the conclusion that we really can use *diminishing* or *increasing* marginal utility and that the "indifference curve" or "utility isoquant" technique has been superfluous after all. This is a dangerous conclusion. The "indifference curve" technique is more general in not requiring measurability of utility up to a linear transformation. But its greatest virtue is that unlike the earlier "partial" analysis of demand of a single commodity the indifference curve analysis by using an extra dimension facilitates intercommodity

[23] Only the reader who chose C should continue, for his choice has revealed irrationality or denial of the axioms. This can be shown easily. He states he prefers C to A and to B. First, suppose he is indifferent between A and B; he doesn't care whether his friend chooses to give him A or B just so long as he gets one or the other. Nor does he care how his friend decides which to give. In particular if his friend tosses a coin and gives A if heads come up, otherwise B, he is still indifferent. This being so, a 50-50 chance to get A or B is equivalent to C, as one can see by realizing that C is really equivalent to a .5 probability of getting A and a .5 probability of getting B. Thus if A and B are indifferent there is no reason for choosing C.

Second, the reader choosing C may have preferred A over B. We proceed as follows. Increase the prize in B until our new B, call it B′, is now indifferent with A. Form the uncertain prospect of A and B′ with probability of .5 for A. This is better than C since C is nothing but an uncertain prospect composed of A and the old B, with probability of .5 for A. Where does this leave us? This says that the new uncertain prospect must be preferred to C. But since the new uncertain prospect is composed of .5 probability for A and .5 for B′, the chooser of C must be indifferent between the uncertain prospect and A. (In axiom 3 let A and B be indifferent, and let C be identically the same thing as A. In other words, if the two entities in the uncertain prospect are equally preferred, then the uncertain prospect is indifferent to one of the entities with certainty.) The upshot is that A is just as desired as the new uncertain prospect which is better than C. Thus A is preferred to C, but the chooser of C denied this. Why? Either he understood and accepted the axioms and was irrational in making a snap judgment, or else he really did not accept the axioms. He may now privately choose his own escape. This example is due to Harry Markowitz.

analyses—the heart of price analyses. But does the more "precise" type of measurement give us more than the ordinal measurement gives? Yes. As we have seen, measurability "up to a linear transform" both implies and is implied by the possibility of predicting choices among uncertain prospects, the universal situation.

2. Nothing in the rehabilitation of measurable utility—or choice-indicating numbers—enables us to predict choices among groups of sure prospects. The "utility" of a group of sure prospects is not dependent on *only* the utility (assigned number) of the *entities* in the combination. It is dependent upon the particular *combination of entities; i.e.,* we do not postulate that the utility of one sure element in a group of sure things is independent of what other entities are included. We think it obviously would not lead to valid predictions of actual choices. Therefore, it must be realized that nothing said so far means that we could measure the total utility of a market basket of different entities by merely adding up the utilities of the individual component entities. No method for aggregating the utilities of the component entities for this purpose has been found; therefore, for this purpose we have to say that utility is not measurable.

3. Is the present discussion more appropriate for a journal in psychology or sociology? If economists analyze the behavior of a system of interacting individuals operating in field of action—called the economic sphere—by building up properties of the system from the behavior aspects of the individuals composing the system, then the economists must have some rationale of behavior applicable to the individuals. An alternative approach is to consider the whole system of individuals and detect predictable properties of the system. The classic example of this distinction is in physics. One approach postulates certain laws describing the behavior of individual molecules, or atom particles, while the other starts with laws describing the observable phenomena of masses of molecules. Apparently, most economists have relied upon the former approach, the building up from individuals—sometimes referred to as the aggregation of micro-economic analysis into macro-economic analysis. On the other hand, those who are skeptical of our ability to build from individual behavior find their haven in postulates describing mass behavior. The current utility analyses aid the former approach.

4. The expression "utility" is common in welfare theory. For demand theory and the theory of prediction of choices made by individuals, measurability of the quantity (called "utility") permits us to make verifiable statements about individual behavior, but there is as yet no such happy development in welfare theory. "Measurability up to a linear transformation" does not provide any theorems for welfare theory beyond those derivable from ordinality. I mention this in order to forestall temptations to assume the contrary. The social welfare

function as synthesized by Hicks and Scitovsky, for example, does not require the "utility" (choice-ordering numbers) of each individual to be measurable up to a linear transformation. It is sufficient that the individual's utility be measurable up to a monotone transformation—or, in other words, that it have merely ordinal properties. Ordinal utility is adequate in this case because orderings are made of positions or states in which, as between the two states compared, everyone is better off in one state than in the other. The welfare function does not enable a ranking of two states in one of which some people are worse off.[24] This would require an entirely different kind of measure of utility for each person because of the necessity of making interpersonal aggregations of utilities. As yet no one has proposed a social welfare function acceptable for this purpose, nor has anyone discovered how, even in principle, to measure utility beyond the linear transformation. Even more important, the various elements in the concept of welfare (as distinct from utility) have not been adequately specified. In effect the utility whose measurement is discussed in this paper has literally nothing to do with individual, social or group welfare, whatever the latter may be supposed to mean.

5. A brief obiter dictum on interpersonal utility comparisons may be appropriate. Sometimes it is said that interpersonal utility comparisons are possible since we are constantly declaring that individual A is better off than individual B. For example, "a rich man is better off than a poor man." But is this really an interpersonal utility comparison? Is it not rather a statement by the declarer that he would prefer to be in the rich man's position rather than in the poor man's? It does not say that the rich *man* is happier or has more "utility" than the poor *man*. Even if the rich man has a perpetual smile and declares himself to be truly happy and the poor man admits he is sorrowful, how do we know that the rich *man* is happier than the poor *man*, even though both men prefer being richer to being poorer? If I were able to experience the totality of the poor man's situation and the rich man's, and preferred the rich man's, it would not constitute an interpersonal comparison; rather it would be an *intrapersonal,* intersituation comparison.

It is hoped that the reader now has at his command enough familiarity with the meanings of measurability to be able to interpret and evaluate the blossoming literature on utility and welfare, and that this exposition has made it clear that welfare analysis gains nothing from the current utility analysis, and conversely.

[24] Absolutely nothing is implied about taxation. For example, justification of progressive income taxation by means of utility analysis remains impossible. The best demonstration of this is still E. D. Fagan, "Recent and Contemporary Theories of Progressive Taxation," *Jour. Pol. Econ.* (Aug. 1938), XLVI, 457-98.

21 Indifference Curves and Uncertainty

K. Borch

Summary

A decision-maker who has to choose between risky prospects, can always select the prospect which offers the greatest expected gain. In practice, however, it seems as if most decision-makers find it necessary to make some "corrections for risk". This may lead to the formulation of a decision rule, which consists of maximizing some function of expected gain and the standard deviation of the gain. It is well known that this role contains contradictions. The author discusses the nature of these contradictions, and gives a number of simple examples.

1. In this paper we shall discuss the inherent contradictions of some very popular models for decision-making under uncertainty. We will start by considering a decision-maker who has to choose an element in a set of "prospects". We shall assume that prospect i will give a monetary payoff, which is a stochastic variable with the distribution $F_i(x)$. It is clear that our decision-maker will need some rule which tells him when one probability distribution is to be considered better than another, i.e. he needs a *preference ordering* over a set of such distributions.

The simplest rule of this kind consists of computing the expected payoff

$$E_i = \int_{-\infty}^{+\infty} x \quad dF_i(x)$$

for each prospect, and choosing the prospect which gives the greatest value of E_i. This rule is often rejected because it is felt that one cannot "ignore the risk" associated with the various prospects. It may then seem natural to take the standard deviation S as a measure of risk, compute

$$S_i^2 = \int_{-\infty}^{+\infty} (x - E_i)^2 dF_i(x)$$

and choose the prospect which gives the best pair (E_i, S_i). This means that the problem of establishing a preference ordering over a set of probability distributions is reduced to that of ordering a set of pairs (E_i, S_i). To an economist, it will then be natural to represent this preference ordering by a family of indifference curves in the ES-plane, and to proceed with the familiar tools of classical economic analysis.

2. The ideas outlined above have been used as building blocks in very gen-

Reprinted from the *Swedish Journal of Economics,* Vol. LXX (March, 1968), pp. 19–24, by permission of the publisher and author.

eral models constructed by Allais [1], Markowitz [2], [3], Tobin [5] and others. These models have proved stimulating, and have led to considerable further research into the economics of uncertainty.

The basic assumption that only the first two moments are considered when ordering prospects is obviously an approximation. It is also well known that the assumption can lead to contradictions of various kinds. The three authors referred to are well aware of this, and they take some care in specifying the conditions under which their results may be valid. The enthusiastic followers of the three pioneers do not always exercise the same amount of caution, and they often seem to assume that the models have a general validity—at least as fair approximations. It may therefore be useful to give a simple demonstration of the contradictions inherent in the assumption.

3. We shall first show that, in general, it is impossible to draw a family of indifference curves in the ES-plane.

Let us consider two points (E_1, S_1) and (E_2, S_2) in this plane, and assume that they lie on the same indifference curve. If $E_1 > E_2$ and $S_1 < S_2$, the points cannot be on the same indifference curve, since the first point will correspond to a prospect with greater expected payoff and smaller risk than the prospect represented by the second point. We can therefore, without loss of generality, assume that $E_1 > E_2$ and $S_1 > S_2$

Let (x_0, p, x), where $x \geqslant x_0$, be the following prospect: Payoff x_0 with probability $q = 1 - p$ or Payoff x with probability p.

If $x_1 > x_2$, the prospect (x_0, p, x_1) is obviously preferred to (x_0, p, x_2), so these two prospects cannot be represented by points on the same indifference curve in the EV-plane.

For the expected payoff and the standard deviation of the prospect (x_0, p, x) we find:

$$E(x) = qx_0 + px$$

$$S(x) = (pq)^{\frac{1}{2}}(x - x_0).$$

Let us now take

$$p = \frac{(E_1 - E_2)^2}{(E_1 - E_2)^2 + (S_1 - S_2)^2}$$

$$x_0 = \frac{S_1 E_2 - S_2 E_1}{S_1 - S_2}$$

$$x = x_1 = E_1 + S_1 \frac{S_1 - S_2}{E_1 - E_2}.$$

We then find

$$E(x_1) = E_1 \text{ and } S(x_1) = S_1.$$

Let us next leave x_0 and p unchanged, and take

$$x = x_2 = E_2 + S_2 \frac{S_1 - S_2}{E_1 - E_2}.$$

We then find

$$E(x_2) = E_2 \text{ and } S(x_2) = S_2.$$

It is obvious that $x_1 > x_2$, so that the points (E_1, S_1) and (E_2, S_2) cannot lie on the same indifference curve. This contradicts our initial assumption, and implies that no indifference curves exist in the ES-plane.

4. Economists often tend to ignore mathematical results of the kind shown in the preceding paragraph. This may be justified as a temporary expedient if it eventually leads to a more rewarding formulation of the problem. Let us therefore consider two prospects with the distributions $F_1(x)$ and $F_2(x)$, corresponding to the points (E_1, S_1) and (E_2, S_2) in the ES-plane, and introduce the following:

Postulate

If a decision-maker is indifferent between the prospects with distributions $F_1(x)$ and $F_2(x)$, he will be indifferent between all prospects with a distribution of the form $F(x) = \alpha\, F_1(x) + (1-\alpha)\, F_2(x)$, where $0 \leqslant \alpha \leqslant 1$.

The postulate means that if a decision-maker is indifferent between both prospects, he does not mind letting chance decide which of them he will obtain. This is little more than a reasonable definition of what we really mean by indifference.

Let $F(x)$ be represented by the point (E, S) in the ES-plane. Since

$$E = \int_{-\infty}^{+\infty} x dF(x)$$

$$S^2 + E^2, = \int_{-\infty}^{+\infty} x^2 dF(x)$$

we have

$$E = \alpha E_1 + (1-\alpha) E_2$$

$$S^2 + E^2 = \alpha(S_1^2 + E_1^2) + (1-\alpha)(S_2^2 + E_2^2).$$

Eliminating α from these equations we obtain:

$$S^2 + (E - \tfrac{1}{2}a)^2 = \tfrac{1}{4}a^2 - b,$$

where

$$a = \frac{S_1^2 + E_1^2 - S_2^2 - E_2^2}{E_1 - E_2}$$

$$b = \frac{(S_1^2 + E_1^2)E_2 - (S_2^2 + E_2^2)E_1}{E_1 - E_2}.$$

Hence all points (E, S) lie on a circle with its center at $(\frac{1}{2}a, 0)$, and passing through points (E_1, S_1) and (E_2, S_2). If we insist on drawing an indifference curve through (E_1, S_1) and (E_2, S_2), it seems as if we have to choose the arc of this circle connecting the two points. If we want a family of indifference curves that do not intersect each other, it seems as if we must choose a family of concentric circles, with centers on the E-axis. This is, indeed, the case, as we shall see in the following paragraph.

5. The starting point of both Markowitz and Tobin is the so-called *Expected Utility Theorem* of von Neumann and Morgenstern [4]. This is not really necessary, since the theorem is deeper than the problem of ordering a two-dimensional set. The theorem does, however, clear up the paradoxes we have encountered.

The Postulate in the preceding paragraph, together with postulates that ensure the existence of an ordering, are equivalent to the consistency conditions of von Neumann and Morgenstern. When these conditions are fulfilled, the preference ordering can be represented by a utility function $u(x)$, so that

$$\int_{-\infty}^{+\infty} u(x)dF_i(x) > \int_{-\infty}^{+\infty} u(x)dF_j(x)$$

if—and only if—$F_i(x)$ is preferred to $F_j(x)$.

If the preference ordering is to depend only on the first two moments of the distributions, the utility function must obviously be a polynominal of the second degree. Since the utility function is determined only up to a positive linear transformation, there is no loss of generality if we write

$$u(x) = x - cx^2.$$

The utility assigned to a prospect with expectation E and standard deviation S is then

$$U = \int_{-\infty}^{+\infty} (x - cx^2)dF(x) = E - cE^2 - cS^2.$$

From this we obtain

$$S^2 + \left(E - \frac{1}{2c}\right)^2 = \frac{1}{4c^2} - \frac{U}{c}.$$

It is then evident that the indifference curves in the ES-plane are concentric semi-circles with the center at the point $(1/2c, 0)$, as indicated in the preceding paragraph.

The function $u(x)$ can be interpreted as the "utility of money". If we are to avoid economic nonsense, we must have $u'(x) \geqslant 0$, i.e. $x \leqslant \frac{1}{2}c$. There are also good reasons for assuming a general risk aversion, so that $u''(x) < 0$, i.e. $c > 0$.

From these considerations it follows that a preference ordering over a set of prospects can be represented by a family of indifference curves in the ES-plane, if the possible payoffs of all prospects in the set are smaller than $\frac{1}{2}c$. If a greater payoff is possible from some prospect, we may run into contradictions due to the implied decreasing utility of money. This was demonstrated in paragraph 3. It is easy to verify that

$$x_1 > \frac{1}{2c} = \frac{a}{2}.$$

It follows that the indifference curves must be circular arcs if the preference ordering satisfies the consistency conditions of von Neumann and Morgenstern. These conditions are very strong. They determine the whole indifference map, once indifference is established between two points (E_1, S_1) and (E_2, S_2). There is only one circle with its center on the E-axis which goes through these two points. Once the center is determined, the whole family of indifference curves is determined, as is the "coefficient of risk aversion" c which in turn determines the set of prospects to which the model can be applied.

6. Few of the authors who have worked with indifference curves in the ES-plane seem to accept the rigid conclusions above. It may therefore be useful to terminate on a tolerant note, and try to bring out the tacit assumptions made by these authors.

If we consider only a finite set of prospects, the set can be ordered, and we can require the prospect corresponding to (E_1, S_1) to be ranked above the prospect corresponding to (E_2, S_2) if

$$E_1 > E_2 \text{ and } S_1 = S_2$$

or

$$E_1 = E_2 \text{ and } S_1 < S_2.$$

There will usually be an infinite number of indifference maps consistent with this ordering. By using the methods in paragraph, 3 we can show that any of these indifference maps contains contradictions. But in order to do so, we have to use prospects of the form (x_0, p, x), which may not be included in the original set. Therefore, it is usually possible to defend any family of indifference curves by excluding a suitable set of prospects from considerations.

Most authors who have worked with these models have taken a finite set of prospects as a basis and generated a larger set, by performing some operation on the elements of the basis. If this operation is a "probability mixture" of the kind considered in paragraph 4, it is hard to escape the conclusion that indifference curves are concentric circles, without contradicting the consistency conditions of von Neumann and Morgenstern.

A more popular operation consists of forming a "portfolio" of the prospects in the basis. A portfolio is defined by a vector $\{\alpha_1, \alpha_2 \ldots\}$, where α_i denotes the fraction of prospect i included in the portfolio. The portfolio itself is a prospect, and its distribution is the convolution of the distributions $F_1(^x/\alpha_1)$, $F_2(^x/\alpha_2)$ .... If the basis chosen is sufficiently narrow, it is clearly impossible to construct a portfolio which will reveal the contradiction inherent in the model.

7. In conclusions let us consider an investor who has selected his optimal portfolio from a set of available prospects, and assume that this portfolio is represented by the point (E, S) in the ES-plane.

We can now offer this investor the opportunity of exchanging his portfolio for the following gamble:

$$\text{Payoff } 0 \qquad \text{with probability } \frac{S^2 - C}{E^2 + S^2 - C}$$

$$\text{Payoff } \frac{E^2 + S^2 - C}{E} \text{ with probability } \frac{E^2}{E^2 + S^2 - C}$$

where $C > 0$.

If the investor accepts the gamble, it is natural to conclude that he is a gambler at heart, and that he was wrong in the first place to seek a diversified portfolio.

If the investor refuses, we can point out that expected payoff from the gamble is E, and that the standard deviation is $(S^2 - C)^{\frac{1}{2}} < S$. The investor should therefore consider the gamble as less risky then the portfolio. It is likely that the investor will then reply that there is more to investment than expectation and standard deviation. The purpose of this paper has been to show that the investor is right—and possibly to help mathematical economics to catch up with common sense.

References

[1]. Allais, M.: "L'Extension des Theories de l'Equilibre Economique Général et du Rendement Social au Cas du Risque", *Econometrica* 1953, pp. 269–290.

[2]. Markowitz, H.: "Portfolio Selection", *The Journal of Finance* 1952, pp. 77–91.

[3]. Markowitz, H.: *Portfolio Selection—Efficient Diversification of Investments*, John Wiley & Sons, New York 1959.

[4]. Neumann, J. von and O. Morgenstern: *Theory of Games and Economic Behavior*, 2nd Edition, Princeton University Press, 1947.

[5]. Tobin, J.: "Liquidity Preference as Behavior Towards Risk", *The Review of Economic Studies*, Vol. XXV (1958), pp. 65–86.

22 Demand Theory Reconsidered

O. Morgenstern

The theory of individual and collective demand is generally believed to be well established. It will be argued in this paper, however, that there are properties of demand that deserve further study and that this results in a recasting of some fundamental notions. In particular, we shall investigate how variations in market price can be treated in demand analysis and what time periods are to be considered. How does demand theory deal with these problems and how useful are the measures of price-and-quantity variation, such as the concept of elasticity of demand? We give only a brief and simple outline, leaving a fuller elaboration of the implications to another occasion.

In general, we make use of the customary concepts of economic theory; in a few instances, however, we shall show how the ideas developed here link up with results obtained in the Theory of Games and Economic Behavior.[1] To the extent to which the following is critical, it is therefore mostly immanent criticism, but we do go well beyond that stage.

I. Individual Demand Schedules

Fundamental properties

1. We start with the individual demand schedule or function. This schedule is generally assumed to express the directly observable fact that the individual, whom we take to be a consumer, will as a rule buy increasing quantities of the same commodity at falling prices. The individual demand of a single firm, rather than a final consumer, is derived demand and raises further problems, which can be attacked only after the simplest cases are settled. However, the following analysis applies even for derived demand, especially regarding the composition of

1. John von Neumann and Oskar Morgenstern: Theory of Games and Economic Behavior, Princeton, 1944, 2d edition, 1947. Cf. also the expositions by L. Hurwicz: The Theory of Economic Behavior, Am. Econ. Review, vol. xxxv (1945), pp. 909–925, and J. Marschak: Neumann's and Morgenstern's New Approach to Static Economics, Journal of Political Economy, vol. LIV (1946), pp. 97–115.

Cf. further O. Morgenstern: Oligopoly, Monopolistic Competition and the Theory of Games, Am. Econ. Assoc. Proceedings (March 1948).

Reprinted with revisions from the *Quarterly Journal of Economics* vol. LXII (February 1948), pp. 165–201, by permission of the publisher and author.

an aggregate demand curve, so that we suffer no loss in generality by not dealing with this case explicitly.

In order to obtain the utmost simplicity, we assume the demand function to be a one-variable function; the individual may be thought to be buying one or several units of only one single commodity, or he may buy several commodities independent of each other (Cournot). The extension of the subsequent arguments to functions of several variables offers no fundamental difficulties. This gives the familiar "demand curve," as a rule falling strictly monotonically from left to right in a Cartesian plane. The ordinate shows quantities (the dependent variable) and the abscissa the price of the commodity in question.[2] This arrangement is the classical one of Cournot and Walras. Marshall changed it, and almost all present textbook expositions follow his practice of showing price on the y- and quantity on the x-axis. This procedure contradicts mathematical usage, which calls for the independent variable to be graphed on the abscissa and to which $q = f(p)$ corresponds exactly. It is definitely awkward because it makes a single-valued function in some cases multi-valued (cf. footnote 11) which is highly undesirable.[3]

With only one possible exception, of little practical significance, the individual demand curve will cut the y-axis at a point $y > 0$, thus fixing the point of complete satiation of demand. (The interesting condition when $y = 0$ at more than one price but $y > 0$ at others, is that of the snob to which we return below in footnote 11.) That such a point must always exist is obvious, since nobody wants infinitely large amounts (which do not even exist in reality!) of anything even if its price should be zero.

Indeed, we can go further: many individual demand curves will have a kink, i.e., for prices lower than a certain price p_i no greater quantity will be demanded than at p_i.[4] (In the above-mentioned graphical representation, the monotonic demand curve will begin perpendicular to the y-axis before falling to the right until it cuts the x-axis.) This will be true of those commodities of which the individual is able to afford an amount satisfying his desire completely at a price higher than zero. If the actually ruling price is within that horizontal part of the demand curve, we call the latter *intramarginal* in respect to that price. Some curves are intramarginal for technical reasons, e.g., when only a fixed amount is

2. A complete description of the function in mathematical terms would be desirable, but our exposition is quite elementary and the above characterization is sufficient. For the same reason we usually speak of "curves," instead of "functions," in spite of the obvious limitations of this term.

3. The graphing of supply curves could also be changed appropriately. When demand curves are combined with cost curves – with costs as the dependent variable, quantity as the independent variable – then no 100 percent correct arrangement is possible. Neither is a harmony to be achieved by the subsequent notations for price and quantity changes. The best is, of course, to free oneself as far as possible from graphs altogether; when functions of more than one variable are considered they become impracticable or impossible at any rate.

4. Cf. Joan Robinson, The Economics of Imperfect Competition, p. 23.

needed, such as one copy of a newspaper, and when the maximum bid is above the market price. If the price falls, a consumer's rent appears or it increases. *Marginal* demand curves are those for commodities of which smaller quantities are bought at the existing price than are needed for complete satiation of the want.[5] The number and the kind of commodities for which marginal demand curves exist at given prices express the degree of affluence of the individual relative to his desires and their capacities. The discussion of demand should not be limited to the marginal curves.[6]

Another assumption is that of the constancy of the marginal utility of money; it is implied in the drawing of decreasing demand curves. If it should happen that additional units of a given commodity have the same (constant) marginal utility, then demand curves in the ordinary sense do not exist. We rule out this important case, in order to leave that part of our observations immanent.[7] We shall not discuss the problem of the marginal utility of money and of income.[8]

Neither do we discuss how the individual correlates prices and quantities; in other words, we take the demand schedule as given. The reader is familiar with demand curves obtained from indifference curves, when the assumption of the non-numerical character of utility prevails. If utility is taken to be numerical (i.e., up to any linear transformation, cf. footnote 49), no problem exists for the individual to obtain that correlation from the numerical utilities. Whichever view is taken, a case can be made for the existence of individual demand functions or curves with the above properties.

Alternative maximum bids

2. The points on the individual demand curve are a series of *simultaneous alternative*[9] *maximum bids* for the quantities associated with each price. This means that each point is valid to the exclusion of all other stated bids at the same or immediately following[10] moment of time. The individual expresses his willingness to buy at a given moment of time either one or any of the other quantities at their respective money prices. The bids are furthermore interrelated – provided there exists a schedule extending over more than one unit – in a manner which

5. In case of complete divisibility, the distinction between the two is not mathematically strict. But this will not matter in what follows.

6. There is, of course, nothing peculiar in using the term "marginal" for entire curves. Besides, the terminology does not matter.

7. This phenomenon occurs necessarily when time is allowed for in the valuation process, so that recurrent wants are included within the same income period.

8. For an exhaustive treatment cf. P. A. Samuelson: Constancy of the Marginal Utility of Income, in Studies in Mathematical Economics and Econometrics (1942), pp. 75–91.

9. Cf. R. G. D. Allen: Mathematical Analysis for Economists (1938), p. 110.

10. This will be further discussed in 12.

requires explicit formulation and, it seems, is lacking in the ordinary expositions of demand theory.

The bids are maximum bids, i.e., it is in keeping with the general assumption that the individual prefers a larger advantage to a smaller one to assume that he would like to obtain any stated quantity at a smaller and even at zero price. This limiting position of the price bid becomes quite clear when the individual demands only one unit of the commodity. For example, only one copy of a newspaper may be desired, for which he might be willing to pay as much as a dollar; but he will also take it, and no more, for nothing. He will not buy if the price is greater than one dollar; hence this is his maximum bid, and the individual's demand is effective whenever the price is at or below it.[11] If the price is higher, he is an *excluded* buyer; he may be (one of) the marginal excluded buyer (s). If a lower price prevails, the difference between the maximum bid and the price paid is an instance of consumer's rent, which here can be expressed unambiguously in monetary terms.[12] If the demand curve expresses the willingness of the individual to buy more than one single definite quantity (e.g., more than one unit only), then consumer's rent is not such a simple concept, as will be shown. But the characteristic of the alternative bids (now for varying quantities), that each is a maximum bid, remains unaltered.

3. The utility function of the individual will, as a rule, call for the acquisition of varying quantities. Then we obtain the usual monotonically downward-sloping demand curve. Now, it is important to realize that the various alternative maximum bids are not independent of each other. In particular, each lower maximum bid (for a larger quantity) depends upon the assumption that a higher maximum bid for a smaller quantity did not materialize "shortly" before the one in question. (About the time intervals to be considered, cf. 12.) The dependency is that of the lower on the (nonmaterialized) higher maximum bids; the higher bids do not depend on the lower in the same sense. This can also be stated as follows: the individual intends to make alternative total outlays that may or may not differ from each other. They will, as a rule, increase and, passing through a maximum, become zero. If they remain constant, the demand curve is, of course, a rectangular hyperbola with unit elasticity.

11. Excepting the case of the snob who cannot buy above a certain figure, but who will not buy if the price is below a certain figure, because then in his eyes socially undesirable consequences are connected with the acquisition of the commodity. This case may, of course, also arise when the snob buys several units. He may stop buying altogether, even then, in case the price should fall below a certain value. The function jumps, as in the previous case, from zero discontinuously to his minimum purchase price; thereafter it may or may not decrease continuously to zero. His demand function is thus a *rising* function and in this respect quite different from all others. In the Marshallian graph the function becomes multivalued. We return to the implications of this whole case below in (a) in 17. This type of rising demand function is different from that studied by Ricci, based on observations by Pantaleoni, Marshall, etc. Cf. also J. Viner, The Utility Concept in Value Theory and its Critics. Journal of Political Economy, vol. 33 (1925), pp. 378–379.

12. Because of the derivation of demand bids from utility, the reverse operation is also possible, but this is immaterial too.

In the case of the actual purchase of the quantity q_i at the price p_i, all higher maximum bids, i.e., $p_i < p_{i-1} < p_{i-2} < \ldots$ disappear completely from the active plan of the individual, at least for the time being. All maximum bids smaller than p_i, i.e., $p_i > p_{i+1} > p_{i+2} > \ldots$, with which were associated the respective quantities, $q_i < q_{i+1} < q_{i+2} < \ldots$, are affected in various manners. In particular, should shortly after p_i was charged the price $p_{i-1} > p_i$ obtain in the market, the individual will now buy nothing, although the original demand curve stated that with p_{i-1} the amount $q_{i-1} < q_i$ would be demanded; should shortly after p_i was charged, the price $p_{i+1} < p_i$ obtain, the individual instead of buying $q_{i+1} > q_i$ may now buy a new quantity $0 \leqslant q'_{i+1} < q_{i+1}$.

Reconstitution of the demand curve

4. This is simply illustrated with a demand curve of unit elasticity.[13] The only sensible interpretation to be given is that if a purchase has been made (at whatever price), the individual clearly will then no longer be in the market.[14] until, as we shall say, his demand curve has been *reconstituted,* i.e. (*a*) either a new income payment and consequently a confirmation of his previous expenditure plan has reproduced a *future* demand curve (identically or with modifications), or (*b*) his expenditure plan has been modified and a new demand curve (which may or may not have the original shape) is set up which describes his *immediate* further intentions in the market under consideration. In the latter case alone is he still in the market when the price variation has occurred. From this it is seen that any individual demand curve, being an arrangement of alternative bids, cannot as it stands describe *successive* actions of the individual, without introducing either or both of the above two adjustments. Their explicit introduction is required. Assumptions of this kind seem to have been made tacitly, but they also go much further, especially in the case of the aggregate demand curve (see Section II), than appears acceptable.

13. Elasticity is defined for the price p and the quantity q in the usual way as $\eta = -dq/dp \cdot p/q$. This is a measure that can be applied to any differentiable real function of one variable. Its formation does not guarantee at all that it has an economic meaning; this has to be established separately.

For a detailed history of demand and its elasticity, see especially A. W. Marget: The Theory of Prices, vol. II (1942), chaps. 4–5, pp. 137–318.

A rectangular hyperbola does not intersect the two axes, so that this demand curve contradicts the relevant observation in 1. But it suffices to consider it only up to that quantity measured along the ordinate which will completely satisfy the individual. At that point the curve will have its kink; if that part is also to be considered, it can easily be done.

14. Assuming that he demands only one single commodity and that $\eta = 1$, i.e., $p_i \cdot q_i = \mu$ (his income), the case is trivially clear that after having spent his entire income he cannot spend anything more, until he has received new income. This holds *mutatis mutandis* even when $\eta \neq 1$. So instead of having the traditional $\eta = 1$ for a rectangular hyperbola *individual* demand curve, we have $\eta = 0$ when a short run variation is considered. Cf. 19 below.

The time interval to which demand curves refer is not uniformly defined in the literature, if at all. Marshall, for example, says: "We may say generally: The elasticity (or responsiveness) of demand in a market is great or small according as the amount *increases* much or little for a *given fall* in price, and *diminishes* much or little for a *given rise* in price.[15] He then proceeds to give the graphical illustration, using the *same* demand curve for these successive operations. H. Schultz writes of the mathematical and the neoclassical laws of demand: "They are both static laws; they relate to a point in time."[16] Such statements could be multiplied. Nothing is said about reconstitution; the same curve is simply used over and over again, and neither individual nor aggregate, neither one-variable nor multivariable functions are differently treated.

An individual demand curve of one variable, then, no matter what its shape, is valid as it stands, only for *one single use*, i.e., for one transaction. Under specific conditions – when the initial total outlay curve (showing total outlay on the y-axis and the quantity bought on the x-axis) has its maximum to the right of the quantity purchased – further transactions at other, lower, prices are possible. There can be no further transaction if the new price is higher than the first one (and if demand functions of one variable only are alone considered).[17]

The reaction function

5. The additional demand, in case of a price fall, will be the quantity q'_{i+1} which can be bought at the new, lower, price for the amount $\Delta = q_{i+1}p_{i+1} - q_ip_i$. When $\Delta \leqslant 0$, there are no transactions; $\Delta > 0$ is the amount that may be spent on additional units.[18] In words, Δ is the difference between the intended outlay at the lower price p_{i+1} and the outlay that has actually occurred at the price p_i.

15. Principles of Economics, 8th Ed. (1925), p. 102. Our italics.

16. Statistical Laws of Demand and Supply (1928), p. 27.

17. This restriction is necessary in order to rule out complementarity and the Giffen paradox. But even if these are admitted, the original demand curve does not show the successive reactions to be expected.

For the theory of demand in general cf. H. Wold: A Synthesis of Pure Demand Analysis (Uppsala 1943–44). Some recognition of limitations to be placed upon the interpretation of demand curves – at least regarding consumers' surplus – is found in A. A. Young's contribution to Ely's Outlines of Economics, 5th ed. (1930), pp. 179–180. Cf. also E. Chamberlin: The Theory of Monopolistic Competition (1933), pp. 27–28, in the same connection.

More recently a brief discussion in the spirit of the argumentation in the text is given by T. Haavelmo: The Probability Approach to Econometrics, Econometrica, Vol. 12, Supplement (1944), pp. 19–21, where a notion similar to our "reaction function," introduced in 5 below, occurs.

18. Whether this additional expenditure for the commodity in question is warranted will really depend on many other factors besides those described by the demand curves. A resetting of preferences by the individual may precede this; it would lead too far to enter upon these matters here. If the individual buys only one single commodity, additional outlay will take place if $\Delta > 0$.

Repeated application will yield a series of what may be called the individual's (short-run) derived *reaction functions.*[19]

We emphasize that this is true only for individual demand curves of one variable. The interpretation of aggregate demand curves, while based on these, must allow for much greater complexity.

Considering, for a moment, more than one demand curve of one variable, we find: Not all demand curves of an individual, valid for a given period, can without further qualifications simultaneously be of $\eta \neq 1$, even if each combination of alternative expenditures for all commodities should add up always, as is necessary, exactly to the same total income to be spent by the individual.

To make this completely clear: just as each single demand curve is a collection of points, each representing alternative maximum bids for that commodity, all points on all demand curves are in some restricted sense alternative to each other. What are these restrictions?

(*a*) The income (or amount of money) to be spent during a unit period is *fixed.* Then all possible combinations of points for all demand curves of the individual must always add up to this same constant sum. If this is the case, we call the demand curves of the individual *compatible.* Static demand theory of the Walrasian type, dealing with functions of several variables, should describe this condition.

(*b*) The income (or amount of money) to be spent during a unit period is *not fixed.* Then the demand curves may have any shape; they are *arbitrary*[20] and the various combinations of possible expenditures need not add up to the same, constant sum.

Under the static assumption a very complicated picture results. Then the reactions of an individual to changes in the price for one commodity can no longer be described in terms of his demand curve, but only in terms of the *compatibility of the induced changes* in expenditure and their *sequences* with all other demand curves (where there might be simultaneous or successive positive or negative price variations with appropriate reactions described by the reaction functions). If all his demand curves were rectangular hyperbolas – and only then – no such problem would arise, provided their sum is equal to the planned total expenditure. In other words: instead of merely requiring the compatibility of the demand functions, the compatibility of all demand and derived reaction functions is necessary.

This means that the ensemble of all the individual demand curves as given before a price fall does not completely describe the future actions in respect to price changes. This would only be the case if for all of them $\eta = 1$ and their sum equals the individual's income: after (simultaneous or successive) transactions no

19. It would be convenient to call them derived demand curves, since they are new demand curves with all the necessary properties. But the term is frequently used for indirectly demanded goods.

20. They will, in the main, still be of negative slope.

further ones would follow within the same income period.[21] It would, in all other instances, obviously be necessary that the demand functions indicate *where* and for what quantities the required withdrawal of money will be made. This is a formidable combinatorial problem.

The "compatibility" of all individual demand curves, i.e., the summation for all possible combinations of prices and quantities demanded, to the same total income is investigated in current theory. The "compatibility" of the second kind, considering also the derived reaction functions as well as the combination of the sequences in which price variations for different commodities follow each other, is neither stated as a problem nor investigated.

For one individual and one commodity we shall summarize briefly as follows:

The individual's demand function, given for one income-(planning) period—before any purchases have been made—can be written as $q(p)$ defined over the interval $0 \leqslant p \leqslant p_m$.

Now assume that a purchase is made at some price p, then the new derived, demand curve will be a function of the price at which the purchase was made, p, and any subsequent price p' that may obtain in the market, where $p' < p$. Mathematically the derived demand curve of our individual will be expressed as $q(p,p'), p' < p \; (0 \leqslant p \leqslant p_m)$.

We can now express $q(p,p')$ in terms of the consumer original demand curve by considering that the consumer will spend $q(p,p')p' = \Delta$ where $\Delta = q(p')p' - q(p)p$ if $\Delta < 0$, and zero otherwise. We may express this as:

$$q(p,p') = \frac{\{\Delta\}^+}{p'} = \frac{\{q(p')p' - q(p)p\}^+}{p'} = \left\{q(p') - q(p)\frac{p}{p'}\right\}^+$$

for $0 \leqslant p \leqslant p_m, p' < p$, where the notation $\{x\}^+$ is defined as

$$\{x\}^+ = x \quad \text{if} \quad x > 0$$

$$\{x\}^+ = 0 \quad \text{if} \quad x \leqslant 0$$

We may illustrate our ideas graphically in the following manner: consider an initial demand curve as illustrated in Figure 1. Generally we may expect that there is some $p = p_m$ above which no quantity will be demanded; similarly, there is some saturation quantity demanded $q = q_m$ as p approaches 0. Between these two points lies the relevant portion of the demand curve. In Figure 1 we have assumed a linear demand curve in the first instance for ease of simplification. Figure 2 shows the theoretically relevant value $p \cdot q$ as a function of p. Let us

21. For the simple reason that for each rectangular hyperbola demand function the reaction functions are all zero.

consider what the derived demand curves will look like for the three cases in which an initial purchase is made at prices p_1, p_2, and p_3. These demand curves are shown in Figures 3, 4, and 5 respectively. The demand curves of Figures 3 and 4 are of a somewhat similar shape to the $p \cdot q$ curve but are skewed somewhat to the left. For $p = p_3$ (Figure 5) we have the limiting case of a finite demand curve for all $p' \leqslant p_3$ the derived demand curve will be null.

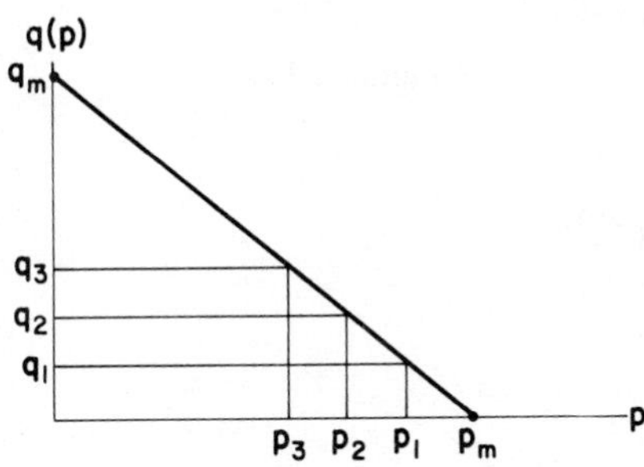

Figure 22–1.

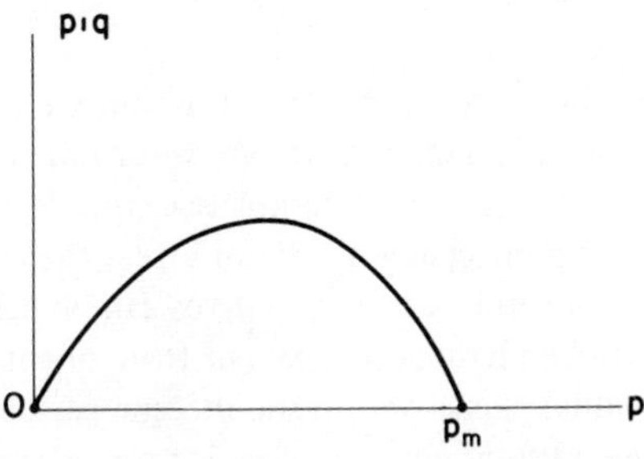

Figure 22–2.

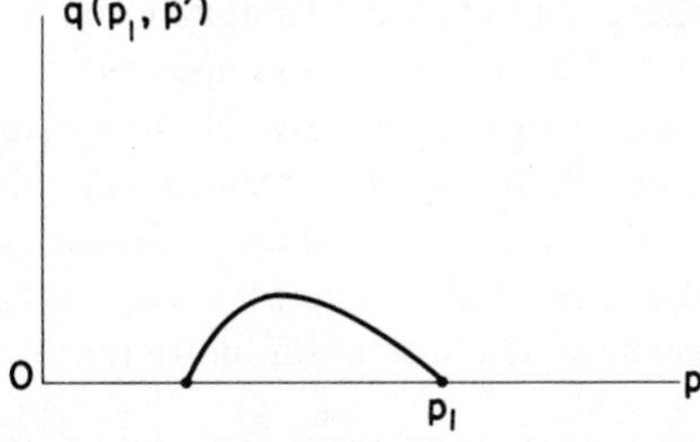

Figure 22–3.

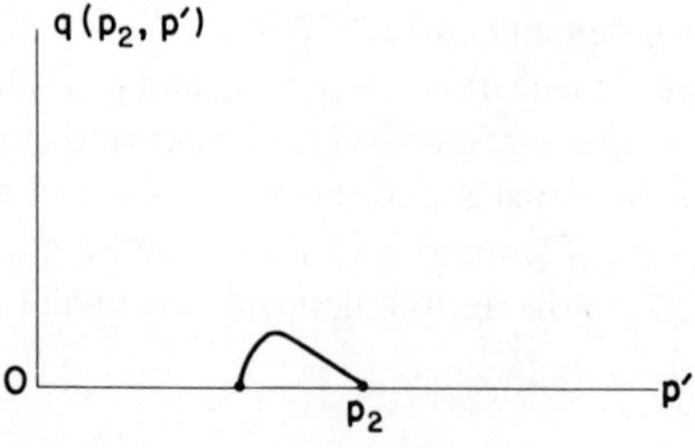

Figure 22–4.

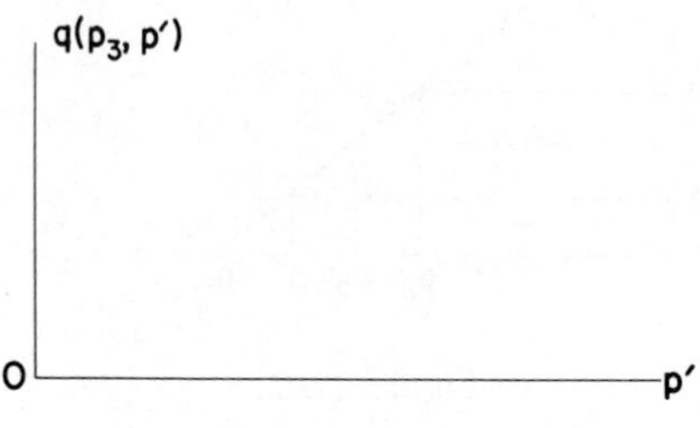

Figure 22–5.

6. It would lead too far to go further into this, but we have to add two more observations. First, individual demand curves are *short run* (cf. 12) except in two senses. (*a*) When goods are bought up to complete extinction of the wants they satisfy and if downward income changes will not affect the amount purchased, then these necessarily intramarginal demand curves can be considered as long run, in the sense that they will be identically *repeated* from one income period to the other.[22] (*b*) If the individual plans over several income periods, i.e., if we allow him to accumulate money during several successive periods and to spend it (e.g., on durable goods of high price relative to his income) in a particular period, then his demand curve for this commodity is, in a certain sense, of long-run character too. It is, however, only *latent* during the time when the accumulation goes on. These questions are already more of a dynamic nature and tend to become very complicated (cf. the reference in footnote 39).

Second, when the individual demand curve of one variable is monotonically falling or strictly monotonically falling but remains single valued (i.e., never becomes parallel to the *y*-axis where the quantity is shown), it requires the assumption of an underlying decreasing marginal utility for additional units bought. This fact can also be stated in terms of indifference curves, preferences,

22. It would be possible to interpret individual demand functions as averages. This deviates from the current conception, but would justify somewhat their use, at least when recurrent wants are involved. Cf. 12 for a further comment.

marginal rates of substitution, etc. If the function should become multivalued,[23] difficulties would arise from the implication of constancy of marginal utility of the commodity and the assumption of constant marginal utility of money, which both cannot hold together.

II. Collective Demand Schedules

Additivity in closed markets

7. The collective or aggregate demand curve presents a much more complicated picture. While not all the characteristics and implications of the individual demand curve will reappear or can be transferred, many new additional features are noticeable. In particular, the various points of the aggregate curve are *not completely alternative* to each other. The extent to which they are depends on the exact form of their composition from the individual curves.

Collective demand is generally understood as a summation of individual demand schedules (for the same commodity). We shall in the following, unless otherwise stated, accept this additivity, but only as a first approximation. It is only valid if the demand functions of the various individuals are independent of each other. This is clearly not true universally. Current theory possesses no methods that allow the construction of aggregate demand curves when the various constituent individual demand curves are not independent of each other. The problem does not even seem to have been put.[24] If there is interdependence among individual demand functions, it is doubtful that aggregate or collective demand functions of the conventional type exist and do not have to be replaced by more complicated concepts. (Cf. the last section.)

It is a serious shortcoming of the current treatment of aggregate demand curves that their study has not been extended to the most important case where additivity is absent. Even if everything were completely known for additive aggregate demand curves and found to be in order, that knowledge would only apply to a small part of aggregate demand; in the majority of empirical cases nonadditivity seems to prevail.[25]

23. Whether it happens is obviously an empirical question.

24. Cf. 26 for the situation regarding aggregate supply curves, where independence of the individual supply curves is a far more artificial, if not an impossible, assumption than for demand curves. In supply theory, however, the problem – still unsolved – was noted.

On the other hand Wicksteed, Wicksell, and others have asserted that the supply curve is only an inverted demand curve, and vice versa, thus indicating an interesting connection.

25. Nonadditivity in this simple sense is given, for example, in the case of fashions, where one person buys because another is buying the same thing, or vice versa. The collective demand curve of snobs is most likely not additive. But the phenomenon of nonadditivity is in fact much deeper. Since virtually all collective supply curves are nonadditive, it follows that the demand of the firms for their labor, raw materials, etc. is also nonadditive. This expands the field of nonadditivity enormously.

However, the question arises whether the summation – even when legitimate – does not obliterate vital information. In other words, in order to judge the significance of an aggregate demand curve[26] it is necessary to know the constituent parts in detail (i.e., the individual demand curves), since exactly the same collective demand curve can be obtained in an infinite number of ways from very different individual demand curves. The fact that it is generally deemed unnecessary to go behind the aggregate curve reflects the assumption that it is irrelevant to know the particular way in which an aggregate demand curve arises (additively or not) from its constituent individual demand curves. To state it differently, the information given by the aggregate demand curve is apparently believed to be invariant with respect to these different constituents.

This view is certainly incorrect, as will be shown. Its replacement will necessarily lead to more complicated notions, even if one wishes to remain within the scope of demand analysis. The belief that the particular way in which aggregates arise is unimportant underlies much of contemporary economic theory (e.g., Keynesian theory, in another field). It involves an idea of simplification which falsifies the very inner structure of economic problems and phenomena. The theory of games, having shown the nature of this situation in a certain basic field, offers a method of overcoming the difficulty. Likewise, it will be seen that it is incorrect to believe, with Marshall, whose opinion probably is generally accepted, that it suffices to know demand curves only in a small neighborhood of a point. A truly general theory cannot be built on such restrictions.

8. We proceed by four stages, dealing at first with a *closed market,* i.e., a market in which the number of buyers and their systems of preferences are supposed to be given for the period under consideration. These are the ordinary assumptions that a static theory must make. The necessary variations to be introduced – in this case price variations – must be of the minor kind compatible with, but necessary for, the essentially static character of the concepts employed.

First, we assume a monopsonistic buyer. Then individual and aggregated curves coincide and nothing more need be said.

Second, we assume that the aggregate demand curve involves a large number of buyers, each of whom desires only one unit, all (or most) having different maximum bids for it, but each willing to buy his one unit at any price below his maximum. Each lower maximum bid is added to all the previous higher individual bids. These, of course, reappear in each successive total,[27] i.e., on each point higher up the y-axis (quantity-axis) and *a fortiori* further to the left on the curve. This aggregate curve will ultimately exhaust all individual demands and cut the y-axis. But this point may be far out on the y-axis, depending on the number of buyers.[28]

26. In the following we speak, of course, only of one arrived at additively.

27. This is due to the assumption that each buyer will buy his one unit also at any price lower than his maximum bid.

28. Instead of showing, on the y-axis, the number of units sold, we can equivalently show, in this case, the number of buyers.

If a price p_i should be charged on the market,[29] the associated quantity q_i will be demanded. All buyers whose maximum bid is $> p_i$ and the marginal buyer(s) for whom it is $= p_i$ will buy one unit each – assuming that sufficient quantity is offered for sale. These buyers are eliminated from the market for further transactions in the short run, i.e., until their individual demand curves have been reconstituted in the sense defined above. That will depend on (*a*) and (*b*) in 6; neglecting (*b*) there, it will be a function of the joint timing of their incomes and their future wants.

There remains, therefore, in the short run in this market only a part of the original demand curve, namely the part that includes the maximum bids lower than p_i and in which the quantities of the original curve must now be reduced by those bought in the transaction. This subtraction is necessary, because all buyers who just have bought must be eliminated with their one unit of demand which reappeared in the original curve at each lower potential price. The part of the demand curve above q_i will thus shift downwards until it touches the x-axis. Otherwise there will be no change, the slope from q_i on being preserved in the new position. A new price $p_{i+1} < p_i$ will now encounter not q_{i+1} but only the very much smaller $q'_{i+1} = q_{i+1} - q_i$ and so forth. Such small quantities were originally demanded with very much higher maximum bids on the original demand curve that now is void. Successive trading at successively lower prices in short-time intervals can, therefore, not be oriented on the first, initial demand curve, but only on successive residual demand curves, again to be called "*derived reaction functions*."

We may generalize the case of one individual, one good to the case of n individuals and one good, by introduction of vector notation. Let $q(\vec{p})$ be the column vector such that $q_i = q_i(p)$ $(i = 1, \ldots, n)$, i.e., the initial demand of the ith individual for the good at price p. Then $q(\vec{p}') \cdot p' - q(\vec{p})p = \vec{\Delta}$ where $\Delta_i = q_i(p')p' - q_i(p)p$ $(i = 1, \ldots, n)$. But

$$q_i(p,p') = \left\{\frac{\Delta_i}{p'}\right\}^+ \qquad (i = 1, \ldots, n)$$

$$\therefore q(\vec{p},p') = \left\{\frac{\vec{1}}{p'}\vec{\Delta}\right\}^+ = \left\{q(\vec{p}') - q(\vec{p}) \cdot \frac{p}{p'}\right\}^+$$

Thus for each consumer from $i = 1, \ldots, n$, we have

$$q_i(p,p') = \left\{q_i(p') - q_i(p)\frac{p}{p'}\right\}$$

if the bracketed expression is positive, otherwise $q_i(p,p') = 0$.

29. In order not to complicate matters more than necessary, we do not inquire how this price comes about. The reader may think of any offer of sale, e.g., in an auction. But cf. the remarks in 13.

If a price rise should occur shortly after p_i has been charged, no sales are to be expected by the seller, who thus cannot take the initial demand curve as a guide in this circumstance. It is, however, possible that buyers who had purchased earlier might feel induced to offer their units for *resale*. This is frequently observed and was treated by Bertrand, Wicksell and others. This possibility – however real or unreal it may be – must not be excluded from a general theory. But it is clear that the original aggregate demand curve cannot possibly offer information about these successive operations without further transformations. These cannot be carried out unless its exact composition is fully known.

If the seller in this market should be a monopolist having no costs and trying to discriminate against the buyers by selling in the short run a strictly homogeneous product successively at lower prices, he would be mistaken if he calculated the successive returns on the basis of the original demand curve.[30] This means that the maximum profit, if it could be realized, would require that at each lower price he could sell exactly the amount which the demand curve indicates, i.e., $p_i q_i$. The sum of these amounts is obviously greater than the area enclosed by the demand curve and the x- and y-axes. However, the monopolist cannot realize this amount since each successively lower price removes from the market those quantities already bought by the stronger buyers until the identical reconstitution of their demand has taken place (which will most likely be randomly distributed throughout time, in which case further complications arise).[31] So the fully discriminating monopolist can do no better than to set successively lower prices such that he sweeps out, in his attempt to maximize his revenue, the area under the demand curve. But this means that the curve is used only for successive additional purchases, not for the sum of the *total* purchases which the demand curve indicates when the conventional interpretation is applied to it.

Price discrimination under monopoly – simultaneous or successive – is known to occur, but the tools of present analysis are not suited for an exhaustive treatment. Instead, it is necessary to establish a theory that will show the phenomenon of discrimination in its basic, elementary forms and comprise it in a truly general manner. Again, we find that the aggregate demand curve – in this case even when its composition is exactly known! – does not necessarily give exhaustive information.

Should the aggregate demand curve not be of this simplest type but of the one to be discussed next (cf. 9), the treatment of the policy of discrimination would have to be modified.[32] The introduction of costs of production does not alter the situation fundamentally; but it certainly does not simplify it.

30. Cf., however, K. E. Boulding: Economic Analysis, New York, 1941, pp. 548–549, where an almost identical case – involving only one buyer – is discussed in the affirmative.

31. This is different from the familiar "splitting" of the given aggregate demand curve. About the merits of that procedure, when as a rule nothing is known or postulated about the composition of the function, cf. 24 below.

32. All this is in the manner of the traditional monopoly theory only. This is, therefore, immanent criticism.

Finally, the collective demand curve may have any monotonic negative slope (cf. (*a*) in 17). This depends entirely upon the numbers of buyers and how much their maximum bids differ from each other. Furthermore, it is clear that for an understanding of the response of demand to successive variations in price, the traditional use of the notion of elasticity of demand is inappropriate for a closed market – unless the variations are separated so much in time that a reconstitution of demand has taken place and that the period is specified within which this happens.

More complex cases and the theory of games

9. *Third,* we assume that the aggregate demand curve is composed only of such demand curves as show repeat bids, i.e., that buyers are willing to buy alternatively various amounts at different prices. One may broadly distinguish two cases: (*a*) there may be a small number of buyers, but each one may reappear along the aggregate demand curve with demand for greatly increasing quantities. In this case the interrelation of the points of this aggregate demand curve is very strong, with consequences presently to be shown; (*b*) there may be a large number of buyers, each intending to buy only a few units at various alternative prices. (This is merely a weakening of the second case in 8.) In both these cases (*a*) and (*b*), the collective demand curve may have exactly the same "elasticity" in the ordinary sense, since this elasticity can be made to depend merely on the number of individual demand curves added together.

Neglecting more complex compositions, downward variations in market price in sufficiently rapid succession will have this result: the transactions at the price p_i will remove from the aggregate demand curve (made up of a total of n potential buyers) for all further transactions (before reconstitution) at prices below p_i certain quantities which now will no longer be demanded by the $m < n$ buyers who have already bought at p_i. The sum of these removed quantities will be $\geqslant q_i$. It would be equal to q_i only if the m individual reaction functions were all zero. There will remain for these m buyers an amount of money

$$\sum_m \Delta \geqslant 0$$

If positive, it will be distributed over additional quantities derived from the original individual demand schedules. The individual demand curves of those buyers who could not buy at p_i remain unaffected, *provided* these excluded buyers had in no way through separate dealings, negotiations, payments of

The theory is artificial, since it does not allow or consider the formation of defensive coalitions among the buyers or coalitions of the monopolist with part of the buyers, which would transform the problem into a vastly more complicated but also more realistic one. This is done by the theory of games, which is free from such unnatural restrictions.

fees, etc., been involved in the transactions. Current theory excludes this, but the possibility exists that such arrangements might have been made, and the theory should be able to deal with that case (cf. 28 below).

From these two groups of curves the next, successive aggregate demand curve is built up. It will be below and probably less elastic than the original curve and will touch the x-axis; for the rest arguments analogous to those of Section I apply. At any rate, for the next transaction the original aggregate demand curve is no longer valid. Should further reductions in price occur in the short run, the same operation has to be repeated for each case.[33] While the notion of elasticity is, of course, perfectly well suited to describing the *slope* of a given demand curve, it is unsuited for the purpose for which it was apparently[34] designed, namely for describing the *reaction* of demand to short-run variations in price.

There is a fundamental difference between the individual derived reaction functions and those derived from aggregate demand functions: in the first case the number – one – of individuals involved is the same for both functions; in the second case, there is, most likely, a different number of potential buyers to be found in the derived function than in the demand function from which it is derived (which need itself not have been the originally-given demand function). *The change in numbers amounts to changing the entire structure of the market,* because – to speak now in terms of the theory of games – an n-person game has been transformed into an m-person game ($m \neq n$) and the theory shows that this entails very important consequences. They can never be described by demand curves.[35] Current price theory does not deal with transitions of this type. This should be kept in mind for the following.

10. *Fourth,* the aggregate demand curve may be a composite of the two types treated in the preceding paragraph and may contain also completely inelastic single-unit demand with different maximum bids, such as was treated in the second category (cf. 8). Now it is obvious that the aggregate demand curve is insufficiently known for practical as well as for theoretical purposes, unless the precise distribution of these various kinds of individual demand schedules of which it is composed is determined. The practical reasons are obvious, as could be seen from the example of monopolistic discrimination given above. The theoretical ones are also clear; they are particularly stringent if it is recalled that

33. We again leave out of account what happens to the supply side during these successive transactions (cf. 26). There similar considerations are indicated, complicating the picture enormously, even within this traditional framework of concepts.

34. It is quite impossible to discover in the literature what the exact assumptions were; but the history of doctrines is not our concern here.

35. We do not wish to imply that the problem of price formation and variation should be put in terms of demand curves. We only state that if it is done, the above described situations arise. Collective demand curves may perhaps be useful when very large numbers are involved because of asymptotic behavior; but this is not known at present. It would certainly have to be established properly.

short-run fluctuations of price, demand, and supply are in the very heart of what theory endeavors to explain. One may, for example, think of the "normal price" of the classics around which the market price fluctuates, or of similar ideas in Marshall and others even more contemporary.[36]

The statements of theory which involve effects of price changes are at least incomplete so long as this inner structure of demand has not been laid bare, or so long as at least an assumption about it is not made explicitly. This seems never to have been done; there is certainly no systematic incorporation of demand structure into the body of accepted theory.

There often exist, however, good grounds for assuming that the demand for a given commodity will over longer periods of time be structurally stable. The reasons are essentially statistical: certain commodities will be purchased by fairly homogeneous income groups; tastes do not, and because of complementarity often cannot, change very often; the income distribution itself is rather stable, etc. These are exceedingly important properties of the various economic systems, still little explored and understood; but even if better known they would not dispense with the necessity of going behind the aggregate demand curve, when dealing with successive adjustments in markets.

Successive adaptation and time intervals

11. We turn now to some further aspects of the process of successive adaptation. Assume that in a static closed market (i.e., one where no new buyers can enter, but existing buyers may refrain from bidding at prices that do not suit them) a "*prix crié*" will be given and transactions occur. If this does not happen to be the equilibrium price (so that we have either excess demand or excess supply) then, say, a downward revision of the price is required. In current theory the consequences of the new price are read from the demand curve which existed in the market at the beginning. It is clear by now, however, that such a procedure is inadmissible. In the second moment of time the market is quite differently constituted,[37] the difference being the larger the lower the (non-equilibrium) price was. Without knowledge of that difference between the original demand curve and the derived reaction curve, the question which price would thereafter establish equilibrium is then no nearer solution. We make the assumption only with great reserve that it could at all be possible to obtain a clearly defined and exhaustively described equilibrium of definite stability properties by the juxtaposition of demand and supply. We make it here, as mentioned before, in order to carry out an essentially immanent discussion.[38]

36. Concerning monopolistic competition, cf. 21–24.

37. Also regarding the supply side, cf. 26; as to barter and the recontracting hypothesis, cf. 13.

38. I.e., one that accepts the premises of the given theory and does not question their validity.

12. Next, we shall delimit more precisely the *time-interval* to which successive trading refers. Consider first again the individual: his alternative maximum bids are the products of a plan which is established (*a*) by his (anticipated) wants – which may be short- or long-run periodic or not periodic at all – and (*b*) by his (past and/or expected) income, which in the majority of cases is periodic. The two periods may differ widely for the same individual, making attempted maximization a very difficult proposition; but we shall not dwell upon this complication.[39] There are sometimes large differences in these periods among different individuals; they are to a high degree dependent upon the level of incomes and consequently on the number and kind of durable goods the individuals acquire, possess, and replace. It is simplest to take the income periods of the individuals as of equal length.[40] Then our previous considerations apply to closed markets with price variations occurring during this standardized time interval.

In the next period the demand curves may again be *reconstituted* – as we have called the process of newly forming demand on the basis of new wants, new income and a possible reshuffling of income distribution. A reconstitution can evidently not take place if successive buying occurs and the market reconvenes or is perpetuated during this same income period, unless money is withdrawn from other purposes,[41] a case that is neglected, however, when one-variable demand functions are considered. Of course, if the first transaction takes place at the end of the first period, a reconstitution of the aggregate demand curve (whether identically or not) may happen immediately, with the beginning of the new period. But this is exceptional and the theory cannot be built on this simplifying assumption.

If a price variation occurs within a unit period and a divisible commodity (milk, gasoline, etc.) is bought continuously in small installments, the individual reaction function can allow for this possibility. The individual demand curve is then composed of as many partial demand curves as there are subdivisions of the unit period, and each one has its own partial reaction function. This requires no change in our main argumentation for individual demand curves, and we need not enter upon further details. The application to aggregate demand curves is easy to see; it follows the same lines. (Cf. also the reference to demand curves as averages in footnote 22.)

If consecutive selling at varying prices extends over more than one period, a new situation arises.

In the current treatment of variations of prices and their significance for demand no such explicit distinctions are made; it is simply tacitly assumed that

39. This is discussed at length in Oskar Morgenstern: Das Zietmoment in der Wertlehre, Zeitsch, f. Nationalökonomie, vol. V (1934), pp. 433–458.

40. For an indication of the consequences if they are not, see Morgenstern, op. cit.

41. Even if there should be a reconstitution of demand curves in this manner, a disturbance of other demand curves is caused.

the demand curve stays where it was,[42] or rather – as we prefer to state more explicitly – that it somehow identically reconstitutes itself automatically after each event. This is clearly a very far-reaching and quite deceptive assumption, especially if only made implicitly. Theories must, instead, be established on the weakest possible assumptions.

As noted at the beginning of 8, a static theory, studying equilibria, must introduce variations of seemingly dynamic character. This is necessary in order to discover whether the equilibrium is conducive to dynamic developments. "An analysis of this feature is, of course, inconceivable without the use of certain rudimentary dynamic concepts. The important point is that they are rudimentary."[43]

Price variations within the same period of a closed economy are of this nature. Those occurring over a greater number of periods and involving, as seen below (cf. 15), indefinite numbers of buyers are of a more dynamic character.

There can be no doubt that successive prices may be "called" within short intervals, i.e., within the same individual income period. Indeed, such descriptions abound in economic theory. One has only to be reminded of discriminating monopoly or of the treatment of variable prices in the theory of duopoly, etc. (We shall turn to the latter in 22–23.)

Recontracting

13. In order to overcome some obvious difficulties caused by successive trading, the notion of "*recontracting*" was introduced. The difficulties were connected with a desire to find an equilibrium price, rather than with the far more elemental (in the sense of preliminary) difficulty shown in respect to the transformation suffered by the original demand curve in the course of successive prices. So recontracting means that if the first price "called" did not happen by chance to be the equilibrium price, the whole transaction was considered to be void and a new one was proposed until finally the desired stable equilibrium established itself. Then the only effective final transaction took place.

With recontracting and voiding of intermediary transactions, the time periods considered are also of no significance. The aim is to find a unique actual price which dispenses with the need (or whatever other reason) for a succession of actual prices. Indeed, the very problem itself has been blotted out: the repeated identical reconstitution of demand into its initial form is postulated. As

42. This is quite clearly the case in the literature on monopolistic competition.

43. John von Neumann and Oskar Morgenstern, op. cit., pp. 45 and 290, where a fuller discussion of the relation between static and dynamic social theory will be found. The surmise in 4.8.3 there, that in economics a dynamic theory may turn out to produce simpler concepts and be quite different from dynamics in mathematical physics, is worth mentioning specifically.

soon as this artificial assumption is dropped, as it must be sooner or later, and actual transactions succeed each other, the situation that we described arises with all its complications. Therefore, even if with the aid of "recontracting" the existence of some particular equilibrium has been proved,[44] we cannot conclude that the problem of successive adaptation has been discussed exhaustively and that the method used is sufficiently general. The idea of recontracting is an interesting and plausible "mental experiment," but it does not correspond to any known markets, or if any do exist, they are certainly insignificant.

Recontracting may still be considered in economic theory, but in an entirely different context, namely, that of the formation of "coalitions," i.e., groups of buyers or sellers acting in unison and settling among themselves the distribution of the advantage gained from combining.[45] We shall not enter upon a discussion of these matters here.

Variations in quantities and prices have been examined when the "*path*" was discussed that successive operations might take, in order to discover its influence upon the final outcome of the exchange. These attempts comprise barter trade involving two participants, i.e., a special case of bilateral monopoly. The contract curve is one way of showing the transactions; it is a formalization of a common-sense approach. However, it has been shown that, though the various formalizations assume that a maximum problem is involved, no ordinary maximum problem is present; instead, one is confronted with a general two-person game involving a so-called minimax problem. The theory of the two-person game is completely known; it takes care of all possible variants of "successive" operations, of all shades of strategies, stages of information, and the like. Thus, it is hardly practicable to extend those older methods to the study of price (not only barter) variations for more complex set-ups. In fact, even that has not been done. We can, therefore, not hope to obtain help from this earlier work in the attempt to understand the influence of short-run price variations upon the structure of demand.

14. A point concerning *consumers' rent* in the case of collective demand curves, supplementing the observations in 3, may be noted here. Since consumers' rent need not always – and in general will not – find a purely monetary expression, but rather be a notion of two components, one money the other utility, and since in an aggregate demand curve as a rule at least two individuals are involved, no statements about consumers' rent are possible at the present level.[46] This is due to our inability to compare utilities of different in-

44. Accepting for the sake of argument the generally prevailing notions of equilibrium in economics to be correct. Cf. 28.

45. Cf. Theory of Games and Economic Behavior, pp. 557, 558.

46. Excepting the cases (*a*) when the aggregate demand curve consists exclusively of totally inelastic individual demand curves, or (*b*) when all demand curves are intramarginal and the price for everyone concerned is at or below the price where the intramarginal character becomes apparent. Then the sum of money saved by the intramarginal buyers can be added up to give a monetary expression. An interpersonal utility comparison, however, is still impossible in the present state of our knowledge.

dividuals. Frequently found wider interpretations of consumers' rent seem inappropriate.

These statements are independent of whether a variation in price actually occurred on the market or not. They derive solely from the basic property of the individual demand curve that it is composed of mutually exclusive alternative maximum bids.

Successive adaptation in open markets

15. We shall now drop the restriction to *closed markets.* This does not affect the statements about the individual demand curve. An *open market* shall be one where the number of buyers does not remain constant during the period considered. We do not examine the separate case of possible variations of wants (preferences) and/or incomes of the buyers initially present. Such variations in the total quantity demanded *cannot be transformed equivalently* into a change in numbers of buyers, or vice versa.[47]

If in successive moments of time new buyers can enter the market, the chances that, in spite of successive price formation the original collective demand curve will be reconstituted, have improved. But recalling 7 it is clear on the one hand that the mere coincidence in numbers between those buyers going out (because they have bought at the various preceding prices) and those coming in is not at all sufficient to produce an "identical reconstitution" of the collective demand curve. On the other hand, if the identical shape and position of the collective demand curve should actually be reestablished, this would still not guarantee that it is fully comparable with the old one. The identity of the shape and position is a necessary but not a sufficient condition.

Very good and convincing reasons must be given if a full congruity between departing and arriving buyers – or, more particularly, between their demand schedules – is to be assumed. According to current views a movement in the number and composition of those buyers who have *not* bought and cannot buy at a given price, excepting those whose maximum bid is immediately below the market price, is irrelevant. These potential but excluded buyers are thought to have no influence on the equilibrium price. Although we are not concerned with the formation of the latter at the moment it is important to point out that this places another, extremely serious, restriction upon price theory: it excludes the possibility that buyers may freely enter into agreements with each other or with the sellers and that therefore very different prices may result and different quantities be traded compared with the single equilibrium price now envisaged. Thus, all not-buying buyers have a decisive influence upon the price and upon

47. This is important in the theory of games, which shows – as already mentioned – that with each change in the number of persons on a market a change of its structure occurs, while the same is not true when a given number of persons vary their individual demand schedules.

the effects of price change.[48] Therefore, movements in numbers and composition of the collective demand curve, even on the part of the thus far or in the future excluded buyers, cannot be neglected. If the above-mentioned atomistic restriction, forbidding coalitions among the participants in the market, is to be enforced, this should be explicitly stated. The resulting theory can then not claim general validity.

We conclude, then, that to demand congruence of parting and arriving buyers for identical reconstitution of the collective demand curve would be making enormous claims on the economic mechanism. One would need far better observations and a much deeper understanding of the interplay of economic forces to make such a convenient and peculiar postulate plausible. It is clear that the best one could hope for are those essentially statistical structural elements mentioned in 10 in a similar context.

There may, finally, be complications regarding the speed with which old buyers leave and new ones enter a market with successive price variations, even if their total number is the same at each beginning period. We mention this only as a further difficulty. At any rate, one is confronted here with a picture vastly more complicated than that so far studied in ecnomics. It is quite in keeping with scientific procedure to leave realistic detail aside until the simplest case is well understood. But simplification can go too far.

16. So far we have discussed what are normally called in economic theory "movements *along* the demand curve." From these are distinguished movements *of* the entire demand curve. The impression may have been created that all along we were actually discussing movements of the second type. This is not so; we were only led to show that what is now considered a movement "along" the demand curve in fact gives rise to new derived demand curves (here called "reaction curves"), and that the classical movement "along" the original demand curve cannot even be carried out unless an identical reconstitution is postulated. The notion of reconstitution is, however, not a part of the ordinary demand theory. Within the latter it has always been important to keep the shifts along the curve and of the curve strictly apart; when this was not done trouble was bound to arise. Yet we now know that this separation is not sufficient, and that still finer distinctions are required.

Shifts of the curve as such are considered to be due to changes in income, in wants, and – in the case of the collective demand curve – in the number of buyers. These shifts of the entire curve are dynamic changes of considerable magnitude. They relate, therefore, to phenomena which must remain outside the domain of this paper, which admits only those minor variations that are compatible with static theory. However, it should be stated that an aggregate demand curve that has shifted will at the same time, in all likelihood, also have changed

48. This is another of the fundamental applications of principles developed in the Theory of Games and Economic Behavior.

its structure considerably. The old and the new demand curves are probably different in more respects than that of change in location. This could obtain, as we now know, even if the shape of the curve has remained unaltered.

If the aggregate demand curve should repeat itself in two points of time in every respect except that the *number* of prospective buyers has changed, an economically vital change would have occurred – but not in the view of current price theory. For this theory nothing has happened! In fact, however, a variation has occurred far more important than a movement of the entire curve resulting from an increase of income accruing to the constant number of buyers. The latter movement present theory would consider "dynamic," while the former would not even register (perhaps excepting the case when the number of buyers is very small, but even of that there is no sure indication). The names given to the changes do not matter, provided that the changes are seen in their proper perspective. The change in numbers is what really is important, because it produces a game of strategy involving a different number of players, with all the attending consequences to which we referred above.

Further properties, nonadditivity

17. We conclude this section with three further observations.

(*a*) We saw in 6 that the negative slope of the individual demand curve requires, or leads to, a hypothesis of decreasing marginal utility or one of its equivalents.[49] No need for such hypothesis arises in the case of the collective demand curve (if and when it is additive).

As the individual function it is as a rule also (but most likely strictly) monotonically decreasing. In order to explain this behavior it is sufficient to assume differences in tastes and/or incomes. The latter alone suffices. To show that inequality of incomes exists is hardly a difficult task, no matter what the sociopolitical organization. It may, however, be more difficult in some instances to demonstrate differences in tastes.

It is appropriate to set forth, in general terms, what the relation of individual and collective or aggregate demand functions is, when the latter arise additively from the former. If all individual functions are monotonically nonincreasing, the aggregate (finite) summation function is too. If among them there is at least one

49. Sometimes these are considered not to be equivalents, as, for example, the increasing marginal rate of substitution, but we think that this is only a terminological affair.

In this paper we have refrained from discussing these and related questions, notably that of the need for the involved indifference curve analysis. We believe that a satisfactory case can be made for numerical ("measurable") utilities. Therefore, we do not follow up the ramifications of our statements about demand for the indifference curves either. Cf. J. von Neumann and O. Morgenstern, op. cit. There an axiomatic formulation of numerical utilities will be found, and in the appendix to the second edition (1947) also the proof that the axioms imply the desired numerical character of utility.

strictly monotonically decreasing, the aggregate function is strictly monotonically decreasing and so it is, *a fortiori,* if all individual functions are strictly monotonic. If among the individual nonincreasing functions one is discontinuous and all others are continuous, the aggregate function is discontinuous. If among the continuous individual functions – where the majority are nonincreasing – there are several discontinuous ones and some of them are rising (e.g., due to the presence of snobs!), the aggregate function may by a remote chance be continuous because of compensation.

As a rule, the additive aggregate demand function will be strictly monotonically falling and discontinuous. It can, of course, also be rising, e.g., when the market consists only of snobs.

(*b*) In Section I individual demand functions of one variable were assumed, but it is easy to see that this constituted no serious limitation. For a given aggregate demand curve it is not necessary to specify whether the individual demand functions are of one variable or not; but it is not unimportant, especially when dealing simultaneously with several commodities between which there may be complementarity, substitution, etc. But we do not deal with these matters here.

(*c*) Finally, we refer once more to the remark in 7 concerning additivity of aggregate demand. The inability of current theory to deal with nonadditivity satisfactorily – still worse, the neglect of this empirically important case – constitutes a most serious limitation of demand theory. It has far-reaching ramifications.

The question of additivity of value – in its broadest forms – necessarily appears also in the theory of games. There additivity is found only in the uninteresting case of "inessential" games, while the really significant "essential"[50] games have a nonadditive characteristic function. Since games of strategy correspond exactly to economic setups, this has implications for the theory of prices.

III. Applications

Elasticity of demand

18. It is clear from previous remarks about elasticity (7–9) that this famous notion of economic theory requires a far more cautious interpretation and use than is customary. It is supposed to be a measure of the reactions of demand to changes in price. Hence it should cover everything that was said in the preceding sections about these reactions. This is obviously not the case, since the present

50. These are games of strategy where a coalition of players acting in unison can obtain more than the same players acting separately.

concept of elasticity requires an unaltered demand curve, and since the expositions[51] say nothing about the time intervals to be considered, although one should have been quite specific about them. In fact, the notion loses all meaning unless the statements about elasticity refer to exactly the same unchanged demand function. The point is that the variation it is supposed to characterize destroys the very foundations upon which it rests.

The normal restriction of the notion of elasticity to small ("infinitesimal"[52]) sections of the demand curve, i.e., to "point elasticity," does not change the situation, because of the interdependence of successive points of the demand curve (which therefore must be considered in its entirety) and because price variations are often great and discontinuous. *A fortiori* the notions of "arc elasticity," covering a larger segment of the same function, and that of "cross elasticity," covering several functions, suffer from the same difficulties.

On the other hand, the information represented, however imperfectly, by the entire (additive) demand curve is absolutely necessary for the determination even of a *single* (static) price. One cannot be satisfied with that point of a demand curve representing the price-quantity relationship that emerges in the market plus the directly adjoining demand showing the immediately following excluded buyers.[53] Thus only two points seem to be needed. But this is, as pointed out above, an entirely unwarranted restriction, because *all* excluded buyers, and not only those directly following, can influence the price, depending on the kind and number of arrangements that may be made among them, on the one hand, and the buyers who will actually be able to buy on the market (by virtue of their maximum bids being greater than those of the excluded buyers), on the other hand.[54] (Cf. 15.)

We shall not dwell upon the implications of this, because they go far beyond the limited character of most of our other observations; but it may be mentioned that the intersection of the demand curve with the supply curve (which would

51. This is true of the originator of the concept (Cournot), of Marshall and of current expositions, e.g., in Allen op. cit. In the last instance it is particularly noteworthy that the hypothetical character of demand curves is stressed, yet elasticity is treated as a concept actually describing successive changes, apparently in the short run (pp. 254–257). The same is true of other textbooks. For a full discussion of the literature cf. A. W. Marget, loc. cit.

52. The "infinitely small" is *not,* as is often believed, a rigorous mathematical notion. It should therefore not be used in economics to "clarify" something.

53. The immediately following point does not even show this clearly, because it shows in reality also the alternative demand of those who are now buying at the higher price that materializes! These bids must first be subtracted in order to obtain the true value of the following point.

54. Interesting observations about the role of the excluded buyers and the necessity for redrawing demand curves in the case of successive variations of price were – apparently for the first time – made by J. Bertrand (Comptes Rendues et Analyses, in Bulletin des Sciences Mathématiques, 1883) discussing Cournot and Walras. As is well known, the remarks of the French mathematician were not appreciated by Edgeworth and others. The fact is that none of them – including Bertrand – was in possession of a method powerful enough to deal with the situation.

have to be similarly treated!) need then describe neither the price nor the quantity of the stable, static transaction.[55] These can perhaps be discovered by means of the techniques recently developed in the Theory of Games and Economic Behavior and already applied to some simple cases; they are designed to take care precisely of these complications, but it would lead too far to attempt a description here.

19. An exact quantitative measure of the nature and extent of the response of demand to price changes is, of course, greatly needed. It can be seen that it would have to express the differences in reaction due to different composition of individual demand curves, although the aggregate demand curve[56] may appear to be the same. In other words, this new measure of elasticity of demand would have to be a quantitative expression of the short-run operation of the factors discussed in the preceding two sections on a more qualitative basis. It need not run in terms of demand curves. The present measure of elasticity would in all these latter cases give the same "elasticity," while the new one would have to show the differences due to the differences in composition, i.e., it would express the proper knowledge of the function. Moreover, for the present concept it does not matter whether one deals with additive or nonadditive aggregate curves, individual or aggregate demand curves, etc. Yet all these differences are essential.

That the neglect of this distinction leads to absurd statements is easily seen from the examples of curves entirely of "unit elasticity" in both cases (cf. 5 and 8). A price variation in the first instance (individual demand curve in the short run) shows the disappearance of the entire curve (this is true "zero elasticity" instead of "unit elasticity"), while for a collective demand curve it shows that as a rule some purchasers remain after deduction of the demand of those buyers who made their purchases, so that another, much reduced, collective demand curve, not necessarily again of "unit elasticity," forms. It is clearly inadmissible to characterize these two widely different kinds of behavior by one and the same measure of "elasticity."[57] It is thus not a very useful measurement at all.

Demand curves entirely of unit elasticity are special but simple forms of individual or collective demand curves. If the accepted measure is unsatisfactory for the simple forms, it is still less suited to describe more complicated cases. These, however, are the rule, since rectangular hyperbolas are highly special functions.

55. The reader will observe that wherever understandings between buyers – whether included in, or excluded from, the final transactions – are possible and actually in progress, the (assumed) additivity of demand curves is lost. It is difficult to see how *ab initio* understandings could have been ruled out by a theory striving for generality.

56. The current notion of elasticity is used for additive collective demand; what would be its fate if it were applied to nonadditive demand curves? And to nonadditive supply curves?

57. It will be observed that the difference obtains for virtually every composition of the aggregate curve. But each different composition gives a different derived reaction curve, each with a different elasticity measure.

20. The efforts which have been made to determine demand curves and their elasticities statistically are well known. This is an important branch of economics; its growth encounters great obstacles arising not least from the time intervals over which data are usually scattered. On the other hand, yearly intervals are conveniently large enough to dispense with the kind of short-run fluctuations that cause some of the difficulties discussed in this paper.

A statistical aggregate demand curve, derived from short-run observations with frequent price changes, is thus not necessarily a representation of "the" (original) demand curve, but more often only one of *successive reaction points* to which a curve may be fitted. How much this historical curve differs from the initial demand curves is impossible to say, unless a study of other factors in the market that have influenced demand has been made, especially the price variations during the year. The initial aggregate demand curve could be statistically determined only by questioning of the prospective buyers *before* any transaction has taken place, and, in the case of an open market, also by appropriate information from the leaving and entering buyers. All markets where statistical curves were ever determined are naturally open. Combining the reasons stated in 10 and 17, it may be assumed that the original aggregate demand curve and the (historical) reaction curve differ far less for open than for closed markets.

Even the statistical determination of individual demand curves might lead to erroneous interpretations. As an example, we mention this case. Suppose a series of observations of an individual's purchases at varying prices and in short intervals allows the interpolation of these points by a rectangular hyperbola. Then the conclusion that his several demand curves at these points were all of the shape of the interpolated curve, i.e., that $\eta = 1$ throughout each curve, is not necessarily true. While it may be true, it is equally possible that these curves were all different from each other, perhaps none ever having $\eta = 1$ for its entire length. Thus, the investigation of the true original demand curves is not exhausted by the study of these statistical data, unless their distribution over the individual's income periods is known. The observed curve consists of successive transaction points, but the (active) demand curve of alternative intentions.

The elasticities derived from empirical aggregate demand curves are, of course, not immediately suited for use in estimating the reaction of demand when the consequences of price variations in shorter intervals than years are to be estimated. We shall not discuss this point any further.

It may be added, however, that in view of the lack of clarity regarding the periods to which demand curves were supposed to apply,[58] this interpretation suggests itself: only broad open markets are meant where shifting masses of people buy repeatedly and continuous pricing goes on. This is, perhaps, what

58. Cf. the reference in footnote 13 to A. W. Marget, and 25 below concerning the cobweb theorem.

Marshall had in mind and what some of our textbooks deal with, though one cannot be sure. In such a market the traditional notion of elasticity of demand has some application because of the probability that the demand curve may reconstitute itself all the time, at least as to slope and position. But this is a field of large, not rudimentary dynamic changes which have also many other characteristics. The current theory of demand, and more specifically of elasticity, is, therefore, not applicable *tel quel* where those conditions do not prevail (e.g., static markets, monopolistic competition, etc.). In short, it does not hold for the cases described in the preceding pages. The freedom with which these notions and measures are now used does not generally exist.[59]

Monopolistic discrimination and monopolistic competition

21. In both of these the elasticity of demand and the shape of various demand curves play an important, if not decisive, role. These fields, especially that of monopolistic competition, are very large and the theories are complicated; so we shall have to be satisfied with a few remarks only.

Monopolistic discrimination has already been mentioned in 8. It consists of the monopolist's attempt to split the demand for his product, either by slight variation in the nature of the commodity (different names, packages, etc.) or by selling consecutively at varying prices (i.e., at gradually lowered prices). The study of these practices leads very naturally to the device of "splitting the demand curve," which enjoys such a great, indeed even fundamental, role in the present theories of monopolistic competition.[60] This "splitting" means, of course, that one believes that the aggregate demand curve for the product provides enough information for the setting of different prices (simultaneously or successively).

22. The best prototype is the theory of *duopoly*. Without entering upon the merits of the accepted doctrine, we observe this much. It is unmistakably assumed – though tacitly – that the demand curve for their common product remains unaltered during the manipulations of the duopolists. These operations are obviously thought to go on in fairly rapid succession,[61] and are not merely

59. One can well imagine what results an analysis of such notions as the "elasticity of expectations" would yield!

60. This brief mention of the theories of monopoly and monopolistic competition should not indicate our acceptance of the theories. Indeed, it is essentially the artificial (though tacit and implicit) restriction to atomistic demand that makes the present theory possible. Once this condition is dropped and appears only as a limiting case, the need for entirely different considerations about monopolistic competition will become clear. Thus that theory will have to undergo profound changes. Cf. the following text for some comments, and my paper quoted in footnote 1.

61. Though nothing very specific can be gleaned from the theories in this respect.

events in the mind of the duopolists. In one version of the theory, first a high price is charged, then the other duopolist undersells. So the first undersells the second, etc. Or a similar upward movement takes place. All the while "the" (aggregate) demand curve confronting the two sellers together is supposed to give all the necessary information, describe the volume of the successive transactions for each, and allow the calculation of the effects of these successive operations on the profits of the duopolists.

23. It is easy to reduce this procedure *ad absurdum* by way of immanent reasoning for the limiting case where the aggregate demand curve is both that of a single buyer and has the shape of a rectangular hyperbola. After the first sale, no matter what the price or the quantity, no further transaction can take place in the same period. The reader can extend this to the case where the aggregate demand curve is also of unit elasticity but composed of more than one buyer, each buying one unit, several units, etc.

If it should be maintained that this limitation of the aggregate demand curve to one buyer transforms the situation also in other respects in an essential way (by making it also monopsonistic), we will gladly concur. But we maintain in general that it is fundamental to know how many individuals are behind the facade of the aggregate demand curve and what the particular characteristics of their individual demand schedules are. With this setup, one is necessarily led far away from the traditional theory, which believes that it has to do with ordinary maximum problems, into the realm of the theory of games with its entirely different conceptual structure.

24. Returning to 21–22, we repeat that, whatever the number of sellers, the "splitting" of the aggregate demand curve for their products[62] – for example by halving it – from every point of view violates the principles that must be observed when theorizing about demand curves. The objection is, of course, not against the idea that a monopolist or one or more of a group of oligopolists try to split the aggregate demand in the market for their (uniform or slightly different) products. The objection is against theory representing these efforts by means of mere shifts or splittings of aggregate demand curves without having shown that the split in precisely the way chosen is correct and possible, that the theory built upon it is exhaustive, etc. But since the legitimacy of this operation was apparently never questioned, these considerations did not arise either.

It should be expressly mentioned that the splitting of demand curves is inadmissible even if the widest interpretation – i.e., that at the end of 20 – is applied to them. No matter how open and large the market, a correct splitting is impossible unless it is known *how many buyers* are involved and what their

62. In the literature one finds sometime the expression: "the demand curve *of* the firm," when one really should speak about the demand curve *faced by* the firm. The first would obviously be the (individual) demand curve of a firm for its raw material, labor, etc. This kind of negligence, seemingly harmless, but repugnant to the scientific mind, is characteristic of verbal economics; it abounds especially in textbooks.

individual demand schedules are. It is clear that as intricate a problem as this must first of all be solved under very simple and truly static conditions.

We leave this important topic of monopolistic competition here, not because nothing more could be said, but on the contrary because it would require an extensive digression from the narrower subject matter of this paper. The chief reason, however, is, as mentioned in 23 and elsewhere, that the entire approach to the problem requires a revision that goes deep into its conceptual structure.[63]

The cobweb theorem

25. This theorem is a prototype for the discussion of successive adaptation of demand and supply to variations in price or vice versa. We make only a few additional observations.[64]

Depending on the slopes of the supply and demand curves there results, according to the theorem, either (α) a tendency towards stable equilibrium (their point of intersection), i.e., a dampening of fluctuations; (β) a continued oscillation of constant amplitude; or finally, (γ) a growing instability (explosion). All this is deduced from the same aggregate demand and supply curves, but nothing is said about why they should remain unaltered throughout the period of variable prices at which changing quantities are sold, what the limits of these variations are, and within which time intervals they may occur.[65]

Now it is clear that, if our previous arguments are accepted, the cobweb theorem in its present form must be laid aside, if only for reasons prevailing on the demand side. If the theorem is upheld on the ground that it is applied chiefly to agricultural products with discontinuous production and hence discontinuous adaptation, the answer is still that the reasoning, as far as demand is concerned, is faulty. It might very well be that the theorem describes correctly some phenomena of adaptation, but the reasoning through which one arrives at this description may nevertheless be at fault. Then a correction is called for.

For example, the translation of the hog cycle from the time-series evidence into the allegedly equivalent (static) demand-and-supply apparatus may give an appearance of correctness which rests, however, only on the basic observation of two pairs of counter moving cycles: those of hog prices and hog production and of corn prices and corn production.

63. In particular, the idea that in the field of monopolistic competition one is confronted with ordinary maximum problems has to be dropped entirely. A far more complicated situation exists.

64. For a discussion of the literature and some pertinent, sceptical observations, cf. Norman S. Buchanan: A Reconsideration of the Cobweb Theorem, Journal of Political Economy, vol. 47, 1939.

65. Buchanan, op. cit., has great difficulty in determining to what periods the demand curves of the various writers on the cobweb theorem refer; he sees clearly that this endangers the whole argument.

An heuristic, or even an objectionable, procedure of arriving at a correct theory can very well be tolerated if the theory thus discussed is otherwise proved in order. But this has not been done, and our exposition casts doubts on the usual arguments about adaptation of demand (and supply) curves.

The supply curve, nonadditivity.

26. The repetition of the basic distinction between an individual and aggregate or collective supply curve is clearly in order. While there seemed to be no a priori objections against the assumption of the additive character of the aggregate demand curve – though doubts evolved in the course of our exposition regarding the interpretation even of the additive type – it is quite different now. Indeed, one can hardly think of a single case where additivity of supply might be given, except when very short runs are considered, and even this is doubtful. Supply would have to be completely atomistic, i.e., the various individual supply curves would have to be totally independent of each other. But an individual supply curve is generally conceived to be nothing else but a qualified individual cost curve. Firms in the same industry, i.e., producers of the practically homogeneous product whose aggregate supply curve one wishes to construct, compete with each other for raw materials and labor. Thus, their costs become interdependent. This removes the possibility of simple addition. There is, further, the still more important likelihood of cooperation among the suppliers.

Discussion of these matters, stimulated by Sraffa's investigations, has not led to any generally accepted method of constructing aggregate supply curves, and the matter rests where it was left almost twenty years ago. Yet one encounters these curves or "functions"[66] everywhere (even aggregate supply curves of money!), as if they were perfectly clear concepts and could be used for extensive further deductions. The virtual dropping of these topics without any solution at all is a most curious feature in economics. Similar instances could be mentioned from other parts of theory. It is hard to see how a consistent and satisfactory economic theory can ever arise when such gaps remain.

27. We saw in 6 that the individual demand curve is a short-run proposition, except when the use of savings is considered or the goods considered are well below the marginal levels of purchase, i.e., are those which will be bought up to the satiation level (staples, such as some foods). The collective demand curve is short run, unless open markets are considered, when it may be, but need not be, long run. Now a supply curve, whether individual or aggregate, may be either short or long run. It is short run when no adaptation of fixed equipment is intended. The line of demarcation is, of course, uncertain. Consequently, if a

66. Obscure "functions" abound in economics. Often neither the number of variables nor their domains are known or indicated, but vast operations are carried out with the aid of the functions thus "defined."

juxtaposition of demand and supply curves is made for the purpose of studying their mutual reactions in the event of price changes, additional information is required for both, in order to make them homogeneous. We shall say only a few words for the case of supply, where we shall also assume that an aggregate supply curve has been satisfactorily constructed.[67]

The individual supply curve either refers to a short-run cost curve in an existing plant or to a planning curve for hypothetical future plants, in which case it is long run. The same quantities will, therefore, be offered at different supply prices, as soon as nonproportionality of costs exists. This is the regular case, thus the principal one needing discussion.

If a price change occurs and is believed to be of short duration, it may produce no effect on output if the latter is dependent upon individual planning cost curves, while a reaction, as indicated by the short-run supply curve, will take place in the short run. So the juxtaposition of demand and supply curves has to specify the probable nature of the price variation if planning curves are used, while for all short-run phenomena the short-run supply curve can be used – with whatever restrictions have to be laid upon all supply curves – by appropriate application of the conclusions arrived at above concerning demand curves.

Conclusions

28. In the preceding sections an idea was given of some of the extraordinarily narrow limitations within which current price theory operates, without, indeed, being aware of these restrictions. Moreover, they are of a kind which, when once seen, call for abandonment, so that a more generally useful theory can be built. One step, staying within the traditional setup, would undoubtedly have to consist in devising techniques for obtaining demand and supply curves that are not additive and investigating the operations that can be carried out with their aid. This will encounter great difficulties. If the task is accomplished, it will not have done away with even more basic restrictive assumptions: the limitation of the theory to those participants in the market who actually carry out the final transactions, while in fact the possibility of all kinds of agreements, negotiations, etc. among *all* actual and prospective buyers and sellers must be admitted and investigated.

As far as can be seen today, a theory of this wider scope shows that one is confronted with market conditions that are strictly identical with certain games of strategy. Thus the theory of games and concepts developed there may

67. This improbable assumption, of course, seriously restricts everything said about the aggregate supply curve. Its real, now unknown, structure is undoubtedly exceedingly complicated and can only be revealed by thorough mathematical investigations on the basis of extensive empirical studies.

become applicable. Among the salient points is that, instead of simple unique equilibria of the type investigated in current economic theory, one has to allow for far more complicated kinds of equilibria,[68] which constitute the solutions of the various market situations. Furthermore, in games of strategy, quite different situations arise than can be described by some supposed maximum problems of economic theory.

Thus, even when using notions of collective demand and supply improved over the present type, the intersection of such curves – if they exist at all – would tell but little. Neither would the necessary extension of individual demand to functions of several variables improve the situation. Even the variation of prices, which may have been found an undesirable feature of our argumentation, can be dropped and still it is seen that the most rigidly static treatment of conventional demand curves is inadequate. Instead of perfecting those tools and pursuing those ideas, it may be necessary to apply and elaborate new concepts and techniques which have already proven their power in a number of specific cases.

68. Called "standards of behavior," made up by (mutually undominated) imputations, i.e., divisions of the proceeds of transactions among all the participants.

23 A Theory of Demand with Variable Consumer Preferences[1]

R. L. Basmann[2]

Existing theory of consumer demand does not contain a body of theorems purporting to explain the consumption behavior of individuals when their preferences are changed, either autonomously or by advertising and other forms of selling effort. The objective of this paper is to present a theory of consumer demand with variable preferences. The assumption that the individual consumer has a unique ordinal utility index function is replaced by the assumption that he has a family of ordinal utility functions; advertising expenditures by the sellers of commodities are assumed to determine which one of these ordinal utility functions is to be maximized. From these assumptions are derived a number of theoretical relations which measurements defining advertising elasticities of demand must satisfy. The relations involving shifts in demand and advertising elasticities of demand are shown to be analogues of the theorems of consumer demand under fixed preferences. For example, a theorem corresponding to the well-known Leontief-Hicks theorem on aggregate commodities has been worked out, thus showing that, under certain advertising conditions, a group of commodities may be treated as a single good.

1. INTRODUCTION

THE MODERN THEORY of consumer demand as formulated by Edgeworth,[3] Antonelli,[4] and Pareto,[5] and worked out by Slutsky,[6] Hicks and Allen,[7] and Hicks,[8] is based on the assumption that the individual consumer allocates expenditures on commodities as if he had a fixed, ordered set of preferences described by an indifference map or by an ordinal utility function which he maximizes subject to restraints imposed by the money income he receives and the prices he must pay. From the point of view of the econometrician, this theory has served well by indicating criteria to govern the construction of aggregate commodity and consumer price indexes,[9] by providing certain plausible a priori constraints to be imposed on estimates of the parameters of empirical demand

[1] Journal Paper No. J-2772 of the Iowa Agricultural Experiment Station, Ames, Iowa. Project No. 1200.

[2] The author is indebted to Professors Gerhard Tintner, John A. Nordin, and Donald R. Kaldor and to Mr. George Elsasser of Iowa State College and to Professor Leonid Hurwicz of the University of Minnesota for their advice and criticism. Responsibility for any errors found in this article belongs to the author alone.

[3] F. Y. Edgeworth, *Mathematical Psychics*, London: Kegan Paul, 1881.

[4] G. B. Antonelli, *Sulla teoria matematica della economia pura*, Pisa: Folchetto, 1886. Reprinted in *Giornale degli Economisti*, N. S., Vol. 10, 1951, pp. 233–263.

[5] V. Pareto. *Manuel d'Économie Politique*, 2d ed., Paris: Giard, 1927.

[6] E. Slutsky, "Sulla teoria del bilancio del consumatore," *Giornale degli Economisti*, Vol. 51, 1915, pp. 1–26.

[7] J. R. Hicks and R. G. D. Allen, "A Reconsideration of the Theory of Value," *Economica*, N. S., Vol. 1, 1934, pp. 52–73, 196–219.

[8] J. R. Hicks. *Value and Capital*, Oxford: Clarendon Press, 1939.

[9] *Cf.* E. von Hofsten, *Price Indexes and Quality Changes*, London: Allen and Unwin, 1952, *passim.*

Reprinted with revisions from *Econometrica*, Vol. XXIV (January, 1956), pp. 47–58, by permission of the publisher and author.

functions,[10] and by suggesting several hypotheses to be subjected to statistical test. Consumer demand theory, however, not having taken variable preferences explicitly into account until very recently, has not asserted any hypothetical laws governing relations among the shifts in demand functions which a change in preference orderings should cause. It is desirable that such hypothetical laws be derived, and that econometricians bring them under empirical test. The logical consequences of the assumption of fixed preferences differs markedly from experience in the modern economy, for in the latter it is commonly observed that the consumption behavior of real individuals and households is changed more or less systematically by advertising and other forms of selling effort, and by changes in social and technological factors exogenous with respect to the consumer economy. In econometric demand analysis, the introduction of time as an independent trend variable to "explain" the effects of changes in taste is at best an expedient it would be better to avoid, if possible, since trend parameters are not capable of causal or legal interpretation.

In recent years two economists have cleared the way for the development of a theory of consumer demand with variable preferences. In two short papers growing out of the Lange-Robertson-Hicks debate over the nature of related goods,[11] Ichimura[12] and Tintner[13] defined a change in preferences by a change in the form of the ordinal utility function or indifference map and derived, for shifts in demand, algebraic expressions which are linear combinations of the Slutsky-Hicks substitution terms[14] which play a central role in existing consumer demand theory. Straightforward linear transformations of the expressions derived by Tintner can be shown to follow the same mathematical rules as the corresponding linear transformations of substitution terms. Economic interpretations of the latter transformations and the rules which govern them constitute all but one of the major analytical laws of existing consumer demand theory; thus, in general, the same mathematical rules that govern the reactions of consumers' expenditure and consumption to income-compensated price changes govern the reactions of consumers' expenditure and consumption to changes in the variables that determine the form of their preference orderings.

In this article the laws of consumer demand with variable preferences are worked out and interpreted. Throughout the theoretical analysis, it is assumed that the form of a representative individual's utility function depends on the

[10] *Cf.* H. Wold. *Demand Analysis: A Study in Econometrics*, New York: John Wiley. 1953. p. 47; and T. C. Koopmans and W. C. Hood, "The Estimation of Simultaneous Linear Economic Relationships," in W. C. Hood and T. C. Koopmans, eds., *Studies in Econometric Method*, New York: John Wiley, 1953, pp. 120–122.

[11] *Cf.* O. Lange, "Complementarity and Interrelations of Shifts in Demand," *Review of Economic Studies*, Vol. 8, 1940, pp. 58–63; and D. H. Robertson, J. R. Hicks, and O. Lange, "The Interrelations of Shifts in Demand," *Review of Economic Studies*, Vol. 12, 1944–45, pp. 71–78.

[12] S. Ichimura, "A Critical Note on the Definition of Related Goods," *Review of Economic Studies*, Vol. 18, 1950–51, pp. 179–183.

[13] G. Tintner, "Complementarity and Shifts in Demand," *Metroeconomica*, Vol. 4, 1952, pp. 1–4.

[14] *Cf.* J. R. Hicks, *Value and Capital*, 2d ed., Oxford: Clarendon Press, 1946, pp. 309–311.

expenditures which sellers make for advertising goods and services. The analysis is entirely in terms of comparative statics; it provides theoretical explanations of the way a hypothetical consumer, who always maximizes his utility function, reallocates a fixed total expenditure to purchases of goods and services when his preference structure (ordinal utility function) is changed by advertising in certain defined ways. From the point of view of the econometrician engaged in empirical demand analysis existing consumer demand theory has shown itself to be essentially adequate for the analysis of effects of prices and income on demand, and it seems plausible that the theory of consumer demand with variable preferences will be equally useful in the empirical analysis of the effects of advertising on demand functions.

2. DEFINITIONS AND ASSUMPTIONS

The point of view adopted here is that advertising costs are incurred by a seller in an effort to secure a favorable change in consumers' subjective evaluations of the commodity he offers for sale; in terms of economic theory, the seller seeks by advertising his goods and services to increase their marginal utilities to consumers with respect to the marginal utilities of the commodities offered by other sellers. This point of view conforms to that expressed in the institutional studies of advertising by Borden[15] and Lever.[16]

In order to express this concept of advertising in terms of ordinal utility theory, it is first assumed that an individual's preferences can be represented by the utility function, $u(x_1, \cdots, x_n; \theta_1, \cdots, \theta_n)$, where the x_i denote the quantities of distinct goods and services he consumes during a given period of time during which he receives money income, M, and pays prices, $p_1, \cdots, p_n$, which he cannot influence. The θ_i denote parameters which describe the form of the ordinal utility function. They are assumed to depend on the variables a_j, where a_j denotes the money expenditure by the seller of x_j in advertising that commodity to the consumer. It is also assumed that the form of the utility function is uniquely determined by the advertising expenditures, i.e., that

$$\theta_j = \theta_j(a_1, \cdots, a_n/x_1, \cdots, x_n) \qquad (j = 1, \cdots, n), \tag{1}$$

are single-valued functions. The utility function is presumed to possess first-order partial derivatives, $u_1, \cdots, u_n$, with respect to the x_i, and these denote the marginal utilities of the commodities, $x_1, \cdots, x_n$. The marginal utilities are presumed to possess in turn the first-order partial derivatives, u_{ij}, and $u_{i\theta_j}$. It is assumed, moreover, that the inverse of transformation (1) exists, so that the second-order partial derivatives, u_{ia_j} and $u_{i\theta_k}$, $i, j, k = 1, \cdots, n$, are related according to

$$\frac{\partial(u_1, \cdots, u_n)}{\partial(\theta_1, \cdots, \theta_n)} \cdot \frac{\partial(\theta_1, \cdots, \theta_n)}{\partial(a_1, \cdots, a_n)} = \frac{\partial(u_1, \cdots, u_n)}{\partial(a_1, \cdots, a_n)}. \tag{2}$$

[15] N. H. Borden, *The Economic Effects of Advertising*, Chicago: Richard D. Irwin, 1947, pp. 162–163.

[16] E. A. Lever, *Advertising and Economic Theory*, London: Oxford University Press, 1947, p. 28.

3. DERIVATION OF THE TINTNER-ICHIMURA RELATION

The derivation of expressions for shifts in demand functions with respect to small changes in advertising expenditures begins here with the assumption that the usual first and second order conditions for individual consumer equilibrium are fulfilled, i.e., that

$$\sum_{i=1}^{n} p_i x_i = M, \tag{3}$$

$$-\lambda p_i + u_i = 0 \qquad (i = 1, \cdots, n), \tag{4}$$

and the matrix

$$U = \begin{bmatrix} o & u_j \\ u_i & u_{ij} \end{bmatrix} \qquad (i, j = 1, \cdots, n), \tag{5}$$

is negative definite. The Lagrangean multiplier, λ, denotes the marginal utility of money income, M, and is positive. Income, M, and all prices, p_i, are assumed to remain constant.

An important invariant derived from the equilibrium conditions is the Slutsky-Hicks[17] substitution term, s_{ij}. It is obtained by differentiating the first order conditions (4), along with the side condition

$$u(x_1, \cdots, x_n; \theta_1, \cdots, \theta_n) = \text{constant}, \tag{6}$$

partially with respect to p_j and solving the resulting system of equations for

$$s_{ij} = \frac{\lambda \mid U_{ij} \mid}{\mid U \mid}, \qquad (i, j = 1, \cdots, n), \tag{7}$$

where $\mid U_{ij} \mid$ is the cofactor of u_{ij} in the matrix U. The substitution term, s_{ij}, denotes the rate of change in demand for x_i with respect to a small change in the price of x_j, all other prices remaining constant, but with income adjusted to maintain a constant level of utility. The mathematical laws governing relations among substitution terms play a central role in the theory of consumer demand with variable preferences, and so are summarized here, though without complete proofs being furnished as these are available elsewhere.[18] The four major theorems are:

$$s_{ii} < 0, \tag{8}$$

$$s_{ij} = s_{ji} \qquad (i, j = 1, \cdots, n), \tag{9}$$

$$\sum_{j=1}^{n} p_j s_{ij} = 0, \tag{10}$$

$$\sum_{i=1}^{m} \sum_{j=1}^{m} s_{ij} z_i z_j < 0, \qquad (m < n), \tag{11}$$

where not all $z_i = 0$.

[17] J. R. Hicks, *Value and Capital*, 2d ed., p. 309.

[18] J. L. Mosak, *General Equilibrium Theory in International Trade*, Bloomington, Ind.: Principia Press, 1944, pp. 9–30.

Expressions for shifts in demand with respect to advertising are obtained from the equilibrium conditions (3) and (4) by differentiating them partially with respect to a_j and solving the resulting system of equations. Denote the shift in demand for x_i and x_{ia_j}, where $x_{ia_j} = \partial x_i/\partial a_j$; then

$$x_{ia_j} = -\sum_{h=1}^{n} \frac{u_{ha_j}}{\lambda} s_{hi}, \qquad (i, j = 1, \cdots, n), \tag{12}$$

or

$$x_{ia_j} = -\sum_{h=1}^{n-1} R_{ha_j} s_{hi} \tag{13}$$

where $R_{ha_j} = \partial R_h/\partial a_j$, $R_h = u_h/u_n$, and $p_n \equiv 1$, x_n being the numéraire. The relation (12) was first derived by Tintner;[19] and a special case of (12) was derived earlier by Ichimura.[20] Ichimura's assumption was that there is a solitary increase in the marginal rate of substitution of (say) x_1 for one of the other commodities, all other marginal rates of substitution remaining constant; thus, the expression he derived is equivalent to (13) when $R_{ja_j} > 0$, and $R_{ia_j} = 0$, for all $i \neq j$.[21]

The expressions (12) and (13), which are called the Tintner-Ichimura Relations, satisfy the criterion of invariance; for if the equally valid utility function, $v = \phi(u)$, where $\phi'(u) > 0$, is substituted for u, $v_h = \phi'(u)u_h$, $v_{ha_j} = \phi'(u)u_{ha_j} + \phi''(u)u_h u_{a_j}$, and the marginal utility of money income, M, is $\phi'(u)\lambda$. Slutsky-Hicks substitution terms are invariant against this transformation.[22] The Tintner-Ichimura Relation, (12), after elementary simplification becomes

$$x_{ia_j} = -\sum_{h=1}^{n} \frac{u_{ha_j}}{x} s_{hi} - \phi''(u)u_{a_j} \sum_{h=1}^{n} \frac{u_h}{\lambda} s_{hi}. \tag{14}$$

According to the first order conditions (4), $u_h/\lambda = p_h$, and so it follows from the linear dependence relation (10) that the second right-hand term of (14) is equal to zero; x_{ia_j} is therefore invariant against the transformation $\phi(u)$.

It follows from the initial assumption that the individual consumer spends his entire money income, M, that the expressions for shifts in demand are related according to the linear dependence

$$\sum_{i=1}^{n} p_i x_{ia_j} = 0. \tag{15}$$

That the Tintner-Ichimura relations satisfy this linear dependence can easily be verified by straightforward substitution of (12) into (15), having regard to the linear dependence rule for Slutsky-Hicks substitution terms.

[19] G. Tintner, "Complementarity and Shifts in Demand," *Metroeconomica*, Vol. 4, 1952, pp. 1–4.

[20] S. Ichimura, "A Critical Note on the Definition of Related Goods," *Review of Economic Studies*, Vol. 18, 1950–51, pp. 179–183.

[21] *Cf.* R. L. Basmann, "A Note on Mr. Ichimura's Definition of Related Goods," *Review of Economic Studies*, Vol. 22, 1954–55, pp. 67–69.

[22] *Cf.* J. R. Hicks, *op. cit.*, pp. 306–307.

The Tintner-Ichimura market relation is obtained by summing over all (say, N) individuals in the market; that is,

$$X_{ia_j} = \sum_{\mu=1}^{N} x_{ia_j}^{(\mu)}. \tag{16}$$

(The notation, X_i, will henceforth denote market demand.) Since each individual is presumed to be charged the same prices for his purchases of commodities, it follows from (15) that the Tintner-Ichimura market relations (16) satisfy the linear dependence

$$\sum_{i=1}^{n} p_i X_{ia_j} = 0. \tag{17}$$

4. INTERRELATIONS OF ELASTICITIES OF DEMAND

The transformations

$$e_{ij} = \frac{a_j}{x_i} x_{ia_j} \qquad (i, j = 1, \cdots, n), \tag{18}$$

$$E_{ij} = \frac{a_j}{X_i} x_{ia_j}, \tag{19}$$

define the empirically useful concepts of individual and market advertising elasticities of demand.[23] e_{ij} is a dimensionless number representing the percentage change in demand for x_i with respect to a one per cent change in advertising expenditure, a_j; E_{ij} represents the corresponding concept for market demand functions. These concepts are closely related to that of the elasticity of substitution sometimes employed in existing consumer demand theory. We define

$$z_{ij} = -s_{ij} p_j/x_i \qquad (i, j = 1, \cdots, n). \tag{20}$$

z_{ij} represents the percentage change in the consumer's demand for x_i with respect to a one per cent income-compensated change in the price of x_j. If $b_{hj}R_h$ is substituted for R_{ha_j} in (13), then, after simplification, the expression for e_{ij} becomes

$$e_{ij} = \sum_{h=1}^{n-1} a_j b_{hj}(-s_{ih} p_h/x_i) = \sum_{h=1}^{n-1} w_{hj} z_{ih}, \tag{21}$$

where $w_{hj} = a_j b_{hj}$ is the elasticity of the marginal rate of substitution of x_n for x_h with respect to the advertising expenditure, a_j, and represents the percentage change in the marginal rate of substitution with respect to a one per cent change in expenditure on advertising x_j. Formula (21) shows that advertising elasticities of demand are linear combinations of substitution elasticities with advertising elasticities of the marginal rates of substitution acting as weights. Since, in empirical demand analysis, it is sometimes possible to obtain inde-

[23] *Cf.* R. Dorfman and P. O. Steiner, "Optimal Advertising and Optimal Quality," *American Economic Review*, Vol. 44, 1954, pp. 826–836.

pendent estimates of substitution elasticities and advertising elasticities of demand, it is also possible to obtain estimates of the advertising elasticities of marginal rates of substitution. Empirical verification of several hypotheses concerning the w_{hj} might then throw some light on problems encountered in the theory of selling costs.[24] Some possibilities will be mentioned below.

Using relations (15) and (17), one can easily verify that advertising elasticities of demand are linearly dependent according to

$$\sum_{i=1}^{n} (p_i x_i) e_{ij} = 0 \qquad (j = 1, \cdots, n), \tag{22}$$

for individual consumers, and

$$\sum_{i=1}^{n} (p_i X_i) E_{ij} = 0 \qquad (j = 1, \cdots, n), \tag{23}$$

for the market demand functions.

The linear dependence relations impose several restrictions on the signs and magnitudes of advertising elasticities of demand. Since the coefficients, $p_i x_i$ and $p_i X_i$, are nonnegative, it follows from (22) and (23) that the elasticity of demand with respect to a_j must be positive for at least one i, and negative for at least one other, except in the logically (but not empirically) trivial case where all advertising elasticities are zero.

Another restriction imposed by the linear dependence relations limits the number of elasticities, e_{ij} and E_{ij} which can be constant. Not all the e_{ij} (or E_{ij}) can be constant unless all are (trivially) zero, for if they were all constant, then expenditures on the several commodities would be determined according to the system of equations

$$[e_{ji}]m = 0 \qquad (j, i = 1, \cdots, n), \tag{24}$$

where m is the column vector $(m_1, \cdots, m_n)$, $m_i = p_i x_i$, and the rank of the matrix $[e_{ji}]$ is $n - 1$. It follows from (24) that the ratios of expenditures, m_i/m_n are constant; hence

$$\frac{\partial}{\partial a_j}\left(\frac{m_i}{m_n}\right) = 0, \tag{25}$$

and this implies

$$\frac{a_j}{m_i}\frac{\partial m_i}{\partial a_j} = \frac{a_j}{m_n}\frac{\partial m_n}{\partial a_j}, \tag{26}$$

i.e.,

$$e_{ij} = e_{nj} \qquad (i = 1, \cdots, n = 1). \tag{27}$$

[24] *Cf.* N. S. Buchanan, "Advertising Expenditures: A Suggested Treatment," *Journal of Political Economy*, Vol. 20, 1942, pp. 537–557.

Thus, if all the elasticities of demand with respect to a_j are constant, and if this is true for all $j = 1, \cdots, n$, then the elasticities of all the demand functions with respect to each a_j are equal; but the only magnitude of the e_{ij} which is consistent with this result is zero.

Some interesting results are obtained when it is assumed that advertising expenditure, a_i, affects only the marginal rate of substitution of x_n for x_i leaving all other marginal utilities unchanged.[25] Let $R_{ia_i} = b_{ii}R_i > 0$, $R_{ja_i} = 0$, for all $j \neq i$. In this case the Tintner-Ichimura relation (13) becomes, after some simplification,

$$x_{ja_i} = -b_{ii}R_i s_{ji} = -b_{ii}s_{ji}p_i, \tag{28}$$

and

$$e_{ji} = w_{ii}z_{ji} \qquad (j = 1, \cdots, n). \tag{29}$$

From (28) and (8) it follows that $x_{ia_i} > 0$; and from (16) that $X_{ia_i} > 0$. According to the definition of related goods given by Hicks,[26] x_i is a substitute for x_j if $s_{ij} > 0$; x_i is a complement of x_j if $s_{ij} < 0$; and x_i and x_j are independent commodities if $s_{ij} = 0$. Accordingly, if x_i is a substitute for x_j, then by (28) $x_{ja_i} < 0$; if x_i is a complement of x_j, then $x_{ja_i} > 0$; that is, if there is an increase in advertising expenditure, a_i, there results an increase in the demand for x_i, a decrease in the demand for commodities which are substitutes for x_i, an increase in the demand for commodities which are complements of x_i, and no change in the demand for commodities which are independent of x_i. From the definition of z_{ji} (formula (20)), the algebraic sign of z_{ji} is opposite to that of s_{ji}. Moreover, the elasticity, w_{ii}, of the marginal rate of substitution of x_m for x_i with respect to advertising expenditure, a_i, is a positive number. It follows, therefore, from the definition of related goods, that the advertising elasticity of demand for x_i with respect to a_i is greater than zero, and that the advertising elasticity of demand for x_j with respect to a_i is less than zero if x_i is a substitute for x_j, is greater than zero if x_i is a complement of x_j, and is zero if x_i is independent of x_j.

In this case where the advertising expenditure, a_i, affects only the marginal rate of substitution of x_n for x_i, the advertising elasticities of demand are directly proportional to the elasticities of substitution. Indeed, the advertising elasticity of demand for x_j with respect to a_i is simply the product of the elasticity of the marginal rate of substitution of x_n for x_i with respect to a_i and the elasticity of substitution of x_i for x_j. If R_i is relatively inelastic, i.e., if $w_{ii} < 1$, then formula (29) indicates that the consumer's demand for x_j responds relatively less to a one per cent increase in advertising expenditure, a_i, than to a one per cent income-compensated decrease in the price of x_i; if R_i is relatively elastic, i.e., if $w_{ii} > 1$, then (29) indicates that the consumer's demand for x_j responds relatively more to a one per cent increase in advertising expenditure, a_i, than to a one per cent income-compensated decrease in the price of x_i. This points to the

[25] *Cf.* G. Tintner, *op. cit.*, p. 3.

[26] J. R. Hicks, *op. cit.*, pp. 309–311. Also see S. Ichimura, *op. cit.*, p. 181 and R. L. Basmann, *op. cit.*, p. 69.

possible convenience of classifying commodities as "necessities" or "luxuries" according as the elasticities, w_{ii}, are either less than or equal to or else greater than unity. Possibly such a classification would agree closely with a corresponding one based on the magnitude of price elasticities.[27]

5. SOME THEOREMS ON COMPOSITE COMMODITIES

From the point of view of empirical demand analysis, one of the most important propositions of existing consumer demand theory is the well-known Leontief-Hicks theorem,[28] which asserts that if the prices of a group of goods all change in equal proportion, then that group of goods can be treated logically as if it were but a single commodity. It is frequently the experience with market data that the prices of individual goods in a general class of commodity undergo approximately uniformly proportionate changes. By using the Leontief-Hicks theorem, one is then able to define the concepts of related commodities as applied to composite goods in exactly the same way as one defines complementarity, substitutability, and independence of single, well-defined goods, and to define the concepts of price elasticity, income elasticity, and substitution elasticity of demand for composite commodities, and to verify that these measures satisfy exactly the same laws as do the corresponding measures defined for single goods.

There is an analogous theorem in the theory of consumer demand with variable preferences, but here it is the marginal rates of substitution of x_n for each good in a group of goods which are assumed to change in equal proportion. If $x_1, \cdots, x_m$, are all sub-commodities of a general class, it may sometimes be plausible to assume that expenditure devoted to advertising the class of commodity will affect the marginal utilities of the sub-commodities more or less uniformly. The theorem asserts that if the marginal rates of substitution are all increased in the same proportion, then the group of goods can be treated logically as a single commodity; specifically, an aggregate quantity, called the composite demand for the group, which is a weighted sum of the demands for individual commodities within the group, can be defined such that this quantity behaves exactly as do the x_{ja_i} in formula (28); and elasticities of composite demand can be defined such that they behave exactly as the e_{ji} in formula (29). The proof of the theorem is essentially equivalent to one of the steps in the proof of the Leontief-Hicks theorem.

Before the proof is undertaken, it is necessary to define the concept of related composite commodities. Suppose that the prices of $x_1, \cdots, x_m$ all increase in the same proportion, and denote this aggregate by v_1; suppose that all other prices remain constant, but partition the remaining commodities into two aggregates, $x_{m+1}, \cdots, x_p$, denoted by v_2, and $x_{p+1}, \cdots, x_n$, denoted by v_3. According to the Leontief-Hicks theorem, each of these groups of goods, v_1, v_2, and v_3, may be treated as if it were a single commodity. In addition, suppose that the equal proportionate changes in the prices, $p_1, \cdots, p_m$, are income-compensated.

[27] *Cf.* H. Wold, *op. cit.*, pp. 114–115.

[28] *Cf.* W. Leontief, "Composite Commodities and the Problem of Index Numbers," *Econometrica*, Vol. 4, 1936, pp. 39–59; J. R. Hicks, *op. cit.*, pp. 312–313; and H. Wold, *op. cit.*, pp. 108–109.

Thus, the change in expenditure on x_j, $j = 1, \cdots, n$, due to the proportionate change in the price of x_i, $i = 1, \cdots, m$, is equal to $s_{ji}p_jp_i$. If x_j is a substitute for x_i, then it follows from the definition of related goods that $s_{ji}p_jp_i > 0$; if x_j is a complement of x_i, it follows that $s_{ji}p_jp_i < 0$; and, in particular,

$$s_{ii}p_i^2 < 0. \tag{30}$$

Summing over the commodities making up the aggregate, v_1, one obtains the result that the change in aggregate expenditure on v_1 with respect to the proportionate increase or decrease in prices, $p_1, \cdots, p_m$, obeys the same law of sign as $s_{ii}p_i$; for, according to the theorem (11), it follows that

$$Q_1' = \sum_{h=1}^{m}\sum_{i=1}^{m} s_{hi}p_hp_i < 0 \tag{31}$$

where the left-hand member is the rate of change in expenditure on the group v_1 with respect to the equal proportionate change in prices.

$$Q_2' = \sum_{j=m+1}^{p}\sum_{i=1}^{m} s_{ji}p_jp_i \tag{32}$$

is the rate of change in expenditure on the aggregate v_2, and

$$Q_3' = \sum_{k=p+1}^{n}\sum_{i=1}^{m} s_{ki}p_kp_i \tag{33}$$

is the rate of change in expenditure on the aggregate v_3 with respect to the proportionate change in prices, $p_1, \cdots, p_m$. If $Q_2' > 0$, the commodities in the aggregate v_2 are said to be predominantly substitutable for the commodities in the aggregate v_1; if $Q_2' < 0$, the commodities in the aggregate v_2 are said to be predominantly complementary with the commodities in v_1. It follows from the linear dependence rule (10) that if $Q_2' < 0$, $Q_3' > 0$, i.e., if v_2 is predominantly complementary with v_1, then v_3 is predominantly substitutable for v_1. This last result is derived ultimately from the assumption that the consumer spends his entire income, M.

Suppose that there is advertising which increases all the marginal rates of substitution, $R_1, \cdots, R_m$, in equal proportion, and denote the proportional increase by b. Denote by a the total advertising on v_1; denote by r_1 the total expenditure on v_1, by r_2 the total expenditure on v_2, and by r_3 the total expenditure on v_3; i.e.,

$$r_1 = \sum_{h=1}^{m} p_hx_h, \tag{34}$$

$$r_2 = \sum_{j=m+1}^{p} p_jx_j, \tag{35}$$

$$r_3 = \sum_{k=p+1}^{n} p_kx_k. \tag{36}$$

From (13) the Tintner-Ichimura relation for the single good, x_j, is given by

$$x_{ja} = -b\sum_{i=1}^{m} s_{ji}p_i \qquad (j = 1, \cdots, n). \tag{37}$$

The rates of change of expenditures, r_1, r_2, and r_3, are given by

$$\frac{\partial r_1}{\partial a} = -b \sum_{h=1}^{m} \sum_{i=1}^{m} s_{hi} p_h p_i, \tag{38}$$

$$\frac{\partial r_2}{\partial a} = -b \sum_{j=m+1}^{p} \sum_{i=1}^{m} s_{ji} p_j p_i, \tag{39}$$

$$\frac{\partial r_3}{\partial a} = -b \sum_{k=p+1}^{n} \sum_{i=1}^{m} s_{ki} p_k p_i. \tag{40}$$

It follows once more from (11) that $\partial r_1/\partial a > 0$. From the definitions of related aggregate commodities given early in this section it follows that $\partial r_2/\partial a < 0$, if v_2 is predominantly substitutable for v_1, and that $\partial r_2/\partial a > 0$, if v_2 is predominantly complementary with v_1. Comparing (34) with (38), one sees that $\partial r_1/\partial a$ obeys the same law of sign as $p_i x_{ia_i}$; and comparing (34) with (39), one sees that $\partial r_2/\partial a$ and $\partial r_3/\partial a$ obey the same law of sign as $p_j x_{ja_i}$, where $j \neq i$.

From the linear dependence rule (15) it follows that

$$\frac{\partial r_1}{\partial a} + \frac{\partial r_2}{\partial a} + \frac{\partial r_3}{\partial a} = 0, \tag{41}$$

from which it follows that

$$\frac{a\partial r_1}{r_1\partial a} r_1 + \frac{a\partial r_2}{r_2\partial a} r_2 + \frac{a\partial r_3}{r_3\partial a} r_3 = 0, \tag{42}$$

which is the linear dependence rule for advertising elasticities of composite commodities. Or, in a more condensed notation,

$$r_1 e_{v_1 a} + r_2 e_{v_2 a} + r_3 e_{v_3 a} = 0, \tag{43}$$

where

$$e_{v_i a} = \frac{a}{r_i} \frac{\partial r_i}{\partial a}$$

is the advertising elasticity of demand for the composite commodity, v_i, $i = 1, 2, 3$, with respect to the aggregate advertising expenditure on v_1. (43) is seen to have exactly the same form as (22). This completes the proof of the theorem that a group of goods, all of whose marginal rates of substitution increase or decrease in equal proportion, can be treated as a single commodity.

6. FURTHER INTERRELATIONS OF ELASTICITIES OF DEMAND: COMPOSITE GOODS

In formulas (21) and (29) the connections between advertising elasticities of demand and substitution elasticities were pointed out. Similar connections exist between advertising elasticities of demand for composite goods and the advertising elasticities of demand for the sub-commodities that make up the aggregates, which elasticities are in turn related to elasticities of substitution between the sub-commodities. In order to show these relations, the concept of elasticity of substitution between two aggregate commodities is first defined.

This is done in a fashion similar to that in which the concept of related composite commodities was defined above. From formula (20) one has

$$z_{ji} = -\frac{s_{ji}p_ip_j}{p_jx_j}. \tag{44}$$

Analogously, in terms of the composite commodities, one may define the elasticity

$$v_{21} = -\frac{1}{r_2}\sum_{j=m+1}^{p}\sum_{i=1}^{m} s_{ji}p_ip_j, \tag{45}$$

and similarly for v_{31} and v_{11}.

It follows from the definitions of elasticities, e_{v_ia}, $i = 1, 2, 3$, and from the formulas (38), (39), and (40) that

$$e_{v_ia} = w_{v_1}v_{i_1} \qquad (i = 1, 2, 3), \tag{46}$$

where $w_{v_1} = ab$ defines the elasticity of the marginal rate of substitution of x_n for the composite commodity v_1 with respect to aggregate advertising expenditure, a. That the relations (46) have the same form as (29) shows that there are the same relations between aggregate elasticities of demand with respect to advertising expenditure and the income-compensated price elasticities of one aggregate commodity for another as there are between elasticities of demand with respect to advertising which affects the marginal rate of substitution of x_n for only one commodity and the income-compensated price elasticities of that one commodity.

7. CONCLUSION

By summing over all individual consumers in a given market, or within a market stratum, market formulas equivalent to (29) through (46) can easily be derived and shown to have the same algebraic form. In empirical demand analysis it is frequently convenient to postulate that aggregate market behavior of individuals can be represented as the market behavior of a conceptual average individual; the formulas then purport to describe the consumption behavior of this statistical individual.

The linear dependence rules (22) and (42) may be employed in empirical demand analysis in essentially two different ways. First, the linear dependence may be imposed a priori, i.e., as side conditions which estimated advertising elasticities of demand are forced to satisfy. One might do this when, for example, one is chiefly interested in testing the hypothesis that an increase in expenditure on advertising a commodity, x_i, affects only the marginal rate of substitution of x_n for x_i. Second, elasticities estimated unconditionally may be "tested" by substitution in the appropriate linear dependence relation.

If independent estimates of elasticities of substitution and advertising elasticities can be obtained, it is possible, using the relations (21), for one to estimate advertising elasticities of marginal rates of substitution and to test hypotheses such as those represented by formula (29).

Postscript: 1971[30]

The editors of this volume have kindly provided space to answer some questions students frequently ask about the foregoing article. The most frequent student questions are:

1. What are some examples of parameters of utility functions?
2. Is it essential to the theory of variable preferences to interpret a_j as the money expenditure by the seller of x_j in advertising that commodity to the consumer?

In order to exemplify the concept of a parameter of a utility function, one must refer to a definite utility function.

The differential equations

$$-\frac{dx_n}{dx_i} = \left[\frac{\beta_n(x_i - \gamma_i)}{\beta_i(x_n - \gamma_n)}\right]^{\frac{1}{(\sigma-1)}} \qquad (i = 1, 2, \ldots, n) \tag{i}$$

where

$$\sigma < 1 \quad \beta_i > 0 \quad \gamma_i > 0 \quad x_i \geqslant \gamma_i \tag{ii}$$

determine a utility function that is characterized by $(2n + 1)$ structural parameters, σ, β_i, γ_i. The marginal rate of substitution R_i of X_n for X_i is defined by

$$R_i = -\frac{dx_n}{dx_i} \qquad R_i = \frac{u_i}{u_n} \tag{iii}$$

Using (i) and the first-order equilibrium conditions (3) and (4) of Section 3 one derives the system of demand functions

$$x_i = \frac{\beta_i p_i^{\sigma-1}}{\sum_{k=1}^{n} \beta_i p_k^{\sigma}}\left[M - \sum_{k=1}^{n} \gamma_k p_k\right] + \gamma_i \tag{iv}$$

30. I am indebted to R. C. Battalio (Texas A & M University) for several helpful suggestions in preparing this postscript.

for all commodity prices $p_1, \ldots, p_n$ and income M such that[31]

$$M - \sum_{k=1}^{n} \gamma_k p_k > 0$$

Any cause a_j whose effect is a change in at least one of the $(2n + 1)$ structural parameters changes at least one of the marginal rates of substitution R_i, and (consequently) shifts the demand functions (iv) in accordance with formula (13). It is not essential that a_j be interpreted by the money expenditure by the seller of x_j in advertising that commodity to the consumer, as is done in Section 2. As a matter of fact, the article was written in response to a Ph.D. preliminary examination question put to me in 1955 by Gerhard Tintner, who asked me to consider (a) the total effect on demand of a solitary change in income M or wealth W when at least one parameter θ of the utility function depends on M or W, and (b) the total effect on demand of a solitary change in a commodity price p_j when at least one parameter θ of the utility function depends on p_j. Those total effects on demand are respectively:

$$\frac{dx_i}{dM} = \left[\frac{\partial x_i}{\partial M}\right]_{\theta=\text{const.}} - \frac{\partial \theta}{\partial M} \sum_{h=1}^{n} \frac{u_{h\theta}}{\lambda} s_{hi} \tag{vi}$$

$$\frac{dx_i}{dW} = - \frac{\partial \theta}{\partial W} \sum_{h=1}^{n} \frac{u_{h\theta}}{\lambda} s_{hi}$$

and

$$\frac{dx_i}{dp_j} = \left[s_{ij} - x_j \frac{\partial x_i}{\partial M}\right]_{\theta=\text{const.}} - \frac{\partial \theta}{\partial p_j} \sum_{h=1}^{n} \frac{u_{h\theta}}{\lambda} s_{hi} \tag{vii}$$

$$i = 1, 2, \ldots, n$$

(See formula (12).) Since no premise of Slutsky-Hicks theory of consumer demand excludes the possibility that both

$$\frac{\partial x_i}{\partial M} > 0 \quad \text{and} \quad \frac{dx_i}{dp_i} > 0$$

– $s_{ii} \leqslant 0$ necessarily – the formula (vii) is capable of accounting for the phenomenon known as *conspicuous consumption.*[32]

31. Cf. R. L. Basmann, "Hypothesis Formulation in Quantitative Economics: A Contribution to Demand Analysis" in Quirk, J. and A. Zarley, editors, *Papers in Quantitative Economics*, Lawrence, Kansas: University Press Kansas, 1968, p. 338.
32. Cf. Gerhard Tintner, "External Economies in Consumption" *Essays in Economics and Econometrics*, Chapel Hill: University of North Carolina Press, 1960.